Mifflin
Harcourt

STECK-VAUGHN

INSTRUCTOR EDITION

TEST PREPARATION FOR THE 2014 GED® TEST

- Reasoning Through Language Arts
- Mathematical Reasoning
- Science
- Social Studies

POWERED BY

PAXEN

Houghton Mifflin Harcourt

POWERED BY

PAXEN

Acknowledgments

For each of the images listed below, grateful acknowledgment is made for permission to reprint original or copyrighted material, as follows:

Images

Cover Bigstock/Diego Cervo. **vi** iStockphoto. **MA 55** Used with permission of Texas Instruments.

Steck-Vaughn Test Preparation for the 2014 GED® Test Instructor Edition

Table of Contents

Title page i
Acknowledgments/Copyright ii
Table of Contents iii
About the GED® Test .... iv–v
About *Steck-Vaughn Test Preparation for the 2014 GED® Test* .... vi–vii
About *Steck-Vaughn Test Preparation*
for the 2014 GED® Test Instructor Edition viii

REASONING THROUGH LANGUAGE ARTS .... RLA 1–RLA 99
UNIT
1: Reading Comprehension .... RLA 3–RLA 29
2: Argument Analysis and Text Comparison .... RLA 31–RLA 46
3: Extended Response .... RLA 47–RLA 55
4: Editing .... RLA 57–RLA 79
APPENDICES .... RLA 80–RLA 94
CORRELATIONS/REASONING THROUGH LANGUAGE ARTS .... RLA 95–RLA 99

MATHEMATICAL REASONING .... MA 1–MA 71
UNIT
1: Number Sense and Operations .... MA 3–MA1 2
2: Data Measurement/Analysis .... MA 13–MA 22
3: Algebra, Functions, and Patterns .... MA 23–MA 42
4: Geometry .... MA 43–MA 54
APPENDICES .... MA 55–MA 61
CORRELATIONS/MATHEMATICS .... MA 62–MA 71

SCIENCE .... SCI 1–SCI 56
UNIT
1: Life Science .... SCI 3–SCI 20
2: Physical Science .... SCI 21–SCI 38
3: Earth and Space Science .... SCI 39–SCI 48
APPENDIX .... SCI 49
CORRELATIONS/SCIENCE .... SCI 50–SCI 56

SOCIAL STUDIES .... SS 1–SS 63
UNIT
1: Geography and the World .... SS 3–SS 9
2: United States History .... SS 11–SS 19
3: Civics and Government .... SS 21–SS 40
4: Economics .... SS 41–SS 47
APPENDICES .... SS 48–SS 53
CORRELATIONS/SOCIAL STUDIES .... SS 54–SS 63

About the GED® Test

Through your work with learners pursuing a General Education Development (GED®) credential, you know that earning a GED® credential takes effort. It always has, and the task may be more challenging now than ever. Today's GED® Test is new, improved, and more rigorous, with content aligned to the Common Core State Standards. For the first time, the GED® Test serves both as a high-school equivalency degree and as a predictor of college and career readiness. The new GED® Test features four subject areas: Reasoning Through Language Arts (RLA), Mathematical Reasoning, Science, and Social Studies. Each subject area is delivered via a computer-based format and includes an array of technology-enhanced item types. The four subject-area exams together comprise a testing time of seven hours.

Studying for the GED® Test may be harder work today than ever before. However, the old saying is true: Hard work pays off. That payoff is significant: more and better career options, higher earnings, and the sense of achievement that comes with a GED® credential. Employers and colleges and universities accept the GED® credential as they would a high school diploma. On average, GED® graduates earn at least $8,400 more per year than those with an incomplete high school education.

The GED® Testing Service has constructed the GED® Test to mirror a high school experience. As such, your learners must be able to answer a variety of questions within and across the four subject areas. Also, they will encounter questions requiring varying levels of cognitive effort, or Depth of Knowledge (DOK) levels. The following table details the content areas, number of items, score points, DOK levels, and total testing time for each subject area.

Subject-Area Test	Content Areas	Items	Raw Score Points	DOK Level	Time
Reasoning Through Language Arts	**Informational Texts—75%** **Literary Texts—25%**	*51	65	80% of items at Level 2 or 3	150 minutes
Mathematical Reasoning	**Algebraic Problem Solving—55%** **Quantitative Problem Solving—45%**	*46	49	50% of items at Level 2	115 minutes
Science	**Life Science—40%** **Physical Science—40%** **Earth and Space Science—20%**	*34	40	80% of items at Level 2 or 3	90 minutes
Social Studies	**Civics/Government—50%** **U.S. History—20%** **Economics—15%** **Geography and the World—15%**	*35	44	80% of items at Level 2 or 3	90 minutes

* Number of items may vary slightly by test.

Because the demands of today's high school education and its relationship to workforce needs differ from those of a decade ago, the GED® Testing Service has moved to a computer-based format. Although multiple-choice questions remain the dominant type of item, the new GED® Test series includes a variety of technology-enhanced item types: drop-down, fill-in-the-blank, drag-and-drop, hot spot, short answer, and extended response items.

The table to the right identifies the various item types and their distribution on the new subject-area exams. As you can see, all four tests include multiple-choice, drop-down, fill-in-the-blank, and drag-and-drop items. Some variation occurs with hot spot, short answer, and extended response items.

2014 ITEM TYPES

	RLA	Math	Science	Social Studies
Multiple-choice	✓	✓	✓	✓
Drop-down	✓	✓	✓	✓
Fill-in-the-blank	✓	✓	✓	✓
Drag-and-drop	✓	✓	✓	✓
Hot spot		✓	✓	✓
Short answer			✓	
Extended response	✓			✓

In addition to changes in item formatting, the relationship of items to today's more demanding educational standards has resulted in a GED® Test with elevated academic rigor. Items align to appropriate assessment targets and to varying DOK levels:

- **Content Topics/Assessment Targets:** These topics and targets describe and detail the content on the GED® Test. They tie to the Common Core State Standards, as well as state standards for Texas and Virginia.
- **Content Practices:** These practices describe the types of reasoning and modes of thinking required to answer specific items on the GED® Test.
- **Depth of Knowledge:** The DOK model details the level of cognitive complexity and steps required to arrive at a correct answer on the test. The new GED® Test addresses three levels of DOK complexity:
  - **Level 1:** Test takers must recall, observe, question, or represent facts or simple skills. Typically, they must exhibit only a surface understanding of text and graphics.
  - **Level 2:** Test takers must process information beyond simple recall and observation to include summarizing, ordering, classifying, identifying patterns and relationships, and connecting ideas. Test takers must scrutinize text and graphics.
  - **Level 3:** Test takers must explain, generalize, and connect ideas by inferring, elaborating, and predicting. Test takers must summarize from multiple sources and use that information to develop compositions with multiple paragraphs. Those paragraphs should feature a critical analysis of sources, include supporting positions from the test takers' own experiences, and reflect editing to ensure coherent, correct writing.

Approximately 80 percent of items across most content areas will be written to DOK Levels 2 and 3, with the remainder at Level 1. Writing portions, such as the extended response item in Social Studies (25 minutes) and Reasoning Through Language Arts (45 minutes), are considered DOK Level 3 items.

Even in a robust testing year, only about 700,000 learners take the GED® Test, a figure far below the actual annual dropout rate. Obviously, we hope that dropout prevention programs bring about decreases in the numbers of students who leave school. Also, we hope that through our mutual efforts, more learners who do drop out of school eventually prepare for and succeed on the GED® Test. As we know, a GED® credential can open a variety of doors. For learners standing at the threshold of success, the GED® Test represents an opportunity for an array of achievement possibilities—academic, career, and otherwise.

About *Steck-Vaughn Test Preparation for the 2014 GED® Test*

As one of the thousands of adult-basic education instructors across the country, you make a difference each day in the lives of learners who need your help the most. To make your job—and the job of your learners—a little easier, we have devoted considerable effort and energy to developing and perfecting the *Steck-Vaughn Test Preparation for the 2014 GED® Test* series, which we hope does for you and learners what jet propulsion did for air travel.

For more than 70 years, the GED® Tests have offered a second chance to people who need it most. To date, more than 19 million Americans have studied for and earned GED® certificates and, in so doing, jump-started their lives and careers. Benefits abound for GED® holders. Recent studies have shown that people with GED® certificates earn more money, enjoy better health, and exhibit greater interest in and understanding of the world around them than those without.

Approximately 65 percent of GED® recipients plan to further their educations, providing them with more and better career options. Postsecondary education has become increasingly important in securing the most sought-after jobs. In fact, the U.S. Department of Labor projections show that 50 percent of the 20 fastest-growing jobs through 2020 will require postsecondary education.

For learners, the pathway to the future—a brighter future—begins with *Steck-Vaughn Test Preparation for the 2014 GED® Test*, an intense, accelerated approach to GED® preparation. Unlike other programs, which take months to prepare potential test takers for the GED® Tests through a content-based approach, *Steck-Vaughn Test Preparation for the 2014 GED® Test* gets to the heart of the GED® Tests—and quickly—by emphasizing key reading and thinking concepts to equip learners with the skills and strategies they'll need to interpret and answer questions correctly on the GED® Test. Learners must be able to read and interpret excerpts, passages, and visuals—tables, diagrams, graphs, timelines, and so on—and then answer questions based on them.

Steck-Vaughn Test Preparation for the 2014 GED® Test shows the way. Learners receive intensive instruction and practice through a series of linked lessons, all of which tie to relevant assessment targets and DOK levels. Two-page micro-lessons in each student book provide focused and efficient instruction, while callout boxes, sample exercises, and tips for test-taking and other thinking strategies aid in understanding complex concepts. Most lessons in the series include a *Spotlighted Item* feature that corresponds to one of the technology-enhanced item types that appear on the GED® Test: drop-down, fill-in-the-blank, drag-and-drop, hot spot, short answer, or extended response. *Spotlighted Item* features provide deeper, richer treatment of these item types, allowing learners ample opportunity to build familiarity with them.

Each unit closes with an eight-page review that includes a representative sampling of items, including technology-enhanced item types, from the lessons that comprise the unit. Learners may use each unit review as a posttest to gauge their mastery of content and skills and readiness for that aspect of the GED® Test. For those who require additional support, we offer the *Steck-Vaughn Test Preparation for the 2014 GED® Test* workbooks, which provide twice the support and practice exercises as the student books.

Unlike other GED® materials, which were designed for the classroom, *Steck-Vaughn Test Preparation for the 2014 GED® Test* materials were designed from the classroom, using proven educational theory and cutting-edge classroom philosophy. For learners who have long had the deck stacked against them, the odds are finally in their favor. And yours.

> The **LEARN THE SKILL** section provides information about the skill to be studied.

> Each lesson includes correlations to subject-area assessment targets, such as **CONTENT TOPICS** and **PRACTICES**, that will help learners focus their studies.

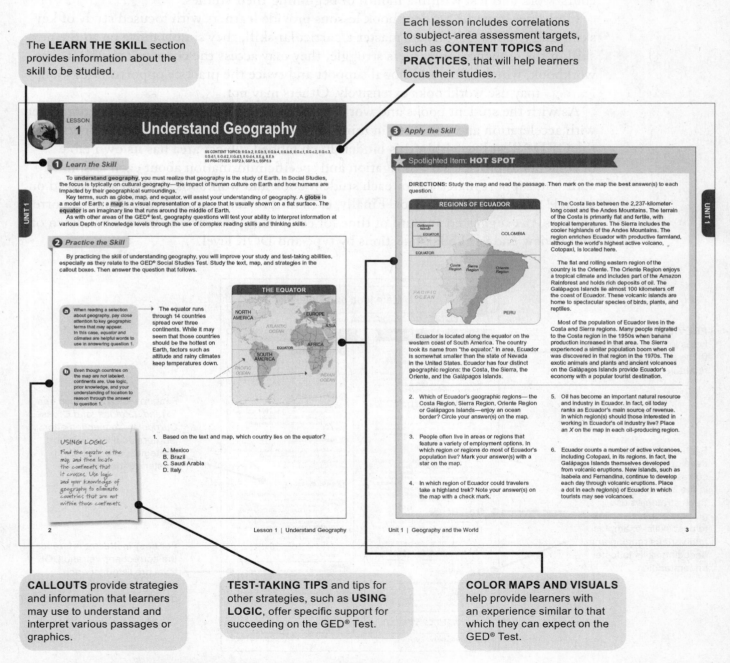

> **CALLOUTS** provide strategies and information that learners may use to understand and interpret various passages or graphics.

> **TEST-TAKING TIPS** and tips for other strategies, such as **USING LOGIC**, offer specific support for succeeding on the GED® Test.

> **COLOR MAPS AND VISUALS** help provide learners with an experience similar to that which they can expect on the GED® Test.

About *Steck-Vaughn Test Preparation for the 2014 GED® Test Instructor Edition*

As you know, the GED® Test series is a comprehensive battery of exams that represent an equivalent high-school experience. Together, the four subject-area tests, which total seven hours, are to testing what marathons are to running. As a result, the average learner may spend months, possibly even years, studying for the GED® Test.

Then there's *Steck-Vaughn Test Preparation for the 2014 GED® Test*. Material in the program emphasizes the development of core reading and thinking skills, meaning learners build and extend their understanding of concepts necessary for success on the GED® Test—and fast. Learners who use this program typically can complete the coursework and test within a month of beginning their studies.

How does it work? Student book lessons provide learners with focused study of key skills and content. If learners master a particular skill, they simply move on to the next skill in the sequence. If learners struggle, they may access the companion subject-area workbook, which offers additional support and twice the practice opportunities. Some learners may use workbooks extensively. Others may not.

As with the student books and workbooks, the instructor edition has been organized with acceleration and efficiency in mind. Everything you need to prepare learners for the GED® Test lies within this binder. Each tabbed subject area has its own table of contents to provide easy navigation and specific information about each lesson. In addition, support materials for each student book and workbook skill are organized on a single page for easy reference. Finally, each unit review features corresponding correct answers, the suggested amount of time for completing the review, and a breakdown of unit review and workbook questions by type and DOK level.

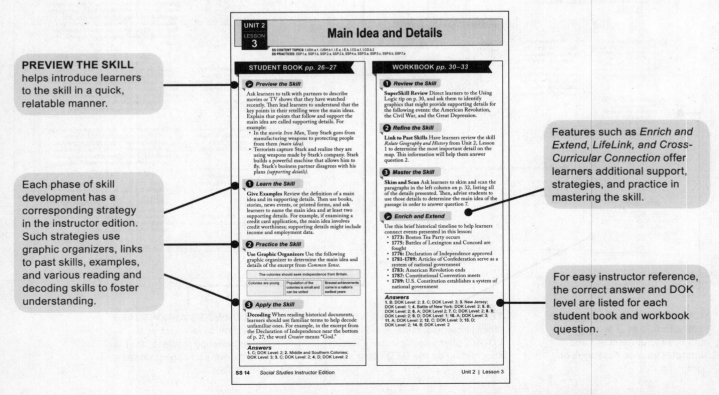

PREVIEW THE SKILL helps introduce learners to the skill in a quick, relatable manner.

Each phase of skill development has a corresponding strategy in the instructor edition. Such strategies use graphic organizers, links to past skills, examples, and various reading and decoding skills to foster understanding.

Features such as *Enrich and Extend, LifeLink,* and *Cross-Curricular Connection* offer learners additional support, strategies, and practice in mastering the skill.

For easy instructor reference, the correct answer and DOK level are listed for each student book and workbook question.

Reasoning Through Language Arts

Instructor Edition

LANGUAGE ARTS

Table of Contents

Table of Contents...RLA 1
About *Steck-Vaughn Test Preparation for the 2014 GED® Test: Reasoning Through Language Arts* ....RLA 2

UNIT 1 *Reading Comprehension*...............RLA 3
LESSON
1: Determine Main Idea and Details ....RLA 4
2: Summarize...RLA 5
3: Determine Sequence......................................RLA 6
4: Categorize ....RLA 7
5: Identify Cause and Effect...............................RLA 8
6: Compare and Contrast ....RLA 9
7: Determine Author's Point of View.................RLA 10
8: Make Inferences...RLA 11
9: Analyze Style and Tone................................RLA 12
10: Draw Conclusions.......................................RLA 13
11: Make Generalizations ....RLA 14
12: Synthesize Information ....RLA 15
13: Use Context Clues......................................RLA 16
14: Identify Cause and Effect in Fiction ....RLA 17
15: Compare and Contrast in Fiction.................RLA 18
16: Analyze Plot Elements ....RLA 19
17: Analyze Character ....RLA 20
18: Analyze Setting ....RLA 21
19: Interpret Figurative Language ....RLA 22
20: Determine Narrative Point of View ....RLA 23
21: Make Inferences in Fiction ....RLA 24
22: Identify Theme ....RLA 25
23: Draw Conclusions in Fiction........................RLA 26
24: Apply Ideas ....RLA 27
Unit 1 Review.............................RLA 28–RLA 29

UNIT 2 *Argument Analysis and Text Comparison* ....RLA 31
LESSON
1: Determine Author's Purpose ....RLA 32
2: Analyze Elements of Persuasion ....RLA 33
3: Identify Evidence ....RLA 34
4: Analyze Visuals and Data............................RLA 35
5: Identify Faulty Evidence ....RLA 36
6: Classify Valid and Invalid Evidence...............RLA 37
7: Analyze the Structure of Arguments..............RLA 38
8: Analyze Rhetorical Devices ....RLA 39
9: Compare and Contrast Texts ....RLA 40

10: Compare Texts in Different Formats............RLA 41
11: Compare Texts in Similar Genres................RLA 42
12: Compare Texts in Different Genres ....RLA 43
13: Gain Information from Multiple Texts...........RLA 44
Unit 2 Review.............................RLA 45–RLA 46

UNIT 3 *Extended Response*......................RLA 47
LESSON
1: Compare Opposing Arguments.....................RLA 48
2: Develop a Thesis..RLA 49
3: Define Points and Gather Evidence ....RLA 50
4: Plan the Extended Response........................RLA 51
5: Write Introduction and Conclusion ....RLA 52
6: Draft the Extended Response.......................RLA 53
7: Review the Extended Response ....RLA 54
Unit 3 Review...RLA 55

UNIT 4 *Editing*...RLA 57
LESSON
1: Nouns ....RLA 58
2: Pronouns ....RLA 59
3: Basic Verb Tenses..RLA 60
4: Verbs with Helping Verbs.............................RLA 61
5: Apostrophes...RLA 62
6: Frequently Confused Words ....RLA 63
7: Basic Subject-Verb Agreement ....RLA 64
8: Standard English ....RLA 65
9: Capitalization ....RLA 66
10: Sentence Fragment Correction ....RLA 67
11: Commas ....RLA 68
12: Sentence Combining ....RLA 69
13: Run-on Sentence Correction ....RLA 70
14: Modifiers ....RLA 71
15: Advanced Pronoun Use ....RLA 72
16: Advanced Subject-Verb Agreement.............RLA 73
17: Parallelism ....RLA 74
18: Transitions..RLA 75
19: Paragraph Organization..............................RLA 76
20: Other Punctuation ....RLA 77
Unit 4 Review.............................RLA 78–RLA 79

APPENDIX.................................RLA 80–RLA 94

CORRELATIONS/REASONING THROUGH LANGUAGE ARTS ....RLA 95–RLA 99

About *Steck-Vaughn Test Preparation for the 2014 GED® Test: Reasoning Through Language Arts*

Steck-Vaughn's student book and workbook help unlock the learning and deconstruct the different elements of the test by helping learners build and develop core reading and thinking skills. The content of our books aligns to the new GED® language arts content standards and item distribution to provide a superior test preparation experience.

Our Spotlighted Item feature offers a deeper, richer treatment for each technology-enhanced item type. On initial introduction, a unique item type—such as drag-and-drop—receives a full page of example items in the student book lesson and three pages in the companion workbook. The length of subsequent features may be shorter depending on the skill, lesson, and requirements.

A combination of targeted strategies, informational callouts, sample questions, assorted tips and hints, and ample assessment help focus study efforts in needed areas.

In addition to the book features, a highly detailed answer key provides the correct answer and the rationale for it so that learners know exactly why an answer is correct. The *Reasoning Through Language Arts* student book and workbook are designed with an eye toward the end goal: Success on the GED® Reasoning Through Language Arts Test.

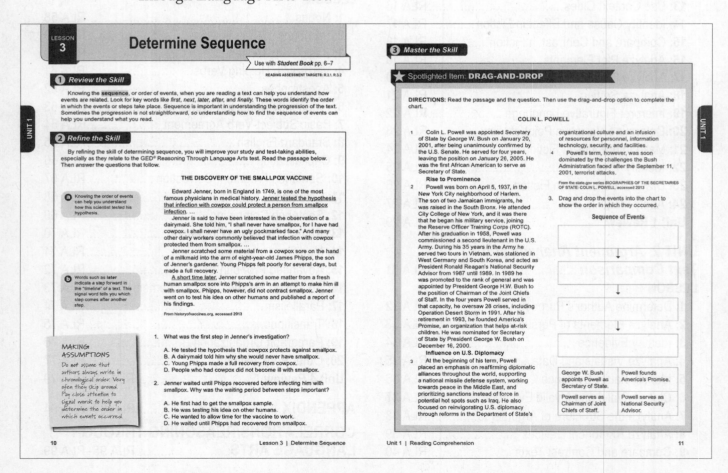

Unit 1

Reading Comprehension

To address the new GED® Reasoning Through Language Arts Test, Unit 1 includes nonfiction and fiction passages for reading comprehension. Although the test will consist of 75 percent nonfiction and 25 percent fiction, this unit provides an equal number of nonfiction and fiction lessons so that learners can focus on all skills to help them understand texts and answer questions correctly.

The passages in Lessons 1–12 are nonfiction; those in Lessons 13–24 are fiction. Some skills are addressed twice: with nonfiction and again with fiction. However, most lessons apply to both and can be adapted as needed.

The nonfiction passages cover a wide range of social studies and science topics, according to the targeted subject areas of the GED® test. Social studies passages address "The Great American Conversation." Science passages address "Human Health and Living Systems" and "Energy and Related Systems." Each lesson focuses on one skill, which serves as a stepping stone to the next. Drag-and drop items are spotlighted in Lesson 3, fill-in-the-blanks in Lesson 13.

Learners should read each passage carefully to answer questions on DOK levels 1, 2, and 3. Most questions address DOK Levels 2 and 3. All questions align with the Common Core State Standards for English Language Arts.

Table of Contents

LESSON	PAGE
1: Determine Main Idea and Details	RLA 4
2: Summarize	RLA 5
3: Determine Sequence	RLA 6
4: Categorize	RLA 7
5: Identify Cause and Effect	RLA 8
6: Compare and Contrast	RLA 9
7: Determine Author's Point of View	RLA 10
8: Make Inferences	RLA 11
9: Analyze Style and Tone	RLA 12
10: Draw Conclusions	RLA 13
11: Make Generalizations	RLA 14
12: Synthesize Information	RLA 15
13: Use Context Clues	RLA 16
14: Identify Cause and Effect in Fiction	RLA 17
15: Compare and Contrast in Fiction	RLA 18
16: Analyze Plot Elements	RLA 19
17: Analyze Character	RLA 20
18: Analyze Setting	RLA 21
19: Interpret Figurative Language	RLA 22
20: Determine Narrative Point of View	RLA 23
21: Make Inferences in Fiction	RLA 24
22: Identify Theme	RLA 25
23: Draw Conclusions in Fiction	RLA 26
24: Apply Ideas	RLA 27
Unit 1 Review	RLA 28–RLA 29

Determine Main Idea and Details

READING ASSESSMENT TARGETS: R.2.1, R.2.4, R.2.5, R.3.5, R.5.1, R.5.2, R.5.4

LANGUAGE ARTS

STUDENT BOOK *pp. 2–3*

▶ *Preview the Skill*

Ask learners to describe a sporting event that they have watched or heard about recently. Lead them to understand that the outcome of the game is the main idea. Explain that supporting details include outstanding performances by particular players or key plays that led to a victory. For example,

- **Main Idea:** *Louisiana State won the College World Series by defeating the Texas Longhorns.*
- **Supporting Detail:** *In the final game, Jared Mitchell's three-run homer gave LSU an early lead.*

❶ *Learn the Skill*

Give Examples Direct learners' attention to a document with an announcement, such as a flyer advertising a meeting, a party, or a service. Have them identify the main idea and supporting details. For example, *The Lead Singers will give a concert next week* is a main idea. Supporting details are the time, place, and cost of the tickets.

❷ *Practice the Skill*

Skim and Scan Tell learners to skim the first paragraph of the passage on p. 2 for sentences and phrases that support the main idea—for example, *"Couple this with long work hours, shift-work, chronic caffeine use and exposure to the glow of computer screens late into the night, and it may be much more than sleep that suffers."* Have learners use these details to help them identify the main idea of the passage.

❸ *Apply the Skill*

Use Graphic Organizers Use this graphic organizer to determine the main idea and details of the passage on p. 3.

There are benefits to using wind energy, which is growing in popularity.		
Wind energy is renewable.	Wind energy produces no air or water pollution.	Operational costs are low.

Answers

1. B; DOK Level: 2; **2.** C; DOK Level: 2; **3.** D; DOK Level: 2;
4. C; DOK Level: 2; **5.** A; DOK Level: 2

WORKBOOK *pp. 2–5*

❶ *Review the Skill*

SuperSkill Review Using the *Test-Taking Tips* note on p. 2, point out that many texts state the main idea in a topic sentence near the beginning of a paragraph. Often the main idea is restated in a conclusion near the end of the text. Have learners examine the first and last paragraphs of magazine articles or other texts to identify topic sentences that include main ideas. Then explain that main ideas can be implicit and require readers to infer them from the ideas and information presented. Offer some examples of implicit main ideas.

❷ *Refine the Skill*

Decoding The passage on p. 2 includes scientific terms that learners may not understand. Have them use familiar words in the passage to decode terms such as *circadian rhythm* and *chronic insomnia*.

❸ *Master the Skill*

Skim and Scan Have learners skim and scan the letter on p. 4 to identify "I" statements, such as *"I sympathize," "I do not understand,"* and *"I only wish."* Advise learners that identifying the author's opinions can reveal the main idea of a text.

▶ *LifeLink*

Remind learners that many of the documents they see each day provide visual clues about the importance of information. Discuss items such as bills, bank statements, or help-wanted ads. Then ask learners to locate the headings, subheadings, and other clues that indicate a main idea. Learners may then examine the way details in the document are organized to support the main idea.

Answers

1. C; DOK Level: 2; **2.** A; DOK Level: 2; **3.** D; DOK Level: 2;
4. A; DOK Level: 2; **5.** C; DOK Level: 2; **6.** B; DOK Level: 3;
7. C; DOK Level: 2; **8.** B; DOK Level: 2; **9.** B; DOK Level: 2;
10. A; DOK Level: 2; **11.** C; DOK Level: 2; **12.** A;
DOK Level: 2; **13.** D; DOK Level: 2; **14.** A; DOK Level: 2

Summarize

READING ASSESSMENT TARGETS: R.2.1, R.2.2, R.5.1, R.5.2, R.5.3, R.5.4, R.6.1, R.6.4

STUDENT BOOK pp. 4–5

▶ Preview the Skill

Discuss with learners how often they ask or answer the question *"So what happened?"* Lead them to understand that summarizing not only restates parts of a story or an event but also highlights the most important ideas. For example,
- *In the movie* The Bourne Ultimatum, *the main character finally discovers how he became an assassin and remembers his true identity.*
- *At the job interview, Kai summarized his work experiences, listing his previous positions in food service, food preparation, and restaurant management.*

① Learn the Skill

Decoding Learners may use more familiar terms to describe the skill of summarizing. In daily conversation, learners may say that they *sum up, recap,* or *give a rundown* of an event.

② Practice the Skill

Give Examples Point out to learners that the passage on p. 4 is a summary of a scientific study on memory. To help learners answer question 1 correctly, have them identify the main idea of the passage. Explain that the main idea of a research study is often a rephrasing of the results of the study.

③ Apply the Skill

Use Graphic Organizers Use this graphic organizer to summarize the excerpt from Nixon's speech on p. 5.

Nixon defends himself against charges of taking money during his political campaign.		
People should be able to trust those who hold high political office.	The best way to address charges made against you is to tell the truth.	Taxpayers should not have to fund personal expenses of those who hold office.

Answers
1. C; DOK Level: 2; **2.** D; DOK Level: 2; **3.** B; DOK Level: 2; **4.** A; DOK Level: 2; **5.** D; DOK Level: 2

WORKBOOK pp. 6–9

① Review the Skill

Use Graphic Organizers Use this graphic organizer to help learners identify what a summary should and should not include.

Summaries should	Summaries should not
highlight a text's main points.	state reader's judgments.
restate the main ideas of a text in the reader's own words.	reveal reader's opinions.
include the most important information from a text.	discuss reader's beliefs.

② Refine the Skill

Skim and Scan Remind learners that the passage on p. 6 is a summary of a study on false memory. Have learners skim and scan the text for the statement that best summarizes the findings of the study. Mention that such a statement is usually found at the end of the passage.

③ Master the Skill

SuperSkill Review Advise learners that summaries may focus on a particular concept or word. Point out the word *indifference* in the passage on p. 9. To help learners answer question 14 correctly, challenge them to write a summary sentence that contains the stem *"Elie Wiesel views indifference as …"*

▶ Language Analysis

Discuss how political speeches often contain formal or eloquent language, such as Johnson's statement "An assassin's bullet has thrust upon me the awesome burden of the Presidency" (p. 8, paragraph 1). Have learners work in pairs to find other places in the speech that show elevated rhetoric. Then have them paraphrase and summarize the ideas.

Answers
1. C; DOK Level: 2; **2.** A; DOK Level: 2; **3.** B; DOK Level: 2; **4.** B; DOK Level: 2; **5.** D; DOK Level: 2; **6.** C; DOK Level: 2; **7.** D; DOK Level: 2; **8.** B; DOK Level: 2; **9.** A; DOK Level: 2; **10.** C; DOK Level: 2; **11.** D; DOK Level: 2; **12.** A; DOK Level: 2; **13.** C; DOK Level: 2; **14.** A; DOK Level: 2

Determine Sequence

READING ASSESSMENT TARGETS: R.3.1, R.3.2, R.5.3

LANGUAGE ARTS

STUDENT BOOK *pp. 6–7*

➤ *Preview the Skill*

Ask learners to tell about an event that takes place over time. Explain that the order in which the parts of the event occur is the sequence. Lead learners to recount the event chronologically, and instruct them to use words that indicate order, such as *first, second, then, after,* and *finally.* For example,
- *When I wake up in the morning, the first thing I do is take a shower.*
- *Second, I eat a piece of toast.*
- *Next I brush my teeth and then get dressed.*
- *Finally, I leave for work.*

1 *Learn the Skill*

Give Examples Remind learners that the sequence may include a beginning, a middle, and an end. Ask them to recall the sequence of a sports event or a television program by using three sentences that begin with the phrases *In the beginning, In the middle,* and *At the end.*

2 *Practice the Skill*

Skim and Scan Ask learners to skim and scan the passage on p. 6. Tell them to look for phrases and sentences that describe specific actions or steps in a process. Point out "Scientific investigations usually begin with an observation" as an example. Using this information, learners can create a sequence chart like the one on p. 7 to help them answer question 1.

3 *Apply the Skill*

Spotlighted Item Type Explain that drag-and-drop item types are interactive and require learners to move words, phrases, or sentences from a list or group into a graphic organizer, such as a timeline, flow chart, Venn diagram, or web. Remind learners that some drag-and-drop items contain more choices than places in the organizer and that learners must eliminate incorrect answers.

Answers
1. B; DOK Level: 1; **2.** 1) Rehearsals for the Christmas play begin in October. 2) The author is shifted to a different fourth-grade class. 3) The author reads poetry to his students. 4) The next day, the author is fired. DOK Level: 1

WORKBOOK *pp. 10–13*

1 *Review the Skill*

SuperSkill Review Draw learners' attention to the *Making Assumptions* note on p. 10. Ask learners to give examples of movies in which the plot does not flow in chronological order. Discuss in what ways an element such as a flashback or a flash forward can change the sequence of events to achieve a particular effect.

2 *Refine the Skill*

Link to Past Skills Review the skill *Summarize* from Unit 1, Lesson 2. Then refer to the passage on p. 10. Point out that the last sentence of the first paragraph indicates that the passage explains how Jenner tested the hypothesis that infection with cowpox could protect people from smallpox infection. Ask learners to summarize the passage to determine the sequence in which Jenner proved the hypothesis correct.

3 *Master the Skill*

Spotlighted Item Type Have learners work with a partner to discuss and decide on the sequence of events that completes the drag-and-drop question on p. 11. Explain that partners should identify transition words in the passage to determine the order of events in Colin Powell's life. Consider extending the activity to have learners list all events mentioned in the passage and to use sequence words to identify each.

Answers
1. B; DOK Level: 1; **2.** C; DOK Level: 2; **3.** 1) Powell serves as National Security Advisor. 2) Powell serves as Chairman of Joint Chiefs of Staff. 3) Powell founds America's Promise. 4) George W. Bush appoints Powell as Secretary of State. DOK Level: 1; **4. October 1987:** The city's garbage pickups cease. **Spring 1988:** A policeman tells a visitor that 40 bags of trash are waiting for removal from his mother's backyard. **March 1989:** Emergency state loans are proposed to pay for garbage collection. **Spring 1989:** Raw sewage overflows into a playground. DOK Level 1: **5.** 1) The bill is referred to committee. 2) The committee holds hearings on the bill. 3) The committee votes to report the bill. 4) The House votes to pass the bill. 5) The Senate votes to pass the bill. 6) The President signs the bill into law. DOK Level: 1

Categorize

READING ASSESSMENT TARGETS: R.2.1, R.2.3, R.2.4, R.2.5, R.2.7, R.2.8, R.5.1, R.5.2, R.5.3, R.5.4

LANGUAGE ARTS

STUDENT BOOK *pp. 8–9*

▶ Preview the Skill

Ask learners to list the names of their favorite sports teams. Lead them to understand that each team fits into a broader category. For example, the Phillies are a baseball team. Explain that some teams may fit into more than one category: The Giants are a football team (the New York Giants), and they are also a baseball team (the San Francisco Giants).

❶ Learn the Skill

Give Examples Have learners give examples of different types of breakfast foods, such as cereal, pancakes, or toast. Then work with learners to sort the list into smaller categories, such as "Nutritious" or "Easy to Prepare." Point out that some examples may fall into more than one category.

❷ Practice the Skill

Skim and Scan Advise learners to skim and scan the passage on p. 8 to identify words and phrases that describe the categories of voters—for example, *age* or *race*. Have learners use this information to help them answer question 1 correctly.

❸ Apply the Skill

Decoding Refer learners to paragraph 5 of the passage on p. 9. Help them decode the words *redolent* and *savory* by explaining that these words must indicate good-tasting food because paragraph 5 describes the pleasant culinary experiences that umami provides. Understanding these words will help learners find the correct answers to questions 3 and 4.

Answers
1. B; DOK Level: 2; **2.** D; DOK Level: 2; **3.** C; DOK Level: 1; **4.** A; DOK Level: 2; **5.** B; DOK Level: 1

WORKBOOK *pp. 14–17*

❶ Review the Skill

SuperSkill Review Ask learners how they would sort work skills into different job categories. For example, computer skills would fit into an office-job category. Remind learners that one skill may fit into several job categories. For example, math skills may be useful for a position in construction or retail.

❷ Refine the Skill

Link to Past Skills Have learners review the skill *Determine Main Idea and Details* from Unit 1, Lesson 1, to help them identify the types of details about the voters described in the passage on p. 14. Learners may use this information to help them compare voter types when explaining why one group votes more often than another.

❸ Master the Skill

Spotlighted Item Type Explain to learners that going over the answer choices and then rereading the passage may help them complete the drag-and-drop web. Suggest that they look for the terms listed in the answer choices in paragraph 1, which mentions umami-rich ingredients.

▶ LifeLink

Have learners create a grocery list that includes everything they might need to stock a pantry and refrigerator. Then organize learners into pairs, and ask them to categorize the items in their lists according to supermarket sections. If time remains, suggest other ways of categorizing, such as by price, necessity, perishability, and so forth. Extend the activity by having small groups categorize everyday items such as clothing (items appropriate for work, items appropriate for the gym, items that fit, and so on) or types of cars (brands, models, SUVs, sedans, gas mileage, and so on).

Answers
1. B; DOK Level: 1; **2.** C; DOK Level: 2; **3.** fish sauce, aged cheese, ham bone, tomato sauce; DOK Level: 1; **4.** D; DOK Level: 1; **5.** A; DOK Level: 1; **6.** B; DOK Level: 3; **7.** A; DOK Level: 2; **8.** B; DOK Level: 3; **9.** D; DOK Level: 2; **10.** A; DOK Level: 2; **11.** C; DOK Level: 3

Identify Cause and Effect

READING ASSESSMENT TARGETS: R.2.1, R.2.2, R.2.3, R.2.5, R.2.7, R.3.4, R.5.1, R.5.2, R.5.3

LANGUAGE ARTS

STUDENT BOOK *pp. 10–11*

➤ Preview the Skill

Explain that nearly every action learners perform has an effect. Have learners create action statements that relate to their work, home, or everyday lives. Ask them to phrase the statements in the form of an *If … then* sentence. For example,
- If *I meet my sales goal for the year* (cause), then *I will get a raise* (effect).
- If *I get a raise* (cause), then *I can buy a new phone* (effect).

❶ Learn the Skill

Give Examples Review with learners the relationship between cause and effect. Give examples of cause statements, such as *I changed the oil in my car.* Ask learners to provide possible effect statements containing the signal words *so, as a result,* or *therefore.* For example, *I changed the oil in my car. As a result, my car is now getting better gas mileage.* Point out that the outcome is the effect of the action that occurred previously.

❷ Practice the Skill

Use Graphic Organizers Use this graphic organizer to show the causes and effects included in the passage on p. 10.

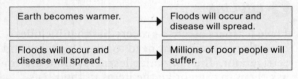

Earth becomes warmer. →	Floods will occur and disease will spread.
Floods will occur and disease will spread. →	Millions of poor people will suffer.

❸ Apply the Skill

Decoding Have learners read aloud the last paragraph of the passage on p. 11, replacing the words *beneficial, eliminate,* and *curbing* with everyday words, such as *helpful, stop eating,* and *reducing.*

Answers
1. D; DOK Level: 2; **2.** B; DOK Level: 2; **3.** C; DOK Level: 2; **4.** A; DOK Level: 2; **5.** A; DOK Level: 1

WORKBOOK *pp. 18–21*

❶ Review the Skill

SuperSkill Review Review the difference between explicit and implicit causes. Then provide learners with an implicit cause statement, and ask them to state the cause explicitly. For example,
- **Implied:** *Barack Obama received the most votes for president in many cities and urban areas. Cities and urban areas tend to be more liberal than rural areas.*
- **Explicit:** *Barack Obama received more votes in cities and urban areas because he was the Democratic candidate and supported more liberal policies.*

❷ Refine the Skill

Link to Past Skills Have learners review the skill *Determine Sequence* from Unit 1, Lesson 3. Explain that a cause must always happen before its effect can occur. Learners can use this skill to determine what was happening before classrooms began "going green."

❸ Master the Skill

Spotlighted Item Type Mention that diseases are often used as examples of causes and effects because they always have one or more causes and one or more effects. Have learners work in pairs to discuss and decide on the appropriate answers to complete the organizer on p. 20.

➤ LifeLink

Remind learners that they often identify causes and effects in their daily lives. Have learners work in pairs to discuss the behavior of friends, family members, or people at work. Help learners get started by having them complete one of these sentence stems:
- *I knew she was angry because* _____.
- *He has been happy lately because* _____.
- *My boss's attitude is causing others to* _____.

Answers
1. C; DOK Level: 1; **2.** B; DOK Level: 1; **3.** A; DOK Level: 2; **4.** C; DOK Level: 1; **5.** B; DOK Level: 3; **6.** heat edema, malfunctioning organs, brain damage; DOK Level:1; **7.** B; DOK Level: 1; **8.** D; DOK Level: 2; **9.** C; DOK Level: 1; **10.** B; DOK Level: 1; 11. A; DOK Level: 3

Compare and Contrast

READING ASSESSMENT TARGETS: R.2.1, R.2.2, R.2.3, R.2.4, R.2.5, R.2.7, R.2.8, R.3.2, R.3.3, R.3.4, R.3.5, R.5.1, R.5.2, R.5.3

LANGUAGE ARTS

STUDENT BOOK pp. 12–13

➤ Preview the Skill

Ask learners to think of two television programs or movies. Lead them to discuss the two together, noting ways in which they are both similar and different. For example,

- *Both* SportsCenter *and* Baseball Tonight *are popular television programs that air on ESPN.* SportsCenter *shows highlights from all sports, but* Baseball Tonight *shows only major league baseball highlights.*
- *Both* Star Wars *and* Star Trek *are popular science-fiction movies; however,* Star Wars *is set in the past, and* Star Trek *is set in the future.*

❶ Learn the Skill

Give Examples Provide learners with two organizations' descriptions of similar jobs. Discuss as a class how the jobs appear both similar and different.

❷ Practice the Skill

Use Graphic Organizers To help learners answer question 1, have them complete a Venn diagram to compare and contrast Generals Lee and Sherman.

General Lee
- Fought for the South
- Forbade looting and needless destruction
- Sought to engage in combat

Both
- High-ranking leaders
- Fought on enemy soil
- Wanted to win the war

General Sherman
- Fought for the North
- Allowed looting and burning
- Aimed to cut off supplies to the South
- Sought to obliterate southerners' will to wage war

❸ Apply the Skill

Decoding To help learners answer question 3, work with them to decode unfamiliar words in paragraph 2; for example, *genetic* means "relating to genes," *uniformity* means "sameness," and *consistent* means "steady" or "constant."

Answers
1. D; DOK Level: 2; **2.** A; DOK Level: 2; **3.** D; DOK Level: 2; **4.** A; DOK Level: 2; **5.** C; DOK Level: 2

WORKBOOK pp. 22–25

❶ Review the Skill

SuperSkill Review Ask learners to identify informal words and phrases that they would use with their friends to compare and contrast items. Comparing phrases might include *exactly the same, almost like twins,* or *hardly any difference.* Contrasting phrases might include *nothing alike* or *totally different.* Work with learners to identify other phrases that they use in everyday speech to compare and contrast.

❷ Refine the Skill

Skim and Scan Have learners skim and scan the passage on p. 22, underlining in each paragraph the statements that explain Lincoln's plan and those that explain the Radical Republicans' plan. Underlining this way should help learners make the contrast between the plans and thus answer question 1 correctly.

❸ Master the Skill

Spotlighted Item Type To help learners answer question 7, review the sections of a Venn diagram. Have student pairs work together to complete the diagram, and ask partners to explain to each other why they chose the items that belong in the overlapping section. As an extension of this activity, suggest that learners reread the passage to find more items that belong in the overlapping section (*baked goods, pie crusts, cookies, margarine, shortening*) and to explain why they belong there.

➤ Cross-Curricular Connection

To familiarize learners with comparing and contrasting in other subject areas, refer them to Unit 1, Lesson 9, in the Science book for more practice, particularly with Venn diagrams, and to applicable lessons in the Social Studies book.

Answers
1. B; DOK Level: 2; **2.** A; DOK Level: 2; **3.** B; DOK Level: 2; **4.** D; DOK Level: 2; **5.** A; DOK Level: 1; **6.** B; DOK Level: 2; **7. Good Fats:** sunflower seeds, nuts, trout; **Bad Fats:** meat, butter, cheese; **May Be Good or Bad:** oil, crackers; DOK Level: 2; **8.** C; DOK Level: 2; **9.** B; DOK Level: 2; **10.** D; DOK Level: 3; **11.** D; DOK Level: 3; **12.** B; DOK Level: 2

Determine Author's Point of View

READING ASSESSMENT TARGETS: R.2.3, R.2.7, R.3.4, R.3.5, R.4.1/L.4.1, R.4.3/L.4.3, R.5.1, R.5.2, R.6.1, R.6.2, R.6.4

LANGUAGE ARTS

STUDENT BOOK pp. 14–15

▶ Preview the Skill

Ask learners to recall a recent sporting event. Have them first relate the outcome of the game from the perspective of the winning team or individual. Then challenge them to tell the same story from the perspective of the losing team or individual. This practice will help illustrate differences in point of view.

❶ Learn the Skill

Give Examples Explain how point of view can influence the way an author forms an argument. Provide or refer learners to letters to the editor or editorials that support a particular issue. Ask learners to identify the opinions that shape each writer's decision to support the issue.

❷ Practice the Skill

Link to Past Skills Have learners review the skill *Determine Main Idea and Details* from Unit 1, Lesson 1. Explain that identifying the main idea is useful in determining an author's point of view. Learners can use this information to help them choose the correct answer to question 1.

❸ Apply the Skill

Use Graphic Organizers Use this graphic organizer to help learners identify different phrases in the passage that indicate the opinion of the author. Learners can use this information to help them answer question 4 correctly.

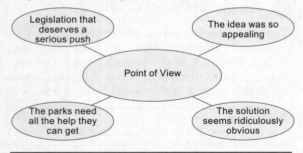

Answers
1. D; DOK Level: 2; **2.** A; DOK Level: 2; **3.** B; DOK Level: 2; **4.** B; DOK Level: 2; **5.** C; DOK Level: 3

WORKBOOK pp. 26–29

❶ Review the Skill

SuperSkill Review Review the *Using Logic* note on p. 26, and discuss the differences between logical and emotional arguments. Point out that some authors base their perspective on facts and data but that others base theirs on emotions. For example, one writer could cite city budget constraints to oppose building a new stadium for the football team. Another writer could argue that a new stadium is necessary to show that the city values the team.

❷ Refine the Skill

Skim and Scan Ask learners to skim and scan the passage on p. 26. Tell them to look for descriptive words and phrases that reveal what the author thinks about federal workers. Explain that emotionally charged phrases, such as "just college dropouts" and "hardly paper-pushing," may indicate an author's point of view. Learners can use this information to find the correct answer to question 1.

❸ Master the Skill

Spotlighted Item Type Have learners work in pairs to read the passage on p. 27 and to look for statements that express what the author supports and opposes. Ask learners to highlight or underline these statements and then match them with the answer choices in question 3.

▶ Enrich and Extend

Often a speaker's point of view can be identified by his or her interests or from other background details. Ask learners to describe their passion for a particular sport, game, or political issue. Then have other learners take the opposite view.

Answers
1. A; DOK Level: 2; **2.** C; DOK Level: 2; **3. Supports** freedom of speech, traditional American ideals, thoughtful political debate; **Opposes** special treatment for political leaders, thought control, making unsupported claims; DOK Level: 2; **4.** A; DOK Level: 2; **5.** C; DOK Level: 2; **6.** B; DOK Level: 2; **7.** D; DOK Level: 2; **8.** C; DOK Level: 2; **9.** B; DOK Level: 2; **10.** D; DOK Level: 2; **11.** A; DOK Level: 2

Make Inferences

READING ASSESSMENT TARGETS: R.2.3, R.2.4, R.2.5, R.3.5, R.4.1/L.4.1, R.4.3,/L.4.3, R.5.1, R.5.4, R.6.1, R.6.3, R.6.4

STUDENT BOOK *pp. 16–17*

➤ Preview the Skill

Describe this scene to learners: *You walk into the house and see an empty bag of chips on the counter and your roommate's backpack on the kitchen table.* Ask learners to use this evidence to make an educated guess about the roommate's activities. For example, *From the evidence I found in the house, I think my roommate came home from class and ate a bag of chips.*

❶ Learn the Skill

Give Examples Point out examples of how learners use clues and incomplete information to make inferences in their daily lives. For instance, if learners see a long line of people at a restaurant, they might infer that the restaurant is popular and serves good food. Ask learners for other possible inferences based on the long line; for example, the restaurant might be featuring special prices or popular entertainment.

❷ Practice the Skill

Skim and Scan To help learners answer question 1, have them skim and scan the passage and list words and phrases that explain how the author's processing of information has changed since the Internet became available.

❸ Apply the Skill

Decoding When reading humorous texts, learners should understand when words are being used for a particular effect. For example, the word *agoraphobia* in the passage means "intense fear of open spaces." However, the author uses this word ironically to support her observation that people stay inside too much. Learners can use this information to help them answer question 4 correctly.

Answers
1. A; DOK Level: 2; **2.** lack purpose and motivation, watch too much television, have few interests; DOK Level: 2; **3.** D; DOK Level: 2; **4.** A; DOK Level: 2

WORKBOOK *pp. 30–33*

❶ Review the Skill

Give Examples Using the *Test-Taking Tips* note on p. 30, discuss with learners how they are often required to make inferences. For example, if a baby is crying, learners can make the inference that the baby needs to be fed or changed or is feeling discomfort or pain. If a cat hisses upon a person's approach, learners can infer that the cat does not want to be touched.

❷ Refine the Skill

Link to Past Skills Review the skill *Compare and Contrast* from Unit 1, Lesson 6. Have learners use the skill to contrast old and new media as a result of the Internet's influence, as discussed in the passage on p. 30, and to answer question 2 correctly.

❸ Master the Skill

Use Graphic Organizers Use this graphic organizer to help learners make an inference to answer question 14 correctly.

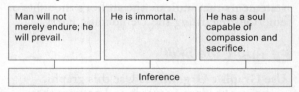

Man will not merely endure; he will prevail.	He is immortal.	He has a soul capable of compassion and sacrifice.

Inference

➤ LifeLink

Have learners make inferences about different everyday situations, such as these:
- *Your girlfriend persuades you to go to a movie, and you aren't sure what the movie will be about. During the previews, you notice that four of the five trailers show romantic comedies.*
- *When you leave for work, the house is clean, and no one is home except your dog. When you return from work, the garbage can is on its side, and trash is scattered over the kitchen floor.*

Answers
1. D; DOK Level: 2; **2.** B; DOK Level: 2; **3.** D; DOK Level: 2; **4.** B; DOK Level: 2; **5.** C; DOK Level: 3; **6.** C; DOK Level: 3; **7.** D; DOK Level: 2; **8.** B; DOK Level: 2; **9.** A; DOK Level: 2; **10.** B; DOK Level: 2; **11.** A; DOK Level: 2; **12.** D; DOK Level: 2; **13.** C; DOK Level: 2; **14.** A; DOK Level: 2; **15.** B; DOK Level: 2

Analyze Style and Tone

READING ASSESSMENT TARGETS: R.3.4, R.4.1/L.4.1, R.4.2/L.4.2, R.4.3/L.4.3, R.5.1, R.5.2, R.5.4, R.6.1, R.6.4

LANGUAGE ARTS

STUDENT BOOK pp. 18–19

➤ Preview the Skill

Have learners describe a comedy act or television show that they have seen recently. Ask, *"What made the show funny?"* Point out different delivery methods, such as a stand-up act or a television comedy series. Have learners share examples of word choice, tone of voice, or body language that can help convey a performer's humorous tone.

❶ Learn the Skill

Give Examples Review the definitions of style and tone. Then help learners recognize different styles and tones used in popular music lyrics. For example, style may be described as formal, informal, repetitious, rhyming, comedic, hip-hop, or pop. Tone may be described as upbeat, mellow, soulful, sad, ironic, or angry.

❷ Practice the Skill

Skim and Scan Ask learners to read the *Using Logic* note on p. 18. To help learners determine the tone of the passage, have them skim and scan for statements that indicate the author's thoughts or emotions regarding the Democratic Party.

❸ Apply the Skill

Use Graphic Organizers Use this graphic organizer to identify words and phrases that contribute to the tone of the passage on p. 19.

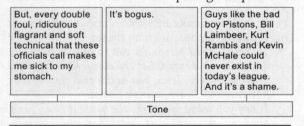

But, every double foul, ridiculous flagrant and soft technical that these officials call makes me sick to my stomach.	It's bogus.	Guys like the bad boy Pistons, Bill Laimbeer, Kurt Rambis and Kevin McHale could never exist in today's league. And it's a shame.
	Tone	

Answers
1. D; DOK Level: 2; **2.** C; DOK Level: 2; **3.** A; DOK Level: 2; **4.** B; DOK Level: 2; **5.** D; DOK Level: 2

WORKBOOK pp. 34–37

❶ Review the Skill

Give Examples Remind learners that style and tone are closely related. Then ask learners to suggest the style and tone most appropriate for various situations, such as a job interview or a first date. For example, the style of an interview may be formal or low-key, and the tone may be positive or neutral.

❷ Refine the Skill

Link to Past Skills Have learners review the skill *Determine Author's Point of View* from Unit 1, Lesson 7, to identify the perspective of the passage on p. 34. Advise learners that recognizing the author's point of view will help them identify the passage's tone and style and thus answer questions 1 and 2 correctly.

❸ Master the Skill

Spotlighted Item Type Organize students in pairs to find the words that contribute most to the tone of the passage at the top of p. 36. Ask students first to discuss what the author's attitude toward personality testing seems to be and then to decide which answer choices best reflect that attitude or tone. Tell students to eliminate the answer choice that has the least impact on the tone of the passage.

➤ Language Analysis

Organize learners into pairs, and have them read through the passages on p. 35, at the bottom of p. 36, and on p. 37. Ask them to underline all words and phrases that express the authors' tone or attitude. After they have finished reading, have partners share their reasons for choosing the words they did. Then have learners replace the words or expressions with others and discuss how the replacements affect the tone.

Answers
1. C; DOK Level: 2; **2.** A; DOK Level: 2; **3.** B; DOK Level: 2; **4.** B; DOK Level: 2; **5.** D; DOK Level: 3; **6.** A; DOK Level: 2; **7.** exhaustive, artsy, devise; DOK Level: 2; **8.** B; DOK Level: 2; **9.** A; DOK Level: 3; **10.** C; DOK Level: 2; **11.** D; DOK Level: 2; **12.** B; DOK Level: 2; **13.** B; DOK Level: 3

Draw Conclusions

READING ASSESSMENT TARGETS: R.2.1, R.2.4, R.2.5, R.2.8, R.3.2, R.3.3, R.3.4, R.3.5, R.4.3/L.4.3, R.5.1, R.5.2, R.5.4, R.6.3

STUDENT BOOK pp. 20–21

▶ Preview the Skill

Explain to learners that they draw conclusions on the basis of what they observe or hear. Ask a volunteer to describe a recent event, such as a date, to the rest of the class. Have learners draw conclusions based on the story. For example, the volunteer may say, *"I went out last Friday night with someone I met at a party. I had a great time, and we had a lot in common, like watching baseball, taking photographs, and cooking Asian dishes."* Another learner could draw the conclusion (in this case a prediction) that the two will go out again and do something involving their similar interests.

❶ Learn the Skill

Give Examples Remind learners that conclusions are based on several educated guesses, or inferences, which, in turn, are based on facts and evidence. Ask learners to name some examples of evidence that would lead to this conclusion: *Maintaining your car saves money on repairs.* A fact that supports this statement is *Failing to change your car's oil regularly may lead to engine failure.*

❷ Practice the Skill

Decoding Tell learners that although there may appear to be more than one correct response to question 1, the question is actually asking them to draw a conclusion, not to identify a fact from the passage. Have learners decode the answer choices carefully to identify and eliminate answers that contain facts but no conclusions.

❸ Apply the Skill

Use Graphic Organizers Use this graphic organizer to help learners answer question 2.

Boys perform better than girls on standardized tests.	Addressing gender bias in co-ed schools hasn't been effective.	Girls get more encouragement in all-girl math classes.
Conclusion		

Answers

1. A; DOK Level: 2; **2.** C; DOK Level: 2; **3.** B; DOK Level: 2; **4.** B: DOK Level: 2; **5.** A; DOK Level: 2

WORKBOOK pp. 38–41

❶ Review the Skill

Give Examples Discuss how learners draw conclusions when they analyze facts about a situation. Present this scenario, or invent your own, and have students draw conclusions based on the facts:
- **Fact 1:** *A worker with a GED® credential earns more money than a worker without one.*
- **Fact 2:** *Most employers require employees to have a GED® credential or a high school diploma.*
- **Conclusion:** *I have a better chance of getting a well-paying job if I have a GED® credential.*

❷ Refine the Skill

Link to Past Skills Have learners review the skill *Identify Cause and Effect* from Unit 1, Lesson 5, to help them find the correct answer to question 1.

❸ Master the Skill

Spotlighted Item Type Have student pairs complete the chart on p. 39. Explain that they first must consider the pros and cons of telecommuting before drawing conclusions about the information in the passage. Remind learners not to include in the chart stated facts from the article

▶ Enrich and Extend

Have learners read the passage on p. 41. Point out that the excerpt is from the book *Up From Slavery.* Ask learners to draw conclusions, on the basis of the title and information in the excerpt, about the author's background and the times during which he lived.

Answers

1. B; DOK Level: 2; **2.** D; DOK Level: 2; **3. Reasons to Encourage Telecommuting**: People have co-workers all around the world, so being required to go to an office does not make sense. New technologies make telecommuting easier and more effective. **Reasons to Restrict Telecommuting**: It is difficult to manage employees when they are not in the office. Employees who telecommute are less obligated to their companies. DOK Level: 2; **4.** D; DOK Level: 2; **5.** C; DOK Level: 2; **6.** C; DOK Level: 2; **7.** A; DOK Level: 2; **8.** A; DOK Level: 3; **9.** C; DOK Level: 2; **10.** D; DOK Level: 2; **11.** B; DOK Level: 2

Make Generalizations

READING ASSESSMENT TARGETS: R.2.1, R.2.4, R.2.5, R.2.7, R.2.8, R.3.5, R.4.3/L.4.3, R.5.2, R.8.3

LANGUAGE ARTS

STUDENT BOOK *pp. 22–23*

▶ Preview the Skill

Ask learners to make a statement about a recent event by using the words *all, everyone, few, none,* or *usually.* For example,
- *Everyone was at Kevin's birthday party on Friday night.*
- *None of my friends wanted to see the new Johnny Depp movie.*

Explain that these statements are examples of generalizations.

❶ Learn the Skill

Give Examples Review with learners the definition of *generalization.* Then ask them to make broad statements about different topics, such as "people who love baseball" or "restaurants that serve buffalo wings." Learners might say *People who love baseball usually watch the World Series* or *Restaurants that serve buffalo wings are always crowded during football games.*

❷ Practice the Skill

Use Graphic Organizers Use this graphic organizer to help learners answer question 1. Remind them that not all generalizations are valid.

As the economy struggles, it becomes more difficult for young people to gain their independence.	Financial difficulties during a recession make living alone a challenge.	With few job openings and more competition for those jobs, recent graduates have a harder time finding meaningful employment.
	Generalization	

❸ Apply the Skill

Link to Past Skills Have learners review the skill *Compare and Contrast* from Unit 1, Lesson 6, to help them answer questions 3 and 5 correctly. Both questions require that learners make a generalization based on a comparison and contrast between food stores in different areas.

Answers
1. D; DOK Level: 2; **2.** B; DOK Level: 1; **3.** A; DOK Level: 2; **4.** A; DOK Level: 2; **5.** D; DOK Level: 3

WORKBOOK *pp. 42–45*

❶ Review the Skill

SuperSkill Review Remind learners that generalizations may be valid or invalid. Then have them make valid or invalid generalizations about the GED® Test. For example,
- *Everyone who takes a GED® prep course passes the GED® Test.*
- *People who enroll in a GED® prep course usually get better results on the GED® Test than people who do not take a prep course.*

❷ Refine the Skill

Skim and Scan Ask learners to skim and scan the passage on p. 42 and list the details that support the main idea of the passage. Advise learners to use these details to arrive at a logical generalization and then answer question 1.

❸ Master the Skill

Link to Past Skills Have learners review the skill *Categorize* from Unit 1, Lesson 4, to identify stereotypes (or unsupported generalizations) about men and women found in the passage on p. 44. Point out that identifying which stereotypes apply to men can help learners answer question 8.

▶ LifeLink

Ask learners to list generalizations about something that they like, dislike, or do frequently. Then have class members name a specific example that falls under the generalization. For example, for the generalization, *"I hate all foods with melted cheese,"* someone could state, *"You wouldn't like anything at Taco Haven."* Encourage learners to discuss whether the generalizations are valid or invalid.

Answers
1. C; DOK Level: 2; **2.** A; DOK Level: 3; **3.** A; DOK Level: 2; **4.** C; DOK Level: 2; **5.** D; DOK Level: 3; **6.** B; DOK Level: 2; **7.** B; DOK Level: 2; **8.** D; DOK Level: 2; **9.** C; DOK Level: 2; **10.** B; DOK Level: 2; **11. Preschool Years:** This group learns a great deal from exposure to media. **The Twelve Years of Formal Education:** Students are labeled by test scores, which determine their formal education. **College:** Students impress teachers to move to the next level of education. **Graduate School:** Students must be shrewd and do what it takes to achieve more than their classmates. DOK Level: 2

Synthesize Information

READING ASSESSMENT TARGETS: R.2.7, R.2.8, R.3.4, R.3.5, R.4.3/L.4.3, R.6.1, R.9.1/R.7.1, R.9.2

STUDENT BOOK pp. 24–25

➤ Preview the Skill

Ask learners to recall an incident in which they used two or more sources to learn or confirm something. For example, a learner might have combined two recipes to make a tastier pizza. Another might have used several maps to determine the best driving directions. Have learners make a generalization about what they gleaned from each source. Then have them combine this information into one statement about what they learned overall. This practice illustrates how to synthesize information.

❶ Learn the Skill

Give Examples Point out examples of how learners synthesize information in daily life. For example, they may learn from the news that their area is under a flood watch and learn from the Internet that the road they take to work is closed. They may use both sources to conclude that this road is closed because of flooding and that they must take another route.

❷ Practice the Skill

Skim and Scan To help learners answer question 1, have them skim and scan both passages on p. 24 and find the author's generalizations. Have learners identify the main idea about the federal government and its employees.

❸ Apply the Skill

Spotlighted Item Type Have learners work in pairs to complete the chart on p, 25. Suggest that they read the question and answer choices before reading the passages. Then, as they read, they can underline or highlight information to help them choose the correct answers. Remind learners that answers must come from at least two of the passages and should not be stated directly in any.

Answers
1. C; DOK Level: 3; **2.** Although the use of renewable energy sources is expected to increase, such energy sources have drawbacks and detractors. The lack of significant growth in hydropower may be reversed. More than half of the electricity generated in the United States from renewable energy sources comes from hydropower. DOK Level: 3

WORKBOOK pp. 46–49

❶ Review the Skill

Give Examples Remind learners that when they synthesize information, they look for the most important ideas from one or more sources to form new, or composite, ideas. For example, students may read two texts about vaccinations. One text may emphasize the necessity and safety, whereas the other text may emphasize incidents in which vaccines caused harm. Learners could then conclude that vaccines are helpful for most people in preventing disease but may not be worth the risk for others.

❷ Refine the Skill

Link to Past Skills Review the skill *Compare and Contrast* from Unit 1, Lesson 6. Have learners use this skill to address the similar message in both the Lincoln and the Johnson speeches. Explain that both speakers describe the issue of civil rights as incomplete in the United States. Then illustrate how a bridge stretching halfway across the river is an unfinished project.

❸ Master the Skill

Decoding When reading scientific texts, learners may encounter unfamiliar words. Have learners work in pairs to decode the meaning of the terms *randomization* and *double-blind*. Point out that the passage contains clues to the meanings of these terms. Ask learners to try to find the clues and define the terms.

➤ LifeLink

Ask learners to discuss situations in which they would need to synthesize information. For example, learners might suggest using the skill to choose a product or prepare for an event. Then have learners explain why synthesizing information is useful when they are looking for information or making a decision.

Answers
1. B; DOK Level: 3; **2.** D; DOK Level: 3; **3.** A; DOK Level: 3; **4.** C; DOK Level: 3; **5.** B; DOK Level: 3; **6.** B; DOK Level: 2; **7.** A; DOK Level: 3; **8.** C; DOK Level: 3; **9.** D; DOK Level: 2; **10.** B; DOK Level: 2; **11.** C; DOK Level: 3; **12.** B; DOK Level: 2

Use Context Clues

READING ASSESSMENT TARGETS: R.4.1/L.4.1, R.4.2/L.4.2, R.4.3/L.4.3

LANGUAGE ARTS

▶ STUDENT BOOK *pp. 26–27*

▶ Preview the Skill

Present learners with a sentence containing an unfamiliar word, such as *The dog looked menacing.* Then add context clues to the sentence: *The dog looked menacing, as if he were ready to attack.* Ask learners to use the clue to decode *menacing.* Explain that because learners know that the dog is ready to attack, they can infer that *menacing* means "threatening" or "frightening."

❶ Learn the Skill

Give Examples Explain how details surrounding an unknown word can help learners determine the meaning of that word. Then direct learners' attention to the passages on pp. 26 and 27. Have learners identify unfamiliar words and use context clues to replace them with more familiar ones; consider using *interminable* (p. 26), *petrified* (p. 27), and *thronged* (p. 27).

❷ Practice the Skill

Skim and Scan Ask learners to skim and scan the passage on p. 26 to identify words and phrases that describe Simon Wheeler's storytelling technique. Examples include "never changed his voice" and "gentle-flowing key." Learners can use this strategy to determine the meaning of the word *monotonous* in question 1.

❸ Apply the Skill

Spotlighted Item Type Explain that fill-in-the-blank questions require test takers to supply their own answers. Demonstrate the types of answers that may be appropriate, focusing on conciseness. Generally, for definitions, a synonym may be sufficient or required. If no synonym comes to mind, learners can write a brief definition. Other questions, such as question 4 on p. 27, may ask for specific information to show that learners understand the word and can supply more than a mere definition.

Answers
1. C; DOK Level: 2; **2.** small village or small town; DOK Level: 2; **3.** the river can be crossed; DOK Level 2; **4.** nothing; it would be empty; DOK Level 2; **5.** moved, walked, or stepped; DOK Level: 2

▶ WORKBOOK *pp. 50–53*

❶ Review the Skill

SuperSkill Review Create a nonsense word, use it in a sentence or scenario, and ask learners to define it by examining context clues. For example: *I was lucky to have had my inflatador with me yesterday when my tire went flat. It pumped up my tire in minutes, and its computer indicated the closest repair shop.*

❷ Refine the Skill

Link to Past Skills Have learners review the skill *Make Inferences* from Unit 1, Lesson 8, to help them infer the meaning of *oases* and answer question 2 correctly.

❸ Master the Skill

Spotlighted Item Type From the passages on pp. 50–53, pull sentences that contain unfamiliar words or homophones, such as these: "**stealing** from a heated plain into some cool, deep glen" (p. 50); "you **adroitly** turn a mystic corner" (p. 50); and "His figure soon **emerged** into view, and showed itself" (p. 52). Have partners determine the meanings of these words and supply possible fill-in-the-blank (FIB) responses. Then select three or four other words from these passages that show a similar range of answer types—from synonyms, to phrases, to applications—and practice answering a fill-in-the-blank question for each. You may supply the questions or have learners suggest their own.

Answers
1. A; DOK Level: 2; **2.** C; DOK Level: 3; **3.** This is the best time for observing nature, just as the best or most popular television shows are those that air during "prime time." DOK Level: 2; **4.** a line, or row; DOK Level: 2; **5.** is harsh or is disturbing to the ear or lacks harmony; DOK Level: 2; **6.** Using the word *government* helps neutralize, or soften, the connotation so that it is less negative. DOK Level: 2; **7.** The connotation of sickliness would not be present or The word *slender* would not have the connotation of extreme thinness or thinness bordering on starvation. DOK Level: 2; **8.** middle-aged; DOK Level: 2; **9.** having more health, beauty, and energy than needed; DOK Level: 2; **10.** has become sick or diseased; DOK Level: 2; **11.** the equivalent of Mr. DOK Level: 1; **12.** Zelig is not entirely whole or not mentally stable or not all there. DOK Level: 2; **13.** very different or seemingly from another planet; DOK Level: 2; **14.** messy or unkempt; DOK Level: 2

READING ASSESSMENT TARGETS: R.2.1, R.2.2, R.2.5, R.2.7, R.2.8, R.3.2, R.3.3, R.3.4, R.3.5, R.4.3/L.4.3, R.5.1, R.5.3

STUDENT BOOK pp. 28–29

➤ Preview the Skill

Explain that before learners read about or experience a real situation, they may be aware of certain information. For example, they might know they feel sick with the flu and spent time recently with a friend who had the flu. Therefore, the cause of their illness seems logical. In contrast, when reading fiction, learners must examine the text to determine causes and effects, basing their ideas only on material provided by the author.

❶ Learn the Skill

Give Examples Ask learners to think of all they know about fictional characters. Suggest simple, well-known characters, like Cinderella or Shrek, or complex characters, like Huckleberry Finn. Have learners give examples of the characters' actions and what resulted.

❷ Practice the Skill

Use Graphic Organizers Use this graphic organizer to establish the sequence of the excerpt on p. 28. Learners can use the sequence to determine why John shuts the window. Explain the gap between 3 and 4, saying that although the result follows the action, John does not close the window specifically because of the narrator's fear.

1	The characters move into an empty house.
2	The narrator states that the house is strange.
3	The narrator tells John she is afraid of the house.
4	John closes a window.

❸ Apply the Skill

Link to Past Skills To help learners answer question 6, have them review the skills *Identifying Cause and Effect* from Unit 1, Lesson 5, and *Drawing Conclusions* from Unit 1, Lesson 10. Tell learners that they have to draw several inferences based on cause-and-effect relationships to reach the most logical conclusion about why Aunt Georgiana goes to bed early.

Answers
1. B; DOK Level: 2; **2.** B; DOK Level: 2; **3.** B DOK Level: 2; **4.** C; DOK Level: 2; **5.** A; DOK Level: 2; **6.** D; DOK Level: 2

WORKBOOK pp. 54–57

❶ Review the Skill

SuperSkill Review Point out that a single cause can lead to a ripple or domino of cascading effects. Provide an example like the one below, and discuss with learners the causes and resulting effects.
- *In a NASCAR race, Jimmy Johnson blew out a tire on the last lap.*
- *As a result, Johnson lost control and crashed into his teammate, Dale Earnhardt, Jr.*
- *Neither driver finished the race, and Earnhardt, Jr., fell out of the top ten in the standings.*

❷ Refine the Skill

Skim and Scan To help learners answer question 1 correctly, have them skim and scan the passage on p. 54 and identify phrases that indicate cause and effect.

❸ Master the Skill

Link to Past Skills Have learners review the skill *Draw Conclusions* from Unit 1, Lesson 10. Explain that to answer question 8, they must make several inferences (or educated guesses) to predict the results of Sylvia's keeping the location of the white heron a secret.

➤ Cross-Curricular Connection

Social Studies Review with learners the lessons in the social studies texts that address the American Revolution. Have learners point out the causes of the war and what happened as a result of it.

Answers
1. C; DOK Level: 2; **2.** B; DOK Level: 2; **3. First box:** Trains have been stalled in the snow. **Second box:** The narrator arrives an hour early at the station. **Third box:** The narrator prepares for extreme conditions. DOK Level: 2; **4.** C; DOK Level: 2; **5.** D; DOK Level: 2; **6.** B; DOK Level: 2; **7.** D; DOK Level: 2; **8.** C; DOK Level: 3; **9.** B; DOK Level: 2; **10.** D; DOK Level: 2; **11.** C; DOK Level: 2; **12.** A; DOK Level: 3; **13.** B; DOK Level: 3

Compare and Contrast in Fiction

READING ASSESSMENT TARGETS: R.2.1, R.2.2, R.2.5, R.2.6, R.2.7, R.2.8, R.3.2, R.3.3, R.3.4, R.3.5, R.4.3/L.4.3, R.5.1, R.5.3, R.6.1

LANGUAGE ARTS

STUDENT BOOK pp. 30–31

▶ Preview the Skill

In nonfiction texts, authors compare and contrast objects or ideas to make a point. In fiction texts, authors compare and contrast people, places, or conflicts to tell a story. Present learners with descriptions of two fictional places or events, and have them list similarities and differences. Ask learners to determine whether the results reflect more similarities or differences.

❶ Learn the Skill

Use Graphic Organizers Ask learners to name two favorite fictional characters from literature, television, or movies. Tell them to list details about the two, such as their appearance, personality, or talents. For example, *Both Leonard and Sheldon from* The Big Bang Theory *are considered "nerds," have high IQs, and are physicists with PhDs. Leonard is outgoing and relaxed, but Sheldon is cold and aloof and stresses over minor details.* Have learners chart this information in a Venn diagram like the one below to determine whether the characters show more similarities or differences.

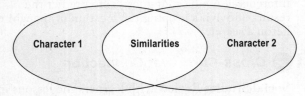

❷ Practice the Skill

Skim and Scan Have learners skim and scan the passage on p. 30 for phrases and sentences that contrast Susan and Emily. This information will help learners answer question 1 correctly.

❸ Apply the Skill

Spotlighted Item Type Explain that the best FIB responses are short and straightforward. For example, the best answer to question 2 is simply *country music.*

Answers
1. D; DOK Level: 1; **2.** country music; DOK Level: 2; **3.** fall, sharp fall, or crash; DOK Level: 3; **4.** A; DOK Level: 2; **5.** C; DOK Level: 2

WORKBOOK pp. 58–61

❶ Review the Skill

SuperSkill Review Referring to the *Making Assumptions* note on p. 58, mention that comparing and contrasting highlights qualities the author thinks are important. Explain that in the passage on this page the narrator uses comparison and contrast to highlight her daughter's problems, which may be a source of conflict in the story.

❷ Refine the Skill

Link to Past Skills Have learners review the skill *Identify Cause and Effect in Fiction* from Unit 1, Lesson 14. Continuing with the *SuperSkill Review* activity, explain that the narrator of the passage on p. 58 compares and contrasts her daughter with other children to explain why she struggles socially and academically. To answer question 2, learners can identify cause-and-effect to understand that the daughter's differences have caused her to be viewed unfavorably.

❸ Master the Skill

Decoding To help learners answer questions 4–7, read the passage together and list similarities and differences between the Burnells and Kelveys. Discuss what the examples reveal about the attitudes of the time in which the story is set.

▶ Enrich and Extend

Ask learners to think of two characters from a recent television show or movie and to list details about each character (appearance, actions, personality traits, and so on). Then have learners use these details to make deeper comparisons and contrasts. For example, both characters have similar goals, but their motivations are different. Ask learners to explain how these similarities and differences drive the plot.

Answers
1. D; DOK Level: 2; **2.** B; DOK Level: 2; **3.** A; DOK Level: 2; **4.** A; DOK Level: 2; **5.** C; DOK Level: 3; **6.** B; DOK Level: 2; **7.** D; DOK Level: 2; **8.** C; DOK Level: 2; **9.** D; DOK Level: 2; **10.** D; DOK Level: 2; **11.** B; DOK Level: 2; **12.** B; DOK Level: 3; **13.** A; DOK Level: 2; **14.** C; DOK Level: 2; **15.** B; DOK Level: 2; **16.** D; DOK Level: 3

Analyze Plot Elements

READING ASSESSMENT TARGETS: R.2.1, R.2.7, R.2.8, R.3.2, R.3.3, R.3.4, R.3.5, R.5.1, R.5.4, R.6.1

STUDENT BOOK pp. 32–33

▶ Preview the Skill

Point out that every good story has a problem, or *complication*, that characters must confront. For example, Katniss Everdeen must survive the Hunger Games, Luke Skywalker must defeat Darth Vader, and Superman must stop Lex Luther from killing. If a character overcomes the complication successfully, the *resolution*, or ending, is usually a happy one. If a character cannot overcome the problem, then the ending is probably unhappy.

❶ Learn the Skill

Give Examples Have students identify plot elements in a recent event in their own lives, such as a date, a party, or another function. For example,
- **Exposition:** *I threw a birthday party for one of my friends on Saturday night.*
- **Complication:** *Everyone was having a great time until my friend's ex-girlfriend showed up uninvited.*
- **Climax:** *The two began arguing while everyone at the party watched.*
- **Resolution:** *Finally, the ex-girlfriend left, and we continued with the party.*

❷ Practice the Skill

Link to Past Skills Review the skill *Summarize* from Unit 1, Lesson 2. Point out that identifying the most important elements of a passage can help learners focus on the passage's conflict. Suggest they use this strategy to answer question 1.

❸ Apply the Skill

Decoding Have learners read the passage on p. 33 and look for context clues to determine what Goodman Parker means when he says that he doesn't have a "word of comfort" for Mary. Learners may note that Mary is already "in trouble" or that Margaret screams at Goodman Parker. This information could indicate that Mary has already received bad news. This strategy should help learners answer questions 3 and 5.

Answers
1. B; DOK Level: 2; **2.** C; DOK Level: 2; **3.** A; DOK Level: 2;
4. D; DOK Level: 3; **5.** B; DOK Level: 2

WORKBOOK pp. 62–65

❶ Review the Skill

SuperSkill Review Provide learners with a model for identifying plot elements, with headings labeled *Somebody, Wanted, But,* and *So.* Point out that these categories can help learners identify a story's exposition, complication(s), climax, and resolution.

❷ Refine the Skill

Skim and Scan Ask learners to skim and scan the passage on p. 62, looking for phrases and sentences that describe heightened emotions. Explain that the characters' emotions give clues to a story's complications, or conflicts. These details will help learners answer questions 1 and 2 correctly.

❸ Master the Skill

Spotlighted Item Type To help learners answer questions 11–14, have them work in pairs to discuss the plot elements of the story on p. 65. Mention that the answers to questions 11–13 should be one word or short phrases; however, the answer to question 14 requires a longer statement.

▶ Language Analysis

List and explain some common terms that authors use to signal plot elements.
- A classic **exposition** is *once upon a time.*
- **Complications** often begin with words such as *however, the problem was,* or *despite.*
- Words such as *suddenly, at last,* or *just in time* often signal the **climax**.
- A familiar **resolution** is *happily ever after.*
Ask learners to use this sample language to construct a four-sentence story containing all four plot elements.

Answers
1. D; DOK Level: 2; **2.** B; DOK Level: 2; **3.** D; DOK Level: 3;
4. A; DOK Level: 2; **5.** C; DOK Level: 2; **6.** B; DOK Level: 3;
7. A; DOK Level: 2; **8.** C; DOK Level: 2; **9.** C; DOK Level: 2;
10. B; DOK Level: 3; **11.** exposition; DOK Level: 2;
12. complication (or conflict); DOK Level: 2; **13.** she is "free, free, free!" DOK Level: 2; **14.** Mrs. Mallard's heart attack at the end connects to the statement about her heart trouble in the exposition. DOK Level: 2

Analyze Character

READING ASSESSMENT TARGETS: R.2.1, R.3.2, R.3.3, R.3.4, R.3.5, R.4.3/L.4.3

LANGUAGE ARTS

STUDENT BOOK pp. 34–35

▶ Preview the Skill

Tell learners that well-developed fictional characters think and behave as real people do. Ask learners to describe a character who seems convincingly real to them, focusing on the character's appearance, thoughts, and actions. Ask learners to explain what makes these characters seem so real.

❶ Learn the Skill

Give Examples Ask learners to name characters from popular television shows. The characters may be funny, serious, or mean. Have learners analyze how these characters' actions, speech, and relationships with other characters reflect these qualities.

❷ Practice the Skill

Skim and Scan Have learners skim and scan the passage on p. 34 to identify phrases or sentences that reveal Tiny's thoughts or actions, such as "She told me about some of the desperate chances she had taken in the gold country, but the thrill of them was quite gone." Advise learners to use these details to answer question 1.

❸ Apply the Skill

Use Graphic Organizers To answer questions 5 and 6, learners can use this graphic organizer to list the traits of the narrator in the passage on p. 35.

Character Trait	Shown By
Mentally ill	He is so afraid of the old man's cataract that he wants to kill the old man to be rid of the eye.
Obsessed	The idea of killing the old man "haunts" the narrator ceaselessly.
Methodical	He goes about killing the old man with much "caution," "foresight," and "dissimulation."
Patient	He enters the old man's room so slowly so as not to wake him that it takes him an entire hour to peek into the doorway.

Answers
1. D; DOK Level: 2; **2.** B; DOK Level: 2; **3.** C; DOK Level: 1; **4.** A; DOK Level: 2; **5.** D; DOK Level: 2; **6.** D; DOK Level: 2

WORKBOOK pp. 66–69

❶ Review the Skill

SuperSkill Review Remind learners that a character's actions reveal much about his or her personality. Ask learners to make inferences about these individuals, given these observations:
- *A man in a business suit busily checks his iPhone while sitting at the dinner table with his family.*
- *A woman walking home from work gives $5 to a homeless person.*

❷ Refine the Skill

Link to Past Skills Have learners review the skill *Make Generalizations* from Unit 1, Lesson 11. From details in the passage on p. 66, learners can make a generalization about the character of Mr. Hooper and use it to help them answer question 1.

❸ Master the Skill

Spotlighted Item Type Help learners complete the character web on p. 67 by reminding them that the narrator considers Nick's appeal to women as a bit of a mystery. His are not traits that most people would necessarily find attractive; therefore, finding the correct answers requires a careful reading of the passage.

▶ Enrich and Extend

Provide the names of well-known fictional characters, and have learners identify the different traits of each character. Then have learners create a story that features one or more existing characters and one or more characters that learners will create for this activity. In the course of their stories, learners should describe each character's appearance, thoughts, and actions. Use these characters or others:
- Wolverine *(X-Men)*
- Tony Stark *(Iron Man)*
- Bella *(Twilight)*

Answers
1. B; DOK Level: 2; **2.** C; DOK Level: 2; **3.** He looks like a surgeon when he works. He is a wizard at driving. His behavior is selfish. He makes no effort with women. DOK Level: 2; **4.** D; DOK Level: 2; **5.** A; DOK Level: 2; **6.** B; DOK Level: 2; **7.** C; DOK Level: 2; **8.** D; DOK Level: 2; **9.** C; DOK Level: 2; **10.** D; DOK Level: 2; **11.** B; DOK Level: 2; **12.** C; DOK Level: 2; **13.** D; DOK Level: 3

Analyze Setting

READING ASSESSMENT TARGETS: R.2.1, R.2.7, R.3.2, R.3.3, R.3.4, R.3.5, R.4.1/L.4.1, R.4.3/L.4.3

STUDENT BOOK pp. 36–37

➤ Preview the Skill

Explain to learners that the setting of a story can be as influential as a main character. Suggest this scenario: *A young man sets off on a trip during which he will face many challenges.* Discuss with learners how the story would change when presented in different settings, such as outer space, the Old West, or downtown Los Angeles.

❶ Learn the Skill

Give Examples Review the ways in which settings may be developed: Authors may describe landscapes, buildings, rooms, or objects such as furniture and decorations. Also, authors may place characters in these settings and describe both together. Offer examples of different events or locations, and have learners describe details of each setting. Examples may include a work space or an office, a sporting event, or the classroom.

❷ Practice the Skill

Link to Past Skills Have learners review the skill *Determine Main Idea and Details* from Unit 1, Lesson 1. Then help them identify the details that describe the setting in the passage on p. 36 in order to answer question 1 correctly.

❸ Apply the Skill

Decoding Have learners read the first passage on p. 37 carefully. Learners probably are familiar with the meaning of *drought* but may not recognize the word when it is written. Lead learners to understand that Hook and his parents must adjust their hunting habits; therefore, his parents bring him down from the nest sooner so that he has a better chance of finding food.

Answers
1. D; DOK Level: 2; **2.** the drought; DOK Level: 2; **3.** D; DOK Level: 2; **4.** D; DOK Level: 3

WORKBOOK pp. 70–73

❶ Review the Skill

Give Examples Remind learners that setting may be shaped by both place and time. Then ask learners to describe the setting for a romantic date. Examples may include *walking on a beach at sunset, sitting in front of a fireplace on a winter evening,* or *dining at an elegant restaurant on Valentine's Day.*

❷ Refine the Skill

Skim and Scan To help learners answer question 1, advise them to skim and scan the passage on p. 70 to identify the type of environment the narrator is describing. Learners should note sensory details—those that appeal to the five senses—to locate descriptions of setting.

❸ Master the Skill

Use Graphic Organizers Have learners complete a graphic organizer like the one below to answer question 11.

Dark and deserted — Iron-shuttered fronts — Chicago's South Side — Loaves of bread given away to stragglers — Given up largely to wholesale stores

➤ LifeLink

Explain that decorators, party planners, and stage designers understand how setting can affect emotions and thus are skilled at creating an environment. Ask learners to recall particular settings or environments that had an emotional effect on them. Examples may include a well-tended garden, a house of worship, or a celebration. Have learners list details about these settings to explain their effects.

Answers
1. A; DOK Level: 3; **2.** C; DOK Level: 3; **3.** D; DOK Level: 1; **4.** A; DOK Level: 2; **5.** A; DOK Level: 2; **6.** C; DOK Level: 2; **7.** C; DOK Level: 2; **8.** B; DOK Level: 2; **9.** D; DOK Level: 2; **10.** A; DOK Level: 3; **11.** A; DOK Level: 2; **12.** C; DOK Level: 2; **13.** D; DOK Level: 2; **14.** C; DOK Level: 2; **15.** B; DOK Level: 2; **16.** B; DOK Level: 2

Interpret Figurative Language

READING ASSESSMENT TARGETS: R.2.7, R.3.2, R.3.5, R.4.1/L.4.1, R.4.2/L.4.2, R.4.3/L.4.3, R.5.1, R.5.2, R.5.4

LANGUAGE ARTS

STUDENT BOOK *pp. 38–39*

➤ Preview the Skill

Ask students to think of ways to describe a household item as if it were human. They may suggest *My computer hates me* or *The refrigerator hums all night long*. Point out that these descriptions are examples of personification. Use similar examples to introduce metaphors, similes, hyperbole, and onomatopoeia:
- **Simile:** *Without glasses, I'm as blind as a bat.*
- **Metaphor:** *It's raining cats and dogs.*
- **Hyperbole:** *I'm so hungry, I could eat a cow.*
- **Onomatopoeia:** *The clock goes "tick-tock."*

❶ Learn the Skill

Give Examples Have learners give an example of a simile, such as *Traffic is so bad today that my street is as crowded as a parking lot on Black Friday morning*. Then tell them to turn the simile into a metaphor by removing the key linking words *like* or *as*: *Traffic is so bad today that my street is a parking lot on Black Friday morning*.

❷ Practice the Skill

Decoding To help learners answer question 1 correctly, explain that a *laceration* is a "deep cut or gash, especially in the skin." This explanation will help them understand the metaphor in question 1.

❸ Apply the Skill

Use Graphic Organizers Ask learners to use a graphic organizer like the one below to identify examples of figurative language in the passage on p. 39 and then to answer question 6 correctly.

Hyperbole	Onomatopoeia	Personification	Similes
He did not move a muscle.	A cricket which has made a single chirp	Death, in approaching him had stalked with his black shadow before him.	A low, dull, quick sound, such as a watch makes when enveloped in cotton
			Increased my fury, as the beating of a drum stimulates the soldier into courage

Answers
1. B; DOK Level: 2; **2.** B; DOK Level: 2; **3.** B; DOK Level: 2; **4.** C; DOK Level: 2; **5.** C; DOK Level: 2; **6.** A; DOK Level: 3

WORKBOOK *pp. 74–77*

❶ Review the Skill

Give Examples On the board or an overhead projector, list the six types of figurative language mentioned in *Review the Skill*. Then assign random topics, such as grocery shopping, gridlock, or computer glitches, and have learners create figurative expressions for all or some of the six types listed. Suggest some key words, if necessary.

❷ Refine the Skill

Decoding To help learners answer question 1, have them rephrase the quotation in familiar terms. Explain that a *dose* is an "amount of medicine," *scored* means "carved," and an *apothecary* is a "pharmacist."

❸ Master the Skill

Spotlighted Item Type Have learners work in pairs to find the correct words that complete the fill-in-the-blank question on p. 75. Remind learners to look for details that describe a human action *(sing)* or feeling *(fear)*. Although animals may be capable of doing or feeling what is described, inanimate objects are not.

➤ Language Analysis

Have learners analyze song lyrics to identify metaphors, similes, hyperbole, personification, or onomatopoeia. Here are some examples:
- *"My heart's a stereo; it beats for you"* (metaphor) —Maroon 5, "My Heart's a Stereo"
- *"Wearing a gown shaped like a pastry"* (simile) —Taylor Swift, "Speak Now"
- *"And when you smile, the whole world stops and stares for a while"* (hyperbole, personification) —Bruno Mars, "Just the Way You Are"
- *"Boom, boom, boom, even brighter than the moon, moon, moon"* (onomatopoeia) —Katy Perry, "Firework"

Answers
1. A; DOK Level: 2; **2.** B; DOK Level: 2; **3.** sing; fear; DOK Level: 2; **4.** B; DOK Level: 2; **5.** C; DOK Level: 3; **6.** B; DOK Level: 2; **7.** D; DOK Level: 2; **8.** A; DOK Level: 3; **9.** C; DOK Level: 2; **10.** A; DOK Level: 2; **11.** C; DOK Level: 2; **12.** C; DOK Level: 2; **13.** A; DOK Level: 2; **14.** B; DOK Level: 2; **15.** B; DOK Level: 2

Determine Narrative Point of View

READING ASSESSMENT TARGETS: R.2.7, R.2.8, R.3.2, R.3.3, R.3.5, R.5.1, R.6.3

STUDENT BOOK pp. 40–41

▶ Preview the Skill

Present the scenario of a fender bender. Ask learners to describe the event from each driver's point of view and then from the Web camera that captured the entire event. Use this analogy to explain point of view in fiction—that a first person narrator (each driver) can relate events from a single viewpoint, whereas an omniscient narrator (camera) sees everything. Consider adding that unlike the camera, however, an omniscient narrator would know the thoughts and feelings of the drivers and may not be completely objective.

❶ Learn the Skill

Give Examples Ask learners to use first-person point of view to explain how they got to class. Then ask them to use an omniscient narrator to tell the same story. For example,
- **First person:** *I often drive down Park Road to get to class. It's faster than taking Lee Street.*
- **Omniscient:** *Max often takes Park Road to class because he thinks it's faster than taking Lee Street.*

❷ Practice the Skill

Decoding To help learners determine point of view and answer question 1, ask them to decode the passage on p. 40 to identify whose thoughts and feelings are revealed. Explain that the shift in pronoun use in the second paragraph comes from a direct quotation; it is not a shift in point of view.

❸ Apply the Skill

Use Graphic Organizers To answer question 2, have learners use details from the passage on p. 41 to complete a graphic organizer like this one.

I would lie in bed awake, and I could hear all the sounds my parents made as they prepared for the day.	As my mother made my father his breakfast, my father would shave.	My mother would always add some hot water to my bathwater to take off the chill.

Point of View

Answers
1. A; DOK Level: 2; **2.** D; DOK Level: 2; **3.** A; DOK Level: 2; **4.** C; DOK Level: 2; **5.** B; DOK Level: 3

WORKBOOK pp. 78–81

❶ Review the Skill

SuperSkill Review Provide learners with two statements about the same event in a story, one told by a first-person narrator and one by an omniscient narrator. Have learners identify the point of view. Remind them that an omniscient narrator is "outside" the story; a first-person narrator is usually a character in the story.

❷ Refine the Skill

Decoding Help learners decode the passage on p. 78 to determine point of view. Identify the characters and the details about them, and explain how each character might describe the scene. For example, the sentinels might describe their discomfort from holding "a formal and unnatural position," and the captain might focus on getting the execution over with quickly.

❸ Master the Skill

Spotlighted Item Type Have partners answer questions 7 and 8. If partners do not agree on an answer, tell them to go back to the text to examine the point of view and how characters are revealed. Then ask partners to rewrite the passage from the other *(first-person)* point of view.

▶ Enrich and Extend

Ask learners to consider how seating at a sporting event or concert affects what the audience can see. For instance, someone who sits at the 50-yard line at a football game has a different perspective from someone who sits in the end zone. Offer this example: *The running back fumbles the ball at the team's own 5-yard line.* Then ask learners to consider what that play looks like from the perspective of the running back, a defense lineman, the officials, and the fans in the end zone.

Answers
1. D; DOK Level: 2; **2.** B; DOK Level: 3; **3.** C; DOK Level: 2; **4.** A; DOK Level: 2; **5.** D; DOK Level: 2; **6.** C; DOK Level: 3; **7.** omniscient; DOK Level: 2; **8.** The narrator reveals Connie's thoughts and actions as well as her mother's. DOK Level: 2; **9.** B; DOK Level: 2; **10.** C; DOK Level: 3; **11.** C; DOK Level: 2; **12.** D; DOK Level: 2; **13.** C; DOK Level: 2; **14.** C; DOK Level: 3; **15.** A; DOK Level: 2

Make Inferences in Fiction

READING ASSESSMENT TARGETS: R.2.4, R.2.7, R.3.2, R.3.3, R.3.4, R.3.5

LANGUAGE ARTS

STUDENT BOOK pp. 42–43

▸ Preview the Skill

Ask learners to imagine that a friend has invited them out to dinner. Explain how they would use clues from the invitation and their knowledge of the friend's likes and dislikes to guess the kind of restaurant the friend would choose. Point out that when reading fiction, learners encounter unknown characters created by the author and must combine the author's details with their own prior knowledge about people to determine the unstated information.

❶ Learn the Skill

Link to Past Skills Review the skill *Make Inferences* from Unit 1, Lesson 8. Remind learners that although some inferences may be obvious, they are unstated. For example, an author may write *He put on his warmest jacket and headed out into the snow.* The inference—unstated but obvious—is that the weather is cold.

❷ Practice the Skill

Decoding Help learners decode the meanings of unfamiliar words in the passage on p. 42, such as *meditate* and *conjectural*. Explain that both relate to thinking and speculating, which relate to imagination. Learners can use this information to find the correct answer to question 1.

❸ Apply the Skill

Use Graphic Organizers To help learners answer question 2, have them use this graphic organizer to make inferences about the passage on p. 43.

Evidence and Clues	What I Know	Inference
Ulrich and Georg, longtime enemies, face each other. Each has a rifle and can shoot the other. Neither is directly threatened or dishonored by the other.	Most civilized people would rather not kill an enemy in a standoff without direct provocation.	Georg and Ulrich are honorable men who follow a code of civilized behavior.

Answers
1. A; DOK Level: 2; **2.** B; DOK Level: 2; **3.** C; DOK Level: 2; **4.** D; DOK Level: 2; **5.** A; DOK Level: 2; **6.** D; DOK Level: 3

WORKBOOK pp. 82–85

❶ Review the Skill

Give Examples Draw learners' attention to the *Test-Taking Tips* note on p. 82. Explain that because conflicts can develop over time, references to past events can help readers understand present conflicts. For example, in an elementary school cafeteria, a child makes a face and says, *"Ew, gross. Not stinky pea soup again for lunch!"* From the comment and gesture, you can infer that the child dislikes pea soup and that it has been served often.

❷ Refine the Skill

Skim and Scan To help learners answer question 1, have them skim and scan the passage on p. 82 and look for clues that indicate why Sarah is eager to improve the condition of her home. Have learners use prior knowledge, or personal experience, to find a detail that explains Sarah's eagerness.

❸ Master the Skill

Spotlighted Item Type Have learners work with a partner to complete the fill-in-the-blank questions on p. 85. Tell learners to focus on the key actions and traits of both the narrator and Pauline and to use these details to make inferences about the characters and plot of the story. Learners can use these details to answer questions 14–17 correctly.

▸ Enrich and Extend

Have partners think of characters from movies, television, or literature that both have encountered recently. Ask learners to list the key actions of these characters and then to use these details to make inferences about the characters' pasts, personalities, relationships, and motivations.

Answers
1. A; DOK Level: 2; **2.** B; DOK Level: 2; **3.** A; DOK Level: 2; **4.** C; DOK Level: 2; **5.** D; DOK Level: 2; **6.** C; DOK Level: 2; **7.** B; DOK Level: 2; **8.** D; DOK Level: 3; **9.** B; DOK Level: 2; **10.** C; DOK Level: 2; **11.** D; DOK Level: 2; **12.** B; DOK Level: 2; **13.** A; DOK Level: 3; **14.** younger; DOK Level: 2; **15.** the ex-husband of the narrator and the current husband of Pauline; DOK Level: 2; **16.** slightly amused, confused, or puzzled; DOK Level: 3; **17.** demanding; someone who worries or is difficult in some way; DOK Level: 2

Identify Theme

READING ASSESSMENT TARGETS: R.2.6, R.2.7, R.3.3, R.3.4, R.3.5, R.4.3/L.4.3, R.5.1, R.5.2, R.5.4

STUDENT BOOK pp. 44–45

▶ Preview the Skill

Explain to learners that *plot* is the series of events that occur in a story and that *theme* is the main idea that the story reveals. Theme statements are usually implied, not directly stated. One of the most common themes is *Good triumphs over evil.* Ask learners to think of books, television shows, or movies that share this theme. If appropriate, repeat the activity with another theme, such as *Good looks may hide a nasty nature.*

1 Learn the Skill

Give Examples Tell learners that familiar fables are simple examples of stories that contain obvious theme statements. For instance, the moral of "The Boy Who Cried Wolf" might be stated as *If a person keeps lying, he or she will not be believed when telling the truth* or *Honesty is the best policy.* Challenge learners to provide more examples of themes of familiar stories. Stress that themes reflect an author's underlying ideas and are not necessarily "moralistic" statements. Add, too, that works of fiction often have more than one theme.

2 Practice the Skill

Skim and Scan Ask learners to skim and scan the passage on p. 44, looking for details that describe Della and Jim's relationship and what they have done for each other. For example, Della has given Jim a watch chain, but Jim tells her that he has "sold the watch to get the money to buy your combs." Have learners use these details to identify the theme of the passage.

3 Apply the Skill

Link to Past Skills Have learners review the skill *Analyze Character* from Unit 1, Lesson 17. Then have them reread the passage on p. 45, looking for words or phrases that describe Donald's character. For example, they may suggest "darkest moods," "depressed," or "moody." Learners can use this information to help them answer question 3.

Answers
1. D; DOK Level: 2; **2.** C; DOK Level: 2; **3.** B; DOK Level: 2; **4.** A; DOK Level: 3; **5.** B; DOK Level: 3; **6.** A; DOK Level: 3

WORKBOOK pp. 86–89

1 Review the Skill

SuperSkill Review Ask learners to explain the plot and theme of a favorite film to illustrate the difference. For example,
- **Plot:** *In the movie* Avatar, *Jake, a paraplegic Marine, is sent in avatar form on a mission to the planet Pandora, where he finds its inhabitants, the Na'vi, at odds with humans from Earth who seek to exploit Pandora.*
- **Theme:** *All living beings are connected; those who try to destroy nature will destroy only themselves.*

2 Refine the Skill

Use Graphic Organizers Use this graphic organizer to help learners identify the theme of the passage on p. 86.

During winter, the children met in the street after dinner.

When they returned from playing, it was dark outside.

The theme of this passage is…

The children ran through alleys behind their houses.

The air was cold, but they played until their "bodies glowed."

3 Master the Skill

Spotlighted Item Type Have pairs work together to answer the questions on p. 88. Suggest that learners find one word to describe what is being challenged in Hadleyburg. Then ask why the old lady would be concerned about an unlocked door if the town is so safe and virtuous. What does her comment suggest?

▶ Enrich and Extend

Have learners identify two possible themes for each event: a parade (could be festive or somber) and a family reunion (could be pleasant if people enjoy being around family or distressing if not).

Answers
1. A; DOK Level: 2; **2.** C; DOK Level: 2; **3.** C; DOK Level: 2; **4.** A; DOK Level: 2; **5.** B; DOK Level: 2; **6.** C; DOK Level: 2; **7.** honesty; DOK Level: 2; **8.** Hadleyburg's honesty will be challenged. DOK Level: 3; **9.** B; DOK Level: 2; **10.** D; DOK Level: 3; **11.** C; DOK Level: 2; **12.** B; DOK Level: 3

Draw Conclusions in Fiction

READING ASSESSMENT TARGETS: R.2.7, R.2.8, R.3.2, R.3.3, R.3.4, R.3.5, R.4.3/L.4.3, R.5.1

LANGUAGE ARTS

STUDENT BOOK *pp. 46–47*

➤ *Preview the Skill*

Remind learners that drawing conclusions is like solving a mystery: Learners must piece together two or more inferences, or clues, to arrive at a logical solution, or conclusion. In reading fiction, learners base their conclusions on the information the author provides as well as on their prior knowledge. For example, they can take details about a character and combine them with what they know about human behavior to draw conclusions about that character's actions or motives.

❶ *Learn the Skill*

Give Examples Present learners with a simple situation that requires them to make several inferences to draw a conclusion. For example, *You turn on the TV in the morning. Nothing happens. Prior knowledge tells you that the TV is powered by electricity. So you infer that the TV is not getting electricity. Prior knowledge tells you that the TV gets electricity from the outlet into which it is plugged. You verify that the TV is connected to the outlet. It is. Then you open the refrigerator. The light is off. Prior knowledge leads you to the same inference, and you check the connection. Knowing that both appliances are connected but not working, you conclude that the electricity in your home is not working.*

❷ *Practice the Skill*

Skim and Scan To help learners answer question 1, ask them to find clues about Laird's condition as they skim and scan the passage and callouts on p. 46. Learners should note statements such as "blankets despite the summer heat" or "people … were shocked to tears by his appearance."

❸ *Apply the Skill*

Spotlighted Item Type Remind learners to use their knowledge of sub-zero weather to draw conclusions about the story and to answer questions 2–4 correctly.

Answers
1. A; DOK Level: 2; **2.** build a fire; warm; DOK Level: 2; **3.** hypothermia or extreme and dangerous exposure to cold; DOK Level: 3; **4.** branch; puts out the fire; DOK Level: 2

WORKBOOK *pp. 90–93*

❶ *Review the Skill*

SuperSkill Review Review how certain details can help learners draw conclusions about a person or situation. These details may include character descriptions, character interaction, setting, or tone. For example,
- **Character description:** *Kate remained in front of the mirror, fussing with her skirt and scarf and spraying copious amounts of hairspray.*
- **Character interaction:** *"Come on," said Paul. "This time, no one's going to notice you." Kate disagreed smugly, "Of course they'll notice me."*
- **Conclusion:** *Kate is vain.*

❷ *Refine the Skill*

Decoding Have learners reread the first 10 lines of the passage on p. 90. Help them paraphrase Gloria's observations to draw conclusions about the woman's behavior and to answer question 1. For example, *ceased to be cherished* means "no longer is loved."

❸ *Master the Skill*

Use Graphic Organizers To answer question 11, have learners use this graphic organizer to draw conclusions about Laird's conversation with his mother.

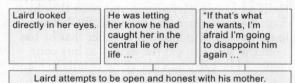

| Laird looked directly in her eyes. | He was letting her know he had caught her in the central lie of her life … | "If that's what he wants, I'm afraid I'm going to disappoint him again …" |

Laird attempts to be open and honest with his mother.

➤ *LifeLink*

Provide small groups with a list of everyday situations. Have group members offer suggestions about and discuss conclusions that they might draw from these topics, which may include *difficulty steering their car, symptoms of an illness, and decisions about major purchases.*

Answers
1. B; DOK Level: 2; **2.** A; DOK Level: 2; **3.** D; DOK Level: 2; **4.** D; DOK Level: 2; **5.** A; DOK Level: 2; **6.** C; DOK Level: 2; **7.** D; DOK Level: 2; **8.** B; DOK Level: 2; **9.** A; DOK Level: 2; **10.** C; DOK Level: 3; **11.** D; DOK Level: 2; **12.** B; DOK Level: 2; **13.** B; DOK Level: 2; **14.** C; DOK Level: 2

Apply Ideas

READING ASSESSMENT TARGETS: R.2.7, R.2.8, R.3.2, R.3.3, R.3.4, R.3.5, R.4.1/L.4.1, R.4.3/L.4.3

STUDENT BOOK pp. 48–49

▶ Preview the Skill

Explain that learners apply ideas when they make predictions based on their own knowledge and on information provided to them. Ask them to think of a movie character, such as Harry Potter, and discuss that character's traits. Learners can use this information to predict what Harry would do on a long summer day. For example,

- *Harry might meet Ron, Hermione, and their friends to practice spells or play quidditch.*
- *At the end of the day, Harry, Ron, and Hermione probably hang out at Hagrid's house.*

① Learn the Skill

Give Examples Ask learners to list the traits and actions of their favorite television characters and give examples of how those characters might behave in different situations. For instance, Jack Bauer (from *24*) would be the first person to stop at the scene of a car accident because he loves action and saving lives.

② Practice the Skill

Use Graphic Organizers Using details about Paul's thoughts and behavior from the passage on p. 48, learners can complete a graphic organizer like the one below to answer question 1.

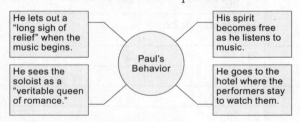

He lets out a "long sigh of relief" when the music begins.

His spirit becomes free as he listens to music.

Paul's Behavior

He sees the soloist as a "veritable queen of romance."

He goes to the hotel where the performers stay to watch them.

③ Apply the Skill

Skim and Scan To help learners answer question 3, have them skim and scan the passage on p. 49 to identify words and phrases that indicate tone. Learners should note words with unpleasant associations, such as *impelled* and *frustration*.

Answers
1. A; DOK Level: 3; **2.** B; DOK Level: 3; **3.** B; DOK Level: 3;
4. C; DOK Level: 3; **5.** A; DOK Level: 3; **6.** C; DOK Level: 3

WORKBOOK pp. 94–97

① Review the Skill

Give Examples Remind learners that they apply ideas each time they make a prediction in both fiction and nonfiction. Ask them to identify predictions they could make, given these details:

- **Details:** *The forecast indicates storms continuing through the evening. It is raining now, an hour before I leave work. Flooding is causing delays on my route home. Traffic is rerouted.*
- **Possible Prediction:** *Traffic on the way home from work will be bad; the drive will take longer.*
- **Application:** *I'll either stay later at work or go home another way.*

② Refine the Skill

Link to Past Skills Review the skill *Analyze Character* from Unit 1, Lesson 17. To help learners answer question 1, ask them to analyze Paul's traits and actions in the passage on p. 94 and to consider what the details reveal about his past as well as present actions.

③ Master the Skill

Spotlighted Item Type Have partners complete the chart on p. 96, noting the specific descriptions of Belinda as hard and cold. Learners should consider how such a person would respond to anger.

▶ LifeLink

Organize learners into small groups. Have one group member suggest a situation, such as going to a horror movie. Have another member predict how a relative or friend would behave in that situation. For example, *My sister would grab my arm and scream for half the film. She'd be angry with me for suggesting the movie and insist I take her out for ice cream to "pay" for my poor judgment.*

Answers
1. B; DOK Level: 2; **2.** D; DOK Level: 3; **3.** C; DOK Level: 3;
4. D; DOK Level: 3; **5.** B; DOK Level: 2; **6.** A; DOK Level: 3;
7. C; DOK Level: 3; **8. Belinda would:** ignore the angry person; listen to the angry person and walk away silently; **Belinda would not** fly into a rage; cry and apologize immediately; DOK Level: 3; **9.** A; DOK Level: 3; **10.** C; DOK Level: 3; **11.** C; DOK Level: 3; **12.** B; DOK Level: 3

Unit 1 Review

READING ASSESSMENT TARGETS: R.2.1, R.2.2, R.2.3, R.2.4, R.2.5, R.2.6, R.2.7, R.2.8, R.3.1, R.3.2, R.3.3, R.3.4, R.3.5, R.4.1/L.4.1, R.4.2/L.4.2, R.4.3/L.4.3, R.5.1, R.5.2, R.5.3, R.5.4, R.6.1, R.6.3

You may choose to use the Unit 1 Review on Student Book pp. 50–57 as a mini–practice test. If you wish to time the test, ask learners to complete all the items in 65 minutes.

Unit 1 Review Answers

1. B; **2.** D; **3.** A; **4.** B; **5.** Old movies often demean women. Old movies are slow paced. Old movies use few special effects. **6.** C; **7.** supports; **8.** old-fashioned, outdated; **9.** A; **10.** B; **11.** preserving the beauty of nature; **12.** D; **13.** B; **14.** C; **15.** A; **16.** C; **17.** D; **18.** D; **19.** C; **20.** Framton's sister stays at the rectory. The "tragedy" takes place. The niece explains why the window remains open. Framton acts as though he has seen a ghost. **21.** D; **22.** C; **23.** C; **24.** D; **25.** B; **26.** C; **27.** D; **28.** Jimmy: Police officer; Sensitive; Honest; Bob: Criminal; Ambitious; Adventurous; Both: From New York; Keeps appointment; **29.** D; **30.** C; **31.** B; **32.** B; **33.** A

Unit 1 Review Item Analysis

SKILL	DOK LEVEL 1	DOK LEVEL 2	DOK LEVEL 3
Determine Main Idea and Details		2, 3, 5, 10, 13, 21	14
Summarize		4, 15, 28	
Determine Sequence	20	30	
Categorize		2	
Identify Cause and Effect		11	5
Compare and Contrast		3	
Determine Author's Point of View		6	
Make Inferences		13	5, 7, 14
Analyze Style and Tone		1	12
Draw Conclusions		15	16, 17,
Make Generalizations		9	7, 16, 17,
Synthesize Information		9	16, 17
Use Context Clues		8, 22	
Identify Cause and Effect in Fiction		24, 29, 31	19
Compare and Contrast in Fiction		28	
Analyze Plot Elements	20	24, 29, 30, 31	19
Analyze Character		23, 24, 26, 28, 29, 31, 32	
Analyze Setting		21	27
Interpret Figurative Language		22	
Determine Narrative Point of View		18, 32	
Make Inferences in Fiction		21, 26, 29	
Identify Theme		25, 32	
Draw Conclusions in Fiction		23, 24	33
Apply Ideas			7, 33

Unit 1 Review

Use workbook lessons, as identified in the following table, to assist learners who require additional remediation with certain skills or items having certain DOK levels.

Unit 1 Workbook Item Analysis

SKILL	DOK LEVEL 1	DOK LEVEL 2	DOK LEVEL 3
Determine Main Idea and Details		1, 2, 3, 4, 5, 7, 8, 9, 10, 11, 12, 13, 14	6
Summarize		1, 2, 3, 4, 5, 6, 7, 8, 9, 10, 11, 12, 13, 14	
Determine Sequence	1, 3, 4, 5	2	
Categorize	1, 3, 4, 5	2, 7, 9, 10	6, 8, 11
Identify Cause and Effect	1, 2, 4, 6, 7, 9, 10	3, 8	5, 11
Compare and Contrast	5	1, 2, 3, 4, 6, 7, 8, 9, 10, 12	11
Determine Author's Point of View		1, 2, 3, 4, 5, 6, 7, 8, 9, 10, 11	
Make Inferences		1, 2, 3, 4, 7, 8, 9, 10, 11, 12, 13, 14, 15	5, 6
Analyze Style and Tone		1, 2, 3, 4, 6, 7, 8, 10, 11, 12	5, 9, 13
Draw Conclusions		1, 2, 3, 4, 5, 6, 7, 9, 10, 11	8
Make Generalizations		1, 3, 4, 6, 7, 8, 9, 10, 11	2, 5
Synthesize Information		6, 9, 10, 12	1, 2, 3, 4, 5, 7, 8, 11
Use Context Clues	11	1, 3, 4, 5, 6, 7, 8, 9, 10, 12, 13, 14	2
Identify Cause and Effect in Fiction		1, 2, 3, 4, 5, 6, 7, 9, 10, 11	8, 12, 13
Compare and Contrast in Fiction		1, 2, 3, 4, 6, 7, 8, 9, 10, 11, 13, 14, 15	5, 12, 16
Analyze Plot Elements		1, 2, 4, 5, 7, 8, 9, 11, 12, 13, 14, 15	3, 6, 10
Analyze Character		1, 2, 3, 4, 5, 6, 7, 8, 9, 10, 11, 12	13
Analyze Setting	3	4, 5, 6, 7, 8, 9, 11, 12, 13, 14, 15, 16	1, 2, 10
Interpret Figurative Language		1, 2, 3, 4, 6, 7, 9, 10, 11, 12, 13, 14, 15	5, 8
Determine Narrative Point of View		1, 3, 4, 5, 7, 8, 9, 11, 12, 13, 15	2, 6, 10, 14
Make Inferences in Fiction		1, 2, 3, 4, 5, 6, 7, 9, 10, 11, 12, 14, 15, 17	8, 13, 16
Identify Theme		1, 2, 3, 4, 5, 6, 7, 9, 11	8, 10, 12
Draw Conclusions in Fiction		1, 2, 3, 4, 5, 6, 7, 8, 9, 11, 12, 13, 14	10
Apply Ideas		1, 5	2, 3, 4, 6, 7, 8, 9, 10, 11, 12

Unit 2

Argument Analysis and Text Comparison

Table of Contents

LESSON	PAGE
1: Determine Author's Purpose	RLA 32
2: Analyze Elements of Persuasion	RLA 33
3: Identify Evidence	RLA 34
4: Analyze Visuals and Data	RLA 35
5: Identify Faulty Evidence	RLA 36
6: Classify Valid and Invalid Evidence	RLA 37
7: Analyze the Structure of Arguments	RLA 38
8: Analyze Rhetorical Devices	RLA 39
9: Compare and Contrast Texts	RLA 40
10: Compare Texts in Different Formats	RLA 41
11: Compare Texts in Similar Genres	RLA 42
12: Compare Texts in Different Genres	RLA 43
13: Gain Information from Multiple Texts	RLA 44
Unit 2 Review	RLA 45–RLA 46

Building on reading and critical thinking skills addressed in Unit 1, Unit 2 offers learners an opportunity to read and analyze written argument and examine relationships in multiple texts. Learners will begin by determining author's purpose in Lesson 1, move through persuasive text analysis in Lessons 2–8, then compare and contrast paired texts in Lessons 9–13.

The skills in Lessons 1–8 follow a logical sequence: from understanding how authors persuade an audience; identifying, classifying, and analyzing valid and invalid evidence; and analyzing passage structure and rhetorical strategies. However, the lessons can be taught in any order appropriate for learners. Some controversial passages, such as "Segregation Now, Segregation Forever" in workbook Lesson 5, exemplify attempts to persuade through invalid evidence and fallacious reasoning and should encourage thoughtful insights.

Lessons 9–13 present different combinations of passages: similar topics, similar formats, different formats, and different genres. Questions address the passages both individually and together. Note that all lessons require learners to compare and contrast even though the lesson title may include the word *compare* only.

The lessons in this unit generally align with Common Core State Standards, Indicators 5–9. Like Unit 1, Unit 2 features drag-and-drop and fill-in-the-blank items. Nearly all questions are written at DOK 2 and 3 levels. After completing Unit 2, learners will have mastered the strategies needed for Trait 1, the reading portion of the extended response.

LANGUAGE ARTS

UNIT 2
LESSON 1

Determine Author's Purpose

READING ASSESSMENT TARGETS: R.2.1, R.2.3, R.2.4, R.2.5, R.2.7, R.2.8, R.3.2, R.3.5, R.4.3/L.4.3, R.5.1, R.5.2, R.5.4, R.6.1, R.6.2, R.6.3, R.6.4, R.8.2

LANGUAGE ARTS

STUDENT BOOK pp. 60–61

▶ Preview the Skill

Point out that when people run errands, they have purposes for doing so. For example, people go to the grocery to buy food or to the post office to mail a package. Explain that an author similarly has a purpose when writing. Discuss why an author might write each of these:

- *a funny story about a trip to the beach* (to entertain)
- *an instruction manual for assembling a piece of furniture* (to inform)
- *a letter to neighbors about a proposed city park that the writer would like to see built* (to inform and persuade)

❶ Learn the Skill

Give Examples Explain that the language an author uses depends on the author's purpose and intended readers. For example, a scientist writing to inform other scientists uses technical language. Ask learners to describe the language an author might use in other examples. You may use these situations as prompts:

- *a recipe for a general audience* (simple, clear language)
- *car review in a magazine for mechanics* (language that includes specialized terms)

❷ Practice the Skill

Link to Past Skills Have learners review the skill *Determine Main Idea and Details* from Unit 1, Lesson 1. Help them understand how the author's purpose relates to the main idea and details of the passage on p. 60. Point out the main idea: *The flu shot is worth getting.* Ask how the main idea relates to the author's purpose. Ask learners to identify persuasive details.

❸ Apply the Skill

Decoding Help learners use context clues to decode unfamiliar words in the passage on p. 61. For example, in paragraph 5, the author gives examples of "mediating institutions."

Answers
1. D; DOK Level: 2; **2.** D; DOK Level: 2; **3.** A; DOK Level: 2; **4.** C; DOK Level: 2; **5.** B; DOK Level: 3

WORKBOOK pp. 98–101

❶ Review the Skill

SuperSkill Review Explain that considering the types of details the author includes can help readers identify the author's purpose and intended audience. For example, to persuade, an author might include only the details that support a particular opinion. Ask learners to suppose that they are reading a passage about adopting a dog. Ask what details an author would include to entertain, inform, and persuade. Ask how the details might differ for an audience of experienced or first-time dog owners.

❷ Refine the Skill

Give Examples Organize learners in pairs, and have them read the passage and callouts on p. 98. To give learners more practice in identifying audience and purpose, ask one partner to suggest another target audience, and then have the other partner suggest how the passage would be different. Then have partners reverse roles.

❸ Master the Skill

Skim and Scan Have students skim the passage on p. 101. Ask what they can infer about the authors' purpose *(to inform)* from the facts and numbers.

▶ Spotlighted Item Type

Have each student in a pair write two fill-in-the-blank items for the passages on p. 100 or p. 101. Have partners exchange and answer each other's items.

Answers
1. A; DOK Level: 2; **2.** D; DOK Level: 2; **3.** generals on opposing sides—Sherman fought for the North and Hood for the South. DOK Level: 1; **4.** to confirm the plans for evacuating Atlanta; DOK Level: 1; **5.** to justify his invasion of Atlanta; DOK Level: 2; **6.** heartless cruelty; DOK Level: 2; **7.** not evacuating women and children would reflect cruelty rather than would the acts of war; DOK Level: 2; **8.** C; DOK Level: 2; **9.** A; DOK Level: 3; **10.** C; DOK Level: 3; **11.** B; DOK Level: 3; **12.** A; DOK Level: 1; **13.** C; DOK Level: 3; **14.** A; DOK Level: 2 ; **15.** C; DOK Level: 3; **16.** A; DOK Level: 3

Analyze Elements of Persuasion

READING ASSESSMENT TARGETS: R.2.2, R.2.7, R.2.8, R.3.1, R.5.1, R.5.2, R.5.3, R.5.4, R.6.1, R.6.2, R.6.3, R.6.4, R.8.1, R.8.2, R.8.6

STUDENT BOOK pp. 62–63

▶ Preview the Skill

State this claim: *It is wise to use sunscreen when working outdoors.* Offer evidence, such as *Too much sun exposure can damage skin.* Ask learners for additional evidence. Then state a conclusion: *Always apply sunscreen before going outside.* Explain that claim, evidence, and conclusion are the bases of argument.

❶ Learn the Skill

Give Examples Point out that commercials are often structured like arguments. For example, a car commercial states that a particular car is the safest *(claim)*, then lists awards the car has won and shows images of it in a crash *(evidence)*. The commercial states that safety-conscious drivers should buy the car *(conclusion)*. Ask learners to share examples of similar commercials.

❷ Practice the Skill

Use Graphic Organizers Use this graphic organizer to identify the claim, evidence, and conclusion of the passage on p. 62.

> **Claim**
> Investment in public transportation generates jobs and boosts the economy.

↓

> **Evidence**
> • Thousands of workers have jobs related to mass transit.
> • Workers and riders spend money throughout a mass transit network.
> • The American Public Transportation Association estimates that for every dollar spent on investment in public transit, six dollars are generated in jobs and public benefits.

↓

> **Conclusion**
> Vote in favor of mass transit projects.

❸ Apply the Skill

Skim and Scan Ask learners to skim the passage on p. 63 and identify the author's position. Ask them what details support their decision.

Answers

1. B; DOK Level: 2; **2.** A; DOK Level: 2; **3.** C; DOK Level: 3; **4.** D; DOK Level: 2; **5.** B; DOK Level: 2

WORKBOOK pp. 102–105

❶ Review the Skill

SuperSkill Review Ask learners to suppose that a mayoral candidate is delivering a campaign speech. State the following lines from the speech, and ask learners to identify the part of the argument.
• *I have a plan to boost high-school attendance by 15 percent.* (evidence)
• *I am the best choice to lead this city.* (claim)
• *Opponents say I lack experience.* (counterclaim)
• *Vote for me!* (conclusion)
• *I led the City Coalition for nine years.* (evidence)

❷ Refine the Skill

Decoding Have learners read callout *a* on p. 102 and then read the entire passage carefully. Have them underline the support in the second and third paragraphs for each claim made in the first.

❸ Master the Skill

Spotlighted Item Type Have learners work in pairs to answer question 3. Suggest that they start by categorizing statements they can easily identify.

▶ Enrich and Extend

Organize learners in pairs. Ask one partner to think of a simple claim. Ask the other partner to think of a counterclaim. Challenge each partner to add evidence that supports the claim. Ask each partner to state his or her claim and evidence for the class. Then invite listeners to state possible conclusions.

Answers

1. B; DOK Level: 2; **2.** A; DOK Level: 3; **3. Claim** It ought to be possible, in short, for every American to enjoy the privileges of being American without regard to his race or his color. **Evidence** The Negro baby born in America today … has about one-half as much chance of completing high school as a white baby. **Evidence** The Negro baby born in America today … [has] twice as much chance of becoming unemployed. **Evidence** Difficulties over segregation and discrimination exist in every city, in every State of the Union. **Conclusion** One hundred years of delay have passed since President Lincoln freed the slaves, yet their heirs, their grandsons, are not fully free. DOK Level: 2; **4.** C; DOK Level: 2; **5.** A; DOK Level: 2; **6.** D; DOK Level: 2; **7.** D; DOK Level: 3; **8.** B; DOK Level: 2; **9.** D; DOK Level: 2; **10.** A; DOK Level: 2; **11.** C; DOK Level: 2

Identify Evidence

READING ASSESSMENT TARGETS: R.2.2, R.2.4, R.2.5, R.2.8, R.3.5, R.4.3/L.4.3, R.5.1, R.5.2, R.5.4, R.6.1, R.6.3, R.8.1, R.8.2, R.8.3, R.8.4

LANGUAGE ARTS

STUDENT BOOK *pp. 64–65*

➤ *Preview the Skill*

To help learners understand different types of evidence and appeals to logic, emotion, and ethics, use these examples of ways an organization might try to persuade readers to support its program to protect endangered whales.
- *To appeal to logic, the organization might list facts about how few whales are left.*
- *To appeal to emotion, the organization might include a photo of a baby whale.*
- *To appeal to ethics, the organization might quote a prominent marine biologist.*

❶ *Learn the Skill*

Link to Past Skills Have students review the skill *Make Inferences* from Unit 1, Lesson 8. Explain that learners may need to make inferences to determine whether evidence successfully supports a claim. For example, if an author appeals only to emotion, learners might infer that no facts support the claim. Similarly, if an author does not include reliable sources for information, facts and other evidence may be questionable.

❷ *Practice the Skill*

Give Examples Review the different types of evidence. Share several common types of persuasive texts (advertisements, editorials, articles, and so on). Ask learners to identify examples of evidence and to explain why each example appeals to logic, emotion, or ethics.

❸ *Apply the Skill*

SuperSkill Review List examples of persuasive texts, such as a newspaper editorial calling for more public parking, an article in a scientific magazine warning about the urgency of climate change, and a flyer advertising a local lawn-care service. Have learners think of evidence to appeal to logic, emotion, and ethics for each text. Provide examples and guidance as needed. Then consider reading the passage and answering the questions on p. 65 as a class.

Answers
1. C; DOK Level: 2; **2.** B; DOK Level: 2; **3.** D; DOK Level: 2; **4.** A; DOK Level: 2; **5.** C; DOK Level: 2

WORKBOOK *pp. 106–109*

❶ *Review the Skill*

Give Examples Write these topics on the board: *professional sports, movies, public transportation.* Ask learners for an opinion about each topic and an example of a fact supporting the opinion. Begin by providing examples.

❷ *Refine the Skill*

Decoding Have learners work in pairs to read the passage, callouts, and answer choices to the questions on p. 106. Then ask them to use the information provided to answer questions 1 and 2 and to explain the reasons for their choices.

❸ *Master the Skill*

Spotlighted Item Type Refer learners to the *Inside the Items* note on p. 106. Point out that question 3 has four statements but six possible places in which to drag and drop them. Organize learners into pairs to consider whether two statements contain emotional language, two statements contain facts and figures, or two statements refer to a reliable source.

➤ *LifeLink*

Have learners examine the three appeals in their daily lives. Have one partner take the role of a parent telling a child why certain safety precautions, like wearing a helmet when riding a bike, are important. Have the partner present the child with an example of each appeal. Then have the other partner do the same with another topic, such as proper nutrition or study habits.

Answers
1. D; DOK Level: 2; **2.** C; DOK Level: 2; **3. Logical:** Each electoral vote in Alaska is equivalent to approximately 112,000 people. Each electoral vote in New York is equivalent to approximately 404,000 eligible people. **Emotional:** Defecting electors in a close race could cause a crisis of confidence in our electoral system. In a nation where voting rights are grounded in the one person, one vote principle, the electoral college is a hopeless anachronism. **Ethical:** I am pleased to be here today to express the League's support for a constitutional amendment. DOK Level: 2; **4.** A; DOK Level: 2; **5.** B; DOK Level: 2; **6.** B; DOK Level: 2; **7.** D; DOK Level: 3; **8.** D; DOK Level: 2; **9.** A; DOK Level: 2; **10.** A; DOK Level: 2; **11.** C; DOK Level: 2

Analyze Visuals and Data

READING ASSESSMENT TARGETS: R.2.7, R.2.8, R.3.5, R.6.1, R.6.2, R.6.3, R.7.2, R.7.4, R.8.2 , R.9.1/R.7.1

LANGUAGE ARTS

STUDENT BOOK pp. 66–67

▶ Preview the Skill

Display a classroom document that pairs text and images, such as a book cover or poster. Read the text, and then explain the information or effect the image adds. For example, a book cover with smiling people working together may imply that learning the material in the book will be satisfying. Repeat the exercise with a document that includes data.

❶ Learn the Skill

Give Examples Explain that manuals commonly include text and visuals. For example, instructions for operating a remote control include images that identify the buttons and text that explains their functions. Ask learners to name other examples of documents that include text and images and to explain how the images add to the text.

❷ Practice the Skill

Use Graphic Organizers Have students use a Venn diagram to analyze the information in the table on p. 66.

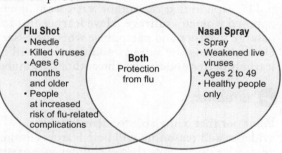

Flu Shot
• Needle
• Killed viruses
• Ages 6 months and older
• People at increased risk of flu-related complications

Both
Protection from flu

Nasal Spray
• Spray
• Weakened live viruses
• Ages 2 to 49
• Healthy people only

❸ Apply the Skill

Decoding Point out that both the passage and image on p. 67 date from 1912. Tell learners that remembering the purpose of the passage—to encourage farmers to move to Oregon—will help them understand the old-fashioned language.

Answers
1. B; DOK Level: 3; **2.** D; DOK Level: 3; **3.** A; DOK Level: 3; **4.** D; DOK Level: 3

WORKBOOK pp. 110–113

❶ Review the Skill

SuperSkill Review On the board or an overhead projector, draw a graph with a line descending from left to right (similar to the one on p. 110). Say, *This graph could show the amount of snowfall over the 12 months of the year.* Label the x- and y-axes appropriately. Have learners work in pairs to think of other information the graph might show.

❷ Refine the Skill

Give Examples Note that authors present data in different ways. Bar graphs compare quantities. Line graphs often show change over time. Bullets convey short statements of fact. Pie charts show quantities that make up a larger whole. Draw a simple bar graph, and explain that it could show how many people drive cars versus trucks. Then ask learners to share other examples of data in bar graphs, line graphs, bullets, and pie charts.

❸ Master the Skill

Skim and Scan Have learners look at the photograph on p. 111. Ask them to think about how the image makes them feel and what they think it depicts. Then have them skim the passage. Ask how their understanding of the photograph has changed after they skimmed the text.

▶ Cross-Curricular Connection

Suggest that learners refer to the applicable lessons in the math, social studies, and science texts for extra support in reading graphs, diagrams, and tables. Remind learners that they will have access to calculators during the actual test.

Answers
1. C; DOK Level: 2; **2.** D; DOK Level: 2; **3.** B; DOK Level: 3; **4.** A; DOK Level: 3; **5.** C; DOK Level: 3; **6.** A; DOK Level: 3; **7.** B; DOK Level: 2; **8.** B; DOK Level: 3; **9.** D; DOK Level: 2; **10.** A; DOK Level: 3; **11.** experience joblessness less frequently than their non-STEM counterparts; DOK Level: 2; **12.** earn more on average than their counterparts in other jobs, regardless of their educational attainment; DOK Level: 3

Identify Faulty Evidence

READING ASSESSMENT TARGETS: R.2.5, R.3.2, R.4.3/L.4.3, R.5.1, R.6.1, R.6.4, R.8.2, R.8.3, R.8.4, R.8.5, R.8.6

LANGUAGE ARTS

STUDENT BOOK pp. 68–69

➤ Preview the Skill

Ask whether learners have ever bought an item of clothing because it was popular or because they saw a celebrity wearing it. Explain that authors may appeal to readers by saying that an idea is popular *(bandwagon)* or that a celebrity supports it *(testimonial)*. These are examples of faulty evidence.

❶ Learn the Skill

Give Examples Share these examples of faulty reasoning. Ask learners to share other examples.
- **Inaccurate Cause and Effect:** *After her election, the town's economy started to go downhill.*
- **Irrelevant Information:** *Garbage collectors deserve higher wages. Very few households recycle!*
- **Inaccurate Either/Or Situation:** *If you support this bill, you are in favor of higher taxes!*

❷ Practice the Skill

Decoding Have pairs read callout *a* carefully and then work together to decode the answer choices in question 1. Have them explain each answer choice to their partner and review it as a possible correct answer. If applicable, have partners paraphrase the options for easier reading.

❸ Apply the Skill

Spotlighted Item Type For drag-and-drop items, such as those in question 2, encourage learners to check that they move each answer to the correct place.

Answers
1. D; DOK Level: 2; **2. Irrelevant Information:** According to the American Pet Products Association, approximately 62 percent of American households own pets. **Inaccurate either/or situation:** But without your financial support, other animals will not be so lucky. **Bandwagon appeal:** Through the generosity of so many people like you, who care deeply about animals, we are able to help unfortunate creatures that cannot help themselves. **Appeal to sympathy:** Can you imagine what it must feel like to find yourself in a strange place, without food or water, completely alone? **Testimonial:** And our own hero, Damian Ferri, says "Supporting helpless animals has given me as much personal satisfaction as it has helped save abused and abandoned animals." DOK Level: 2

WORKBOOK pp. 114–117

❶ Review the Skill

Give Examples Write the following claim on the board or an overhead projector: *Federal taxes should be used fund to local school districts.* Then use an example of faulty evidence or reasoning to support this claim. For example, *Our children are our most precious resource, and every American has a duty to pay for their education* (emotional appeal/language). Ask learners to think of other examples of faulty evidence and reasoning that could support this claim.

❷ Refine the Skill

Link to Past Skills Have pairs of learners review the skill *Identify Evidence* from Unit 2, Lesson 3. Have them look for examples of similar evidence in the passage on p. 114 and list what they find. To help them answer questions 1 and 2, ask learners to explain why the evidence is faulty.

❸ Master the Skill

Decoding To help learners understand the somewhat antiquated language in the passage on p. 117, explain that the author was a woman who opposed women's suffrage. Have learners read the passage together and paraphrase when necessary. Understanding the author's point of view will help learners better understand the author's argument.

➤ LifeLink

Point out that being able to identify faulty evidence and reasoning will help learners evaluate persuasive documents they encounter in everyday life, such as political advertisements, arguments related to local issues, newspaper editorials, advertisements for products and services, and so on. Share a print advertisement, and ask learners to evaluate the support provided to persuade the reader to purchase the product or service.

Answers
1. C; DOK Level: 2; **2.** C; DOK Level: 2; **3.** C; DOK Level: 2; **4.** A; DOK Level: 3; **5.** B; DOK Level: 2; **6.** A; DOK Level: 2; **7.** B; DOK Level: 2; **8.** C; DOK Level: 2; **9.** D; DOK Level: 2; **10.** C; DOK Level: 2; **11.** D; DOK Level: 3; **12.** A; DOK Level: 3; **13.** B; DOK Level: 3

Classify Valid and Invalid Evidence

READING ASSESSMENT TARGETS: R.2.8, R.4.3/L.4.3, R.5.1, R.5.4, R.6.3, R.6.4, R.8.2, R.8.3, R.8.4, R.8.5, R.8.6

STUDENT BOOK pp. 70–71

Preview the Skill

Point out that crime shows often feature an unlikable character who turns out not to be the criminal. Discuss with learners why being unlikable is not valid, or reliable, evidence. However, DNA found at a crime scene is valid evidence.

❶ Learn the Skill

Link to Past Skills Have learners review the skill *Categorize* from Unit 1, Lesson 4, to help them understand how to categorize evidence as valid or invalid. Explain that categorizing evidence will help learners evaluate the strength of an argument.

❷ Practice the Skill

Use Graphic Organizers Have learners use this graphic organizer to classify evidence in the passage on p. 70.

Valid	Invalid
• The solar industry added 13,872 jobs from 2011 to 2012. • Employment grew 13%.	• If we do not switch to energy sources such as solar, we could find ourselves with unpredictable weather, unstable food supply, and political upheaval. • "Going solar" is a strategy with no downside!

❸ Apply the Skill

Spotlighted Item Type Review the parts of the drag-and-drop question on p. 71. Point out that drag-and-drop items can be configured in different ways, so learners must be sure they understand the layout of each item.

Answers
1. C; DOK Level: 2; **2. Valid.** Dog trainer and author Brian Kilcommons explains, "mixed breed dogs are often healthier, longer-lived, more intelligent, and of more stable temperament than purebreds." Shelter workers have often observed that many shelter animals seem to sense what they were up against and become among the most devoted and grateful companions. **Invalid.** According to the Humane Society of the United States, mutts are America's dog of choice, accounting for nearly 60 percent of all pet dogs. Dogs, cats, and small mammals like guinea pigs, rabbits, and rats end up in shelters because of circumstances beyond their control. DOK Level: 2

WORKBOOK pp. 118–121

❶ Review the Skill

SuperSkill Review Ask learners to name experts in various fields, such as doctors or automobile mechanics. Challenge learners to explain why these people would be reliable sources of information and why others outside the fields may not. Then provide a brief list of valid and invalid evidence pertaining to these fields, and have learners classify each item as likely or unlikely to have come from a reliable source.

❷ Refine the Skill

Decoding Have partners read the callouts and *Test-Taking Tips* note on p. 118. Ask learners to state the author's claim and to read the passage carefully to gather evidence, listing their findings as "valid" and "invalid." Then have them decode questions 1 and 2 and choose the best answers according to the evidence they have gathered.

❸ Master the Skill

Skim and Scan Have learners skim the passage on p. 120. Ask them to pick out two examples of valid evidence in the passage. Ask learners to explain what makes the evidence valid.

Cross-Curricular Connection

Explain that as learners read for social studies and science, they will continue to use the skill of classifying evidence. In social studies, they must consider whether the author is knowledgeable and has done research about the history or events that he or she is writing about. If an author witnessed events, learners should consider whether the author is presenting more than one side of a story. When reading scientific texts, learners should consider whether the author has sufficient data supporting his or her claims.

Answers
1. D; DOK Level: 2; **2.** A; DOK Level: 3; **3.** C; DOK Level: 2; **4.** B; DOK Level: 2; **5.** C; DOK Level: 2; **6.** D; DOK Level: 2; **7.** A; DOK Level: 2; **8.** D; DOK Level: 3; **9.** C; DOK Level: 2; **10.** B; DOK Level: 3; **11.** B; DOK Level: 3; **12.** D; DOK Level: 2; **13.** A; DOK Level: 2; **14.** C; DOK Level: 3

Analyze the Structure of Arguments

READING ASSESSMENT TARGETS: R.2.5, R.2.8, R.4.3/L.4.3, R.5.1, R.5.2, R.5.3, R.5.4, R.6.1, R.6.2, R.6.3, R.8.1, R.8.2, R.8.3, R.8.5, R.8.6

LANGUAGE ARTS

STUDENT BOOK *pp. 72–73*

➤ Preview the Skill

Explain that authors construct arguments in a number of ways. Draw a sandwich on the board or an overhead projector. Label the top slice of bread *Introduction*. Label the fillings *Evidence*. Label the bottom slice *Conclusion*. Explain the parts of the traditional "sandwich" structure. To help learners understand other structures, draw a two-column chart with the headings + and – (positive and negative) to represent the pro/con structure. A pyramid or inverted pyramid can represent a structure that lists evidence in order of importance.

❶ Learn the Skill

Give Examples Explain that the "sandwich" and order-of-importance structures are common in advertisements or sales pitches. For example, a flyer might begin with a claim, such as *The Townville Flea Market is the best place for bargains!* The flyer could then list evidence, such as number of vendors, types of items for sale, and willingness of vendors to bargain. The flyer might end with this conclusion: *Come to the Townville Flea Market to score a great deal!* Have learners work in pairs to develop sample advertisements that use a sandwich or order-of-importance structure.

❷ Practice the Skill

SuperSkill Review List these situations, and ask learners to identify the most effective argument structure. Have them explain their choices.

- *A researcher disagrees with a claim that elementary students should eat breakfast in school, as opposed to at home, to improve attention spans.*
- *A magazine writer is reviewing a new cell phone.*

❸ Apply the Skill

Spotlighted Item Type Organize learners into pairs to answer question 2. Point out that fill-in-the-blank items may require analysis, synthesis, or a complete sentence response, as on p. 73.

Answers

1. C; DOK Level: 2; **2.** It provides a definition and explanation or background information. DOK Level: 2; **3.** B; DOK Level: 2; **4.** D; DOK Level: 3

WORKBOOK *pp. 122–125*

❶ Review the Skill

Give Examples Ask a volunteer to describe a familiar TV commercial. On the board, write a summary of the commercial, and review its structure. Be sure that learners can identify its parts.

❷ Refine the Skill

Use Graphic Organizers Have learners use this graphic organizer to analyze the structure of the passage on p. 122.

Pros	Cons
• Students paid for behaviors do better on standardized tests. • Economist Roland Fryer Jr. found that second-graders paid for each book they read performed better on reading tests.	• When the rewards are for results rather than behaviors, test scores do not improve. • Payment systems teach students to value education for only short-term gains.

❸ Master the Skill

Link to Past Skills Have students review the skill *Draw Conclusions* from Unit 1, Lesson 10, to analyze and evaluate the passages in this lesson. Point out that even if the structure of an argument is effective, learners still must draw conclusions about whether the evidence supports the claim.

➤ Enrich and Extend

Display this claim: *Investing in energy-efficient appliances and energy-efficiency improvements is a smart move for homeowners and renters.* Have partners pull a type of structure—"sandwich," pro/con, refutation/proof, or order of importance—from a hat and write a paragraph that uses the selected structure to support the claim. Explain that if partners select the refutation/proof structure, they should refute the idea that investing in energy efficiency is not a smart move.

Answers

1. A; DOK Level: 2; **2.** D; DOK Level: 2; **3.** C; DOK Level: 2; **4.** D; DOK Level: 2; **5.** B; DOK Level: 2; **6.** A; DOK Level: 3; **7.** A; DOK Level: 2; **8.** D; DOK Level: 2; **9.** B; DOK Level: 2; **10.** C; DOK Level: 2; **11.** D; DOK Level: 2; **12.** C; DOK Level: 2

Analyze Rhetorical Devices

READING ASSESSMENT TARGETS: R.4.3/L.4.3, R.5.1, R.5.2, R.6.1, R.6.3, R.6.4

STUDENT BOOK pp. 74–75

➤ Preview the Skill

Provide students with a short political speech or excerpts from a longer one. Be sure the text contains rhetorical devices. Read it aloud, and ask learners to identify the language that shows it is a speech. Then explain the function of rhetorical devices, particularly in persuasive writing.

❶ Learn the Skill

Give Examples Explain that rhetorical devices are language choices an author uses to emphasize a point or create a particular effect. For example, repetition and parallelism create rhythm that can move or inspire readers. Mention the movie *Lincoln*, which dramatizes Lincoln's second inaugural address and in which he states *"Fondly do we hope, fervently do we pray, that this mighty scourge of war may speedily pass away."* The parallelism adds rhythm and emphasizes how deeply people wanted an end to the war.

❷ Practice the Skill

Skim and Scan Write a topic on the board, such as dental hygiene, and ask learners to skim and scan the chart on p. 74. When they have finished, ask volunteers or partners to think of other rhetorical devices, listed in the chart, applicable to the topic. For example, an analogy could be *"Failing to brush and floss regularly is like refusing to change your car's oil. At first, the harm might be negligible, but over time, your whole vehicle could be destroyed."*

❸ Apply the Skill

Decoding Students may not recognize all the words in the Churchill quotation in the passage on p. 75. Explain that a paradox is a statement or situation in which two things that seem as though they cannot exist together are said to exist at the same time. Point out that because Churchill is discussing a paradox, the pairs of words are generally opposite in meaning. Encourage learners to use context clues as needed.

Answers

1. B; DOK Level: 2; **2.** qualifying statement; DOK Level: 2;
3. C; DOK Level: 3; **4.** D; DOK Level: 2; **5.** A; DOK Level: 2

WORKBOOK pp. 126–129

❶ Review the Skill

Use Graphic Organizers Have learners use the graphic organizer to develop rhetorical devices related to a claim.

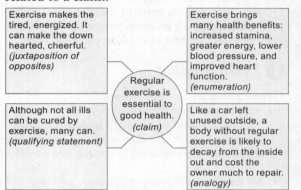

Exercise makes the tired, energized. It can make the down hearted, cheerful. *(juxtaposition of opposites)*

Exercise brings many health benefits: increased stamina, greater energy, lower blood pressure, and improved heart function. *(enumeration)*

Regular exercise is essential to good health. *(claim)*

Although not all ills can be cured by exercise, many can. *(qualifying statement)*

Like a car left unused outside, a body without regular exercise is likely to decay from the inside out and cost the owner much to repair. *(analogy)*

❷ Refine the Skill

Link to Past Skills Have learners review the skill *Analyze Style and Tone* from Unit 1, Lesson 9, to help them understand how rhetorical devices relate to style and tone. To help learners answer questions 1 and 2, ask how different devices affect the style and tone of the passage on p. 126.

❸ Master the Skill

Skim and Scan Have partners scan the passage on p. 127 and note repeated words or phrases. Ask learners to choose one example, examine it, and explain how parallelism or repetition helps the author accomplish her purpose.

➤ Enrich and Extend

Read aloud or play a recording of Kennedy's inaugural address on p. 129. Tell learners to note rhetorical devices. After you read, ask learners how hearing the speech changed their understanding of it. Discuss the rhetorical devices, and ask how the speech might differ without them.

Answers

1. C; DOK Level: 2; **2.** A; DOK Level: 2; **3.** D; DOK Level: 2;
4. B; DOK Level: 2; **5.** C; DOK Level: 3; **6.** A; DOK Level: 2;
7. D; DOK Level: 2; **8.** B; DOK Level: 2; **9.** A; DOK Level: 2;
10. C; DOK Level: 2; **11.** A; DOK Level: 2; **12.** A; DOK Level: 2; **13.** C; DOK Level: 2

Compare and Contrast Texts

READING ASSESSMENT TARGETS: R.2.1, R.2.2, R.4.2/L.4.2, R.4.3/L.4.3, R.5.1, R.5.4, R.6.1, R.6.3, R.7.3, R.9.1/R.7.1, R.9.2

STUDENT BOOK *pp. 67–68*

➤ Preview the Skill

Present learners with two newspaper or magazine articles that address the same topic. As a class, list the similarities and differences between the articles, focusing on content, perspective, style, and tone. Then ask learners to decide which article is more effective and to explain their decision.

❶ Learn the Skill

Give Examples Present these examples, and ask learners to contrast the authors' styles:
- *Clad in full-dress uniform of purple leaves edged in rose and cream, the slow-growing tricolor beech withstands the onslaught of winter, like a stalwart soldier.*
- *The tricolor beech tree grows slowly and can withstand cold. The tree has purple leaves with pink and white edges.*

❷ Practice the Skill

Use Graphic Organizers Use this graphic organizer to compare and contrast the passages on p. 76. Consider mentioning that Shriver was the first director of the Peace Corps.

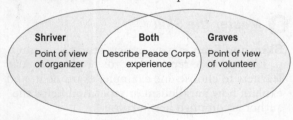

Shriver	Both	Graves
Point of view of organizer	Describe Peace Corps experience	Point of view of volunteer

❸ Apply the Skill

Spotlighted Item Type Have learners work in pairs to complete question 2. Remind them to compare and contrast the perspectives of the authors. To help learners complete the drag-and-drop chart, suggest they use the callouts on p. 76.

Answers
1. C; DOK Level: 3; **2. Shriver:** emphasizes that the Peace Corps represents American ideals and ingenuity; promotes the Peace Corps by providing an overview of the program; appeals to American patriotism; **Graves:** appeals to human sympathy; has gained knowledge and experience from the Peace Corps; describes the Peace Corps by providing aspects of a specific experience; DOK Level: 2

WORKBOOK *pp. 130–133*

❶ Review the Skill

SuperSkill Review Review the *Test-Taking Tips* note on p. 130, and discuss ways to determine, and then compare and contrast, authors' perspectives. Provide several nouns or verbs, and ask learners to suggest descriptive words or phrases with similar meanings but with negative or positive connotations. For example, an *overbearing* parent as opposed to a *helpful* parent.

❷ Refine the Skill

Link to Past Skills Review the skills *Determine Author's Point of View* from Unit 1, Lesson 7, and *Analyze Style and Tone* from Unit 1 Lesson 9. To help learners answer question 1 correctly, ask them to analyze the authors' word choice to determine their points of view. Remind learners to pay particular attention to words that show emotions, such as anger or humor.

❸ Master the Skill

Skim and Scan To help learners answer question 3 correctly, have them skim and scan the passages on p. 131 to identify the thoughts and feelings of each author. Advise them to look for emotionally charged language and for uses of the pronoun *I, me,* or *my.*

➤ Language Analysis

Discuss how authors use language. For example, a speech intended to persuade or motivate likely will contain inspirational, emotional language, whereas an article intended to inform likely will use fact-based reasoning and often formal, academic language. Have pairs work together to compare and contrast the purpose of the Riley letter and Spacey article on p. 132 and to explain how language supports each purpose.

Answers
1. 1. D; DOK Level: 3; **2.** A; DOK Level: 2; **3.** D; DOK Level: 3; **4.** B; DOK Level: 3; **5.** D; DOK Level: 2; **6.** C; DOK Level: 2; **7.** A; DOK Level: 1; **8.** B; DOK Level: 2; **9.** A; DOK Level: 2; **10.** B; DOK Level: 2; **11.** C; DOK Level: 3; **12.** D; DOK Level: 3; **13.** D; DOK Level: 3

Compare Texts in Different Formats

READING ASSESSMENT TARGETS: R.5.1, R.5.4, R.6.1, R.6.3, R.6.4, R.7.2, R.7.3, R.7.4, R.9.1/R.7.1

LANGUAGE ARTS

STUDENT BOOK *pp. 78–79*

▶ Preview the Skill

Present two texts that cover the same topic and present similar information, but in different formats. For example, consider a set of driving directions, one in paragraph format and the other in simplified map format. Ask learners to compare and contrast the two texts and explain which is more useful. Similarly, present a job performance review in simple or abbreviated bullet points and one that combines the bullet points with explanatory paragraphs. Discuss with learners which format would be more effective when delivering or receiving such a review. Lead learners to conclude that different formats are appropriate for different situations and that some formats contain more information or greater detail, which may or may not be useful or necessary.

❶ Learn the Skill

Give Examples Point out examples of how learners use various text formats every day to share information. For instance, they might write a formal letter, an informal e-mail, or an abbreviated text message. They also may write lists or draw simple visuals to present information. Have learners compare and contrast these formats, discussing their purposes, ease of readability, and effectiveness in presenting information.

❷ Practice the Skill

Skim and Scan To help learners answer question 1, have them skim and scan the letter and floor plan on p. 78 for details about the early White House. Ask what both texts reveal about its construction. Point out that learners will need to synthesize details to answer the question.

❸ Apply the Skill

Decoding To help learners answer questions 2–4, explain that *scope* refers to what a text covers, or the range of the material that it includes. Both the passage and the timeline describe events during a certain period in Rosa Parks's life.

Answers
1. B; DOK Level: 3; **2.** C; DOK Level: 3; **3.** A; DOK Level: 3; **4.** B; DOK Level: 3

WORKBOOK *pp. 134–137*

❶ Review the Skill

Give Examples To review the skill of comparing and contrasting texts in different formats, write a list of formats and topics on the board—for example, write *paragraph format: instructions for putting together a prefabricated shelving unit* and *table: review of a recent movie*. Discuss with the class the information provided by these or other formats and when they are most useful to readers, noting that both formats are inappropriate for the purposes mentioned. Focus on how audience, purpose, scope, and emphasis influence format choice. Lead learners to explain why writers use certain formats.

❷ Refine the Skill

Use Graphic Organizers Have learners use this graphic organizer to compare and contrast the texts on p. 134.

Moon Mining article
• Uses quotations as evidence
• Presents opinions

Both
• Tell what is on the moon
• Tell that the moon contains important resources

What's on the Moon table
• Lists facts
• Fast to read

❸ Master the Skill

Spotlighted Item Type Have learners work in pairs to complete the fill-in-the-blank questions on p. 135. To answer questions 2-4, learners must compare and contrast the information in the passage and the table.

Answers
1. D; DOK Level: 3; **2.** listing the requirements for holding office; DOK Level: 3; **3.** Only the passage explains that these requirements come from Articles I and II of the U.S. Constitution and includes information about term lengths, number of Senators, and the Vice President's role in the Senate. DOK Level: 3; **4.** U.S. Representative; two; DOK Level: 3; **5.** A; DOK Level: 2; **6.** C; DOK Level: 2; **7.** A; DOK Level: 2; **8.** D; DOK Level: 3; **9.** B; DOK Level: 3; **10.** C; DOK Level: 3; **11.** A; DOK Level: 3; **12.** B; DOK Level: 3

Compare Texts in Similar Genres

READING ASSESSMENT TARGETS: R.2.7, R.4.3/L.4.3, R.5.1, R.5.2, R.5.3, R.6.1, R.6.3, R.6.4, R.9.1/R.7.1, R.9.2

LANGUAGE ARTS

STUDENT BOOK pp. 80–81

▶ Preview the Skill

Ask learners to recall a recent awards show and two memorable speeches presented at it. Have learners compare and contrast the speeches. For example, one speech might have been short and humorous, the other repetitive and sentimental. Tell learners to list similarities and differences and to explain why they found one more effective than the other. As an alternative, ask learners to name two sports announcers and to list similarities and differences in the ways they follow the game.

❶ Learn the Skill

Decoding With learners, read the instruction in the *Learn the Skill* section on p. 80. Ask volunteers to define the highlighted terms and to explain what to look for when answering questions that include these terms. Supplement the instruction by providing definitions and explanations as needed.

❷ Practice the Skill

Skim and Scan Have learners skim and scan the *Making Assumptions* note on p. 80. Ask them to conclude what situations Roosevelt addresses but Kennedy omits *(work and security)* because they do not concern his audience. This conclusion will help learners answer question 1.

❸ Apply the Skill

Spotlighted Item Type Have small groups complete the Venn diagram on p. 81. Remind them that some answer choices may describe both passages. For example, both *Style* options belong in the overlapping section.

Answers
1. B; DOK Level: 3; **2. Roosevelt:** Perspective: Local and federal government must aid the American people in times of need.; Structure: solution to current problems; Overall Impact: Audience is hopeful for the end to distress. **Kennedy:** Perspective: Federal government must lead in areas of technology, foreign relations, and human rights. Structure: implied comparison with pioneer spirit; Overall impact: Audience is excited by new challenges. **Both:** Style: parallelism; repetition of key words; strong, patriotic language; Style: strong, stirring language; Long-range purpose: to be elected president; Long-range purpose: to persuade audience to support candidate and his ideas; Tone: forceful, optimistic; patriotic; DOK Level: 3

WORKBOOK pp. 138–141

❶ Review the Skill

Give Examples Remind learners that when they compare and contrast texts in similar genres, they look for similarities and differences in author's perspective, tone, purpose, style and structure. Ask learners to consider how these elements would differ to suit the different purposes for these examples:
- *a speech written to persuade people to donate money to a children's charity*
- *a speech written to honor those who served in a recent war*
- *a speech given at a graduation ceremony to celebrate students' achievements*

❷ Refine the Skill

Decoding Refer to the passages on p. 138. Help learners decode the message of each text by explaining that Reagan and Johnson belonged to different political parties and that *they*, to whom Reagan refers, are the members of the Democratic Party.

❸ Master the Skill

Link to Past Skills Review the skill *Analyze Style and Tone* from Unit 1, Lesson 9. Then ask learners to compare and contrast the styles and tones of Reagan's and Johnson's speeches on p. 139. Doing so will help learners answer questions 4 and 5.

▶ Enrich and Extend

Provide pairs or small groups with two public service announcements that contain a considerable amount of text. Ask learners to compare and contrast the messages, tones, styles, and purposes of the announcements. Then have groups or pairs decide which announcement would have greater impact on the public and explain the reason for their choice.

Answers
1. A; DOK Level: 3; **2.** D; DOK Level: 2; **3.** B; DOK Level: 2; **4.** A; DOK Level: 2; **5.** C; DOK Level: 3; **6.** D; DOK Level: 3; **7.** A; DOK Level: 2; **8.** D; DOK Level: 2; **9.** B; DOK Level: 2; **10.** C; DOK Level: 2; **11.** D; DOK Level: 3; **12.** A; DOK Level: 3; **13.** B; DOK Level: 3; **14.** C; DOK Level: 3; **15.** D; DOK Level: 3

Compare Texts in Different Genres

READING ASSESSMENT TARGETS: R.2.7, R.2.8, R.4.3/L.4.3, R.5.1, R.5.3, R.5.4, R.6.1, R.6.2, R.6.3, R.7.3, R.7.4, R.8.2

STUDENT BOOK pp. 82–83

▶ Preview the Skill

Discuss with learners the differences in purpose and point of view between these statements:

- *Modern parenting practices recommend parents allow infants to "cry it out" so that infants will learn to self-soothe and sleep longer and better, faster. However, recent research suggests this practice may hinder infant brain development.*
- *Any mother who allows her baby to "cry it out" should be charged with neglect! This selfish, barbaric practice is creating a generation of children with emotional and mental deficiencies.*

Have learners suggest appropriate genres for each.

❶ Learn the Skill

Give Examples Present two passages on the same topic or issue—an editorial and a news article, a biography and an editorial, or any combination of genres. Work with learners to compare and contrast the purpose, audience, scope, and overall impact of the texts.

❷ Practice the Skill

Skim and Scan To help learners answer question 1, have them skim and scan the passages on p. 82 for details that reveal each author's purpose. Point out that both passages use strong language, but only one tries to motivate readers to take action.

❸ Apply the Skill

Use Graphic Organizers Have learners use this graphic organizer to compare and contrast the article and editorial on p. 83.

Article
- General audience
- Reports fluoride debate

Both
- Address issue of fluoridating Portland's water
- Use direct quotations
- Offer researched evidence

Editorial
- Audience of Portland voters
- Argues against fluoride in water
- Offers data about health concerns from fluoride use

Answers
1. A; DOK Level: 3; **2.** A; DOK Level: 3; **3.** D; DOK Level: 2; **4.** B; DOK Level: 3

WORKBOOK pp. 142–145

❶ Review the Skill

SuperSkill Review Using callouts *a* and *b* on p. 142, discuss with learners how they can distinguish the genres of various texts. Name various genres, such as speeches, news articles, FAQ, memoirs, etc., and ask volunteers to identify specific characteristics of each. For example, a timeline lists events in chronological order; a speech addresses a specific audience and often contains emotional or inspirational language.

❷ Refine the Skill

Link to Past Skills Have learners review the skill *Synthesize Information* from Unit 1, Lesson 12, to help them answer question 1 on p. 142. To draw the most logical conclusion about Parks's arrest, learners must consider details from both passages.

❸ Master the Skill

Spotlighted Item Type Have learners work in small groups to complete the chart on p. 143. Explain that by completing the chart, they are contrasting the perspectives of the author of each passage. If group members disagree on answers, have them skim and scan the passages for key ideas until they reach a consensus.

▶ Enrich and Extend

Provide learners with a speech and an interview given by the same person. Have learners compare and contrast the passages, focusing on the audience and ways in which language and style are related to purpose. Ask learners to answer these questions: *Which passage is more entertaining and successful in engaging readers? Which passage is more informative? Which has the greater impact?*

Answers
1. A; DOK Level: 3; **2. Obama Honors Parks**: An act of civil disobedience changed a nation. Courageous acts by ordinary people lead to change. **Rosa Parks FAQ**: People should believe in themselves and their ideals. All people deserve the same opportunities. DOK Level: 2; **3.** D; DOK Level: 2; **4.** B; DOK Level: 3; **5.** C; DOK Level: 2; **6.** B; DOK Level: 3; **7.** A; DOK Level: 3; **8.** C; DOK Level: 2; **9.** A; DOK Level: 3; **10.** B; DOK Level: 3; **11.** B; DOK Level: 3

Gain Information from Multiple Texts

READING ASSESSMENT TARGETS: R.7.3, R.7.4, R.9.1/R.7.1

LANGUAGE ARTS

STUDENT BOOK *pp. 84–85*

▶ Preview the Skill

Ask learners to share experiences in making a decision for which they had to do research in more than one source. For example, in buying a new phone plan, they might have begun the decision-making process by knowing what they wanted and did not want, continued by researching different companies' offerings, and then consulted comments about customer satisfaction. Then they made their decision. Explain that this process is similar to synthesizing information, drawing conclusions, using prior knowledge, and applying information to form a new idea.

❶ Learn the Skill

Give Examples Present learners with two details from separate texts on the same topic. For example,
- *It is common for fussy babies to have soy or dairy intolerances that they outgrow within a few months.*
- *With improved understanding of food allergies, colic is less likely to be blamed for babies' fussiness.*

Have learners synthesize this information into one statement: *Today, babies are commonly diagnosed with soy and dairy intolerances rather than colic.*

❷ Practice the Skill

Link to Past Skills Have learners review the skill *Synthesize Information* from Unit 1, Lesson 12, to help them answer question 1. Explain that combining information from multiple texts can lead to a new idea that goes beyond the text.

❸ Apply the Skill

Skim and Scan Ask learners to skim and scan the passages on p. 85, looking for details that describe the culture and mentality of football. Have learners use these details to draw conclusions about head injuries and the sport itself and then synthesize the information to answer questions 2–4.

Answers
1. A; DOK Level: 3; **2.** C; DOK Level: 3; **3.** B; DOK Level: 3; **4.** D; DOK Level: 3

WORKBOOK *pp. 146–149*

❶ Review the Skill

Link to Past Skills Have learners review the skill *Apply Ideas* from Unit 1, Lesson 24. Although the lesson focuses on fiction, work with learners to adapt the instruction to nonfiction so that they understand how to draw conclusions, make generalizations, make predictions about outcomes, and draw parallels. Consider using weather or behavior patterns as a topic.

❷ Refine the Skill

Decoding Have learners reread the passages on p. 146. Then help them look for clues in the passages to draw conclusions about why the recipient of the letter would accept the position offered. Point out that the offer letter indicates that the recipient already has experience as an editor. This support will help learners answer question 1 correctly.

❸ Master the Skill

Spotlighted Item Type Have learners work in small groups to complete the chart on p. 147. Explain that by completing the chart, they are synthesizing information, or drawing on both passages to determine the pros and cons of part-time jobs. Suggest that learners use prior knowledge in completing the activity.

▶ LifeLink

Ask learners to think of everyday situations that would require them to draw on different sources of information, as well as prior knowledge, to help them make a decision. For example, they might mention reading an article about what to look for in day care, then read an ad for a day-care center, and use prior knowledge about cost and convenience to make a decision. Other situations might include making costly purchases or repairs.

Answers
1. D; DOK Level: 3; **2. Pros:** experience in field, leads to letters of recommendation, acquisitions of professional contacts; **Cons:** no insurance benefits, low pay, no paid vacation; DOK Level: 3; **3.** C; DOK Level: 3; **4.** B; DOK Level: 3; **5.** A; DOK Level: 3; **6.** C; DOK Level: 3; **7.** B; DOK Level: 3; **8.** C; DOK Level: 3; **9.** D; DOK Level: 3; **10.** A; DOK Level: 3; **11.** B; DOK Level: 3; **12.** C; DOK Level: 3

Unit 2 Review

You may choose to use the Unit 2 Review on Student Book pp. 86–93 as a mini–practice test. If you wish to time the test, ask learners to complete all the items in 60 minutes.

Unit 2 Review Answers

1. B; **2.** A; **3.** A; **4.** D; **5.** C; **6. Supported:** Ocean acidity has increased rapidly in the past 250 years. Human activity is the likely cause of increased CO2 emissions. Humans must act quickly to save the coral reefs and shellfish. **Unsupported:** The "tipping point" for coral reefs could happen as soon as 2050. **7.** A; **8.** D; **9.** C; **10.** B; **11.** A; **12.** A; **13.** B; **14.** the new energy policy; **15.** selfish, timid, grandchildren, catastrophe; **16.** light; **17.** will indicate the costs of different light bulbs, thus completing the answer to the FAQ about costs. **18.** C; **19.** C; **20.** B; **21.** D; **22.** C; **23.** C; **24.** B; **25.** stress, misfortune, or difficulty; **26.** A; **27.** late Memorial Day, today, and this time next year; **28.** C; **29. Speech:** specific audience; first-person point of view; **News Article:** third-person point of view; general audience; **30.** B; **31.** B; **32.** D

Unit 2 Review Item Analysis

SKILL	DOK LEVEL 1	DOK LEVEL 2	DOK LEVEL 3
Determine Author's Purpose		1, 5, 9, 13, 14, 17, 26	20, 30
Analyze Elements of Persuasion		1, 9, 13, 15, 18, 26	
Identify Evidence		2, 7, 15, 18, 26	
Analyze Visuals and Data		2, 7	
Identify Faulty Evidence		8	6, 11
Classify Valid and Invalid Evidence		15, 18	6, 11
Analyze the Structure of Arguments		1, 4, 9. 13, 17, 26, 27	11, 12, 21
Analyze Rhetorical Devices		10, 13, 15	3
Compare and Contrast Texts		19, 29	20, 21, 22, 23, 24, 28, 30, 31, 32
Compare Texts in Different Formats		19	20, 21, 22, 23, 24
Compare Texts in Different Genres		29	28, 30, 31, 32
Gain Information from Multiple Texts			23, 24, 31, 32

LANGUAGE ARTS

Unit 2 Review

Use workbook lessons, as identified in the following table, to assist learners who require additional remediation with certain skills or items having certain DOK levels.

Unit 2 Workbook Item Analysis

SKILL	DOK LEVEL 1	DOK LEVEL 2	DOK LEVEL 3
Determine Author's Purpose	3, 4, 10	1, 2, 5, 6, 7, 11, 12	8, 9, 13, 14
Analyze Elements of Persuasion		1, 3, 4, 5, 6, 8, 9, 10, 11	2, 7
Identify Evidence		1, 2, 3, 4, 5, 6, 8, 9, 10, 11	7
Analyze Visuals and Data		1, 2, 6, 7, 9, 11	3, 4, 5, 8, 10, 12
Identify Faulty Evidence		1, 2, 3, 5, 6, 7, 8, 9, 10	4, 11, 12, 13
Classify Valid and Invalid Evidence		1, 3, 4, 5, 6, 7, 9, 12, 13	2, 8, 10, 11, 14
Analyze the Structure of Arguments		1, 2, 3, 4, 5, 7, 8, 9, 10, 11, 12	6
Analyze Rhetorical Devices		1, 2, 3, 4, 6, 7, 8, 9, 10, 11, 12, 13	5
Compare and Contrast Texts	7	2, 5, 6, 8, 9, 10	1, 3, 4, 11, 12, 13
Compare Texts in Different Formats		5, 6, 7	1, 2, 3, 4, 8, 9, 10, 11, 12
Compare Texts in Similar Genres		2, 3, 4, 7, 8, 9, 10	1, 5, 6, 11, 12, 13, 14, 15
Compare Texts in Different Genres		2, 3, 5, 8	1, 4, 6, 7, 9, 10, 11
Gain Information from Multiple Texts			1, 2, 3, 4, 5, 6, 7, 8, 9, 10, 11, 12

Unit 3

Extended Response

In the 45-minute extended response section of the GED® Reasoning Through Language Arts Test, candidates will provide a written analysis supporting an opinion with appropriate textual evidence drawn from one or two passages. Extended responses will be scored according to a three-trait rubric.

- Trait 1: Analysis of Arguments and Use of Evidence *(the ability to read closely)*
- Trait 2: Development of Ideas and Structure *(the ability to write clearly)*
- Trait 3: Clarity and Command of Standard English Conventions *(the ability to use, edit, and understand standard written English)*

Unit 3 integrates reading and writing as assessed in this section of the test. Lesson 1 focuses solely on analytical reading. Then, using these passages as the sources of their extended responses, learners progress to Lesson 2, which introduces the writing prompt and provides instruction on developing a comprehensive thesis. Each lesson builds on previous ones so that when learners write their drafts in Lesson 6, they will have written a clear thesis, an introduction, and a conclusion and will have their main points and evidence well phrased and in order.

Unit 3 is closely connected with Unit 4. Consider using them simultaneously or teaching all or some Unit 4 material before beginning Unit 3. If applicable, practice keyboarding skills—such as copy, paste, delete, and undo—that learners will use when taking the test.

Table of Contents

LESSON	PAGE
1: Compare Opposing Arguments	RLA 48
2: Develop a Thesis	RLA 49
3: Define Points and Gather Evidence	RLA 50
4: Plan the Extended Response	RLA 51
5: Write Introduction and Conclusion	RLA 52
6: Draft the Extended Response	RLA 53
7: Review the Extended Response	RLA 54
Unit 3 Review	RLA 55

Compare Opposing Arguments

READING ASSESSMENT TARGETS: R.5.1, R.5.3, R.5.4, R.6.1, R.6.2, R.6.4, R.9.1/R.7.1, R.9.2, R.9.3

LANGUAGE ARTS

STUDENT BOOK pp. 96–97

▶ Preview the Skill

Read aloud or use an overhead projector to show learners an editorial, a letter to the editor, or a speech. For each passage, ask learners to think of opposing arguments or something that a writer with another opinion might add or omit. Then remind learners that authors writing on the same topic often have different opinions about it. As learners prepare to compare and contrast the arguments on p. 98, have them answer these questions:

- *What is each author's purpose?*
- *What is each author's main claim?*
- *What support does each author provide?*

❶ Learn the Skill

Link to Past Skills Have learners review the skill *Analyze the Structure of Arguments* from Unit 2, Lesson 7. Applying the information from this lesson to the excerpts on p. 96, have learners explain how both authors introduce their claims. (*Clift refers to her teaching experience, whereas Jones uses an anecdote about an adult returning to school.*) Ask learners which introduction they think is stronger and to explain the reason for their choice.

❷ Practice the Skill

Skim and Scan To help learners answer question 1, have them skim and scan both passages for statements that indicate the authors' points of view about online education. For example, Clift states that she will "never do it again," whereas Jones says that online education has its "benefits" for working adults. Have learners use these and other statements to contrast the authors' points of view.

❸ Apply the Skill

Decoding To help learners answer question 3, review how to use context clues to decode unfamiliar words. For example, in paragraph 2, Clift mentions the *anonymity* students experience with online education, resulting in "no face … no body language, no in-the-moment exchange."

Answers
1. B; DOK Level: 3; **2.** D; DOK Level: 3; **3.** A; DOK Level: 3

WORKBOOK pp. 150–153

❶ Review the Skill

SuperSkill Review Explain to learners that when they compare and contrast arguments, they not only find similarities and differences but they also evaluate each argument to decide which is stronger. Advise learners to consider the type of evidence as well as the way in which it is used when they determine which argument is stronger. For example, Clemmitt cites research on social media's impact on thinking and multitasking, whereas Leung cites research about the impact of texting on communication skills.

❷ Refine the Skill

Use Graphic Organizers Have learners use this graphic organizer to compare and contrast the arguments introduced on p. 150.

Passage 1	Passage 2
Claim: Social media is distracting and negatively affects thinking and learning.	Claim: Social media can improve communication skills and literacy.
Evidence: Many people spend a great deal of time checking mobile-devices for messages and give "continuous partial attention" to everything.	Evidence: Texting offers people more exposure to the written word, thus improving literacy.

▶ Master the Skill

Spotlighted Item Type Have student pairs work together to complete the drag-and-drop chart for one passage. Then have them complete the second chart individually and explain their choices to each other.

▶ Enrich and Extend

Have students discuss their views of texting (they can address texting while driving) or another controversial issue, such as genetically modified foods. Ask them to list arguments in support of and against the issue. Then ask class members to determine which argument seems stronger.

Answers
1. A; DOK Level: 3; **2.** B; DOK Level: 3; **3.** D; DOK Level: 3. See the workbook Annotated Answer Key, p. 313, for answers and explanations for the charts on pp. 152 and 153.

Develop a Thesis

READING ASSESSMENT TARGETS: R.5.3, R.6.2, R.6.4, R.8.1, R.8.2, R.8.3, R.9.1/R.7.1, R.9.2, R.9.3
WRITING ASSESSMENT TARGETS: W.1, W.2

LANGUAGE ARTS

STUDENT BOOK *pp. 98–99*

➤ Preview the Skill

Work with learners to develop a thesis on sample topics phrased as questions or prompts. Have learners narrow each topic to reach a thesis that answers all parts of the question. For example, a thesis for the question *Do cats or dogs make better pets?* could be *Cats make better pets than dogs because cats are more independent and less expensive to own.* Remind learners that a response that does not answer the prompt, no matter how well written and supported, is still wrong. Remind them, too, that all parts of their extended responses must address the thesis, which must be narrow enough to focus on their point of view and broad enough to include supporting ideas.

❶ Learn the Skill

Give Examples Read aloud examples of introductory paragraphs from magazine articles, editorials, or speeches. Ask learners to identify the claim or thesis and identify the issue(s) it will address. If any paragraphs are unclear, discuss ways to improve clarity.

❷ Practice the Skill

Decoding Help learners decode the answer choices to determine which claim makes the best thesis statement for the prompt on p. 98. Explain that the best claim should answer the prompt by including both articles and indicating which author's position is better supported.

❸ Apply the Skill

Spotlighted Item Type Have learners work in pairs to complete the organizer on p. 99. Explain that partners may not agree about which position is better supported. However, as they answer questions 4 and 5, they must be able to explain their choices to their partners. As an extension, consider having each partner provide support for the other's point of view.

Answers

See the student book Annotated Answer Key, p. 206, for answers and explanations.

WORKBOOK *pp. 154–157*

❶ Review the Skill

SuperSkill Review Referring to the *Using Logic* note on p. 154, remind learners that their thesis statement in response to the prompt must not only state which author better supports her claim but also briefly explain why. Ask learners to consider their own opinions about social media and to explain how either article might have persuaded them to think differently. If neither article changed their minds, ask learners to explain why their opinions have remained the same. Use their comments to form a sample thesis.

❷ Refine the Skill

Decoding To help learners answer question 1, have them decode the answer choices carefully and choose the answer that indicates one claim is better supported than the other. Only such a thesis statement addresses the extended response prompt.

❸ Master the Skill

Spotlighted Item Type First have learners work individually to complete the graphic organizer on p. 155. Explain that the organizer will help them answer questions 2 and 3. Then organize learners into pairs, and have them answer questions 2 and 3 together. Ask each partner to explain the reasons for his or her choice about the strengths and weakness of the authors' arguments. Then have each learner develop a thesis statement to complete the organizer on p. 157.

➤ Language Analysis

Have students work in pairs or small groups to complete the activity on page 156. Learners can work together for the first passage, then individually for the second. After they have completed both passages, have learners share their work with their partners or group.

Answers

See the workbook Annotated Answer Key, p. 314, for answers and explanations.

LANGUAGE ARTS

Define Points and Gather Evidence

READING ASSESSMENT TARGETS: R.5.3, R.9.1/R.7.1, R.9.2, R.9.3
WRITING ASSESSMENT TARGETS: W.1, W.2

STUDENT BOOK pp. 100–101

▸ Preview the Skill

Remind learners that they first will compare and contrast the passages before deciding which argument is better supported. Explain that they will focus not only on the differences and similarities in claims and supporting evidence but also on tone and rhetorical techniques. Read aloud two paragraphs that address the same issue. You can find these in a newspaper or magazine or write them yourself. Have students identify the claims made by each author. As a group, discuss both authors' tone and rhetorical techniques and how they strengthen or weaken the arguments.

❶ Learn the Skill

Give Examples Read aloud these sentences:
- *Travis works out regularly.*
- *Travis lifts weights at the gym five days a week and runs four miles every morning.*

Ask learners to identify the major difference between the two sentences. (*The first sentence provides no details about Travis's workout, but the second sentence reveals how often and in what ways Travis works out.*) Remind learners to include all necessary details to support their thesis. Emphasize that the strongest responses include such necessary details and do not read as summaries, as does the first sentence.

❷ Practice the Skill

Link to Past Skills Have learners review the skill *Analyze Style and Tone* from Unit 1, Lesson 9, to determine each author's tone. Students may note that Clift's tone is more negative or resentful whereas Jones's is more positive.

❸ Apply the Skill

Spotlighted Item Type Have learners work in pairs to complete the chart on p. 101. Remind them to refer to the web diagram on p. 100 to identify possible points of comparison or contrast. Learners will use these points of comparison and contrast in their extended responses.

Answers
See the student book Annotated Answer Key, p. 206, for answers and explanations.

WORKBOOK pp. 158–161

❶ Review the Skill

SuperSkill Review If needed, remind learners how counterarguments strengthen an author's claims. Then, referring to the *Using Logic* note on p. 158, advise learners to focus on three points of comparison between the passages. Explain that they should focus only on the points that support their thesis. Examples may include these:
- *Leung opens with a humorous anecdote, but Clemmitt begins by referring to a common annoyance.*
- *Clemmitt's tone is apprehensive, but Leung's tone is more positive and friendly.*

❷ Refine the Skill

Skim and Scan To answer question 1, have learners skim and scan the answer choices to look for the answer that addresses a common point in both passages. Encourage learners to go back to the passages to find the answer choice that applies to both passages.

❸ Master the Skill

Spotlighted Item Type Have learners complete the graphic organizers on pp. 159–160 by using the points of comparison listed in the Venn diagram on p. 158. After learners have finished, ask them to exchange organizers with a partner and to provide feedback on the relevance and strength of the evidence supporting each point of comparison.

▸ LifeLink

Ask learners to relate a recent experience in which they compared and contrasted two items or ideas to decide which was better. For example, they may have decided between two job offers or between two apartments to rent. Have learners create a list of pros and cons that helped them decide. Then ask them to write a thesis statement in which they state which option they chose and why they chose it.

Answers
See the workbook Annotated Answer Key, pp. 314–315, for answers and explanations.

Plan the Extended Response

WRITING ASSESSMENT TARGETS: W.1, W.2

STUDENT BOOK *pp. 102–103*

▶ Preview the Skill

Discuss with learners the organizational structures for writing, such as cause-and-effect, chronological order, and compare-and-contrast. Provide appropriate examples from essays, books, magazines, or Units 1 and 2 of this book or the workbook. Discuss the structures that each paragraph or passage displays. Remind learners that most passages have an overall structure but that individual paragraphs or sections usually reflect other structures, such as cause-and-effect or sequence.

❶ Learn the Skill

Link to Past Skills Have learners review the skill *Analyze the Structure of Arguments* from Unit 2, Lesson 7. Discuss, as a class, the differences among the structures mentioned in the Unit 2 lesson. Then take the discussion a step further to focus on how these structures apply to the point-by-point and subject-by-subject organization as explained in this lesson.

❷ Practice the Skill

Give Examples Provide learners with examples of possible topics or actual passages for comparison and contrast. As a class, decide on points of comparison or contrast. Then, with the class, create a chart similar to those on p. 102 outlining the structure of a point-by-point and subject-by-subject structure for each topic or passage.

❸ Apply the Skill

Spotlighted Item Type Have learners work in small groups to complete the charts on p. 103. Remind learners to refer to the evidence chart in Lesson 3, p. 101. Learners will use these points of comparison and contrast in their extended responses.

Answers
See the student book Annotated Answer Key, pp. 206–207, for answers and explanations.

WORKBOOK *pp. 162–165*

❶ Review the Skill

SuperSkill Review Point out that authors often use more than one structure to organize ideas. For example, an author may describe an event by using both chronological order and a cause-and-effect structure, thus relating events as they happened and at the same time explaining how one event led to another. These structures also may be part of an overall point-by-point or subject-by-subject comparison. Ask learners to brainstorm for other ways in which writers may combine organizational structures.

❷ Refine the Skill

Give Examples To help learners decide how to organize their ideas, point out the *Using Logic* note on p. 162. With learners organized into small groups, suggest possible topics, purposes, and audiences. For example, suggest the topic of stores charging extra for plastic bags. Possible audiences might be plastic bag manufacturers, paper bag manufacturers, environmentalists, small business owners, or a general audience. Ask group members to decide which order and overall structure would be most effective for each target audience and to explain their decisions.

❸ Master the Skill

Spotlighted Item Type Have learners work in pairs to complete the activity on p. 163. Ask them to evaluate their partners' answers and offer tips on how best to organize the extended response.

▶ Enrich and Extend

Ask learners, organized into small groups, to think of a food item, such as a hamburger, featured at two different restaurants. Have learners list points of comparison and contrast to determine which restaurant serves a better hamburger. Then ask them to arrange the points in order of importance according to different audiences (for example, health-conscious adults or restaurant owners) and to make appropriate adjustments.

Answers
See the workbook Annotated Answer Key, p. 315, for answers and explanations.

Write Introduction and Conclusion

READING ASSESSMENT TARGET: R.5.4
WRITING ASSESSMENT TARGETS: W.1, W.2, W.3
LANGUAGE ASSESSMENT TARGETS: L.1.9, L.2.4

LANGUAGE ARTS

STUDENT BOOK *pp. 104–105*

➤ Preview the Skill

Remind learners that an engaging introduction is necessary to hook readers. Mention, too, that an effective response usually does not begin with the thesis as the first sentence. Explain that authors may begin with an interesting story, or anecdote, that includes specific details and examples reflecting their position on an issue. Then, as a class, write an opening sentence for an essay about the advantages of obtaining the GED® certificate. Continue the activity by creating an attention-getting introductory paragraph that supports the opening sentence.

❶ Learn the Skill

Give Examples From magazine or newspaper articles or from speeches, provide learners with examples of introductory paragraphs that use an action, dialogue/quotation, or reaction strategy. Then provide examples of conclusions that use an anecdote, connection, or facts or statistics strategy. Ask learners to identify the introduction or conclusion strategies and to explain which strategies they find most effective.

❷ Practice the Skill

Decoding To help learners answer question 1, remind them that an action lead starts with a scenario in which a person is doing something. The author then uses this action as a transition to the thesis. Have students decode the answer choices to find which best describes such a scenario.

❸ Apply the Skill

Spotlighted Item Type Have learners work in pairs to complete the charts on p. 105. Remind learners to use the thesis statement they developed in Lesson 2. Tell partners to help each other choose effective strategies for writing engaging introductions and thought-provoking or motivating conclusions.

Answers
See the student book Annotated Answer Key, p. 207, for answers and explanations.

WORKBOOK *pp. 166–169*

❶ Review the Skill

Link to Past Skills Have learners review the skill *Summarize* from Unit 1, Lesson 2. Explain that a conclusion is like a summary. By reviewing what they learned about summarizing, learners should be better equipped to write concluding paragraphs that summarize their extended responses.

❷ Refine the Skill

Decoding Have learners read the *Review the Skill* section and the Introduction and Conclusion paragraphs on p. 166. Ask learners to underline transitions and circle the thesis statement in the Introduction and thesis restatement in the Conclusion. Then, as a class, discuss the forceful way in which the writer has begun and ended the response. Lead learners to recognize words and expressions that appeal to emotions in the conclusion—*disturbing effects, charmed,* and *dumbing down*—and discuss whether this strategy makes the conclusion more effective than it would be otherwise.

❸ Master the Skill

SuperSkill Review Have learners complete the charts on p. 167 individually or in pairs. Refer learners to Unit 4, Lesson 20, if they are not sure how to punctuate dialog or quotations. Then, as a class, discuss which strategies appeal most to them and why certain strategies work better than others. For example, some students may find the action strategy engaging or humorous whereas others may find that the quotation from Mark Zuckerberg gives credibility.

➤ Language Analysis

Ask learners to think of transitional words and phrases to use as they lead into their thesis restatements and open their conclusions. For example, learners may suggest *nevertheless, however, in conclusion,* or *as a result.* Create a list of transitions, and encourage learners to use them in their extended responses.

Answers
See the workbook Annotated Answer Key, p. 316, for answers and explanations.

Draft the Extended Response

READING ASSESSMENT TARGET: R.5.3
WRITING ASSESSMENT TARGETS: W.1, W.2, W.3
LANGUAGE ASSESSMENT TARGET: L.1.9

STUDENT BOOK pp. 106–109

➤ Preview the Skill

Explain that as learners draft their extended responses, they must keep in mind their audience, their purpose—which is to persuade—and their thesis—which should fully answer the extended response prompt. Suggest that learners stop after each paragraph they write and ask these questions:
- *Do the main idea and supporting details support the thesis and help answer the prompt?*
- *Does each paragraph follow a logical and appropriate order with the other paragraphs?*
- *Do transitions between and within paragraphs show the relationships between ideas?*

❶ Learn the Skill

Give Examples Provide learners with samples of student writing that fail to answer the prompt, that contain irrelevant or insufficient information, that do not consider the audience consistently, and that lack effective transitions. Ask learners to identify and suggest corrections for each problem.

❷ Practice the Skill

Skim and Scan To help learners answer question 1, have them consider the passages. Ask: *Do the authors' points of view agree? Are they similar or different?* Have learners skim and scan the answer choices for words or phrases that show comparison or contrast. Tell learners to choose the answer that best explains how the authors' claims relate to each other.

❸ Apply the Skill

Spotlighted Item Type Have learners work individually to draft their extended responses on pp. 107–109. Explain that if they use a subject-by-subject structure, they first must create an outline similar to the one on p. 106. They can use the Subject By Subject chart on p. 103 for guidance. After they have completed their responses, organize learners into small groups to exchange drafts for peer reviews. If applicable, refer learners to the rubrics on pp. 182–184.

Answers
See the student book Annotated Answer Key, p. 207, for answers and explanations.

WORKBOOK pp. 170–173

❶ Review the Skill

SuperSkill Review Remind learners that their drafts should stay focused on answering the prompt and stay true to their purpose, which is not merely to compare and contrast but to persuade readers to agree with their analysis of the passages. Share with learners two drafts, one that reveals such an analysis and one that reveals only comparison and contrast.

❷ Refine the Skill

Decoding To help learners answer question 1, have them decode the answer choices for the types of transitions that writers use to compare or contrast points of view. Explain that the transition must introduce the second author's point of view and show how it relates to the first author's point of view.

❸ Master the Skill

Spotlighted Item Type Ask students to work in pairs to draft their extended responses on pp. 171-173. Partners should review each other's work in progress to ensure that each point of comparison and contrast is supported and that transitions are used in a way that makes sense. Partners also should check each other's work for clarity and word choice, avoiding vague language.

➤ Enrich and Extend

Have students work in pairs (different from the partners they worked with while drafting) to read each other's drafts. Ask "readers" to explain to "writers" what does and does not make sense, what needs clarifying, and where transitions could be improved. Also, have partners explain how successfully the draft answers the prompt and how well all claims are supported with textual evidence. Encourage readers to comment on at least three positive aspects of each response. If applicable, refer learners to the rubrics on pp. 270–272.

Answers
See the workbook Annotated Answer Key, p. 316, for answers and explanations.

Review the Extended Response

WRITING ASSESSMENT TARGETS: W.1, W.2, W.3
LANGUAGE ASSESSMENT TARGETS: L.1.1, L.1.2, L.1.3, L.1.4, L.1.5, L.1.6, L.1.7, L.1.8, L.1.9, L.2.1, L.2.2, L.2.3, L.2.4

LANGUAGE ARTS

STUDENT BOOK pp. 110–111

➤ Preview the Skill

If you have not already done so, consider assigning or working through Unit 4, Lesson 19 (*Paragraph Organization*) and other applicable lessons in Unit 4. To determine specific problems with material covered in Unit 4, have learners participate in an "Everything You Always Wanted to Know About Revising But Never Got a Chance to Ask" session in which each learner asks a question about usage, punctuation, mechanics, and so forth. Expect questions such as *I'm not sure what a run –on sentence is* or *How do I know whether a sentence fits into a paragraph?* If applicable, use learners' questions to guide the review process.

① Learn the Skill

Link to Past Skills As learners prepare to review and revise their extended responses, point out that they have learned skills critical to this process by having completing Units 1 and 2. In addition, learners can advance individually, if appropriate, to Unit 4 to learn or review grammar, punctuation, and usage. Remind learners to check not only for grammatical errors and use of language but for content as well and to revise accordingly.

② Practice the Skill

Give Examples Provide learners with examples of wordiness and omitted transitions. As a class, consider ways of eliminating wordy expressions, such as *at this point in time* instead of *now*, and add transitions as needed for clarity and logic.

③ Apply the Skill

Skim and Scan Have learners work in pairs to complete the Review Chart on p. 111. Tell them to skim and scan their drafts for examples of word choice, transition, wordiness, sentence structure, and mechanical errors that require correction. Remind students to think critically about what they have learned about writing an effective response and to refer to the rubrics on pp. 182–184 and Unit 4 lessons as needed.

Answers
See the student book Annotated Answer Key, pp. 207–208 for answers and explanations.

WORKBOOK pp. 174–177

① Review the Skill

SuperSkill Review As a class, review and revise either a short news item or a writing sample that contains deliberate errors. Have learners discuss ways to improve word choice for interest and clarity and to eliminate wordiness by using concise language and limiting descriptive words. Learners also should identify errors in punctuation, spelling, usage, and mechanics.

② Refine the Skill

Give Examples Read aloud vague word choices such as *stuff, things, go, did, it,* and similar items. Use each example in a sentence:
- *I did it.*
- *You can look up stuff on the computer.*
- *She was great at making things.*
- *He got it.*
- *David was good at it.*

Ask learners to suggest descriptive words to replace the vague ones, and advise learners to use strong, active verbs instead of adverbs and adjectives, when possible. Learners may use an online or print thesaurus to find alternatives.

③ Master the Skill

Decoding To help learners complete the review charts on pp. 175-177, explain the types of errors listed in the review categories. For example, show learners the following run-on sentence: *I went to the store I bought ice cream for the party.* Demonstrate correct ways to write the sentence: *I went to the store and bought ice cream for the party* or *I went to the store to buy ice cream for the party.*

➤ Language Analysis

Have student partners exchange the introductory paragraph and a body paragraph from their extended responses. Ask each partner to underline points at which the writer has used vague or incorrect words. This activity will help learners revise their extended responses.

Answers
See the workbook Annotated Answer Key, pp. 317–318, for answers and explanations.

Unit 3 Review

You may choose to use the Unit 3 Review on Student Book pp. 112–119 as a mini–practice test. If you wish to time the test, ask learners to complete all the items in 150 minutes.

Unit 3 Review Answers

1. A; **2.** C; **3.** C; **4.** A; **5.** A; **6.** D; **7.** B; **8.** however; **9.** See the student book Annotated Answer Key for answers and explanations. **10.** See the student book Annotated Answer Key for answers and explanations. **11.** See the student book Annotated Answer Key for answers and explanations.

Unit 3 Review Item Analysis

SKILL	DOK LEVEL 1	DOK LEVEL 2	DOK LEVEL 3
Compare Opposing Arguments		1, 2, 4, 7, 8	3, 5, 6, 9, 10, 11
Develop a Thesis		1, 2, 4, 7, 8	3, 9, 10, 11
Define Points and Gather Evidence		1, 2, 3, 4, 7, 8	6, 9, 10, 11
Plan the Extended Response			9, 10, 11
Write Introduction and Conclusion			9, 10, 11
Draft the Extended Response			9, 10, 11
Review the Extended Response			9, 10, 11

Use workbook lessons, as identified in the following table, to assist learners who require additional remediation with certain skills or items having certain DOK levels.

Unit 3 Workbook Item Analysis

SKILL	DOK LEVEL 1	DOK LEVEL 2	DOK LEVEL 3
Compare Opposing Arguments		Chart 1, Chart 2	1, 2, 3
Develop a Thesis		Chart 1, Chart 2, Text Mark-Up	1, 2, 3, Web Diagram
Define Points and Gather Evidence		1, 2	Graphic Organizer 1, Graphic Organizer 2, 3, 4
Plan the Extended Response		1, Web Diagram	2, 3, 4, 5, Organizational Flow Chart 1, Organizational Flow Chart 2
Write Introduction and Conclusion		1, Introduction Chart, Conclusion Chart, 7	2, 3, 4, 5, 6, 8, 9, 10, 11, 12
Draft the Extended Response		1	Frame
Review the Extended Response		1, Revision Chart 1, Revision Chart 2, Revision Chart 3	

RLA 56 *Reasoning Through Language Arts* Instructor Edition

Unit 4

Editing

Unit 4 focuses on two areas of editing: the command of Standard English conventions and the ability to write and edit for clarity, conciseness, and coherence. The GED® Reasoning Through Language Arts Test will assess these skills as individual test questions and as part of Traits 2 and 3 of the extended response.

Introduced in this unit, drop-down items—embedded in workplace or community-related passages—contain four answer options and allow test takers to view answer choices in context, closely simulating the actual editing process. Most drop-down items assessing conventions of standard English are Depth of Knowledge Level 1 and are based on Indicators L1 and L2 of the Common Core State Standards.

Elements more closely connected to writing—modifiers, sentence construction, parallelism, transitions, and paragraph structure will be assessed on the test primarily as part of Trait 2 of the extended response. However, to give learners more opportunity to practice these elements, Unit 4 covers modifiers, sentence combining, transitions, and parallelism in drop-down format and covers paragraph organization in both multiple-choice and drag-and-drop formats.

Because Units 3 and 4 are interdependent, consider teaching all or part of Unit 4 at the same time as Unit 3 or teaching Unit 4 first. For further instruction and convenient reference, use the Appendices to supplement lessons, and, when appropriate, encourage learners to memorize irregular verb conjugations, frequently confused words, and grammar rules in problem areas.

Table of Contents

LESSON	PAGE
1: Nouns	RLA 58
2: Pronouns	RLA 59
3: Basic Verb Tenses	RLA 60
4: Verbs with Helping Verbs	RLA 61
5: Apostrophes	RLA 62
6: Frequently Confused Words	RLA 63
7: Basic Subject-Verb Agreement	RLA 64
8: Standard English	RLA 65
9: Capitalization	RLA 66
10: Sentence Fragment Correction	RLA 67
11: Commas	RLA 68
12: Sentence Combining	RLA 69
13: Run-on Sentence Correction	RLA 70
14: Modifiers	RLA 71
15: Advanced Pronoun Use	RLA 72
16: Advanced Subject-Verb Agreement	RLA 73
17: Parallelism	RLA 74
18: Transitions	RLA 75
19: Paragraph Organization	RLA 76
20: Other Punctuation	RLA 77
Unit 4 Review	RLA 78–RLA 79

LANGUAGE ARTS

Nouns

LANGUAGE ASSESSMENT TARGET: L.2.1
WRITING ASSESSMENT TARGET: W.3

LANGUAGE ARTS

STUDENT BOOK *pp. 122–123*

▶ Preview the Skill

Write the following list for learners to see:
- *Comedian*
- *Chris Rock*
- *New York Jets*
- *Team*
- *Law*
- *Constitution of the United States*

Tell learners that proper nouns are specific titles or names of specific people, places, or things. Proper nouns are always capitalized. Ask learners to identify the proper nouns in the list provided.

❶ Learn the Skill

Use Graphic Organizers Ask learners to use the rules displayed in the graphic organizers on p. 122 to complete the chart below. In some cases, learners will make a singular noun plural. In others, they will convert the plural noun to its singular form.

Singular	Plural	Singular	Plural
baby			lives
	tomatoes	man	
	calves		mixes
car			mice
ranch		glass	

❷ Practice the Skill

Decoding To help learners answer question 1, have them decode the graphic organizers on p. 122 for rules on changing singular nouns to plural nouns.

❸ Apply the Skill

Spotlighted Item Type Explain that when learners are faced with a drop-down item type that completes a sentence, they should read the sentence with each answer choice inserted. For example, have students practice this approach when answering question 2.4.

Answers
1. C; DOK Level: 1; **2.1** D; DOK Level: 1; **2.2** B; DOK Level: 1; **2.3** C; DOK Level: 1; **2.4** A; DOK Level: 1

WORKBOOK *pp. 178–181*

❶ Review the Skill

Give Examples Provide learners with one page each from a newspaper or magazine. Have them underline all proper nouns or collective nouns that they find. Then have learners explain why the nouns are proper nouns; state whether they name a person, place, thing, or idea; and suggest an example of a corresponding common noun. For example, *New Jersey/place/state.*

❷ Refine the Skill

Skim and Scan To help learners answer question 1, ask them to skim and scan the callouts in the *Refine the Skill* section on p. 178. These callouts show ways to form the plural versions of certain kinds of nouns.

❸ Master the Skill

Spotlighted Item Type Tell learners that drop-down items are similar to multiple-choice items without question stems. Encourage students to use the rules they have learned regarding plural nouns, proper nouns, and collective nouns to eliminate answer choices from the drop-down menus as they would in multiple-choice items.

▶ Enrich and Extend

Explain that, at times, identifying collective nouns can be challenging. Ask learners to think of groups or categories to which they belong that are collective nouns, such as *family, club, audience, squad, brigade, jury, panel, staff, class,* or *team.* Then have students work in pairs to write a paragraph or brief anecdote, containing at least four different collection nouns, about a real or invented situation. Suggest more collective nouns, if necessary.

Answers
1. D; DOK Level: 1; **2.** B; DOK Level: 1; **3.1** D; DOK Level: 1; **3.2** C; DOK Level: 1; **3.3** A; DOK Level: 1; **3.4** C; DOK Level: 1; **4.1** A; DOK Level: 1; **4.2** B; DOK Level: 1; **4.3** D; DOK Level: 1; **4.4** C; DOK Level: 1; **5.1** C; DOK Level: 1; **5.2** A; DOK Level: 1; **5.3** D; DOK Level: 1; **5.4** A; DOK Level: 1

Pronouns

STUDENT BOOK pp. 124–125

➤ Preview the Skill

Read aloud the following sentences: *Jen loves to eat out. If Jen has time on Jen's way to work, Jen stops at the Early Bird Diner to get breakfast. Sometimes Jen goes to lunch with coworkers. Jen and the coworkers like to eat at the Chinese buffet. If Jen is running late, Jen will stop on Jen's way home and pick up a pizza for Jen's dinner.* Ask learners whether the sentences you have just read sound awkward. When learners notice the repetition, explain that everyone uses pronouns naturally, without thinking about doing so. Continue explaining that the sentences sound repetitive because speakers normally would replace several of the nouns with pronouns: *Jen loves to eat out. If she has time on her way to work, Jen stops at the Early Bird Diner to get breakfast. Sometimes she goes to lunch with coworkers. They like to eat at the Chinese buffet. If Jen is running late, she will stop on her way home and pick up a pizza for her dinner.*

❶ Learn the Skill

Give Examples Provide learners with examples of pronouns, such as *I, his,* and *me.* Then have learners give examples of other subject, object, and possessive pronouns. Have class members suggest nouns that the pronouns could replace.

❷ Practice the Skill

Skim and Scan To help learners answer question 1, have them skim and scan the sentence for the nouns that should be replaced by a pronoun. Then have learners explain why those nouns should be replaced.

❸ Apply the Skill

Decoding To help learners answer question 2.3, have them decode the second paragraph to determine which noun is replaced by the pronoun.

Answers
1. B; DOK Level: 1; **2.1** D; DOK Level: 1; **2.2** C; DOK Level: 1; **2.3** C; DOK Level: 1; **2.4** B; DOK Level: 1

WORKBOOK pp. 182–185

❶ Review the Skill

Give Examples Write the following sets of sentences for learners to see. The second sentence includes a pronoun that replaces the subject or object of the first sentence. Underline each pronoun, and tell learners whether it is a subject pronoun or an object pronoun.
- *Joanne finished the paper on time.*
- ***She** finished the paper on time.* (subject pronoun)
- *Randy helped Francesca choose a new car.*
- *Randy helped **her** choose a new car.* (object pronoun)

Have students give examples of other subject and object pronouns.

❷ Refine the Skill

Decoding To help learners answer question 1, ask them to decode the graphic organizer to determine whether a subject, an object, or a possessive pronoun is the best fit.

❸ Master the Skill

Spotlighted Item Type Have learners work in pairs to review the answer choices for one or more drop-down items. Have partners choose the correct answer and explain why the other choices are incorrect.

➤ Language Analysis

Provide student pairs with a few paragraphs from various writing samples, such as a short story, a human interest piece from a newspaper, or a magazine article. Ask partners to review these materials for pronoun use. Ask learners to underline each pronoun and then match each pronoun with the noun it replaces.

Answers
1. C; DOK Level: 1; **2.** D; DOK Level: 1; **3.1** A; DOK Level: 1; **3.2** D; DOK Level: 1; **3.3** D; DOK Level: 1; **3.4** A; DOK Level: 1; **4.1** A; DOK Level: 1; **4.2** D; DOK Level: 1; **4.3** C; DOK Level: 1; **4.4** B; DOK Level: 1; **5.1** B; DOK Level: 1; **5.2** D; DOK Level: 1; **5.3** A; DOK Level: 1; **5.4** A; DOK Level: 1

Basic Verb Tenses

LANGUAGE ARTS

▶ Preview the Skill

Read these sentences aloud: *For my birthday, I received a DVD player from my parents. I hooked it up right away, and then my friend and I watched a movie.* Explain that the past tense of most verbs is formed by adding *–d* or *–ed* to the end of the verb. In the sentences above, *received*, *hooked*, and *watched* are past-tense verbs. Ask learners to write a few sentences about a gift they once received. Then have each learner read the sentences to a partner. Each learner should identify the past-tense verbs in his or her partner's sentences.

❶ Learn the Skill

Use Graphic Organizers Ask learners to look at the verbs in the *Present* column of the graphic organizer. Have students complete the organizer by filling in the past and future tenses of each verb.

Past	Present	Future
	watch	
	cook	
	listen	
	push	

❷ Practice the Skill

Give Examples To help learners answer question 1, explain that in some cases, they must double the final consonant before adding the past-tense ending *–d* or *–ed* to a verb. Cite this rule: *If a single-syllable verb ends in a consonant that follows a single vowel, then double the consonant before adding* –ed *or* –ing. Provide these examples: *stop* becomes *stopped*, and *rub* becomes *rubbed*. Ask learners to provide additional examples.

❸ Apply the Skill

Decoding Ask learners to decode each sentence that contains a drop-down list to determine the tense of the missing verb. Learners should identify details from the text that helped them decide.

Answers
1. A; DOK Level: 1; **2.1** B; DOK Level: 1; **2.2** D; DOK Level: 1; **2.3** C; DOK Level: 1; **2.4** A; DOK Level: 1

❶ Review the Skill

Give Examples Distribute samples of writing from a newspaper, a magazine, a newsletter, or some other material. Identify several past-tense, present-tense, and future-tense verbs for learners. Then have class members identify additional verbs in these tenses.

❷ Refine the Skill

Skim and Scan To help learners answer question 1, have them skim and scan the sentence for clues as to when the action is taking place.

❸ Master the Skill

Decoding To help learners answer questions 3.1–3.4, ask them to read the passage carefully. Tell them to indicate next to each sentence when the information contained in that sentence is taking place. This exercise will help learners determine which verb tense to use.

▶ Enrich and Extend

Provide learners with these incomplete sentences:
- *I will buy the pizza, and Charles _____ the soft drinks.*
- *Last Saturday, Shawna _____ the new rollercoaster.*

Have learners work in pairs. One learner should focus on the first sentence, and the other on the second. Have learners choose a verb to complete the sentence. Remind learners to choose the correct verb tense. Then have them create a multiple-choice test item by creating three distracters for each sentence. Have partners test each other by exchanging test questions.

Answers
1. A; DOK Level: 1; **2.** C; DOK Level: 1; **3.1** A; DOK Level: 1; **3.2** C; DOK Level: 1; **3.3** D; DOK Level: 1; **3.4** D; DOK Level: 1; **4.1** D; DOK Level: 1; **4.2** C; DOK Level: 1; **4.3** A; DOK Level: 1; **4.4** C; DOK Level: 1; **5.1** B; DOK Level: 1; **5.2** B; DOK Level: 1; **5.3** C; DOK Level: 1; **5.4** D; DOK Level: 1

Verbs with Helping Verbs

WRITING ASSESSMENT TARGET: W.3

STUDENT BOOK pp. 128–129

Preview the Skill

Read aloud this sentence to learners: *I had boiled the water before I realized that I was out of pasta.* Explain that in this sentence, the word *had* is a helping verb. The appearance of *had* with the main verb, *boiled*, indicates the past perfect tense; that is, the action in this part of the sentence took place in the past before another past action was completed.

❶ Learn the Skill

Give Examples Have learners copy these sentences. Then ask learners to determine when the action took place and to label each item with the appropriate tense.

- *Mario will have finished painting the room by tomorrow.* (future perfect tense)
- *He has worked there for three months.* (present perfect tense)
- *Beth had seen the movie before she watched it again with friends.* (past perfect tense)

Have learners work in pairs to create their own sentences, using the future perfect, present perfect, and past perfect tenses.

❷ Practice the Skill

Skim and Scan Have learners skim and scan the *Learn the Skill* paragraph for instruction that will help them answer question 1. Learners should indicate which instruction applies to the sentence in question 1.

❸ Apply the Skill

Link to Past Skills Refer learners to the skill *Determine Sequence* from Unit 1, Lesson 3. Ask them to use helping verbs and transitions to create a logical sequence for the sentences in question 2.

Answers
1. B; DOK Level: 1; **2.1** C; DOK Level: 1; **2.2** A; DOK Level: 1; **2.3** B; DOK Level: 1; **2.4** D; DOK Level: 1

WORKBOOK pp. 190–193

❶ Review the Skill

SuperSkill Review Emphasize that helping verbs indicate actions that take place at different times. Read these sentences aloud, and explain the purpose of each helping verb.

- *Jon had washed his car before he met his friends.* (past perfect tense)
- *Luis has participated in the blood drive for years.* (present perfect tense)
- *By next week, she will have raised over $100 for cancer research.* (future perfect tense)

Then have learners use helping verbs to create sentences based on events in their lives. To do this activity as a class, begin by asking volunteers to share their sentences with the class.

❷ Refine the Skill

Skim and Scan To help learners answer question 1, have them skim and scan the graphic organizer to look for examples that are similar to the sentence in question 1.

❸ Master the Skill

Decoding For question 3.2, have learners identify the part of the sentence that shows when the action is taking place.

Cross-Curricular Connection

Have learners refer to the social studies workbook lesson on *Sequence* from Unit 1, Lesson 4. Ask partners to rewrite the answer choices in questions 1, 3, 5, 12, 13, 14, and/or 15 to create a short paragraph composed of sentences that demonstrate the correct use of tenses formed with helping verbs.

Answers
1. D; DOK Level: 1; **2.** C; DOK Level: 1; **3.1** D; DOK Level: 1; **3.2** B; DOK Level: 1; **3.3** C; DOK Level: 1; **3.4** A; DOK Level: 1; **4.1** D; DOK Level: 1; **4.2** C; DOK Level: 1; **4.3** B; DOK Level: 1; **4.4** D; DOK Level: 1; **5.1** C; DOK Level: 1; **5.2** A; DOK Level: 1; **5.3** D; DOK Level: 1; **5.4** B; DOK Level: 1

Apostrophes

LANGUAGE ASSESSMENT TARGETS: L.1.1, L.1.3, L.2.3
WRITING ASSESSMENT TARGET: W.3

LANGUAGE ARTS

STUDENT BOOK pp. 130–131

▷ Preview the Skill

Explain that an apostrophe may show possession; that is, it indicates to whom or what something or someone belongs. Apostrophes also take the place of missing letters when words are combined to form a contraction. Read these sentences aloud, and ask volunteers to identify the possessive words and the contractions.

- *I **can't** go to the concert because I have to work.*
- *The **players'** equipment belongs in the recreation facility.*
- ***Devon's** uniform **isn't** clean.*
- *Our cat **won't** go near **Carla's** dog.*

❶ Learn the Skill

Give Examples Ask learners to suggest examples of commonly used contractions, such as *won't*, *couldn't*, and *you're*. Then, as a group, have learners use those contractions in sentences.

❷ Practice the Skill

Skim and Scan To help learners answer question 1, have them skim and scan the *Test-Taking Tips* note for a hint about identifying and using contractions.

❸ Apply the Skill

Spotlighted Item Type Have learners work in pairs to examine the drop-down lists. For each drop-down list, have learners use specific instruction from p. 130 to help them determine the correct answer choices.

Answers

1. D; DOK Level: 1; **2.1** B; DOK Level: 1; **2.2** A; DOK Level: 1; **2.3** D; DOK Level: 1; **2.4** B; DOK Level: 1

WORKBOOK pp. 194–197

❶ Review the Skill

Give Examples Review the rules of possessives. Point out that adding an apostrophe and the letter *s* after a singular noun indicates that something belongs to that noun. Provide the following example: *my brother's video game*. Also, point out that if a plural noun ends in the letter *s*, then only an apostrophe is added to the end of that noun. Provide the following example: *the workers' rights*. Have learners suggest additional possessives that demonstrate each rule. Then review the rules for forming contractions, and provide examples.

❷ Refine the Skill

Decoding To help learners answer question 1, have them rephrase the sentence with each answer choice, replacing the contraction with its original words. For example, in answer B, *you're* becomes *you are*, and learners will notice that it makes no sense in the sentence. Reading these sentences for sense will help learners determine the correct answers.

❸ Master the Skill

Link to Past Skills Have learners review the information in *Nouns* from Unit 4, Lesson 1. Remind learners that a collective noun refers to people acting as a group. This information will help them answer question 3.4.

▷ Enrich and Extend

Have learners write a paragraph describing or reviewing a movie or television program that they have seen recently. Ask them to find ways to include several possessive nouns and contractions. Then have learners exchangeparagraphs; have them underline possessive nouns and circle contractions.

Answers

1. B; DOK Level: 1; **2.** A; DOK Level: 1; **3.1** D; DOK Level: 1; **3.2** C; DOK Level: 1; **3.3** B; DOK Level: 1; **3.4** C; DOK Level: 1; **4.1** C; DOK Level: 1; **4.2** B; DOK Level: 1; **4.3** C; DOK Level: 1; **4.4** A; DOK Level: 1; **5.1** A; DOK Level: 1; **5.2** C; DOK Level: 1; **5.3** A; DOK Level: 1; **5.4** B; DOK Level: 1

Frequently Confused Words

LANGUAGE ASSESSMENT TARGETS: L.1.1, L.1.3

STUDENT BOOK *pp. 132–133*

➤ *Preview the Skill*

Explain that homonyms are words that sound alike or nearly alike but are spelled differently and have different meanings. Select a magazine or newspaper passage that contains several frequently confused words, including homonyms, and point out these words. For example, point out the homonyms *to*, *too*, and *two* and the words *then* and *than*. Have students examine the context of the words in each sentence to determine the definition of each frequently confused word.

❶ *Learn the Skill*

Give Examples Have learners give examples of some other frequently confused words, such as *write/right*, *cell/sell*, *pain/pane*, *be/bee*, *great/grate*, *ate/eight*, *our/hour*, *meet/meat*, *fare/fair*, *bred/bread*, and *advice/advise*. Then have learners write sentences that demonstrate the use of each frequently confused word, using each pair in a single sentence. Consider suggesting a topic for their sentences, such as restaurants or products that learners like or dislike.

❷ *Practice the Skill*

SuperSkill Review Have learners work with a partner to choose a pair of homonyms on pp. 174–175. Have partners create a sentence for each homonym. Then have partners test the class by reading their sentences aloud, allowing class members to choose the correct homonym for each sentence. Once again, consider suggesting several general topics for the sentences—for example, hardware stores, doctors' offices, public transportation, the street on which they live or work.

❸ *Apply the Skill*

Decoding To help learners answer question 2.1, have them decode the sentence containing the drop-down list. Have them identify the part of the sentence that allows them to choose the correct word.

Answers
1. B; DOK Level: 1; **2.1** C; DOK Level: 1; **2.2** D; DOK Level: 1; **2.3** B; DOK Level: 1; **2.4** C; DOK Level: 1

WORKBOOK *pp. 198–201*

❶ *Review the Skill*

SuperSkill Review Share these sentences with learners:
- *The restaurant was busy, sew wee where told too except a long weight.*
- *Nikki didn't no weather her sell phone was ringing because the mane area of the station were she was sitting was two noisy.*

Ask learners to identify the misused words in these sentences and to explain what the sentences actually mean with the incorrect words. Then explain the meaning of each word. Have learners correct the sentences and think of others using these words.

❷ *Refine the Skill*

Decoding To help learners answer question 1, have them decode the answer choices and define the words to determine which correction best fits the sentence.

❸ *Master the Skill*

Skim and Scan To help learners answer question 4.4, instruct them to skim and scan the third paragraph and determine the context that provides the correct answer.

➤ *Language Analysis*

Explain that knowing the correct definitions of homonyms and other frequently confused words will help learners avoid errors. Knowing definitions and when to use these words may be challenging—for example, *affect* and *effect*. *Affect* means "to influence," as in *The time change affected his mood*. *Effect* has several meanings as a noun, but the meaning "result" is at the core of all the definitions, as in *The movie had quite an effect on him*. Tell learners that, in general, if a verb is needed, they should use *affect*. If a noun is needed, they should use *effect*.

Answers
1. C; DOK Level: 1; **2.** D; DOK Level: 1; **3.1** D; DOK Level: 1; **3.2** A; DOK Level: 1; **3.3** C; DOK Level: 1; **3.4** B; DOK Level: 1; **4.1** A; DOK Level: 1; **4.2** C; DOK Level: 1; **4.3** B; DOK Level: 1; **4.4** B; DOK Level: 1; **5.1** B; DOK Level: 1; **5.2** D; DOK Level: 1; **5.3** A; DOK Level: 1; **5.4** C; DOK Level: 1

Basic Subject-Verb Agreement

LANGUAGE ASSESSMENT TARGETS: L.1.2, L.1.7

STUDENT BOOK *pp. 134–135*

➤ Preview the Skill

Read aloud this sentence: *Amy are going on a camping trip.* Ask learners whether the sentence sounds correct. Explain that the sentence is incorrect because the subject and verb do not agree: *Amy* is a singular subject, but *are* is a plural verb. Read aloud these corrections to the sentence:
• *Amy is going on a camping trip.*
• *Amy and DeShaun are going on a camping trip.*
The first sentence is correct because the singular verb *is* agrees with the singular subject *Amy.* The second sentence is correct because the plural subject *Amy and DeShaun* agrees with the plural verb *are.*

❶ Learn the Skill

Use Graphic Organizers Ask learners to correct the sentences in the graphic organizer to ensure subject-verb agreement. As a group, have learners create the new sentences that belong in the empty boxes.

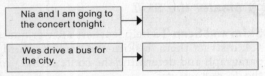

Nia and I am going to the concert tonight.	→
Wes drive a bus for the city.	→

❷ Practice the Skill

Skim and Scan To help learners answer question 1, have them skim and scan the graphic organizer on p. 134 for examples of subject-verb agreement and disagreement. Remind learners that third-person singular verbs end in *s* and not to confuse the *s* ending with a plural.

❸ Apply the Skill

Decoding To help learners answer question 2.4, ask them to decode the sentence containing the drop-down list. Guide learners to recognize that the verb must agree with the subject that is closer to the verb. The word *or* indicates that the subject is compound.

Answers
1. A; DOK Level: 1; **2.1** B; DOK Level: 1; **2.2** C; DOK Level: 1; **2.3** A; DOK Level: 1; **2.4** D; DOK Level: 1

WORKBOOK *pp. 202–205*

❶ Review the Skill

Give Examples Review the definition of subject-verb agreement. Read aloud from a book, magazine, or newspaper to illustrate examples of subject-verb agreement. After reading the first example, point out the subject and verb, and explain why they agree. Ask volunteers to do the same for other examples as you continue to read aloud.

❷ Refine the Skill

SuperSkill Review Review the rules and examples in the graphic organizer on p. 202. Then provide learners with an event or activity about which to create five of their own sentences that illustrate the rules in the chart. For example, have students focus their sentences on a party or meeting they attended or on taking care of a pet.

❸ Master the Skill

Decoding Whether or not the subject and verb in a sentence are separated by other words, they still must agree. To help learners answer question 5.4, have them decode the sentence containing the drop-down list to determine the appropriate subject.

➤ Enrich and Extend

Tell learners to copy the sentences below. Then have learners work in pairs to correct the sentences in which the subject and verb disagree.
• *Kendall and Robin goes to the gym every week.*
• *Isabelle and Felipe is watching movies.*
• *Beth or her parents get the mail every afternoon.*
• *Michael and Sumit grows vegetables every year.*
• *Harry and I are good friends.*
• *My brother belong to a bowling league.*
• *Rita or Connie buy the groceries after work.*

Answers
1. C; DOK Level: 1; **2.** A; DOK Level: 1; **3.1** D; DOK Level: 1; **3.2** A; DOK Level: 1; **3.3** C; DOK Level: 1; **3.4** B; DOK Level: 1; **4.1** C; DOK Level: 1; **4.2** D; DOK Level: 1; **4.3** A; DOK Level: 1; **4.4** B; DOK Level: 1; **5.1** D; DOK Level: 1; **5.2** B; DOK Level: 1; **5.3** D; DOK Level: 1; **5.4** A; DOK Level: 1

STUDENT BOOK *pp. 136–137*

▶ Preview the Skill

Emphasize that writers may use slang or informal speech when they are writing dialogue for characters in short stories, books, movies, or television shows. In these cases, writers are portraying how the characters would actually speak, rather than adhering to the rules of Standard English. Explain that when learners write formally, such as when writing a cover letter, they should follow the rules of Standard English rather than accurately reflect the way they or anyone else speaks.

❶ Learn the Skill

Use Graphic Organizers Ask learners to look at the two versions of each sentence in the graphic organizer. Then have them choose the version that reflects Standard English. Have learners use the last row in the graphic organizer to create two versions of a sentence, one containing *ain't* and the other following Standard English.

Version 1	Version 2
He should of made dinner.	He should have made dinner.
We should try to finish the project today.	We should try and finish the project today.
My costume it is original.	My costume is original.

❷ Practice the Skill

Skim and Scan To help learners answer question 1, have them skim and scan the graphic organizer on p. 136 for the example and explanation that provide guidance.

❸ Apply the Skill

Decoding To help learners decode the answer choices for questions 2.2 and 2.3, explain that when looking for double negatives, they should examine contractions that contain a form of *not*, such as *don't*. Also emphasize that *never*, *no*, and *not* are negative words.

Answers
1. C; DOK Level: 1; **2.1** D; DOK Level: 1; **2.2** D; DOK Level: 1; **2.3** A; DOK Level: 1; **2.4** B; DOK Level: 1

WORKBOOK *pp. 206–209*

❶ Review the Skill

Give Examples Provide learners with these sentences, and ask them to revise the sentences to follow Standard English.
- *Merrick he wants to rescue an animal, but he dunno whether to get a dog or cat.*
- *We're suppose to buy extra supplies, but we don't have no time to stop at the store.*

❷ Refine the Skill

SuperSkill Review Review the content of the graphic organizer on p. 206. Then explain that learners should memorize these types of mistakes so that they can easily recognize them when editing. Emphasize that if learners are familiar with basic spelling and grammar rules, they can use this knowledge to recognize incorrect use of language.

❸ Master the Skill

Decoding To help learners answer question 3.4, have them write the sentence four times, interchanging answer choices. Then have learners circle the negative words in each sentence so that they can easily identify double negatives.

▶ Enrich and Extend

Have learners write a paragraph about a childhood experience, such as a trip to an amusement park or a sporting event. Challenge them to provide at least three instances of slang or informal language in their paragraphs. The examples could be dialog that they recall or invent. Some examples might even contain mistakes that a child would make. Encourage learners to review the graphic organizer in the *Refine the Skill* section for guidance. If appropriate, have partners read their paragraphs quietly to each other. Then have partners exchange paragraphs and correct intentional and any unintentional mistakes.

Answers
1. B; DOK Level: 1; **2.** C; DOK Level: 1; **3.1** C; DOK Level: 1; **3.2** A; DOK Level: 1; **3.3** C; DOK Level: 1; **3.4** B; DOK Level: 1; **4.1** C; DOK Level: 1; **4.2** B; DOK Level: 1; **4.3** B; DOK Level: 1; **4.4** D; DOK Level: 1; **5.1** D; DOK Level: 1; **5.2** C; DOK Level: 1; **5.3** B; DOK Level: 1; **5.4** C; DOK Level: 1

Capitalization

LANGUAGE ARTS

STUDENT BOOK *pp. 138–139*

▶ Preview the Skill

Remind learners that a proper noun is the name of a specific person, place, or thing, as well as a title preceding a person's name, such as *Professor Rojas* or *Captain Wade*. Also point out that proper adjectives are descriptive words based on proper nouns. Proper nouns and proper adjectives begin with capital letters. Ask learners to identify the proper nouns and adjectives in this paragraph. *Logan and his wife, Jenny, will observe Memorial Day by placing flags along the front walk of their home. Later that day, Logan has an appointment to see Dr. Brown. After the appointment, Jenny will meet Logan for dinner at the new Italian restaurant in town.*

❶ Learn the Skill

Use Graphic Organizers Ask learners to fill in the graphic organizer by listing four proper nouns and four proper adjectives. One example of each is provided.

Proper Noun	Proper Adjective
United States Constitution	Siamese cat

❷ Practice the Skill

Link to Past Skills To help learners answer question 1, suggest that they review *Nouns* from Unit 4, Lesson 1. Then explain how to capitalize titles of works, distinguishing main words from articles and short prepositions. Mention, too, that the first and last words are always capitalized no matter what they are.

❸ Apply the Skill

Spotlighted Item Type Advise learners to check that they have made the selection they intended. If learners rush through their selections, they may accidentally click the wrong option.

Answers
1. D; DOK Level: 1; **2.1** A; DOK Level: 1; **2.2** C; DOK Level: 1; **2.3** D; DOK Level: 1; **2.4** B; DOK Level: 1

WORKBOOK *pp. 210–213*

❶ Review the Skill

SuperSkill Review Explain that some aspects of capitalization are easy to remember, such as the capitalization of people's names. Other capitalization rules can be tricky. Proper adjectives, like *French* in *French fries*, should be capitalized. Tell learners that when a title comes before someone's name, the title should be capitalized: for example, *Senator Windler*. A title should not be capitalized when used in place of a name: *The senators met.* Also, directions such as *south* or *east* should be capitalized only when a certain region is specified: *We were in the South. I drove south to Texas.*

❷ Refine the Skill

Skim and Scan To help learners answer questions 1 and 2, direct them to skim and scan the *Review the Skill* paragraphs to look for information about proper nouns.

❸ Master the Skill

Decoding Guide volunteers to explain the appropriate capitalization of prepositions and articles in titles. Then have learners decode the answer choices for question 5.3, noting the correct or incorrect capitalization of prepositions and articles.

▶ LifeLink

Have learners create a calendar for one week and fill in events (such as going to the store or getting a haircut) for each day. Encourage learners to add a movie, television show, or other title. When the calendars are complete, have learners underline common nouns and common adjectives, circle proper nouns and proper adjectives, and check that title capitalization is correct.

Answers
1. A; DOK Level: 1; **2.** C; DOK Level: 1; **3.1** C; DOK Level: 1; **3.2** C; DOK Level: 1; **3.3** A; DOK Level: 1; **3.4** B; DOK Level: 1; **4.1** A; DOK Level: 1; **4.2** D; DOK Level: 1; **4.3** B; DOK Level: 1; **4.4** B; DOK Level: 1; **5.1** A; DOK Level: 1; **5.2** C; DOK Level: 1; **5.3** B; DOK Level: 1; **5.4** A; DOK Level: 1

Sentence Fragment Correction

LANGUAGE ASSESSMENT TARGETS: L.2.1, L.2.2, L.2.4

STUDENT BOOK pp. 140–141

► Preview the Skill

Ask learners to think about a time when they heard a toddler speaking. Explain that toddlers often use sentence fragments. A sentence fragment represents an incomplete idea and cannot stand alone. Usually, a fragment is missing either a subject or verb. For example, a toddler who says, *Want up,* is using a fragment, which is missing some of the components necessary to form a sentence, or complete thought. The correct sentence is *I want to be picked up.*

❶ Learn the Skill

Give Examples Provide learners with example sentence fragments, some missing subjects and others missing verbs. Then have learners revise the fragments to make them complete sentences. Remind learners that the first word in a sentence must begin with a capital letter.

❷ Practice the Skill

Link to Past Skills Have learners review the information in *Basic Subject-Verb Agreement* from Unit 4, Lesson 7. A review of subjects and verbs in sentences will help learners find the missing parts in sentence fragments and help them answer question 1.

❸ Apply the Skill

Decoding Have learners work in pairs to decode the answer choices for question 2.1. For each answer choice, have pairs determine why the choice is correct or incorrect. Then have volunteers state and explain their choices aloud.

Answers
1. C; DOK Level: 1; **2.1** B; DOK Level: 1; **2.2** C; DOK Level: 1; **2.3** D; DOK Level: 1; **2.4** B; DOK Level: 1

WORKBOOK pp. 214–217

❶ Review the Skill

Give Examples Explain that one way to identify sentence fragments is to read them aloud for sense. Fragments often sound awkward because they lack one or more sentence components. Read aloud these examples, and ask learners to determine whether each is a fragment or a sentence.
* *Although she was excited.* (fragment)
* *I like going to the library and the coffee shop by myself.* (complete)
* *Fantastic customer service.* (fragment)
* *Yes, I do.* (complete)
* *The children in the playground.* (fragment)
* *Eat this.* (complete)

❷ Refine the Skill

Skim and Scan To help learners answer questions 1 and 2, have them skim and scan the instructions in the *Refine the Skill* section to find examples that illustrate how to correct the sentence fragments.

❸ Master the Skill

Spotlighted Item Type To help them answer questions with lengthy answer choices, such as question 5.4, encourage learners to click each answer choice so that it displays on the screen in its entirety as it would appear in context. Seeing the text in this format should help learners choose the correct answer.

► Enrich and Extend

Provide several samples of advertisements that contain sentence fragments, and explain that copy writers use fragments very often in advertising. Consider having a brief discussion about why this practice is common. Then have learners work in pairs to correct the fragments and discuss differences in tone and impact.

Answers
1. A; DOK Level: 1; **2.** C; DOK Level: 1; **3.1** A; DOK Level: 1; **3.2** C; DOK Level: 1; **3.3** B; DOK Level: 1; **3.4** D; DOK Level: 1; **4.1** D; DOK Level: 1; **4.2** B; DOK Level: 1; **4.3** B; DOK Level: 1; **4.4** C; DOK Level: 1; **5.1** D; DOK Level: 1; **5.2** A; DOK Level: 1; **5.3** B; DOK Level: 1; **5.4** C; DOK Level: 1

Commas

LANGUAGE ARTS

➤ Preview the Skill

Obtain a newspaper or magazine article on an engaging topic for learners, such as a popular sports team or movie. Be sure that the article contains several commas. Read aloud an excerpt. Tell learners that a comma indicates a pause in reading, which reflects sentence parts or word groups that belong either together or separate from the rest of the sentence. Reread the excerpt line by line, and ask volunteers to identify places in which commas are (or should be) used.

❶ Learn the Skill

Give Examples Have learners copy the sentences provided below. Then ask them to insert commas in the appropriate places, reminding them to use the graphic organizer on p. 142 as a guide.

- *Ivan liked to sing dance and act.*
- *To arrive at the airport on time for her flight Shaylah had to get up earlier than usual.*
- *The farmers' market offered bright crisp fresh vegetables.*
- *Vinnie who is a great basketball player himself met his favorite professional player.*

❷ Practice the Skill

Skim and Scan To help learners answer question 1, suggest that they skim and scan the *Practice the Skill* section for information about intervening phrases. Point out that the commas change the meaning of the sentence.

❸ Apply the Skill

Spotlighted Item Type When learners answer questions 2.2 and 2.3, suggest they pay very close attention to all words in the drop-down menu choices so that they do not overlook the punctuation following the last word in the option. This punctuation or lack of it may make the sentence correct or incorrect.

Answers
1. B; DOK Level: 1; **2.1** D; DOK Level: 1; **2.2** C; DOK Level: 1; **2.3** B; DOK Level: 1; **2.4** A; DOK Level: 1

❶ Review the Skill

SuperSkill Review With learners, list some objects found in the room. Then use the listed items to create sentences that demonstrate various comma uses. For example, if some of the items include a pen, a marker, and a book, learners could construct a sentence like this one: *I borrowed the pen and book, but I didn't need the marker.* To set off an introductory phrase or clause, construct a sentence like this: *Before I sat down, I grabbed a book from the shelf.*

❷ Refine the Skill

Decoding Remind learners that commas show the division of sentence parts into meaningful units. Have student pairs work together to answer questions 1 and 2 and to explain the use of each comma—that is, what it divides within the sentence.

❸ Master the Skill

Skim and Scan Before they answer questions 3.1–3.4, have learners skim and scan these questions to determine which comma rule applies to each question.

➤ LifeLink

Have learners write a paragraph—containing no commas—about what they would like to or what they must do over the weekend. When they have finished writing, ask learners to work in pairs to review the paragraphs. Using the rules in this lesson as a guide, partners should add commas to each other's paragraph and explain the reasons for doing so.

Answers
1. C; DOK Level: 1; **2.** A; DOK Level: 1; **3.1** C; DOK Level: 1; **3.2** B; DOK Level: 1; **3.3** C; DOK Level: 1; **3.4** A; DOK Level: 1; **4.1** C; DOK Level: 1; **4.2** A; DOK Level: 1; **4.3** B; DOK Level: 1; **4.4** A; DOK Level: 1; **5.1** D; DOK Level: 1; **5.2** C; DOK Level: 1; **5.3** D; DOK Level: 1; **5.4** B; DOK Level: 1

Sentence Combining

LANGUAGE ASSESSMENT TARGETS: L.1.6, L.1.8, L.1.9, L.2.4

STUDENT BOOK pp. 144–145

➤ Preview the Skill

Read these sentences aloud.
- *I woke up.*
- *I got dressed.*
- *The sun was shining outside.*
- *I mowed my lawn.*
- *My neighbor stopped by.*

Ask learners what they think about this series of short, choppy sentences. What could be done to improve them? Explain that readers expect varied sentence length and that these short sentences would sound smoother combined in one of several ways.

❶ Learn the Skill

Give Examples Emphasize that learners can combine sentences by eliminating needless repetition and using connecting words. Then read aloud these two sentences, and ask learners to write a new, longer sentence.
- *Maya loves playing video games.*
- *Maya loves playing Frisbee.*

The new sentence should read *Maya loves playing video games and Frisbee.* Guide students to create examples of two sentences that could be combined with the connecting word *but*.

❷ Practice the Skill

Skim and Scan Explain that one technique for combining sentences involves looking for repeated words and phrases in sentences that are near each other and closely related. Have learners skim and scan the sentences in question 1, looking for needlessly repeated words and phrases that they can eliminate when combining.

❸ Apply the Skill

Decoding Explain to learners that effective writing involves stating ideas clearly and concisely. Tell learners that when they decode answer choices, they should think about which choice best relates the writer's ideas without unnecessary repetition or useless words.

Answers
1. D; DOK Level: 2; **2.1** B; DOK Level: 2; **2.2** D; DOK Level: 2; **2.3** B; DOK Level: 2; **2.4** B; DOK Level: 2

WORKBOOK pp. 222–225

❶ Review the Skill

Use Graphic Organizers Have learners review the graphic organizer below. Explain why context matters when they select the connecting word to join two sentences.

send a text	and	write an e-mail
send a text	or	write an e-mail
send a text	but	write an e-mail
send a text	yet	write an e-mail
send a text	so	write an e-mail
send a text	however	write an e-mail

❷ Refine the Skill

Decoding To help learners answer question 2, emphasize that when choosing a connecting word to combine two sentences, they have to think about how the sentences' ideas are related.

❸ Master the Skill

Link to Past Skills Have learners review the information about *Commas* in Unit 4, Lesson 11. Explain that when combining sentences, learners often will use commas to bring the sentences' ideas together.

➤ Language Analysis

Point out that when people speak, they tend to combine sentences automatically, without paying attention to how they are connecting ideas. Have each student use a few sentences to describe his or her morning routine to a partner. Ask the listening partner to write what is being said. Direct partners to go through the transcribed version and identify points at which sentences have been combined with a comma, a connecting word and a comma, or a semicolon.

Answers
1. B; DOK Level: 2; **2.** C; DOK Level: 2; **3.1** C; DOK Level: 2; **3.2** B; DOK Level: 2; **3.3** A; DOK Level: 2; **3.4** B; DOK Level: 2; **4.1** A; DOK Level: 2; **4.2** C; DOK Level: 2; **4.3** B; DOK Level: 2; **4.4** D; DOK Level: 2; **5.1** C; DOK Level: 2; **5.2** A; DOK Level: 2; **5.3** D; DOK Level: 2; **5.4** B; DOK Level: 2

Run-on Sentence Correction

LANGUAGE ASSESSMENT TARGETS: L.2.2, L.2.4

STUDENT BOOK *pp. 146–147*

➤ *Preview the Skill*

Discuss with learners how when people are nervous, they can speak on and on without pausing or making a comprehensible point. Provide examples of this kind of speaking, such as a very nervous person speaking in front of a group or being interviewed for a job. Explain that such speech is difficult to understand and that the context may be unclear or even absent. In writing, a run-on sentence causes difficulties similar to rambling speech. Tell learners that a run-on sentence contains two or more complete sentences that are not distinguished by appropriate connecting words or punctuation. Remind learners that a run-on sentence is not necessarily long, nor is a long sentence a run-on.

1 *Learn the Skill*

Link to Past Skills Have learners review the skill *Sentence Combining* from Unit 4, Lesson 12. Explain to learners that they can draw on their knowledge of combining sentences to correct run-on sentences.

2 *Practice the Skill*

Decoding Have learners read aloud the wrong sentences from the *Practice the Skill* section. Explain that when they read a run-on sentence aloud, they usually can recognize the point at which a sentence ends. To correct the run-on sentence, learners should add a connecting word, add a comma and connecting word, add a semicolon, or create separate sentences.

3 *Apply the Skill*

Skim and Scan To determine the best way to answer question 2.1, direct learners to skim and scan each answer choice, looking for reasons to eliminate incorrect answers. For example, learners should recognize that answer choices A and D do not separate the two ideas adequately. Remind learners that the subject of an imperative sentence is usually *you* and is understood rather than stated.

Answers
1. C; DOK Level: 2; **2.1** C; DOK Level: 2; **2.2** A; DOK Level: 2; **2.3** D; DOK Level: 2; **2.4** C; DOK Level: 2

WORKBOOK *pp. 226–229*

1 *Review the Skill*

Give Examples Emphasize that a comma alone is not enough to correct a run-on sentence. Show learners this sentence as an example: *When Jana dresses for cold weather, she does not forget anything, she wears gloves, a scarf, a hat, boots, and a heavy jacket.* Then ask learners to identify the point at which the idea of the first sentence is complete. Ask them to suggest the best way to correct the error.

2 *Refine the Skill*

Decoding To help learners answer question 1, explain that, at times, the best way to determine the correct answer is to write out all possible choices. Tell learners to use each answer option to rewrite the sentence.

3 *Master the Skill*

SuperSkill Review Provide a review of the ways to correct run-on sentences. As a class, discuss the answer options for question 3.1. Guide learners to explain why each option is correct or incorrect. For example, guide learners to explain that the connecting word in answer C does not reflect the relationship of the two ideas.

➤ *Enrich and Extend*

Provide learners with a selection of magazine articles. Have each learner choose a paragraph. Then direct learners to rewrite the paragraph, purposely creating two or more run-on sentences. Have learners exchange paragraphs and make corrections, without looking at the original.

Answers
1. A; DOK Level: 2; **2.** C; DOK Level: 2; **3.1** A; DOK Level: 2; **3.2** C; DOK Level: 2; **3.3** B; DOK Level: 2; **3.4** A; DOK Level: 2; **4.1** D; DOK Level: 2; **4.2** B; DOK Level: 2; **4.3** A; DOK Level: 2; **4.4** C; DOK Level: 2; **5.1** B; DOK Level: 2; **5.2** D; DOK Level: 2; **5.3** C; DOK Level: 2; **5.4** D; DOK Level: 2

Modifiers

LANGUAGE ASSESSMENT TARGET: L.1.5

STUDENT BOOK *pp. 148–149*

▶ Preview the Skill

Explain that modifiers provide details about or clarify other words in a sentence. Point out that when reading sentences, learners may find it helpful to identify each modifier and the word it modifies. Review these examples:

- *Morgan was **very** good at volleyball.*
  (How good was Morgan? Very good.)
- *She drove **only** four miles to work each day.*
  (How many miles? Only four miles. The author believes that four miles is not a long drive.)

Select an item in the room, and ask learners to use modifiers to describe the item.

❶ Learn the Skill

Give Examples Have learners identify modifiers and words they modify in these sentences. Then have learners correct the sentences.

- *On his walk, Jason found a silver woman's ring.*
  (**Incorrect:** This sentence implies that Jason found a ring belonging to a silver woman.)
- **Correct:** *On his walk, Jason found a woman's silver ring.*
- *Very late for the flight, the tickets were misplaced.*
  (**Incorrect:** Who was running late? Who misplaced the tickets?)
- **Correct:** *Very late for the flight, Ava misplaced the tickets* or *Because Ava was very late for the flight, she misplaced the tickets.*

❷ Practice the Skill

Skim and Scan Have learners skim and scan the chart on p.148 to identify questions they can ask to identify misplaced or dangling modifiers. Then have learners answer question 1. For example, *What was nearly over?* Remind learners that in this type of constructions, the modified word must follow the modifier directly.

❸ Apply the Skill

Decoding To help learners answer question 2.4, guide them to understand that the introductory phrase modifies the understood subject *you.*

Answers
1. D; DOK Level: 2; **2.1** B; DOK Level: 2; **2.2** B; DOK Level: 2; **2.3** A; DOK Level: 2; **2.4** B; DOK Level: 2

WORKBOOK *pp. 230–233*

❶ Review the Skill

Give Examples Refer learners to the *Using Logic* note on p. 230. Explain that a verb + *-ing*, a verb + *-ed*, and *to* + a verb often become dangling modifiers. To correct a dangling modifier, learners must insert a subject and rewrite the sentence. Have volunteers correct each sentence below.

- *After going to the post office, dinner was served.*
- **Correct:** *After going to the post office, Matt served dinner* or *After Matt went to the post office, he served dinner.*
- *To forecast the weather, radar technology is used.*
- **Correct:** *To forecast the weather, meteorologists use radar technology.*

❷ Refine the Skill

Decoding To help learners answer question 1, have them write the sentence, circle the misplaced modifier, and underline the word that the modifier describes.

❸ Master the Skill

Skim and Scan Explain that learners may have difficulty identifying misplaced adverbs. Remind learners that they should place an adverb after the direct object in a sentence containing a direct object. Then have learners skim and scan answer choices for adverbs and determine whether they are misplaced.

▶ Language Analysis

Provide writing samples (such as a company's newsletter or a brochure), and ask student pairs to review the materials for dangling and misplaced modifiers. If learners find errors, ask them to correct and rewrite the sentences on a separate sheet of paper. If learners do not find errors, ask them to circle each modifier and underline the word it modifies.

Answers
1. D; DOK Level: 2; **2.** B; DOK Level: 2; **3.1** B; DOK Level: 2; **3.2** B; DOK Level: 2; **3.3** C; DOK Level: 2; **3.4** C; DOK Level: 2; **4.1** D; DOK Level: 2; **4.2** B; DOK Level: 2; **4.3** A; DOK Level: 2; **4.4** B; DOK Level: 2; **5.1** C; DOK Level: 2; **5.2** A; DOK Level: 2; **5.3** C; DOK Level: 2; **5.4** D; DOK Level: 2

Advanced Pronoun Use

LANGUAGE ASSESSMENT TARGETS: L.1.3, L.1.7

LANGUAGE ARTS

STUDENT BOOK *pp. 150–151*

➤ Preview the Skill

Explain to learners that people often misuse pronouns in conversational language. For example, people might say, *Who are you calling?* instead of *Whom are you calling?* People also might use a pronoun that is unclear—for example, *This is unreasonable!* rather than indicating what "this" is: *This regulation is unreasonable!* Learners often will hear incorrect pronoun case in plural subjects or objects—for example, the sentence *Jorge asked Omar and I for help* is incorrect. *I* should be *me*. Emphasize that learners should not rely on conversational language to identify correct pronoun use.

❶ Learn the Skill

Link to Past Skills Have learners review the information in *Pronouns* from Unit 4, Lesson 2. Explain that understanding basic pronoun use provides a solid foundation for advanced pronoun use.

❷ Practice the Skill

Skim and Scan To help learners answer question 1, have them skim and scan the graphic organizer on p. 150 to find the examples and explanations that provide guidance for the question. Have learners determine whether the appropriate pronoun is a subject or an object pronoun. Add further explanation of subjects and objects as needed, particularly when pronouns are part of a compound subject or object. Add that when learners are unsure, they can block out the compound and use a singular subject or object to guide their choice.

❸ Apply the Skill

Decoding For questions 2.1–2.4, assign an answer choice to each learner to determine whether it is correct and to provide reasoning for his or her decision. For each answer choice, have a learner share his or her determination and reasoning with the rest of the class.

Answers
1. D; DOK Level: 2; **2.1** B; DOK Level: 2; **2.2** C; DOK Level: 2; **2.3** A; DOK Level: 2; **2.4** B; DOK Level: 2

WORKBOOK *pp. 234–237*

❶ Review the Skill

Use Graphic Organizers Have learners use this graphic organizer to write sentences that show correct and incorrect use of each pronoun. Have volunteers share sentences with the class.

Pronoun	Correct Use	Incorrect Use
whom		
this		
whoever		
myself		

❷ Refine the Skill

Give Examples Provide these examples; have learners determine whether the sentences illustrate correct use. Then have learners make corrections.
- *Each artist must bring their own supplies.* (**Correct**: *Each artist must bring his or her own supplies* or *All artists must bring their own supplies.*)
- *Whom do you think sent the package?* (**Correct**: *Who do you think sent the package?*)

❸ Master the Skill

Spotlighted Item Type Have student pairs discuss and decide on an answer for each drop-down item or specific drop-down items you have chosen. Explain that if partners suggest different answers, they should review the graphic organizer on p. 234 to eliminate one or more answers.

➤ Enrich and Extend

Ask learners to identify the pronouns that cause the most trouble. Pair learners who identify the same pronouns, have them review usage rules, and then have them write a short anecdote showing correct use. Topics may include a trip during which someone got lost, a misunderstanding about returning something at a store, or a child's birthday party.

Answers
1. B; DOK Level: 2; **2.** C; DOK Level: 1; **3.1** A; DOK Level: 1; **3.2** C; DOK Level: 1; **3.3** C; DOK Level: 2; **3.4** B; DOK Level: 2; **4.1** B; DOK Level: 2; **4.2** D; DOK Level: 2; **4.3** C; DOK Level: 2; **4.4** A; DOK Level: 2; **5.1** D; DOK Level: 1; **5.2** D; DOK Level: 1; **5.3** B; DOK Level: 1; **5.4** A; DOK Level: 2

Advanced Subject-Verb Agreement

LANGUAGE ASSESSMENT TARGET: L.1.7

STUDENT BOOK pp. 152–153

 Preview the Skill

Explain that certain subject-verb agreement rules are considered advanced because some subject-verb agreement is more difficult to discern. For example, if a sentence contains several words between a subject and a verb, or if the verb precedes the subject, learners may struggle to identify correct agreement. Provide these examples of subject-verb disagreement, and ask volunteers to correct the sentences.

- *Carl and the new girl with the pink, wavy hair and high-pitched voice is going to a movie.*
- *One of the experienced delivery drivers take that route.*
- *In the bag is your sandwich, fruit, and drink.*

❶ Learn the Skill

Link to Past Skills Have learners review the information in *Basic Subject-Verb Agreement* from Unit 4, Lesson 7. To assess their knowledge of the rules in the graphic organizer on p. 134, ask one student partner to suggest applicable singular, plural, and compound subjects and the other partner supply the correct verb. Then have partners reverse roles.

❷ Practice the Skill

Decoding To help learners answer question 1, explain that if the verb precedes the subject, they can rearrange the sentence by placing the subject before the verb. Have learners rearrange question 1 as follows: *A pencil, a piece of cheese, and a phone was in his pocket.* Ask learners whether this strategy helped them select the correct answer.

❸ Apply the Skill

Skim and Scan To help learners answer questions 2.1–2.4, encourage them to skim and scan each sentence containing a drop-down list and to identify the subject. Then have them identify the subject as singular or plural, according to the guidelines on p. 152.

Answers
1. B; DOK Level: 1; **2.1** D; DOK Level: 1; **2.2** B; DOK Level: 1; **2.3** C; DOK Level: 1; **2.4** C; DOK Level: 1

WORKBOOK pp. 238–241

❶ Review the Skill

SuperSkill Review Have learners write a summary of what they have learned about advanced subject-verb agreement. You may choose to have them use their books or write from memory. Tell learners that their audience is composed of students who are unfamiliar with the topic. As learners write, walk around the classroom, and offer assistance to learners who are struggling. Have volunteers present their summaries to the class.

❷ Refine the Skill

Skim and Scan To help learners answer questions 1 and 2, have them skim and scan the graphic organizer in the *Refine the Skill* section to identify the examples and explanations that provide guidance for each question. After learners answer the questions, have volunteers explain the reasoning behind their answer choices.

❸ Master the Skill

Decoding Encourage learners to ask themselves these questions as they answer the drop-down items:
- *What is the subject of the sentence?*
- *Does the subject appear before or after the verb?*
- *Does the sentence contain an aside that appears between the subject and the verb?*
- *Is the subject compound? If so, which part of the subject determines the appropriate verb?*
- *Is the subject a collective noun? If so, does the group act as a whole?*

LifeLink

Have learners write a brief review of a local store, service, or restaurant. In their reviews, have learners include at least three instances of correct advanced subject-verb agreement.

Answers
1. B; DOK Level: 1; **2.** B; DOK Level: 1; **3.1** C; DOK Level: 2; **3.2** A; DOK Level: 1; **3.3** C; DOK Level: 1; **3.4** C; DOK Level: 1; **4.1** D; DOK Level: 1; **4.2** B; DOK Level: 2; **4.3** A; DOK Level: 2; **4.4** C; DOK Level: 2; **5.1** D; DOK Level: 1; **5.2** D; DOK Level: 2; **5.3** C; DOK Level: 2; **5.4** D; DOK Level: 2

Parallelism

LANGUAGE ASSESSMENT TARGETS: L.1.6, L.1.8

LANGUAGE ARTS

STUDENT BOOK pp. 154–155

▶ Preview the Skill

Read aloud a section from a speech—for example, Lincoln's Gettysburg Address (workbook p. 125), Lyndon Johnson's speech (student book, p. 52), or Roosevelt's or Kennedy's nomination speech (student book pp. 80–81)—that contains parallel structure. Then read it again, rephrasing it to eliminate the parallel structure and create wordiness. Ask learners to explain their reactions to both versions, and discuss as a class how the parallel version is clearer, is more concise, draws attention to the words, and reinforces meaning. Then explain that *parallelism* simply means "stating closely related ideas in the same grammatical structure." Reinforce the idea that sentences or paragraphs lacking parallel structure sound awkward because parallelism creates a rhythmic pattern that draws listeners' and readers' attention. In fact, listeners and readers expect similar ideas to be stated in similar fashion.

❶ Learn the Skill

Link to Past Skills Review the information about connecting words in *Sentence Combining* from Unit 4, Lesson 12. Emphasize that *and*, *but*, or *or* in a series often indicates that connected elements are of equal importance. Explain that when seeing these connecting words, learners should determine whether parallel structure is present and correct.

❷ Practice the Skill

Decoding To help learners answer question 1, have them read the sentence aloud as it is written. Then ask volunteers to read the answer choice options. As each volunteer reads aloud, instruct learners to listen for the rhythm of the parallel structure to select the best answer.

❸ Apply the Skill

Skim and Scan To help learners answer question 4, encourage them to skim and scan the answer choices for wordy repetition.

Answers
1. A; DOK Level: 2; **2.** C; DOK Level: 2; **3.** D; DOK Level: 2; **4.** A; DOK Level: 2; **5.** C; DOK Level: 2

WORKBOOK pp. 242–245

❶ Review the Skill

Give Examples Show learners an example résumé that is wordy and lacks parallelism. Organize learners in pairs or small groups, and ask them to revise the sections that are wordy or not parallel. Review several volunteers' revisions, and ask learners to explain their changes.

❷ Refine the Skill

SuperSkill Review Emphasize that parallelism prevents the wordiness of inefficient writing and draws attention to important points. Discuss how the awkward sentences in the graphic organizer on p. 242 are wordy and inefficient and how the revisions improve the writing. If applicable, answer questions 1 and 2 as a class.

❸ Master the Skill

Decoding Before learners answer questions 3–6, test their ability to recognize sentences that they need to revise for parallelism. To do so, have learners cover questions 3–6 and read the passage to choose which sentences they need to revise for parallelism.

▶ LifeLink

Explain that when learners try to make a good impression, such as during a job interview, they try to avoid excessive wordiness and rambling. Advise them to follow the rules of parallelism when they plan and practice how to present ideas for these events. Consider having pairs of learners role play interviewer and interviewee, with the interviewer asking questions and the interviewee framing answers stated concisely and in parallel structure. After partners have asked and answered several questions, have learners exchange roles.

Answers
1. B; DOK Level: 2; **2.** D; DOK Level: 2; **3.** C; DOK Level: 2; **4.** C; DOK Level: 2; **5.** B; DOK Level: 2; **6.** A; DOK Level: 2; **7.** C; DOK Level: 2; **8.** A; DOK Level: 2; **9.** B; DOK Level: 2; **10.** B; DOK Level: 2; **11.1** A; DOK Level: 2; **11.2** D; DOK Level: 2; **11.3** B; DOK Level: 2; **11.4** C; DOK Level: 2

Transitions

LANGUAGE ASSESSMENT TARGET: L.1.9

STUDENT BOOK pp. 156–157

➤ Preview the Skill

Ask a volunteer to recount aloud the events that took place during the morning. Then point out the transitions the volunteer used. Explain that transitions show connections between ideas and often indicate time, causal relationship, similarity, or contrast. Identify the types of transitions used in the narrative.

❶ Learn the Skill

Use Graphic Organizers Explain that transitions often suggest a sequence of events. The first box of the graphic organizer provides a topic sentence. Ask learners to fill in the remaining boxes by creating sentences containing transitions that show sequence. When combined, the sentences will form a paragraph. Ask volunteers to read aloud their completed work.

1	Amika is preparing to go on a date.
2	
3	
4	

❷ Practice the Skill

Decoding To help learners answer question 1, suggest that they ask themselves these questions:
- *How are the two sentences related?*
- *Do the sentences need a transition that shows time, similarity, contrast, or cause-and-effect?*

❸ Apply the Skill

Spotlighted Item Type Explain that even though drop-down items usually focus on one sentence, learners need to examine surrounding sentences to gain context. For example, point out that to answer question 2.1, learners need to read the sentence that precedes the sentence with the drop-down list to understand the kind of transition needed. Emphasize that understanding the context of the sentence within the passage will help them answer individual questions.

Answers
1. B; DOK Level: 1 **2.1** A; DOK Level: 1; **2.2** C; DOK Level: 1; **2.3** D; DOK Level: 1; **2.4** B; DOK Level: 1

WORKBOOK pp. 246–249

❶ Review the Skill

Use Graphic Organizers Using the examples in the graphic organizer below, work with learners to fill in the center box with a transition that connects the sentences.

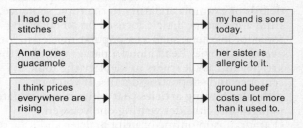

❷ Refine the Skill

SuperSkill Review Emphasize the importance of transitions in smooth writing. Provide learners with a writing sample that contains several transitions. Have learners delete some of the transitions and read the text without them. Then discuss how transitions affect the clarity and fluidity of the writing sample.

❸ Master the Skill

Decoding Encourage learners to decode answer options to determine whether the transition in each option signifies time, similarity, or contrast. As learners decode the sentences in the passages and recognize the types of transitions needed, they can eliminate incorrect options.

➤ Language Analysis

As a class, list some common transitions. Ask volunteers to create sentences for a paragraph that begins with this topic sentence: *Learning how to change the oil in your car is a good idea.* Encourage students to use the listed transitions as the paragraph takes shape. Ask a volunteer to read the completed paragraph aloud.

Answers
1. B; DOK Level: 1; **2.** C; DOK Level: 1; **3.1** C; DOK Level: 1; **3.2** B; DOK Level: 1; **3.3** C; DOK Level: 1; **3.4** A; DOK Level: 1; **4.1** A; DOK Level: 1; **4.2** D; DOK Level: 1; **4.3** C; DOK Level: 1; **4.4** A; DOK Level: 1; **5.1** C; DOK Level: 1; **5.2** C; DOK Level: 1; **5.3** B; DOK Level: 1; **5.4** A; DOK Level: 1

Paragraph Organization

LANGUAGE ASSESSMENT TARGET: L.1.9
WRITING ASSESSMENT TARGET: W.2

LANGUAGE ARTS

STUDENT BOOK pp. 158–159

➤ Preview the Skill

Explain that a paragraph must follow a pattern of organization that allows the text to flow smoothly and logically. A paragraph consists of a topic sentence and supporting sentences that provide details or examples relating to the topic sentence. Find a magazine article focused on an engaging topic for learners, such as a popular musician, local event, or movie. Read aloud a paragraph from the article, and ask learners to identify the topic sentence and supporting details. If you have difficulty finding articles that contain appropriate paragraphs, consider writing one yourself. (Paragraphs in online or print articles and newspapers may be too short, and topic sentences may be implied rather than stated.)

1 Learn the Skill

Give Examples Have learners write supporting detail sentences for the topic sentence below. Then, as a class activity, use students' sentences to construct a full paragraph.
• *Getting our first apartment took a lot of work.*

2 Practice the Skill

Skim and Scan To help learners answer question 1, have them skim and scan the *Using Logic* note on p. 158 for strategies on analyzing the organization of the paragraph. After learners have chosen answers, ask volunteers to explain the reasoning behind their decisions.

3 Apply the Skill

Decoding Before learners answer questions 2–5, have them read the passage and note sentences that seem out of place. Tell learners to think about whether to remove these sentences or to keep them and move them to other places within the paragraphs. Then have learners answer the questions to see whether they dealt correctly with the misplaced sentences.

Answers
1. B; DOK Level: 2; **2.** B; DOK Level: 2; **3.** A; DOK Level: 2;
4. C; DOK Level: 2; **5.** D; DOK Level: 2

WORKBOOK pp. 250–253

1 Review the Skill

SuperSkill Review Provide learners with copies of magazine articles. Have student partners work together to circle the topic sentence of each paragraph and to underline the supporting details. If the topic sentence is implicit, have learners write an appropriate topic sentence. Each learner should be prepared to explain how the details support the stated or implied topic sentence.

2 Refine the Skill

Decoding As a class activity, have learners determine the main idea of the paragraph in the *Refine the Skill* section. Then have partners work together to answer questions 1 and 2 and to provide reasoning for their choices. Have volunteers share their answers and reasoning.

3 Master the Skill

Spotlighted Item Type Explain that when answering drag-and-drop items, learners should examine the question and move items to the appropriate positions. Then they should read the displayed choices to double-check their reasoning. Emphasize that learners can move the items again if they rethink their first choices or accidentally drop answers into the wrong places.

➤ Enrich and Extend

Have each learner write a paragraph explaining his or her opinion of a celebrity. Remind learners to write one sentence that states the main idea and several sentences that support it. After learners have written their paragraphs, have them insert a sentence that discusses the celebrity but does not support the main idea and should not be in the paragraph. Have student partners exchange paragraphs and identify sentences that do not belong.

Answers
1. B; DOK Level: 2; **2.** C; DOK Level: 2; **3.** Sentences belong in this order: C, B, E, A, D; DOK Level: 2; **4.** A; DOK Level: 2;
5. B; DOK Level: 2; **6.** D; DOK Level: 2; **7.** D; DOK Level: 2;
8. C; DOK Level: 2; **9.** D; DOK Level: 2; **10.** D; DOK Level: 2;
11. B; DOK Level: 2

Other Punctuation

LANGUAGE ASSESSMENT TARGETS: L.2.2, L.2.4

STUDENT BOOK pp. 160–161

Preview the Skill

Explain that learners will use hyphens, parentheses, quotation marks, colons, and semicolons in all types of writing. Provide writing samples from daily life, such as a cover letter, a résumé, and an e-mail message. Point out hyphens, parentheses, quotation marks, colons, and semicolons. Emphasize that all punctuation has a purpose and that using punctuation correctly makes a good impression on people, especially prospective employers or supervisors.

1 Learn the Skill

Use Graphic Organizers The center circle of this graphic organizer contains a hyphenated word, a phrase in parentheses, a quotation, and a three-item list. Ask learners to use each in a sentence.

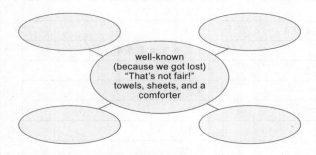

well-known
(because we got lost)
"That's not fair!"
towels, sheets, and a
comforter

2 Practice the Skill

Skim and Scan To help learners answer question 1, ask them to skim and scan the graphic organizer in the *Practice the Skill* section to find the example that best matches the sentence in the question.

3 Apply the Skill

Spotlighted Item Type Emphasize the importance of reviewing the context of sentences that contain drop-down lists. Learners may recognize some incorrect options without referring to the passage but always should check the context to ensure that they have chosen correctly.

Answers
1. B; DOK Level: 1; **2.1** D; DOK Level: 1; **2.2** B; DOK Level: 1; **2.3** A; DOK Level: 1; **2.4** C; DOK Level: 1

WORKBOOK pp. 254–257

1 Review the Skill

Use Graphic Organizers Use this graphic organizer to demonstrate proper punctuation use. Have learners explain why the examples are correct.

Punctuation Mark	Example
Hyphen	The media provided up-to-date information.
Parentheses	Toby saw *Jaws* (his favorite movie) for the tenth time.
Quotation Marks	Cameron cried, "My dog ran away!"
Colon	Kyle bought the following furnishings: a chair, a lamp, and a rug.
Semicolon	Callie went to the bank; she had to deposit a paycheck.

2 Refine the Skill

Skim and Scan Explain that if a sentence contains two complete ideas that are closely related, learners can use a semicolon to connect the ideas. Have learners skim and scan the sentences in questions 1 and 2 to determine whether they can revise either sentence with a semicolon.

3 Master the Skill

Link to Past Skills Have learners review the information in *Commas* from Unit 4, Lesson 11. Explain that learners need to understand proper comma use before they use colons, quotation marks, and semicolons correctly.

Enrich and Extend

Ask learners to write sentences about things they do on a typical evening. Consider providing sentence starters so that learners have an opportunity to include all the punctuation covered in this lesson. For example, a learner might write or complete a sentence about greeting his or her family: *When I open the door, I ask, "Is anyone home?"*

Answers
1. B; DOK Level: 1; **2.** C; DOK Level: 1; **3.1** B; DOK Level: 1; **3.2** D; DOK Level: 1; **3.3** B; DOK Level: 1; **3.4** A; DOK Level: 1; **4.1** B; DOK Level: 1; **4.2** C; DOK Level: 1; **4.3** A; DOK Level: 1; **4.4** D; DOK Level: 1; **5.1** A; DOK Level: 1; **5.2** C; DOK Level: 1; **5.3** B; DOK Level: 1; **5.4** D; DOK Level: 1

Unit 4 Review

LANGUAGE ASSESSMENT TARGETS: L.1.1, L.1.2, L.1.3, L.1.4, L.1.5, L.1.6, L.1.7, L.1.8, L.1.9, L.2.1, L.2.2, L.2.3, L.2.4
WRITING ASSESSMENT TARGETS: W.2, W.3

You may choose to use the Unit 4 Review on Student Book pp. 162–169 as a mini–practice test. If you wish to time the test, ask learners to complete all the items in 60 minutes.

Unit 4 Review Answers

1.1 C; **1.2** D; **1.3** B; **1.4** A; **2.1** D; **2.2** C; **2.3** B; **2.4** B; **3.1** D; **3.2** A; **3.3** B; **3.4** A; **4.1** C; **4.2** D; **4.3** B; **4.4** A; **5.1** C; **5.2** D; **5.3** B; **5.4** A; **6.1** D; **6.2** B; **6.3** A; **6.4** D; **7.1** B; **7.2** C; **7.3** D; **7.4** B; **8.** C; **9.** D; **10.** A; **11.** D

Unit 4 Review Item Analysis

SKILL	DOK LEVEL 1	DOK LEVEL 2
Nouns	4.2	
Pronouns	1.3, 1.4, 4.1, 5.1, 6.2	
Basic Verb Tenses	6.3	
Verbs with Helping Verbs	6.1, 7.1	
Apostrophes	4.2, 6.2	
Frequently Confused Words	1.3, 3.1, 4.1, 6.2	7.3
Basic Subject-Verb Agreement	4.1	1.1
Standard English	4.1, 6.1, 7.2	
Capitalization	2.2, 2.3, 6.4	
Sentence Fragment Correction	5.2	
Commas	2.1, 2.3, 3.1, 3.3, 3.4	
Sentence Combining	2.1	2.4, 7.4
Run-on Sentence Correction	2.1, 3.1, 3.2, 6.4, 7.4	
Modifiers		1.2, 4.3, 4.4, 5.4, 7.1
Advanced Pronoun Use	1.4, 5.1, 5.2, 5.3	7.3
Advanced Subject-Verb Agreement	4.1	4.3. 5.4, 6.3
Parallelism	3.4	11
Transitions	2.4, 8	7.4
Paragraph Organization		9, 10
Other Punctuation	2.4, 3.1, 3.2, 3.3, 3.4, 6.4, 7.4	

Unit 4 Review

Use workbook lessons, as identified in the following table, to assist learners who require additional remediation with certain skills or items having certain DOK levels.

Unit 4 Workbook Item Analysis

SKILL	DOK LEVEL 1	DOK LEVEL 2
Nouns	1, 2, 3.1, 3.2, 3.3, 3.4, 4.1, 4.2, 4.3, 4.4, 5.1, 5.2, 5.3, 5.4	
Pronouns	1, 2, 3.1, 3.2, 3.3, 3.4, 4.1, 4.2, 4.3, 4.4, 5.1, 5.2, 5.3, 5.4	
Basic Verb Tenses	1, 2, 3.1, 3.2, 3.3, 3.4, 4.1, 4.2, 4.3, 4.4, 5.1, 5.2, 5.3, 5.4	
Verbs with Helping Verbs	1, 2, 3.1, 3.2, 3.3, 3.4, 4.1, 4.2, 4.3, 4.4, 5.1, 5.2, 5.3, 5.4	
Apostrophes	1, 2, 3.1, 3.2, 3.3, 3.4, 4.1, 4.2, 4.3, 4.4, 5.1, 5.2, 5.3, 5.4	
Frequently Confused Words	1, 2, 3.1, 3.2, 3.3, 3.4, 4.1, 4.2, 4.3, 4.4, 5.1, 5.2, 5.3, 5.4	
Basic Subject-Verb Agreement	1, 2, 3.1, 3.2, 3.3, 3.4, 4.1, 4.2, 4.3, 4.4, 5.1, 5.2, 5.3, 5.4	
Standard English	1, 2, 3.1, 3.2, 3.3, 3.4, 4.1, 4.2, 4.3, 4.4, 5.1, 5.2, 5.3, 5.4	
Capitalization	1, 2, 3.1, 3.2, 3.3, 3.4, 4.1, 4.2, 4.3, 4.4, 5.1, 5.2, 5.3, 5.4	
Sentence Fragment Correction	1, 2, 3.1, 3.2, 3.3, 3.4, 4.1, 4.2, 4.3, 4.4, 5.1, 5.2, 5.3, 5.4	
Commas	1, 2, 3.1, 3.2, 3.3, 3.4, 4.1, 4.2, 4.3, 4.4, 5.1, 5.2, 5.3, 5.4	
Sentence Combining		1, 2, 3.1, 3.2, 3.3, 3.4, 4.1, 4.2, 4.3, 4.4, 5.1, 5.2, 5.3, 5.4
Run-on Sentence Correction		1, 2, 3.1, 3.2, 3.3, 3.4, 4.1, 4.2, 4.3, 4.4, 5.1, 5.2, 5.3, 5.4
Modifiers	5.1, 5.2, 5.4	1, 2, 3.1, 3.2, 3.3, 3.4, 4.1, 4.2, 4.3, 4.4, 5.3
Advanced Pronoun Use	2, 3.1, 3.2, 5.1, 5.2, 5.3	1, 3.3, 3.4, 4.1. 4.2, 4.3, 4.4, 5.4
Advanced Subject-Verb Agreement	1, 2, 3.1, 3.2, 3.3, 3.4, 4.1, 4.2, 4.3, 5.1, 5.2, 5.3, 5.4	4.4
Parallelism		1, 2, 3, 4, 5, 6, 7, 8, 9, 10,11.1, 11.2, 11.3, 11.4
Transitions	1, 2, 3.1, 3.2, 3.3, 3.4, 4.1, 4.2, 4.3, 4.4, 5.1, 5.2, 5.3, 5.4	
Paragraph Organization		1, 2, 3, 4, 5, 6, 7, 8, 9, 10, 11
Other Punctuation	1, 2, 3.1, 3.2, 3.3, 3.4, 4.1, 4.2, 4.3, 4.4, 5.1, 5.2, 5.3, 5.4	

Appendix

Table of Contents

Glossary   RLA 81
Grammar Rules   RLA 82–83
Frequently Confused Words   RLA 84–85
Frequently Misspelled Words   RLA 86–87
Verb Conjugation Tables   RLA 88–91
Extended Response Rubrics   RLA 92–94

Glossary

Adjective: modifies or describes a noun or a pronoun: *fast, pretty, new, old*

Adverb: modifies a verb, an adjective, or another adverb: *A deliciously ripe apple fell quickly from the tree.*

Apostrophe: (') used to indicate possession: *Chandra's jeans;* also used to form a contraction: *They're hungry.*

Colon: (:) used to separate phrases and to introduce lists or examples: *We knew what would happen next: the band would play an encore. I asked three people to come over: John, Melissa, and Mike.*

Comma: (,) used within a sentence to represent a pause or to connect clauses or phrases: *However you look at it, the team won fair and square.*

Complete sentence: contains a subject and a verb and conveys a complete idea

Connecting words: used to combine sentences: *and, or, but, nor, for, so, yet*

Contractions: used in informal writing to combine words:
will + not = won't, you + are = you're, they + have = they've

Homonyms: sound alike or nearly alike but are spelled differently and have different meanings: *acts are a deed; an ax is a tool;* also include words that sound and are spelled alike but have different meanings: *a bat is both a flying animal and a stick for hitting a ball*

Modifiers: describe, clarify, and provide more detail about another word: *I ate only two cookies.*

Nouns: name people, places, or things, such as *mother, home, Asia, book, car, Frisbee*

Object: receives or completes the subject's action: *Dan drove the truck.*

Paragraph: group of sentences that form a complete idea

Parallel structure: using the same pattern of words to indicate that two or more ideas have equal importance: *I like football, baseball, and basketball.*

Plural: indicates more than one thing or person: *five books, two sodas*

Possessive: indicates ownership: *It was Dan's truck.*

Pronouns: take the place of nouns: *you, he, she, it, they, we, them, him, her, myself, whoever, whomever, each, somebody*

Proper nouns: specific names of people, places, or things; must always be capitalized: *Mr. President, Alabama, Bill of Rights*

Punctuation marks: provide structure within written text, such as periods (.), commas (,), question marks (?), and exclamation marks (!)

Quotation marks: (" . . . ") appear immediately before and after something that someone has said: *"Don't forget your cell phone," she said.*

Run-on sentence: formed when two or more complete sentences are combined without the use of a comma and a connecting word:

   run-on: *Dan drove the van the rest of us took the subway.*

   correct: *Dan drove the van, and the rest of us took the subway.*

Semicolon: (;) used between two complete ideas: *I was running late; I missed the bus to work.*

Sentence fragment: does not express a complete idea: *Two days after we broke up*

Singular: indicates just one thing or person: *one book, one army*

Subject: person or thing doing the action: *Dan drove the truck.*

Supporting details: support the topic sentence in a logical way

Topic sentence: explains the main idea of a paragraph; usually the first sentence in a paragraph

Transitions: show connections between ideas: *First, I brush my teeth. Next, I take a shower.*

Verb: states an action or state of being: *Dan drove the truck.*

Grammar Rules

LANGUAGE ARTS

Capitalization: Proper nouns, proper adjectives, titles, holidays, days of the week, and months of the year are capitalized.

➤ **proper noun:** a name that identifies a particular person, place, or thing
  - the <u>C</u>leveland <u>C</u>avaliers

➤ **proper adjective:** a description based on a proper name
  - <u>G</u>erman sausages

Comma: A comma separates a sentence into meaningful units.

➤ **to form a series:** I made roast chicken, mashed potatoes, and a salad for dinner.

➤ **after an introductory phrase:** To get to the restaurant, she had to take the bus.

➤ **to set off an interrupting or descriptive phrase:** My sister, who is in the Air Force, came home for Christmas.

➤ **when combining sentences:** We went to the game, and we stopped for burgers on the way home.

➤ **when using two or more adjectives:** She ran a long, hard race.

Combining sentences: Short, related sentences can be combined to make writing more cohesive.

➤ **use connecting words:** I drove to the gas station. I drove to the mall.
  - I drove to the gas station *and* the mall.

➤ **create a list:** My son likes baseball. My son likes cars. My son likes ice cream.
  - My son likes baseball, cars, and ice cream.

➤ **use a semicolon:** They went to see a movie. It was a scary one.
  - They went to see a movie; it was a scary one.

Complete sentence: A complete sentence must contain a subject, a verb, and appropriate end punctuation. A complete sentence will present a complete idea.

➤ Nick loved to skateboard.

Contraction: A contraction occurs when two words are shortened to one word by replacing a letter or letters with an apostrophe. Contractions are used in informal writing.

➤ Examples: they + have = they've, it + is = it's

Helping verbs: Helping verbs indicate that actions have occurred at various points in time.

➤ **past perfect tense:** used to indicate that an action took place in the past before another past action was completed. The word *had* appears before the main verb.
  - We *had* driven for more than three hours before we arrived at my aunt's house.

➤ **present perfect tense:** used to indicate that an action began in the past and continues into the present. The words *has* or *have been* appear before the main verb.
  - He *has been* working there for more than a year.

➤ **future perfect tense:** used to indicate that an action will be completed at a specific time in the future. The words *will have* or *will have been* appear in front of the main verb.
  - By the end of the month, we *will have* saved enough money for a DVD player.

Modifiers: A modifier describes, clarifies, or provides details about other words in a sentence. Avoid a **misplaced modifier,** which misleads readers by describing the wrong word in the sentence, or a **dangling modifier,** which does not apply logically to any word in the sentence.

➤ **misplaced modifier:** I only ran one mile. **correct:** I ran only one mile.

➤ **dangling modifier:** Running down the street, my long scarf blew across my face. **correct:** While I was running down the street, my long scarf blew across my face.

Parallel structure: A sentence with parallel structure displays the same pattern to indicate that two or more ideas are of equal importance.

➤ **wrong:** Both my boyfriend's mom and the cousin of my friend work at the mall.

➤ **correct:** Both my boyfriend's mom and my friend's cousin work at the mall.

Parentheses: Parentheses are used to separate text and often contain nonessential information—the sentence is intact without the parenthetical material.

➤ After work, Ryan drove to the gym (on Jefferson Road).

Plural nouns: Often, nouns are made plural simply by the addition of -s or -es.

- ➤ add -s to most nouns: bottles, books
- ➤ add -es to nouns ending in o: tomatoes (tomato), heroes (hero)
- ➤ add -es to nouns ending in ch, sh, ss, z, or x: taxes (tax), churches (church)
- ➤ for nouns that end in y after a consonant, drop the y and add -ies: puppies (puppy), cities (city)
- ➤ for nouns that end in f or fe, drop the f(e) and add -ves: wives (wife), thieves (thief)
- ➤ some nouns change form: women (woman), teeth (tooth)
- ➤ some nouns don't change at all: fish, sheep

Possession: Possession, indicated by the use of an apostrophe and s ('s) or by an s followed by an apostrophe (s'), shows ownership.

- ➤ for singular nouns, use an apostrophe and add s: **dog's** bone
- ➤ for most singular nouns ending in s, use an apostrophe and add s: **Mars's** moon
- ➤ for plural nouns ending in s, use only an apostrophe: **players'** meeting

Pronouns: Pronouns are words that take the place of nouns. Pronouns must agree in gender and number with the nouns they replace.

- ➤ Sharon drove Keith home after work. **Replace nouns with pronouns:** _She_ drove _him_ home after work.

Regular and irregular verbs: Regular verbs indicate past, present, and future tenses when -ed, -s, or -ing is added to the base verb. Irregular verbs are less consistent; the spelling of such verbs often changes to indicate a particular tense.

Run-on sentence: A run-on sentence occurs when two or more sentences are joined incorrectly. A run-on sentence can be corrected by adding a connecting word, adding a comma and a connecting word, or creating two separate sentences.

- ➤ **wrong:** I met a friend at the movies we had a good time.
- ➤ **correct:** I met a friend at the movies, and we had a good time.

Subject-verb agreement: In a sentence, subjects and verbs must agree in person and number.

- ➤ **wrong:** Amber and I am going out to eat Friday.
- ➤ **right:** Amber and I _are_ going out to eat Friday.

Verb tenses: The three basic verb tenses are _past, present,_ and _future._ Using the correct tense of the verb lets your readers know whether events have occurred in the past, are happening now, or will happen in the future. In the **past tense,** regular verbs will end in -d or -ed (_walk_ becomes _walked_). Irregular verbs often indicate the past tense by a spelling change (_eat_ becomes _ate_). In the **present tense,** the verb maintains its root form (_make, walk, come_). In **future tense,** the helping verb _will_ appears in front of the main verb (_move_ becomes _will move_).

Frequently Confused Words

Some frequently confused words are homonyms. These are words that sound the same or nearly the same but are spelled differently and have different meanings. Sometimes the two words may be spelled alike but have different meanings. Below is a list of frequently confused words. Learn these words and you will be sure of using the right word every time.

accept: *to receive; to endure; to approve*
except: *to exclude*

affect: *to influence*
effect: *a result*

ate: *past tense of <u>eat</u>*
eight: *the number <u>8</u>*

be: *to exist*
bee: *an insect*

beat: *to strike or hit*
beet: *a type of root vegetable*

board: *a piece of wood*
bored: *uninterested*

brake: *to stop*
break: *to damage or destroy; a rest period*

buy: *to get by paying money*
by: *near; according to*

capital: *city that is the seat of government; money to invest; very important*
capitol: *building in which the legislature meets*

cell: *a small room, as in a prison*
sell: *to offer for sale*

cent: *a penny*
scent: *to smell*
sent: *to cause to go or be transmitted*

close: *to shut; to finish*
clothes: *something to wear on the body, usually made of cloth*

complement: *to go with*
compliment: *flattering words*

coarse: *rough or harsh*
course: *a path or track; part of a meal*

dear: *much loved; sweet*
deer: *an animal*

desert: *a dry, barren, sandy region*
dessert: *the final, usually sweet, course of a meal*

feat: *an accomplishment*
feet: *plural of <u>foot</u>*

flour: *ground grain used in making bread*
flower: *the bloom or blossom on a plant*

for: *to be used as; meant to belong to*
four: *the number <u>4</u>*

grate: *to shred*
great: *very good*

hear: *to listen*
here: *in this place*

hole: *opening*
whole: *entire*

hour: *60 minutes*
our: *belonging to us*

its: *possessive of <u>it</u>*
it's: *contraction of <u>it is</u>*

knew: *was certain of*
new: *modern; recent*

know: *to have information*
no: *not at all; opposite of <u>yes</u>*

lessen: *to decrease*
lesson: *something that is taught*

leave: *to go away*
let: *to allow*

loose: *not tight*
lose: *to fail to keep or win*

made: *created*
maid: *a person who cleans*

mail: *letters or packages delivered by the post office*
male: *the opposite of <u>female</u>*

main: *most important*
mane: *the hair of a horse or lion*

meat: *animal flesh that is eaten*
meet: *to get together*

one: *the number 1*
won: *past tense of win*

pail: *a bucket or tub*
pale: *light in color*

pain: *soreness, aching*
pane: *the glass in a window*

passed: *went by*
past: *a time before; opposite of future*

patience: *ability to wait*
patients: *plural of patient*

peace: *freedom from war; harmony; calm*
piece: *a part of something*

plain: *ordinary; simple*
plane: *airplane; a flat surface*

pole: *a long piece of wood or metal*
poll: *a listing of people; a vote*

principal: *first in rank; the head of a school*
principle: *a rule or belief*

quiet: *silent; still*
quite: *completely; really; positively*

right: *correct; opposite of left*
write: *to form visible words*

road: *a path or street*
rode: *past tense of the verb ride*

role: *a part played*
roll: *to turn over; a type of bread*

scene: *a view; part of a play or movie*

seen: *past participle of see*

sea: *the ocean*
see: *to look at*

set: *to put or lay something in a place*
sit: *to rest oneself on a chair or perch*

sight: *the ability to see*
site: *a place or location*

some: *a few*
sum: *the total amount*

stake: *a pointed piece of metal or wood for driving into the ground*

steak: *a slice of beef or fish for cooking*

steal: *to take dishonestly or unlawfully*
steel: *a hard, tough metal*

than: *a conjunction used to compare two things, as in larger than or more than*
then: *an adverb meaning at that time, next, or after*

their: *belonging to them*
there: *at or in that place*
they're: *a contraction of the words they are*

threw: *past tense of throw*
through: *in one side and out the other side*

to: *in the direction of*
too: *in addition; very*
two: *the number 2*

wait: *to stay until something happens; to serve food at a meal*
weight: *how heavy something is*

weak: *opposite of strong*
week: *seven days*

wear: *to have clothing on the body*
where: *referring to a place*

weather: *the climate*
whether: *in case; in either case*

who's: *contraction of who is or who has*
whose: *possessive of who*

wood: *what trees are made of*
would: *helping verb; also, the past tense of will*

you're: *contraction of you are*
your: *belonging to you*

Frequently Misspelled Words

Although most word processing programs include a spell-checker, you won't be able to count on that feature when you write your essay for the GED® Reasoning Through Language Arts Test. Below is a list of some commonly misspelled words for you to study.

A

a lot
absence
accept
accident
achieve (*When in doubt, think i before e, except after c, and words that say "hey!" as in neighbor and weigh.*)
accommodate
address
again
against
agree
all right
almost
already
although
always
appear
approach
argue
attention
August
author
awful
awkward

B

balloon
beautiful
because
beginning
being
believe
benefit
between
bicycle
borrow
business

C

calendar
captain
career
cereal
chief
coffee

college
congratulate
curiosity

D

daily
daughter
definitely
delicious
describe
difference
different
discover
disease
distance
dollar
doubt

E

easy
education
effect
eight
either
embarrass
emergency
English (The *E* is always capitalized.)
enough
environment
equipment
especially
excellent
except
exercise
extreme

F

familiar
February
financial
forehead
foreign
former
fourteen
fourth
friend
further

G

gallon
general
genius
government
governor
grammar
grateful
great
grocery
guard
guess

H

half
happiness
healthy
heard
heavy
height
heroes
holiday
hopeless
hospital
hurrying

I

immediately
increase
independence
independent
innocence
instead
interrupt
invitation
island

J

January
jealous

K

kitchen
knowledge

L

language
laugh
library
license
light
likely
losing
loyal

M

maintenance
marriage
mathematics
measure
medicine
million
muscle
mystery

N

natural
necessary
neighbor
neither
niece
night

O

o'clock
occasion
ocean
often
operate
opinion

P

parallel
particular
patience
people
perfect
perform
perhaps
permanent
personal
personality
picture
piece
poison
political
positive

possess
potatoes
prepare
prescription
probably
produce
professional
profit
promise
pronounce

Q

quality
quiet
quite

R

raise
realize
reason
receipt
receive
recipe
recognize
recommend
relieve
responsible
restaurant
rhythm
ridiculous
right
roommate

S

sandwich
scene
schedule
science
season
secretary
sense
separate
service
sight
signal
similar
since
soldier
sophomore
soul
source
special

stomach
strength
stretch
succeed
successful
supposedly
surprise
sweat
sympathy

T

technical
though
through
together
tomorrow
tongue
toward
tragedy
tries
twelfth
twelve

U

unnecessary
unusual
usual

V

vacuum
valuable
variety
vegetable
view
voice
volume

W

weather
Wednesday
weird
whether
which
while

Verb Conjugation Tables

to be	past	present	future	past perfect	present perfect	future perfect
I	was	am	will be	had been	have been	will have been
you	were	are	will be	had been	have been	will have been
he/she/it	was	is	will be	had been	has been	will have been
we	were	are	will be	had been	have been	will have been
they	were	are	will be	had been	have been	will have been

to say	past	present	future	past perfect	present perfect	future perfect
I	said	say	will say	had said	have said	will have said
you	said	say	will say	had said	have said	will have said
he/she/it	said	says	will say	had said	has said	will have said
we	said	say	will say	had said	have said	will have said
they	said	say	will say	had said	have said	will have said

to make	past	present	future	past perfect	present perfect	future perfect
I	made	make	will make	had made	have made	will have made
you	made	make	will make	had made	have made	will have made
he/she/it	made	makes	will make	had made	has made	will have made
we	made	make	will make	had made	have made	will have made
they	made	make	will make	had made	have made	will have made

to become	past	present	future	past perfect	present perfect	future perfect
I	became	become	will become	had become	have become	will have become
you	became	become	will become	had become	have become	will have become
he/she/it	became	becomes	will become	had become	has become	will have become
we	became	become	will become	had become	have become	will have become
they	became	become	will become	had become	have become	will have become

to come	past	present	future	past perfect	present perfect	future perfect
I	came	come	will come	had come	have come	will have come
you	came	come	will come	had come	have come	will have come
he/she/it	came	comes	will come	had come	has come	will have come
we	came	come	will come	had come	have come	will have come
they	came	come	will come	had come	have come	will have come

to live	past	present	future	past perfect	present perfect	future perfect
I	lived	live	will live	had lived	have lived	will have lived
you	lived	live	will live	had lived	have lived	will have lived
he/she/it	lived	lives	will live	had lived	has lived	will have lived
we	lived	live	will live	had lived	have lived	will have lived
they	lived	live	will live	had lived	have lived	will have lived

to have	past	present	future	past perfect	present perfect	future perfect
I	had	have	will have	had had	have had	will have had
you	had	have	will have	had had	have had	will have had
he/she/it	had	has	will have	had had	has had	will have had
we	had	have	will have	had had	have had	will have had
they	had	have	will have	had had	have had	will have had

to read	past	present	future	past perfect	present perfect	future perfect
I	read	read	will read	had read	have read	will have read
you	read	read	will read	had read	have read	will have read
he/she/it	read	reads	will read	had read	has read	will have read
we	read	read	will read	had read	have read	will have read
they	read	read	will read	had read	have read	will have read

to bring	past	present	future	past perfect	present perfect	future perfect
I	brought	bring	will bring	had brought	have brought	will have brought
you	brought	bring	will bring	had brought	have brought	will have brought
he/she/it	brought	brings	will bring	had brought	has brought	will have brought
we	brought	bring	will bring	had brought	have brought	will have brought
they	brought	bring	will bring	had brought	have brought	will have brought

to write	past	present	future	past perfect	present perfect	future perfect
I	wrote	write	will write	had written	have written	will have written
you	wrote	write	will write	had written	have written	will have written
he/she/it	wrote	writes	will write	had written	has written	will have written
we	wrote	write	will write	had written	have written	will have written
they	wrote	write	will write	had written	have written	will have written

Verb Conjugation Tables

to begin	past	present	future	past perfect	present perfect	future perfect
I	began	begin	will begin	had begun	have begun	will have begun
you	began	begin	will begin	had begun	have begun	will have begun
he/she/it	began	begins	will begin	had begun	has begun	will have begun
we	began	begin	will begin	had begun	have begun	will have begun
they	began	begin	will begin	had begun	have begun	will have begun

to take	past	present	future	past perfect	present perfect	future perfect
I	took	take	will take	had taken	have taken	will have taken
you	took	take	will take	had taken	have taken	will have taken
he/she/it	took	takes	will take	had taken	has taken	will have taken
we	took	take	will take	had taken	have taken	will have taken
they	took	take	will take	had taken	have taken	will have taken

to lay	past	present	future	past perfect	present perfect	future perfect
I	laid	lay	will lay	had laid	have laid	will have laid
you	laid	lay	will lay	had laid	have laid	will have laid
he/she/it	laid	lays	will lay	had laid	has laid	will have laid
we	laid	lay	will lay	had laid	have laid	will have laid
they	laid	lay	will lay	had laid	have laid	will have laid

to sell	past	present	future	past perfect	present perfect	future perfect
I	sold	sell	will sell	had sold	have sold	will have sold
you	sold	sell	will sell	had sold	have sold	will have sold
he/she/it	sold	sells	will sell	had sold	has sold	will have sold
we	sold	sell	will sell	had sold	have sold	will have sold
they	sold	sell	will sell	had sold	have sold	will have sold

to leave	past	present	future	past perfect	present perfect	future perfect
I	left	leave	will leave	had left	have left	will have left
you	left	leave	will leave	had left	have left	will have left
he/she/it	left	leaves	will leave	had left	has left	will have left
we	left	leave	will leave	had left	have left	will have left
they	left	leave	will leave	had left	have left	will have left

to run	past	present	future	past perfect	present perfect	future perfect
I	ran	run	will run	had run	have run	will have run
you	ran	run	will run	had run	have run	will have run
he/she/it	ran	runs	will run	had run	has run	will have run
we	ran	run	will run	had run	have run	will have run
they	ran	run	will run	had run	have run	will have run

to sit	past	present	future	past perfect	present perfect	future perfect
I	sat	sit	will sit	had sat	have sat	will have sat
you	sat	sit	will sit	had sat	have sat	will have sat
he/she/it	sat	sits	will sit	had sat	has sat	will have sat
we	sat	sit	will sit	had sat	have sat	will have sat
they	sat	sit	will sit	had sat	have sat	will have sat

to lose	past	present	future	past perfect	present perfect	future perfect
I	lost	lose	will lose	had lost	have lost	will have lost
you	lost	lose	will lose	had lost	have lost	will have lost
he/she/it	lost	loses	will lose	had lost	has lost	will have lost
we	lost	lose	will lose	had lost	have lost	will have lost
they	lost	lose	will lose	had lost	have lost	will have lost

to know	past	present	future	past perfect	present perfect	future perfect
I	knew	know	will know	had known	have known	will have known
you	knew	know	will know	had known	have known	will have known
he/she/it	knew	knows	will know	had known	has known	will have known
we	knew	know	will know	had known	have known	will have known
they	knew	know	will know	had known	have known	will have known

Extended Response Scoring Rubrics

Score	Description
	**Trait 1: Creation of Arguments and Use of Evidence**
2	Generates text-based argument(s) and establishes a purpose that is connected to the prompt
	Cites relevant and specific evidence from source text(s) to support argument (may include few irrelevant pieces of evidence or unsupported claims)
	Analyzes the issue and/or evaluates the validity of the argumentation within the source texts (e.g., Distinguishes between supported and unsupported claims, makes reasonable inferences about underlying premises or assumptions, identifies fallacious reasoning, evaluates the credibility of sources, etc.)
1	Generates an argument and demonstrates some connection to the prompt
	Cites some evidence from source text(s) to support argument (may include a mix of relevant and irrelevant citations or a mix of textual and non-textual references)
	Partially analyzes the issue and/or evaluates the validity of the argumentation within the source texts; may be simplistic, limited, or inaccurate
0	May attempt to create an argument or lacks purpose or connection to the prompt or does neither
	Cites minimal or no evidence from source text(s) (sections of text may be copied from source)
	Minimally analyzes the issue and/or evaluates the validity of the argumentation within the source texts; may completely lack analysis or demonstrate minimal or no understanding of the given argument(s)

Non-scorable Responses (Score of 0/Condition Codes)
- Response exclusively contains text copied from source text(s) or prompt
- Response shows no evidence that test-taker has read the prompt or is off-topic
- Response is incomprehensible
- Response is not in English
- Response has not been attempted (blank)

Courtesy of the GED® Testing Service

Score	Description
	Trait 2: Development of Ideas and Organizational Structure
2	Contains ideas that are well developed and generally logical; most ideas are elaborated upon
	Contains a sensible progression of ideas with clear connections between details and main points
	Establishes an organizational structure that conveys the message and purpose of the response; applies transitional devices appropriately
	Establishes and maintains a formal style and appropriate tone that demonstrate awareness of the audience and purpose of the task
	Chooses specific words to express ideas clearly
1	Contains ideas that are inconsistently developed and/or may reflect simplistic or vague reasoning; some ideas are elaborated upon
	Demonstrates some evidence of a progression of ideas, but details may be disjointed or lacking connection to main ideas
	Establishes an organization structure that may inconsistently group ideas or is partially effective at conveying the message of the task; uses transitional devices inconsistently
	May inconsistently maintain a formal style and appropriate tone to demonstrate an awareness of the audience and purpose of the task
	May occasionally misuse words and/or choose words that express ideas in vague terms
0	Contains ideas that are insufficiently or illogically developed, with minimal or no elaboration on main ideas
	Contains an unclear or no progression of ideas; details may be absent or irrelevant to the main ideas
	Establishes an ineffective or no discernable organizational structure; does not apply transitional devices, or does so inappropriately
	Uses an informal style and/or inappropriate tone that demonstrates limited or no awareness of audience and purpose
	May frequently misuse words, overuse slang or express ideas in a vague or repetitive manner

Non-scorable Responses (Score of 0/Condition Codes)
- Response exclusively contains text copied from source text(s) or prompt
- Response shows no evidence that test-taker has read the prompt or is off-topic
- Response is incomprehensible
- Response is not in English
- Response has not been attempted (blank)

Courtesy of the GED® Testing Service

Extended Response Scoring Rubrics

Score	Description
	Trait 3: Clarity and Command of Standard English Conventions
2	Demonstrates largely correct sentence structure and a general fluency that enhances clarity with specific regard to the following skills: 1) varied sentence structure within a paragraph or paragraphs 2) correct subordination, coordination and parallelism 3) avoidance of wordiness and awkward sentence structures 4) usage of transitional words, conjunctive adverbs and other words that support logic and clarity 5) avoidance of run-on sentences, fused sentences, or sentence fragments Demonstrates competent application of conventions with specific regard to the following skills: 1) frequently confused words and homonyms, including contractions 2) subject-verb agreement 3) pronoun usage, including pronoun antecedent agreement, unclear pronoun references, and pronoun case 4) placement of modifiers and correct word order 5) capitalization (e.g., proper nouns, titles, and beginnings of sentences) 6) use of apostrophes with possessive nouns 7) use of punctuation (e.g., commas in a series or in appositives and other non-essential elements, end marks, and appropriate punctuation for clause separation) May contain some errors in mechanics and conventions, but they do not interfere with comprehension; overall, standard usage is at a level appropriate for on-demand draft writing.
1	Demonstrates inconsistent sentence structure; may contain some repetitive, choppy, rambling, or awkward sentences that may detract from clarity; demonstrates inconsistent control over skills 1-5 as listed in the first bullet under trait 3, score point 2 above Demonstrates inconsistent control of basic conventions with specific regard to skills 1 – 7 as listed in the second bullet under trait 3, score point 2 above May contain frequent errors in mechanics and conventions that occasionally interfere with comprehension; standard usage is at a minimally acceptable level of appropriateness for on-demand draft writing.
0	Demonstrates consistently flawed sentence structure such that meaning may be obscured; demonstrates minimal control over skills 1-5 as listed in the first bullet under Trait 3, Score point 2 above Demonstrates minimal control of basic conventions with specific regard to skills 1 – 7 as listed in the second bullet under Trait 3, Score point 2 above Contains severe and frequent errors in mechanics and conventions that interfere with comprehension; overall, standard usage is at an unacceptable level for on-demand draft writing OR Response is insufficient to demonstrate level of mastery over conventions and usage

*Because test-takers will be given only 45 minutes to complete Extended Response tasks, there is no expectation that a response should be completely free of conventions or usage errors to receive a score of 2.

Non-scorable Responses (Score of 0/Condition Codes)
- Response exclusively contains text copied from source text(s) or prompt
- Response shows no evidence that test-taker has read the prompt or is off-topic
- Response is incomprehensible
- Response is not in English
- Response has not been attempted (blank)

Courtesy of the GED® Testing Service

Correlations/Reasoning Through Language Arts

Indicator Codes	Reasoning Through Language Arts Indicators	*Reasoning Through Language Arts* Book Pages
Reading Assessment Targets		
R.2	**Determine central ideas or themes of texts and analyze their development; summarize the key supporting details and ideas.**	
R.2.1	Comprehend explicit details and main ideas in text.	**Student Book:** 2, 3, 4, 8, 9, 10, 11, 13, 21, 23, 29, 31, 32, 35, 51, 53 **Workbook:** 2, 3, 4, 5, 6, 7, 9, 14, 15, 16, 17, 18, 19, 20, 21, 22, 23, 24, 25, 56, 58, 60, 71, 99, 133
R.2.2	Summarize details and ideas in text.	**Student Book:** 4, 5, 11, 29, 51, 53, 57, 65 **Workbook:** 6, 7, 8, 9, 25, 61, 105, 133
R.2.3	Make sentence level inferences about details that support main ideas.	**Student Book:** 9, 11, 16, 17, 51, 53 **Workbook:** 17, 24, 26, 27, 30, 31, 32, 33, 98
R.2.4	Infer implied main ideas in paragraphs or whole texts.	**Student Book:** 2, 3, 12, 16, 17, 42, 51, 53 **Workbook:** 2, 4, 5, 16, 17, 25, 31, 32, 33, 41, 43, 99, 108, 109, 124
R.2.5	Determine which detail(s) support(s) a main idea.	**Student Book:** 2, 3, 9, 21, 30, 51, 53, 60, 61, 65, 73 **Workbook:** 2, 3, 4, 5, 15, 16, 17, 18, 23, 25, 31, 40, 41, 43, 55, 56, 60, 65, 101, 109, 114, 116
R.2.6	Identify a theme, or identify which element(s) in a text support a theme.	**Student Book:** 44, 45, 55, 57 **Workbook:** 61, 86, 87, 88, 89
R.2.7	Make evidence-based generalizations or hypotheses based on details in text, including clarifications, extensions, or applications of main ideas to new situations.	**Student Book:** 15, 22, 23, 24, 25, 41, 43, 44, 45, 47, 48, 49, 51, 53, 57, 66, 67, 72 **Workbook:** 16, 17, 21, 25, 28, 42, 43, 44, 45, 46, 47, 48, 49, 56, 57, 59, 63, 64, 69, 72, 78, 83, 84, 89, 94, 95, 96, 97, 98, 100, 101, 102, 139, 145
R.2.8	Draw conclusions or make generalizations that require synthesis of multiple main ideas in text.	**Student Book:** 20, 21, 23, 24, 25, 46, 47, 48, 53, 55, 57, 72, 113 **Workbook:** 16, 25, 38, 39, 40, 41, 43, 46, 47, 48, 49, 57, 61, 63, 79, 90, 91, 92, 93, 94, 95, 96, 97, 101, 102, 108, 112, 120, 121, 145
R.3	**Analyze how individuals, events, and ideas develop and interact over the course of a text.**	
R.3.1	Order sequences of events in texts.	**Student Book:** 6, 7, 55, 57, 93 **Workbook:** 10, 11, 12, 13, 105
R.3.2	Make inferences about plot/sequence of events, characters/people, settings, or ideas in texts.	**Student Book:** 12, 29, 32, 33, 34, 35, 36, 37, 40, 41, 42, 43, 55, 57 **Workbook:** 10, 22, 41, 54, 55, 56, 57, 58, 59, 60, 61, 62, 63, 64, 65, 66, 67, 68, 69, 70, 71, 72, 73, 77, 78, 79, 80, 81, 82, 83, 84, 85, 90, 91, 93, 94, 95, 101, 115, 116
R.3.3	Analyze relationships within texts, including how events are important in relation to plot or conflict; how people, ideas, or events are connected, developed, or distinguished; how events contribute to theme or relate to key ideas; or how a setting or context shapes structure and meaning.	**Student Book:** 12, 29, 31, 33, 35, 36, 37, 40, 42, 43, 44, 45, 47, 49, 55, 57 **Workbook:** 41, 57, 59, 60, 61, 63, 64, 65, 67, 68, 69, 70, 71, 73, 77, 79, 80, 81, 82, 84, 85, 87, 91, 92, 93, 95, 96, 97
R.3.4	Infer relationships between ideas in a text (e.g., an implicit cause and effect, parallel, or contrasting relationship).	**Student Book:** 10, 11, 12, 13, 21, 28, 29, 31, 33, 34, 37, 42, 43, 44, 45, 47, 49, 51, 53, 55, 57 **Workbook:** 19, 21, 22, 23, 24, 25, 29, 35, 38, 40, 41, 48, 49, 54, 55, 56, 57, 58, 59, 60, 61, 62, 65, 68, 69, 70, 71, 72, 82, 84, 85, 95

Correlations/Reasoning Through Language Arts

Indicator Codes	Reasoning Through Language Arts Indicators	Reasoning Through Language Arts Book Pages
R.3.5	Analyze the roles that details play in complex literary or informational texts.	**Student Book:** 29, 33, 34, 35, 36, 41, 43, 47, 48, 49, 55, 57, 65 **Workbook:** 3, 4, 23, 29, 31, 41, 43, 48, 57, 60, 61, 64, 66, 67, 68, 69, 70, 72, 73, 77, 78, 79, 81, 82, 83, 84, 89, 90, 91, 92, 93, 97, 101, 108, 112, 124
R.4/L.4	**Interpret words and phrases that appear frequently in texts from a wide variety of disciplines, including determining connotative and figurative meanings from context and analyzing how specific word choices shape meaning or tone.**	
R.4.1 / L.4.1	Determine the meaning of words and phrases as they are used in a text, including determining connotative and figurative meanings from context.	**Student Book:** 14, 15, 16, 18, 26, 27, 49, 51, 55, 89, 91, 93 **Workbook:** 30, 31, 33, 34, 35, 36, 37, 50, 51, 52, 53, 70, 75, 95
R.4.2 / L.4.2	Analyze how meaning or tone is affected when one word is replaced with another.	**Student Book:** 19, 39, 51 **Workbook:** 34, 35, 37, 51, 52, 75, 130
R.4.3 / L.4.3	Analyze the impact of specific words, phrases, or figurative language in text, with a focus on an author's intent to convey information or construct an argument.	**Student Book:** 14, 15, 16, 18, 19, 23, 31, 35, 36, 37, 38, 39, 43, 45, 49, 53, 55, 57, 75, 76, 87, 89 **Workbook:** 26, 28, 29, 30, 31, 33, 34, 35, 36, 37, 41, 46, 48, 50, 51, 57, 59, 60, 66, 68, 69, 70, 73, 74, 75, 76, 77, 89, 90, 91, 92, 93, 94, 95, 98, 101, 106, 115, 116, 119, 124, 126, 128, 129, 130, 138, 139, 145
R.5	**Analyze the structure of texts, including how specific sentences or paragraphs relate to each other and to the whole.**	
R.5.1	Analyze how a particular sentence, paragraph, chapter, or section fits into the overall structure of a text and contributes to the development of the ideas.	**Student Book:** 9, 10, 11, 12, 19, 31, 45, 53, 55, 57, 61, 62, 63, 65, 87, 91, 93 **Workbook:** 2, 3, 4, 5, 6, 7, 8, 14, 17, 23, 26, 30, 32, 33, 35, 36, 41, 54, 60, 65, 76, 79, 87, 88, 91, 92, 93, 103, 105, 106, 109, 116, 120, 121, 122, 123, 124, 125, 128, 130, 133, 137, 139, 145, 152, 153
R.5.2	Analyze the structural relationship between adjacent sections of text (e.g., how one paragraph develops or refines a key concept or how one idea is distinguished from another).	**Student Book:** 3, 9, 11, 12, 21, 45, 53, 55, 61, 63, 73, 87, 89 **Workbook:** 5, 7, 8, 14, 19, 21, 23, 26, 35, 36, 43, 76, 104, 108, 122, 123, 124, 125, 128, 139, 141
R.5.3	Analyze transitional language or signal words (words that indicate structural relationships, such as consequently, nevertheless, otherwise) and determine how they refine meaning, emphasize certain ideas, or reinforce an author's purpose.	**Student Book:** 3, 6, 12, 13, 22, 28, 30, 89, 91, 93, 106, 113 **Workbook:** 7, 10, 14, 22, 54, 59, 105, 122, 125, 141, 145, 152, 153, 156, 158, 166, 170
R.5.4	Analyze how the structure of a paragraph, section, or passage shapes meaning, emphasizes key ideas, or supports an author's purpose.	**Student Book:** 9, 19, 20, 39, 55, 61, 63, 65, 72, 73, 89, 91, 113 **Workbook:** 4, 5, 8, 17, 33, 35, 65, 87, 98, 99, 100, 104, 105, 120, 122, 123, 124, 125, 133, 137, 141, 152, 153, 158, 167, 168
R.6	**Determine an author's purpose or point of view in a text and explain how it is conveyed and shapes the content and style of a text.**	
R.6.1	Determine an author's point of view or purpose of a text.	**Student Book:** 5, 14, 15, 19, 24, 33, 51, 55, 60, 61, 62, 63, 64, 75, 87, 113 **Workbook:** 9, 26, 27, 28, 29, 33, 60, 98, 99, 100, 101, 102, 106, 110, 116, 122, 123, 125, 127, 128, 131, 133, 134, 135, 138, 139, 141, 145, 150, 152, 153

Correlations/Reasoning Through Language Arts

Indicator Codes	Reasoning Through Language Arts Indicators	*Reasoning Through Language Arts* Book Pages
R.6.2	Analyze how the author distinguishes his or her position from that of others or how an author acknowledges or responds to conflicting evidence or viewpoints.	**Student Book:** 61, 83, 89, 113 **Workbook:** 28, 29, 99, 104, 110, 123, 124, 125, 152, 153, 156
R.6.3	Infer an author's implicit as well as explicit purposes based on details in text.	**Student Book:** 41, 51, 53, 57, 75, 87, 89, 93 **Workbook:** 33, 40, 79, 98, 99, 100, 101, 102, 108, 109, 111, 112, 119, 121, 125, 127, 128, 133, 137, 139, 141, 145
R.6.4	Analyze how an author uses rhetorical techniques to advance his or her point of view or achieve a specific purpose (e.g., analogies, enumerations, repetition and parallelism, juxtaposition of opposites, qualifying statements).	**Student Book:** 18, 19, 63, 74, 75, 87, 89, 93, 113 **Workbook:** 8, 26, 32, 99, 100, 115, 119, 126, 127, 128, 129, 137, 138, 152, 153, 156
R.8	**Delineate and evaluate the argument and specific claims in a text, including the validity of the reasoning as well as the relevance and sufficiency of the evidence.**	
R.8.1	Delineate the specific steps of an argument the author puts forward, including how the argument's claims build on one another.	**Student Book:** 62, 63, 65, 72, 73, 87, 89, 98, 99, 113 **Workbook:** 103, 104, 105, 122, 123, 124, 125, 155, 156
R.8.2	Identify specific pieces of evidence an author uses in support of claims or conclusions.	**Student Book:** 60, 61, 63, 64, 65, 66, 67, 68, 69, 70, 83, 87, 98, 99, 113 **Workbook:** 99, 101, 102, 103, 106, 107, 108, 109, 111, 114, 116, 118, 119, 120, 121, 123, 155, 156
R.8.3	Evaluate the relevance and sufficiency of evidence offered in support of a claim.	**Student Book:** 68, 69, 70, 71, 87, 89, 91, 98, 99 **Workbook:** 42, 108, 114, 115, 118, 119, 120, 121, 123, 155
R.8.4	Distinguish claims that are supported by reasons and evidence from claims that are not.	**Student Book:** 68, 70, 87, 91 **Workbook:** 42, 109, 117, 118, 120, 121
R.8.5	Assess whether the reasoning is valid; identify fallacious reasoning in an argument and evaluate its impact.	**Student Book:** 68, 69, 70, 71, 89 **Workbook:** 114, 115, 116, 117, 118, 119, 121, 123
R.8.6	Identify an underlying premise or assumption in an argument and evaluate the logical support and evidence provided.	**Student Book:** 63, 72, 73, 87 **Workbook:** 104, 116, 117, 119, 120
R.7, R.9	**Analyze how two or more texts address similar themes or topics.**	
R.9.1 / 7.1	Draw specific comparisons between two texts that address similar themes or topics or between information presented in different formats (e.g., between information presented in text and information or data summarized in a table or timeline).	**Student Book:** 25, 76, 77, 78, 79, 80, 81, 84, 85, 91, 93, 100, 101 **Workbook:** 46, 49, 110, 111, 112, 113, 130, 131, 133, 134, 135, 137, 138, 139, 141, 147, 149, 150, 151, 154, 157, 158, 159, 160
R.9.2	Compare two passages in similar or closely related genre that share ideas or themes, focusing on similarities and/or differences in perspective, tone, style, structure, purpose, or overall impact.	**Student Book:** 24, 25, 80, 81, 93, 96, 97, 98, 99, 100, 101, 113 **Workbook:** 48, 49, 130, 131, 133, 138, 139, 141, 150, 151, 154, 155, 158, 159, 160

Correlations/Reasoning Through Language Arts

Indicator Codes	Reasoning Through Language Arts Indicators	Reasoning Through Language Arts Book Pages
R.9.3	Compare two argumentative passages on the same topic that present opposing claims (either main or supporting claims) and analyze how each text emphasizes different evidence or advances a different interpretations of facts.	**Student Book:** 96, 97, 98, 99, 100, 101, 113 **Workbook:** 150, 151, 154, 156, 158, 159, 160
R.7.2	Analyze how data or quantitative and/or visual information extends, clarifies, or contradicts information in text, or determine how data supports an author's argument.	**Student Book:** 66, 67, 78, 87 **Workbook:** 110, 111, 112, 113, 134, 135
R.7.3	Compare two passages that present related ideas or themes in different genres or formats (e.g., a feature article and an online FAQ or fact sheet) in order to evaluate differences in scope, purpose, emphasis, intended audience, or overall impact when comparing.	**Student Book:** 76, 77, 78, 79, 82, 83, 91, 93 **Workbook:** 134, 135, 137, 142, 143, 145, 149
R.7.4	Compare two passages that present related ideas or themes in different genre or formats in order to synthesize details, draw conclusions, or apply information to new situations.	**Student Book:** 66, 84, 85, 91, 93 **Workbook:** 111, 112, 113, 135, 137, 142, 145, 146, 147, 149
Writing Assessment Targets		
R.1		
W.1	Determine the details of what is explicitly stated and make logical inferences or valid claims that square with textual evidence.	**Student Book:** 98, 99, 100, 101, 102, 103, 104, 105, 106, 107, 108, 109, 110, 111, 113, 115, 117, 119 **Workbook:** 154, 155, 157, 158, 159, 160, 161, 162, 163, 164, 165, 166, 167, 168, 169, 170, 171, 172, 173, 174
W.1, W.2, W.4		
W.2	Produce an extended analytic response in which the writer introduces the idea(s) or claim(s) clearly, creates an organization that logically sequences information, develops the idea(s) or claim(s) thoroughly with well-chosen examples, facts, or details from the text, and maintains a coherent focus.	**Student Book:** 98, 99, 100, 101, 102, 103, 104, 105, 106, 107, 108, 109, 110, 111, 113, 115, 117, 119, 158, 159, 169 **Workbook:** 154, 155, 157, 158, 159, 160, 161, 162, 163, 164, 165, 166, 167, 168, 169, 170, 171, 172, 173, 174, 250, 251, 252, 253
W.5, L.1, L.2, L.3		
W.3	Write clearly and demonstrate sufficient command of standard English conventions.	**Student Book:** 104, 105, 106, 107, 110, 111, 115, 117, 119, 122, 123, 126, 127, 128, 129, 165, 186, 187, 188, 189, 190, 191, 192, 193, 195, 197 **Workbook:** 168, 169, 170, 171, 172, 173, 174, 175, 176, 177, 178, 179, 180, 181, 195, 197, 250, 251, 252, 253
Language Assessment Targets		
L.1	Demonstrate command of the conventions of standard English grammar and usage when writing or speaking.	
L.1.1	Edit to correct errors involving frequently confused words and homonyms, including contractions (passed, past; two, too, to; there, their, they're; knew, new; it's its).	**Student Book:** 110, 130, 131, 132, 133, 162, 164, 165, 167, 168 **Workbook:** 177, 194, 196, 197, 198, 199, 200, 201

Correlations/Reasoning Through Language Arts

Indicator Codes	Reasoning Through Language Arts Indicators	Reasoning Through Language Arts Book Pages
L.1.2	Edit to correct errors in straightforward subject-verb agreement.	**Student Book:** 110, 115, 134, 135, 162 **Workbook:** 177, 202, 203, 204, 205
L.1.3	Edit to correct errors in pronoun usage, including pronoun- antecedent agreement, unclear pronoun references, and pronoun case.	**Student Book:** 110, 124, 125, 130, 133, 150, 151, 162, 165, 166, 167, 168 **Workbook:** 177, 182, 183, 184, 185, 197, 201, 234, 235, 236, 237
L.1.4	Edit to eliminate non-standard or informal usage (e.g., correctly use try to win the game instead of try and win the game).	**Student Book:** 110, 111, 136, 137, 165, 167, 168 **Workbook:** 174, 175, 206, 207, 208, 209
L.1.5	Edit to eliminate dangling or misplaced modifiers or illogical word order (e.g., correctly use to meet almost all requirements instead of to almost meet all requirements).	**Student Book:** 110, 148, 149, 162, 165, 166, 168 **Workbook:** 177, 230, 231, 232, 233
L.1.6	Edit to ensure parallelism and proper subordination and coordination.	**Student Book:** 115, 117, 144, 145, 154, 155, 163, 164, 169 **Workbook:** 176, 222, 223, 224, 225, 242, 243, 244, 245
L.1.7	Edit to correct errors in subject-verb or pronoun-antecedent agreement in more complicated situations (e.g., with compound subjects, interceding phrases, or collective nouns).	**Student Book:** 110, 134, 135, 150, 151, 152, 153, 165, 166, 167, 168 **Workbook:** 177, 202, 203, 204, 234, 235, 236, 237, 238, 239, 240, 241
L.1.8	Edit to eliminate wordiness or awkward sentence construction.	**Student Book:** 110, 111, 144, 145, 154, 155, 163, 169 **Workbook:** 175, 176, 222, 223, 224, 225, 242, 243, 244, 245
L.1.9	Edit to ensure effective use of transitional words, conjunctive adverbs, and other words and phrases that support logic and clarity.	**Student Book:** 105, 106, 110, 111, 115, 117, 119, 144, 145, 156, 157, 158, 159, 163, 164, 168, 169 **Workbook:** 166, 168, 169, 170, 171, 172, 173, 174, 175, 176, 222, 223, 224, 225, 246, 247, 248, 249, 250, 251, 252, 253
L.2	**Demonstrate command of the conventions of standard English capitalization and punctuation when writing.**	
L.2.1	Edit to ensure correct use of capitalization (e.g., proper nouns, titles, and beginnings of sentences).	**Student Book:** 110, 122, 123, 138, 139, 140, 141, 163, 167 **Workbook:** 177, 178, 179, 180, 210, 211, 212, 213, 215, 216, 217
L.2.2	Edit to eliminate run-on sentences, fused sentences, or sentence fragments.	**Student Book:** 110, 111, 140, 141, 146, 147, 160, 161, 163, 164, 167, 168 **Workbook:** 176, 214, 215, 216, 217, 226, 227, 228, 229, 254, 255, 256
L.2.3	Edit to ensure correct use of apostrophes with possessive nouns.	**Student Book:** 110, 130, 131, 165 **Workbook:** 177, 194, 195, 196, 197
L.2.4	Edit to ensure correct use of punctuation (e.g., commas in a series or in appositives and other non-essential elements, end marks, and appropriate punctuation for clause separation).	**Student Book:** 110, 119, 140, 141, 142, 143, 144, 145, 146, 147, 160, 161, 163, 164, 167, 168 **Workbook:** 177, 214, 215, 216, 217, 218, 219, 220, 221, 222, 223, 224, 225, 226, 229, 254, 255, 256, 257

LANGUAGE ARTS

Table of Contents

Table of Contents... MA 1
About *Steck-Vaughn Test Preparation for the 2014 GED® Test: Mathematical Reasoning* .... MA 2

UNIT 1 *Number Sense and Operations* ...... MA 3
LESSON
1: Whole Numbers... MA 4
2: Operations .... MA 5
3: Integers .... MA 6
4: Fractions .... MA 7
5: Ratios and Proportions .... MA 8
6: Decimals .... MA 9
7: Percent .... MA 10
Unit 1 Review................................. MA 11–MA 12

UNIT 2 *Data Measurement/Analysis* .... MA 13
LESSON
1: Measurement and Units of Measure.............. MA 14
2: Length, Area, and Volume .... MA 15
3: Mean, Median, and Mode .... MA 16
4: Probability .... MA 17
5: Bar and Line Graphs .... MA 18
6: Circle Graphs .... MA 19
7: Dot Plots, Histograms, and Box Plots............ MA 20
Unit 2 Review.................................... MA 21–MA 22

UNIT 3 *Algebra, Functions, and Patterns*.. MA 23
LESSON
1: Algebraic Expressions and Variables .... MA 24
2: Equations.. MA 25
3: Squaring, Cubing, and Taking Roots .... MA 26
4: Exponents and Scientific Notation .... MA 27
5: Patterns and Functions............................... MA 28
6: One-Variable Linear Equations .... MA 29
7: Two-Variable Linear Equations...................... MA 30
8: Factoring...MA 31
9: Rational Expressions and Equations.............. MA 32
10: Solving and Graphing Inequalities................. MA 33
11: The Coordinate Grid .... MA 34
12: Graphing Linear Equations .... MA 35
13: Slope.. MA 36
14: Using Slope to Solve Geometric Problems ... MA 37
15: Graphing Quadratic Equations .... MA 38

16: Evaluation of Functions............................... MA 39
17: Comparison of Functions .... MA 40
Unit 3 Review....................................... MA 41–MA 42

UNIT 4 *Geometry* .... MA 43
LESSON
1: Triangles and Quadrilaterals .... MA 44
2: Pythagorean Theorem.................................. MA 45
3: Polygons .... MA 46
4: Circles... MA 47
5: Composite Plane Figures.............................. MA 48
6: Scale Drawings .... MA 49
7: Prisms and Cylinders................................... MA 50
8: Pyramids, Cones, and Spheres .... MA 51
9: Composite Solids .... MA 52
Unit 4 Review... MA 53–MA 54

APPENDICES
A: Calculator Directions......................... MA 55–MA 56
B: Formulas for the GED® Mathematical Reasoning Test .... MA 57
C: Glossary... MA 58–MA 61

CORRELATIONS/MATHEMATICS MA 62–MA 71

About *Steck-Vaughn Test Preparation for the 2014 GED® Test: Mathematical Reasoning*

Steck-Vaughn's student book and workbook help unlock the learning and deconstruct the different elements of the test by helping learners build and develop core mathematics skills. The content of our books aligns to the new GED® math content standards and item distribution to provide learners with a superior test preparation experience.

Our *Spotlighted Item* feature provides a deeper, richer treatment for each technology-enhanced item type. On initial introduction, a unique item type—such as drag-and-drop—receives a full-page of example items in the student book lesson and three pages in the companion workbook. The length of subsequent features may be shorter depending on the skill, lesson, and requirements.

A combination of targeted strategies, informational call-outs and sample questions, assorted tips and hints, and ample assessment help to clearly focus study efforts in needed areas.

In addition to the book features, a highly detailed answer key provides the correct answer and the rationale for it so that learners know exactly why an answer is correct. The *Mathematical Reasoning* student book and workbook are designed with an eye toward the end goal: Success on the GED® Mathematical Reasoning Test.

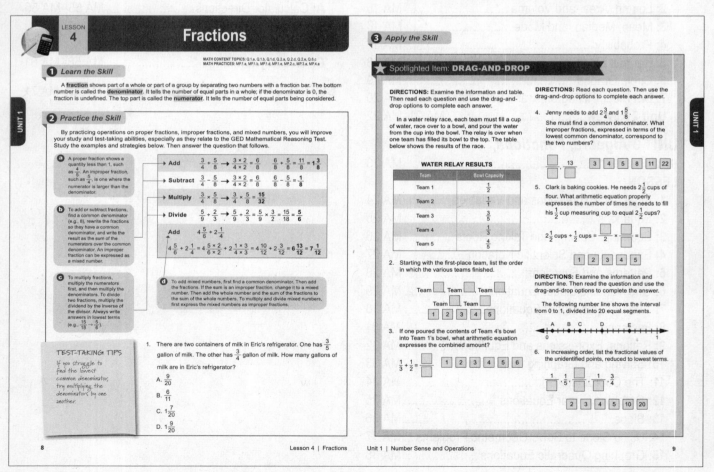

Unit 1

Number Sense and Operations

For many learners, mathematical reasoning may be the most intimidating of all the GED® Test subject areas. To help put learners' minds at ease, remind them that problems on the GED® Mathematical Reasoning Test can be solved by using the four basic operations of addition, subtraction, multiplication, and division. The key comes in determining the components to multiply, for example, and how. For that reason, students must gain a strong foundation in those four operations in Unit 1.

Operations using whole numbers, fractions, decimals, and percentages make up a significant amount of questions on the GED® Mathematical Reasoning Test. While many students may be familiar with the concept of decimals (especially as represented in a financial context, such as on a paycheck or a price tag), fractions and percentages may seem more daunting. Remind students that fractions and percentages are just different ways of expressing a decimal (and vice versa). Through such connections, the material in this unit may seem more accessible and less overwhelming to learners.

Table of Contents

LESSON	PAGE
1: Whole Numbers	MA 4
2: Operations	MA 5
3: Integers	MA 6
4: Fractions	MA 7
5: Ratios and Proportions	MA 8
6: Decimals	MA 9
7: Percent	MA 10
Unit 1 Review	**MA 11– MA 12**

MATHEMATICS

Whole Numbers

MATH CONTENT TOPICS: Q.1, Q.2.a, Q.2.e, Q.6.c
MATH PRACTICES: MP.1.a, MP.1.b, MP.1.c, MP.1.e, MP.2.c, MP.3.a, MP.4.a, MP.5.c

MATHEMATICS

STUDENT BOOK pp. 2–3

▶ Preview the Skill

Discuss with learners the following scenario: The cost of a tire at Store A is $132. The cost of that same tire at Store B is $123. Ask learners at which store, A or B, they would buy the tire. Elicit that most learners would compare the two prices and choose the store—in this case, Store B—with the most affordable price. Point out that even though both numbers contain the same digits, the placement of those digits is different. As a result, the value of each number is different. For example, the *3* in $132 has a value of $30 and the *3* in $123 has a value of $3. Tell learners that since both numbers have a 1 in the hundreds place, they can use the tens place to compare the numbers.

❶ Learn the Skill

Decoding Prompt learners to think of the word "whole" as "unbroken." Explain that numbers that are whole lack decimal or fractional parts. Explain that even the number 0 is a whole number.

❷ Practice the Skill

Use Graphic Organizers Refer learners to the place-value chart on p. 2 and ask them about digit values, comma locations, and rounding strategies.

❸ Apply the Skill

SuperSkill Review Inform learners that to successfully answer question 4, learners must know that the numbers are in ranges. Elicit that Shelf I contains numbers greater than or equal to 1337 and less than or equal to 1420. Learners first must identify which range of numbers contains the number 1384. So, 1384 will be equal to one of the two numbers in the range or it will be between the two numbers. Once they identify the correct range, then they can identify the letter of the shelf with the correct range of numbers.

Answers
1. D; DOK Level: 1; **2.** B; DOK Level: 1; **3.** C; DOK Level: 1; **4.** A; DOK Level: 1; **5.** C; DOK Level: 2; **6.** B; DOK Level: 2; **7.** A; DOK Level: 2; **8.** A; DOK Level: 2; **9.** A; DOK Level: 2; **10.** B; DOK Level: 2

WORKBOOK pp. 2–5

❶ Review the Skill

SuperSkill Review Use an example to explain the differences between place, place value, and value. Use the number 342 as an example. The digit *3* is in the hundreds *place*. The *place value* of this digit is *100*. The *value* of the *3* is *300*. Next, provide learners with a series of two-, three- and four-digit numbers and have them determine place, place value, and value for each.

❷ Refine the Skill

Problem-Solving Strategy Have students write the numbers from the table in a place-value chart. To answer question 1, they then should scan across the chart from left to right, beginning at the thousands place. Lead learners to note that 5,683 is the greatest number because it is the only one with a 5 in its thousands place. Then direct learners to scan the table on p. 2 to identify the day of the week that drew 5,683 people to the amusement park. To extend the learning, request that learners order the daily sales for the table on p. 2 according to increasing sales.

❸ Master the Skill

Skim and Scan This lesson introduces skills associated with interpreting tables. Tables often require identification of relevant rows or columns, scanning to find information, and performance of additional arithmetic operations. Explain to learners that tables also often include more data than necessary to answer problems, such as those in items 13 through 15.

Answers
1. D; DOK Level: 1; **2.** C; DOK Level: 1; **3.** C; DOK Level: 1; **4.** B; DOK Level: 2; **5.** A; DOK Level: 2; **6.** C; DOK Level: 1; **7.** D; DOK Level: 2; **8.** B; DOK Level: 1; **9.** D; DOK Level: 1; **10.** A; DOK Level: 1; **11.** D; DOK Level: 2; **12.** B; DOK Level: 1; **13.** C; DOK Level: 1; **14.** C; DOK Level: 2; **15.** A; DOK Level: 2; **16.** D; DOK Level: 2; **17.** C; DOK Level: 3; **18.** B; DOK Level: 1; **19.** B; DOK Level: 1; **20.** D; DOK Level: 3; **21.** B; DOK Level: 3; **22.** D; DOK Level: 2; **23.** D; DOK Level: 2; **24.** D; DOK Level: 2; **25.** C; DOK Level: 2

Operations

MATH CONTENT TOPICS: Q.1.b, Q.2.a, Q.2.e, Q.3.a, Q.6.c, Q.7.a
MATH PRACTICES: MP.1.a, MP.1.b, MP.1.c, MP.1.d, MP.1.e, MP.2.c, MP.3.a, MP.4.a, MP.5.c

STUDENT BOOK pp. 4–5

➤ Preview the Skill

Discuss everyday situations that require the use of addition, subtraction, multiplication, and division. For example, a trip to the grocery store may involve adding to find total cost, multiplying to find the total cost of several of the same item, and subtracting to find the change that you receive from a purchase. Have volunteers provide other examples and the operations needed to solve them.

❶ Learn the Skill

Decoding Many people have trouble distinguishing the terms *divisor* and *dividend*. The suffix *-or* often helps to indicate something or someone who does an action or serves in a particular role. This suffix appears in words such as *director*, *mentor*, and *negotiator*. The *divisor* divides the *dividend* into groups. The dividend is the number that appears on the left side of the ÷ symbol, or the number that appears inside of a division bracket. The divisor is always the number on the right side of the ÷ symbol, or it is the number that appears outside of the division bracket.

❷ Practice the Skill

SuperSkill Review Encourage learners to remember place value when performing operations. For example, to add 482 + 208, encourage learners to think "2 ones + 8 ones, 8 tens + 0 tens + 1 ten, and 4 hundreds + 2 hundreds," rather than just "2 + 8, 8 + 0 + 1, and 4 + 2." Using grid paper can help learners to line up numbers by place value.

❸ Apply the Skill

Spotlighted Item: Fill-in-the-Blank Explain that, when learners take the GED® Mathematical Reasoning Test, they will do so via computer. As a result, they will need to use basic keyboarding skills—such as use of a mouse, placement of a cursor, and basic typing skills—to enter responses to fill-in-the-blank questions.

Answers
1. B; DOK Level: 1; **2.** 1,050; DOK Level: 1; **3.** 288; DOK Level: 1; **4.** $360; DOK Level: 1; **5.** $540; DOK Level: 1; **6.** $16; DOK Level: 1; **7.** 10; DOK Level: 3; **8.** $11,340; DOK Level: 1; **9.** 241; DOK Level: 3; **10.** 4; DOK Level: 3; **11.** 18; DOK Level: 3; **12.** 42; DOK Level: 1

WORKBOOK pp. 6–9

❶ Review the Skill

Decoding Explain to learners that success on the GED® Mathematical Reasoning Test depends on their understanding of operations, their order, and their place value. Reinforce that learners will work from right to left when adding, subtracting, and multiplying numbers, and from left to right when dividing them.

❷ Refine the Skill

Decoding Explain to learners that it can be challenging to determine the proper operation. Guide learners to identify keywords in each question that can lead them to correctly perform a specific operation or series of operations. For example, the phrase *find the difference* means learners should subtract a smaller number from a larger one. In question 1, the phrase *the total number of boxes of cereal* should prompt learners to add the cereal totals from Monday and Tuesday.

❸ Master the Skill

Spotlighted Item: Fill-in-the-Blank Explain that fill-in-the-blank items often provide a stronger measure of learners' understanding than traditional multiple-choice items. Learners must be able to calculate the response without clues. Then have learners review item 25, and write their answers as they would key them on the actual test. Explain that any items, such as this one, will require the use of multiple operations. Also lead learners to understand the importance of accurate placement of commas as they relate to place value.

Answers
1. D; DOK Level: 1; **2.** B; DOK Level: 1; **3.** $1,950; DOK Level: 1; **4.** $1,190; DOK Level: 1; **5.** $864; DOK Level: 1; **6.** $270; DOK Level: 1; **7.** 9; DOK Level: 3; **8.** $826,700; DOK Level: 1; **9.** 48; DOK Level: 1; **10.** 608; DOK Level: 1; **11.** $108; DOK Level: 2; **12.** $756; DOK Level: 2; **13.** $1,330; DOK Level: 1; **14.** $106; DOK Level: 1; **15.** $2,148; DOK Level: 1; **16.** $2,640; DOK Level: 2; **17.** $564; DOK Level: 2; **18.** $1,560; DOK Level: 2; **19.** $1,023; DOK Level: 2; **20.** $1,347; DOK Level: 1; **21.** 62; DOK Level: 1; **22.** 3; DOK Level: 3; **23.** 15; DOK Level: 2; **24.** 740; DOK Level: 2; **25.** $4,578; DOK Level: 1; **26.** $5; DOK Level: 1; **27.** $372; DOK Level: 2; **28.** $18,900; DOK Level: 2; **29.** 18; DOK Level: 1; **30.** $175; DOK Level: 1; **31.** 6; DOK Level: 3; **32.** 60; DOK Level: 3

MATHEMATICS

MATH CONTENT TOPICS: Q.1.d, Q.2.a, Q.2.e, Q.6.c
MATH PRACTICES: MP.1.a, MP.1.b, MP.1.c, MP.1.d, MP.1.e, MP.2.c, MP.3.a, MP.4.a

STUDENT BOOK pp. 6–7

➤ Preview the Skill

Draw a number line on the board. Pass a six-sided die around, allowing learners to roll the die. On the first roll, write the result on the number line as a positive integer. On the second roll, write the result as a negative integer and move the first point on the number line appropriately. Repeat this process a variety of times, alternating between positive and negative integers for rolls. Lead learners to understand that positive rolls move the point to the right on a number line, while negative rolls move it to the left.

❶ Learn the Skill

Give Examples Help learners practice adding integers by providing the example of balancing a checkbook. Explain that deposits are positive numbers and that checks, withdrawals, and banking fees are negative numbers. For an account that begins with $30, have learners calculate the balance after each of the following transactions: $200 deposit ($230); $112 check ($118); $70 cash withdrawal ($48); $59 check (−$11); $20 overdraft fee (−$31); $50 deposit ($19); and $2 fee ($17).

❷ Practice the Skill

Link to Past Skills Have learners revisit the skill of operations in Unit 1, Lesson 2, for help in deciding whether to add, subtract, multiply, or divide integers. To answer question 1, learners must find the change in temperature, or the *difference* of the new temperature minus the old, or $12 - (-3)$.

❸ Apply the Skill

Decoding Use problem 4 as a basis to lead learners through the process of translating words such as *enrolled*, *graduated*, and *left* into the appropriate arithmetic operations.

Answers
1. D; DOK Level: 1; 2. $114; DOK Level: 1; 3. +7 spaces; DOK Level: 2; 4. 3,368; DOK Level: 2; 5. 26; DOK Level: 2; 6. A; DOK Level: 1; 7. D; DOK Level: 2; 8. D; DOK Level: 2; 9. B; DOK Level: 2

WORKBOOK pp. 10–13

❶ Review the Skill

Decoding Explain that a set of whole numbers includes positive whole numbers, their opposites, and zero. Tell learners that negative numbers are less than 0, that 0 is neither positive nor negative, and that positive numbers are greater than 0. Explain that, although a negative sign and a subtraction sign may look the same, they have different meanings. A negative sign appears left of a numeral and describes a number as being negative, or less than 0. It also can indicate that number's opposite. For example, $-(-3)$ can mean the opposite of negative 3 (positive 3). A subtraction sign indicates that one amount is being subtracted from another. It appears between two numbers.

❷ Refine the Skill

Give Examples Explain that negative numbers are used to show a decrease, and positive numbers are used to show an increase. For example, if an employee's paycheck was changed by $-\$5.00$, this indicates a loss of 5 dollars. To help learners with question 1, ask, "Did the temperature increase or decrease?" If the temperature increased, then the answer is positive. If the temperature decreased, then the answer is negative.

❸ Master the Skill

Skim and Scan Select a subset of problems and, for each, have the students skim them to see whether they can identify extraneous information. Question 14, for example, features an unnecessary fact. Explain to learners that they must evaluate all of the information in an item, and then decide which parts of it to use in arriving at a solution.

Answers
1. A; DOK Level: 1; 2. D; DOK Level: 1; 3. D; DOK Level: 1; 4. −43; DOK Level: 2; 5. C; DOK Level: 2; 6. D; DOK Level: 2; 7. B; DOK Level: 2; 8. A; DOK Level: 2; 9. D; DOK Level: 2; 10. B; DOK Level: 2; 11. D; DOK Level: 2; 12. D; DOK Level: 2; 13. A; DOK Level: 2; 14. D; DOK Level: 2; 15. A; DOK Level: 2; 16. A; DOK Level: 3; 17. 20 miles; DOK Level: 3; 18. A; DOK Level: 1; 19. B; DOK Level: 1; 20. D; DOK Level: 1; 21. A; DOK Level: 2; 22. D; DOK Level: 1; 23. C; DOK Level: 1; 24. B; DOK Level: 2; 25. A; DOK Level: 2; 26. B; DOK Level: 2; 27. C; DOK Level: 2; 28. D; DOK Level: 1; 29. B; DOK Level: 2

Fractions

MATH CONTENT TOPICS: Q.1.a, Q.1.b, Q.1.d, Q.2.a, Q.2.d, Q.2.e, Q.6.c, Q.3.a
MATH PRACTICES: MP.1.a, MP.1.b, MP.1.d, MP.1.e, MP.2.c, MP.3.a, MP.4.a

STUDENT BOOK *pp. 8–9*

▶ Preview the Skill

Inform learners that fractions show parts of a whole. For example, explain that if you sleep 8 hours each night, then you sleep 8 out of 24 hours per day. Your amount of time each day spent sleeping can be represented by the fraction $\frac{8}{24}$ or $\frac{1}{3}$. This means you spend $\frac{1}{3}$ of your day sleeping. Have learners calculate fractions for the parts of their days in which they sleep, work, attend class, or read.

❶ Learn the Skill

Decoding Inform learners that to *numerate* means to count. The *numerator* of a fraction counts the number of parts. Explain that the *denomination* of a bill tells the number of dollars that make up the whole bill. Likewise, the denominator of a fraction tells the number of parts that make up the whole. Use these definitions to help learners remember the difference between a fraction's *numerator* and *denominator*.

❷ Practice the Skill

Decoding Inform learners that they may estimate the value of a fraction, but they will do so differently than they would with a whole number. Explain that when two fractions, such as those in question 1, have the same numerator, the larger fraction will have the smaller denominator. Lead learners to understand that, although it has a 5 in the denominator, $\frac{3}{5}$ is less than $\frac{3}{4}$.

❸ Apply the Skill

Spotlighted Item: Drag-and-Drop Explain that, on the GED® Mathematical Reasoning Test, drag-and-drop items require learners to drag, or move, small images to designated drop targets on the screen. Learners will use drag-and-drop items to complete expressions or to order series of numbers.

Answers
1. C; DOK Level: 1; **2.** Team 2, Team 5, Team 3, Team 1, and Team 4; DOK Level: 3; **3.** $\frac{1}{3} + \frac{1}{2} = \frac{2}{6} + \frac{3}{6} = \frac{5}{6}$; DOK Level: 1; **4.** $\frac{22}{8}, \frac{13}{8}$; DOK Level: 1; **5.** $\frac{5}{2} \times \frac{2}{1} = 5$; DOK Level: 1; **6.** $\frac{1}{20}, \frac{1}{5}, \frac{3}{10}, \frac{1}{2}, \frac{3}{4}$; DOK Level: 2

WORKBOOK *pp. 14–17*

❶ Review the Skill

Give Examples Explain to learners that a mixed number actually indicates addition of a whole number part and a fraction part. For example, $3 + \frac{1}{4}$ actually means $3\frac{1}{4}$.

❷ Refine the Skill

SuperSkill Review As learners seek a common denominator to answer question 1, encourage them to find the *lowest* common denominator. Explain that, to do so, they first must identify the greatest denominator in the problem. If all other denominators divide evenly into the greatest denominator, then learners should use that denominator. If not, then learners should multiply the greatest denominator in that problem by 2. If that fails to provide the lowest common denominator, learners should multiply by increasing numbers (3, 4, 5, and so on) until they find a number divisible by all of the other denominators.

❸ Master the Skill

Decoding Question 10 introduces, for the first time in a mathematical context, the word *undefined*. While learners may have a sense of what the word means, use this as an opportunity to introduce and preview its mathematical meaning (a denominator of 0).

Answers
1. B; DOK Level: 1; **2.** $\frac{2}{5}$; DOK Level: 1; **3.** $\frac{1}{4}$; DOK Level: 1; **4.** $\frac{4}{15}$; DOK Level: 1; **5.** $\frac{11}{25}$; DOK Level: 1; **6.** Ethan, Walt, Natalia, Miguel, and Dara; DOK Level: 2; **7.** Miguel and Dara; DOK Level: 2; **8.** $\frac{1}{4}$; DOK Level: 1; **9.** 7; DOK Level: 1; **10.** A; DOK Level: 3; **11.** $1\frac{1}{2}$ hours; DOK Level: 1; **12.** $43\frac{1}{2}$ miles; DOK Level: 1; **13.** He rode $13\frac{1}{40}$ fewer miles on Wednesday than on Monday; DOK Level: 1; **14.** $2\frac{8}{9}$ hours; DOK Level: 1; **15.** $\frac{9}{10}, \frac{7}{10}, \frac{9}{20}, \frac{3}{20}$; DOK Level: 2; **16.** $\frac{9}{20}$; DOK Level: 1; **17.** (5)(21 − 8)/5 = 13; DOK Level: 3; **18.** $\frac{(7)(3 + 8 - 4)}{7} = 7$; DOK Level: 3; **19.** $12\frac{23}{24}$; DOK Level: 1

MATHEMATICS

Ratios and Proportions

MATH CONTENT TOPICS: Q.2.a, Q.2.e, Q.3.a, Q.3.b, Q.3.c, Q.6.c
MATH PRACTICES: MP.1.a, MP.1.b, MP.1.d, MP.1.e, MP.2.c, MP.3.a, MP.4.a

MATHEMATICS

STUDENT BOOK pp. 10–11

▶ Preview the Skill

Ask learners whether they have heard the phrase "blown out of proportion." Explain that this phrase means that an event received greater significance than it deserved. Encourage learners to give examples, such as the media "blowing out of proportion" a minor incident in an athlete's or a celebrity's life. Explain that, in mathematics, proportions maintain equality between two ratios so that they will not be "out of proportion."

❶ Learn the Skill

Link to Past Skills Remind learners that in the Unit 1, Lesson 4, skill *Fractions*, they learned that a fraction compares parts to a whole. Explain that a ratio can be written as a fraction, but that ratio also can compare parts to a whole or parts to other parts, such as quarters to nickels or boys to girls.

❷ Practice the Skill

Give Examples Explain that not all relationships are proportional. For example, suppose a store was selling shirts for $20 apiece. However, the store offered a sale price of $35 (instead of $40) to encourage people to purchase two shirts. These ratios—1/20 and 2/35—are unequal. To determine whether two ratios are equal, multiply the cross products. In this case, the cross products would be 35×1 and 20×2. If cross products are equal, then the ratios are equal.

❸ Apply the Skill

Decoding Explain that ratio questions on the GED® Mathematical Reasoning Test may provide a ratio, proportion, or rate relating two quantities, plus a specific instance of one quantity, and require learners to find the value of the other quantity. Or they may give values of both quantities and ask learners for the ratio, proportion, or rate.

Answers
1. C; DOK Level: 2; **2.** B; DOK Level: 2; **3.** A; DOK Level: 2;
4. A; DOK Level: 2; **5.** C; DOK Level: 1; **6.** A; DOK Level: 2;
7. B; DOK Level: 2; **8.** C; DOK Level: 2; **9.** D; DOK Level: 2;
10. D; DOK Level: 2; **11.** B; DOK Level: 2

WORKBOOK pp. 18–21

❶ Review the Skill

Give Examples Remind learners that a ratio compares two amounts, such as miles and hours, and can be written as a fraction. For example, 120 miles in 3 hours can be written as 120 miles/3 hours. If we simplify the ratio as 40 miles/1 hour, the ratio represents a unit rate because the denominator is 1. Point out to learners that this represents a whole, rather than parts of a whole.

❷ Refine the Skill

Link to Past Skills Remind learners that in the Unit 1, Lesson 4, skill *Fractions*, they studied mixed numbers. Next, ask learners to repeat question 1 for the remaining instruments in the band. Have them reduce improper fractions to mixed numbers as necessary.

❸ Master the Skill

Give Examples Distribute news articles that reference proportions or ratios, and ask learners to identify the instances. Then pose questions based on the material and discuss.

▶ Optional Activity

LifeLink Ask learners to estimate the dimensions of the rooms and the pieces of furniture within them in their homes. Then, distribute graph paper, and have each learner select a scale to use as a basis to produce scale drawings of their rooms.

Answers
1. B; DOK Level: 2; **2.** D; DOK Level: 2; **3.** A; DOK Level: 2; **4.** D; DOK Level: 2; **5.** C; DOK Level: 1;
6. D; DOK Level: 2; **7.** C; DOK Level: 1; **8.** A; DOK Level: 2;
9. B; DOK Level: 2; **10.** C; DOK Level: 2; **11.** B; DOK Level: 2; **12.** A; DOK Level: 2; **13.** $\frac{5}{15} = \frac{275}{x}$; x = $825; DOK Level: 2; **14.** $\frac{14}{[1]} = \frac{[406]}{[x]}$; x = 29; DOK Level: 2; **15.** B; DOK Level: 2; **16.** A; DOK Level: 1; **17.** B; DOK Level: 2;
18. C; DOK Level: 2; **19.** B; DOK Level: 2; **20.** C; DOK Level: 2; **21.** A; DOK Level: 2; **22.** B; DOK Level: 2; **23.** B; DOK Level: 2; **24.** C; DOK Level: 2; **25.** B; DOK Level: 2; **26.** D; DOK Level: 2; **27.** C; DOK Level: 2; **28.** A; DOK Level: 2

Decimals

MATH CONTENT TOPICS: Q.1.a, Q.2.a, Q.2.e, Q.3.a, Q.6.c
MATH PRACTICES: MP.1.a, MP.1.b, MP.1.e, MP.2.c, MP.3.a, MP.4.a, MP.3.c

STUDENT BOOK *pp. 12–13*

▶ Preview the Skill

Ask learners to compare $2500 and $25.00. Elicit that both numbers contain the same digits. However, explain that the placement of the decimal point in the second number affects its value. Ask learners to compare the value of the 2 in both numbers. Elicit that the 2 in the first number is *2000* because it is in the thousands place and that the 2 in the second number is *20* because it is in the tens place. Point out that since the decimal point in the second number is two places to the left of the understood decimal point in the first number, the second number is less than the first number by a factor of 100.

❶ Learn the Skill

Give Examples Distribute copies of a sales receipt for approximately 10 items, including several duplicates of one item, and some discounts or coupon deductions. Redact any subtotals and the final total, and have learners work in pairs to calculate the subtotals and final total. Discuss the results as a group and resolve discrepancies. Make use of discounts to illustrate decimal subtraction, and multiple items to show decimal multiplication and division.

❷ Practice the Skill

Link to Past Skills Emphasize that the four operations, especially multiplication and division, are variations of previous operations with whole numbers that learners studied in Unit 1, Lesson 2.

❸ Apply the Skill

Decoding Use question 6 as a focal point in explaining how to convert a word problem into an arithmetic expression. Highlight the fact that more than one expression may result from a single word problem. In this case, depending on how learners think of the problem, they may write either $(15)(\$5.25) - (15)(\$3.99)$ or $(15)(\$5.25 - \$3.99)$. Emphasize that both approaches are correct and lead to the same answer.

Answers
1. A; DOK Level: 2; **2.** D; DOK Level: 2; **3.** B; DOK Level: 2; **4.** A; DOK Level: 1; **5.** D; DOK Level: 1; **6.** B; DOK Level: 2; **7.** D; DOK Level: 3; **8.** C; DOK Level: 1

WORKBOOK *pp. 22–25*

❶ Review the Skill

Use Graphic Organizers Use the organizer below to reinforce learner understanding of decimals.

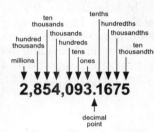

Decimal	Fraction	Place Value
5.2	$5\frac{2}{10}$	5 plus 2 tenths
27.36	$27\frac{36}{100}$	27 plus 36 hundredths
0.004	$\frac{4}{1000}$	4 thousandths

❷ Refine the Skill

Decoding Reinforce to learners the importance of carefully reading each question to determine what it is asking. For example, question 1 asks for the number of bowling balls with masses greater than 6.25 kg. It does not, however, ask for the difference between each ball's mass and the mass of 6.25.

❸ Master the Skill

Decoding Explain that certain items, such as questions 6 and 24, require careful interpretation of the text by learners so that they may identify the multiple steps necessary to solve such problems.

▶ Enrich and Extend

Have learners gain further practice by answering the following questions:
- How many tenths are in 1? *(10)*
- How many hundredths are in two-tenths? *(20)*
- Compare 10 and one-tenth. Which is larger, and by how much? *(10 is greater than one-tenth by a factor of 100)*

Answers
1. B; DOK Level: 2; **2.** B; DOK Level: 2; **3.** Monday; DOK Level: 2; **4.** 189.4; DOK Level: 2; **5.** 0.8; DOK Level: 2; **6.** $75.60; DOK Level: 3; **7.** C; DOK Level: 2; **8.** A; DOK Level: 2; **9.** C; DOK Level: 2; **10.** A; DOK Level: 2; **11.** C; DOK Level: 2; **12.** B; DOK Level: 2; **13.** A; DOK Level: 2; **14.** B; DOK Level: 2; **15.** D; DOK Level: 2; **16.** D; DOK Level: 2; **17.** B; DOK Level: 2; **18.** B; DOK Level: 2; **19.** C; DOK Level: 2; **20.** B; DOK Level: 2; **21.** C; DOK Level: 2; **22.** D; DOK Level: 2; **23.** B; DOK Level: 2; **24.** C; DOK Level: 3; **25.** B; DOK Level: 3

MATHEMATICS

Percent

MATH CONTENT TOPICS: Q.2.a, Q.2.e, Q.3.c, Q.3.d, Q.6.c
MATH PRACTICES: MP.1.a, MP.1.b, MP.1.d, MP.1.e, MP.2.c, MP.3.a, MP.4.a

MATHEMATICS

STUDENT BOOK *pp. 14–15*

Preview the Skill

Suppose a store rack is labeled "25% off the marked price," and you find a pair of jeans marked $20. Inform learners that it can be helpful to quickly calculate the sales price of the jeans. In this case, learners can divide 20 by 4 (since 25% is one-fourth, and one-fourth times 20 is the same as dividing by 4) to get a sales savings of $5. They then can subtract $5 from the retail price of $20 to get a sales price of $15.

❶ Learn the Skill

Give Examples To help learners understand the difference between the base (whole), rate (percent), and part (piece), discuss this example:

There are 20 dogs in a pet store; 5 are brown.

$$\frac{\text{part}}{\text{base}} = \frac{5 \text{ brown dogs}}{20 \text{ dogs}} \qquad \frac{\text{rate}}{100} = \frac{25}{100}$$

Here, the base is the number of dogs in the pet store, the part is the number of brown dogs, and the rate is 25%.

❷ Practice the Skill

Problem-Solving Strategy Have students construct a table like the one below with steps for converting fractions, decimals, and percent.

From	To	Steps
Fraction	Decimal	Divide numerator by denominator
Fraction	Percent	First change to decimal. Then multiply by 100 (move decimal point 2 places to the right). Add percent sign.

❸ Apply the Skill

Spotlighted Item: Drop-Down Build learners' comfort level with drop-down items by explaining their similarity to multiple-choice items. Encourage learners to use strategies similar to those they use in answering multiple-choice items, such as eliminating options they know to be incorrect.

Answers
1. C; DOK Level: 2; **2.** A; DOK Level: 1; **3.** C; DOK Level: 2;
4. B; DOK Level: 2; **5.** C; DOK Level: 2; **6.** D; DOK Level: 2;
7. C; DOK Level: 2; **8.** B; DOK Level: 2; **9.** C; DOK Level: 2;
10. B; DOK Level: 2; **11.** B; DOK Level: 2; **12.** D; DOK Level: 2

WORKBOOK *pp. 26–29*

❶ Review the Skill

Give Examples Review the terms *base*, *rate*, and *part*. Discuss the following scenario with students: Orlando earns 15% commission on his furniture sales. On Monday, he sold $3,500 worth of furniture and earned $525. Have learners identify the base (*$3,500*), rate (*15%*), and part (*$525*) for this situation. Encourage learners to set up and solve the problem to check. (*15% × $3,500 = $525*)

❷ Refine the Skill

Problem Solving Strategy Point out that learners must use base, rate, and part to solve the sample items. Explain that the tax that appears on the bill is an example of a part determined from an unknown rate.

❸ Master the Skill

Spotlighted Item: Drop-Down Spotlight question 22 to illustrate how drop-down items may include a different amount of answer options than typical multiple-choice items. Note how drop-down items also allow for deeper understanding of complex concepts.

Enrich and Extend

Organize learners into pairs, and provide each pair with two regular dice. Have them roll the dice 20 times, and tabulate the number of times the various totals (ranging from 2 to 12) come up. When finished, have each group calculate percentages for its total. Then, calculate percentages for aggregate totals.

Answers
1. B; DOK Level: 1; **2.** D; DOK Level: 2; **3.** C; DOK Level: 1;
4. D; DOK Level: 2; **5.** B; DOK Level: 1; **6.** B; DOK Level: 2;
7. C; DOK Level: 2; **8.** B; DOK Level: 2; **9.** B; DOK Level: 2;
10. C; DOK Level: 3; **11.** A; DOK Level: 2; **12.** B; DOK Level: 2; **13.** B; DOK Level: 2; **14.** A; DOK Level: 2; **15.** C; DOK Level: 2; **16.** B; DOK Level: 2; **17.** C; DOK Level: 2; **18.** B; DOK Level: 2; **19.** D; DOK Level: 2; **20.** D; DOK Level: 2; **21.** B; DOK Level: 2; **22.1** B; **22.2.** B; DOK Level: 2; **23.** C; DOK Level: 2; **24.** B; DOK Level: 2; **25.** A; DOK Level: 2

Unit 1 Review

MATH CONTENT TOPICS: Q.1, Q.1.a, Q.1.b, Q.1.d, Q.2.a, Q.2.d, Q.2.e, Q.3.a, Q.3.c, Q.3.d, Q.4.a, Q.6.c
MATH PRACTICES: MP.1.a, MP.1.b, MP.1.c, MP.1.d, MP.1.e, MP.2.c, MP.3.a, MP.4.a, MP.5.c

You may choose to use the Unit 1 Review on Student Book pp. 16–23 as a practice test. If you wish to time the test, ask learners to complete all the items in 140 minutes.

Unit 1 Review Answers

1. D; **2.** C; **3.** A; **4.** C; **5.** C; **6.** B; **7.** C; **8.** C; **9.** D; **10.** D; **11.** B; **12.** A; **13.** C; **14.** A; **15.** C; **16.** B; **17.** D; **18.** 67; **19.** $180; **20.** 7; **21.** −20; **22.** 7; **23.** 5; **24.** $28; **25.** 6; **26.** B; **27.** B; **28.** C; **29.** D; **30.** B; **31.** C; **32.** A; **33.** D; **34.** A; **35.** D; **36.** B; **37.** C; **38.** A; **39.** B; **40.** D; **41.** C; **42.** A; **43.** C; **44.** B; **45.** D; **46.** A; **47.** A; **48.** C; **49.** B; **50.** C; **51.** D; **52.** A; **53.** D; **54.** A; **55.** B; **56.** C; **57.** D; **58.** A; **59.** D; **60.** B; **61.** C; **62.** D; **63.** C; **64.** 13°F; **65.** −6°F; **66.** Any choice in top box, 3 in bottom; **67.** Number 1 in the numerator, 5 in the denominator; **68.** $\frac{2}{5}, \frac{7}{10}$, and $\frac{5}{4}$; **69.** $\frac{11}{20}$; **70.** $\frac{93}{100} \cdot \frac{\text{\#circuits}}{4,000} = 3,720$

Unit 1 Review Item Analysis

SKILL	DOK LEVEL 1	DOK LEVEL 2	DOK LEVEL 3
Whole Numbers	6, 29	12, 13, 47, 48, 51	49
Operations	59, 60	19, 20, 30, 35, 46, 50, 55	5, 7, 25
Integers	62	21, 52, 53, 54, 57, 58, 63, 64, 65	
Fractions	1	4, 8, 9, 11, 15, 16, 24, 32, 44, 67, 68, 69	66
Ratios and Proportions	18, 23	22, 31, 38, 39, 70	
Decimals	3	2, 14, 26, 27, 28, 36, 43, 45	56
Percent		10, 17, 33, 34, 37, 40, 41, 42, 61	

Unit 1 Review

Use workbook lessons, as identified in the following table, to assist learners who require additional remediation with certain skills or items having certain DOK levels.

Unit 1 Workbook Item Analysis

SKILL	DOK LEVEL 1	DOK LEVEL 2	DOK LEVEL 3
Whole Numbers	1, 2, 3, 6, 8, 9, 10, 12, 13, 18, 19	4, 5, 7, 11, 14, 15, 16, 22, 23, 24, 25	17, 20, 21
Operations	1, 2, 3, 4, 5, 6, 8, 9, 10, 13, 14, 15, 20, 21, 25, 26, 29, 30	11, 12, 16, 17, 18, 19, 23, 24, 27, 28	7, 22, 31, 32
Integers	1, 2, 3, 18, 19, 20, 23, 28	4, 5, 6, 7, 8, 9, 10, 11, 12, 13, 14, 15, 21, 22, 24, 25, 26, 27, 29	16, 17
Fractions	1, 2, 3, 4, 5, 8, 9, 11, 12, 13, 14, 16, 19	6, 7, 15	10, 17, 18
Ratios and Proportions	5, 7, 16	1, 2, 3, 4, 6, 8, 9, 10, 11, 12, 13, 14, 15, 17, 18, 19, 20, 21, 22, 23, 24, 25, 26, 27, 28	
Decimals		1, 2, 3, 4, 5, 7, 8, 9, 10, 11, 12, 13, 14, 15, 16, 17, 18, 19, 20, 21, 22, 23	6, 24, 25
Percent	1, 3, 5	2, 4, 6, 7, 8, 9, 11, 12, 13, 14, 15, 16, 17, 18, 19, 20, 21, 22, 23, 24, 25	10

Unit 2

Data Measurement/Analysis

As with Unit 1, the material in Unit 2 requires learners to use the four basic operations, albeit in a different—and deeper—way. Inform learners that they use rulers, tape measures, scales, and other instruments to measure materials in everyday life. In Unit 2, however, explain that they will study and learn different means and methods of measurement. Some of them, such as length, area, and volume and probability involve higher-order thinking skills that will require students to grasp concepts beyond what they can observe (such as the amount of water necessary to fill a fish tank or the surface of a wall to paint).

Solving problems in this unit may require learners to use multiple steps. In such cases, learners first must interpret and even decode visuals such as two- and three-dimensional figures, tables, line, bar, and circle graphs, and dot plots, histograms, and box plots. Next, learners may need to first successfully solve a smaller problem in order to find the necessary figures to complete a second, or even a third, part of a larger equation. The key to students' success will involve their ability to learn—and apply—the correct order with which to solve a given problem.

Table of Contents

LESSON	PAGE
1: Measurement and Units of Measure	MA 14
2: Length, Area, and Volume	MA 15
3: Mean, Median, and Mode	MA 16
4: Probability	MA 17
5: Bar and Line Graphs	MA 18
6: Circle Graphs	MA 19
7: Dot Plots, Histograms, and Box Plots	MA 20
Unit 2 Review	**MA 21–MA 22**

MATHEMATICS

Measurement and Units of Measure

MATH CONTENT TOPICS: Q.1.a, Q.1.b, Q.2.a, Q.2.d, Q.2.e, Q.3.a, Q.3.b Q.3.c, Q.6.c
MATH PRACTICES: MP.1.a, MP.1.b, MP.1.d, MP.1.e, MP.2.c, MP.3.a, MP.4.a

MATHEMATICS

STUDENT BOOK pp. 26–27

➤ Preview the Skill

Ask learners to think about the last time they cooked or baked something. Discuss units of measure that they used in the recipe. Explain that these are examples of units of capacity in the customary system of measurement. Ask learners to name other units of capacity with which they are familiar (*liters, milliliters*). Explain that these are units in the metric system of measurement.

❶ Learn the Skill

Give Examples Explain that certain units measure length, others measure weight or mass, and still others measure capacity. Draw a table on the board, showing items that could use each unit of measurement. Have learners provide additional examples to it.

Measurement	U.S. Units	Metric units
Length	Inches—Width of a book	Meters—Length of a run
Capacity	Gallons—Milk	Liters—Beverage, such as water
Weight/mass	Pounds—Weight of a bag of apples	Grams—Weight of a baby

❷ Practice the Skill

Skim and Scan Explain that when adding measurements, the units must be the same. When units are different, some renaming must occur before they can be combined or subtracted. Have learners skim question 1 for the units mentioned. They should convert 30 milliliters to centiliters before adding.

❸ Apply the Skill

Spotlighted Item: Fill-in-the-Blank Have each learner complete items individually and compare answers with a partner. Explain that, if partners compute different answers for an item, they should collaborate to discover possible errors.

Answers
1. A; DOK Level: 2; **2.** 30 feet; DOK Level: 2; **3.** 640 g; DOK Level: 2; **4.** 5,500 m; DOK Level: 3; **5.** .0966 s; DOK Level: 2; **6.** D; DOK Level: 2; **7.** C; DOK Level: 2; **8.** A; DOK Level: 2; **9.** D; DOK Level: 2

WORKBOOK pp. 30–33

❶ Review the Skill

Review units of measure in each system of measurement. Discuss U.S. customary and metric units of length, capacity, time, and mass or weight. Have students work in small groups to order each set of units from smallest to largest. Discuss results and clarify any issues that students might have about the relative sizes of units.

❷ Refine the Skill

Decoding Explain to learners that the conversion chart on p. 30 shows whether to multiply or divide to convert to a certain unit, along with the power of ten to use. The chart shows that to convert from kilometers to meters, for example, the number of kilometers should be multiplied by 1,000. However, to answer question 1, the number of milligrams should be divided by 10×100, or 1,000. This means that, since there are 3 zeros in 1,000, the decimal should move 3 places to the left.

❸ Master the Skill

Decoding Students should look for key words or phrases to help them determine how to approach word problems. For example, in question 5, the phrase "combined mass" indicates the need to add masses together and "how much greater" indicates the need to subtract.

➤ Optional Activity

Language Analysis To reinforce relationships among units in the metric system, have students brainstorm words they know that use the same prefixes, such as *centi*, *kilo*, and *milli*. For example, *century* means 100 years, a *kilobyte* is 1,000 bytes of data, and a *millipede* has 1,000 legs.

Answers
1. C; DOK Level: 2; **2.** C; DOK Level: 2; **3.** D; DOK Level: 2; **4.** D; DOK Level: 2; **5.** B; DOK Level: 2; **6.** D; DOK Level: 2; **7.** B; DOK Level: 2; **8.** B; DOK Level: 3; **9.** D; DOK Level: 2; **10.** B; DOK Level: 2; **11.** A; DOK Level: 2; **12.** C; DOK Level: 2; **13.** A; DOK Level: 2; **14.** C; DOK Level: 2; **15.** B; DOK Level: 3; **16.** C; DOK Level: 2; **17.** C; DOK Level: 2; **18.** C; DOK Level: 2; **19.** A; DOK Level: 2; **20.** A; DOK Level: 2; **21.** C; DOK Level: 2; **22.** B; DOK Level: 2; **23.** D; DOK Level: 3; **24.** D; DOK Level: 2

Length, Area, and Volume

MATH CONTENT TOPICS: Q.2.a, Q.2.e, Q.3.b, Q.4.a, Q.4.c, Q.4.d, Q.5.a, Q.5.c, Q.5.f
MATH PRACTICES: MP.1.a, MP.1.b, MP.1.c, MP.1.d, MP.1.e, MP.2.c, MP.3.a, MP.4.a

STUDENT BOOK pp. 29–30

➤ Preview the Skill

Ask learners if they have worked on a project such as installing a fence or flooring. Discuss how they determine the length of fencing or the amount of flooring. (*The length of fencing is the distance around the area to be enclosed; the amount of flooring is the amount of surface that needs to be covered.*) Inform students that the length of the fence is equal to the perimeter of the enclosure, and that the amount of flooring is equal to the area of the floor.

1 Learn the Skill

Give Examples Draw a rectangle, and then draw a grid within the rectangle that divides it into squares with side lengths of 1 unit. Demonstrate perimeter by counting the number of units along each side. Then, find the perimeter by adding the side lengths. Show that the result is the same. Next, demonstrate the area by counting the number of unit squares within the rectangle. Then, find the area by multiplying the length and width. Show that the result is the same. Repeat with other rectangles as needed.

2 Practice the Skill

Decoding Explain that learners should read word problems carefully, and that it sometimes can be helpful to diagram the information. Demonstrate by sketching a rectangular prism with length 5 cm, width 2 cm, and height 4 cm. Explain that 1 cm represents 3 feet. Finally, re-label the diagram with length 15 feet, width 6 feet, and height 12 feet.

3 Apply the Skill

Decoding A figure may have missing side lengths. If a side length lacks a label, it may be inferred from the information presented in the figure or the problem. In a rectangle, opposite (parallel) sides have the same length, and only one side length may be labeled. Encourage students to provide missing side lengths before attempting the problem.

Answers
1. C; DOK Level: 2; **2.** D; DOK Level: 2; **3.** D; DOK Level: 2;
4. B; DOK Level: 2; **5.** A; DOK Level: 3; **6.** D; DOK Level: 2;
7. B; DOK Level: 2; **8.** D; DOK Level: 2; **9.** C; DOK Level: 2;
10. B; DOK Level: 2

WORKBOOK pp. 34–37

1 Review the Skill

Review the meanings of *perimeter*, *area*, *volume*, and *surface area*. Next, ask a volunteer to measure the dimensions of a rectangle or a rectangular prism in the classroom (for example, a tissue box) and have learners use those dimensions to calculate its surface area and volume. Remind learners that they will have access to various formulas—including surface area—on the GED® Mathematical Reasoning Test.

2 Refine the Skill

SuperSkill Review Using the diagram on p. 34, have students practice the skill of calculating area by finding the area of the house (40 yd × 40 yd = 1,600 square yd) the plot of land (80 yd × 120 yd = 9,600 square yd), and the field (9,600 square yd − 1,600 square yd = 8,000 square yd).

3 Master the Skill

Spotlighted Item: Drop-Down Build learners' comfort level with the drop-down item type by explaining that drop-down answer options are like multiple-choice answer options. Since answer choices will not be visible until learners enable them, encourage students to formulate their own responses before reading the choices.

➤ Optional Activity

Language Analysis Discuss words or phrases in word problems on pp. 35–37 that students may have difficulty interpreting, such as cost-effective (item 12) and "combined volume" (item 21).

Answers
1. D; DOK Level: 2; **2.** D; DOK Level: 2; **3.** A; DOK Level: 2;
4. C; DOK Level: 1; **5.** D; DOK Level: 1; **6.** A; DOK Level: 2;
7. C; DOK Level: 3; **8.** A; DOK Level: 1; **9.** B; DOK Level: 1;
10. D; DOK Level: 2; **11.** C; DOK Level: 2; **12.** D; DOK Level: 3; **13.** B; DOK Level: 3; **14.** C; DOK Level: 2; **15.** D; DOK Level: 2; **16.** B; DOK Level: 2; **17.** C; DOK Level: 2; **18.** B; DOK Level: 3; **19.** D; DOK Level: 2; **20.** B; DOK Level: 2; **21.** C; DOK Level: 2; **22.** A; DOK Level: 2

MATH CONTENT TOPICS: Q.1.a, Q.2.a, Q.2.e, Q.6.c, Q.7.a
MATH PRACTICES: MP.1.a, MP.1.b, MP.1.d, MP.1.e, MP.2.c, MP.3.a, MP.4.a

MATHEMATICS

STUDENT BOOK pp. 30–31

▶ Preview the Skill

Ask learners to think about sports that they follow. With learners, list sports terms that include the word "average," such as *earned run average* (ERA) in baseball, *goals against average* in hockey, *average points per game* in basketball, and *rushing average* in football. Ask learners to explain the meaning of the measures they name. Explain that an average is a value that represents a set of numbers, such as the number of yards rushed in each game or the number of points scored in each game. Tell learners that an average is also known as a mean, and, along with median and mode, it helps describe data in data sets.

❶ Learn the Skill

Give Examples Reinforce the instruction by providing additional data sets and having learners find the mean, median and mode. For example, the data set 2, 4, 5, 5, 8 has a mean of 4.8, a median of 5, and a mode of 5. To challenge learners, list data values out of sequence so that they first must perform the additional step of ordering data values from least to greatest before finding the median.

❷ Practice the Skill

Link to Past Skills Remind learners that they studied decimals in Unit 1, Lesson 6, and explain that when dividing an even number by 2, they will get a whole-number quotient. However, when dividing an odd number by 2, the quotient will be a decimal that ends in .5 (e.g., $5 \div 2 = 2.5$; $13 \div 2 = 6.5$). Therefore, the median of a data set must be either a whole number or a decimal ending in .5.

❸ Apply the Skill

Skim and Scan As learners attempt to answer questions relating to mean, median, mode, and range, explain that these values will not exceed the highest value in a data set or be less than the lowest value in a data set.

Answers
1. C; DOK Level: 2; **2.** B; DOK Level: 2; **3.** C; DOK Level: 2; **4.** B; DOK Level: 2; **5.** A; DOK Level: 2; **6.** C; DOK Level: 2; **7.** B; DOK Level: 2; **8.** A; DOK Level: 2

WORKBOOK pp. 38–41

❶ Review the Skill

Give Examples Relate the concepts of mean, median, mode, and range to learners' everyday lives by asking them to provide data, such as the number of hours they sleep per day. Write data on the board, and have learners determine the mean, median, mode, and range of the data set. Learners can discuss the results and determine whether the mean or median best describes the data. If the range is large, the median might better describe the data. If the range is small, the mean might provide the best description of the data.

❷ Refine the Skill

SuperSkill Review Ask learners to find the median of the data set shown in the table on p. 38. First, learners should order the numbers from least to greatest, taking care to include each value. To help learners find the middle number, encourage them to cross out numbers at each end, pair-by-pair, until only one or two numbers remain in the middle. If only one value remains, that number is the median. If two values remain, learners should circle those numbers and then determine their mean. This is the median.

❸ Master the Skill

Spotlighted Item: Fill-in-the-Blank Have learners work in pairs to discuss and decide on an appropriate answer for each fill-in-the-blank item. Explain that, if partners suggest different answers for an item, they should share their computations and attempt to identify any errors or misconceptions. Guide learners to understand that they will need to determine the answer to item 20 in order to determine the range of the data set for item 21.

Answers
1. D; DOK Level: 2; **2.** C; DOK Level: 2; **3.** A; DOK Level: 2; **4.** C; DOK Level: 2; **5.** C; DOK Level: 2; **6.** A; DOK Level: 2; **7.** A; DOK Level: 2; **8.** C; DOK Level: 2; **9.** D; DOK Level: 2; **10.** B; DOK Level: 2; **11.** D; DOK Level: 2; **12.** C; DOK Level: 2; **13.** B; DOK Level: 2; **14.** D; DOK Level: 2; **15.** C; DOK Level: 2; **16.** C; DOK Level: 2; **17.** B; DOK Level: 2; **18.** D; DOK Level: 2; **19.** C; DOK Level: 2; **20.** $150; DOK Level: 2; **21.** $150; DOK Level: 2; **22.** B; DOK Level: 2; **23.** C; DOK Level: 2; **24.** A; DOK Level: 3; **25.** A; DOK Level: 2; **26.** D; DOK Level: 2

Probability

MATH CONTENT TOPICS: Q.1.b, Q.2.a, Q.2.e, Q.3.c, Q.3.d, Q.6.c, Q.8.a, Q.8.b
MATH PRACTICES: MP.1.a, MP.1.b, MP.1.d, MP.1.e, MP.2.c, MP.3.a, MP.3.b, MP.3.c, MP.4.a, MP.5.a, MP.5.b, MP.5.c

STUDENT BOOK *pp. 32–33*

▶ Preview the Skill

Discuss the weather with learners. Ask learners if they have checked the weather forecast for today or for the upcoming week. Discuss whether there is a chance of precipitation in the forecast. Elicit from learners or explain that the chance of precipitation, usually expressed as a percent, is the likelihood or probability of precipitation, based on weather conditions.

❶ Learn the Skill

Link to Past Skills Have learners review the skill *Ratios and Proportions* from Unit 1, Lesson 5. Explain that, in any probability ratio, the first number in the ratio is the number of favored, or desired outcomes, and the second number in the ratio is the total number of outcomes.

❷ Practice the Skill

Use Graphic Organizers Tables are an effective way to organize information about probability events. Draw a table with rows labeled *Black Marbles* and *Striped Marbles*. Label the columns: *Start* | *1ˢᵗ Event* | *2ⁿᵈ* Event | *3ʳᵈ* Event | *4ᵗʰ* Event | *5ᵗʰ* Event. Work with learners to complete the table and show the number of black marbles and striped marbles left in the bag after each draw. Guide students to read the last column of the table to determine the number of black marbles (*2*) and the total number of marbles (*2 + 4 = 6*) left in the bag for the fifth event.

❸ Apply the Skill

Draw learners' attention to item 8 on p. 33. Have learners find the probability that a call concerns the electronics department (*6:15 = 0.4*). Next, have learners find the probability that a call concerns one of the other departments (*4 + 2 + 3 = 9; 9:15 = 0.6*). Guide learners to understand that the two probabilities have a sum of 1, so the probability of "not electronics" is equal to 1 − (probability of "electronics").

Answers
1. B; DOK Level: 2; **2.** A; DOK Level: 1; **3.** C; DOK Level: 2;
4. A; DOK Level: 1; **5.** B; DOK Level: 3; **6.** A; DOK Level: 2;
7. D; DOK Level: 2; **8.** C; DOK Level: 2; **9.** C; DOK Level: 1

WORKBOOK *pp. 42–45*

❶ Review the Skill

Give Examples Organize learners in small groups. Have each group flip a coin 20 times, recording the number of heads and tails. Have each group find the experimental probability of flipping heads. Discuss the results from each group and compare to the theoretical probability (1:2) of flipping heads. Discuss whether the outcome of each coin flip is a dependent event or an independent event (*independent*).

❷ Refine the Skill

Explain that learners may express probability as a fraction, decimal, ratio, or percent. In addition to the correct answer of C for item 2, they could respond by noting the probability as 1/5, .2, or 20%.

❸ Master the Skill

Link to Past Skills Have learners review the skill *Fractions* from Unit 1, Lesson 4, to refresh their understanding of fraction operations. Explain that, to find the probability of two consecutive events, as in item 6 on p. 43, learners must multiply the probability of the first event by the probability of the second event.

▶ Enrich and Extend

Inform learners that the probability of randomly selecting a red marble from a certain bag of red and black marbles is 2 out of 5. However, explain that there are more than 5 marbles in the bag. Ask learners to draw or describe the probable marble contents of the bag.

Answers
1. C; DOK Level: 2; **2.** C; DOK Level: 1; **3.** B; DOK Level: 2;
4. D; DOK Level: 2; **5.** C; DOK Level: 2; **6.** A; DOK Level: 3;
7. B; DOK Level: 2; **8.** D; DOK Level: 2; **9.** B; DOK Level: 2;
10. D; DOK Level: 2; **11.** C; DOK Level: 2; **12.** C; DOK
Level: 2; **13.** A; DOK Level: 1; **14.** A; DOK Level: 2; **15.** B;
DOK Level: 2; **16.** B; DOK Level: 2; **17.** A; DOK Level: 2;
18. B; DOK Level: 2; **19.** C; DOK Level: 2; **20.** C; DOK
Level: 2; **21.** D; DOK Level: 2; **22.** B; DOK Level: 2; **23.** C;
DOK Level: 3

MATHEMATICS

Bar and Line Graphs

MATH CONTENT TOPICS: Q.2.a, Q.2.e, Q.6.a, Q.6.c
MATH PRACTICES: MP.1.a, MP.1.b, MP.1.e, MP.2.c, MP.3.a, MP.4.a, MP.4.c, MP.5.a

MATHEMATICS

STUDENT BOOK pp. 34–35

➤ Preview the Skill

Take a brief survey of learners. For example, ask for each learner's favorite color and record it in a table. Sketch a bar graph that illustrates the data and tell learners that a bar graph is one way by which to display data in categories. Discuss other examples of bar graphs that learners have seen.

① Learn the Skill

Give Examples As learners study the types of data displays, sketch examples or draw their attention to examples of each type of data display on pp. 34 (line graph) and 35 (bar graph and scatter plot). How are they similar? How are they different? Explain that each graph has at least one numerical scale that increases in equal intervals.

② Practice the Skill

Skim and Scan Have learners read the answer choices and quickly examine the line graph for question 1. Elicit from learners that choice C, June, can be eliminated by visual inspection because the gap between the two data points is clearly smaller than the gaps between the other pairs of data points. Discuss whether any other answer choices may be reasonably eliminated by visual inspection.

③ Apply the Skill

Spotlighted Item: Hot-Spot The hot-spot item type may be least familiar to learners. Explain that a hot-spot item tests both a learner's mousing and mathematical skills. On the GED® Mathematical Reasoning Test, learners may need to drag a star or a circle, click a point on a grid, or manipulate a graph to show data. As learners attempt items on p. 35, ensure that they understand what to do and how to proceed.

Answers

1. B; DOK Level: 2; **2.** The bar for Contestant B should be circled; DOK Level: 2; **3.** The distance of 15 feet should be circled; DOK Level: 2; **4.** An X should be placed in the bar for Contestant D; DOK Level: 2; **5.** The bar for Contestant C should be extended to a distance of 15 feet on the graph; DOK Level: 2; **6.** 17; DOK Level: 1; **7.** Either 8 or 10 hours should be circled; DOK Level: 2; **8.** Students should circle 5 levels: associate's degree, bachelor's degree, master's degree, professional degree, and doctoral degree; DOK Level: 2

WORKBOOK pp. 46–49

① Review the Skill

Skim and Scan Preview with learners the various types of graphs that appear on pp. 46–49. Ask volunteers for examples of data they might present in each type of graph.

② Refine the Skill

Decoding Guide learners to understand that the key on the bar graph on p. 46 describes the information in the data set. Draw learners' attention to the vertical scale of the graph. Elicit from learners that the grid lines are in increments of $100. Guide learners to estimate the heights and values of bar that fall between grid lines.

③ Master the Skill

Spotlighted Item: Hot-Spot Draw students' attention to p. 48. Explain that there are two components to a hot-spot answer: the answer itself, and the manner in which the answer should be indicated. Point out that there are two different types of directions in the six items on this page: circling an answer and placing a star next to an answer. Discuss other ways in which learners must indicate answers on pp. 46–49 (*placing a dot; placing an X; drawing a bar on graph*).

Answers

1. B; DOK Level 2; **2.** C; DOK Level: 2; **3.** 1960 and 2000; DOK Level: 2; **4.** Bar showing a 2010 population of 3,500; DOK Level: 3; **5.** 55; DOK Level: 2; **6.** $60,000; DOK Level: 2; **7.** Dot placed directly above age 30 and directly on the line for $80,000; DOK Level: 3; **8.** Raleigh, N.C.; Dallas, Texas; Boston, Mass.; Houston, Texas; San Francisco, Calif.; Seattle, Wash.; San Jose, Calif.; Denver, Colo.; and Salt Lake City, Utah; DOK Level: 3; **9.** (25, 50); DOK Level: 1; **10.** Don Meredith; DOK Level: 3; **11.** Circles around the names Mike Tirico, Jon Gruden, and Lisa Salters; DOK Level: 2; **12.** Students should place stars next to the names of Keith Jackson, Fred Williamson, Joe Namath, Lisa Guerrero, Sam Ryan, and Joe Theismann; DOK Level: 2; **13.** Circle around the name Frank Gifford; DOK Level: 2; **14.** Star next to the name of Lynn Swann; DOK Level: 2; **15.** Circle around the name of Al Michaels; DOK Level: 2; **16.** Gray Squirrels; DOK Level: 2; **17.** The opossum; DOK Level: 1; **18.** Computer Specialist; DOK Level: 2; **19.** September; DOK Level: 1; **20.** May; DOK Level: 2; **21.** June, July, August; DOK Level: 2

Circle Graphs

MATH CONTENT TOPICS: Q.2.a, Q.2.e, Q.6.a
MATH PRACTICES: MP.1.a, MP.1.b, MP.1.d, MP.1.e, MP.2.c, MP.3.a, MP.4.a, MP.4.c

➤ Preview the Skill

Sketch a bar graph to show a simple data set, such as the number of male and female learners in class. Elicit conclusions about the data set; for example, a comparison of the number of males and females. Then sketch a circle graph to show the same data. Explain that both circle and bar graphs can compare categories, but that circle graphs also show how the categories make up the whole.

❶ Learn the Skill

Give Examples Some learners may have difficulty understanding the abstract concepts of "whole" and "part" in a circle graph. Support learners by providing concrete numbers for each category and explaining how they relate to the whole budget. For example, if Jerry's monthly budget is $2,000, *car maintenance* and *gasoline* each would account for $500, *food* for about $600, *clothing* for about $225, *school supplies* for about $125, and *other* for about $50.

❷ Practice the Skill

Skim and Scan Tell learners that they can use visual inspection to eliminate unreasonable answer choices. In question 1 on p. 36, choice D is unreasonable because 45% is about half of the circle. Discuss whether other answer choices can be eliminated.

❸ Apply the Skill

Spotlighted Item: Drag-and-Drop In question 2 on p. 37, learners must drag percent labels to each category on the circle graph. Have learners solve the problem in pairs or small groups, and then ask each group to share its solution strategies. Try to elicit more than one strategy. For example, learners might estimate the percent shown by each sector in the graph and then match that percent to the key, or learners might list categories in the key from least to greatest percent and then match the greatest percent to the largest sector, the least percent to the smallest sector, and so on.

Answers
1. C; DOK Level: 2; **2.** Clockwise from top right: *Parents* (gray section); *Financial Aid* (blue section); *Salary* (green section); *Scholarships* (yellow section); DOK Level: 2; **3.** D; DOK Level: 2; **4.** A; DOK Level: 2

❶ Review the Skill

Give Examples Review with learners the definition of a circle graph and how circle graphs represent data. Next, ask learners to describe examples in their daily lives in which circle graphs are used and explain why a circle graph is an effective display of data. For example, a circle graph of a household budget shows what part of the total budget is used for each category.

❷ Refine the Skill

Link to Past Skills Guide learners to review the skill *Percent* from Unit 1, Lesson 7, for help in converting among fractions, decimals, and percent with circle graphs. To answer question 1 on p. 50, some students may find it helpful to estimate the fraction of the circle that represents "ice cream," and then convert that fraction to a percent.

❸ Master the Skill

SuperSkill Review Learners can check their logic or determine how to approach a question about circle graphs by remembering that a circle represents a whole. For example, on question 5 (p. 51), the part of the whole that uses a source other than gas is equal to the whole minus the part of the whole that does use gas. For question 10 (also p. 51), the whole is 200 people, so the number of people who voted Independent is the percent shown in the graph multiplied by 200.

➤ Optional Activity

Enrich and Extend Challenge learners to use data in one of the circle graphs on pp. 50–53 to create a bar graph showing the same information and data.

Answers
1. B; DOK Level: 2; **2.** B; DOK Level: 2; **3.** D; DOK Level: 2; **4.** D; DOK Level: 2; **5.** A; DOK Level: 2; **6.** C; DOK Level: 2; **7.** C; DOK Level: 1; **8.** C; DOK Level: 2; **9.** B; DOK Level: 2; **10.** B; DOK Level: 3; **11.** C; DOK Level: 2; **12.** C; DOK Level: 2; **13.** D; DOK Level: 2; **14.** B; DOK Level: 3; **15.** A; DOK Level: 2; **16.** C; DOK Level: 1; **17.** D; DOK Level: 2; **18.** C; DOK Level: 2; **19.** D; DOK Level: 2; **20.** A; DOK Level: 2; **21.** C; DOK Level: 2; **22.** C; DOK Level: 2; **23.** D; DOK Level: 2

Dot Plots, Histograms, and Box Plots

MATH CONTENT TOPICS: Q.1, Q.2.a, Q.2.e, Q.6.b, Q.7.a
MATH PRACTICES: MP.1.a, MP.1.b, MP.1.e, MP.2.c, MP.3.a, MP.4.a, MP.4.c

MATHEMATICS

STUDENT BOOK *pp. 38–39*

➤ Preview the Skill

Have learners think about a sporting event or concert they attended or watched on TV. Ask them to estimate the number of people who attended the event. Next, ask them to think about how they could use a data display to show the ages of the people who attended the event. Elicit from learners that it would be impractical to use one category for each age. Explain that histograms and box plots can represent data sets with a large quantity of values.

❶ Learn the Skill

Explain that, along with line graphs, bar graphs, and circle graphs, there are other types of graphs that represent data sets and values. Inform learners that dot plots tend to be used with smaller data sets, while there are no such limitations on the use of histograms. Box plots display data using five characteristics: the median, the lower (25%) and upper (75%) quartile values, and the maximum and minimum values.

❷ Practice the Skill

Compare and contrast the dot plot and the box plot on p. 38. Elicit from students that both plots show a least and greatest value; however, the dot plot clearly shows the mode, while the box plot clearly shows the first quartile, median, and third quartile values.

❸ Apply the Skill

Link to Past Skills Have learners review the skill *Mean, Median, and Mode* from Unit 2, Lesson 3. Prior to completing the items on p. 39, ask learners to explain the meaning of median, mode, and range. Discuss how these values are represented in a dot plot. (*The median is the dot that represents the middle value; the mode is the value with the most dots; the range is the difference between the values shown by the first dot and the last dot.*)

Answers
1. B; DOK Level: 3; **2.** C; DOK Level: 3; **3.** B; DOK Level: 1; **4.** D; DOK Level: 1; **5.** A; DOK Level: 1; **6.** C; DOK Level: 3; **7.** A; DOK Level: 1

WORKBOOK *pp. 54–57*

❶ Review the Skill

Ask a volunteer to name the type of data representation shown on p. 54 (*dot plot*). Discuss how the same set of data could be shown using a histogram (*combine data values into intervals and use bars to show the number of data points in each interval*) or a box plot (*use the data values shown in the dot plot to find the minimum, first quartile, median, third quartile, and maximum values*).

❷ Refine the Skill

After learners have completed items 1 and 2 on p. 54, organize them into three small groups. Have each group find the minimum and maximum, the median, and the quartiles for a value of 4, 5, or 6 for the circled student. Discuss their findings.

❸ Master the Skill

Explain that box plots can compare data sets by placing the box plots along the same number line. The box plots may be oriented horizontally, with single box plots, or vertically, as shown on pp. 55–57.

➤ Optional Activity

Spotlighted Item: Hot-Spot Remind learners that hot-spot items require them to interact with grids or graphs. To complete the hot-spot items on p. 56, learners must place dots on open circles. Encourage learners to build dot plots by starting at the bottom circle in each column.

Answers
1. B; DOK Level: 1; **2.** A; DOK Level: 2; **3.** D; DOK Level: 2; **4.** B; DOK Level: 2; **5.** D; DOK Level: 2; **6.** B; DOK Level: 2; **7.** A; DOK Level: 2; **8.** A; DOK Level: 2; **9.** C; DOK Level: 3; **10.** Dot plot with 2 dots placed above 6, 2 dots placed above 7, 2 dots placed above 8, 1 dot placed above 9, and 1 dot placed above 10; DOK Level: 2; **11.** Dot plot with 2 dots placed above each of 6, 7, 8, 9, and 10; DOK Level: 3; **12.** C; DOK Level: 3; **13.** A; DOK Level: 1; **14.** C; DOK Level: 2; **15.** D; DOK Level: 2; **16.** C; DOK Level: 2; **17.** A; DOK Level: 2; **18.** C; DOK Level: 2; **19.** D; DOK Level: 2; **20.** A; DOK Level: 2

Unit 2 Review

MATH CONTENT TOPICS: Q.1.a, Q.2.a, A.2.e, Q.3.a, Q.3.b, Q.3.c, Q.5.a, Q.6.a, Q.6.c
Q.7.a Q.8.a, Q.8.b
MATH PRACTICES: MP.1.a, MP.1.b, MP.1.c, MP.1.d, MP.1.e, MP.1.c, MP.3.a, MP.4.a, MP.5.c

You may choose to use the Unit 2 Review on Student Book pp. 40–47 as a practice test. If you wish to time the test, ask learners to complete all the items in 100 minutes.

Unit 2 Review Answers

1. B; **2.** D; **3.** D; **4.** C; **5.** A; **6.** A; **7.** D; **8.** C; **9.** A; **10.** B; **11.** A; **12.** C; **13.** C; **14.** B; **15.** B; **16.** D; **17.** C; **18.** A; **19.** B; **20.** D; **21.** Negative; **22.** 20; **23.** A; **24.** D; **25.** B; **26.** C; **27.** D; **28.** A; **29.** C; **30.** B; **31.** C; **32.** C; **33.** B; **34.** 0.4; **35.** 1; **36.** Dot plot in which there is 1 filled dot above −2, 6 filled dots above −1, 7 filled dots above 0, 8 filled dots above 1, 4 filled dots above 2, and 1 filled dot above 3; **37.** Box plot in which the minimum value is −2, the first quartile value is −1, the third quartile value is 1, and the maximum value is 3; **38.** 17.6; **39.** 5.7; **40.** D; **41.** Bar graph with categories labeled (from left to right) Fish, Chicken, Steak, Pasta, Vegetarian; **42.** Circle graph with sectors labeled (clockwise from top right): Fish (25%), Chicken (18%), Steak (28%), Pasta (20%), Vegetarian (8%); **43.** Bar/Circle; **44.** C; **45.** B; **46.** B; **47.** A; **48.** Dot plot with 1 filled dot above 19, 23, 26, 27, 29, 30, and 35; 2 filled dots above 14, 16, 17, 20, 22, and 24; and 3 filled dots above 18 and 21; **49.** Histogram with 2 data points in the 12−16 range, 8 data points in the 16−20 range, 8 data points in the 20−24 range, 4 data points in the 24−28 range, 2 data points in the 28−32 range, and 1 data point in the 32−36 range; **50.** C; **51.** A

Unit 2 Review Item Analysis

SKILL	DOK LEVEL 1	DOK LEVEL 2	DOK LEVEL 3
Measurement and Units of Measure	1	2, 5, 6, 16, 17, 18, 38, 39	
Length, Area, and Volume		3, 4, 7, 8, 9, 23	
Mean, Median, and Mode	31, 32	10, 11, 12, 33, 34, 35	30
Probability		13, 14, 28	15, 24, 25, 26, 27, 29, 40
Bar and Line Graphs		19, 20, 21, 22, 41, 43, 44, 45	
Circle Graphs		42, 43, 46, 47	
Dot Plots, Histograms, and Box Plots		36, 37, 48, 49, 50	51

MATHEMATICS

Unit 2 Review

Use workbook lessons, as identified in the following table, to assist learners who require additional remediation with certain skills or items having certain DOK levels.

Unit 2 Workbook Item Analysis

SKILL	DOK LEVEL 1	DOK LEVEL 2	DOK LEVEL 3
Measurement and Units of Measure		1, 2, 3, 4, 5, 6, 7, 9, 10, 11, 12, 13, 14, 15, 16, 17, 18, 19, 20, 21, 22, 24	8, 15, 23
Length, Area, and Volume	4, 5, 8, 9	1, 2, 3, 6, 10, 11, 14, 15, 16, 17, 19, 20, 21, 22	7, 12, 13, 18
Mean, Median, and Mode		1, 2, 3, 4, 5, 6, 7, 8, 9, 10, 11, 12, 13, 14, 15, 16, 17, 18, 19, 20, 21, 22, 23, 25, 26	24
Probability	2, 11, 13	1, 3, 4, 5, 7, 8, 9, 10, 12, 14, 15, 16, 17, 18, 19, 20, 21, 22	6, 23
Bar and Line Graphs	9, 17, 19	1, 2, 3, 5, 6, 11, 12, 13, 14, 15, 16, 18, 20, 21	4, 7, 8, 10
Circle Graphs	7, 16	1, 2, 3, 4, 5, 6, 8, 9, 11, 12, 13, 15, 17, 18, 19, 20, 21, 22, 23	10, 14
Dot Plots, Histograms, and Box Plots	1, 13	2, 3, 4, 5, 6, 7, 8, 10, 14, 15, 16, 17, 18, 19, 20	9, 11, 12

Unit 3

Algebra, Functions, and Patterns

With its numerous operations and variables, algebra at first may seem overwhelming to learners. Attempt to ease such sentiments by explaining that algebra shares certain characteristics with other areas of mathematics. Learners should attempt to solve algebraic equations as they do other complex mathematical items: by first determining the proper steps (order of operations) and then using basic operations (addition, subtraction, multiplication, and division) to do so.

Algebraic equations often involve conceptual information, such as negative numbers, variables, exponents, and changes to figures on a grid, which may require learners to use higher-order thinking skills to solve them. To foster understanding of these increasingly complex skills, you may wish to break down each formula in the Practice the Skill section. Then work through sample items and other examples with learners to ensure mastery of the proper steps to use in solving a particular equation, pattern, or grid problem. For example, you may wish to introduce variables through the equation $4x = 12$. Ask students which number, when multiplied by 4, equals 12. Most students will know that $3 \times 4 = 12$, so they will understand the relationship. By properly modeling the correct steps (first isolating the variable and then dividing 12 by 4), you will deconstruct for students the correct way in which to solve the problem.

Table of Contents

LESSON	PAGE
1: Algebraic Expressions and Variables	MA 24
2: Equations	MA 25
3: Squaring, Cubing, and Taking Roots	MA 26
4: Exponents and Scientific Notation	MA 27
5: Patterns and Functions	MA 28
6: One-Variable Linear Equations	MA 29
7: Two-Variable Linear Equations	MA 30
8: Factoring	MA 31
9: Rational Expressions and Equations	MA 32
10: Solving and Graphing Inequalities	MA 33
11: The Coordinate Grid	MA 34
12: Graphing Linear Equations	MA 35
13: Slope	MA 36
14: Using Slope to Solve Geometric Problems	MA 37
15: Graphing Quadratic Equations	MA 38
16: Evaluation of Functions	MA 39
17: Comparison of Functions	MA 40
Unit 3 Review	MA 41–MA 42

MATHEMATICS

Algebraic Expressions and Variables

MATH CONTENT TOPICS: Q.1.b, Q.2.a, Q.2.e, Q.4.a, A.1.a, A.1.c, A.1.d, A.1.e, A.1.g, A.1.i, A.1.j
MATH PRACTICES: MP.1.a, MP.1.b, MP.1.e, MP.2.a, MP.2.c, MP.3.a, MP.4.a, MP.4.b, MP.5.c

MATHEMATICS

STUDENT BOOK pp. 50–51

➤ Preview the Skill

Ask learners to describe a situation in which the cost of a product or a service depended on the number of units purchased. For example, the cost of deli meat includes the number of pounds multiplied by the price per pound. Likewise, the charge for a visit by a plumber might involve a service fee plus an hourly rate multiplied by the number of hours. Explain that these situations may be represented by an expression with a variable.

❶ Learn the Skill

Decoding Ask learners to list expressions they have heard that include the word "variable," or a related word such as *variable cloudiness*, *various*, or *variability*. Elicit from learners that the meanings of these words and phrases relate to the concept of change. Explain that, in math, a variable is a quantity whose value can change.

❷ Practice the Skill

Decoding Call learners' attention to the table of words and symbols on p. 50. Explain that math phrases that include *more than* or *less than* suggest the operations of addition and subtraction, respectively, while *product* means multiplication and *quotient* means division. Further explain that *3 times* means to multiply by 3, whereas *3 times itself* means to square the number 3.

❸ Apply the Skill

Spotlighted Item: Fill-in-the-Blank Inform learners that they may wish to write key words from questions 2 through 5 on a separate sheet of paper so that they understand what is being asked. From there, learners may construct and solve equations.

Answers

1. A; DOK Level: 1; **2.** The algebraic expression for the plumber's earnings for one day is $55x - 20$; DOK Level: 1; **3.** The algebraic expression for the width of the football field is $w + 30$; DOK Level: 1; **4.** In simplest terms, the algebraic expression is $15x2 - 30x$; DOK Level: 3; **5.** The algebraic expression is $6x2 - 30x$; DOK Level: 3; **6.** D; DOK Level: 2; **7.** B; DOK Level: 1; **8.** C; DOK Level: 1; **9.** A; DOK Level: 1

WORKBOOK pp. 58–61

❶ Review the Skill

Give Examples Review the order of operations by providing examples of expressions with more than one operation. Remind learners to begin with operations within parentheses, then perform multiplication and division from left to right, and finally, perform addition and subtraction from left to right. For example, to simplify $5(3 + 1) - 2$, begin with addition within the parentheses, then multiply by 5 and finally subtract 2 from the product: $5(4) - 2 = 20 - 2 = 18$.

❷ Refine the Skill

Ask learners to write an expression to represent the scenario ($3x$). Then, for question 1 on p. 58, have learners substitute the distance of 39 miles for the value of x ($3 \cdot 39 = 117$).

❸ Master the Skill

Link to Past Skills Items 7 and 13 on pp. 59–60 require learners to write expressions to represent the perimeter or area of a figure. Have learners review the skill *Length, Area, and Volume* from Unit 2, Lesson 2, to refresh their understanding of these concepts.

➤ Optional Activity

Language Analysis As learners seek to complete the items on Workbook pp. 59–61, guide them to circle or underline words or phrases that help indicate the operations they should use.

Answers

1. D; DOK Level: 1; **2.** B; DOK Level: 2; **3.** D; DOK Level: 2
4. B; DOK Level: 2; **5.** D; DOK Level: 2; **6.** C; DOK Level: 2;
7. C; DOK Level: 2; **8.** A; DOK Level: 2; **9.** B; DOK Level: 2;
10. B; DOK Level: 2; **11.** B; DOK Level: 1; **12.** C; DOK Level: 1;
13. C; DOK Level: 2; **14.** A; DOK Level: 3; **15.** C; DOK Level: 2;
16. D; DOK Level: 2; **17.** C; DOK Level: 2; **18.** B; DOK Level: 2;
19. B; DOK Level: 2; **20.** A; DOK Level: 2; **21.** B; DOK Level: 3;
22. A; DOK Level: 3; **23.** B; DOK Level: 2; **24.** A; DOK Level: 2;
25. D; DOK Level: 2; **26.** A; DOK Level: 3; **27.** C; DOK Level: 3;
28. B; DOK Level: 2

Equations

MATH CONTENT TOPICS: Q.2.a, Q.2.e, Q.3.a, A.1.a, A.1.b, A.1.c, A.1.j, A.2.a, A.2.c
MATH PRACTICES: MP.1.a, MP.1.b, MP.1.e, MP.2.a, MP.2.c, MP.3.a, MP.4.a, MP.4.b

STUDENT BOOK *pp. 52–53*

➤ Preview the Skill

Ask learners if they have seen a balance scale. Elicit from learners that the same weight must be added to or subtracted from both sides of the scale to keep it balanced. Explain to learners that an equation is like a balance scale: the same operations must be performed to both sides of the equation to keep it equal.

❶ Learn the Skill

Decoding Help learners connect algebraic equations with their understanding of arithmetic equations. Write on the board the equation $4 + 5 = 9$. Elicit from learners that the equals sign means both sides have the same value. Next, write the equation $4 + x = 9$. Discuss how the equation can be solved to find the value of x. Elicit that since $9 - 4 = 5$, $x = 5$. Explain that the value of x can be found by subtracting 4 from each side of the equation, because addition and subtraction are inverse operations.

❷ Practice the Skill

Give Examples Explain to learners that *like terms* have the same variable raised to the same power. Constants are also like terms. Provide examples of like terms (x and $2x$, 8 and 4, $-3y$ and $\frac{y}{2}$). To combine like terms on the same side of the equation, add the coefficients, which are the numbers that are multiplied by the variables. For example, $2x + 3x = (2 + 3)x = 5x$.

❸ Apply the Skill

Decoding When reading word problems, learners should seek to translate verbal descriptions into mathematical expressions and equations. Read item 2 on p. 53 with learners. Guide learners to understand that "consecutive integers" means that the second integer is one greater than the first integer, so the integers can be represented as x and $(x + 1)$.

Answers

1. D; DOK Level: 2; **2.** B; DOK Level: 2; **3.** C; DOK Level: 3;
4. B; DOK Level: 2; **5.** D; DOK Level: 2; **6.** A; DOK Level: 2;
7. A; DOK Level: 2; **8.** B; DOK Level: 2; **9.** B; DOK Level: 2;
10. B; DOK Level: 2

WORKBOOK *pp. 62–65*

❶ Review the Skill

SuperSkill Review Organize learners in small groups, and have each group write a word problem with an unknown quantity. Next, on a separate sheet of paper, groups should write a solution to the problem. Finally, have groups exchange word problems and write and solve an equation. Discuss the results.

❷ Refine the Skill

Link to Past Skills In order to successfully write and solve equations, learners must be comfortable with translating words into expressions. Have learners review the skill *Algebraic Expressions and Variables* from Unit 3, Lesson 2, for additional support. Then have learners examine item 2 on p. 62. Ask them to write an equation in which the variable is the cost of the three lobster tails $[2(8) + x = 70]$.

❸ Master the Skill

Spotlighted Item: Drop-Down Remind learners that, as with multiple-choice items, drop-down questions include one correct answer and a variety of distractor responses. Encourage learners to use strategies such as elimination to help them identify the correct answer.

Answers

1. B; DOK Level: 2; **2.** D; DOK Level: 2; **3.** D; DOK Level: 2;
4. B; DOK Level: 2; **5.** D; DOK Level: 2; **6.** B; DOK Level: 2;
7. A; DOK Level: 2; **8.** B; DOK Level: 2; **9.** C; DOK Level: 2;
10. C; DOK Level: 2; **11.** A; DOK Level: 2; **12.** D; DOK Level: 2;
13. B; DOK Level: 2; **14.** B; DOK Level: 2; **15.** C; DOK Level: 2;
16. D; DOK Level: 2; **17.** B; DOK Level: 2; **18.** B; DOK Level: 2;
19. C; DOK Level: 2; **20.** B; DOK Level: 3; **21.** A; DOK Level: 2;
22. B; DOK Level: 2; **23.** A; DOK Level: 2; **24.** D; DOK Level: 2;
25. B; DOK Level: 2; **26.** B; DOK Level: 2; **27.** B; DOK Level: 2;
28. A; DOK Level: 2; **29.** C; DOK Level: 2

Squaring, Cubing, and Taking Roots

MATH CONTENT TOPICS: Q.1.c, Q.2.a, Q.2.b, Q.2.c, Q.2.d, Q.2.e, Q.4.a, Q.4.c, A.1.E
MATH PRACTICES: MP.1.a, MP.1.b, MP.1.e, MP.2.c, MP.3.a, MP.4.a, MP.4.b, MP.5.a, MP.5.b, MP.5.c

MATHEMATICS

STUDENT BOOK pp. 54–55

▶ Preview the Skill

Review the properties of the geometric figures *square* and *cube*. Elicit from students that a square is a two-dimensional (plane) figure that has four equal side lengths, and that a cube is a three-dimensional (solid) figure with six congruent square faces.

❶ Learn the Skill

Give Examples Draw a square and a cube. Discuss how to find the area of the square (multiply side × side) and the volume of the cube (multiply edge × edge × edge). Help learners connect these formulas with the concepts of "square" (multiply a number by itself) and "cube" (multiply a number by itself an additional time).

❷ Practice the Skill

Link to Past Skills To successfully square, cube, or take the root of an integer, learners must be comfortable with multiplying and dividing integers. Have students review the skill *Integers* from Unit 1, Lesson 3, to refresh their understanding of how to determine the sign of the product or quotient of integers.

❸ Apply the Skill

Spotlighted Item: Drag-and-Drop Build learners' confidence with drag-and-drop items by explaining that they are similar to multiple-choice questions. Both item types, for example, include one correct response and various incorrect answer options. Explain that drag-and-drop items will require learners to click and drag the correct answer to the proper drop zone.

Answers
1. C; DOK Level: 1; **2.** [>0; <0; undefined; <0]; DOK Level: 1;
3. 8; DOK Level: 2; **4.** D; DOK Level: 1; **5.** A; DOK Level: 1;
6. A; DOK Level: 2; **7.** C; DOK Level: 2; **8.** B; DOK Level: 2;
9. C; DOK Level: 3; **10.** B; DOK Level: 2

WORKBOOK pp. 66–69

❶ Review the Skill

Give Examples Have learners find the square and square root of the following numbers: 4, 9, 16, 25. Have learners find the cube and cube root of the following numbers: −8, 27, 64. Discuss the results.

❷ Refine the Skill

For question 2, have learners find the solution both by multiplying the original area by 2^2 and by doubling each side length and finding the new area. Discuss the results. Write the equation $(2)(11) \times (2)(11) = (2)(2) \times (11)(11)$ and elicit from learners that multiplying each dimension by 2 is equivalent to multiplying the original area by 2^2.

❸ Master the Skill

Link to Past Skills Several items on pp. 66–69 involve the area or volume of a figure. Have students review the skill *Length, Area, and Volume* from Unit 2, Lesson 2, to refresh their understanding of these concepts.

▶ Optional Activity

Enrich and Extend Challenge learners to find the square and square root of a number between 0 and 1. Then, challenge learners to compare the square and the square root of the number itself and explain the results.

Answers
1. B; DOK Level: 1; **2.** C; DOK Level: 2; **3.** C; DOK Level: 1;
4. B; DOK Level: 2; **5.** C; DOK Level: 1; **6.** B; DOK Level: 1;
7. B; DOK Level: 2; **8.** C; DOK Level: 1; **9.** A; DOK Level: 3;
10. B; DOK Level: 2; **11.** C; DOK Level: 3; **12.** B; DOK Level: 3;
13. D; DOK Level: 3; **14.** A; DOK Level: 2; **15.** D; DOK Level: 2;
16. B; DOK Level: 2; **17.** C; DOK Level: 3; **18.** A; DOK Level: 2;
19. D; DOK Level: 3; **20.** D; DOK Level: 2; **21.** C; DOK Level: 3;
22. B; DOK Level: 3; **23.** C; DOK Level: 1; **24.** C; DOK Level: 2;
25. D; DOK Level: 2; **26.** A; DOK Level: 2; **27.** B; DOK Level: 2;
28. D; DOK Level: 1; **29.** B; DOK Level: 1; **30.** B; DOK Level: 3;
31. A; DOK Level: 3; **32.** B; DOK Level: 3; **33.** D; DOK Level: 3;
34. C; DOK Level: 3; **35.** C; DOK Level: 1

Exponents and Scientific Notation

MATH CONTENT TOPICS: Q.1.c, Q.2.a, Q.2.b, Q.2.c, Q.2.d, Q.2.e, Q.4.a, Q.6.c, A.1.a, A.1.d, A.1.e, A.1.f, A.1.i
MATH PRACTICES: MP.1.a, MP.1.b, MP.1.e, MP.2.c, MP.3.a, MP.3.c, MP.4.a, MP.4.b, MP.5.a, MP.5.c

MATHEMATICS

STUDENT BOOK *pp. 56–57*

▶ Preview the Skill

Give Examples Ask learners to identify items, quantities, or distances of extreme sizes or lengths (either very large or long or very small or short). Provide examples such as the world's population, the distance from Earth to a star or another planet, and the width of a hair, and ask learners how the use of exponents or scientific notation could help simplify and convey complex measurements.

❶ Learn the Skill

Link to Past Skills Refer learners to the Unit 3, Lesson 3, skill *Squaring, Cubing, and Taking Roots*. Then write 4^2 and 2^3 on the board and ask volunteers to evaluate the expressions (16; 8). Ensure that learners understand that the superscript numeral tells them how many times to multiply the factor by itself.

❷ Practice the Skill

Link to Past Skills Remind learners of the Unit 1, Lesson 6, skill *Decimals* in which they learned that multiplying or dividing a decimal by 10 is equivalent to moving the decimal point to the left or to the right, respectively. Explain that large numbers can be divided by a power of 10 and small numbers can be multiplied by a power of 10 to move the decimal point to the desired place. The number of times the decimal point is moved is recorded as a power of 10.

❸ Apply the Skill

Decoding Explain to learners that if they cannot remember the rules for multiplying and dividing exponents, they can expand the powers, perform the operation, and then simplify the power. For question 3, the product of $2^6 \times 2^5$ is equivalent to $(2 \times 2 \times 2 \times 2 \times 2 \times 2) \times (2 \times 2 \times 2 \times 2 \times 2)$. Since 2 is multiplied by itself 11 times, the product is 2^{11}.

Answers
1. B: DOK Level: 1; **2.** B: DOK Level: 1; **3.** B: DOK Level: 2;
4. D: DOK Level: 2; **5.** C: DOK Level: 2; **6.** A: DOK Level: 2;
7. C: DOK Level: 3; **8.** C: DOK Level: 2; **9.** D: DOK Level: 2;
10. A: DOK Level: 2; **11.** B: DOK Level: 3; **12.** A: DOK Level: 2

WORKBOOK *pp. 70–73*

❶ Review the Skill

Link to Past Skills Remind learners that they worked with algebraic expressions in the Unit 3, Lesson 1, skill *Algebraic Expressions and Variables*. Unlike that lesson, however, learners in this one will work with variables that raise to a power.

❷ Refine the Skill

Decoding Explain that, in order to correctly answer question 2, learners must use information from question 1. Inform learners that they can compute the answer to question 2 in two ways: by first performing the calculation and then writing the result in scientific notation, or by first writing the numbers in scientific notation and then performing the calculation.

❸ Master the Skill

SuperSkill Review Guide learners to recognize that, when they perform operations with scientific notation, they are applying the rules of operations with exponents. For example, in question 10 on p. 71, learners may subtract the exponents $(10^{27} - 10^{23})$ to find the power of 10 for the quotient. When learners are adding or subtracting in scientific notation, as in question 11, they first must rewrite the addends with the same power of 10, so that they are combining like terms (the same base, 10, and the same exponent).

Answers
1. C: DOK Level: 1; **2.** B: DOK Level: 2; **3.** A: DOK Level: 1;
4. C: DOK Level: 1; **5.** C: DOK Level: 1; **6.** A: DOK Level: 2;
7. D: DOK Level: 2; **8.** C: DOK Level: 2; **9.** A: DOK Level: 2;
10. B: DOK Level: 2; **11.** A: DOK Level: 2; **12.** B: DOK Level: 3;
13. D: DOK Level: 3; **14.** C: DOK Level: 3; **15.** C: DOK Level: 2;
16. D: DOK Level: 2; **17.** D: DOK Level: 2; **18.** C: DOK Level: 1;
19. B: DOK Level: 2; **20.** C: DOK Level: 1; **21.** B: DOK Level: 1;
22. D: DOK Level: 1; **23.** C: DOK Level: 1; **24.** C: DOK Level: 2;
25. D: DOK Level: 1; **26.** C: DOK Level: 2; **27.** B: DOK Level: 3;
28. C: DOK Level: 3; **29.** D: DOK Level: 3; **30.** B: DOK Level: 2

Patterns and Functions

MATH CONTENT TOPICS: Q.2.a, Q.2.b, Q.2.c, Q.2.e, Q.3.d, Q.6.c, A.1.b, A.1.e, A.1.i, A.2.c, A.7.a, A.7.b, A.7.c
MATH PRACTICES: MP.1.a, MP.1.b, MP.1.e, MP.2.a, MP.2.c, MP.3.a, MP.4.a, MP.4.b, MP.5.b, MP.5.c

MATHEMATICS

STUDENT BOOK pp. 58–59

▶ Preview the Skill

Ask learners to describe a pattern they have seen at home (for example, floor tiles with a certain pattern) or can spot in the classroom (the number of learners in each row). Next, discuss how learners identified the pattern, and how they could describe it to someone else.

❶ Learn the Skill

Give Examples Provide examples of simple numerical patterns, such as 2, 4, 6, 8 … and 5, 10, 20, 40. Explain that each value in the pattern is called a *term*, and the list of terms may be called a *sequence*. Ask learners to determine the rule for each pattern (in the first pattern, add 2; in the second pattern, multiply by 2) and then determine the next term in each pattern (16; 80).

❷ Practice the Skill

Link to Past Skills Guide learners to recognize that finding the value of $f(x)$ for a given value of x is similar to evaluating an expression for a given value of the variable. Have learners review the skill *Algebraic Expressions and Variables* from Unit 3, Lesson 1, for additional support.

❸ Apply the Skill

Spotlighted Item: Fill-in-the-Blank After learners have completed question 2 on p. 59, discuss their results. Ask volunteers to describe how they determined the amount of sales tax owed on $25. Encourage learners to share different strategies, such as solving the equation for $x = 25$ or examining the table to realize that, for every $5 increase in purchase amount, the sales tax increases by $0.40.

Answers
1. C; DOK Level: 1; **2.** $2.00; DOK Level: 1; **3.** D; DOK Level: 2;
4. C; DOK Level: 3; **5.** C; DOK Level: 3; **6.** A; DOK Level: 3;
7. C; DOK Level: 2; **8.** A; DOK Level: 3

WORKBOOK pp. 74–77

❶ Review the Skill

SuperSkill Review Have learners work in groups to generate patterns according to a particular rule. Discuss the patterns that learners produce and guide learners to understand that the same rule can generate different patterns, depending on its starting number. Next, have each group write a function to represent its pattern and use the rule to find the value of the function for a particular input.

❷ Refine the Skill

Decoding Have learners work in pairs to determine a pattern rule that represents the information in the table (start with 20 and add 60). Tell learners that the relationship can be represented with the equation $d = 60t + 20$, because at $t = 0$ the train will be 60 miles closer to the station that it was at $t = 1$.

❸ Master the Skill

Problem-Solving Strategy Explain to learners that they should examine more than two terms in order to determine the pattern rule, since two numbers can be related in more than one way. For example, in question 7 on p. 75, the first figure has 1 square and the second figure has 4 squares, so the pattern could be *add 3 squares* or *multiply the number of squares by 4*. When considering the third figure, which has 9 squares, neither rule applies. Next, discuss possible rules for the pattern (*add two more squares than what were added to the previous figure; take the square of the number of the figure in the sequence*).

Answers
1. D; DOK Level: 2; **2.** A; DOK Level: 2; **3.** A; DOK Level: 2;
4. C; DOK Level: 1; **5.** B; DOK Level: 3; **6.** D; DOK Level: 2;
7. B; DOK Level: 2; **8.** A; DOK Level: 2; **9.** C; DOK Level: 2;
10. C; DOK Level: 2; **11.** B; DOK Level: 3; **12.** B; DOK Level: 3;
13. D; DOK Level: 2; **14.** C; DOK Level: 3; **15.** A; DOK Level: 2;
16. A; DOK Level: 1; **17.** D; DOK Level: 1; **18.** A; DOK Level: 2;
19. D; DOK Level: 2; **20.** D; DOK Level: 2; **21.** C; DOK Level: 2;
22. A; DOK Level: 1; **23.** C; DOK Level: 2; **24.** A; DOK Level: 3;
25. D; DOK Level: 2; **26.** B; DOK Level: 2; **27.** B; DOK Level: 2

One-Variable Linear Equations

MATH CONTENT TOPICS: Q.2.a, Q.2.e, A.2.a, Q.3.a, Q.3.d, Q.4.a, A.2.b, A.2.c
MATH PRACTICES: MP.1.a, MP.1.b, MP.1.e, MP.2.a, MP.3.a, MP.3.b, MP.4.a, MP.4.b, MP.5.a, MP.5.c

STUDENT BOOK *pp. 60–61*

▶ Preview the Skill

Ask learners to consider situations in which they have heard words that end in the suffix –*verse*, such as *inverse*, *reverse*, and *converse*. Then, ask learners to explain the meaning of the word in the particular context. Elicit from students that words ending with –*verse* tend to refer to the concept of "going against." For example, an *inverted* dive is upside-down; driving in *reverse* means going backwards; *conversely* means "on the other hand." Tell learners that, in this lesson, they will use *inverse* operations to solve one-variable linear equations.

❶ Learn the Skill

Decoding Elicit from learners that an equation shows that two expressions are equal. Explain that, in a one-variable equation, learners must isolate the variable on one side of the equals (=) sign and the constant terms on the other. To do so, learners will inverse operations (addition and subtraction, multiplication and division).

❷ Practice the Skill

Link to Past Skills In the Unit 3, Lesson 1, skill *Algebraic Expressions and Variables*, learners evaluated numerical expressions by following the order of operations. Elicit from learners that, in order to evaluate or simplify an expression, they first must perform operations within parentheses, then multiply and divide from left to right, and finally add and subtract from left to right.

❸ Apply the Skill

SuperSkill Review Explain that, if learners struggle with multiple-choice items that feature one-variable equations, they can substitute each answer choice to determine the value that makes the equation true.

Answers
1. A; DOK Level: 1; **2.** D; DOK Level: 1; **3.** D; DOK Level: 1;
4. A; DOK Level: 1; **5.** C; DOK Level: 2; **6.** B; DOK Level: 2;
7. C; DOK Level: 3; **8.** C; DOK Level: 3; **9.** D; DOK Level: 1;
10. D; DOK Level: 1; **11.** A; DOK Level: 1

WORKBOOK *pp. 78–81*

❶ Review the Skill

SuperSkill Review After reading the instruction on p. 78, discuss the solution to the equation $3x + 3 = 9$. Elicit from learners that addition was undone first, followed by the multiplication. Draw learners' attention to the coefficient and the constants and elicit that all three values are divisible by 3. Have learners solve the equation by undoing multiplication before undoing addition ($x + 1 = 3$; $x = 3 - 1 = 2$). Point out that, if numeric values in an equation have a common factor, dividing by that common factor can make later computations easier.

❷ Refine the Skill

Give Examples To support learners' understanding of the distributive property, provide an arithmetic example such as $4(2 + 5) = 4(2) + 4(5)$. Have learners evaluate each side of the equation to demonstrate that both expressions are equal to 28. Elicit from students that finding the product of a factor and a sum of two addends is the same as multiplying each addend by the factor and then taking the sum of the products.

❸ Master the Skill

Spotlighted Item: Fill-in-the-Blank After learners have completed the fill-in-the-blank items on p. 80, ask them to check their work by substituting answers into the original equations to ensure they make the equations true.

Answers
1. A; DOK Level: 2; **2.** B; DOK Level: 2; **3.** C; DOK Level: 2;
4. A; DOK Level: 2; **5.** C; DOK Level: 1; **6.** B; DOK Level: 2;
7. A; DOK Level: 2; **8.** A; DOK Level: 2; **9.** B; DOK Level: 2;
10. A; DOK Level: 3; **11.** B; DOK Level: 2; **12.** 1; DOK Level: 2;
13. −24; DOK Level: 2; **14.** 2.5; DOK Level: 2; **15.** −2.2;
DOK Level: 2; **16.** 6; DOK Level: 2; **17.** 1.25; DOK Level: 2;
18. D; DOK Level: 1; **19.** B; DOK Level: 3; **20.** D; DOK Level: 2;
21. A; DOK Level: 1; **22.** C; DOK Level: 2; **23.** C; DOK Level: 2;
24. C; DOK Level: 2; **25.** A; DOK Level: 2; **26.** A; DOK Level: 2;
27. C; DOK Level: 2; **28.** B; DOK Level: 2

MATHEMATICS

Two-Variable Linear Equations

MATH CONTENT TOPICS: Q.2.a, Q.2.e, Q.6.c, A.2.a, A.2.b, A.2.d
MATH PRACTICES: MP.1.a, MP.1.b, MP.1.e, MP.2.a, MP.2.c, MP.3.a, MP.4.a, MP.4.b, MP.5.a, MP.5.c

MATHEMATICS

STUDENT BOOK pp. 62–63

➤ Preview the Skill

Briefly review the skill *One-Variable Linear Equations* from Unit 3, Lesson 6. During the discussion, elicit from learners the following key concepts about a one-variable linear equation:
- It is made up of terms that are numbers and products of variables and numbers.
- Only one variable appears, although it can appear in more than one term.
- To solve a one-variable linear equation, isolate the variable using inverse operations.
- The solution is the value of the variable that makes the equation true.

1 Learn the Skill

Give Examples Learners may find the substitution method to be more intuitive than the linear combination method. Explain to learners that multiplying each term in an equation by the same factor does not change its solution. Demonstrate this concept with a pair of simple equations such as $2x = 6$ and $4x = 12$. Elicit from learners that each term in the second equation is equal to twice the corresponding term in the first equation. Have learners solve each equation ($x = 3$) and discuss the results.

2 Practice the Skill

Decoding Encourage learners to solve the system in question 1 by using the approach described in Callout B. Here, for example, learners can multiply $x + 3y = 1$ by -2 to help solve the system.

3 Apply the Skill

Spotlighted Item: Fill-in-the-Blank Invite learners to share their solutions for fill-in-the-blank items on p. 63. Try to elicit a solution that uses the substitution method and a solution that uses the linear combination method for the same item. Reinforce the importance of checking the solution with both of the original equations when completing fill-in-the-blank item types.

Answers
1. C; DOK Level: 2; **2.** 3; −1; DOK Level: 2; **3.** 2; 3; DOK Level: 2; **4.** 8; −1; DOK Level: 2; **5.** 12; 8; DOK Level: 2; **6.** −2; 4; DOK Level: 2; **7.** D; DOK Level: 2; **8.** B; DOK Level: 2

WORKBOOK pp. 82–85

1 Review the Skill

Link to Past Skills In the Unit 1, Lesson 4, skill *Fractions*, learners found a common denominator to add or subtract fractions. Elicit from learners that a common denominator is a number that is a multiple of each denominator. Explain to learners that, in order to perform a linear combination, they must find a common multiple of the coefficients of one of the variables.

2 Refine the Skill

Give Examples To provide additional practice and support with solving systems by linear combination, have learners solve the system using one of the two methods described in Callout B. Discuss the results and guide learners to understand that different linear combinations of a system lead to the same solution.

3 Master the Skill

SuperSkill Review Draw learners' attention to question 20 on p. 85. Explain that to solve a problem in which you must identify an error, learners should perform each step. If learners get a different result than that which is listed, that step very well may include the error.

➤ Optional Activity

Enrich and Extend Challenge learners to write a system of two linear equations. Learners should first choose the values of the variables and then write equations using those values. Have learners exchange systems with a partner and solve one another's systems.

Answers
1. A; DOK Level: 2; **2.** C; DOK Level: 2; **3.** D; DOK Level: 2; **4.** C; DOK Level: 2; **5.** A; DOK Level: 2; **6.** D; DOK Level: 1; **7.** B; DOK Level: 2; **8.** A; DOK Level: 2; **9.** C; DOK Level: 2; **10.** A; DOK Level: 2; **11.** D; DOK Level: 2; **12.** C; DOK Level: 2; **13.** B; DOK Level: 2; **14.** A; DOK Level: 2; **15.** D; DOK Level: 2; **16.** D; DOK Level: 2; **17.** C; DOK Level: 2; **18.** C; DOK Level: 3; **19.** A; DOK Level: 2; **20.** B; DOK Level: 3; **21.** D; DOK Level: 2; **22.** B; DOK Level: 2; **23.** A; DOK Level: 2; **24.** D; DOK Level: 2; **25.** D; DOK Level: 3

MATH CONTENT TOPICS: Q.1.b, Q.2.a, Q.2.e, Q.3.a, Q.4.a, Q.4.c, A.1.a, A.1.d, A.1.f, A.1.g, A.4.a, A.4.b
MATH PRACTICES: MP.1.a, MP.1.b, MP.1.e, MP.2.a, MP.2.c, MP.3.a, MP.4.a, MP.4.b

MATHEMATICS

STUDENT BOOK *pp. 64–65*

➤ Preview the Skill

Inform learners that they likely are already familiar with one form of factoring. Explain that, in multiplication, the numbers that are multiplied together to form a product are known as its factors. For example, $4 \times 3 = 12$, so 3 and 4 are factors of 12. Inform learners they now will use factoring when solving equations that have an x^2 term and an x term.

❶ Learn the Skill

Give Examples Remind learners that factors are numbers or expressions that, when multiplied together, form a product. In the term $8y$, explain that both 8 and y are factors. Ask volunteers to supply additional factors that result in a product. Next, explain that a factor may have two terms, such as $(x + 7)$, and those terms either may be multiplied using the FOIL method or split into factors.

❷ Practice the Skill

Problem Solving Strategy Explain that to find the factors of a quadratic expression of the form $x^2 + bx + c$, the first step involves identifying the values of b and c. Next, find two integers whose sum is equal to b and whose product is equal to c. Draw students' attention to the expression $x^2 - 2x - 8$. Elicit that b is equal to -2 and c is equal to -8. By listing the factors of -8, you can identify the pair of factors that have a sum of -2. Then, add each of those factors to x to find the two factors of the quadratic expression.

❸ Apply the Skill

SuperSkill Review If learners encounter difficulty with the FOIL method, suggest that they instead think of the distributive property when multiplying binomials. For question 2, learners must find the product of $(x + 5)$ $(x - 7)$. Explain that learners should distribute the first x to $(x - 7)$, and then distribute the 5 to $(x - 7)$. Then they can simplify by combining like terms.

Answers
1. 1. C; DOK Level: 2; **2.** D; DOK Level: 2; **3.** A; DOK Level: 2; **4.** D; DOK Level: 2; **5.** A; DOK Level: 2; **6.** B; DOK Level: 2; **7.** A; DOK Level: 2; **8.** B; DOK Level: 2; **9.** A; DOK Level: 3; **10.** D; DOK Level: 2; **11.** C; DOK Level: 2

WORKBOOK *pp. 86–89*

❶ Review the Skill

Give Examples The skills in this lesson build on one another, so a learner's comfort level with one skill will affect his or her development of another skill. Once learners have mastered the skill of multiplying binomials, such as $(x - 4)(x + 9)$, they may move on to factoring. Have learners factor $x^2 + 5x - 6$ to get $(x - 1)(x + 6)$. Encourage learners to check factoring by multiplying to ensure that the product results in the original expression.

❷ Refine the Skill

For question 2 on p. 86, guide students to understand that the product of the length and width, $(w)(w - 2)$, is equal to the area of the rug, 48 square feet. So, $(w)(w - 2) = 48$. To write the equation in standard form, subtract 48 from both sides: $(w)(w - 2) - 48 = 0$.

❸ Master the Skill

Link to Past Skills To correctly complete questions 22 and 23 on p. 89, learners must substitute for x and solve the equation for R. Since R is isolated on one side of the equation, this is comparable to evaluating an expression for a given value of the variable. Have learners review the skill *Algebraic Expressions and Variables* from Unit 3, Lesson 1, for additional support in evaluating expressions.

➤ Common Errors and Misconceptions

When problems involve algebra and geometry or require several steps, some learners might perform calculations correctly but actually answer the question *incorrectly*. For example, question 15 involves consecutive integers. Learners must read carefully to learn that the problem is only asking for the second, or greater, integer.

Answers
1. C; DOK Level: 2; **2.** D; DOK Level: 2; **3.** B; DOK Level: 2; **4.** D; DOK Level: 2; **5.** D; DOK Level: 2; **6.** A; DOK Level: 2; **7.** C; DOK Level: 2; **8.** B; DOK Level: 2; **9.** A; DOK Level: 2; **10.** A; DOK Level: 2; **11.** B; DOK Level: 2; **12.** B; DOK Level: 2; **13.** D; DOK Level: 2; **14.** D; DOK Level: 2; **15.** A; DOK Level: 2; **16.** D; DOK Level: 2; **17.** C; DOK Level: 2; **18.** B; DOK Level: 2; **19.** C; DOK Level: 2; **20.** D; DOK Level: 2; **21.** 809 kg; DOK Level: 2; **22.** $300; DOK Level: 2; **23.** $11,700; DOK Level: 2; **24.** B; DOK Level: 3; **25.** D; DOK Level: 3; **26.** B; DOK Level: 2; **27.** B; DOK Level: 2

UNIT 3

LESSON 9

Rational Expressions and Equations

MATH CONTENT TOPICS: Q.1.b, Q.2.a, Q.2.e, A.1.a, A.1.d, A.1.f, A.1.h, A.4.a
MATH PRACTICES: MP.1.a, MP.1.b, MP.1.d, MP.1.e, MP.2.a, MP.2.c, MP.3.a, MP.3.b, MP.3.c, MP.4.a, MP.4.b, MP.5.a, MP.5.c

MATHEMATICS

STUDENT BOOK *pp. 66–67*

Preview the Skill

Give Examples Pose this situation to learners: Suppose you and some friends want to rent a van to take a road trip. The van costs $500. The cost per person depends on the number of people sharing the cost. Discuss how the cost-per-person can be expressed using the variable x for the number of friends [$\frac{500}{x}$]. Explain that this expression is an example of a rational expression.

1 Learn the Skill

SuperSkill Review Review the meaning of *ratio*. Elicit from students that a ratio is a comparison of two quantities that may be written as a fraction. Explain that a rational number is another name for a fraction, because it is the ratio of the numerator to the denominator. Similarly, a rational expression is a ratio of two polynomials.

2 Practice the Skill

Link to Past Skills Explain that performing operations with rational numbers is comparable to performing operations with fractions. Have learners review the skill *Fractions* from Unit 1, Lesson 4, for strategies in adding and subtracting fractions with unlike denominators, as well as strategies for multiplying and dividing fractions.

3 Apply the Skill

Spotlighted Item: Drop-Down When seeking to solve drop-down problems, encourage learners to use strategies similar to those they employ in answering multiple-choice items, such as eliminating options they know to be incorrect. In item 3 on p. 67, for example, option B cannot be correct because if $x = 1$, the denominator of the first rational expression would be 0.

Answers

1. A; DOK Level: 2; **2.** C; DOK Level: 2; **3.** D; DOK Level: 2; **4.** C; DOK Level: 2; **5.** A; C; DOK Level: 2; **6.** C; DOK Level: 2; **7.** C; DOK Level: 1; **8.** A; DOK Level: 2; **9.** A; DOK Level: 2

WORKBOOK *pp. 90–93*

1 Review the Skill

Decoding Review the vocabulary terms for this lesson by eliciting examples of rational numbers, rational expressions, and rational equations. Discuss why each example on p. 90 fulfills the criteria for a rational number, expression, or equation.

2 Refine the Skill

Link to Past Skills Call learners' attention to the *Making Assumptions* boxed support feature. Elicit from learners that $\frac{a}{b} = \frac{c}{d}$ is a proportion and the equation $ad = cb$ shows that the crossproducts are equal. Have learners review the skill *Ratios and Proportions* from Unit 1, Lesson 5, to determine the cross products of a proportion. In addition, to successfully solve rational expressions and equations, learners must possess a strong understanding of factoring quadratics. If necessary, have learners review the skill *Factoring* from Unit 3, Lesson 8, before proceeding with items in this lesson.

3 Master the Skill

Content Topics Draw learners' attention to questions 8, 14, and 28. Explain that each of these items requires learners to think—and problem solve—at a higher level. Items 8 and 28 ask learners to identify errors, whether in simplifying an equation or solving an equation. Item 14, meanwhile, asks learners to determine the correct lowest common denominator. Because of their complexity, all three items carry a Depth of Knowledge level of 3—the highest level that appears on the GED® Mathematical Reasoning Test.

Answers

1. C; DOK Level: 2; **2.** A; DOK Level: 2; **3.** C; DOK Level: 2; **4.** A; DOK Level: 2; **5.** A; DOK Level: 2; **6.** B; DOK Level: 2; **7.** A; DOK Level: 2; **8.** B; DOK Level: 3; **9.** C; DOK Level: 2; **10.** B; DOK Level: 2; **11.** A; DOK Level: 2; **12.** C; DOK Level: 2; **13.** B; DOK Level: 2; **14.** A; DOK Level: 3; **15.** C; DOK Level: 2; **16.** A; DOK Level: 2; **17.** A; DOK Level: 2; **18.** C; DOK Level: 2; **19.** A; DOK Level: 2; **20.** D; DOK Level: 2; **21.** A; DOK Level: 2; **22.** D; DOK Level: 1; **23.** A; DOK Level: 3; **24.** B; DOK Level: 2; **25.** C; DOK Level: 2; **26.** C; DOK Level: 2; **27.** C; DOK Level: 2; **28.** B; DOK Level: 3

Solving and Graphing Inequalities

MATH CONTENT TOPICS: A.3.a, A.3.b, A.3.c, A.3.d
MATH PRACTICES: MP.1.a, MP.1.b, MP.1.e, MP.2.a, MP.2.c, MP.3.a, MP.4.a, MP.4.b

STUDENT BOOK pp. 68–69

▶ Preview the Skill

Present this situation to learners: Anna must score at least 1,000 points on a video game to beat the high score. She would be successful if she scored 1,000 points. She also would be successful if she scored 1,500 points, or 1,100 points, or even 1,001 points. Learners are accustomed to finding one or two solutions when solving equations. However, explain that an inequality can have infinite solutions.

❶ Learn the Skill

Give Examples Guide learners to look at the first example in the instructional area on p. 68. Explain the difference between $x \geq 4$ and $x > 4$. *(The first inequality includes 4 as a solution, whereas the second inequality does not).* Point out that the graph of $x \geq 4$ has a closed circle at 4 because 4 is included in the solution. The graph of $x > 4$ has an open circle because 4 is not included in the solution set.

❷ Practice the Skill

Decoding Emphasize the importance of writing an inequality that accurately represents a problem situation. Help learners decode question 1 and write a correct inequality by drawing the following on the board:

5 times a number	is less than or equal to	2 times the number plus 9
↓	↓	↓
$5x$	$\leq$	$2x + 9$

❸ Apply the Skill

Decoding Emphasize the need for learners to carefully translate word problems into inequalities using the correct sign ($<$, $>$, $\leq$, $\geq$). Note that a phrase like *not greater than* is the same as *less than or equal to* ($\leq$); the same is true when a problem speaks of a maximum or a greatest possible value. Item 6 is an example of a problem using the phrase *cannot be greater than*; item 8 refers to the *greatest number*.

Answers
1. D; DOK Level: 2; **2.** D: DOK Level: 1; **3.** A; DOK Level: 1;
4. B; DOK Level: 1; **5.** D; DOK Level: 2; **6.** D; DOK Level: 2;
7. A; DOK Level: 2; **8.** C; DOK Level: 2; **9.** B; DOK Level: 2;
10. B; DOK Level: 2; **11.** D; DOK Level: 2; **12.** C; DOK Level: 2

WORKBOOK pp. 94–97

❶ Review the Skill

Give Examples Tell learners that solving inequalities is similar to solving equations. However, a major difference is that learners must reverse the inequality symbol when multiplying or dividing by a negative. To help learners solve $10 > -2x$, show them that they will reverse the sign because they will need to divide both sides of the inequality by -2, which is a *negative* number. However, they will not reverse the sign when solving $-10 > 2x$ because they can divide both sides by *positive* 2.

❷ Refine the Skill

Skim and Scan When writing an inequality to model a situation, learners should scan the problem for keywords to determine the correct inequality to use. *More than* means that the $>$ symbol should be used, and *less than* means $<$. Other keywords such as *at least* and *no less than* indicate $\geq$, while *at most* and *no more than* indicate $\leq$. Questions 21 and 23 on p. 96 contain *at least*, so the symbol $\geq$ should be used.

❸ Master the Skill

Link to Past Skills Encourage learners to review the Unit 2, Lesson 2, skill *Mean, Median, and Mode* for help in answering question 21. Explain that learners should divide the sum of 45, 38, 47, and the value x by 4, because there will be a total of 4 quizzes. This will help them to set up an inequality that correctly models the situation.

Answers
1. D; DOK Level: 2; **2.** C; DOK Level: 1; **3.** B; DOK Level: 1;
4. D; DOK Level: 1; **5.** C; DOK Level: 1; **6.** D; DOK Level: 2;
7. B; DOK Level: 2; **8.** D; DOK Level: 1; **9.** A; DOK Level: 2;
10. A; DOK Level: 2; **11.** C; DOK Level: 2; **12.** C; DOK Level: 2;
13. A; DOK Level: 2; **14.** $x > -1$; DOK Level: 1; **15.** $x \leq 2$; DOK
Level: 1; **16.** $x > -3$; DOK Level: 2; **17.** $y \geq -4$; DOK Level: 2;
18. $30c \leq 1,000$; DOK Level: 2; **19.** $3m > 18$; DOK Level: 2;
20. 16; DOK Level: 2; **21.** D; DOK Level: 2; **22.** D; DOK
Level: 2; **23.** D; DOK Level: 2; **24.** A; DOK Level: 2; **25.** D; DOK
Level: 2; **26.** B; DOK Level: 2; **27.** A; DOK Level: 2; **28.** B; DOK
Level: 2; **29.** D; DOK Level: 2; **30.** B; DOK Level: 2; **31.** D; DOK
Level: 2; **32.** C; DOK Level: 2

MATHEMATICS

The Coordinate Grid

MATH CONTENT TOPICS: Q.2.e, Q.6.c, A.1.e, A.5.a
MATH PRACTICES: MP.1.a, MP.1.b, MP.1.d, MP.1.e, MP.2.c, MP.3.a, MP.4.c

MATHEMATICS

STUDENT BOOK pp. 70–71

▶ Preview the Skill

Place an object (such as a bucket or a book) a certain diagonal distance away from you. Tell learners that you need to walk to the object but cannot move diagonally—you can only move left or right, and then forward or backward. Ask learners to describe how many steps—and in which directions—you should walk to reach the object.

❶ Learn the Skill

Decoding Explain that the two values in each ordered pair work together to represent a single location on a coordinate grid. Using a coordinate grid, show the difference between (3, 0) and (0, 3). Explain to learners that the order of numbers in an ordered pair is important, hence the term *ordered pair*. Tell students they must memorize that the first coordinate of an ordered pair is the x-coordinate and indicates horizontal distance. The second coordinate is the y-coordinate and indicates vertical distance.

❷ Practice the Skill

Skim and Scan On a coordinate grid, *right* and *up* imply positive values, and *left* and *down* imply negative values. Explain that, in the instructional area, point C is right and up from the origin; therefore, both its x- and y-values should be positive. To answer question 1, instruct learners to skim answer choices for an ordered pair with two positive values.

❸ Apply the Skill

Spotlighted Item Type: Hot-Spot Learners will respond to hot-spot items on the GED® Mathematical Reasoning Test that will assess their abilities to plot points electronically on a coordinate grid. Explain that, in doing so, learners will click on that portion of a grid to provide their answer.

Answers
1. A; DOK Level: 1; **2.** A point is plotted at (5,−3); DOK Level: 1; **3.** A point is plotted at (5, 3); DOK Level: 2; **4.** A point is plotted at (4,0); DOK Level: 1; **5.** A point is plotted at (1,0); DOK Level: 2; **6.** A point is plotted at (2,4); DOK Level: 2; **7.** A point is plotted at (−4,−3); DOK Level: 2; **8.** A point is plotted at (−1,−1); DOK Level: 2; **9.** B; DOK Level: 1; **10.** A; DOK Level: 1; **11.** A; DOK Level: 1; **12.** B; DOK Level: 1

WORKBOOK pp. 98–101

❶ Review the Skill

SuperSkill Review Emphasize to the learners that, when a figure is translated, every point in the figure is translated exactly the same way. For example, illustrate by translating the rectangle formed by points (1, 0), (5, 0), (5, 3), and (1, 3) up by 2 units and left by 5 units. Make the translation point by point, showing that the result, formed by the points (−4, 2), (0, 2), (0, 5), and (−4, 5), is also a rectangle with exactly the same dimensions as the original.

❷ Refine the Skill

Decoding Explain to learners that, when a figure is translated, directions must be properly translated into mathematical operations. Downward translations imply the addition of a negative quantity to the y values of all points in the figure. Similarly, upward implies addition of positive quantities to y values, leftward the addition of negative quantities to x values, and rightward the addition of positive quantities to x values.

❸ Master the Skill

Link to Past Skills Have learners revisit the use of number lines in the Unit 1, Lesson 3, skill *Integers* and note the parallels to how points are translated in the x- and y-directions.

▶ Optional Activity

Common Errors and Misconceptions Learners may encounter difficulty with coordinate pairs when one of the values is zero. Emphasize that an ordered pair always begins with the horizontal distance. Give learners extra practice with locating and plotting points on the x-axis or y-axis.

Answers
1. D; DOK Level: 1; **2.** A; DOK Level: 2; **3.** A; DOK Level: 1; **4.** D; DOK Level: 2; **5.** D; DOK Level: 2; **6.** A. DOK Level: 2; **7.** D; DOK Level: 2; **8.** C; DOK Level: 1; **9.** B; DOK Level: 2; **10.** C; DOK Level: 2; **11.** B; DOK Level: 2; **12.** C; DOK Level: 2; **13.** A; DOK Level: 3; **14.** C; DOK Level: 1; **15.** C; DOK Level: 2; **16.** D; DOK Level: 2; **17.** B; DOK Level: 2; **18.** C; DOK Level: 2; **19.** A; DOK Level: 3; **20.** A; DOK Level: 1; **21.** D; DOK Level: 2; **22.** B; DOK Level: 2; **23.** A; DOK Level: 2

Graphing Linear Equations

MATH CONTENT TOPICS: Q.2.a, Q.2.e, Q.6.c, A.1.b, A.2.d, A.5.a, A.5.d
MATH PRACTICES: MP.1.a, MP.1.b, MP.1.d, MP.1.e, MP.2.c, MP.3.a, MP.4.a, MP.4.b, MP.4.c

STUDENT BOOK pp. 72–73

➤ Preview the Skill

Distribute graph paper, and ask learners to draw on it an *x*- and *y*-axis and a long, diagonal line. Have students create a table of *x*- and *y*-values for about 5 to 10 coordinate pairs that fall on the diagonal line. Explain that all pairs of values have the same relationship, which is why they form a line.

❶ Learn the Skill

Give Examples Sketch a cross-sectional representation of a house formed by a rectangle 50 feet wide and 20 feet high capped by an isosceles triangle 50 feet wide and 10 feet high. Lead learners in developing a graph of roof height as a function of horizontal distance from one wall, and determine the distance from the bottom of the roof to its peak.

❷ Practice the Skill

Link to Past Skills To determine points on a line, learners must use skills from Unit 3, Lessons 1 and 2, *Algebraic Expressions and Variables* and *Equations*. To plot points on a grid, learners must use skills from Unit 3, Lesson 11, *The Coordinate Grid*. To help learners answer question 1, they must test each answer choice by substituting the first value for *x* and the second value for *y*. If a pair of values causes the equation to make a true statement, then that pair of values is the solution to the equation.

❸ Apply the Skill

Decoding Emphasize that items that ask about length or distance typically will involve the distance formula. Those that ask for solutions to an equation often will involve substitution of an ordered pair, either given explicitly as a choice or read from a point on a graph.

Answers
1. B; DOK Level: 1; **2.** C; DOK Level: 1; **3.** A; DOK Level: 1;
4. C; DOK Level: 2; **5.** B; DOK Level: 2; **6.** D; DOK Level: 2;
7. D; DOK Level: 1; **8.** C; DOK Level: 3; **9.** B; DOK Level: 2

WORKBOOK pp. 102–105

❶ Review the Skill

Link to Past Skills Have learners recall what they learned about function rules in *Patterns and Functions* from Unit 3, Lesson 5. Explain that a pair of values that satisfies a function rule forms an ordered pair, and a line is the collection of all ordered pairs that satisfy a certain equation or function rule.

❷ Refine the Skill

Give Examples Draw a graph with lines representing the two functions $y = 3x + 2$ and $y = -x - 2$. Lead learners to understand that the point at which the two lines cross, $(-1, -1)$, is the one and *only* point that solves both equations simultaneously. Provide additional examples for students to plot and solve.

❸ Master the Skill

Spotlighted Item: Drag and Drop Use items 9 through 11 to emphasize that, while drag-and-drop items allow questions of increased complexity, the same basic skills are required. For example, item 9 requires learners to substitute ordered pairs from a graph into equations to test for consistency. Similarly, items 10 and 11 require substitution of supplied ordered pairs into equations.

Answers
1. B; DOK Level: 1; **2.** C; DOK Level: 2; **3.** C; DOK Level: 1;
4. A; DOK Level: 2; **5.** C; DOK Level: 2; **6.** D; DOK Level: 1;

7. C; DOK Level: 2; **8.** C; DOK Level: 2; **9.** PR: $y = -\frac{1}{2}x - 2$,

QR: $y = \frac{3}{2}x - 2$, PQ: $y = \frac{1}{2}x + 2$; DOK Level: 2;

10. First pair: (4,4), second pair: (0,−2), third pair: (4,0); DOK Level: 2; **11.** First line: (−6, −1) and (0,2), second line: (2,1) and (6,7), third line: (2,−3) and (8,−6); DOK Level: 1; **12.** D; DOK Level: 2; **13.** A; DOK Level: 2; **14.** A; DOK Level: 1; **15.** B; DOK Level: 2; **16.** A; DOK Level: 2; **17.** C; DOK Level: 2; **18.** C; DOK Level: 2; **19.** B; DOK Level: 2

MATHEMATICS

Slope

MATH CONTENT TOPICS: Q.2.a, Q.2.d, Q.2.e, Q.6.c, A.1.i, A.5.b, A.5.c, A.6.a, A.6.b
MATH PRACTICES: MP.1.a, MP.1.b, MP.1.e, MP.2.a, MP.2.c, MP.3.a, MP.4.a, MP.4.c

MATHEMATICS

STUDENT BOOK pp. 74–75

➤ Preview the Skill

Have learners create a table of coordinate pairs for the line $y = 4x - 3$ when $x = -2, -1, 0, 1, 2,$ and 3. Point out to learners that the x-values increase by 1 each time. Ask learners to work in pairs to identify a similar pattern in the y-values. Explain that the value of y increases by 4 for each increase of 1 in x. Explain that the relationship between the change in x and the change in y helps to create the graph of a line.

1 Learn the Skill

Decoding Relate the slope of a line to the slope of a hill. Explain that some hills are relatively flat, while others are fairly steep. Depending on one's position, some hills decline, while others rise. Explain that the slope between any two points on a line is always the same, which is why all points fall on one line.

2 Practice the Skill

Link to Past Skills Refer learners to the Unit 1, Lesson 3, skill *Integers* for a refresher in subtracting integers. Explain that to subtract two integers, learners should add the opposite—meaning they should change the subtraction sign to an addition sign and also change the sign of the second number. Inform learners that they will need to be proficient with subtracting integers when using the slope formula. For help with finding slope, guide learners to review the test-taking tip on p. 74. It shows that both $\frac{-1}{2}$ and $\frac{1}{-2}$ equal $-\frac{1}{2}$. The first is a negative divided by a positive, and the second is a positive divided by a negative; both yield a negative.

3 Apply the Skill

Decoding Spotlight that item 2 contains more information than needed to solve the problem. However, learners may use the extra information to check the answer. Also demonstrate how slopes could prove that the three points all fall on the same line.

Answers
1. C; DOK Level: 2; **2.** A; DOK Level: 2; **3.** C; DOK Level: 2;
4. C; DOK Level: 2; **5.** D; DOK Level: 2; **6.** C; DOK Level 2;
7. D; DOK Level: 2; **8.** A; DOK Level: 2; **9.** D; DOK Level: 3

WORKBOOK pp. 106–109

1 Review the Skill

Skim and Scan Encourage learners to skim the lines on a coordinate grid before determining slope. Explain that, if a line climbs from left to right, the slope is positive. If a line falls from left to right, then the slope is negative. If the line is flat and horizontal, the slope is 0. If the line is vertical, the slope is undefined.

2 Refine the Skill

Link to Past Skills Remind learners that the slopes in the answer choices will be expressed in lowest terms. This means that learners may want to review the Unit 1, Lesson 4, lesson *Fractions*. Learners will probably find a slope of $\frac{3}{6}$ for question 1. Ensure that they simplify to get $\frac{1}{2}$.

3 Master the Skill

Decoding Explore with learners item 22 and the multiple steps required to solve it. Learners first must determine the temperature and the extent by which the temperature dropped at 4:30 A.M. *(The temperature was 48 degrees Fahrenheit, or 42 degrees less than the temperature at 6 P.M.).* From there, learners must determine the temperature and the extent by which it dropped two hours prior to that time, at 2:30 A.M. *(The temperature at 2:30 A.M. was 56 degrees Fahrenheit, or 34 degrees less than the temperature at 6 P.M.).* Then, learners must determine whether the temperature dropped below 60 degrees Fahrenheit for two consecutive hours. *(It did, which led to the death of Maria's plant.)*

Answers
1. D; DOK Level: 2; **2.** C; DOK Level: 2; **3.** A; DOK Level: 2;
4. D; DOK Level: 2; **5.** B; DOK Level: 2; **6.** C; DOK Level: 2;
7. A; DOK Level: 3; **8.** D; DOK Level: 2; **9.** C; DOK Level: 2;
10. D; DOK Level: 2; **11.** D; DOK Level: 2; **12.** C;
DOK Level: 2; **13.** A; DOK Level: 2; **14.** B; DOK Level: 3;

15. 4.5 feet; DOK Level: 2; **16.** 2; DOK Level: 2; **17.** $\frac{4}{5}$;

DOK Level: 2; **18.** B; DOK Level: 2; **19.** C; DOK Level: 2;
20. D; DOK Level: 2; **21.** A; DOK Level: 2; **22.** Q; DOK
Level: 3

UNIT 3 / LESSON 14

Using Slope to Solve Geometric Problems

MATH CONTENT TOPICS: Q.2.a, Q.2.d, Q.2.e, Q.6.c, A.5.a, A.5.b, A.6.a, A.6.b, A.6.c
MATH PRACTICES: MP.1.a, MP.1.b, MP.1.c, MP.1.d, MP.1.e, MP.2.c, MP.3.a, MP.4.a, MP.4.b, MP.5.c

MATHEMATICS

STUDENT BOOK pp. 76–77

➤ Preview the Skill

Ask learners what it means for two lines to be parallel. Guide them to understand that, because parallel lines neither approach nor diverge from one another, they never cross. Follow with a discussion of what it means for two lines to be perpendicular, drawing on learners' experiences with squares or rectangles in everyday life.

➊ Learn the Skill

Give Examples Ask learners to consider where two lines with the same slope (e.g., $y = mx + a$ and $y = mx + b$) cross one another. By setting the equations equal to one another ($mx + a = mx + b$), lead learners to understand that they can never cross if $a \neq b$. Next, illustrate the rule that perpendicular lines have slopes that are negative inverses of one another. Point out, for example, that lines with large, positive slopes (e.g., $y = 5x$) will have perpendiculars with small, negative slopes. Reinforce by using two special cases: the perpendicular to $y = x$ is $y = -x$, and perpendiculars to $y = 0$ (the x axis) have slopes that are undefined.

➋ Practice the Skill

Link to Past Skills Remind learners that, in this lesson, they will build on concepts introduced in Unit 2, Lesson 2, *Length, Area, and Volume*. Ensure that learners understand that opposite sides are parallel and that adjacent sides are perpendicular.

➌ Apply the Skill

Decoding Explain that the slopes required to answer items 7 and 8 can be determined from the graph. Point out to learners that, as a check, the slopes also must be negative inverses of each other.

Answers

1. C; DOK Level: 2; **2.** D; DOK Level: 1; **3.** C; DOK Level: 1; **4.** D; DOK Level: 2; **5.** B; DOK Level: 2; **6.** A; DOK Level: 3; **7.** C; DOK Level: 3; **8.** B; DOK Level: 3; **9.** C; DOK Level: 3; **10.** D; DOK Level: 3

WORKBOOK pp. 110–113

➊ Review the Skill

SuperSkill Review Explain that two geometric rules about slope may be of help to learners on the GED® Mathematical Reasoning Test. First, if two lines are parallel, any line perpendicular to one will be perpendicular to the other. Second, if two lines are both perpendicular to a third line, they are parallel to one another. Demonstrate these rules to learners using slope rules for parallel and perpendicular lines.

➋ Refine the Skill

Problem-Solving Strategy Explain that, if two lines have the same slope, they are considered to be parallel to one another. Two lines are considered to be perpendicular if they have slopes that are the negative inverses, or opposites, of one another. Explain that learners may check whether two lines are perpendicular by determining whether the product of the two slopes equals −1.

➌ Master the Skill

Decoding In dealing with multi-step problems such as those in items 17 through 19, learners may have difficulty determining the intermediate steps necessary to complete the solution. If this happens, urge them to fill in pieces of information they *can* find using the given information. For example, a student could list the slopes of all four sides of the lines defining the rug, along with the distance from point B to the upper left corner of the room (14 ft − 6 ft = 8 ft). By doing so, the solution to item 19 will be more evident.

Answers

1. A; DOK Level: 1; **2.** A; DOK Level: 1; **3.** B; DOK Level: 1; **4.** C; DOK Level: 1; **5.** A; DOK Level: 2; **6.** D; DOK Level: 2; **7.** B; DOK Level: 2; **8.** D; DOK Level: 2; **9.** $y = 2x$; DOK Level: 3; **10.** −0.5; DOK Level: 2; **11.** (1.6, 3.2); DOK Level: 3; **12.** (−0.4,−0.8); DOK Level: 3; **13.** A; DOK Level: 3; **14.** D; DOK Level: 3; **15.** D; DOK Level: 3; **16.** C; DOK Level: 3; **17.** B; DOK Level: 2; **18.** A; DOK Level: 2; **19.** B; DOK Level: 3

Graphing Quadratic Equations

MATH CONTENT TOPICS: Q.2.a, Q.2.e, Q.6.c, A.1.e, A.1.f, A.1.g, A.4.a, A.4.b, A.5.a, A.5.e
MATH PRACTICES: MP.1.a, MP.1.b, MP.1.c, MP.1.d, MP.1.e, MP.2.a, MP.2.c, MP.3.a, MP.4.a, MP.4.b, MP.4.c, MP.5.c

MATHEMATICS

STUDENT BOOK pp. 78–79

▶ Preview the Skill

Have learners sketch paths taken by a baseball thrown at different speeds and angles. Help learners identify parameters that could describe the paths (for example, the initial height, the horizontal distance thrown, the peak height, and so on). Inform students that the paths can be approximated by quadratic equations with parameters related to concepts that learners have identified, such as the force of gravity, the ball's initial speed and angle, and so forth.

❶ Learn the Skill

Give Examples Have the learners sketch the function $y = (x - 1)(x - 2) = x^2 - 3x + 2$ after substituting a few values of x. Use the fact that the equation is already in factored form to easily find where the curve crosses the x axis ($x = 1, 2$). Show, by substituting $x = 0$, that the curve crosses the y axis at $y = 2$. Point out that the minimum is at $x = -\frac{b}{2a} = \frac{3}{2} = 1.5$ and, by substitution, $y = -0.25$. Relate the fact that $a = 1$ to the orientation of the curve.

❷ Practice the Skill

Decoding Explain that curves cross the x axis when $y = 0$, and that curves cross the y axis when $x = 0$. Inform learners that the number along the y axis that intersects with the x curve is the y-intercept.

❸ Apply the Skill

Decoding Questions involving a curve crossing axes or achieving a maximum/minimum usually involve the parameters a, b, and/or c. Highlight the fact that item 5 is different because it involves symmetry.

Answers
1. D; DOK Level: 2; **2.** B; DOK Level: 2; **3.** A; DOK Level: 1;
4. B; DOK Level: 2; **5.** C; DOK Level: 3; **6.** D; DOK Level: 2;
7. A; DOK Level: 2; **8.** C; DOK Level: 2; **9.** D; DOK Level: 2

WORKBOOK pp. 114–117

❶ Review the Skill

SuperSkill Review Provide learners with hints about how to use symmetry to identify missing points. For example, moving a pencil or cursor vertically from a minimum so that it is level with a given point, and then noting the amount of horizontal units there are to that given point, will tell you the number of units to move horizontally in the opposite direction to find the corresponding point by symmetry.

❷ Refine the Skill

Decoding Explain that, in order to answer question 1, learners must reference the equation rather than the points on the coordinate grid. Inform them that, in the equation of $y = -2x^2 + 16x - 24$, $a = -2$, $b = 16$, and $c = -24$. Therefore, -24 is the answer to question 1.

❸ Master the Skill

Spotlighted Item: Hot-Spot Emphasize to learners that the hot-spot items that appear on p. 116 require learners to mark points where a curve goes through a maximum or minimum, crosses the x- or y-axes, or marks points of symmetry on a graph. Explain that, on the GED® Mathematical Reasoning Test, learners will perform the same function by clicking areas of an interactive coordinate grid.

Answers
1. B; DOK Level: 1; **2.** A; DOK Level: 2; **3.** C; DOK Level: 1;
4. D; DOK Level: 2; **5.** A; DOK Level: 3; **6.** D; DOK Level: 2;
7. B; DOK Level: 2; **8.** A; DOK Level: 2; **9.** A; DOK Level: 3;
10. (−2,0), (2,0), (0,−2); DOK Level: 2; **11.** (0,3), (−1,0),
(−3,0), (−2,−1); DOK Level: 2; **12.** (0,3), (3,0), (−1,0), (1,4);
DOK Level: 2; **13.** (−1,−3), (0,2), (1,0), (2,3); DOK Level: 3;
14. (1,4), (4,1), (−1,−4); DOK Level: 3; **15.** (0,−4), (−3,−1),
(2,4); DOK Level: 3; **16.** D; DOK Level: 2; **17.** D; DOK Level:
1; **18.** C; DOK Level: 2; **19.** B; DOK Level: 3; **20.** D; DOK
Level: 3; **21.** B; DOK Level: 2; **22.** C; DOK Level: 1; **23.** C;
DOK Level: 3

Evaluation of Functions

MATH CONTENT TOPICS: Q.2.a, Q.6.c, A.1.e, A.1.f, A.1.i, A.5.e, A.7.b, A.7.c
MATH PRACTICES: MP.1.a, MP.1.b, MP.1.e, MP.2.c, MP.3.a, MP.4.a, MP.4.c, MP.5.b, MP.5.c

MATHEMATICS

STUDENT BOOK pp. 80–81

➤ Preview the Skill

Provide learners with examples of various inputs and outputs. For example, a powered computer or tablet is the output of an electrical current or charge. Next, explain that the length of the charge is the relationship between the current/charge and the powered device.

❶ Learn the Skill

Decoding Remind learners that a mathematical function includes three parts—the input, the relationship, and the output. Explain that functions generally have one output (y-value) for each input (x-value). The relationship describes the effect that the input, in combination with another term, has on the output. In the equation $1 \times 2 = 2$, *1* is the input, *2* is the output, and the relationship is $x\,2$.

❷ Practice the Skill

Content Topics Inform learners that Content Topic A.5.e includes the concept of periodic behavior, so there may be a likelihood that they see it in an item or items on the GED® Mathematical Reasoning Test. Explain that periodic behavior means that a function repeats various times.

❸ Apply the Skill

SuperSkill Review Lead learners to realize that the functions graphed in the lesson have exactly one output for each input. Next, lead learners in plotting the curve for the equation $x = y^2$. Point out that, for an input of $x = 1$, there are two outputs: $y = -1$ and $y = 1$. Similarly, there are two outputs for each value of x greater than 0. Use this exercise as a lead-in to item 9.

Answers
1. D; DOK Level: 2; **2.** C; DOK Level: 1; **3.** D; DOK Level: 2;
4. B; DOK Level: 2; **5.** B; DOK Level: 2; **6.** A. DOK Level: 2;
7. A; DOK Level: 3; **8.** C; DOK Level: 2; **9.** C; DOK Level: 3

WORKBOOK pp. 118–121

❶ Review the Skill

SuperSkill Review To ensure understanding of *input*, *output*, and *relationship*, ask learners to identify the input, output, and relationship of a learner studying for his or her GED® credential (*The input is that the learner is studying for the GED® credential, the output might be that the learner passes and receives his credential, and the relationship might be the amount of time he or she spends studying.*).

❷ Refine the Skill

Decoding Remind learners that an undefined function means one with a denominator of 0. With that in mind, ask learners to solve the question 2. Guide learners to understand that, in order to have a denominator of 0, x must equal -1.

❸ Master the Skill

Spotlighted Item: Drag-and-Drop Explain to learners that, as with multiple-choice and drop-down items, drag-and-drop items include a variety of distractor options. Inform learners that they first may want to eliminate answer options they know to be incorrect before selecting one they believe to be correct. On p. 120, learners may opt to use a similar strategy by selecting those items for which they know the answers, eliminate those from the drag-and-drop list, and then attempt to complete those for which they are less certain.

Answers
1. D; DOK Level: 1; **2.** B; DOK Level: 2; **3.** D; DOK Level: 3;
4. B; DOK Level: 3; **5.** A; DOK Level: 1; **6.** C; DOK Level: 2;
7. D; DOK Level: 2; **8.** C; DOK Level: 2; **9.** D; DOK Level: 2;
10. B: $y = \dfrac{x(x-1)}{(x+1)}$; DOK Level: 3; **11.** A: $y = \dfrac{(x+1)(x-1)}{x}$; DOK Level: 3; **12.** C: $y = -\dfrac{1}{x}$; DOK Level: 3;
13. F: $y = \dfrac{-x(x-1)}{(x+1)}$; DOK Level: 3;
14. E: $y = \dfrac{x(x+1)}{(x-1)}$; DOK Level: 3;
15. D: $y = -\dfrac{(x+1)(x-1)}{x}$; **16.** C; DOK Level: 3;
17. C; DOK Level: 3; **18.** B; DOK Level: 3; **19.** D; DOK Level: 3;
20. C; DOK Level: 3

Comparison of Functions

MATH CONTENT TOPICS: Q.2.a, Q.2.e, Q.6.c, A.5.e, A.7.a, A.7.b. A.7.c, A.7.d
MATH PRACTICES: MP.1.a, MP.1.b, MP.1.d, MP.1.e, MP.2.c, MP.3.a, MP.4.a, MP.4.c, MP.5.a

MATHEMATICS

STUDENT BOOK *pp. 82–83*

▶ Preview the Skill

Have learners provide examples of the various types of functions they've worked with in Unit 3. From each, develop a list of the characteristics they used to describe functions: slopes, intercepts, relative and absolute maxima and minima, periods, undefined points, and limiting behavior as x becomes very positive or very negative.

❶ Learn the Skill

Give Examples Inform learners of the various ways in which functions may be represented—via ordered pairs, in tables, in graphs, algebraically, or through verbal descriptions—and that they'll see or use various examples of them on the GED® Mathematical Reasoning Test.

❷ Practice the Skill

Link to Past Skills Emphasize to learners that success in this lesson presumes a solid understanding of Unit 3, Lesson 16, *Evaluation of Functions*. Urge students to review the previous lesson for additional support.

❸ Apply the Skill

Decoding If learners struggle with comparing different representations of a different function, urge them to recast one of the representations. For example, some students might find that a rough sketch of the four ordered pairs in item 3 or the tabular data prior to item 5 helps them to visualize the function. Others might find jotting down slopes or intercepts, based on graphs for items 2 or 6, to be of help.

Answers
1. C; DOK Level: 2; **2.** C; DOK Level: 2; **3.** B; DOK Level: 2; **4.** D; DOK Level: 2; **5.** A; DOK Level: 2; **6.** A; DOK Level: 2

WORKBOOK *pp. 122–125*

❶ Review the Skill

SuperSkill Review While learners know what slope means in the context of straight lines, they will be less familiar with the concept of average slope or average rate of change for non-linear curves. Illustrate using the curve $y = x^2$. Point out that the slope changes continually with x. Next, illustrate for learners how an average slope exists between any two points on the curve, such as (0, 0) and (2, 4), equal to the slope of the line connecting the two points. Explain that learners will use this knowledge to solve item 16.

❷ Refine the Skill

Link to Past Skills Explain that items 11 and 15 both involve finding the maximum or minimum of quadratic functions. Remind learners that they may accomplish this by finding the x value as explained in Unit 3, Lesson 13 $(x = -\frac{b}{2a})$, and substituting to find the corresponding y value.

❸ Master the Skill

Spotlighted Item: Drop-Down Explain that many drop-down items include numerals as response options. Items on p. 123, for example, feature options that compare numerical values. Learners must exhibit an understanding of y-intercepts and rates of change to successfully answer the items.

Answers
1. B; DOK Level: 2; **2.** A; DOK Level: 2; **3.** B; DOK Level: 1; **4.** B; DOK Level: 2; **5.** C; DOK Level: 2; **6.** A; DOK Level: 2; **7.** A; DOK Level: 2; **8.** C; DOK Level: 2; **9.** D; DOK Level: 1; **10.** C; DOK Level: 2; **11.** D; DOK Level: 2; **12.** B; DOK Level: 3; **13.** D; DOK Level: 3; **14.** B; DOK Level: 3; **15.** D; DOK Level: 2; **16.** C; DOK Level: 2; **17.** D; DOK Level: 2; **18.** B; DOK Level: 2; **19.** B; DOK Level: 2

Unit 3 Review

MATH CONTENT TOPICS: Q.1.c, Q.2.a, Q.2.b, Q.2.c, Q.2.d, Q.2.e, Q.5.a, Q.6.c, A.1.b, A.1.c, A.1.f, A.1.j, A.2.a, A.2.b, A.2.c, A.3.a, A.3.b, A.4.a, A.5.a, A.5.b, A.5.d
MATH PRACTICES: MP.1.a, MP.1.b, MP.1.c, MP.1.d, MP.1.e, MP.2.a, MP.2.c, MP.3.a, MP.4.a, MP.4.b, MP.4.c

You may choose to use the Unit 3 Review on Student Book pp. 84–91 as a practice test. If you wish to time the test, ask learners to complete all the items in 140 minutes.

Unit 3 Review Answers

1. A; **2.** D; **3.** C; **4.** A; **5.** B; **6.** A; **7.** B; **8.** B; **9.** 3, −2; **10.** C; **11.** B; **12.** C; **13.** C; **14.** D; **15.** D; **16.** C; **17.** C; **18.** B; **19.** A; **20.** A; **21.** D; **22.** A; **23.** C; **24.** C; **25.** A; **26.** D; **27.** A; **28.** A; **29.** (2,1); **30.** C; **31.** C; **32.** D; **33.** A; **34.** D; **35.** B; **36.** D; **37.** D; **38.** B; **39.** D; **40.** B; **41.** B; **42.** A; **43.** D; **44.** 2; **45.** −1.5; **46.** 3; **47.** D; **48.** C; **49.** The plot will show four points corresponding to the following ordered pairs: (1,2.5), (2,5), (3,7.5), (4,10); **50.** A; **51.** D; **52.** B; **53.** C; **54.** A; **55.** C; **56.** D; **57.** A; **58.** B; **59.** A; **60.** C; **61.** A; **62.** D; **63.** A; **64.** B; **65.** C; **66.** C; **67.** D; **68.** Point *A:* (2,1), Point *B:* (4,1), Point *C:* (3,−2); **69.** A; **70.** D; **71.** B

Unit 3 Review Item Analysis

SKILL	DOK LEVEL 1	DOK LEVEL 2	DOK LEVEL 3
Algebraic Expressions and Variables		5, 11, 23, 33	
Equations	15	1, 3, 45, 46, 47, 48	14, 17
Squaring, Cubing, and Taking Roots		2, 24, 60, 63	65, 66
Exponents and Scientific Notation		12, 16, 35, 36	
Patterns and Functions		4, 19, 21, 69, 70	
One-Variable Linear Equations		6, 13, 20, 34, 39, 51, 52, 53, 54, 56, 61, 64	55
Two-Variable Linear Equations		57, 59	58
Factoring		71	27, 32
Rational Expressions and Equations		67	
Solving and Graphing Inequalities		22, 25, 26, 28, 38	37
The Coordinate Grid	40	9, 49, 68	
Graphing Linear Equations		30, 31, 41, 42	
Slope	43	7, 8, 10, 44, 50	
Using Slope to Solve Geometric Problems		29	
Graphing Quadratic Functions		57	
Evaluation of Functions		18	
Comparison of Functions		64	

MATHEMATICS

Unit 3 Review

Use workbook lessons, as identified in the following table, to assist learners who require additional remediation with certain skills or items having certain DOK levels.

Unit 3 Workbook Item Analysis

SKILL	DOK LEVEL 1	DOK LEVEL 2	DOK LEVEL 3
Algebraic Expressions and Variables	1, 11, 12	2, 3, 4, 5, 6, 7, 8, 9, 10, 13, 15, 16, 17, 18, 19, 20, 23, 24, 25, 28	14, 21, 22, 26, 27
Equations		1, 2, 3, 4, 5, 6, 7, 8, 9, 10, 11, 12, 13, 14, 15, 16, 17, 18, 19, 21, 22, 23, 24, 25, 26, 27, 28, 29	20
Squaring, Cubing, and Taking Roots	1, 3, 5, 6, 8, 23, 28, 29, 35	2, 4, 7, 10, 14, 15, 16, 18, 20, 24, 25, 26, 27	9, 11, 12, 13, 17, 19, 21, 22, 30, 31, 32, 33, 34
Exponents and Scientific Notation	1, 3, 4, 5, 18, 20, 21, 22, 23, 25	2, 6, 7, 8, 9, 10, 11, 15, 16, 17, 19, 24, 26, 30	12, 13, 14, 27, 28, 29
Patterns and Functions	4, 16, 17, 22	1, 2, 3, 6, 7, 8, 9, 10, 13, 15, 18, 19, 20, 21, 23, 25, 26, 27	5, 11, 12, 14, 24
One-Variable Linear Equations	5, 18, 21	1, 2, 3, 4, 6, 7, 8, 9, 11, 12, 13, 14, 15, 16, 17, 20, 22, 23, 24, 25, 26, 27, 28	10, 19
Two-Variable Linear Equations	6	1, 2, 3, 4, 5, 7, 8, 9, 10, 11, 12, 13, 14, 15, 16, 17, 19, 21, 22, 23, 24	18, 20, 25
Factoring		1, 2, 3, 4, 5, 6, 7, 8, 9, 10, 11, 12, 13, 14, 15, 16, 17, 18, 19, 20, 21, 22, 23, 26, 27	24, 25
Rational Expressions and Equations	22	1, 2, 3, 4, 5, 6, 7, 9, 10, 11, 12, 13, 15, 16, 17, 18, 19, 20, 21, 24, 25, 26, 27	8, 14, 23, 28
Solving and Graphing Inequalities	2, 3, 4, 5, 8, 14, 15	1, 6, 7, 9, 10, 11, 12, 13, 16, 17, 18, 19, 20, 21, 22, 23, 24, 25, 26, 27, 28, 29, 30, 31, 32	
The Coordinate Grid	1, 3, 8, 14, 20	2, 4, 5, 6, 7, 9, 10, 11, 12, 15, 16, 17, 18, 21, 22, 23	13, 19
Graphing Linear Equations	1, 3, 6, 11, 14	2, 4, 5, 7, 8, 9, 10, 12, 13, 15, 16, 17, 18, 19	
Slope		1, 2, 3, 4, 5, 6, 8, 9, 10, 11, 12, 13, 15, 16, 17, 18, 19, 20, 21	7, 14, 22
Using Slope to Solve Geometric Problems	1, 2, 3, 4	5, 6, 7, 8, 10, 17, 18	9, 11, 12, 13, 14, 15, 16, 19
Graphing Quadratic Functions	1, 3, 17, 22	2, 4, 6, 7, 8, 10, 11, 12, 16, 18, 21	5, 9, 13, 14, 15, 19, 20, 23
Evaluation of Functions	1, 5	2, 6, 7, 8, 9	3, 4, 10, 11, 12, 13, 14, 15, 16, 17, 18, 19, 20
Comparison of Functions	3, 9	1, 2, 4, 5, 6, 7, 8, 10, 11, 15, 16, 17, 18, 19	12, 13, 14

Unit 4

Geometry

The subject area of geometry differs considerably from that of algebra. For starters, geometry is a more visual discipline in which learners must identify relationships between shapes, scale drawings, and solids. As a result, visual-spatial learners may have less difficulty with geometry than with algebra. You may notice this distinction among your students. However, because learners in some cases must solve algebraic equations in order to solve geometric problems, the two disciplines are interconnected.

In this unit, learners must work and master multi-step problem solving to calculate the perimeter, area, volume, and surface area of various complex figures. Formulas for the Pythagorean relationship, as well as area, volume, surface area, and others, are available in the frontmatter of the Student Book and Workbook.

Table of Contents

LESSON	PAGE
1: Triangles and Quadrilaterals	MA 44
2: Pythagorean Theorem	MA 45
3: Polygons	MA 46
4: Circles	MA 47
5: Composite Plane Figures	MA 48
6: Scale Drawings	MA 49
7: Prisms and Cylinders	MA 50
8: Pyramids, Cones, and Spheres	MA 51
9: Composite Solids	MA 52
Unit 4 Review	**MA 53–MA 54**

MATHEMATICS

Triangles and Quadrilaterals

MATH CONTENT TOPICS: Q.2.a, Q.2.e, Q.4.a, Q.4.c, Q.4.d, A.2.a, A.2.b, A.2.c
MATH PRACTICES: MP.1.a, MP.1.b, MP.1.d, MP.1.e, MP.2.a, MP.2.b, MP.2.c, MP.4.a, MP.4.b, MP.5.a, MP.5.b

MATHEMATICS

STUDENT BOOK pp. 94–95

➤ Preview the Skill

Briefly review the meanings of *perimeter* and *area*. Ask learners to describe a situation in their daily lives in which they might need to find the perimeter or area of three- or four-sided figures. For example, to tile a floor they would need to know its area, or to build a fence they would need to know the perimeter of the area to be fenced.

① Learn the Skill

Link to Past Skills In the Unit 2, Lesson 1, skill *Length, Area, and Volume*, students learned how to find the perimeter and area of squares and rectangles. Explain that, in this lesson, students will build on that understanding as they find the perimeter and area of triangles and other quadrilaterals and find missing side lengths when given perimeter or area.

② Practice the Skill

Decoding Reinforce to learners the importance of carefully reading each question so that they may correctly respond to it. For example, question 1 asks learners to find both the area *and* the perimeter of the square. Remind learners that they will use different formulas—and operations—to determine each measurement.

③ Apply the Skill

Decoding Explain that a figure on the GED® Mathematical Reasoning Test, such as those that appear with question 2 and question 6, may be missing certain side lengths. If so, have learners use the formula $P = 2(l + w)$ or their own understanding that rectangles and parallelograms have two pairs of congruent sides to determine the missing side lengths.

Answers
1. D; DOK Level: 1; **2.** D; DOK Level: 1; **3.** B; DOK Level: 1; **4.** A; DOK Level: 1; **5.** C; DOK Level: 1; **6.** B; DOK Level: 1; **7.** A; DOK Level: 2; **8.** B; DOK Level: 2; **9.** B; DOK Level: 2; **10.** C; DOK Level: 2

WORKBOOK pp. 126–129

① Review the Skill

SuperSkill Review Understanding the reasoning behind the formula for the area of a triangle may help learners remember it. Elicit from learners that the area of a rectangle is lw. Draw a rectangle and divide it in half diagonally. Elicit from learners that each half of the rectangle is a triangle with area $\frac{1}{2}lw$, or $\frac{1}{2}bh$. Repeat, this time drawing a parallelogram and dividing it into triangles with area $\frac{1}{2}bh$. Guide students to understand that the area of any triangle is equal to one-half the area of a rectangle or parallelogram with the same base and height.

② Refine the Skill

Decoding Draw learners' attention to Callout B. Emphasize that the height of a triangle must be perpendicular to its base. Elicit that only in a right triangle do the base and height form two sides of the triangle.

③ Master the Skill

Explain that when two or more questions relate to the same figure, learners should answer those questions in sequence, since the first question may provide information that they can use to answer the second question. For example, to complete question 11 on p. 128, learners first must know the length of one side, which they determined with item 10.

Answers
1. A; DOK Level: 2; **2.** B; DOK Level: 2; **3.** 24; DOK Level: 2; **4.** 16; DOK Level: 2; **5.** 4; DOK Level: 2; **6.** 8; DOK Level: 3; **7.** 22; DOK Level: 3; **8.** C; DOK Level: 1; **9.** A; DOK Level: 2; **10.** B; DOK Level: 2; **11.** C; DOK Level: 2; **12.** B; DOK Level: 2; **13.** A; DOK Level: 2; **14.** A; DOK Level: 2; **15.** B; DOK Level: 2; **16.** A; DOK Level: 2; **17.** A; DOK Level: 2; **18.** B; DOK Level: 2; **19.** C; DOK Level: 2; **20.** D; DOK Level: 2; **21.** A; DOK Level: 3; **22.** D; DOK Level: 2; **23.** B; DOK Level: 2; **24.** B; DOK Level: 2; **25.** D; DOK Level: 3

MATH CONTENT TOPICS: Q.2.b, Q.4.a, Q.4.e, A.4.a, A.4.b
MATH PRACTICES: MP.1.a, MP.1.b, M.P.2.b, MP.3.c, MP.4.b, MP.5.a

STUDENT BOOK pp. 96–97

➤ Preview the Skill

Display an 8.5 × 11 sheet of paper. Cut the paper diagonally from one corner to another, forming two triangles. Display the triangles to learners, and tell them that both triangles are right triangles because each contains a right angle. Explain that, in this lesson, students will learn how to determine the length of the diagonal side without measuring it.

❶ Learn the Skill

Give Examples Draw a triangle on the board. Have learners practice naming an opposite side when given an angle. Explain that, in a right triangle, the right angle is the greatest angle in the triangle. Therefore, the side that is opposite the right angle is always the longest side. Tell learners that this side is called the hypotenuse, and that the other sides are called *legs*.

❷ Practice the Skill

SuperSkill Review Have students examine the variables in $a^2 + b^2 = c^2$. Explain that it does not matter which leg is called a and which leg is called b. This is because the squares of these measurements will be added together, and numbers can be added in any order. However, the hypotenuse, or longest side, always should be represented by c. For question 1, help learners create a labeled sketch. Draw a vertical line that represents the wall (labeled x), and then draw a diagonal line that represents the ladder (labeled 10 feet). Lead learners to understand that, in this case, the ladder represents the hypotenuse.

❸ Apply the Skill

Decoding Have learners examine the graphic that accompanies question 2. Help them decode that the side labeled "30 ft" represents the pole, the side labeled "15 ft" is the distance between the bottom of the cable and the bottom of the pole, and the unlabeled side represents the length of the cable.

Answers

1. C: DOK Level: 2; **2.** D: DOK Level: 2; **3.** B: DOK Level: 2;
4. C: DOK Level: 3; **5.** C: DOK Level: 2; **6.** A: DOK Level: 2;
7. D: DOK Level: 2

WORKBOOK pp. 130–133

❶ Review the Skill

Skim and Scan Students already have learned that the hypotenuse is always the longest side of a right triangle. Have learners skim the figures on pp. 130–133, noting the hypotenuse in each instance. After learners solve a problem, they should scan the three side-length measurements to ensure that the hypotenuse has the greatest measure.

❷ Refine the Skill

Problem-Solving Strategy Remind learners that checking their answers is a very important part of the problem-solving process. After learners use the Pythagorean Theorem to find missing measures, they should substitute each side length into $a^2 + b^2 = c^2$ to ensure that the sum $a^2 + b^2$ equals c^2.

❸ Master the Skill

SuperSkill Review Students already have learned how to use the distance formula to calculate distance between two ordered pairs. However, they may prefer to instead use the Pythagorean Theorem. Have learners examine the grid on p. 131. To help learners find the distance between A and B, tell them to imagine that $\overline{AB}$ is the hypotenuse of a right triangle with legs of 2 units and 8 units. Then they can use $a^2 + b^2 = c^2$ to find the missing length. To help learners answer question 4, tell them to plot a point at (5, −3) to create a right triangle with $\overline{AC}$ as the hypotenuse.

➤ Optional Activity

Spotlighted Item: Fill-in-the-Blank Draw students' attention to the fill-in-the-blank items on p. 131. Point out that the questions specify to round answers to the nearest hundredth. Explain to learners that, for fill-in-the-blank items, they should give answers to the specified decimal place. Briefly review place value through hundredths, as needed.

Answers

1. D; DOK Level: 2; **2.** B; DOK Level: 2; **3.** 8.25; DOK Level: 2;
4. 10.05; DOK Level: 2; **5.** 7.21; DOK Level: 2; **6.** 6; DOK Level:
2; **7.** 17.21; DOK Level: 2; **8.** D; DOK Level: 3; **9.** A; DOK Level:
2; **10.** C; DOK Level: 2; **11.** D; DOK Level: 2; **12.** C; DOK Level:
2; **13.** B; DOK Level: 2; **14.** D; DOK Level: 2; **15.** B; DOK Level:
2; **16.** C; DOK Level: 3; **17.** A; DOK Level: 2; **18.** B; DOK Level:
2; **19.** B; DOK Level: 2; **20.** A; DOK Level: 2; **21.** C; DOK Level:
2; **22.** D; DOK Level: 2; **23.** A; DOK Level: 2; **24.** B; DOK Level: 3

MATHEMATICS

Polygons

MATH CONTENT TOPICS: Q.2.a, Q.2.e, Q.4.a, Q.4.c, Q.4.d, A.2.a, A.2.b, A.2.c
MATH PRACTICES: MP.1.a, MP.1.b, MP.1.d, MP.1.e, MP.2.a, MP.2.b, MP.2.c, MP.3.a, MP.3.b, MP.4.c, MP.5.b

STUDENT BOOK *pp. 98–99*

▶ Preview the Skill

Ask learners to think of street signs they have seen. Discuss the shapes of the signs. Elicit that a stop sign is an octagon (eight sides) and a school-zone sign is a pentagon (five sides). Explain that these also are examples of polygons.

① Learn the Skill

Decoding Many questions involving geometry will require learners to know the number of sides in some common polygons. Help learners develop strategies for remembering that a pentagon has five sides (e.g., the pentathlon event in the Olympics has five events), a hexagon has six sides (e.g., *hex* and *six* both contain the letter *x*), and an octagon has eight sides (e.g., an octopus has eight legs).

② Practice the Skill

Link to Past Skills Ask learners to discuss their solutions to question 1. Try to elicit a solution that involved multiplication (e.g., $6 \times 5 = 30$) and a solution that used addition ($5 + 5 + 5 + 5 + 5 + 5 = 30$). Remind learners that they studied both addition and multiplication in the Unit 1, Lesson 2, skill *Operations*. Then guide learners to understand that multiplying the number of sides by the side length is equivalent to adding the number of sides with a given side length.

③ Apply the Skill

Draw learners' attention to question 5 on p. 99. Have learners compute the perimeter by adding together the six side lengths. Then, discuss the figure and elicit from learners that there are four sides that each measure 7 cm and two sides that each measure 4 cm. Guide learners to understand that, if there are multiple sides with the same length, they can use multiplication in combination with addition to find the perimeter. For example, $4 + 4 + 7 + 7 + 7 + 7 = 2(4) + 4(7) = 8 + 28 = 36$. Explain that reducing the number of steps can reduce the chance of a computational error.

Answers
1. C; DOK Level: 1; **2.** B; DOK Level: 1; **3.** C; DOK Level: 1; **4.** A; DOK Level: 2; **5.** C; DOK Level: 1; **6.** C; DOK Level: 1; **7.** C; DOK Level: 1; **8.** B; DOK Level: 2; **9.** C; DOK Level: 2

WORKBOOK *pp. 134–137*

① Review the Skill

SuperSkill Review Review the skill of calculating the perimeter of a polygon by providing examples. If possible, have learners find and measure the perimeters of polygon-shaped objects in the classroom. Discuss the results and clarify any errors or misconceptions.

② Refine the Skill

Link to Past Skills By representing an unknown quantity as a variable, explain that learners may use the perimeter of an irregular polygon and known side lengths to determine the missing side length. Similarly, explain that they may use the perimeter of a regular polygon and its side length to determine the number of sides, or the perimeter and its number of sides to find side length. Have learners review the skill *Equations* from Unit 3, Lesson 2, to solve an equation and find the value of the variable in question 2.

③ Master the Skill

Spotlighted Item: Drag-and-Drop Explain to learners that drag-and-drop items may require deeper, more complex problem solving than multiple-choice items. For example, the drag-and-drop items on p. 137 require learners to determine two missing pieces of information about regular polygons. For question 16, learners must determine which side length, multiplied by eight, will result in the perimeter. For question 19, learners must determine which combination of side length and number of sides has a product equal to the given perimeter.

Answers
1. B; DOK Level: 2; **2.** B; DOK Level: 2; **3.** A; DOK Level: 1; **4.** C; DOK Level: 2; **5.** A; DOK Level: 2; **6.** A; DOK Level: 2; **7.** B; DOK Level: 2; **8.** C; DOK Level: 2; **9.** B; DOK Level: 2; **10.** C; DOK Level: 1; **11.** A; DOK Level: 1; **12.** A; DOK Level: 2; **13.** C; DOK Level: 3; **14.** B; DOK Level: 3; **15.** D; DOK Level: 3; **16.** 40; 5; DOK Level: 2; **17.** hexagon; 54; DOK Level: 2; **18.** octagon; 1.5; DOK Level: 2; **19.** 7; 4.5; DOK Level: 2; **20.** A; DOK Level: 2; **21.** B; DOK Level: 3; **22.** B; DOK Level: 3

MATHEMATICS

Circles

MATH CONTENT TOPICS: Q.2.a, Q.2.e, Q.4.b, A.2.a, A.2.b, A.2.c
MATH PRACTICES: MP.1.a, MP.1.b, MP.1.d, MP.1.e, MP.2.c, MP.4.a, MP.4.b

MATHEMATICS

STUDENT BOOK pp. 100–101

➤ Preview the Skill

Have learners identify a circular object or objects in the classroom. Review the definition of a polygon (a closed, plane figure with three or more sides). Discuss whether a circle is a polygon (no, because it lacks sides). Elicit from learners that, since a circle lacks sides, they cannot find the distance around a circle by adding its side lengths, as they would to find the distance around a polygon.

1 Learn the Skill

Give Examples Draw a circle on the board. Next, draw a diameter in the circle. Finally, draw a radius in the circle that overlaps the diameter. Label both segments and elicit from learners that the radius is half the distance, and that the diameter is twice the radius. Write $d = 2r$ and $r = \dfrac{d}{2}$. Provide learners with circles of different diameter and radius, and have them find the other measure.

2 Practice the Skill

Problem-Solving Strategies Tell learners that many geometry items are multi-step problems, and incorrect answer choices often are the result of neglecting to perform one of the steps. For example, choice B in question 1 on p. 100 gives the circumference of the *swimming pool*, rather than the circumference of the *fence*.

3 Apply the Skill

Skim and Scan Elicit from learners that problems involving the area of a circle also involve the radius, while problems involving the circumference of a circle also involve the diameter. Encourage learners to quickly skim and scan items involving circles to determine whether they are given the appropriate information or whether they will need to change radius to diameter or vice versa.

Answers
1. C; DOK Level: 2; **2.** D; DOK Level: 2; **3.** C; DOK Level: 2; **4.** B; DOK Level: 1; **5.** C; DOK Level: 2; **6.** B; DOK Level: 2; **7.** B; DOK Level: 2; **8.** C; DOK Level: 1; **9.** C; DOK Level: 1; **10.** A; DOK Level: 2

WORKBOOK pp. 138–141

1 Review the Skill

Link to Past Skills Encourage learners to review the skill *Squaring, Cubing, and Taking Roots* in Unit 3, Lesson 3. Explain that, in the formula for the area of a circle, the radius is the base. The exponent 2 indicates that the base (radius) should be used as a factor two times.

2 Refine the Skill

Link to Past Skills Explain that, as with question 1, learners must use available information—in this case, the known measure of circumference—to answer question 2. First, learners must find the diameter of a paving stone (8.25 in.). Next, they must multiply by the number of paving stones (35). Then, they must convert units of measurement from inches to feet (288.75 in. divided by 12 in. = 24 ft). To aid learners in mastering this final step, refer them to *Measurement and Units of Measure* on pp. 30–33.

3 Master the Skill

Decoding Draw learners' attention to the figure in the left column on p. 140. Elicit from learners that the radius of the frame is 2 inches greater than the radius of the mirror in every direction. Guide learners to understand that, if the radius is 2 inches greater, the diameter will be 4 inches greater, so the diameter of the mirror alone is 11 − 4 = 7 inches.

➤ Optional Activity

Spotlighted Item: Fill-in-the-Blank Have learners work in pairs to answer each fill-in-the-blank item on p. 139. Explain that if partners suggest different answers for an item, they should discuss their solutions and help one another identify any potential errors or misconceptions.

Answers
1. D; DOK Level: 2; **2.** A; DOK Level: 3; **3.** 18.84; DOK Level: 1; **4.** 43.96; DOK Level: 2; **5.** 94.2; DOK Level: 1; **6.** 4; DOK Level: 2; **7.** 6; DOK Level: 2; **8.** C; DOK Level: 1; **9.** D; DOK Level: 2; **10.** A; DOK Level: 2; **11.** A; DOK Level: 1; **12.** B; DOK Level: 1; **13.** C; DOK Level: 2; **14.** A; DOK Level: 1; **15.** B; DOK Level: 3; **16.** C; DOK Level: 1; **17.** B; DOK Level: 3; **18.** B; DOK Level: 2; **19.** D; DOK Level: 2; **20.** B; DOK Level: 2; **21.** C; DOK Level: 2; **22.** B; DOK Level: 2; **23.** D; DOK Level: 2; **24.** D; DOK Level: 2; **25.** D; DOK Level: 2; **26.** A; DOK Level: 3

Composite Plane Figures

MATH CONTENT TOPICS: Q.4.a, Q.4.b, Q.4.c, Q.4.d
MATH PRACTICES: MP.1.a, MP.1.b, MP.1.c, MP.1.d, MP.1.e, MP.3.a, MP.5.c

MATHEMATICS

STUDENT BOOK pp. 102–103

▶ Preview the Skill

Give Examples Ask learners to describe figures they have seen, both inside and outside of the classroom, that are made up of more than one shape (for example, a rectangular window with a semi-circular window above it, a picture frame that holds a collection of photos, and so on). Explain that these figures are called composite figures, because they are composed, or made up, of two or more figures.

❶ Learn the Skill

Link to Past Skills In order to find the areas of composite plane figures, learners must calculate the areas of plane figures. Have learners review the skills *Length, Area, and Volume* from Unit 2, Lesson 2, *Triangles and Quadrilaterals* from Unit 4, Lesson 1, and *Circles* from Unit 4, Lesson 4.

❷ Practice the Skill

Explain that, just as with an irregular polygon, the perimeter of a composite plane figure reflects the sum of the lengths of its sides. Elicit from learners that there are three unknown side lengths in the figure on p. 102. Discuss how to find the length of the horizontal side (*subtract the lengths of the top sides from the length of the bottom: $15 - 4 - 6 = 5$*). Discuss how to find the lengths of the unknown vertical sides (*subtract the given length from the total length: $10 - 6 = 4$*).

❸ Apply the Skill

Decoding Explain to learners that there may be more than one way to determine the area of a composite plane figure. Ask learners to share their solutions to question 5 on p. 103. Try to elicit more than one different solution. For example, the figure can be decomposed into a 10×10 square and two 5×6 rectangles, into three horizontal rectangles, or into three vertical rectangles. Guide learners to understand that each method will yield the same total area for the figure.

Answers
1. C; DOK Level: 3; **2.** D; DOK Level: 3; **3.** A; DOK Level: 3; **4.** D; DOK Level: 3; **5.** A; DOK Level: 3; **6.** D; DOK Level: 2

WORKBOOK pp. 142–145

❶ Review the Skill

Briefly review how to find the area of circles, squares, rectangles, and triangles by eliciting the formulas from learners. Ask learners to explain how to find the area of a semi-circle (*find the area of the whole circle and divide by 2*).

❷ Refine the Skill

Decoding Discuss the figure on p. 142. Ask learners to identify dimensions on the figure (length and width of rectangular section; diameter of semi-circular section). Elicit from learners that they first must find the radius of the semi-circle before they can find its area.

❸ Master the Skill

SuperSkill Review Learners can separate irregular figures into several regular figures and then determine the sum of their areas or volumes. For example, guide learners through the following multi-step process to answer question 7. To find the area of the irregular figure, learners can subtract the top rectangular figure (40×64) from the bottom rectangular figure (40×104). (To answer question 7, learners will need to divide this difference by 64, since they are to find the amount of 8 by 8 tiles that will fit on the floor.)

Answers
1. D; DOK Level: 3; **2.** A; DOK Level: 2; **3.** C; DOK Level: 3; **4.** B; DOK Level: 3; **5.** D; DOK Level: 3; **6.** C; DOK Level: 3; **7.** B; DOK Level: 3; **8.** C; DOK Level: 3; **9.** B; DOK Level: 3; **10.** C; DOK Level: 3; **11.** B; DOK Level: 3; **12.** C; DOK Level: 3; **13.** B; DOK Level: 3; **14.** B; DOK Level: 3; **15.** B; DOK Level: 3; **16.** C; DOK Level: 3; **17.** D; DOK Level: 3; **18.** A; DOK Level: 2; **19.** C; DOK Level: 3; **20.** C; DOK Level: 3; **21.** A; DOK Level: 3; **22.** C; DOK Level: 3; **23.** B; DOK Level: 3; **24.** C; DOK Level: 3; **25.** C; DOK Level: 3

Scale Drawings

MATH CONTENT TOPICS: Q.3.b, Q.3.c
MATH PRACTICES: MP.1.a, MP.1.b, MP.1.d, M.P.4.b

STUDENT BOOK *pp. 104–105*

➤ Preview the Skill

Ask learners to consider maps they have used, such as road maps or atlases. Discuss how learners may have determined the distance between two locations on the map. Elicit from learners that the distance on a map is proportional to its actual distance, and the scale on the map shows the relationship between the map distance and the actual distance.

❶ Learn the Skill

Decoding Draw two congruent triangles and label their corresponding angles and sides with equal measures. Explain that the two figures are congruent because the corresponding sides and angles have equal measure. Next, draw two similar triangles and label their corresponding angles with equal measures and their corresponding sides with proportional measures. For example, make each side of the larger triangle twice the length of the corresponding side on the smaller triangle. Elicit from learners that the ratios of corresponding side lengths are the same.

❷ Practice the Skill

Link to Past Skills In order to determine unknown measures in scale diagrams and similar figures, learners must possess a solid understanding of proportions. Have learners review the skill *Ratios and Proportions* from Unit 1, Lesson 5, to write and solve proportions.

❸ Apply the Skill

Spotlighted Item: Fill-in-the-Blank Since fill-in-the-blank items lack answer choice options, learners should carefully check their work by approaching the problem in a different way. For example, to check their answer on question 2 on p. 105, learners can use the calculated length of $\overline{FG}$ to find the length of $\overline{GH}$. If they get an answer of 10 m, their length of $\overline{FG}$ is reasonable.

Answers

1. C; DOK Level: 2; **2.** 10.8 m; DOK Level: 2; **3.** 24.8 m; DOK Level: 2; **4.** B; DOK Level: 2; **5.** D; DOK Level: 2; **6.** A; DOK Level: 3; **7.** A; DOK Level: 3

WORKBOOK *pp. 146–149*

❶ Review the Skill

Give Examples Explain to learners that if a certain distance appears to be longer than another distance on a map, then that relationship also holds true in real life. This is because maps are drawn to scale. Have learners consider how much more difficult map reading would be if maps were not drawn to scale. Explain that it would be much more difficult to determine distances and areas.

❷ Refine the Skill

Problem Solving Strategy Explain that one way to find the scale of a drawing involves writing the ratio of the measure in the diagram to the actual measure, and then simplifying the ratio. Elicit from learners that, to simplify the ratio, they first must divide each quantity in the ratio by a common factor.

❸ Master the Skill

Decoding Remind learners that the numerators of the ratios in a proportion describe the same part, as do the denominators. So, if a scale is written as the ratio $\dfrac{\text{length in drawing}}{\text{actual length}}$, then the second ratio must be written in the same way.

➤ Optional Activity

Analyze Visuals Explain that, in order to use similar figures to find a missing measure, learners must correctly identify corresponding sides. Then discuss strategies that learners can use to identify corresponding sides. For example, on question 3 on p. 147, the longer sides of each rectangle correspond, as do the shorter sides of each rectangle. In question 20 on p. 149, since $\overline{CB}$ corresponds to $\overline{GF}$, $\overline{AC}$ must correspond to $\overline{HG}$ because each forms the second leg of the right triangle.

Answers

1. C; DOK Level: 2; **2.** B; DOK Level: 2; **3.** D; DOK Level: 3; **4.** C; DOK Level: 2; **5.** A; DOK Level: 2; **6.** C; DOK Level: 2; **7.** D; DOK Level: 2; **8.** D; DOK Level: 2; **9.** B; DOK Level: 2; **10.** D; DOK Level: 2; **11.** A; DOK Level: 2; **12.** A; DOK Level: 2; **13.** B; DOK Level: 3; **14.** D; DOK Level: 2; **15.** A; DOK Level: 2; **16.** C; DOK Level: 2; **17.** C; DOK Level: 2; **18.** B; DOK Level: 2; **19.** D; DOK Level: 2; **20.** C; DOK Level: 2; **21.** B; DOK Level: 3

Prisms and Cylinders

MATH CONTENT TOPICS: Q.2.a, Q.2.e, Q.4.b, Q.5.a, Q.5.b, Q.5.c, A.2.a, A.2.b, A.2.c
MATH PRACTICES: MP.1.a, MP.1.b, MP.1.d, MP.1.e, MP.2.a, MP.2.c, MP.3.a, MP.3.b, MP.4.a, MP.4.b, MP.5.b

MATHEMATICS

STUDENT BOOK *pp. 106–107*

▶ Preview the Skill

Give Examples Tell learners that many everyday items have the shapes of prisms and cylinders. Provide examples of rectangular prisms (e.g., tissue boxes, file cabinets, textbooks) and cylinders (e.g., soup cans, fluorescent tube lights). Then, ask learners to provide additional examples.

❶ Learn the Skill

Give Examples Display to learners an empty box and explain that volume is the amount of space within the box. Then explain that surface area is the amount of paper or cardboard needed to make the box. To facilitate understanding, disassemble the box to illustrate to learners its surfaces.

❷ Practice the Skill

Decoding To help learners connect the surface area of a cylinder with its formula, have them work in small groups to construct cylinders from paper. Elicit from learners that the width of the rectangle that they use to make the lateral surface is equal to the circumference of the base, because the lateral surface wraps exactly once around the base. Then have learners calculate the surface area of the cylinder described in question 1 on p. 106 (207.24 in.²)

❸ Apply the Skill

Draw learners' attention to question 3 on p. 107. Explain that a triangular prism has two congruent triangular bases. Next, elicit from learners that the area of each triangular base is $\frac{1}{2}bh = \frac{1}{2}(4 \times 8)$. Guide learners to recognize that, since the bases are congruent, the total area of the bases is

$$2 \times \frac{1}{2}bh = bh = 4 \times 8$$

Answers
1. C; DOK Level: 1; **2.** D; DOK Level: 2; **3.** B; DOK Level: 2;
4. B; DOK Level: 2; **5.** C; DOK Level: 2; **6.** C; DOK Level: 2;
7. B; DOK Level: 3

WORKBOOK *pp. 150–153*

❶ Review the Skill

SuperSkill Review Organize learners in small groups, and have them measure the dimensions of a rectangular prism you provide or that they locate in the classroom. Next, have groups calculate the surface area and volume of a prism. Discuss the results. Ensure that learners understand the difference between volume and surface area.

❷ Refine the Skill

Link to Past Skills Explain to learners that formulas are like equations. Just as an equation can be solved for a variable, explain that a formula can be solved for an unknown quantity by first substituting the known quantities. Have learners review the skill *Equations* from Unit 3, Lesson 2, to refresh their understandings of equations and the strategies for solving them.

❸ Master the Skill

Problem Solving Strategy Elicit from learners that the formula for the area of the curved surface (lateral area) of a cylinder is $2\pi rh$. Next, elicit from learners that $2\pi r$ is the circumference of the circular base, so the area of the curved surface is the circumference multiplied by the height. Draw learners' attention to question 11 on p. 152. Guide learners to understand that, if the circumference of a cylinder is provided, they can use that circumference to find the lateral area.

▶ Optional Activity

Spotlighted Item: Drop-Down Remind learners that drop-down answer options are like multiple-choice answer options. Encourage learners to use strategies similar to those they use in answering multiple-choice questions, such as eliminating options they know to be incorrect.

Answers
1. C; DOK Level: 1; **2.** B; DOK Level: 2; **3.** A; DOK Level: 1;
4. B; DOK Level: 2; **5.** D; DOK Level: 1; **6.** A; DOK Level: 2;
7. B; DOK Level: 2; **8.** C; DOK Level: 2; **9.** D; DOK Level: 2;
10. C; DOK Level: 2; **11.** D; DOK Level: 2; **12.** B; DOK Level: 2; **13.** D; DOK Level: 2; **14.** C; DOK Level: 2; **15.** C; DOK Level: 2; **16.** A; DOK Level: 2; **17.** D; DOK Level: 2; **18.** B; DOK Level: 3; **19.** B; DOK Level: 2; **20.** C; DOK Level: 3; **21.** A; DOK Level: 3

Pyramids, Cones, and Spheres

MATH CONTENT TOPICS: Q.2.a, Q.2.e, Q.5.d, Q.5.e, A.2.a, A.2.b, A.2.c
MATH PRACTICES: MP.1.a, MP.1.b, MP.1.d, MP.1.e, MP.2.a, MP.2.c, MP.3.a, MP.3.b, MP.4.a, MP.4.b, MP.5.b

STUDENT BOOK *pp. 108–109*

➤ Preview the Skill

Inform learners that, the next time they enjoy an ice cream cone or an orange, they are using solid figures. In particular, ask students how they would measure the contents (volume) of that ice cream cone or orange. Explain that different formulas are used for the various solid figures about which they will learn.

❶ Learn the Skill

Problem Solving Strategy Ensure that learners understand the difference between the height, *h*, of a pyramid or cone, and the slant height, *s*, of a pyramid or cone. Explain that learners will need the height of a solid to determine its volume, and its slant height to determine its surface area.

❷ Practice the Skill

Link to Past Skills Have learners review the skill *Squaring, Cubing, and Taking Roots* from Unit 3, Lesson 3, for help in determining the square or cube of the radius of a sphere.

❸ Apply the Skill

Decoding Direct students' attention to p. 109 for help in learning and decoding the parts of solid figures. Tell students that faces can be polygons or circles. Show that a vertex is a single point, as in the vertex of an angle. (The term *vertices* describes more than one vertex.) Explain that a base is also a face. Use the illustrated figures to demonstrate that the height of a figure is perpendicular to that figure's base. Then discuss similarities and differences between pyramids, cones, and spheres. For example, explain that pyramids, cones, and spheres each have one base.

Answers
1. A; DOK Level: 1; **2.** B; DOK Level: 1; **3.** B; DOK Level: 2;
4. C; DOK Level: 1; **5.** B; DOK Level: 3; **6.** C; DOK Level: 1;
7. B; DOK Level: 2; **8.** D; DOK Level: 2

WORKBOOK *pp. 154–157*

❶ Review the Skill

Skim and Scan Have learners identify images of pyramids, cones, and spheres on pp. 154–157. Then, discuss the dimensions learners need to determine the surface area and volume of each type of figure.

❷ Refine the Skill

Skim and Scan Encourage learners to use logic to eliminate unreasonable answer choices. Draw learners' attention to question 2 on p. 154. Elicit from learners that, if the sheds hold the same amount of grain, they have the same volume. Guide learners to understand that if Shed B's height is less than Shed A's height, then Shed B must be wider than Shed A. Therefore, choice C must be correct.

❸ Master the Skill

Spotlighted Item: Drag-and-Drop Have learners work in pairs to discuss and decide on appropriate answers for each drag-and-drop item. Explain that if partners suggest different answers for an item, they should explain their reasoning to help one another identify any errors.

➤ Optional Activity

Enrich and Extend Explain that the slant height of a pyramid or cone can be thought of as the hypotenuse of a right triangle whose legs are the height of the figure and one-half the base of the figure. Have learners calculate the slant heights of Pyramids A and B on p. 156. (Pyramid A: 7.62 ft; Pyramid B: 7.81 ft)

Answers
1. A; DOK Level: 1; **2.** C; DOK Level: 2; **3.** B; DOK Level: 2;
4. A; DOK Level: 1; **5.** A; DOK Level: 2; **6.** B; DOK Level: 2;
7. C; DOK Level: 2; **8.** A; DOK Level: 2; **9.** B; DOK Level: 2;
10. C; DOK Level: 2; **11.** A; DOK Level: 2;

12. $V = \frac{1}{3} \times \pi \times 5^2 \times 8 = 209$; DOK Level: 3;

13. $V = \frac{1}{3} \times 144 \times 15 = 720$ ft³; DOK Level: 1;

14. C; DOK Level: 1; **15.** D; DOK Level: 1; **16.** A; DOK Level: 2;
17. A; DOK Level: 3; **18.** D; DOK Level: 2; **19.** B; DOK Level: 2;
20. C; DOK Level: 2; **21.** B; DOK Level: 2; **22.** C; DOK Level: 1;
23. D; DOK Level: 2; **24.** D; DOK Level: 2

MATHEMATICS

Composite Solids

MATH CONTENT TOPICS: Q.2.a, Q.2.e, Q.5.a, Q.5.b, Q.5.c, Q.5.d, Q.5.e, Q.5.f, A.1.a, A.1.c, A.1.g, A.2.c, A.4.b
MATH PRACTICES: MP.1.a, MP.1.b, MP.1.c, MP.1.d, MP.1.e, MP.2.c, MP.3.a, MP.4.a, MP.4.b, MP.5.c

MATHEMATICS

STUDENT BOOK pp. 110–111

▶ Preview the Skill

Ask learners to think about the shape of the building in which you're holding class. Next, work with the class to generate a rough 3-D sketch of the building. Discuss the solid figures that make up the building. For example, the building may be comprised of several rectangular prisms arranged in wings. Alternately, if the building is a simple prism, provide an image or a sketch of a more complicated structure.

❶ Learn the Skill

Problem Solving Strategy Ensure that learners understand that a cross-section is the result of cutting through a solid. For example, the cross-section of a sphere is a circle. Since the volume of a solid is equal to the area of its base times its height, one way to find the volume of a composite figure is to find the area of its cross-section and multiply by its height.

❷ Practice the Skill

Give Examples Ask learners to share their solutions for question 1 on p. 110. Try to elicit several different solutions. For example, the volume can be found by taking the area of the square and four semi-circles and then multiplying by the height; taking the area of the square and two circles and then multiplying by the height; or taking the volume of a rectangular prism and the volume of two cylinders. Discuss the results and elicit from learners that volume is the same regardless of the method used to determine it.

❸ Apply the Skill

Link to Past Skills To find surface area and volume of composite solids, learners first must understand how to find the surface area and volume of simple solids. Have learners review the skill *Prisms and Cylinders* from Unit 4, Lesson 7, and *Pyramids, Cones, and Spheres* from Unit 4, Lesson 8.

Answers
1. B; DOK Level: 2; **2.** 25; DOK Level: 2; **3.** 100; DOK Level: 2; **4.** A; DOK Level: 3; **5.** A; DOK Level: 3; **6.** C; DOK Level: 3; **7.** D; DOK Level: 2

WORKBOOK pp. 158–161

❶ Review the Skill

SuperSkill Review Review the formulas for surface area and volume of prisms, cylinders, pyramids, cones, and spheres in the book's frontmatter. Ensure that learners understand the difference between surface area and volume and can explain the meanings of variables in each formula. In particular, ensure that learners understand that s is the slant height of a pyramid or cone.

❷ Refine the Skill

SuperSkill Review Organize learners in small groups, and have each group find the surface area of the storage shed, not including its floor (*2,612 ft²*). Learners must find the area of the four walls ($4 \times 12 \times 20 = 960$), the area of the four sides of the roof

$(s = \sqrt{12^2 + 15^2} \approx 19.2 : 4 \times \frac{1}{2} \times 30 \times 19.2 = 1,152)$,

and the area of the underside of the roof that overhangs the shed ($30^2 - 20^2 = 900 - 400 = 500$).

❸ Master the Skill

Decoding Explain to learners that some composite solids involve taking parts away, as well as adding parts together. Draw learners' attention to question 18 on p. 161. Discuss the components that make up the water tower. Elicit from learners that the water tower is composed of a cylinder, a hemisphere, and a cone from which the tip has been removed. Elicit from learners that, to find the volume of the conical part, they first must find the volume of the complete cone and then subtract the volume of the smaller, removed cone.

Answers
1. C; DOK Level: 1; **2.** B; DOK Level: 2; **3.** C; DOK Level: 2; **4.** D; DOK Level: 2; **5.** B; DOK Level: 2; **6.** D; DOK Level: 2; **7.** B; DOK Level: 3; **8.** A; DOK Level: 3; **9.** C; DOK Level: 2; **10.** D; DOK Level: 2; **11.** A; DOK Level: 2; **12.** C; DOK Level: 2; **13.** B; DOK Level: 3; **14.** C; DOK Level: 3; **15.** D; DOK Level: 2; **16.** C; DOK Level: 2; **17.** D; DOK Level: 3; **18.** C; DOK Level: 2; **19.** A; DOK Level: 3; **20.** C; DOK Level: 2; **21.** B; DOK Level: 3

Unit 4 Review

MATH CONTENT TOPICS: Q.2.a, Q.2.e, Q.3.b, Q.3.c, Q.4.a, Q.4.b, Q.4.d, Q.5.a, Q.5.b, Q.5.c, Q.5.d, Q.5.e, A.2.a, A.2.b, A.2.c, A.4.a, A.4.b
MATH PRACTICES: MP.1.a, MP.1.b, MP.1.d, MP.1.e, MP.2.a, MP.2.b, MP.2.c, MP.3.a, MP.3.b, MP.4.a, MP.4.b, MP.5.a, MP.5.b, MP.5.c

You may choose to use the Unit 4 Review on Student Book pp. 112–119 as a practice test. If you wish to time the test, ask learners to complete all the items in 110 minutes.

Unit 4 Review Answers
1. B; **2.** B; **3.** C; **4.** B; **5.** 4; **6.** 7.1; **7.** 39.2 or 39.6; **8.** 22.3; **9.** 1st, 2nd and 4th figures; **10.** D; **11.** B; **12.** B; **13.** C; **14.** C; **15.** B; **16.** C; **17.** B; **18.** 9.9; **19.** B; **20.** D; **21.** C; **22.** A; **23.** B; **24.** Parallelogram: 5 cm; Triangle: 10 cm; Rectangle: 8 cm; **25.** C; **26.** C; **27.** A; **28.** C; **29.** B; **30.** C; **31.** A; **32.** B; **33.** A; **34.** B; **35.** B; **36.** A; **37.** D; **38.** C; **39.** C; **40.** 48; **41.** 10; **42.** A; **43.** D; **44.** A; **45.** 8; **46.** 89.1; **47.** C; **48.** B; **49.** B; **50.** C; **51.** 1,413 cm²; **52.** 3,140; **53.** C; **54.** A; **55.** A

Unit 4 Review Item Analysis

SKILL	DOK LEVEL 1	DOK LEVEL 2	DOK LEVEL 3
Triangles and Quadrilaterals	10	1, 5, 12, 16, 17, 24, 40, 41	
Pythagorean Theorem		3, 4, 13, 18, 32, 47	21, 33
Polygons	36	2, 9, 26	
Circles		11, 20, 22, 27, 42, 43, 49, 50	6, 7, 8, 44
Composite Plane Figures		23, 25, 29, 30	45, 46
Scale Drawings		14, 15, 28, 55	34, 54
Prisms and Cylinders	48	35, 51, 52	
Pyramids, Cones, and Spheres		31	
Composite Solids			19, 37, 38, 39, 53

Use workbook lessons, as identified in the following table, to assist learners who require additional remediation with certain skills or items having certain DOK levels.

Unit 4 Workbook Item Analysis

SKILL	DOK LEVEL 1	DOK LEVEL 2	DOK LEVEL 3
Triangles and Quadrilaterals	8	1, 2, 3, 4, 5, 9, 10, 11, 12, 13, 14, 15, 16, 17, 18, 19, 20, 22, 23, 24	6, 7, 21, 25
Pythagorean Theorem		1, 2, 3, 4, 5, 6, 7, 9, 10, 11, 12, 13, 14, 15, 17, 18, 19, 20, 21, 22, 23	8, 16, 24
Polygons	3, 10, 11	1, 2, 4, 5, 6, 7, 8, 9, 12, 16, 17, 18, 19, 20	13, 14, 15, 21, 22
Circles	3, 5, 11, 12, 14, 16	1, 4, 6, 7, 8, 9, 10, 13, 18, 19, 20, 21, 22, 23, 24, 25	2, 15, 17, 26
Composite Plane Figures	13	2, 18	1, 3, 4, 5, 6, 7, 8, 9, 10, 11, 12, 14, 15, 16, 17, 19, 20, 21, 22, 23, 24, 25
Scale Drawings		1, 2, 4, 5, 6, 7, 8, 9, 10, 11, 12, 14, 15, 16, 17, 18, 19, 20	3, 13, 21
Prisms and Cylinders	1, 3	2, 4, 5, 6, 7, 8, 9, 10, 11, 12, 13, 14, 15, 16, 17, 19	18, 20, 21
Pyramids, Cones, and Spheres	1, 4, 13, 14, 15, 22	2, 3, 5, 6, 7, 8, 9, 10, 11, 16, 18, 19, 20, 21, 23, 24	12, 17
Composite Solids	1	2, 3, 4, 5, 6, 9, 10, 11, 12, 15, 16, 18, 20	7, 8, 13, 14, 17, 19, 21

Calculator Directions

Certain items on the GED® Mathematical Reasoning Test allow for the use of a calculator to aid in answering questions. That calculator, the TI-30XS, is embedded within the testing interface. The TI-30XS calculator will be available for most items on the GED® Mathematical Reasoning Test and for some items on the GED® Science Test and GED® Social Studies Test. The TI-30XS calculator is shown below, along with callouts of some of its most important keys. A button that will enable the calculator reference sheet will appear in the upper right corner of the testing screen.

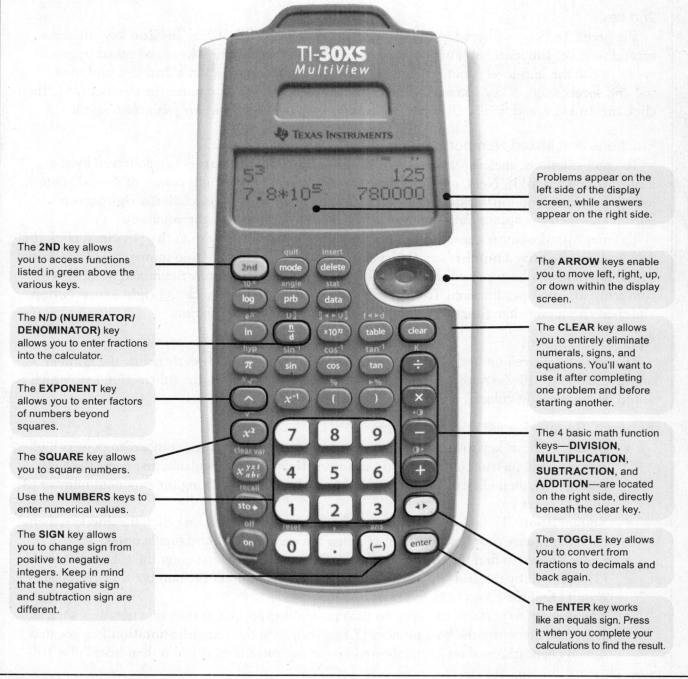

The **2ND** key allows you to access functions listed in green above the various keys.

The **N/D (NUMERATOR/ DENOMINATOR)** key allows you to enter fractions into the calculator.

The **EXPONENT** key allows you to enter factors of numbers beyond squares.

The **SQUARE** key allows you to square numbers.

Use the **NUMBERS** keys to enter numerical values.

The **SIGN** key allows you to change sign from positive to negative integers. Keep in mind that the negative sign and subtraction sign are different.

Problems appear on the left side of the display screen, while answers appear on the right side.

The **ARROW** keys enable you to move left, right, up, or down within the display screen.

The **CLEAR** key allows you to entirely eliminate numerals, signs, and equations. You'll want to use it after completing one problem and before starting another.

The 4 basic math function keys—**DIVISION**, **MULTIPLICATION**, **SUBTRACTION**, and **ADDITION**—are located on the right side, directly beneath the clear key.

The **TOGGLE** key allows you to convert from fractions to decimals and back again.

The **ENTER** key works like an equals sign. Press it when you complete your calculations to find the result.

Calculator Directions

Getting Started

To enable the calculator on a question that allows it, click on the upper left-hand portion of the testing screen. If the calculator displays over top of a problem, you may move it by clicking and dragging it to another part of the screen. Once enabled, the calculator will be ready for use (no need to push the **on** key).

- Use the **clear** key to clear all numbers and operations from the screen.
- Use the **enter** key to complete all calculations.

2nd key

The green **2nd** key is located in the upper left corner of the TI-30XS. The **2nd** key enables a second series of function keys, which are located above other function keys and noted in green type. To use the 2nd-level function, first click the numeral, next click the **2nd** key, and then click the 2nd-level function key you need. For example, to enter **25%**, first enter the number [**25**]. Then click the **2nd** key, and finally click the 2nd-level **%** key (1st-level *beginning parenthesis* sign).

Fractions and Mixed Numbers

To enter fractions, such as $\frac{3}{4}$, click the **n/d** (**numerator/denominator**) key, followed by the numerator quantity [**3**]. Next, click the **down arrow** button (upper right corner of the calculator), followed by the denominator quantity [**4**]. To calculate with fractions, click the **right arrow** button and then the appropriate function key and other numerals in the equation.

To enter mixed numbers, such as $1\frac{3}{8}$, first enter the whole number quantity [**1**]. Next, click the **2nd** key and the **mixed number** key (1st level **n/d**). Then enter the fraction numerator [**3**], followed by the **down arrow** button, and the denominator [**8**]. If you click **enter**, the mixed number will convert to an improper fraction. To calculate with mixed numbers, click the **right arrow** button and then the appropriate function key and other numerals in the equation.

Negative Numbers

To enter a negative number, click the **negative sign** key (located directly below the number **3** on the calculator). Please note that the negative sign key differs from the subtraction key, which is found in the far right column of keys, directly above the plus (+) key.

Squares, Square Roots, and Exponents

- **Squares:** The x^2 key squares numbers. The **exponent** key (^) raises numbers to powers higher than squares, such as cubes. To find the answer to 5^3 on the calculator, first enter the base number [**5**], then click the exponent key (^), and follow by clicking the exponent number [**3**], and the **enter** key.
- **Square Roots:** To find the square root of a number, such as 36, first click the **2nd** key, then click the **square root** key (1st-level x^2), then the number [**36**], and finally **enter**.
- **Cube Roots:** To find the cube root of a number, such as **125**, first enter the cube as a number [**3**], followed by the **2nd** key and **square root** key. Finally, enter the number for which you want to find the cube [**125**], followed by **enter**.
- **Exponents:** To perform calculations with numbers expressed in scientific notation, such as 7.8×10^9, first enter the base number [**7.8**]. Next, click the **scientific notation** key (located directly beneath the **data** key), followed by the exponent level [**9**]. You then have 7.8×10^9.

Formulas

Formulas for the GED® Mathematical Reasoning Test

Following are formulas that will be used on the new GED® Mathematical Reasoning Test. A button that will enable a formula reference sheet will appear in the upper left corner of the testing screen itself.

Area of a ...

Parallelogram:	$A = base \times height\ (bh)$
Trapezoid:	$A = \frac{1}{2}h\ (base_1 + base_2)$

Surface Area and Volume of a ...

Rectangular / Right Prism:	$SA = Ph + 2B$	$V = Bh$
Cylinder:	$SA = 2\pi rh + 2\pi r^2$	$V = \pi r^2 h$
Pyramid:	$SA = \frac{1}{2}Ps + B$	$V = \frac{1}{3}Bh$
Cone:	$SA = \pi rs + \pi r^2$	$V = \frac{1}{3}\pi r^2 h$
Sphere:	$SA = 4\pi r^2$	$V = \frac{4}{3}\pi r^3$

(P = perimeter of base B; π = 3.14)

Algebra

Slope of a line:	$m =$
Slope-intercept form of equation of a line:	$y = mx + b$ $\frac{y_2 - y_1}{x_2 - x_1}$
Point-slope form of equation of a line:	$y - y_1 = m(x - x_1)$
Standard form of a quadratic equation:	$y = ax^2 + bx + c$
Quadratic formula:	$x = \dfrac{-b \pm \sqrt{b^2 - 4ac}}{2a}$
Pythagorean Theorem:	$a^2 + b^2 = c^2$
Simple interest:	$I = prt$

(I = interest, p = principal, r = rate, t = time)

Glossary

UNIT 1

Absolute value: an integer's distance from zero

Base: the whole amount in a percent problem

Common denominator: when two or more fractions share the same bottom number ($\frac{3}{8}$ and $\frac{1}{8}$)

Decimal: another way to write a fraction based on the base-ten place value system; for example, $\frac{1}{4}$ would become .25

Denominator: the bottom number in a fraction

Difference: the answer to a subtraction problem

Dividend: the initial quantity in a division problem (the number being divided)

Divisor: the number by which you divide the initial quantity

Factors: numbers that can be multiplied together to get another number

Fraction: part of a whole or part of a group

Improper fraction: a fraction in which the top number (numerator) is larger than the bottom number (denominator); this should be written as a mixed number (from $\frac{5}{4}$ to $1\frac{1}{4}$)

Integers: include positive whole numbers, their opposites or negative numbers, and zero

Mixed number: a fraction that includes a whole number ($1\frac{2}{5}$)

Numerator: the top number in a fraction

Part: a piece of the whole or base in a percent problem

Percent: another way to show part of a whole; always compares amounts to 100, with 50% meaning 50 out of 100

Product: the answer to a multiplication problem

Proper fraction: a fraction, such as $\frac{3}{4}$, in which the bottom number (denominator) is larger than the top number (numerator)

Proportion: an equation with equal ratios on each side

Quotient: the answer to a division problem

Rate: tells how the base and the whole are related in a percent problem

Ratio: a comparison of two numbers; can be written as a fraction, by using the word to, or with a colon (:)

Sum: the answer to an addition problem

Whole numbers: numbers written with the digits 0 through 9

MATHEMATICS

UNIT 2

Area: the space within a two-dimensional figure

Bar graph: visual means of displaying and comparing data through either horizontal or vertical bars

Base: the bottom line segment of a figure (forms a 90° angle when paired with a height segment)

Box Plot: convenient way to show and compare sets of data using 5 characteristics of each data set: the median value, the lower (25%0 and upper (75%) quartile values, and the maximum and minimum values

Circle graph: visual means of showing how parts compare to a whole

Circumference: the distance around a circle

Congruent: exactly the same; line segments that have the same length or angles that have the same measurement

Correlation: the relationship between two or more sets of data; it may be positive, negative, or not exist at all

Cube: a three-dimensional figure with six congruent (exactly the same) square faces

Dot Plot: an easy way to organize sets of data with modest number of values (less than 50)

Elapsed time: the amount of time that has passed from one time to another

Experimental probability: establishing a probability outcome by completing an actual experiment (such as rolling a die or spinning a wheel)

Height: a line segment rising from the base on a figure (forms a 90° angle when paired with a base segment)

Histogram: are made up of adjoining bars of width to graphically demonstrate data sets

Line graph: visual means of showing changes in a data set over time

Mean: the average value of a set of data

Median: the middle number in a set of data when the values are ordered from least to greatest

Metric system: means of measurement that includes length (such as centimeter and meter), mass (such as gram and kilogram), and capacity (such as milliliter and liter)

Mode: the value that occurs most often in a set of data

Parallelogram: a four-sided figure with two congruent sides and two parallel sides

Parallel: similar line segments that are the same distance apart

Perimeter: the distance around a polygon (a multi-sided figure with straight sides)

Range: the total value covered by the data set; figure it by subtracting the least value from the greatest value

Rectangle: a four-sided figure in which the corners all are 90° angles; has two pairs of parallel sides

Rectangular prism: a three-dimensional figure shaped like a box

Scatterplot: type of line graph that shows how one set of dat affects another

Surface area: the sum of the areas of its two bases and the area of its lateral surfaces

Table: visual means of organizing information through clearly labeled columns and rows

Theoretical probability: establishing a probability outcome by using a mathematical formula

Trapezoid: a four-sided figure with only one pair of parallel sides

Triangle: a three-sided figure with three angles

U.S. customary systems: means of measurement that includes length (such as inch and foot), weight (such as ounce and pound), and capacity (such as pint and quart)

Volume: the amount of space inside a three-dimensional figure (such as a cube)

Glossary

UNIT 3

Algebra: a branch of mathematics that uses letters to represent unknown numbers; the order of operations used to solve problems to identify the unknown numbers

Algebraic expression: a set of letters, numbers, and operation signs used to solve a problem ($4x + 8x$)

An inequality: states that two algebraic expressions are not equal

Coordinate grid: a graph with an x-axis (a horizontal line) and a y-axis (a vertical line); a visual representation of points; features both positive and negative numbers

Cube root: is that number which, when cubed, equals the given number

Cube: when a number or variable is multiplied by itself three times

Equation: a mathematical statement that shows two equal quantities; shown as being on either side of an equal sign ($4x + 8x = 36$)

Exponents: when a number (the base) is multiplied by itself many times; the number of times to multiply the base number is represented as a superscript number (for example, 4^3 would be the same as $4 \times 4 \times 4$)

Factors: numbers or algebraic expressions multiplied together; represented as $4y$, meaning *4 times y*, or as ($4 + y$), meaning the sum of *4 plus y* should be multiplied by the number or expression outside the parentheses

FOIL method: a system for multiplying factors with two terms, such as ($x + 2$)($x − 4$); FOIL stands for the order in which you should multiply—the *First* two terms in each expression, then the two *Outer* terms (x and 4 in the above example), followed by the two *Inner* terms (in the above example, 2 and x), and finally the *Last* two terms

Function: an algebraic rule that defines the relationship between one variable and another; represented as $f(x)$, or simply x or y

Inequality: two algebraic expressions that are not equal; represented using the greater than (>) and less than (<) symbols (for example: $x > 3$); also used to express "greater than or equal to" (≥) or "less than or equal to" (≤)

Integers: positive or negative whole numbers (. . . 3, 2, 1, 0, −1, −2, −3. . .) used to solve algebraic problems; positive numbers sometimes written as *+3* or more often just as *3*

Inverse operation: are operations that undo each other

linear combination: is a method, or elimination, in which one or both equations are multiplied by a constant to produce new coefficients that are opposites, so that one variable may be cancelled out and the resulting equation may be solved for the other variable

Linear equation: an equation that forms a straight line when graphed

Mathematical pattern: A mathematical pattern is an arrangement of numbers and terms created by following a specific rule.

One-variable linear equation: an equation that consists of expressions involving only number values and products of constants and a variable

Ordered pair: a pair of values (an x-value and a y-value) placed on the x-axis and y-axis on a coordinate grid; represented, for example, as (5, −3)

Origin: the point on a coordinate grid at which the x-axis and the y-axis meet (0 on both axes)

Parallel: extending in the same direction, but never meeting

Perpendicular: meeting at right angles

Plot: to place a dot on a coordinate grid to represent a certain number (could be a positive or a negative number); the dot on the grid is called a *point*

Power: tells how many times a number is multiplied by itself

Quadrants: the four sections on a coordinate grid; the top two quadrants are where positive numbers are plotted and the bottom two are where negative numbers are plotted

Quadratic equation: equation in which one of the terms is squared, such as $3x^2 − y + 13x$

Rational equation: an equation that contains rational expressions

Rational expression: a fraction whose numerator, denominator, or both are nonzero polynomials

Rational number: a number that can be written in the form a/b, where a and b are integers and b does not equal 0

Rise: the number of points you must climb from one point to reach another point; becomes the numerator (top number) when slope is represented as a fraction

Run: the number of points you must move left or right to reach another point; becomes the denominator (bottom number) when the slope is represented as a fraction

Scientific notation: ability to write very large or very small numbers through the use of exponents and powers of 10

Slope: the number that measures the steepness of a line

Square root: a number that, when multiplied by itself, equals a given number

Squaring: multiplying a number by itself one time (2×2); represented as 2^2

Substitution: the method in which one of the equations is solved for one variable, and the value of that variable is substituted into the original equation to solve for the second variable

Two-variable linear equation: a mathematical, sentence that equates two expressions, whose terms are made up of number values and products of constants and variables

Variable: a letter used to represent an unknown number ($b + 6 = 10$; $3x - 8 = 4$)

y-intercept: the point on the y-axis where a line crosses

UNIT 4

Acute triangle: a triangle whose largest angle is less than 90°

Circle: a completely round shape in which all points on the perimeter (outside) are the same distance from the center

Circumference: the distance around a circle

Composite plane figure: is made up of two or more other 2-dimensional , or 2-D, shapes

Composite solids: a solid formed by two or more solids

Cone: has one circular base

Congruent figures: two or more figures that have the same shape and size

Diameter: the distance across the center of a circle, from one side to the other

Equilateral triangle: a triangle with three congruent sides

Hypotenuse: the longest side of a right triangle

Incongruent: unequal

Irregular figures: figures made up of several plane or solid shapes

Irregular polygon: has congruent sides and angles that are incongruent or unequal

Isosceles triangle: a triangle with two congruent sides

Legs: the two shorter sides of a right triangle (can be different lengths)

Obtuse triangle: a triangle whose largest angle is greater than 90°

Pyramid: a 3-dimensional figure that has a polygon as its base and triangular faces

Pythagorean theorem: named for an ancient Greek mathematician, this process describes the relationship between the sides of a right triangle; in order to find the length of the hypotenuse (the longest side of a right triangle), add the squares of the two smaller legs ($a^2 + b^2$) and then divide that sum by the square of the hypotenuse ($a^2 + b^2 = c^2$)

Polygon: is any closed figure with three or more sides

Quadrilateral: a closed four-sided figure with four angles

Radius: the distance from the center of a circle to any point on the perimeter

Regular polygon: has congruent sides and angles

Right triangle: a triangle whose largest angle is 90°

Scale drawing: a drawing that represents an actual, larger object

Scale factor: the ratio of a dimension in a scale drawing to the corresponding dimension in an actual drawing or in reality

Scalene triangle: a triangle with no congruent sides

Similar figures: two or more figures that have the same shape and congruent angles, but have proportional sides (such as two right triangles, with one being 2 inches high and one being 1 inch high)

Solid figures: three-dimensional figures, such as cubes, pyramids, and cones

Sphere: is shaped like a ball and has no bases or faces

Surface are: the sum of the areas of its two bases and the area of its lateral surfaces

Triangle: a closed three-sided figure with three angles or corners

Volume: the amount of space inside a three-dimensional figure (such as a cube)

Correlations/Mathematics

Indicator Codes	Mathematical Reasoning Practices	*Mathematical Reasoning* Book Pages
MP.1	**Building Solution Pathways and Lines of Reasoning**	
MP.1.a	Search for and recognize entry points for solving a problem.	**Student Book:** 2, 3, 4, 5, 6, 7, 8, 9, 10, 11, 12, 13, 14, 15, 26, 27, 28, 29, 30, 31, 32, 33, 34, 35, 36, 37, 50, 51, 52, 53, 54, 55, 56, 57, 58, 59, 60, 61, 62, 63, 64, 65, 66, 67, 68, 69, 70, 71, 72, 73, 74, 75, 76, 77, 78, 79, 80, 81, 82, 83, 94, 95, 96, 97, 98, 99, 100, 101, 102, 103, 104, 105, 106, 107, 108, 109, 110, 111 **Workbook:** 2, 3, 4, 5, 6, 7, 8, 9, 10, 11, 12, 13, 14, 15, 16, 17, 18, 19, 20, 21, 22, 23, 24, 25, 26, 27, 28, 29, 30, 31, 32, 33, 34, 35, 36, 37, 38, 39, 40, 41, 42, 43, 44, 45, 46, 47, 48, 49, 50, 51, 52, 53, 54, 55, 56, 57, 58, 59, 60, 61, 62, 63, 64, 65, 66, 67, 68, 69, 70, 71, 72, 73, 74, 75, 76, 77, 78, 79, 80, 81, 82, 83, 84, 85, 86, 87, 88, 89, 90, 91, 92, 93, 94, 95, 96, 97, 98, 99, 100, 101, 102, 103, 104, 105, 106, 107, 108, 109, 110, 111, 112, 113, 114, 115, 116, 117, 118, 119, 120, 121, 122, 123, 124, 125, 126, 127, 128, 129, 130, 131, 132, 133, 134, 135, 136, 137, 138, 139, 140, 141, 142, 143, 144, 145, 146, 147, 148, 149, 150, 151, 152, 153, 154, 155, 156, 157, 158, 159, 160, 161
MP.1.b	Plan a solution pathway or outline a line of reasoning.	**Student Book:** 2, 3, 4, 5, 6, 7, 8, 9, 10, 11, 12, 13, 14, 15, 26, 27, 28, 29, 30, 31, 32, 33, 34, 35, 36, 37, 50, 51, 52, 53, 54, 55, 56, 57, 58, 59, 60, 61, 62, 63, 64, 65, 66, 67, 68, 69, 70, 71, 72, 73, 74, 75, 76, 77, 78, 79, 80, 81, 82, 83, 94, 95, 96, 97, 98, 99, 100, 101, 102, 103, 104, 105, 106, 107, 108, 109, 110, 111 **Workbook:** 2, 3, 4, 5, 6, 7, 8, 9, 10, 11, 12, 13, 14, 15, 16, 17, 18, 19, 20, 21, 22, 23, 24, 25, 26, 27, 28, 29, 30, 31, 32, 33, 34, 35, 36, 37, 38, 39, 40, 41, 42, 43, 44, 45, 46, 47, 48, 49, 50, 51, 52, 53, 54, 55, 56, 57, 58, 59, 60, 61, 62, 63, 64, 65, 66, 67, 68, 69, 70, 71, 72, 73, 74, 75, 76, 77, 78, 79, 80, 81, 82, 83, 84, 85, 86, 87, 88, 89, 90, 91, 92, 93, 94, 95, 96, 97, 98, 99, 100, 101, 102, 103, 104, 105, 106, 107, 108, 109, 110, 111, 112, 113, 114, 115, 116, 117, 118, 119, 120, 121, 122, 123, 124, 125, 126, 127, 128, 129, 130, 131, 132, 133, 134, 135, 136, 137, 138, 139, 140, 141, 142, 143, 144, 145, 146, 147, 148, 149, 150, 151, 152, 153, 154, 155, 156, 157, 158, 159, 160, 161
MP.1.c	Select the best solution pathway, according to given criteria.	**Student Book:** 6, 7, 28, 29, 76, 77, 102, 103, 110, 111 **Workbook:** 2, 3, 4, 5, 6, 7, 8, 9, 10, 11, 12, 13, 110, 111, 112, 113, 114, 115, 116, 117, 142, 143, 144, 145, 158, 159, 160, 161

Correlations/Mathematics

Indicator Codes	Mathematical Reasoning Practices	*Mathematical Reasoning* Book Pages
MP.1.d	Recognize and identify missing information that is required to solve a problem.	**Student Book:** 26, 27, 106, 107, 110, 111 **Workbook:** 6, 7, 8, 9, 10, 11, 12, 13, 14, 15, 16, 17, 18, 19, 20, 21, 26, 27, 28, 29, 30, 31, 32, 33, 34, 35, 36, 37, 38, 39, 40, 41, 42, 43, 44, 45, 50, 51, 52, 53, 90, 91, 92, 93, 98, 99, 100, 101, 102, 103, 104, 105, 110, 111, 112, 113, 114, 115, 116, 117, 122, 123, 124, 125, 126, 127, 128, 129, 134, 135, 136, 137, 138, 139, 140, 141, 142, 143, 144, 145, 146, 147, 148, 149, 150, 151, 152, 153, 154, 155, 156, 157, 158, 159, 160, 161
MP.1.e	Select the appropriate mathematical technique(s) to use in solving a problem or a line of reasoning.	**Student Book:** 2, 3, 8, 9, 10, 11, 12, 13, 14, 15, 26, 27, 28, 29, 30, 31, 32, 33, 34, 35, 38, 39, 50, 51, 52, 53, 54, 55, 56, 57, 58, 59, 60, 61, 62, 63, 64, 65, 66, 67, 68, 69, 70, 71, 72, 73, 74, 75, 76, 77, 80, 81, 82, 83, 94, 95, 98, 99, 100, 101, 102, 103, 106, 107, 108, 109, 110, 111 **Workbook:** 2, 3, 4, 5, 6, 7, 8, 9, 10, 11, 12, 13, 14, 15, 16, 17, 18, 19, 20, 21, 22, 23, 24, 25, 26, 27, 28, 29, 30, 31, 32, 33, 34, 35, 36, 37, 38, 39, 40, 41, 42, 43, 44, 45, 46, 47, 48, 49, 50, 51, 52, 53, 54, 55, 56, 57, 58, 59, 60, 61, 62, 63, 64, 65, 66, 67, 68, 69, 70, 71, 72, 73, 74, 75, 76, 77, 78, 79, 80, 81, 82, 83, 84, 85, 86, 87, 88, 89, 94, 95, 96, 97, 98, 99, 100, 101, 102, 103, 104, 105, 106, 107, 108, 109, 110, 111, 112, 113, 114, 115, 116, 117, 118, 119, 120, 121, 122, 123, 124, 125, 126, 127, 128, 129, 134, 135, 136, 137, 138, 139, 140, 141, 150, 151, 152, 153, 154, 155, 156, 157, 158, 159, 160, 161
MP.2	**Abstracting Problems**	
MP.2. a	62, 63, 64, 65,	**Student Book:** 50, 51, 52, 53, 58, 59, 60, 61, 62, 63, 64, 65, 66, 67, 68, 69, 94, 95, 106, 107, 108, 109 **Workbook:** 58, 59, 60, 61, 74, 75, 76, 77, 78, 79, 80, 81, 82, 83, 84, 85, 86, 87, 88, 89, 90, 91, 92, 93, 94, 95, 96, 97, 106, 107, 108, 109, 114, 115, 116, 117, 126, 127, 128, 129, 134, 135, 136, 137, 150, 151, 152, 153, 154, 155, 156, 157
MP.2. b	Represent real world problems visually.	**Student Book:** 94, 95, 96, 97, 98, 99 **Workbook:** 126, 127, 128, 129, 130, 131, 132, 133, 134, 135, 136, 137

MATHEMATICS

Correlations/Mathematics

Indicator Codes	Mathematical Reasoning Practices	*Mathematical Reasoning* Book Pages
MP.2.c	Recognize the important and salient attributes of a problem.	**Student Book:** 2, 3, 4, 5, 6, 7, 8, 9, 10, 11, 12, 13, 14, 15, 26, 27, 28, 29, 30, 31, 32, 33, 34, 35, 36, 37, 38, 39, 50, 51, 52, 53, 54, 55, 56, 57, 58, 59, 62, 63, 64, 65, 66, 67, 68, 69, 70, 71, 72, 73, 74, 75, 76, 77, 78, 79, 80, 81, 82, 83, 94, 95, 98, 99, 100, 101, 106, 107, 108, 109, 110, 111 **Workbook:** 2, 3, 4, 5, 6, 7, 8, 9, 14, 15, 16, 17, 18, 19, 20, 21, 22, 23, 24, 25, 26, 27, 28, 29, 30, 31, 32, 33, 34, 35, 36, 37, 38, 39, 40, 41, 42, 43, 44, 45, 46, 47, 48, 49, 50, 51, 52, 53, 54, 55, 56, 57, 58, 59, 60, 61, 62, 63, 64, 65, 66, 67, 68, 69, 70, 71, 72, 73, 74, 75, 76, 77, 82, 83, 84, 85, 86, 87, 88, 89, 90, 91, 92, 93, 94, 95, 96, 97, 98, 99, 100, 101, 102, 103, 104, 105, 106, 107, 108, 109, 110, 111, 112, 113, 114, 115, 116, 117, 118, 119, 120, 121, 122, 123, 124, 125, 126, 127, 128, 129, 134, 135, 136, 137, 138, 139, 140, 141, 150, 151, 152, 153, 154, 155, 156, 157, 158, 159, 160, 161
MP.3	**Furthering Lines of Reasoning**	**54, 55, 56, 57**
MP.3.a	Build steps of a line of reasoning or solution pathway, based on previous step or givens.	**Student Book:** 4, 5, 6, 7, 8, 9, 10, 11, 12, 13, 14, 15, 26, 27, 28, 29, 32, 33, 34, 35, 36, 37, 38, 39, 50, 51, 52, 53, 54, 55, 56, 57, 58, 59, 60, 61, 62, 63, 64, 65, 66, 67, 68, 69, 70, 71, 72, 73, 74, 75, 76, 77, 78, 79, 80, 81, 82, 83, 98, 99, 102, 103, 106, 107, 108, 109, 110, 111 **Workbook:** 2, 3, 4, 5, 6, 7, 8, 9, 10, 11, 12, 13, 18, 19, 20, 21, 22, 23, 24, 25, 26, 27, 28, 29, 34, 35, 36, 37, 38, 39, 40, 41, 42, 43, 44, 45, 46, 47, 48, 49, 50, 51, 52, 53, 54, 55, 56, 57, 58, 59, 60, 61, 62, 63, 64, 65, 66, 67, 68, 69, 70, 71, 72, 73, 74, 75, 76, 77, 78, 79, 80, 81, 82, 83, 84, 85, 86, 87, 88, 89, 90, 91, 92, 93, 94, 95, 96, 97, 98, 99, 100, 101, 102, 103, 104, 105, 106, 107, 108, 109, 110, 111, 112, 113, 114, 115, 116, 117, 118, 119, 120, 121, 122, 123, 124, 125, 134, 135, 136, 137, 142, 143, 144, 145, 150, 151, 152, 153, 154, 155, 156, 157, 158, 159, 160, 161
MP.3.b	Complete the lines of reasoning of others.	**Student Book:** 98, 99, 106, 107 **Workbook:** 42, 43, 44, 45, 78, 79, 80, 81, 90, 91, 92, 93, 134, 135, 136, 137, 150, 151, 152, 153, 154, 155, 156, 157
MP.3.c	Improve or correct a flawed line of reasoning.	**Student Book:** 12, 13, 56, 57, 66, 67 **Workbook:** 42, 43, 44, 45, 130, 131, 132, 133

Correlations/Mathematics

Indicator Codes	Mathematical Reasoning Practices	*Mathematical Reasoning* Book Pages
MP.4	**Mathematical Fluency**	
MP.4.a	Manipulate and solve arithmetic expressions.	**Student Book:** 4, 5, 6, 7, 8, 9, 10, 11, 12, 13, 14, 15, 26, 27, 28, 29, 50, 51, 52, 53, 54, 55, 56, 57, 58, 59, 62, 63, 66, 67, 70, 71, 78, 79, 80, 81, 98, 99, 100, 101, 106, 107, 108, 109, 110, 111 **Workbook:** 10, 11, 12, 13, 14, 15, 16, 17, 18, 19, 20, 21, 22, 23, 24, 25, 26, 27, 28, 29, 30, 31, 32, 33, 34, 35, 36, 37, 38, 39, 40, 41, 42, 43, 44, 45, 46, 47, 48, 49, 50, 51, 52, 53, 54, 55, 56, 57, 58, 59, 60, 61, 62, 63, 64, 65, 66, 67, 68, 69, 70, 71, 72, 73, 74, 75, 76, 77, 78, 79, 80, 81, 82, 83, 84, 85, 86, 87, 88, 89, 90, 91, 92, 93, 94, 95, 96, 97, 102, 103, 104, 105, 106, 107, 108, 109, 110, 111, 112, 113, 114, 115, 116, 117, 118, 119, 120, 121, 122, 123, 124, 125, 126, 127, 128, 129, 138, 139, 140, 141, 150, 151, 152, 153, 154, 155, 156, 157, 158, 159, 160, 161
MP.4.b	Transform and solve algebraic expressions.	**Student Book:** 50, 51, 52, 53, 56, 57, 58, 59, 60, 61, 62, 63, 64, 65, 68, 69, 72, 73, 76, 77, 78, 79, 94, 95, 96, 97, 100, 101, 104, 105, 106, 107, 108, 109, 110, 111 **Workbook:** 58, 59, 60, 61, 62, 63, 64, 65, 66, 67, 68, 69, 70, 71, 72, 73, 74, 75, 76, 77, 82, 83, 84, 85, 86, 87, 88, 89, 90, 91, 92, 93, 94, 95, 96, 97, 102, 103, 104, 105, 114, 115, 116, 117, 126, 127, 128, 129, 130, 131, 132, 133, 138, 139, 140, 141, 146, 147, 148, 149, 150, 151, 152, 153, 154, 155, 156, 157, 158, 159, 160, 161
MP.4.c	Display data or algebraic expressions graphically.	**Student Book:** 34, 35, 36, 37, 38, 39, 70, 71, 72, 73, 74, 75, 80, 81, 82, 83 **Workbook:** 46, 47, 48, 49, 50, 51, 52, 53, 54, 55, 56, 57, 98, 99, 100, 101, 102, 103, 104, 105, 106, 107, 108, 109, 114, 115, 116, 117, 118, 119, 120, 121, 122, 123, 124, 125, 134, 135, 136, 137
MP.5	**Evaluating Reasoning and Solution Pathways**	
MP.5.a	Recognize flaws in others' reasoning.	**Student Book:** 34, 35, 54, 55, 60, 61, 66, 67 **Workbook:** 42, 43, 44, 45, 70, 71, 72, 73, 78, 79, 80, 81, 82, 83, 84, 85, 90, 91, 92, 93, 122, 123, 124, 125, 126, 127, 128, 129, 130, 131, 132, 133
MP.5.b	Recognize and use counterexamples.	**Student Book:** 54, 55 **Workbook:** 42, 43, 44, 45, 118, 119, 120, 121, 126, 127, 128, 129, 134, 135, 136, 137, 150, 151, 152, 153, 154, 155, 156, 157
MP.5.c	Identify the information required to evaluate a line of reasoning.	**Student Book:** 2, 3, 4, 5, 50, 51, 54, 55, 56, 57, 58, 59, 60, 61, 62, 63, 66, 67, 76, 77, 78, 79, 80, 81, 102, 103, 110, 111 **Workbook:** 6, 7, 8, 9, 42, 43, 44, 45, 70, 71, 72, 73, 82, 83, 84, 85, 90, 91, 92, 93, 110, 111, 112, 113, 114, 115, 116, 117, 118, 119, 120, 121, 142, 143, 144, 145, 158, 159, 160, 161

MATHEMATICS

Correlations/Mathematics

Indicator Codes	Mathematical Reasoning Content Topics	*Mathematical Reasoning* Book Pages
Quantitative Problem Solving Indicators		
Q.1	**Apply number sense concepts, including ordering rational numbers, absolute value, multiples, factors, and exponents**	
Q.1.a	Order fractions and decimals, including on a number line.	**Student Book:** 8, 9, 12, 13, 30, 31 **Workbook:** 14, 15, 16, 17, 22, 23, 24, 25, 30, 31, 32, 33, 38, 39, 40, 41
Q.1.b	Apply number properties involving multiples and factors, such as using the least common multiple, greatest common factor, or distributive property to rewrite numeric expressions.	**Student Book:** 4, 5, 8, 9, 32, 33, 64, 65, 66, 67 **Workbook:** 6, 7, 8, 9, 14, 15, 16, 17, 30, 31, 32, 33, 58, 59, 60, 61
Q.1.c	Apply rules of exponents in numerical expressions with rational exponents to write equivalent expressions with rational exponents.	**Student Book:** 56, 57 **Workbook:** 66, 67, 68, 69, 70, 71, 72, 73
Q.1.d	Identify absolute value or a rational number as its distance from 0 on the number line and determine the distance between two rational numbers on the number line, including using the absolute value of their difference.	**Student Book:** 6, 7, 8, 9 **Workbook:** 10, 11, 12, 13
Q.2	**Add, subtract, multiply, divide, and use exponents and roots of rational, fraction and decimal numbers**	
Q.2.a	Perform addition, subtraction, multiplication, and division on rational numbers.	**Student Book:** 4, 5, 6, 7, 8, 9, 10, 11, 12, 13, 14, 15, 26, 27, 28, 29, 30, 31, 38, 39, 50, 51, 52, 53, 54, 55, 56, 57, 58, 59, 62, 63, 66, 67, 74, 75, 76, 77, 78, 79, 80, 81, 94, 95, 98, 99, 100, 101, 106, 107, 108, 109, 110, 111 **Workbook:** 2, 3, 4, 5, 6, 7, 8, 9, 10, 11, 12, 13, 14, 15, 16, 17, 18, 19, 20, 21, 22, 23, 24, 25, 26, 27, 28, 29, 30, 31, 32, 33, 34, 35, 36, 37, 38, 39, 40, 41, 42, 43, 44, 45, 46, 47, 48, 49, 50, 51, 52, 53, 54, 55, 56, 57, 58, 59, 60, 61, 62, 63, 64, 65, 66, 67, 68, 69, 70, 71, 72, 73, 74, 75, 76, 77, 78, 79, 80, 81, 82, 83, 84, 85, 86, 87, 88, 89, 90, 91, 92, 93, 98, 99, 100, 101, 102, 103, 104, 105, 110, 111, 112, 113, 114, 115, 116, 117, 118, 119, 120, 121, 122, 123, 124, 125, 126, 127, 128, 129, 134, 135, 136, 137, 138, 139, 140, 141, 150, 151, 152, 153, 154, 155, 156, 157, 158, 159, 160, 161
Q.2.b	Perform computations and write numerical expressions with squares and square roots of positive, rational numbers.	**Student Book:** 54, 55, 56, 57, 58, 59, 60, 61, 96, 97 **Workbook:** 66, 67, 68, 69, 70, 71, 72, 73, 74, 75, 76, 77
Q.2.c	Perform computations and write numerical expressions with cubes and cube roots of rational numbers	**Student Book:** 54, 55, 56, 57 **Workbook:** 66, 67, 68, 69, 70, 71, 72, 73, 74, 75, 76, 77
Q.2.d	Determine when a numerical expression is undefined.	**Student Book:** 8, 9, 54, 55, 56, 57 **Workbook:** 14, 15, 16, 17, 30, 31, 32, 33, 66, 67, 68, 69, 70, 71, 72, 73, 106, 107, 108, 109, 110, 111, 112, 113

MATHEMATICS

Correlations/Mathematics

Indicator Codes	Mathematical Reasoning Content Topics	*Mathematical Reasoning* Book Pages
Q.2.e	Solve one-step or multi-step arithmetic, real world problems involving the four operations with rational numbers, including those involving scientific notation	**Student Book:** 4, 5, 6, 7, 8, 9, 10, 11, 12, 13, 14, 15, 26, 27, 28, 29, 30, 31, 50, 51, 52, 53, 54, 55, 56, 57, 58, 59, 60, 61, 62, 63, 66, 67,74, 75, 94, 95, 98, 99, 100, 101, 106, 107, 108, 109, 110, 111 **Workbook:** 6, 7, 8, 9, 10, 11, 12, 13, 14, 15, 16, 17, 18, 19, 20, 21, 22, 23, 24, 25, 26, 27, 28, 29, 34, 35, 36, 37, 38, 39, 40, 41, 42, 43, 44, 45, 46, 47, 48, 49, 50, 51, 52, 53, 54, 55, 56, 57, 58, 59, 60, 61, 62, 63, 64, 65, 66, 67, 68, 69, 70, 71, 72, 73, 74, 75, 76, 77, 78, 79, 80, 81, 82, 83, 84, 85, 86, 87, 88, 89, 90, 91, 92, 93, 98, 99, 100, 101, 102, 103, 104, 105, 106, 107, 108, 109, 110, 111, 112, 113, 114, 115, 116, 117, 122, 123, 124, 125, 126, 127, 128, 129, 134, 135, 136, 137, 138, 139, 140, 141, 150, 151, 152, 153, 154, 155, 156, 157, 158, 159, 160, 161
Q.3	**Calculate and use ratios, percents and scale factors**	
Q.3.a	Compute unit rates. Examples include but are not limited to: unit pricing, constant speed, persons per square mile, BTUs per cubic foot.	**Student Book:** 10, 11, 26, 27, 6, 7, 8, 9 **Workbook:** 14, 15, 16, 17, 18, 19, 20, 21, 22, 23, 24, 25, 30, 31, 32, 33, 62, 63, 64, 65, 78, 79, 80, 81, 86, 87, 88, 89
Q.3.b	Use scale factors to determine the magnitude of a size change. Convert between actual drawings and scale drawings.	**Student Book:** 104, 105 **Workbook:** 18, 19, 20, 21, 30, 31, 32, 33, 34, 35, 36, 37,146, 147, 148, 149
Q.3.c	Solve multistep, arithmetic, real-world problems using ratios or proportions including those that require converting units of measure.	**Student Book:** 10, 11, 14, 15, 26, 27, 104, 105 **Workbook:** 18, 19, 20, 21, 26, 27, 28, 29, 42, 43, 44, 45, 146, 147, 148, 149
Q.3.d	Solve two-step, arithmetic, real world problems involving percents. Examples include but are not limited to: simple interest, tax, markups and markdowns, gratuities and commissions, percent increase and decrease.	**Student Book:** 14, 15, 58, 59, 60, 61 **Workbook:** 26, 27, 28, 29, 42, 43, 44, 45, 62, 63, 64, 65, 74, 75, 76, 77
Q.4	**Solve multistep, arithmetic, real-world problems using ratios or proportions including those that require converting units of measure.Calculate dimensions, perimeter, circumference, and area of two-dimensional figures**	
Q.4.a	Compute the area and perimeter of triangles and rectangles. Determine side lengths of triangles and rectangles when given area or perimeter.	**Student Book:** 28, 29, 56, 57, 64, 65, 94, 95, 98, 99, 102, 103 **Workbook:** 34, 35, 36, 37, 58, 59, 60, 61, 66, 67, 68, 69, 78, 79, 80, 81, 86, 87, 88, 89, 126, 127, 128, 129, 130, 131, 132, 133, 142, 143, 144, 145
Q.4.b	Compute the area and circumference of circles. Determine the radius or diameter when given area or circumference	**Student Book:** 100, 101, 102, 103, 106, 107 **Workbook:** 138, 139, 140, 141, 142, 143, 144, 145
Q.4.c	Use the Pythagorean theorem to determine unknown side lengths in a right triangle	**Student Book:** 28, 29, 94, 95, 98, 99, 102, 103 **Workbook:** 34, 35, 36, 37, 66, 67, 68, 69,86, 87, 88, 89, 126, 127, 128, 129, 134, 135, 136, 137
Q.4.d	Compute perimeter and area of 2-D composite geometric figures, which could include Compute perimeter and area of 2-D composite geometric figures, which could include circles, given geometric formulas as needed.	**Student Book:** 28, 29, 98, 99, 102, 103 **Workbook:** 34, 35, 36, 37, 126, 127, 128, 129, 142, 143, 144, 145

Correlations/Mathematics

Indicator Codes	Mathematical Reasoning Content Topics	*Mathematical Reasoning* Book Pages
Q.4.e	Use the Pythagorean theorem to determine unknown side lengths in a right triangle	**Student Book:** 97 **Workbook:** 130, 131, 132, 133
Q.5	**Calculate dimensions, surface area, and volume of three-dimensional figures**	
Q.5.a	When given geometric formulas, compute volume and surface area of rectangular prisms. Solve for side lengths or height, when given volume or surface area.	**Student Book:** 28, 29,106, 107, 110, 111 **Workbook:** 34, 35, 36, 37, 150, 151, 152, 153, 158, 159, 160, 161
Q.5.b	When given geometric formulas, compute volume and surface area of cylinders. Solve for height, radius, or diameter when given volume or surface area.	**Student Book:** 106, 107, 110, 111 **Workbook:** 150, 151, 152, 153, 158, 159, 160, 161
Q.5.c	When given geometric formulas, compute volume and surface area of right prisms. Solve for side lengths or height, when given volume or surface area.	**Student Book:** 106, 107, 110, 111 **Workbook:** 34, 35, 36, 37, 150, 151, 152, 153, 158, 159, 160, 161
Q.5.d	When given geometric formulas, compute volume and surface area of right pyramids and cones. Solve for side lengths, height, radius, or diameter when given volume or surface area.	**Student Book:** 108, 109, 110, 111 **Workbook:** 154, 155, 156, 157, 158, 159, 160, 161
Q.5.e	When given geometric formulas, compute volume and surface area of spheres. Solve for radius or diameter when given the surface area.	**Student Book:** 108, 109 **Workbook:** 154, 155, 156, 157, 158, 159, 160, 161
Q.5.f	Compute surface area and volume of composite 3-D geometric figures, given geometric formulas as needed	**Student Book:** 28, 29, 110, 111 **Workbook:** 34, 35, 36, 37, 158, 159, 160, 161
Q.6	**Interpret and create data displays**	
Q.6.a	Represent, display, and interpret categorical data in bar graphs or circle graphs.	**Student Book:** 34, 35, 36, 37 **Workbook:** 46, 47, 48, 49, 50, 51, 52, 53
Q.6.b	Represent, display, and interpret data involving one variable plots on the real number line including dot plots, histograms, and box plots.	**Student Book:** 38, 39 **Workbook:** 54, 55, 56, 57
Q.6.c	Represent, display, and interpret data involving two variables in tables and the coordinate plane including scatter plots and graphs	**Student Book:** 2, 3, 6, 7, 8, 9, 10, 11, 12, 13, 14, 15, 26, 27, 30, 31, 32, 33, 34, 35, 58, 59, 70, 71, 74, 75, 76, 77, 78, 79, 80, 81, 82, 83 **Workbook:** 2, 3, 4, 5, 6, 7, 8, 9, 10, 11, 12, 13, 14, 15, 16, 17, 18, 19, 20, 21, 22, 23, 24, 25, 26, 27, 28, 29, 30, 31, 32, 33, 38, 39, 40, 41, 42, 43, 44, 45, 46, 47, 48, 49, 70, 71, 72, 73, 74, 75, 76, 77, 82, 83, 84, 85, 98, 99, 100, 101, 102, 103, 104, 105, 110, 111, 112, 113, 114, 115, 116, 117, 118, 119, 120, 121, 122, 123, 124, 125
Q.7	**Calculate and use mean, median, modeand weighted average**	
Q.7.a	Calculate the mean, median, mode and range. Calculate a missing data value, given the average and all the missing data values but one, as well as calculating the average, given the frequency counts of all the data values, and calculating a weighted average.	**Student Book:** 4, 5, 30, 31,38, 39 **Workbook:** 38, 39, 40, 41

Correlations/Mathematics

Indicator Codes	Mathematical Reasoning Content Topics	*Mathematical Reasoning* Book Pages
Q.8	**Utilize counting techniques and determine probabilities**	
Q.8.a	Use counting techniques to solve problems and determine combinations and permutations.	**Student Book:** N/A **Workbook:** 42, 43, 44, 45
Q.8.b	Determine the probability of simple and compound events	**Student Book:** 32,33 **Workbook:** 42, 43,44, 45
Algebraic Problem Solving		
A.1	**Write, evaluate, and compute with expressions and polynomials**	
A.1.a	Add, subtract, factor, multiply and expand linear expressions with rational coefficients.	**Student Book:** 50, 51, 52, 53, 64, 65, 66, 67, 110, 111 **Workbook:** 58, 59, 60, 61, 62, 63, 64, 65, 70, 71, 72, 73, 86, 87, 88, 89, 90, 91, 92, 93, 158, 159, 160, 161
A.1.b	Evaluate linear expressions by substituting integers for unknown quantities.	**Student Book:** 52, 53, 58, 59, 72, 73 **Workbook:** 58, 59, 60, 61, 66, 67, 68, 69, 74, 75, 76, 77, 102, 103, 104, 105
A.1.c	Write linear expressions as part of word-to-symbol translations or to represent common settings.	**Student Book:** 50, 51, 52, 53 **Workbook:** 58, 59, 60, 61, 158, 159, 160, 161
A.1.d	Add, subtract, multiply polynomials, including multiplying two binomials, or divide factorable polynomials.	**Student Book:** 56, 57, 64, 65, 66, 67 **Workbook:** 58, 59, 60, 61, 70, 71, 72, 73
A.1.e	Evaluate polynomial expressions by substituting integers for unknown quantities.	**Student Book:** 54, 55, 56, 57, 58, 59 **Workbook:** 58, 59, 60, 61, 70, 71, 72, 73, 74, 75, 76, 77, 114, 115, 116, 117, 118, 119, 120, 121
A.1.f	Factor polynomial expressions	**Student Book:** 56, 57, 64, 65, 66, 67 **Workbook:** 70, 71, 72, 73, 86, 87, 88, 89, 90, 91, 92, 93, 114, 115, 116, 117, 118, 119, 120, 121
A.1.g	Write polynomial expressions as part of word-to-symbol translations or to represent common settings.	**Student Book:** 50, 51, 110, 111 **Workbook:** 58, 59, 60, 61, 86, 87, 88, 89, 114, 115, 116, 117, 158, 159, 160, 161
A.1.h	Add, subtract, multiply and divide rational expressions.	**Student Book:** 66, 67 **Workbook:** 90, 91, 92, 93
A.1.i	Evaluate rational expressions by substituting integers for unknown quantities.	**Student Book:** 58, 59 **Workbook:** 58, 59, 60, 61, 70, 71, 72, 73, 106, 107, 108, 109, 118, 119, 120, 121
A.1.j	Write rational expressions as part of word-to-symbol translations or to represent common settings.	**Student Book:** 52, 53 **Workbook:** 58, 59, 60, 61, 62, 63, 64, 65
A.2	**Write, manipulate, and solve linear equations**	
A.2.a	Solve one-variable linear equations with rational number coefficients, including equations whose solutions require expanding expressions using the distributive property and collecting like terms or equations with coefficients represented by letters.	**Student Book:** 52, 53, 60, 61, 62, 63, 94, 95 **Workbook:** 62, 63, 64, 65, 78, 79, 80, 81, 126, 127, 128, 129, 138, 139, 140, 141, 150, 151, 152, 153, 154, 155, 156, 157
A.2.b	Solve real-world problems involving linear equations.	**Student Book:** 60, 61, 62, 63, 94, 95 **Workbook:** 78, 79, 80, 81, 82, 83, 84, 85, 126, 127, 128, 129, 150, 151, 152, 153, 154, 155, 156, 157

Correlations/Mathematics

Indicator Codes	Mathematical Reasoning Content Topics	*Mathematical Reasoning* Book Pages
A.2.c	Write one-variable and multi-variable linear equations to represent context.	**Student Book:** 52, 53, 60, 61, 110, 111 **Workbook:** 62, 63, 64, 65, 74, 75, 76, 77, 126, 127, 128, 129, 138, 139, 140, 141, 150, 151, 152, 153, 154, 155, 156, 157, 158, 159, 160, 161
A.2.d	Solve a system of two simultaneous linear equations by graphing, substitution, or linear combination. Solve real-world problems leading to a system of linear equations.	**Student Book:** 62, 63 **Workbook:** 82, 83, 84, 85, 102, 103, 104, 105
A.3	**Write, manipulate, solve, and graph linear inequalities**	
A.3.a	Solve linear inequalities in one variable with rational number coefficients.	**Student Book:** 68, 69 **Workbook:** 94, 95, 96, 97
A.3.b	Identify or graph the solution to a one variable linear inequality on a number line.	**Student Book:** 68, 69 **Workbook:** 94, 95, 96, 97
A.3.c	Solve real-world problems involving inequalities	**Student Book:** 68, 69 **Workbook:** 94, 95, 96, 97
A.3.d	Write linear inequalities in one variable to represent context.	**Student Book:** 68, 69 **Workbook:** 94, 95, 96, 97
A.4	**Write, manipulate, and solve quadratic equations**	
A.4.a	Solve quadratic equations in one variable with rational coefficients and real solutions, using appropriate methods. (e.g., quadratic formula, completing the square, factoring, inspection)	**Student Book:** 64, 65, 66, 67, 78, 79 **Workbook:** 86, 87, 88, 89, 114, 115, 116, 117, 130, 131, 132, 133
A.4.b	Write one-variable quadratic equations to represent context	**Student Book:** 64, 65, 110, 111 **Workbook:** 86, 87, 88, 89, 114, 115, 116, 117, 130, 131, 132, 133, 158, 159, 160, 161
A.5	**Connect and interpret graphs and functions**	
A.5.a	Locate points in the coordinate plane.	**Student Book:** 70, 71, 72, 73, 76, 77, 78, 79 **Workbook:** 98, 99, 100, 101, 102, 103, 104, 105, 110, 111, 112, 113, 114, 115, 116, 117
A.5.b	Determine the slope of a line from a graph, equation, or table.	**Student Book:** 74, 75, 76, 77 **Workbook:** 106, 107, 108, 109, 110, 111, 112, 113
A.5.c	Interpret unit rate as the slope in a proportional relationship.	**Student Book:** N/A **Workbook:** 106, 107, 108, 109
A.5.d	Graph two-variable linear equations.	**Student Book:** 72, 73 **Workbook:** 102, 103, 104, 105
A.5.e	For a function that models a linear or nonlinear relationship between two quantities, interpret key features of graphs and tables in terms of quantities, and sketch graphs showing key features of graphs and tables in terms of quantities, and sketch graphs showing key features given a verbal description of the relationship. Key features include: intercepts; intervals where the function is increasing, decreasing, positive, or negative; relative maximums and minimums; symmetries; end behavior, and periodicity.	**Student Book:** 78, 79, 80, 81, 82, 83 **Workbook:** 114, 115, 116, 117, 118, 119, 120, 121, 122, 123, 124, 125
A.6	**Connect coordinates, lines, and equations**	
A.6.a	Write the equation of a line with a given slope through a given point.	**Student Book:** 36, 37, 74, 75, 76, 77 **Workbook:** 106, 107, 108, 109, 110, 111, 112, 113

MATHEMATICS

Correlations/Mathematics

Indicator Codes	Mathematical Reasoning Content Topics	*Mathematical Reasoning* Book Pages
A.6.b	Write the equation of a line passing through two given distinct points.	**Student Book:** 74, 75, 76, 77 **Workbook:** 106, 107, 108, 109, 110, 111, 112, 113
A.6.c	Use slope to identify parallel and perpendicular lines and to solve geometric problems. Compare, represent, and evaluate functions.	**Student Book:** 76, 77 **Workbook:** 110, 111, 112, 113
A.7	**Compare, represent, and evaluate functions**	
A.7.a	Compare two different proportional relationships represented in different ways. Examples include but are not limited to: compare a distance-time graph to a distance-time equation to determine which of two moving objects has a greater speed.	**Student Book:** 58, 59, 82, 83 **Workbook:** 74, 75, 76, 77, 122, 123, 124, 125
A.7.b	Represent or identify a function in a table or graph as having exactly one output (one element in the range) for each input (each element in the domain).	**Student Book:** 58, 59, 80, 81 **Workbook:** 74, 75, 76, 77, 118, 119, 120, 121, 122, 123, 124, 125
A.7.c	Evaluate linear and quadratic functions for values in their domain when represented using function notation.	**Student Book:** 80, 81, 82, 83 **Workbook:** 74, 75, 76, 77, 122, 123, 124, 125
A.7.d	Compare properties of two linear or quadratic functions each represented in a different way (algebraically, numerically in tables, graphically or by verbal descriptions). Examples include but are not limited to: given a linear function represented by a table of values and a linear function represented by an algebraic expression, determine which function has the greater rate of change	**Student Book:** 82, 83 **Workbook:** 122, 123, 124, 125

MATHEMATICS

MATHEMATICS

Table of Contents

Table of Contents..SCI 1
About *Steck-Vaughn Test Preparation for the 2014
GED® Test: Science*..SCI 2

UNIT 1 *Life Science*...SCI 3
LESSON
1: Interpret Illustrations...SCI 4
2: Identify Main Idea and Details.......................SCI 5
3: Interpret Tables..SCI 6
4: Identify Cause and Effect...............................SCI 7
5: Interpret Graphs and Maps.............................SCI 8
6: Interpret Diagrams...SCI 9
7: Categorize and Classify................................SCI 10
8: Generalize...SCI 11
9: Compare and Contrast..................................SCI 12
10: Relate Text and Visuals..............................SCI 13
11: Understand Content-Based Tools................SCI 14
12: Use Context Clues.......................................SCI 15
13: Understand Scientific Evidence...................SCI 16
14: Make and Identify Inferences......................SCI 17
15: Draw Conclusions..SCI 18
Unit 1 Review............................... SCI 19–SCI 20

UNIT 2 *Physical Science*............................SCI 21
LESSON
1: Understand Scientific Models.........................SCI 22
2: Interpret Complex Visuals..............................SCI 23
3: Interpret Complex Tables...............................SCI 24
4: Understand Chemical Equations....................SCI 25
5: Predict Outcomes..SCI 26
6: Calculate to Interpret Outcomes....................SCI 27
7: Understand Vector Diagrams.........................SCI 28
8: Apply Scientific Laws.....................................SCI 29
9: Access Prior Knowledge................................SCI 30
10: Link Microscopic and Observable Events.....SCI 31
11: Interpret Observations.................................SCI 32
12: Link Content from Varied Formats................SCI 33
13: Draw Conclusions from Mixed Sources........SCI 34
14: Understand Investigation Techniques...........SCI 35
15: Evaluate Scientific Information.....................SCI 36
Unit 2 Review....................................... SCI 37–SCI 38

UNIT 3 *Earth and Space Science*..............SCI 39
LESSON
1: Understand Scientific Theories......................SCI 40
2: Summarize Complex Material........................SCI 41
3: Understand Patterns in Science.....................SCI 42
4: Interpret Three-Dimensional Diagrams..........SCI 43
5: Apply Science Concepts................................SCI 44
6: Express Scientific Information........................SCI 45
7: Identify Problem and Solution.......................SCI 46
8: Analyze and Present Arguments....................SCI 47
Unit 3 Review...SCI 48

APPENDIX...SCI 49
Glossary..SCI 49

CORRELATIONS/SCIENCE............ SCI 50–SCI 56

SCIENCE

About *Steck-Vaughn Test Preparation for the 2014 GED® Test: Science*

Steck-Vaughn's student book and workbook help unlock the learning and deconstruct the different elements of the test by helping learners build and develop core reading and thinking skills. The content of our books aligns to the new GED® science content standards and item distribution to provide learners with a superior test preparation experience.

Our *Spotlighted Item* feature provides a deeper, richer treatment for each technology-enhanced item type. On initial introduction, a unique item type—such as drag-and-drop—receives a full page of example items in the student book lesson and three pages in the companion workbook. The length of subsequent features may be shorter depending on the skill, lesson, and requirements.

A combination of targeted strategies, informational callouts and sample questions, assorted tips and hints, and ample assessment help clearly focus study efforts in needed areas.

In addition to the book features, a highly detailed answer key provides the correct answer and the rationale for it so that learners know exactly why an answer is correct. The *Science* student book and workbook are designed with an eye toward the end goal: success on the GED® Science Test.

Along with mastering key content and reading and thinking skills, learners will build familiarity with alternate item types that mirror in print the nature and scope of the technology-enhanced items included on the GED® Test.

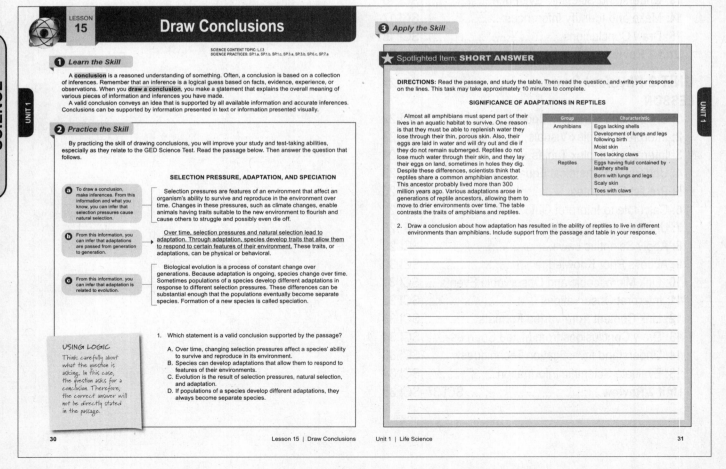

Unit 1

Life Science

As with the GED® Science Test, material in *Steck-Vaughn Test Preparation for the 2014 GED® Test: Science* has been organized across the three main units of life science, physical science, and Earth and space science. Further, the *amount* of content in those three subject areas has been organized according to the percentage of questions that appear on the GED® Science Test. For example, because life science items represent 40 percent of the questions on the GED® Science Test, a like percentage of space has been set aside for life science in the student materials of this program.

Unit 1 lessons progress from simpler to more complex skills. The unit begins with core tasks such as interpreting various types of visuals and identifying main ideas and continues to higher-level undertakings such as interpreting content-based tools and analyzing scientific evidence.

Many life science concepts—such as transmission of disease, relationships among living things, and heredity—may seem familiar to your learners. Other concepts may not. The key to learners' mastery of unfamiliar content lies in their ability to read and analyze the information that accompanies each question. To do this, learners must understand and apply key reading and thinking skills presented in this unit, such as identifying cause and effect, categorizing and classifying, comparing and contrasting, using context clues, making inferences, and drawing conclusions.

Table of Contents

LESSON	PAGE
1: Interpret Illustrations	SCI 4
2: Identify Main Idea and Details	SCI 5
3: Interpret Tables	SCI 6
4: Identify Cause and Effect	SCI 7
5: Interpret Graphs and Maps	SCI 8
6: Interpret Diagrams	SCI 9
7: Categorize and Classify	SCI 10
8: Generalize	SCI 11
9: Compare and Contrast	SCI 12
10: Relate Text and Visuals	SCI 13
11: Understand Content-Based Tools	SCI 14
12: Use Context Clues	SCI 15
13: Understand Scientific Evidence	SCI 16
14: Make and Identify Inferences	SCI 17
15: Draw Conclusions	SCI 18
Unit 1 Review	**SCI 19–SCI 20**

SCIENCE

Interpret Illustrations

SCIENCE CONTENT TOPICS: L.b.1, L.d.1, L.d.2, L.d.3
SCIENCE PRACTICES: SP.1.a, SP.1.b, SP.1.c, SP.7.a

SCIENCE

STUDENT BOOK pp. 2–3

▶ Preview the Skill

Ask learners to think of electrical devices that they use (for example, coffeepot, toaster, flashlight). Have them select one and draw a simple illustration of it with labels indicating parts such as an on/off switch and control buttons. Ask volunteers to describe their illustrations to the class. Have each volunteer discuss how the illustration may help explain the device to someone who is unfamiliar with it.

① Learn the Skill

Decoding Using examples from the *Preview the Skill* activity, discuss the type of information included in the illustration labels. Lead learners to understand that the labels name the parts that make up the device but that they also may provide information about how the various parts function.

② Practice the Skill

Skim and Scan Ask learners to scan the illustration on p. 2, noting in particular the type of information provided in the labels. Ask learners whether the labels indicate the names of parts, the functions of parts, or both *(both).*

③ Apply the Skill

Give Examples Explain that illustrations can convey complex information that otherwise would require lengthy text descriptions. For example, an illustration of a car engine might help someone unfamiliar with auto mechanics locate various engine parts. Illustrations of stages in the process of assembling a media cabinet might help someone put together the cabinet more efficiently. Ask learners to suggest other illustrations they have seen and the role that those illustrations have played in helping foster their understanding of a particular object or activity. Then have learners read the passages, study the illustrations, and answer questions 2–4 on p. 3.

Answers
1. C; DOK Level: 1; **2.** C; DOK Level: 2; **3.** B; DOK Level: 2; **4.** D; DOK Level: 2

WORKBOOK pp. 2–5

① Review the Skill

Skim and Scan Have learners scan the illustration of a lysosome digesting food on p. 2 to determine the meaning of the arrows in the illustration.

② Refine the Skill

Decoding Have learners revisit the illustration on p. 2. Ask them to decode the types of information conveyed in the illustration and to determine whether a sequence of events is shown.

③ Master the Skill

SuperSkill Review Explain that one important purpose of illustrations can be to show how microscopic objects look. Have the class study the illustration shown in the left column of p. 4. Ask a volunteer to describe what the illustration shows *(a magnified cross-section of a leaf).* Starting with the cuticle and moving down, discuss each cell type. Ask learners which aspects of the illustration help them understand each cell type.

▶ LifeLink

Discuss with learners instances in their daily lives in which they use the skill of interpreting illustrations. For example, learners at some point may use the Internet to find information about a health problem or attempt to assemble something, such as a bicycle or a grill. Explain that performing such tasks can involve understanding illustrations. Reinforce the importance of reading accompanying labels as a key strategy in interpreting illustrations.

Answers
1. B; DOK Level: 1; **2.** C; DOK Level: 2; **3.** A; DOK Level: 2; **4.** C; DOK Level: 2; **5.** D; DOK Level: 2; **6.** D; DOK Level: 2; **7.** B; DOK Level: 2; **8.** D; DOK Level: 2; **9.** A; DOK Level: 3; **10.** B; DOK Level: 2; **11.** A; DOK Level: 2; **12.** C; DOK Level: 2; **13.** A; DOK Level: 2; **14.** D; DOK Level: 3; **15.** B; DOK Level: 2; **16.** B; DOK Level: 2; **17.** D; DOK Level: 2

Identify Main Idea and Details

SCIENCE CONTENT TOPICS: L.a.1, L.d.2
SCIENCE PRACTICES: SP.1.a, SP.1.b, SP.1.c, SP.7.a

STUDENT BOOK pp. 4–5

▶ Preview the Skill

Ask learners to write one phrase that explains the main idea of their favorite pastime without revealing the name of the pastime. Ask learners to take turns reading their phrases aloud while other members of the class attempt to identify each pastime by its main idea. Review the concept of a main idea as the major point of a topic. Emphasize that both text and visuals have main ideas and that supporting details provide additional information about main ideas.

1 Learn the Skill

Give Examples Build on the *Preview the Skill* activity by selecting one example that learners found difficult to identify. Write the phrase expressing the main idea of the pastime on the board, and ask the class to provide supporting details that help clarify it.

2 Practice the Skill

Use Graphic Organizers Sketch on the board a graphic organizer like the one shown. Have learners fill in the main idea and supporting details conveyed in the last paragraph of the passage on p. 4.

The heart, blood vessels, and arteries move blood.	Systems work together to perform life functions.

Organs work together to form systems that have specific functions.

3 Apply the Skill

Link to Past Skills Have learners review the skill *Interpret Illustrations* from Lesson 1 of this unit to determine the main idea and details in the illustration of the digestive system on p. 5.

Answers
1. C; DOK Level: 1; **2.** A; DOK Level: 2; **3.** D; DOK Level 3; **4.** C; DOK Level: 2; **5.** B; DOK Level: 2

WORKBOOK pp. 6–9

1 Review the Skill

Give Examples Review with learners the definition of a main idea and its supporting details. Present learners with a title of an article, and ask them to predict the details that might be included in the article.

2 Refine the Skill

Skim and Scan Ask learners to skim and scan the visual about levels of organization on p. 6. Have them highlight all the details presented and use those details to write a main idea for the visual.

3 Master the Skill

Decoding Explain that when an illustration appears in conjunction with text, learners should use clues from the text to decode information in the illustration, and vice versa. Have them study the illustration and read the passage on p. 8 and then identify information in the passage that provides details about sensory neurons and motor neurons.

▶ Analyze Visuals

Draw learners' attention to the illustration of feedback mechanisms involved in the production of growth hormone on p. 9. Analyze the visual with learners to be sure they understand what is depicted. Have a volunteer paraphrase the ideas that the illustration communicates. Then read question 13, and help learners determine which details from the visual are essential to answer the question.

Answers
1. A; DOK Level: 2; **2.** C; DOK Level: 2; **3.** A; DOK Level: 2; **4.** D; DOK Level: 2; **5.** C; DOK Level: 2; **6.** D; DOK Level: 2; **7.** A; DOK Level: 3; **8.** C; DOK Level: 3; **9.** B; DOK Level: 2; **10.** B; DOK Level: 2; **11.** A; DOK Level: 2; **12.** D; DOK Level: 2; **13.** C; DOK Level: 3

SCIENCE

STUDENT BOOK *pp. 6–7*

▶ Preview the Skill

Ask learners to think about ways to organize their activities on a weekly basis. Lead learners to think of an organizational tool that can be used to group activities by days of the week. Write the name for each day of the week along a horizontal line on the board. Leave space underneath for listing activities. Point out that you have created headings for a seven-column table. Ask learners to suggest advantages of using a table as an organizational tool *(examples: conveys main points more efficiently than text in paragraphs, groups pieces of information in ways that make the information clear)*.

❶ Learn the Skill

Decoding Have learners study the table on p. 6. Then ask how information within each column is related. Ensure that learners recognize that each column contains information of a single type and that a column heading identifies the type of information in each column. Then ask learners to suggest information to include in the leftmost column of the table that they began in the *Preview the Skill* activity.

❷ Practice the Skill

Give Examples Have the class read callouts *a*, *b*, and *c* on p. 6, and ask a volunteer to describe the purposes of columns and rows in a table. Then ask learners to think about information presented to customers at an auto service center and how that information might be organized in a table. Ask volunteers to give suggestions for headings for a service center's menu of services. As a class, create a table of options and prices that could be placed above the area where customers drop off their cars.

❸ Apply the Skill

Skim and Scan Have learners skim and scan the information in the tables on p. 7. Allow partners to work together to determine the main idea or purpose of each table based on the information presented in the table.

Answers
1. B; DOK Level: 1; **2.** B; DOK Level: 2; **3.** A; DOK Level: 2; **4.** D; DOK Level: 3; **5.** A; DOK Level: 2

WORKBOOK *pp. 10–13*

❶ Review the Skill

SuperSkill Review Referring to the *Making Assumptions* box on p. 10, have learners analyze the information in the table to explain why it cannot be assumed based on the table that someone who is 80 needs fewer calories than someone who is 70.

❷ Refine the Skill

Skim and Scan Reinforce interpretation skills by asking learners to skim and scan the table on p. 10. Have them identify the information given in each column. Stress that because this table has several different but similar categories, they must read it carefully to find the information they need.

❸ Master the Skill

Decoding Have learners study the table in the left column of p. 11. Help learners decode the main ideas of the table by brainstorming with the class ways in which someone might use the information in the table. Lead learners to consider the possibility of using the table to determine which foods to eat to achieve a desired health goal. Then invite volunteers to answer questions 3–4, and discuss the responses as a class.

▶ Cross-Curricular Connection

Learners often must use math skills to interpret data in tables. For example, on p. 12, question 7 requires that learners add, and question 9 requires that they subtract. Have learners study the tables on p. 12 and write related questions that require the use of math to answer. Then have partners answer each other's questions.

Answers
1. A; DOK Level: 2; **2.** C; DOK Level: 2; **3.** B; DOK Level: 2; **4.** A; DOK Level: 3; **5.** B; DOK Level: 2; **6.** B; DOK Level: 1; **7.** C; DOK Level: 2; **8.** D; DOK Level: 2; **9.** B; DOK Level: 2; **10.** C; DOK Level: 2; **11.** A; DOK Level: 2; **12.** D; DOK Level: 2; **13.** B; DOK Level: 2; **14.** D; DOK Level: 2

SCIENCE

Identify Cause and Effect

SCIENCE CONTENT TOPIC: L.a.2
SCIENCE PRACTICES: SP.1.a, SP.1.b, SP.1.c, SP.3.b, SP.7.a

STUDENT BOOK pp. 8–9

▶ Preview the Skill

Ask learners whether they have ever accidentally exposed a cell phone to water. Then ask what happened to the cell phone. Note that this scenario offers an example of a cause-and-effect relationship.

1 Learn the Skill

Use Graphic Organizers On the board, draw a graphic organizer such as the one shown. Next, ask a volunteer to read the first two sentences in the *Learn the Skill* section on p. 8. Then have learners copy the graphic organizer you drew and complete it to represent the cell phone scenario described in the *Preview the Skill* activity.

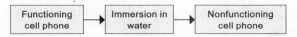

Functioning cell phone → Immersion in water → Nonfunctioning cell phone

2 Practice the Skill

Give Examples Provide another everyday example of cause and effect (for example, heavy morning thunderstorms leading to cancellation of an afternoon activity), and ask learners to suggest their own examples. Use the graphic organizer from the *Learn the Skill* activity to record each example on the board. Then discuss whether each example accurately represents a cause-and-effect relationship. Suggest that learners use this approach to analyze the information presented in the illustration on p. 8 before answering question 1.

3 Apply the Skill

Spotlighted Item Type Point out the *Spotlighted Item* box on p. 9. Build learners' comfort level with the drop-down item type by noting that drop-down answer options are like multiple-choice answer options. Explain that when taking the GED® Science Test, learners will click a blank box in a passage or visual to display drop-down answer options and then click the desired answer choice. Encourage learners to use strategies similar to those they use in answering multiple-choice questions when answering drop-down items.

Answers
1. C; DOK Level: 2; **2.1** B; **2.2** C; **2.3** D; **2.4** A; DOK Level: 2

WORKBOOK pp. 14–17

1 Review the Skill

Skim and Scan Have learners scan the passage about maintaining appropriate body temperature on p. 14 to look for causes and effects. Have them identify at least two causes and their effects, and ask volunteers to share their findings with the class.

2 Refine the Skill

SuperSkill Review Draw learners' attention to callout *b* on p. 14, and review the key words that can signal causes and effects. Next, read the last two sentences of the passage. Invite volunteers to explain the cause-and-effect relationship signaled by the words *as a result*. Finally, have learners provide example sentences, using the key words to convey cause-and-effect relationships.

3 Master the Skill

Spotlighted Item Type Have learners work in pairs to discuss and decide on an appropriate answer for each drop-down box on p. 15. Explain that if partners suggest different answers for an item, they should reread the incomplete passage from the beginning and refer to the illustration to determine the correct answer.

▶ Language Analysis

To complete drop-down items such as those on pp. 16–17, learners need to comprehend and synthesize information from a passage and a visual. Have them work in groups to identify unfamiliar language in the stimulus passages and illustrations for items 4–5. Then have them analyze the words and phrases they identified to determine their meanings, looking up terms in a dictionary as needed.

Answers
1. B; DOK Level: 1; **2.** A; DOK Level: 2; **3.1** B; **3.2** A; **3.3** D; **3.4** C; DOK Level: 2; **4.1** B; **4.2** A; **4.3** B; **4.4** D; DOK Level: 2; **5.1** A; **5.2** C; **5.3** A; **5.4** D; DOK Level: 2

SCIENCE

Interpret Graphs and Maps

SCIENCE CONTENT TOPIC: L.a.4
SCIENCE PRACTICES: SP.1.a, SP.1.b, SP.1.c, SP.3.a, SP.3.b, SP.3.c, SP.3.d

SCIENCE

STUDENT BOOK pp. 10–11

▶ Preview the Skill

Take a quick survey of learners' preferred sport to watch—football, basketball, or soccer. Draw a simple bar graph to show the data. Discuss the data on the graph with learners, making sure that they understand that the height of each bar corresponds to a number of learners.

❶ Learn the Skill

Skim and Scan Ask learners to review the bar graph on p. 10 and determine how it is similar to the graph you developed during the *Preview the Skill* activity. Make sure that learners understand that both graphs show a total number in each category, whether it is number of learners or number of cases and whether the category is a preferred sport or a year.

❷ Practice the Skill

SuperSkill Review Have learners look at the graph for acute hepatitis cases on p. 11, and then ask how the bar graph on p. 10 differs from the line graph on p. 11. Lead a discussion about the strengths and limitations of certain types of graphs. For example, although both bar graphs and line graphs can show change over time, bar graphs often provide more specific information, whereas line graphs often better illustrate trends or patterns.

❸ Apply the Skill

Decoding Ask learners to study the map on p. 11. Help them decode the key by defining the terms *local, regional, sporadic,* and *widespread* in this context. Discuss uses of a thematic map such as this one. Have learners work in pairs to formulate additional questions that can be answered by using data from the map so that they become comfortable with this format of data presentation.

Answers
1. C; DOK Level: 2; **2.** D; DOK Level: 2; **3.** A; DOK Level: 2;
4. C; DOK Level: 3

WORKBOOK pp. 18–21

❶ Review the Skill

Use Graphic Organizers As a class, construct a simple table that identifies major types of graphs and maps and the best uses for each kind.

❷ Refine the Skill

Give Examples Ask the class to examine the graph on p. 18. Have learners think about how the two lines are different and identify the information that each represents. Then ask volunteers to draw graphs on the board that show general trends over the course of a year for scenarios involving seasonal changes, such as population change on a beach that closes in winter or changes in inventory levels at a store that receives new merchandise every quarter. Discuss differences in the graphs.

❸ Master the Skill

SuperSkill Review Before learners answer questions 3–10 on pp. 19–20, review the purposes of various kinds of graphs. Read aloud the following examples, and have learners determine the type of graph that would best convey the information for each example:
• Heights of a group of 10 people *(bar graph)*
• Percentages of U.S. adults having a height below 5 feet, a height from 5 feet to 6 feet, and a height above 6 feet *(circle graph)*
• Change in height over a 10-year period for two growing children *(line graph)*

▶ Enrich and Extend

Remind learners that the same data can be displayed in several different types of graphs. Have them work in groups to choose a graph from the lesson and represent the data in at least one other type of graph. Discuss with them which graph best displays the data and why.

Answers
1. C; DOK Level: 1; **2.** A; DOK Level: 2; **3.** B; DOK Level: 1;
4. A; DOK Level: 1; **5.** D; DOK Level: 2; **6.** C; DOK Level: 3;
7. B; DOK Level: 2; **8.** D; DOK Level: 2; **9.** A; DOK Level: 2;
10. C; DOK Level: 3; **11.1** D; **11.2** C; **11.3** A; **11.4** B;
DOK Level: 3

Interpret Diagrams

SCIENCE CONTENT TOPICS: L.c.1, L.c.2
SCIENCE PRACTICES: SP.1.a, SP.1.b, SP.1.c, SP.3.b, SP.3.d, SP.7.a

STUDENT BOOK pp. 12–13

▷ Preview the Skill

Explain that you want to diagram the procedure for grilling a steak. Have volunteers suggest the actions you must take. As they do, write their suggestions on the board, and include arrows to connect the ideas. Emphasize that the procedure is linear and occurs in ordered steps.

❶ Learn the Skill

Link to Past Skills Have learners look at the diagrams in the lesson. Then review the skill *Interpreting Illustrations* from Lesson 1 of this unit. Explain that like illustrations, diagrams provide information about parts of a whole. However, diagrams typically indicate how parts are related or interact or how an event happens, and they may or may not show how something looks.

❷ Practice the Skill

Use Graphic Organizers Have learners study the diagram on p. 12 while you read callout *b* aloud. Then work with the class to identify species that live together in a body of water. Have the class use a graphic organizer such as the one shown to diagram energy movement in an aquatic ecosystem.

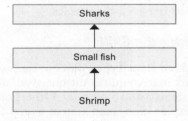

❸ Apply the Skill

Skim and Scan Ask learners to skim and scan the diagrams on p. 13. Discuss how they are alike and different. Lead learners to note that relationships represented by diagrams can be linear or cyclic.

Answers
1. C; DOK Level: 2; **2.** B; DOK Level: 2; **3.** C; DOK Level: 2; **4.** A; DOK Level: 2; **5.** D; DOK Level: 3

WORKBOOK pp. 22–25

❶ Review the Skill

Decoding Help learners decode the information conveyed by the arrows in the diagram on p. 22. Ensure that learners recognize the two ways in which arrows in a diagram are used: to indicate sequence or to show relationships.

❷ Refine the Skill

Give Examples Provide the following example: John plans a barbecue for his friends George, Bob, and Susan, who all know each other. Bob brings his girlfriend Pam, who is a good friend of Susan's. Pam has never met John or George. Ask the class to diagram the social network of this group, using arrows to connect those who know one another. Discuss with learners how the diagram is helpful in showing relationships. Then have learners work in pairs to answer questions 1–2 on p. 22.

❸ Master the Skill

Use Graphic Organizers Write three students' names on the board, and ask each person to come to the board and list four or five grilled foods that he or she enjoys. Then ask the class to help construct a Venn diagram similar to the one on p. 24. Use the learners' names as headings for the three parts of the diagram. Have learners compare and contrast the completed diagram to the one on p. 24.

▷ Analyze Visuals

Explain that although the Venn diagram on p. 24 may look simple, it contains a good deal of information. As a class, discuss and interpret the information presented.

Answers
1. C; DOK Level: 2; **2.** A; DOK Level: 2; **3.** A; DOK Level: 2; **4.** B; DOK Level: 2; **5.** D; DOK Level: 2; **6.** C; DOK Level: 3; **7.1** B; **7.2** B; **7.3** D; **7.4** A; DOK Level: 2; **8.** C; DOK Level: 2; **9.** C; DOK Level: 2; **10.** D; DOK Level: 2; **11.** B; DOK Level: 2

SCIENCE

Categorize and Classify

SCIENCE CONTENT TOPIC: L.c.4
SCIENCE PRACTICES: SP.1.a, SP.1.b, SP.1.c, SP.3.a, SP.3.b, SP.6.a, SP.6.c

STUDENT BOOK *pp. 14–15*

▶ Preview the Skill

Ask learners to suppose that they are setting up an online movie rental business. Lead them to understand that creating groups of movies involves categorization and that placing a particular movie into an existing group involves classification.

❶ Learn the Skill

Give Examples Ask learners to provide examples of categorization and classification in a grocery store. For example, categories might include *produce, dairy, frozen foods, meats,* and *deli.* Yogurt would be classified as dairy; carrots would be classified as produce.

❷ Practice the Skill

Use Graphic Organizers Have learners read the passage and study the diagram on p. 14. Then ask what category of symbiotic relationship the passage identifies *(predator-prey)*, and fill in the large box on a graphic organizer like the one shown. Complete the graphic organizer by having the class brainstorm specific animal relationships that can be classified as predator-prey.

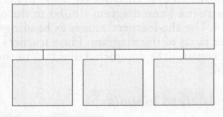

❸ Apply the Skill

Spotlighted Item Type Explain that while taking the GED® Science Test, learners will respond to fill-in-the-blank items by typing an answer in a designated space. Then have learners work in pairs to discuss the differences between parasites and hosts and to decide on the appropriate answer for each fill-in-the-blank item on p. 15. If partners suggest different answers for an item, have them review together the characteristics of the categories.

Answers
1. A; DOK Level: 2; **2.** the canine is a host; the tapeworm is a parasite; the vole is a host; DOK Level: 2; **3.** commensalism and mutualism; DOK Level: 2

WORKBOOK *pp. 26–29*

❶ Review the Skill

Give Examples Use a table like the one below to reinforce the skills of categorizing and classifying. Have volunteers suggest musical groups or artists that are part of each genre (category).

Country	Rock	Rap	Alternative

❷ Refine the Skill

Link to Past Skills Have learners review the skill *Identify Cause and Effect* from Lesson 4 of this unit. Then identify a cause and its effects for one relationship category listed in the table on p. 26. For example, when a flea feeds on a dog (cause), the flea obtains needed nutrients (a positive effect on Species A), and the dog receives a harmful bite (a negative effect on Species B). Ask learners to use the cause-and-effect relationship you have described and the information in the table to identify the type of relationship the flea and the dog have *(parasitic)*. Emphasize that understanding a cause and its effects on Species A and Species B will help them determine the type of relationship that exists between the species.

❸ Master the Skill

Spotlighted Item Type Point out that some fill-in-the-blank items require only one-word answers, such as items 3 and 5 on p. 27. Others require a longer explanation, such as item 6 on p. 27.

Answers
1. C; DOK Level: 2; **2.** A; DOK Level: 2; **3.** predators; DOK Level: 2; **4.** humans, sheep, fish, pigeons; DOK Level: 2; **5.** mutualism; DOK Level: 2; **6.** Both organisms benefit in each relationship. DOK Level: 2; **7.** parasitism; DOK Level: 2; **8.** predator-prey; DOK Level: 2; **9.** mutualistic; DOK Level: 2; **10.** parasitic; DOK Level: 2; **11.** predator-prey or predation; DOK Level: 3; **12.** One species benefits, and the other is not affected. DOK Level: 2; **13.** parasitism; DOK Level: 2; **14.** predator-prey or predation; DOK Level: 2; **15.** predator-prey or predation; DOK Level: 2; **16.** Possible answers: commensalism—animals coming to the hole benefit, but the alligator does not; predation—alligators may return looking for food. DOK Level: 3

SCIENCE

Generalize

SCIENCE CONTENT TOPICS: L.c.3, L.c.4, L.c.5
SCIENCE PRACTICES: SP.1.a, SP.1.b, SP.1.c, SP.3.a, SP.3.b, SP.3.d, SP.6.c

STUDENT BOOK pp. 16–17

➤ Preview the Skill

Provide the following scenario: Two of Tom's friends, Marco and Desiree, recently visited New York City. Marco told Tom that several cabs passed him before one stopped. Desiree noticed a stain on a dress she purchased but said the store manager wouldn't allow her to return it. Tom, who has never visited New York City, generalized that New Yorkers are unfriendly. Ask learners whether his generalization is valid *(the generalization is likely invalid; Marco's experience could have been the result of full cabs, and Desiree's experience might have been the result of a no-return policy)*.

❶ Learn the Skill

Give Examples Explain that a statement that defines a group is not a generalization. Ask learners to identify which of the following statements are generalizations: Most birds fly *(yes)*. Birds are the only animals that have feathers *(no; defining)*. Many Americans are patriotic *(yes)*. Flags are symbols of the countries of the world *(no; defining)*.

❷ Practice the Skill

Skim and Scan Direct learners to callout *b* on p. 16, and have a volunteer read the text. Explain that facts support generalizations. Have learners skim and scan the passage to determine whether each answer choice for question 1 is a fact or a generalization based in fact.

❸ Apply the Skill

Spotlighted Item Type Point out the importance of reading the entire sentence when answering fill-in-the-blank items. For example, items 2–3 on p. 17 could have multiple answers if learners ignore the last part of each sentence.

Answers
1. B; DOK Level: 2; **2.** increases in size; DOK Level: 3; **3.** increasing rapidly; DOK Level: 3; **4.** carrying capacity; DOK Level: 3; **5.** A; DOK Level: 3

WORKBOOK pp. 30–33

❶ Review the Skill

Give Examples Point out that a generalization can have exceptions yet still be valid as a general statement. Often, an invalid generalization is made from observations of only a small number of group members whose specific characteristics are not applicable to all (or most) group members. For example, an observation of a tiger swimming at a zoo might lead a zoo visitor to make an invalid generalization that cats like water. Ask learners to develop other examples of scenarios that could lead to invalid generalizations.

❷ Refine the Skill

Skim and Scan Ask a volunteer to read the text in the *Test-Taking Tech* box on p. 30. Discuss the usefulness of the electronic highlighting feature in helping learners make generalizations. Then have learners read the passage on p. 30 and study the graph. Ask them to highlight details in the passage or graph to support a valid generalization among the answer choices for question 1.

❸ Master the Skill

Link to Past Skills Have learners review the skill *Interpret Graphs and Maps* from Lesson 5 of this unit to interpret the graphs on pp. 32–33. Emphasize that interpreting graphs correctly is the first step in making valid generalizations based on the data they contain.

➤ LifeLink

Have learners work in small groups to list invalid generalizations that people often make. Identify groups of people—for example, adults, kids, and professional athletes—to get them started. As a class, discuss the potential dangers of invalid generalizations.

Answers
1. B; DOK Level: 2; **2.** D; DOK Level: 2; **3.** C; DOK Level: 3; **4.** B; DOK Level: 3; **5.** A; DOK Level: 3; **6.** A; DOK Level: 2; **7.** C; DOK Level: 2; **8.** D; DOK Level: 2; **9.** D; DOK Level: 3; **10.** B; DOK Level: 2; **11.** A; DOK Level: 2; **12.** D; DOK Level: 3; **13.** A; DOK Level: 3

SCIENCE

Compare and Contrast

SCIENCE CONTENT TOPICS: L.c.2, L.c.5
SCIENCE PRACTICES: SP.1.a, SP.1.b, SP.1.c, SP.3.a, SP.6.a, SP.6.c

STUDENT BOOK *pp. 18–19*

➤ Preview the Skill

Note the importance of comparing and contrasting in everyday life. When planning to purchase a car, for example, a buyer typically considers several cars to identify the similarities and differences among them. This strategy of comparing and contrasting determines which car the buyer ultimately chooses.

❶ Learn the Skill

Use Graphic Organizers Extend the example from the *Preview the Skill* activity by displaying a table that compares and contrasts three cars, such as the one shown. Ask learners to determine the car that represents the best value.

	Car A	Car B	Car C
Price	$15,500	$18,900	$21,500
Gas mileage	34 mpg	28 mpg	35 mpg
Engine	6-hp	6-hp	6-hp
Repair record	Poor	Very good	Excellent

❷ Practice the Skill

Skim and Scan Have learners skim and scan the table on p. 18 to look for ways that the animals can be compared and contrasted *(examples: all are vertebrates, all groups include threatened species, different groups have different numbers of threatened species).*

❸ Apply the Skill

Spotlighted Item Type Explain to learners that drag-and-drop items provide information that they are to place correctly in an illustration, a table, or a diagram. Have learners work in pairs to determine where to place the drag-and-drop options in question 2 on p. 19. Have them refer to the passage about healthy and unhealthy ecosystems if they disagree on placement of an option.

Answers
1. C; DOK Level: 2; **2.** healthy—correct proportions of nutrients and sunlight, high level of biodiversity; unhealthy—nonnative species, loss of habitat, polluted water; both—living and nonliving parts; DOK Level: 2

WORKBOOK *pp. 34–37*

❶ Review the Skill

Link to Past Skills Have learners review the skill *Interpret Graphs and Maps* from Lesson 5 of this unit before studying the bar graph on p. 34. Ask how interpreting a bar graph relates to the skill of comparing and contrasting *(when you interpret a bar graph, you compare and contrast data in different categories).*

❷ Refine the Skill

Decoding Help learners decode the information shown in the graph on p. 34. Point out that although the passage compares and contrasts different types of cats, the graph applies only to the African cheetah population. Explain that the graph still can be used to compare and contrast by analyzing information about how the population has changed over time.

❸ Master the Skill

Spotlighted Item Type Have learners discuss the meanings of the arrows in the diagram on p. 36. Emphasize that drag-and-drop items often require them to interpret illustrations, tables, and diagrams in which they will place information.

➤ Analyze Visuals

Draw learners' attention to each visual in the lesson, and discuss how each one allows two or more things to be compared and contrasted. Point out the value of using a visual to compare and contrast.

Answers
1. A; DOK Level: 1; **2.** C; DOK Level: 2; **3.** before desertification—is forested, has greater biodiversity, has smaller numbers of grazing animals; after desertification—is used to grow crops, is at greater risk of soil erosion, has less biodiversity; DOK Level: 2; **4.** sea urchin, mussel, and clam populations will increase; kelp and algae populations will decrease; sea lion population will have no change; DOK Level: 2; **5.** native plants—are native to ecosystem, contribute positively to habitat; invasive species—grow uncontrollably, spread quickly, choke out other plants; both—prevent erosion; DOK Level: 2

SCIENCE

Relate Text and Visuals

SCIENCE CONTENT TOPICS: L.d.3, L.e.1
SCIENCE PRACTICES: SP.1.a, SP.1.b, SP.1.c, SP.6.a, SP.6.c, SP.7.a, SP.8.b

STUDENT BOOK pp. 20–21

▶ Preview the Skill

Ask learners to recall advertisements that make claims that are supported by some kind of visual. For example, a television ad for a cleaning product may show a person using the product to clean a messy kitchen countertop and the resulting sparkling countertop. Lead learners to understand how a complementary combination of text and visuals can enhance the presentation of information.

❶ Learn the Skill

Skim and Scan Explain that because passages on the GED® Science Test often lack titles, one strategy for decoding them involves first examining and interpreting any accompanying graphic. Explain that unlike the passages, the graphics on the GED® Science Test often do contain titles. Ask learners to preview the lesson content by scanning the graphics on pp. 20–21.

❷ Practice the Skill

SuperSkill Review Point out the information in the *Test-Taking Tips* box on p. 20. Then have learners read question 1 and use the visual to eliminate answer choices, such as *all human chromosomes are identical*. Note that questions requiring integration of information from text and a visual can be time consuming and that looking over a visual to eliminate answer choices can help them move through such questions more efficiently.

❸ Apply the Skill

Decoding Have learners read the passage in the left column of p. 21 and study the accompanying illustration. Ask a volunteer to decode the various letters in the illustration. Then have learners use that information to answer question 2. Finally, ask a volunteer to describe the structure of a DNA molecule on the basis of the text and illustration.

Answers
1. B; DOK Level: 2; **2.** D; DOK Level: 2; **3.** A; DOK Level: 2

WORKBOOK pp. 38–41

❶ Review the Skill

SuperSkill Review Tell learners that an efficient way to answer questions requiring them to relate text and visuals is to read the question before reading the text and looking at the visual. For example, after reading question 2, they can read the text to find that the two parts created when a chromosome replicates are chromatids. Then they can look at the visual to find the label for the point at which the chromatids are joined.

❷ Refine the Skill

Decoding Help learners decode the information shown in the illustration on p. 38. Point out that the terms *centromere* and *telomere* are not explained in the text and that they need to use the visual to understand the functions of these structures. Have volunteers describe in their own words each labeled part of the illustration.

❸ Master the Skill

Skim and Scan Ask learners to scan the diagrams on pp. 39–41, noting any common characteristics. Point out that they all contain arrows. Discuss what the arrows represent in the diagrams. Explain that by understanding the purposes of the arrows, learners will better comprehend the information in each diagram and its relationship to information provided in the accompanying text.

▶ Analyze Visuals

Emphasize the importance of analyzing visuals when relating text and visuals. Have learners work in pairs to analyze each visual in the lesson by discussing its illustrated parts, arrows, and labels and summarizing the information the visual provides.

Answers
1. C; DOK Level: 2; **2.** A; DOK Level: 2; **3.** A; DOK Level: 2; **4.** B; DOK Level: 2; **5.** D; DOK Level: 2; **6.** DNA replicates during interphase; chromosomes are visible during prophase; chromatids separate during anaphase; two individual daughter cells form during cytokinesis; DOK Level: 3; **7.** B; DOK Level: 2; **8.** C; DOK Level: 2

SCIENCE

Understand Content-Based Tools

SCIENCE CONTENT TOPIC: L.e.2
SCIENCE PRACTICES: SP.1.a, SP.1.b, SP.1.c, SP.3.d, SP.8.b, SP.8.c

SCIENCE

STUDENT BOOK pp. 22–23

▶ Preview the Skill

On the board, draw a table like the one shown. Ask volunteers to record the colors of their parents' eyes and their own eye color. Ask learners to look for similarities in the data. Explain that tools introduced in this lesson will help them organize information about inheritable traits, such as eye color.

Parents' Eye Colors	Offspring's Eye Color

❶ Learn the Skill

Link to Past Skills Note that content-based tools in science can take many forms. Explain that learners may understand a content-based tool more easily if they connect it with a familiar tool. Review the skill *Interpret Tables* from Lesson 3 of this unit. Then direct learners to preview the Punnett square on p. 23, and discuss the similarities between a Punnett square and a table.

❷ Practice the Skill

Decoding Help learners find meaning in the diagram on p. 22. Have volunteers form data from the diagram into sentences, such as, "In the parent generation, a plant having purple flowers was crossed with a plant having white flowers."

❸ Apply the Skill

Spotlighted Item Type Point out questions 2–3 on p. 23. Explain that hot spot items often involve a graphic representation of information. Tell learners that they will respond to hot spot items on the GED® Science Test by clicking the graphic in a manner that is similar to marking an *X* on a graphic on a printed page.

Answers
1. B; DOK Level: 1; **2.** purple flower color; DOK Level: 3;
3. Molly; DOK Level: 3

WORKBOOK pp. 42–45

❶ Review the Skill

Give Examples To help learners better understand how a Punnett square works, relate Punnett squares to the trait of human eye color. Explain that *B* represents the allele for brown eye color, which is dominant, and *b* represents the allele for blue eye color, which is recessive. Then draw several Punnett squares on the board for learners to complete. Give examples—such as, "One parent has two dominant alleles, and the other parent has one dominant allele and one recessive allele"—and have learners work out the phenotypes of different crossings of *BB*, *Bb*, and *bb*.

❷ Refine the Skill

SuperSkill Review Emphasize that content-based tools are important because of the purposes they serve. Explain that Punnett squares can be used to determine the chance of offspring inheriting a certain trait. Direct learners to the Punnett square on p. 42, and help them calculate the probabilities of the parent plants producing the genotypes *YY*, *Yy*, and *yy*. Then help them calculate the probabilities of the parent plants producing a plant with yellow seeds and a plant with green seeds. Be sure learners understand that question 2 requires that they identify the chance of the parent plants producing a particular phenotype, not genotype.

❸ Master the Skill

Spotlighted Item Type Have learners work through questions 5–6 on p. 44 with a partner. Remind them that for some hot spot items, more than one answer may be correct.

▶ LifeLink

Have learners create a pedigree chart for a particular trait, such as eye color or hair color, in their family. Tell them to refer to the pedigree charts on p. 44 as examples.

Answers
1. D; DOK Level: 2; **2.** C; DOK Level: 3; **3.** offspring in the left column; DOK Level: 2; **4.** green Punnett square; DOK Level: 2; **5.** individuals represented by white shapes; DOK Level: 3; **6.** all individuals with the genotype *rr*; DOK Level: 2; **7.** blue Punnett square; DOK Level: 3; **8.** green Punnett square; DOK Level: 3

Use Context Clues

SCIENCE CONTENT TOPICS: L.d.3, L.e.3
SCIENCE PRACTICES: SP.1.a, SP.1.b, SP.1.c, SP.3.b, SP.7.a

STUDENT BOOK pp. 24–25

▶ Preview the Skill

Ask class members whether they have ever used clues to find their way to an unfamiliar place. An example might involve the experience of arriving at an unfamiliar airport, train station, or bus station and searching for the exit. Because other passengers also are looking for the exit, an individual may be able to determine where to go from the group's direction of movement. Another example might involve using clues from traffic movement to change lanes safely on a highway. Explain that clues are indirect pieces of information that can assist in understanding and that context clues can be useful in clarifying the meanings of unfamiliar words or complicated ideas in passages.

❶ Learn the Skill

Skim and Scan Have learners skim the passage about genetic variation on p. 24 for any unfamiliar words, such as *gametes*. Then have learners underline or highlight any context clues in the text that help them understand each term.

❷ Practice the Skill

Link to Past Skills Have learners review the skill *Identify Main Idea and Details* from Lesson 2 of this unit. Discuss how identifying the main idea of a passage or visual element provides background, or a context, for information in the passage or visual. Explain that learners can use this context to look for clues that will help them understand pieces of unfamiliar information. Then have learners read the passage on p. 24 and answer question 1.

❸ Apply the Skill

Spotlighted Item Type Have learners work in pairs to determine which illustration or illustrations show a mutation in question 2 on p. 25. Remind them that there may be more than one correct answer for hot spot items.

Answers
1. B; DOK Level: 2; **2.** illustration of DNA replication on the right; DOK Level: 3; **3.** D; DOK Level: 2; **4.** C; DOK Level: 2

WORKBOOK pp. 46–49

❶ Review the Skill

Give Examples Remind learners that we encounter unfamiliar words (or familiar words used in unfamiliar ways) in our everyday lives. Often, we can understand these words through the use of context clues. Give an example by using a word in a sentence and then asking a volunteer to explain its meaning. Have learners contribute some of their own examples.

❷ Refine the Skill

SuperSkill Review Have learners read the passage about genetic recombination on p. 46, underlining unfamiliar words as they encounter them. Write each word on the board, and then ask volunteers to explain whether context clues are present in the passage to aid them in defining the word.

❸ Master the Skill

Decoding Have learners look at the table about genetic mutations on p. 47. Ask them to describe how the examples in the right column of the table provide context clues to decode the meanings of the terms *substitution*, *insertion*, *deletion*, and *frameshift* in the left column of the table.

▶ Enrich and Extend

Provide articles from a science-oriented magazine. Have learners working in groups choose an article, identify unfamiliar words or complicated ideas in the article, and then use context clues, where possible, to determine their meanings. For any terms or ideas not explained by context clues, allow learners to use additional resources to determine their meanings.

Answers
1. A; DOK Level: 2; **2.** C; DOK Level: 2; **3.** D; DOK Level: 2;
4. B; DOK Level: 2; **5.** A; DOK Level: 2; **6.** B; DOK Level: 3;
7. A; DOK Level: 3; **8.** C; DOK Level: 2; **9.** B; DOK Level: 3;
10. D; DOK Level: 2; **11.** B; DOK Level: 2; **12.** A; DOK Level: 2; **13.** D; DOK Level: 3; **14.** C; DOK Level: 3

SCIENCE

Understand Scientific Evidence

SCIENCE CONTENT TOPIC: L.f.1
SCIENCE PRACTICES: SP.1.a, SP.1.b, SP.1.c, SP.3.a, SP.3.b, SP.4.a, SP.6.a, SP.6.c, SP.7.a, SP.8.b

STUDENT BOOK pp. 26–27

▷ Preview the Skill

Tell learners that you think that sugar dissolves in water faster than salt does but that you need scientific evidence to support your idea. Explain that scientific evidence is objective and unbiased. Then ask the class to suggest a way in which you could test your idea (by adding the same amount of salt as sugar to equal amounts of water and timing how long it takes for each substance to dissolve). Ask learners what scientific evidence would support your idea. Lead them to understand that an observation that the sugar dissolves faster than the salt in the investigation would be scientific evidence to support your idea.

① Learn the Skill

Skim and Scan Have learners skim and scan the information about common ancestry on p. 26, including the visual. Have them underline or highlight any scientific evidence that supports the idea that very different animals alive today have common ancestors.

② Practice the Skill

Link to Past Skills Have learners review the skill *Compare and Contrast* from Lesson 9 of this unit. Have them use this skill to compare and contrast the forelimbs of the four animals in the visual on p. 26. Explain that the scientific evidence for common ancestors depends on the skill of comparing and contrasting structures.

③ Apply the Skill

Decoding Help learners decode the cladogram on p. 27. Have them determine the meanings of the labels along the trunk and the meanings of the labels at the ends of the branches. Then ask them to summarize how ferns, conifers, and flowering plants are related.

Answers
1. C; DOK Level: 1; **2.** B; DOK Level: 2; **3.** C; DOK Level: 2;
4. D; DOK Level: 3

WORKBOOK pp. 50–53

① Review the Skill

Give Examples Identify a scientific idea and an applicable piece of evidence—for example, the idea that Earth attracts objects through the force of gravity is supported by the observation that objects on Earth stay in place rather than float around. Then challenge learners working in small groups to brainstorm other basic scientific ideas and list scientific evidence that supports the ideas. Have them share their ideas and scientific evidence, and discuss each as a class.

② Refine the Skill

SuperSkill Review In addition to the two questions about the cladogram on p. 50, have learners write two or three more questions about scientific evidence represented by the cladogram (along with answers on a separate sheet of paper). Ask them to exchange questions with a partner and answer each other's questions to gain further practice in understanding cladograms.

③ Master the Skill

Spotlighted Item Type Direct learners to question 6 on p. 52. Have them work in pairs to complete the drag-and-drop question. Point out that to complete any cladogram, they may wish to begin with the box for the organism with the most traits and work backward.

▷ Analyze Visuals

Review the skill *Relate Text and Visuals* from Lesson 10 of this unit. Then have learners work in pairs or small groups to determine the meaning of the visual on p. 53 and to understand the text about DNA sequences. Explain that they should read the text carefully and pause regularly to relate the text to the visual. Remind them that they should refer to the text and the visual as they answer the questions to ensure that they are answering correctly.

Answers
1. D; DOK Level: 1; **2.** A; DOK Level: 2; **3.** C; DOK Level: 1;
4. B; DOK Level: 1; **5.** B; DOK Level: 3; **6.** (order from lowest to highest on cladogram) tiger, gorilla, human; DOK Level: 2;
7. C; DOK Level: 2; **8.** C; DOK Level: 2; **9.** D; DOK Level: 3;
10. A; DOK Level: 3

SCIENCE

Make and Identify Inferences

SCIENCE CONTENT TOPIC: L.f.2
SCIENCE PRACTICES: SP.1.a, SP.1.b, SP.1.c, SP.3.a, SP.3.b, SP.3.c, SP.6.c, SP.7.a

STUDENT BOOK pp. 28–29

➤ Preview the Skill

Explain that an inference is a logical guess based on information or reasoning. Discuss the tendency to use first impressions, such as someone's handshake, appearance, or job, to make inferences about people.

1 Learn the Skill

Use Graphic Organizers Display a graphic organizer like the one shown. Then provide this scenario: A person approaches a desk. On the desk is a sign that says "Receptionist." Behind the desk is a person wearing business clothing and talking on the phone. As a class, complete the graphic organizer to determine what can be inferred from this situation.

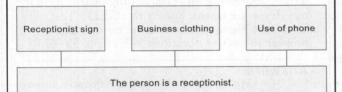

2 Practice the Skill

Give Examples Have learners read the passage on p. 28. Then discuss other advantageous traits that are inheritable. One example is coloration in butterflies that allows them to blend in with tree bark so that they are camouflaged from predators. Challenge learners to think of other examples.

3 Apply the Skill

Spotlighted Item Type Point out the *Spotlighted Item* box on p. 29. Note that for this drag-and-drop item, they are given four drag-and-drop options but will use only two of them. Tell them to begin by eliminating choices that are not appropriate inferences given the information provided. Then explain that they need to place the two correct choices in order according to Darwin's observations.

Answers

1. B; DOK Level: 2; **2.** Inference 1—competition for resources keeps many individuals from surviving to reproduce; Inference 2—traits that help individuals acquire and use resources are important to survival; DOK Level: 2; **3.** A; DOK Level: 3

WORKBOOK pp. 54–57

1 Review the Skill

Give Examples Point out that some inferences can turn out to be incorrect and that additional observations or data can supply evidence to refute an earlier inference. For example, recall the *Learn the Skill* activity about the person in the business clothing sitting at the desk. Note that the person could be a co-worker of the receptionist, who might be on the phone calling in sick. Discuss other similar scenarios.

2 Refine the Skill

Link to Past Skills Emphasize that the ability to make and identify inferences relies on an understanding of information that is presented. Have learners review the skill *Use Context Clues* from Lesson 12 of this unit before reading the passage and answering the questions on p. 54. Encourage them to apply this skill when reading the passages and examining the visuals in the rest of the lesson as well.

3 Master the Skill

Skim and Scan Have learners scan the table in the right column of p. 55. Make sure learners recognize that information such as that presented in the table can provide direct opportunities for comparing and contrasting, allowing inferences to be drawn. Emphasize that an inference is not a proven fact, but a plausible explanation based on information and reasoning.

➤ LifeLink

Have learners work in pairs, with one member of each pair describing a set of observations about a given situation. The other partner then should make an inference based on the observations. Next, have partners switch roles and repeat the activity.

Answers

1. C; DOK Level: 1; **2.** B; DOK Level: 1; **3.** C; DOK Level: 2; **4.** D; DOK Level: 2; **5.** A; DOK Level: 2; **6.** B; DOK Level: 2; **7.** D; DOK Level: 2; **8.** A; DOK Level: 2; **9.** A; DOK Level: 2; **10.** D; DOK Level: 3; **11.** C; DOK Level: 2; **12.** B; DOK Level: 3; **13.** A; DOK Level: 3

SCIENCE

Draw Conclusions

SCIENCE CONTENT TOPICS: L.c.5, L.f.3
SCIENCE PRACTICES: SP.1.a, SP.1.b, SP.1.c, SP.3.a, SP.3.b, SP.6.c, SP.7.a

SCIENCE

STUDENT BOOK *pp. 30–31*

▶ Preview the Skill

Provide learners with this scenario: A birdwatcher puts a mixture of seeds in his birdfeeder but finds squirrels, not birds, eating the seeds. Later, he sees that although the squirrels have eaten various seeds, some remain untouched. Ask what conclusion he can draw.

❶ Learn the Skill

Give Examples Emphasize that a conclusion relies on more evidence than an inference. For example, homeowners who hear noises coming from their cabinets may *infer* that they have mice. However, they can *conclude* that mice are present if they also find clear evidence, such as mouse droppings.

❷ Practice the Skill

Skim and Scan Ask a volunteer to read the information in the *Using Logic* box on p. 30. Have partners rule out answer choices by skimming and scanning the passage to determine whether each answer choice expresses facts stated directly in the passage.

❸ Apply the Skill

Spotlighted Item Type Introduce learners to the short answer item type by previewing the item on p. 31. Read the directions, and emphasize that learners should take their time in crafting responses to short answer items. Have a volunteer read question 2. Point out that short answers require support, and suggest that learners review any related text and visuals before, during, and after writing their responses. Also, note that on the GED® Science Test, they will type short answer responses in designated spaces.

Answers

1. C; DOK Level: 2; **2.** Possible answer: Through adaptation, reptiles have developed several traits that allow them to live in environments in which amphibians cannot survive. Reptiles have scaly skin that does not need to be kept moist. Their eggs stay moist because they have shells that hold in their fluids. Reptiles are born with legs to walk on land, and they have claws that allow them to dig land. They have lungs their entire lives, allowing them to obtain oxygen by taking in air. Amphibians have none of these traits and, therefore, cannot survive in the drier environments in which reptiles live. DOK Level: 3

WORKBOOK *pp. 58–61*

❶ Review the Skill

Give Examples Have partners brainstorm everyday examples that can be expressed as "If... then" statements. Note that making connections is important in drawing conclusions.

❷ Refine the Skill

Link to Past Skills Have learners use the skill *Identify Cause and Effect* from Lesson 4 of this unit to draw conclusions from the passage on p. 58.

❸ Master the Skill

Spotlighted Item Type Tell learners that they will be able to use an erasable note board, similar to a dry-erase board, during the GED® Test. Then have them practice taking notes as they prepare to answer questions 3–5 on pp. 59–61.

Answers

1. B; DOK Level: 2; **2.** A; DOK Level: 2; **3.** Possible answer: The fruit flies on the island could develop into a distinct species if the factors required for speciation to occur were present. The island would have to be far enough from the mainland that the two populations could not reach each other to interbreed. The environmental conditions of the island and mainland would have to be different enough that the two populations would experience different selection pressures. The processes of natural selection and adaptation would have to cause the population of fruit flies on the island to develop unique traits that would make them unwilling or unable to breed with the mainland fruit flies if individuals were returned to the mainland. DOK Level: 3; **4.** Possible answer: Natural selection is critical in the development of drug-resistant microbes. Natural selection results from selection pressures. A selection pressure is a feature of an environment that changes an organism's ability to survive and reproduce in the environment over time. When introduced into a population of microbes, a drug intended to kill or limit the growth of the microbes exerts a selection pressure. Through natural selection, organisms having the trait of resistance to the drug pass that trait on to future generations until the trait becomes common in the population. DOK Level: 3; **5.** Possible answer: By changing the environment, humans exert selection pressures that affect the rate of extinction. The environmental changes humans bring about include habitat destruction and alteration of the climate through global warming. When the environment in which a population lives is changed, the selection pressures on the population change. If members of the population are unable to develop traits needed to survive and reproduce in the changed habitat, the population may die off. When all populations of a species die off, the species becomes extinct. DOK Level: 3

Unit 1 Review

SCIENCE CONTENT TOPICS: L.a.1, L.a.2, L.a.3, L.a.4, L.b.1, L.c.1, L.c.2, L.c.3, L.c.4, L.c.5, L.d.1, L.d.2, L.d.3, L.e.1, L.e.2, L.e.3, L.f.1, L.f.2, L.f.3
SCIENCE PRACTICES: SP.1.a, SP.1.b, SP.1.c, SP.3.a, SP.3.b, SP.6.a, SP.6.c, SP.7.a, SP.8.b, SP.8.c

You may choose to use the Unit 1 Review on student book pp. 32–39 as a mini–practice test. If you wish to time the test, ask learners to complete all items in 75 minutes.

Unit 1 Review Answers

1. C; **2.** A; **3.** D; **4.** D; **5.** C; **6.** B; **7.** A; **8.** telophase; **9.** A; **10.** the mutant allele; **11.** B; **12.** D; **13.** B; **14.** A; **15.** D; **16.** B; **17.** A; **18.** B; **19.** C; **20.** B; **21.** D; **22.** D; **23.** the shark represents the introduction of the derived trait of jaws; the rabbit represents the introduction of the derived trait of hair; **24.** A; **25.1** C; **25.2** C; **25.3** A; **25.4** D; **26.** B; **27.** Possible answer: The passage explains that evolutionary theory suggests that species living today share a common ancestor and that one form of evidence scientists use to support this theory is similarities in stages of embryonic development. The illustration shows that during their embryonic development, both chickens and gorillas have gill-like structures and tails. These traits are evidence that both animals have an ancestor that had gills and a tail, suggesting that the animals share a common ancestor. **28.** B

Unit 1 Review Item Analysis

SKILL	DOK LEVEL 1	DOK LEVEL 2	DOK LEVEL 3
Interpret Illustrations	22		
Identify Main Idea and Details		19	
Interpret Tables	11, 12	6	
Identify Cause and Effect		2, 3, 7	
Interpret Graphs and Maps		1	
Interpret Diagrams		8	
Categorize and Classify	15	10	
Generalize		24	
Compare and Contrast		9, 28	
Relate Text and Visuals	4	5, 25	
Understand Content-Based Tools		16, 17, 18, 23	
Use Context Clues	20		
Understand Scientific Evidence			27
Make and Identify Inferences		14, 26	
Draw Conclusions		13	21

SCIENCE

Unit 1 Review

Use workbook lessons, as identified in the following table, to assist learners who require additional remediation with certain skills or items having certain DOK levels.

Unit 1 Workbook Item Analysis

SKILL	DOK LEVEL 1	DOK LEVEL 2	DOK LEVEL 3
Interpret Illustrations	1	2, 3, 4, 5, 6, 7, 8, 10, 11, 12, 13, 15, 16, 17	9, 14
Identify Main Idea and Details		1, 2, 3, 4, 5, 6, 9, 10, 11, 12	7, 8, 13
Interpret Tables	6	1, 2, 3, 4, 5, 7, 8, 9, 10, 11, 12, 13, 14	
Identify Cause and Effect	1	2, 3, 4, 5	
Interpret Graphs and Maps	1, 3, 4	2, 5, 7, 8, 9	6, 10, 11
Interpret Diagrams		1, 2, 3, 4, 5, 7, 8, 9, 10, 11	6
Categorize and Classify		1, 2, 3, 4, 5, 6, 7, 8, 9, 12, 13, 14, 15	10, 11, 16
Generalize		1, 2, 6, 7, 8, 10, 11	3, 4, 5, 9, 12, 13
Compare and Contrast	1	2, 3, 4, 5	
Relate Text and Visuals		1, 2, 3, 4, 5, 7, 8	6
Understand Content-Based Tools		1, 3, 4, 6	2, 5, 7, 8
Use Context Clues		1, 2, 3, 4, 5, 8, 10, 11, 12	6, 7, 9, 13, 14
Understand Scientific Evidence	1, 3, 4	2, 6, 7, 8	5, 9, 10
Make and Identify Inferences	1, 2	3, 4, 5, 6, 7, 8, 9, 11	10, 12, 13
Draw Conclusions		1, 2	3, 4, 5

SCIENCE

Unit 2

Physical Science

The physical science topics in Unit 2, such as properties of matter, chemical reactions, laws of motion, and energy transfer, may represent some of the most difficult content for your learners to master. However, reassure learners that the text and graphics in this unit will prepare them for physical science questions they will encounter on the GED® Science Test. As with life science, physical science items represent 40 percent of the questions on the GED® Science Test, and a proportionate amount of space has been allotted for physical science in *Steck-Vaughn Test Preparation for the 2014 GED® Test: Science*

Throughout Unit 2, lesson skills grow more complex. Building on such Unit 1 concepts as interpreting simple visuals and relating text and visuals, students will learn how to interpret complex visuals and draw conclusions from mixed sources. If learners struggle with the more complex visuals in Unit 2, you may wish to revisit similar lessons in Unit 1 to help build their skills and confidence.

Higher-order skills, such as those involved in predicting and interpreting outcomes, applying scientific laws, and evaluating scientific information, are a major focus of Unit 2. Because concepts involving atoms and molecules, motion, forces, and energy are less tangible than those involving plants and animals, learners may need to exercise greater abstract thinking when reading material and answering questions in this unit. To that end, *Steck-Vaughn Test Preparation for the 2014 GED® Test: Science* provides illustrations and diagrams that aid in understanding such complex concepts. In addition, this unit addresses techniques used in scientific investigation.

Table of Contents

LESSON	PAGE
1: Understand Scientific Models	SCI 22
2: Interpret Complex Visuals	SCI 23
3: Interpret Complex Tables	SCI 24
4: Understand Chemical Equations	SCI 25
5: Predict Outcomes	SCI 26
6: Calculate to Interpret Outcomes	SCI 27
7: Understand Vector Diagrams	SCI 28
8: Apply Scientific Laws	SCI 29
9: Access Prior Knowledge	SCI 30
10: Link Microscopic and Observable Events	SCI 31
11: Interpret Observations	SCI 32
12: Link Content from Varied Formats	SCI 33
13: Draw Conclusions from Mixed Sources	SCI 34
14: Understand Investigation Techniques	SCI 35
15: Evaluate Scientific Information	SCI 36
Unit 2 Review	SCI 37–SCI 38

SCIENCE

Understand Scientific Models

SCIENCE CONTENT TOPIC: P.c.1
SCIENCE PRACTICES: SP.1.a, SP.1.b, SP.1.c, SP.6.b, SP.7.a

STUDENT BOOK pp. 42–43

▶ Preview the Skill

Introduce the concept of scientific models by referring to model airplanes or trains. Point out that such models are much smaller than the real airplanes or trains they mimic. Lead learners in a discussion of what they might learn about the real-life objects by examining the models.

❶ Learn the Skill

Link to Past Skills Have learners review the skill *Interpret Graphs and Maps* from Unit 1, Lesson 5. Note that although the two-dimensional map on p. 11 is useful for identifying state boundaries, a three-dimensional model of the United States, such as a physical map with mountains and valleys, would provide information that the two-dimensional map cannot portray.

❷ Practice the Skill

Decoding Focus learners' attention on the model of a hydrogen atom and a helium atom on p. 42. Reinforce the idea that models such as these can represent objects that are much smaller in actual size. Help learners decode the symbols used in the models by having them find information about protons, neutrons, and electrons in the second paragraph of the passage. Then ask a volunteer to answer question 1.

❸ Apply the Skill

Give Examples Point out that the models of molecules on p. 43 provide a means for representing atoms, electrons, and protons, which are particles that are too small and move too fast to be seen with the unaided eye. As a class, identify other examples of objects or phenomena that might be modeled because they are too large, too small, too fast, or too slow to be observed directly *(examples: the solar system, cellular functions, the movement of sound waves, weathering and erosion of landforms)*.

Answers
1. D; DOK Level: 2; **2.** A; DOK Level: 2; **3.** B; DOK Level: 3; **4.** D; DOK Level: 2; **5.** B; DOK Level: 2

WORKBOOK pp. 62–65

❶ Review the Skill

SuperSkill Review Organize learners in pairs. Have one partner in each pair describe a model that he or she has seen on the news, on the Internet, or in some other source. Then have the other partner in each pair attempt to draw the model from the supplied description.

❷ Refine the Skill

Skim and Scan Draw attention to the model of the atom on p. 62. Have learners skim and scan pp. 63–65 to find a similar model *(the model of the carbon atom on p. 63)* and to note other ways that atoms and molecules can be depicted. Invite a volunteer to explain why various types of models are used to depict atoms and molecules. Ensure that learners understand that the structure and level of detail of any model relate directly to the characteristics of the object or process being depicted.

❸ Master the Skill

Decoding Discuss the fact that some models are constructed in the form of chemical and structural formulas. Have learners study the chemical and structural formulas for the three compounds depicted at the top of p. 65. Guide learners in decoding the meanings of the letters and subscript numerals used in the chemical formulas as well as the letters and bar symbols used in the structural formulas.

▶ Spotlighted Item Type

Draw learners' attention to the drag-and-drop item at the top of p. 65, and note that this type of item is a form of matching. Explain that they will use certain criteria to match the chemical formula to the structural formula for the same compound.

Answers
1. B; DOK Level: 2; **2.** A; DOK Level: 2; **3.** C; DOK Level: 3; **4.** A; DOK Level: 3; **5.** D; DOK Level: 2; **6.** B; DOK Level: 2; **7.** C; DOK Level: 3; **8.** D; DOK Level: 2; **9.** D; DOK Level: 3; **10.** A; DOK Level: 3; **11.** carbon dioxide—CO_2, hydrogen peroxide—H_2O_2, ozone—O_3; DOK Level: 2; **12.** B; DOK Level: 3

SCIENCE

Interpret Complex Visuals

SCIENCE CONTENT TOPIC: P.c.2
SCIENCE PRACTICES: SP.1.a, SP.1.b, SP.1.c, SP.3.b, SP.6.c, SP.7.a

STUDENT BOOK pp. 44–45

➤ Preview the Skill

Have learners imagine two diagrams, one illustrating battery placement in a flashlight and the other illustrating the workings of an automobile engine. Ask volunteers to describe how the two diagrams would differ in terms of detail, leading them to use the words *simple* and *complex* in their descriptions.

❶ Learn the Skill

Skim and Scan Have learners scan the title and pullout illustrations in the visual on p. 44 to identify information that can be determined by quick inspection. On the basis of this activity, ask learners to predict what they will learn from the diagram *(how the spacing of molecules in matter differs by state).*

❷ Practice the Skill

Link to Past Skills Review the skill *Compare and Contrast* from Unit 1, Lesson 9. Lead learners in contrasting the spacing of water molecules in the three states of matter depicted on p. 44.

❸ Apply the Skill

Use Graphic Organizers Challenge learners to turn a complex visual into a simpler one by transforming the heating curve diagram at the bottom of p. 45 into a four-step flowchart such as the one shown.

Adding energy raises ice temperature to 0°C.

Ice melts into liquid water.

Adding more energy raises water temperature to 100°C.

Water vaporizes into gaseous water vapor.

Answers
1. C; DOK Level: 2; **2.** added; DOK Level: 3; **3.** from liquid to solid; DOK Level: 3; **4.** gas; DOK Level: 3; **5.** B; DOK Level: 3

WORKBOOK pp. 66–69

❶ Review the Skill

Give Examples Ask learners to sketch an example of a complex visual that uses symbols, such as a football play or a family tree. Have several volunteers present their sketches to the class, identify what they have sketched, and explain how a complex visual helps convey information about it.

❷ Refine the Skill

Decoding Help learners decode the information provided in the complex visual on p. 66. Ask what the arrows in the diagram represent *(the directions of changes in state)* and what the pullout illustrations show *(spacing of molecules).* Then ask a volunteer to explain the advantage of using symbols and pullouts to represent information in a diagram *(they can show complex information efficiently, without the use of text).*

❸ Master the Skill

Link to Past Skills Have learners review the skill *Compare and Contrast* from Unit 1, Lesson 9. Point out that the Venn diagram in the left column of p. 67 and the three-part illustration in the right column of p. 67 are used to compare and contrast information. Encourage learners to digest the comparisons and contrasts identified by each visual before answering the associated questions.

➤ Analyze Visuals

Organize the class into four groups. Have each group analyze one of the visuals on pp. 68–69 and then explain the main ideas of the visual to the rest of the class. Then ask learners to work individually to answer questions 8–14.

Answers
1. A; DOK Level: 3; **2.** C; DOK Level: 3; **3.** A; DOK Level: 2; **4.** B; DOK Level: 2; **5.** D; DOK Level: 3; **6.** D; DOK Level: 2; **7.** B; DOK Level: 3; **8.** C; DOK Level: 2; **9.** D; DOK Level: 3; **10.** B; DOK Level: 3; **11.** D; DOK Level: 3; **12.** A; DOK Level: 3; **13.** D; DOK Level: 3; **14.** B; DOK Level: 3

SCIENCE

Interpret Complex Tables

SCIENCE CONTENT TOPIC: P.c.2
SCIENCE PRACTICES: SP.1.a, SP.1.b, SP.1.c, SP.3.a, SP.3.b, SP.3.d, SP.6.a, SP.7.a, SP.7.b, SP.8.b

STUDENT BOOK pp. 46–47

▶ Preview the Skill

Help learners recognize that they regularly encounter sophisticated tables. As an example, explain that the 1040 EZ tax form is made complex by having options for the type of taxpayer (single, married and filing jointly, married and filing separately) and sections for dependents, taxable income, and deductions. Explain that because the information to be entered in certain cells on the 1040 EZ can relate to information entered in previous cells, users must read and understand each line to interpret and complete the form. Ask volunteers to name instances in which they have created or used a complex table.

❶ Learn the Skill

Skim and Scan Review the basic structural elements of a table: title, column headings, and information organized in columns and across rows. Have learners skim and scan the tables on pp. 46–47 to identify those elements in each one.

❷ Practice the Skill

Decoding Direct learners' attention to the table on p. 46, and help them decode the meanings of the symbols related to the numerals in the "Boiling Point (°C)" column. Note that the C indicates that the temperatures are Celsius rather than Fahrenheit and that the minus sign indicates that one temperature is below freezing. Have learners discuss why analyzing a table for this type of information is important and how doing so can help them answer question 1.

❸ Apply the Skill

Spotlighted Item Type Have learners read the passage titled "Physical Properties" at the top of p. 47, and then invite a volunteer to read question 2. Encourage learners to make sure they understand exactly what response is required for a hot spot item. Clarify that for this item, learners are to mark an X in the "Yes" column for any substance that is a metal.

Answers
1. D; DOK Level: 1; **2.** "Yes" column for Substance B, "Yes" column for Substance C; DOK Level: 2; **3.** C; DOK Level: 2; **4.** B; DOK Level: 3

WORKBOOK pp. 70–73

❶ Review the Skill

Give Examples Explain to learners that a restaurant menu is essentially a series of tables. Organize learners in groups, and assign each group a portion of a standard menu, such as appetizers, main courses, desserts, and beverages. Direct each group to construct a simple table of food items and prices. Groups then should add other elements and information, such as item descriptions or nutrition information, to make their tables more complex. Allow learners 10 minutes to create their menus. Then have each group present its menu to the class.

❷ Refine the Skill

Decoding Help learners understand the information provided by the footnotes in the table on p. 70. Then ask whether the information provided in the footnotes is necessary to understand the content of the table *(yes)* and whether it is necessary to answer questions 1 and 2 *(yes for question 1, no for question 2).*

❸ Master the Skill

Skim and Scan Have learners scan the periodic table on p. 71 and skim the passage on p. 72 to identify relationships among the columns and rows of the table and patterns in the information provided by the table. Guide learners in a discussion of their interpretations.

▶ Analyze Visuals

Provide an activity to allow learners to analyze the periodic table further. Assign each class member one element from the table, and have each person identify the following information about his or her assigned element: its symbol; its atomic weight; and whether it is a metal, a nonmetal, or a metalloid. Allow the class two or three minutes to complete the assignment. Then work as a class to discuss uses for the elements they investigated.

Answers
1. D; DOK Level: 1; **2.** A; DOK Level: 2; **3.** D; DOK Level: 1;
4. B; DOK Level: 1; **5.** C; DOK Level: 2; **6.** A; DOK Level: 2;
7. D; DOK Level: 2; **8.** C; DOK Level: 3; **9.** A; DOK Level: 1;
10. B; DOK Level: 2; **11.** D; DOK Level: 2

SCIENCE

Understand Chemical Equations

SCIENCE CONTENT TOPICS: Pa.2, P.c.2, P.c.3
SCIENCE PRACTICES: SP.1.a, SP.1.b, SP.1.c, SP.3.b, SP.6.b, SP.7.a, SP.8.b

STUDENT BOOK *pp. 48–49*

▶ Preview the Skill

Write this mathematical equation on the board: $500 + 200 = 700$. Ask learners to explain how the two parts of the equation, on either side of the equal sign, are alike *(they are equal amounts)*. Note that chemical equations are like mathematical equations in that the number of atoms on one side of the equation (atoms in the reactants) must equal the number of atoms on the other side (atoms in the products).

❶ Learn the Skill

Decoding Ask a volunteer to read the first sentence in the *Learn the Skill* section on p. 48. Help learners understand its meaning by directing the class to examine the three versions of a chemical equation shown in the middle of the page. Have learners identify the version that uses words *(the first version)*, the version that uses symbols *(the second version)*, and the version that uses other components—in this case, models *(the third version)*. Note that learners most often will encounter chemical equations using symbols, such as the second version.

❷ Practice the Skill

Skim and Scan Have learners skim and scan the information on p. 48 to determine the names of the reactants and products in the chemical reaction shown in the middle of the page.

❸ Apply the Skill

Link to Past Skills Review the skills *Interpret Tables* from Unit 1, Lesson 3 and *Categorize and Classify* from Unit 1, Lesson 7. Then direct learners' attention to the "Types of Reactions" passage on p. 49. To strengthen understanding of chemical reactions and chemical equations, guide learners in using the passage to create a table that provides information about types of chemical reactions. Column headings might be "Type of Reaction," "What Occurs," and "General Form Equation."

Answers
1. D; DOK Level: 2; **2.** B; DOK Level: 1; **3.** D; DOK Level: 1; **4.** C; DOK Level: 2

WORKBOOK *pp. 74–77*

❶ Review the Skill

SuperSkill Review Note the chemical equation models in the right column of p. 75. Explain that they are designed to show types of chemical reactions in a way that might be easier to comprehend than the usual format using chemical formulas. Have volunteers describe in general terms what is occurring in the chemical reaction represented by each model (for example, Equation 1 represents a chemical reaction in which one element replaces another in a compound).

❷ Refine the Skill

Link to Past Skills Ask a volunteer to read the information in the *Using Logic* box on p. 74, and draw learners' attention to the chemical equation in the passage on that page. Then have learners use the skill *Compare and Contrast* from Unit 1, Lesson 9 to compare the number of atoms of each element in the reactants and product represented by the equation *(reactants—four hydrogen atoms and two oxygen atoms, product—four hydrogen atoms and two oxygen atoms)*. Ask the class to identify the scientific law that governs their finding *(conservation of mass)*.

❸ Master the Skill

Spotlighted Item Type Have partners work together to complete the fill-in-the-blank item on p. 76. Point out that like this item, fill-in-the-blank items on the GED® Science Test may have parts, requiring test takers to provide multiple answers.

▶ LifeLink

Ask learners to recall that chemical equations obey the law of conservation of mass. Have them brainstorm other instances in which what one has at the beginning of an event must equal what one has at the end, such as getting change for a $10 bill.

Answers
1. A; DOK Level: 1; **2.** B; DOK Level: 1; **3.** A; DOK Level: 3; **4.** C; DOK Level: 1; **5.** B; DOK Level: 1; **6.** C; DOK Level: 2; **7.** Step 1—$CH_4 + O_2 \rightarrow CO_2 + H_2O$, Step 2—$CH_4 + O_2 \rightarrow CO_2 + 2H_2O$, Step 3—$CH_4 + 2O_2 \rightarrow CO_2 + 2H_2O$, Step 4—$CH_4 + 2O_2 \rightarrow CO_2 + 2H_2O$; DOK Level: 2; **8.** D; DOK Level: 2; **9.** B; DOK Level: 2; **10.** A; DOK Level: 3

Predict Outcomes

SCIENCE CONTENT TOPIC: P.c.4
SCIENCE PRACTICES: SP.1.a, SP.1.b, SP.1.c, SP.3.b, SP.3.c, SP.3.d, SP.6.c, SP.7.a

SCIENCE

STUDENT BOOK pp. 50–51

➤ Preview the Skill

Discuss with learners the fact that we often attempt to predict outcomes in everyday life. As an example, ask what prediction a driver might make if his gas gauge shows that his tank is near empty and he is caught in a traffic jam.

❶ Learn the Skill

Give Examples Help learners understand that the skill of predicting outcomes has important real-world applications. Ask how someone might rely on the skill of predicting outcomes to avoid a situation such as the scenario described in the *Preview the Skill* activity *(by keeping an adequate amount of gas in an automobile at all times)*. Challenge learners to identify real-world issues that scientists address by predicting outcomes (for example, scientists predicted that a hole in the ozone layer would increase, so governments made laws to limit the release of hazardous materials into the air).

❷ Practice the Skill

Skim and Scan Have learners read question 1 on p. 50 and then skim the passage for the information needed to answer the question. Then discuss as a class the scenario described in the question, what outcome can be predicted, and what information from the passage is needed to arrive at that response.

❸ Apply the Skill

Link to Past Skills Encourage learners to review the skill *Interpret Graphs and Maps* from Unit 1, Lesson 5 to analyze the graph on p. 51. Discuss as a class how each solution represented by the graph changes as it is heated. Next, read question 3, and invite a volunteer to explain the term *saturated solution (a solution in which no more solute can be dissolved at the current temperature)*. Then ask a volunteer to answer the question and explain the reasoning behind his or her answer.

Answers
1. C; DOK Level: 3; **2.** B; DOK Level: 3; **3.** A; DOK Level: 3; **4.** B; DOK Level: 3; **5.** D; DOK Level 3

WORKBOOK pp. 78–81

❶ Review the Skill

SuperSkill Review Note the general reaction scheme for acid-base reactions in the left column of p. 80. Ask how understanding such a pattern is useful in predicting outcomes *(when an acid and a base are combined, you can predict that water and a salt will be produced)*. Stress the importance of recognizing and understanding patterns in mastering the skill of predicting outcomes.

❷ Refine the Skill

Skim and Scan Have learners skim the passage and scan the accompanying table on p. 78. Suggest that they look for patterns that will help them identify the types of chemical reactions that form acid, base, and salt solutions as well as the types of products that are parts of these solutions.

❸ Master the Skill

Spotlighted Item Type Note that previous short answer items have required learners to draw conclusions but that for question 3 on p. 79, they are to describe a series of events and make a prediction. Suggest that learners complete a flowchart as a prewriting activity for responding to such a question.

➤ LifeLink

Ask each class member to describe in writing a real-life scenario, minus the outcome. Then have each person pass his or her scenario to another class member, who, in turn, will write a one-sentence prediction of the scenario's outcome. Repeat the process until each student has made a prediction for each scenario. As a class, analyze why some scenarios have many possible outcomes whereas others may have only one or two.

Answers
1. C; DOK Level: 3; **2.** D; DOK Level: 3; **3.** Possible answer: When 30 g NaCl are added to the water, an unsaturated solution forms. As the additional 10 g NaCl are added, the solution becomes more concentrated. When 36 g NaCl have been added, the solution reaches saturation. The additional 4 g NaCl cannot dissolve in the solution. DOK Level: 3; **4.** C; DOK Level: 3; **5.** A; DOK Level: 3; **6.** A; DOK Level: 3; **7.** B; DOK Level: 3; **8.** C; DOK Level: 3; **9.** C; DOK Level: 3; **10.** A; DOK Level: 3; **11.** B; DOK Level: 3

Calculate to Interpret Outcomes

SCIENCE CONTENT TOPICS: P.b.1, P.b.2
SCIENCE PRACTICES: SP.1.a, SP.1.b, SP.1.c, SP.6.b, SP.7.b, SP.8.b

STUDENT BOOK pp. 52–53

▷ Preview the Skill

Introduce the skill by describing how someone might save enough money each month to afford a large purchase eventually. Provide the example of setting aside $100 each month. Ask how long it would take at that rate to accumulate enough money to buy a used car for $2,500. Write an equation on the board to show learners that 2,500 divided by 100 equals 25, meaning that it would take 25 months, or a little over two years, to save enough money to buy the car.

❶ Learn the Skill

Give Examples Create a timeline on the board for the example from the *Preview the Skill* activity. Use it to map out the proposed savings in $100 increments. Ask learners to predict how much money will be accumulated after one year. Show how this calculation can be performed on the timeline and by using the following equation:

monthly savings × time in months = total money saved

❷ Practice the Skill

Skim and Scan Have learners skim and scan the passage and diagram on p. 52. Ask what variables are represented in the diagram. Lead learners to recognize that although this example deals with distance and time, it is similar to the money-and-time example discussed during the *Preview the Skill* and *Learn the Skill* activities.

❸ Apply the Skill

Decoding Work with learners to decode the meanings of the words *speed* and *velocity* so that they can answer questions 2–3 on p. 53. Ask why it is important to understand the difference between speed and velocity when calculating outcomes *(to recognize the need to know direction when identifying the displacement of an object).*

Answers
1. C; DOK Level: 1; **2.** C; DOK Level: 2; **3.** A; DOK Level: 2; **4.** A; DOK Level: 2; **5.** D; DOK Level: 2

WORKBOOK pp. 82–85

❶ Review the Skill

Give Examples Have learners read the information presented on p. 82. Review the basic equation for calculating speed. Explain that speed is the rate of distance traveled over a certain amount of time, or distance per time. Then ask learners to suggest other rates *(examples: earnings as money per time, growth as height per time).*

❷ Refine the Skill

Decoding Write the equation $d = st$ on the board. Then note that to solve certain problems, an equation must be rearranged. Point out that the words *how long* in question 1 on p. 82 indicate that learners must solve for the variable of time. Have learners determine how to rearrange the equation to solve for time. Then as a class, use the rearranged equation to answer the question.

❸ Master the Skill

Link to Past Skills Have learners review the skill *Interpret Diagrams* from Unit 1, Lesson 6. Then point out that acceleration of a falling object, as depicted by the diagram in the left column of p. 85, is a complex process but that breaking it into smaller intervals can make it easier to understand. As a class, calculate the velocity of the falling object at each one-second interval, and use a flowchart to record the results.

▷ Cross-Curricular Connection

Learners who struggle with math skills or have math anxiety may feel challenged by the items in this lesson. Note that most of the items involve simple functions: addition, subtraction, multiplication, and division. Allow learners to use calculators to answer the questions or to check their answers, and remind them that they will have access to a calculator function during the GED® Science Test.

Answers
1. B; DOK Level: 1; **2.** B; DOK Level: 2; **3.** C; DOK Level: 1; **4.** C; DOK Level: 2; **5.** C; DOK Level: 1; **6.** A; DOK Level: 2; **7.** +2.0 m/s; DOK Level: 2; **8.** +1.5 m/s; DOK Level: 2; **9.** +2.0 m/s; DOK Level: 2; **10.** C; DOK Level: 2; **11.** D; DOK Level: 2; **12.** B; DOK Level: 2; **13.** A; DOK Level: 3; **14.** B; DOK Level: 3

SCIENCE

Understand Vector Diagrams

SCIENCE CONTENT TOPIC: P.b.2
SCIENCE PRACTICES: SP.1.a, SP.1.b, SP.1.c, SP.3.a, SP.7.a, SP.7.b, SP.8.b

STUDENT BOOK pp. 54–55

▶ Preview the Skill

Ask learners to visualize an adult pushing one side of a door while a small child pushes the other side. Draw a vertical line on the board to represent the door. Then draw an arrow pointing toward one side of the door, and explain that the arrow stands for the force the adult exerts on the door. Explain that you want to add an arrow to represent the force exerted by the child, and ask how that arrow should look compared to the first one *(shorter and pointing in the opposite direction)*. Ask a volunteer to draw that arrow on the diagram.

❶ Learn the Skill

Skim and Scan Emphasize that a force is a quantity that has a magnitude and a direction. Have partners preview the diagrams in the lesson and make statements about the magnitudes and directions of the forces represented based on the arrows in the diagrams.

❷ Practice the Skill

SuperSkill Review Note that like the arrows in the diagram from the *Preview the Skill* activity, the arrows in the diagram on p. 54 represent forces of differing strengths. Explain that the unit of measurement for the magnitude of a force is the newton, and convey the information from question 1 that the magnitudes of the forces represented in the diagram are 2 newtons, 7 newtons, 9 newtons, and 15 newtons. As a class, determine which measurement applies to each arrow in the vector diagram, and then answer question 1.

❸ Apply the Skill

Decoding Draw attention to the equation $F = ma$ in the left column of p. 55. Write the equation on the board, and ask learners to interpret the diagram to help you identify the values for mass *(3 kg)* and acceleration *(5 m/s²)*. Lead learners to understand that they can use the equation to find the value of the force represented by the diagram and answer question 2.

Answers
1. B; DOK Level: 1; **2.** D; DOK Level: 1; **3.** B; DOK Level: 3;
4. D; DOK Level: 2; **5.** C; DOK Level: 2

WORKBOOK pp. 86–89

❶ Review the Skill

SuperSkill Review Point out that the vector diagrams in the lesson are accompanied by passages that help explain what they represent. Emphasize that one purpose of the passages is to teach science concepts learners will need to understand when they take the GED® Science Test. Note that on the test itself, an item about forces might simply depict a vector diagram with little or no accompanying text. Have learners working in groups preview the lesson, attempting to answer questions by first looking at the diagrams and then checking the accompanying passages for any necessary additional information.

❷ Refine the Skill

Decoding Direct learners' attention to question 1 on p. 86. Ask what determining the net force on the object will tell them about the object *(whether it will move, which direction it will move)*. Have learners analyze the question to identify the calculation they will have to carry out to determine the net force *(subtract opposite forces from each other)*.

❸ Master the Skill

Spotlighted Item Type Lead learners to recall that drop-down items are basically multiple-choice questions and that they must choose the best of four possible answers to complete several sentences in a passage. Then allow learners to work in pairs to complete the drop-down item on p. 87.

▶ Enrich and Extend

Have each class member draw a vector diagram representing two forces acting on a box. One force has a value of 50 newtons east; the other has a value of 75 newtons west. Ask volunteers to share their diagrams. Have learners discuss whether they are correct and why or why not. Then ask whether the box will move and, if so, in which direction *(yes; it will move west)*.

Answers
1. C; DOK Level: 1; **2.** B; DOK Level: 1; **3.1** C; **3.2** D; **3.3** A;
DOK Level: 1; **4.** B; DOK Level: 2; **5.** C; DOK Level: 1;
6. D; DOK Level: 1; **7.** B; DOK Level: 2; **8.** A; DOK Level: 1;
9. D; DOK Level: 1; **10.** B; DOK Level: 2; **11.** C; DOK
Level: 2; **12.** D; DOK Level: 3

SCIENCE

Apply Scientific Laws

SCIENCE CONTENT TOPICS: P.b.1, P.b.2
SCIENCE PRACTICES: SP.1.a, SP.1.b, SP.1.c, SP.3.a, SP.3.c, SP.6.c, SP.7.a, SP.7.b, SP.8.b

STUDENT BOOK pp. 56–57

➤ Preview the Skill

Tell learners that, in general, a law is a rule that governs conduct. For example, litter laws state that it is illegal to throw trash on the street. Next, explain that scientific laws are statements that describe how something in the natural environment behaves. For example, the law of conservation of matter states that matter cannot be created or destroyed. So when someone burns wood in a fireplace, the wood does not disappear. It becomes ash, carbon dioxide, water vapor, and various aerosol particles contained in smoke.

❶ Learn the Skill

Give Examples Write Newton's second law of motion on the board: *The acceleration of a body is in direct proportion to and in the same direction as the net force acting on the body.* Guide learners in restating the law in their own words *(example: when a force is applied to an object, it will accelerate or move in the direction of the force; the greater the force, the greater the acceleration).* Next, ask learners to apply the law to predict the movement of a soccer ball when kicked downfield by a 120-pound man and then by a 270-pound man *(the ball will move downfield a greater distance when kicked by the 270-pound man because he can apply greater force).*

❷ Practice the Skill

Decoding Direct learners' attention to the passage on p. 56. Have them look for the section that restates the law of universal gravitation in plainer language. Have learners review the meaning of the law with a partner in preparation for answering question 1.

❸ Apply the Skill

Spotlighted Item Type Emphasize the importance of understanding the drag-and-drop options when responding to a drag-and-drop item. Have learners list the four laws that make up the drag-and-drop options on p. 57, write a summary of each, and use their summaries as an aid in answering question 2.

Answers
1. C; DOK Level: 2; **2.** Scenario A—law of universal gravitation, Scenario B—third law of motion, Scenario C—second law of motion, Scenario D—first law of motion; DOK Level: 3; **3.** B; DOK Level: 2

WORKBOOK pp. 90–93

❶ Review the Skill

SuperSkill Review Write these three definitions on the board: *a statement that describes the rules of scientific investigation, a statement that describes the way forces act on objects, a statement that describes how matter and energy behave.* Point to the definitions one by one. Have the class discuss each one to determine which correctly explains what a scientific law is.

❷ Refine the Skill

Decoding Review the difference between mass and weight. Explain that the mass of an average car could be about 1,100 kilograms, which would be a weight on Earth's surface of 10,780 newtons. Note that the moon has one-sixth Earth's gravity. Ask whether the car's mass would be different on the moon *(no)* and whether its weight would be different *(yes).* Lead learners to recall that the amount of matter (mass) does not change whereas the gravitational force acting on the matter (weight) does.

❸ Master the Skill

Skim and Scan Have learners scan the graph on p. 91 to identify the data on the two axes. Guide learners in understanding the relationship shown between momentum and time.

➤ LifeLink

Have each learner describe in writing a time when he or she observed one of the laws described in this lesson at work in real life. Learners should briefly describe the scenario, explaining how the law was applied. Give learners about five minutes to complete the task, and ask volunteers to share what they have written. Discuss the examples as a class.

Answers
1. A; DOK Level: 2; **2.** A; DOK Level: 2; **3.** A; DOK Level: 2; **4.** B; DOK Level: 3; **5.** C; DOK Level: 2; **6.** B; DOK Level: 2; **7.** D; DOK Level: 2; **8.** A; DOK Level: 2; **9.** C; DOK Level: 2; **10.** D; DOK Level: 2; **11.** A; DOK Level: 2; **12.** B; DOK Level: 2; **13.** D; DOK Level: 3; **14.** D; DOK Level 2; **15.** C; DOK Level: 2; **16.** A; DOK Level: 2; **17.** A; DOK Level: 2; **18.** C; DOK Level: 2; **19.** B; DOK Level: 2

SCIENCE

Access Prior Knowledge

SCIENCE CONTENT TOPIC: P.b.3
SCIENCE PRACTICES: SP.1.a, SP.1.b, SP.1.c, SP.3.b, SP.7.a, SP.7.b, SP.8.b

SCIENCE

STUDENT BOOK pp. 58–59

▶ Preview the Skill

Describe this scenario to learners: A woman puts a small kettle of water on the stove to boil to make a cup of tea and then realizes she is out of tea bags. Ask whether it would be a good idea for her to go to the supermarket to get tea bags while waiting for the water to boil. After learners answer "no," ask them to explain why *(the water will boil before she returns)*. Tell learners that they have just accessed prior science knowledge. They know from past observation that a small kettle of water when heated will reach its boiling point in just a few minutes—not enough time to shop.

❶ Learn the Skill

Skim and Scan Have learners working in groups skim and scan the lesson content. Instruct group members to share with one another what they know about forces, machines, mechanical advantage, and power.

❷ Practice the Skill

Decoding Help learners decode the word *work* as it is used in this lesson. Note that the meaning of *work* as they commonly use the word in everyday life is different from its meaning in science. Discuss as a class how simple machines make work easier. Then have a volunteer answer question 1 on p. 58 and explain the reasoning used to arrive at the correct answer.

❸ Apply the Skill

SuperSkill Review Explain that asking questions about known facts or information can help in accessing prior knowledge and applying that knowledge to new situations. Have learners look at the information and questions on p. 59 and ask themselves these questions:
- What is being described or explained?
- To what situations might the information relate?
- How can I access what I already know to answer the questions correctly?

Answers
1. C; DOK Level: 1; **2.** arrows pointing out from ax blade; DOK Level: 2; **3.** D; DOK Level: 2; **4.** A; DOK Level: 2; **5.** A; DOK Level: 2

WORKBOOK pp. 94–97

❶ Review the Skill

Give Examples Remind learners that they often access prior science knowledge in their everyday lives—as in the example about boiling water from the *Preview the Skill* activity. Organize learners in small groups, and have them relate other examples of ways in which they have accessed prior science knowledge and applied it to everyday situations.

❷ Refine the Skill

Use Graphic Organizers Have learners use a table such as the one shown to record what they know about forces, tools, and machines. Remind them to include information that they have learned in class. Suggest that they refer to the table if they are challenged by a question in the lesson.

Knowledge Acquired Through Formal Learning	Knowledge Acquired Through Experience

❸ Master the Skill

Skim and Scan Explain to learners that they will apply prior knowledge when analyzing visuals to answer questions on the GED® Science Test. Suggest that they scan the diagrams on pp. 95–97 and predict the kinds of knowledge they might need to apply to answer the related questions.

▶ Cross-Curricular Connection

Emphasize that prior knowledge related to science may come from other areas, such as language arts, math, and social studies. Have groups brainstorm examples of prior knowledge in each subject area that they might use to strengthen their understanding of science topics.

Answers
1. D; DOK Level: 2; **2.** C; DOK Level: 2; **3.** B; DOK Level: 2; **4.** B; DOK Level: 2; **5.** C; DOK Level: 2; **6.** A; DOK Level: 2; **7.** C; DOK Level: 3; **8.** A; DOK Level: 2; **9.** D; DOK Level: 2; **10.** D; DOK Level: 2; **11.** A; DOK Level: 1; **12.** B; DOK Level: 1; **13.** D; DOK Level: 1; **14.** A; DOK Level: 2; **15.** D; DOK Level: 2; **16.** C; DOK Level: 3

SCIENCE CONTENT TOPICS: P.a.1, P.a.3, P.a.5
SCIENCE PRACTICES: SP.1.a, SP.1.b, SP.1.c, SP.3.b, SP.3.c, SP.4.a, SP.7.a

STUDENT BOOK pp. 60–61

➤ Preview the Skill

Show a photo of a piece of cake, and lead learners to observe that the cake has tiny holes. Explain that a cake is made with leavening, such as baking powder, which releases a gas into the batter as it bakes, causing the cake to rise. Ask learners to infer how the gas and the small holes they observed are related *(areas of gas create holes in the batter as it bakes)*. Tell learners that the holes in the cake are an observable result of a microscopic event.

1 Learn the Skill

Give Examples Challenge learners to analyze the observable events listed below and suggest the microscopic cause of each:

- Water in an ice cube tray becomes frozen in a freezer *(molecules in the water lose energy)*.
- A chemical reaction produces water *(atoms of hydrogen and oxygen join to form water molecules)*.

2 Practice the Skill

Decoding To ensure that learners can answer question 1 on p. 60, review the difference between a substance's temperature and its thermal energy. Emphasize that because thermal energy is the total kinetic energy in a substance, two substances having different masses but the same temperature contain different amounts of thermal energy. Ask which has more thermal energy—dishwater in a sink at 80°F or water in a filled backyard pool at the same temperature *(the water in the pool)*.

3 Apply the Skill

SuperSkill Review As a class, discuss everyday events that model the types of heat transfer identified in the passage at the top of p. 61 *(examples: conduction—burning feet on hot beach sand, convection—a radiator heating a room, radiation—the sun's energy traveling through space to Earth)*.

Answers
1. D; DOK Level: 2; **2.** convection—blue arrows, conduction—green arrows, radiation—yellow arrows; DOK Level: 2; **3.** B; DOK Level: 3

WORKBOOK pp. 98–101

1 Review the Skill

Skim and Scan Organize learners in groups, and assign a visual from the lesson to each group. Have learners scan the visuals and predict how they depict observable events related to activity occurring at microscopic levels.

2 Refine the Skill

Decoding On the board, write this statement based on the passage on p. 98: *When a glass thermometer comes in contact with a warmer substance, the vibrating particles in the substance cause the vibrating particles in the glass to move faster.* Ask learners to use the information you have written to determine in which direction heat moves—from warmer matter to cooler matter or from cooler matter to warmer matter.

3 Master the Skill

Use Graphic Organizers Have learners read the passage and examine the diagram in the right column of p. 100. Then display the sequence diagram shown to prepare learners for answering question 6. As learners identify the type of heat transfer that occurs at each step, fill in the blanks in the diagram *(convection, conduction, radiation)*.

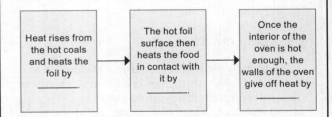

| Heat rises from the hot coals and heats the foil by _____. | → | The hot foil surface then heats the food in contact with it by _____. | → | Once the interior of the oven is hot enough, the walls of the oven give off heat by _____. |

➤ Analyze Visuals

Draw learners' attention to the diagram in the left column of p. 101. Before learners answer question 7, ask a volunteer to explain what the pullout illustration shows *(particles in the coffee, the mug, and the air outside the mug)*.

Answers
1. C; DOK Level: 2; **2.** A; DOK Level 2; **3.** C; DOK Level: 2; **4.** D; DOK Level: 3; **5.** A; DOK Level: 2; **6.** B; DOK Level: 2; **7.** D; DOK Level: 2; **8.** D; DOK Level 3

SCIENCE

Interpret Observations

SCIENCE CONTENT TOPICS: P.a.2, P.a.3
SCIENCE PRACTICES: SP.1.a, SP.1.b, SP.1.c, SP.3.a, SP.3.b, SP.3.c, SP.6.a, SP.7.a

STUDENT BOOK pp. 62–63

➤ Preview the Skill

Ask learners to imagine holding a cup of liquid and observing that the liquid is light brown and that steam is rising from it. Then have them imagine drinking the liquid and finding that it has a sweet flavor. Ask a volunteer to identify the liquid *(hot, sweetened tea)* and explain how the observations you described led to that interpretation.

❶ Learn the Skill

Give Examples Ask learners what they would observe if a bicyclist were to run over a nail, a child were to throw a rock into a pond, or a chef were to place a stick of butter in a hot pan. Remind learners to focus only on what their five senses might detect, not on what they assume, due to prior knowledge, *should* happen. Point out that they should attach meaning to an observation only after describing it.

❷ Practice the Skill

Decoding Walk learners through an analysis of the graph on p. 62. Ask what the two lines on the graph represent *(two types of energy—kinetic and potential)*. Make sure that learners understand how to read the graph to determine how kinetic energy and potential energy are changing as the toy car moves along the ramp.

❸ Apply the Skill

Link to Past Skills Have learners review the skill *Cause and Effect* from Unit 1, Lesson 4. Point out that interpreting observations involves understanding causes and effects. As an example, explain that to answer question 2 on p. 63, learners must determine the effect of the turbine on the wind, as illustrated in the diagram.

Answers
1. A; DOK Level: 2; **2.** A; DOK Level: 2; **3.** B; DOK Level: 2; **4.** C; DOK Level: 2

WORKBOOK pp. 102–105

❶ Review the Skill

Link to Past Skills Ask learners to review the skill *Compare and Contrast* from Unit 1, Lesson 9. Then recall the *Preview the Skill* activity, and have learners imagine a second cup, one containing a steaming liquid that is very dark brown and does not taste sweet (hot, black coffee). Ask learners to explain on the basis of the observations you have described how preparation of the second liquid likely was similar to and different from preparation of the first liquid. Explain that interpreting observations often involves comparing and contrasting the effects of manipulating variables.

❷ Refine the Skill

Skim and Scan Ask a volunteer to read the information in the *Using Logic* box on p. 102. Have learners keep the information from the box in mind as they scan the graph to determine how potential energy and kinetic energy are related in the scenario described in the passage.

❸ Master the Skill

SuperSkill Review Have pairs read the passage and examine the graph in the left column of p. 103. Then read aloud question 3 but not the answer choices. Ask partners to brainstorm interpretations they can make about the potential energy and kinetic energy of the toy car. Finally, have partners read the answer choices and determine the correct answer on the basis of their discussion. Have learners repeat this activity for question 6.

➤ Spotlighted Item Type

Emphasize the importance of connecting any related text with the graphic used to answer a hot spot item. Then allow learners to work in pairs to complete questions 7–8 on p. 104.

Answers
1. C; DOK Level: 2; **2.** D; DOK Level: 2; **3.** B; DOK Level: 2; **4.** A; DOK Level: 2; **5.** C; DOK Level: 2; **6.** A; DOK Level: 2; **7.** at the peak of the first hill; DOK Level: 2; **8.** at the bottom of each hill; DOK Level: 2; **9.** B; DOK Level: 2; **10.** D; DOK Level: 2; **11.** A; DOK Level: 2; **12.** D; DOK Level: 2; **13.** B; DOK Level: 3; **14.** A; DOK Level: 3

SCIENCE

Link Content from Varied Formats

SCIENCE CONTENT TOPIC: P.a.5
SCIENCE PRACTICES: SP.1.a, SP.1.b, SP.1.c, SP.3.b, SP.6.a, SP.6.c, SP.7.a

STUDENT BOOK *pp. 64–65*

▶ Preview the Skill

Display a written recipe that is accompanied by a color photo of the completed dish. Ask learners why the photo—in addition to the written text—would be useful to someone trying to prepare the dish. Emphasize that we often need to link content from varied formats to complete a task or draw a conclusion.

1 Learn the Skill

Give Examples Have learners brainstorm as a class to identify instances in which visual information and textual information can complement one another to help explain a science topic. Ask those who volunteer examples to explain the value of both the visual information and the textual information.

2 Practice the Skill

Link to Past Skills Revisit with learners the skill *Interpret Complex Visuals* from Lesson 2 of this unit. Remind learners that diagrams, such as the one on p. 64, show relationships. Ask learners to identify relationships shown in the diagram *(examples: the movement of particles is perpendicular to the movement of the wave, crests and troughs are equidistant from the resting positions of particles).*

3 Apply the Skill

Spotlighted Item Type Have learners work in pairs to determine the correct answers to question 2 on p. 65. Suggest that they first skim and scan the passage and the diagram to determine the meanings of the four terms that make up the drag-and-drop options. Have learners then look at the diagram to determine how they can apply each definition visually. Emphasize that the key to understanding the diagram is locating text that helps explain it.

Answers
1. B; DOK Level: 2; **2.** top wave is a longitudinal wave and unlabeled part is rarefaction; bottom wave is a transverse wave, and unlabeled part is amplitude; DOK Level: 2; **3.** D; DOK Level: 2

WORKBOOK *pp. 106–109*

1 Review the Skill

SuperSkill Review Tell learners that after a night baseball game, the next morning's newspaper includes an article about the game. Also, it provides the box score for the game. Ask volunteers to explain how the newspaper article and the box score work together to give a more complete understanding of the game.

2 Refine the Skill

Skim and Scan Have learners scan the diagram on p. 106 to determine the types of electromagnetic radiation and how their wavelengths compare. Ask the class to skim the passage and identify information not presented by the diagram. Explain that one such piece of information—the fact that waves with longer wavelengths have less energy than waves with shorter wavelengths—will help them decipher the diagram to answer questions 1 and 2.

3 Master the Skill

Use Graphic Organizers To help learners comprehend the differences between a transverse wave and a longitudinal wave, have them use the passage and the diagram in the left column of p. 107 to fill out a table such as the one shown. Suggest that they refer to their tables when answering questions 3–5.

Type of Wave	Type of Energy	Particle Movement	Repeating Pattern
longitudinal	sound	in the direction of wave movement	areas where particles are squished and spread apart
transverse	light	perpendicular to wave movement	high and low points

Answers
1. A; DOK Level: 1; **2.** D; DOK Level: 2; **3.** D; DOK Level: 2; **4.** D; DOK Level: 2; **5.** A; DOK Level: 2; **6.** B; DOK Level: 2; **7.** A; DOK Level: 2; **8.** D; DOK Level: 2; **9.** A; DOK Level: 2; **10.** C; DOK Level: 2; **11.** B; DOK Level: 1; **12.** A; DOK Level: 2; **13.** B; DOK Level: 3; **14.** D; DOK Level: 2

SCIENCE

Draw Conclusions from Mixed Sources

SCIENCE CONTENT TOPIC: P.a.4
SCIENCE PRACTICES: SP.1.a, SP.1.b, SP.1.c, SP.3.a, SP.3.b, SP.4.a, SP.5.a, SP.6.c, SP.7.a

STUDENT BOOK pp. 66–67

▶ Preview the Skill

Introduce the skill by asking learners to think of a time when they consulted a variety of sources for input before making an important decision. Give the example of a person who wants to go into business for herself but worries about whether her idea will succeed. Ask learners what kinds of information the prospective business owner may want to gather before investing time and money in the business venture. Explain that gathering information from multiple sources can be useful in many situations.

❶ Learn the Skill

Link to Past Skills Have learners review the skill *Draw Conclusions* from Unit 1, Lesson 15. Lead a class discussion about strategies to apply to draw conclusions from diagrams and graphs. Guide learners to view information provided in the labels of diagrams or data represented in graphs as they would facts stated in texts. Emphasize that they can reason from information in diagram labels or data in graphs to draw conclusions.

❷ Practice the Skill

Skim and Scan Ask a volunteer to read the information in callout *a* on p. 66. Then work as a class to follow the suggestion provided in the callout. Ask learners to scan the flowchart to determine the source of coal (*plants*) and then skim the passage to determine the source of the energy in coal (*the sun*).

❸ Apply the Skill

SuperSkill Review Ask a volunteer to read question 2 on p. 67. Next, have learners examine the information in the graphs and determine what additional information they need to answer the question. Ask what they need to know that is not clear from the graphs (*the criteria that would have led to a state's having to submit a pollution-reduction plan in 2010*). Then have learners read the passage to find this information.

Answers
1. B; DOK Level: 2; **2.** D; DOK Level: 2; **3.** C; DOK Level: 3

WORKBOOK pp. 110–113

❶ Review the Skill

SuperSkill Review In a class discussion, have learners describe experiences in which they used multiple sources of information to draw conclusions.

❷ Refine the Skill

Skim and Scan Remind learners that they have to use information from all sources to answer questions such as those on p. 110. Have learners skim and scan the passage and the graph on the page to determine the types of information each contains.

❸ Master the Skill

Link to Past Skills Note that the information needed to answer question 3 on p. 111 comes from two diagrams. Have learners review the skill *Interpret Complex Visuals* from Lesson 2 of this unit for keys to understanding complex diagrams such as these. Allow learners to work in pairs to analyze the workings of the two power plants. Note that concentrating on differences between the power plants will help them answer question 3.

▶ Spotlighted Item Type

Draw attention to the *Spotlighted Item* box on p. 113. Suggest that learners read question 8 before reading the passage and studying the graph. Advise them to pre-write by recording a conclusion followed by a bulleted list of details from the passage and graph that support the conclusion. Encourage them to apply this tactic to draw more than one conclusion from the information.

Answers
1. B; DOK Level: 2; **2.** D; DOK Level: 2; **3.** D; DOK Level: 2; **4.** C; DOK Level: 2; **5.** C; DOK Level: 2; **6.** D; DOK Level: 2; **7.** B; DOK Level: 2; **8.** Possible answer: The data on the graph show that global emissions of carbon dioxide have risen drastically since the 1960s. The passage explains that carbon dioxide is a greenhouse gas that helps retain Earth's heat. Also, it states that the warmest 12-month periods between 1895 and 2012 have occurred since 2000—with five having occurred during the most recent years. With this information, the conclusion can be reached that the increase in carbon dioxide in the air, due in part to burning fossil fuels, has given Earth a greater capacity to hold in heat and made it a warmer planet. DOK Level: 3

SCIENCE

Understand Investigation Techniques

SCIENCE CONTENT TOPICS: P.a.1, P.a.4, P.b.1, P.b.2, P.c.1, P.c.2, P.c.3, P.c.4
SCIENCE PRACTICES: SP.2.a, SP.2.b, SP.2.c, SP.2.d, SP.2.e, SP.3.b, SP.3.c, SP.3.d, SP.5.a, SP.6.c, SP.7.a, SP.8.a, SP.8.b

STUDENT BOOK pp. 68–69

➤ Preview the Skill

Write this sentence on the board: *What color will I get if I mix yellow paint and blue paint?* Then write this sentence: *If I mix yellow paint and blue paint, I will get green paint.* Ask learners what you should do to test your idea *(mix yellow paint and blue paint)*. Explain that scientists use a process similar to the one you just demonstrated to conduct scientific investigations.

❶ Learn the Skill

Use Graphic Organizers To understand investigation techniques, learners must understand the steps in the scientific method. Write these steps on the board: *develop a hypothesis, analyze and interpret data, design and perform an investigation, ask a question.* Note that they are out of sequence. Have each learner fill in the steps in sequence on a graphic organizer such as the one shown. Discuss the correct order of steps as a class.

1	Ask a question.
2	Develop a hypothesis.
3	Design and perform an investigation.
4	Analyze and interpret data.

❷ Practice the Skill

Skim and Scan Point out that question 1 on p. 68 relates to actions investigators take after analyzing and interpreting data. Have learners skim the passage to find information that will help them answer the question.

❸ Apply the Skill

Decoding Ensure that learners comprehend the difference between a dependent variable and an independent variable. Note that a dependent variable changes depending on how an investigator manipulates the factors of an investigation.

Answers
1. B; DOK Level: 1; **2.** C; DOK Level: 2; **3.** B; DOK Level: 2;
4. A; DOK Level: 2; **5.** B; DOK Level: 2; **6.** A; DOK Level: 3

WORKBOOK pp. 114–117

❶ Review the Skill

Give Examples Share this scenario with learners: A man observes that a certain type of plant in his yard is taller near a fence where no trees grow than near his house where there are tall trees. Challenge learners to work as a class to come up with steps the man could use to investigate his observation.

❷ Refine the Skill

Skim and Scan Have learners scan the flowchart on p. 114 to review the steps of the scientific method and then read callouts *a* and *b* to gather additional information.

❸ Master the Skill

SuperSkill Review Have groups preview and discuss the passages and graphics on pp. 115–116. Instruct them to take notes about investigation techniques related to the scenarios described. Encourage learners to refer to their notes as they answer questions on the pages.

Answers
1. D; DOK Level: 2; **2.** B; DOK Level: 2; **3.** D; DOK Level: 2;
4. C; DOK Level: 3; **5.** A; DOK Level: 2; **6.** B; DOK Level: 2;
7. A; DOK Level: 2; **8.** C; DOK Level: 1; **9.** D; DOK Level: 1;
10. B; DOK Level: 3; **11.** Possible answer: Set a starting point and an ending point for the water temperature (for example, 20°C and 90°C), and control for the amount of water used; that is, maintain the same volume of water throughout the investigation. Next, slowly add salt to the water at the coolest temperature to determine the saturation point for the solution. Record the figure for the applicable amount of salt and the water temperature. Then raise the temperature of the water a predetermined increment, add the same amount of salt to the warmer water, and observe whether all the salt goes into solution. Continue the process until reaching a temperature at which all the salt does not go into solution. At that point, strain the precipitate out of the water and measure it to determine what percentage of the salt did not go into solution. The dependent variable is the amount of salt that dissolves before the saturation point is reached; the independent variable is the amount of increase in water temperature. After the investigation, plot data on a line graph, graphing the relationship between saturation point and water temperature. If the investigation results demonstrate that warmer water dissolves less salt, the hypothesis is validated. DOK Level: 3; **12.** B; DOK Level: 2

SCIENCE

Evaluate Scientific Information

SCIENCE CONTENT TOPICS: P.a.1, P.a.3, P.a.5, P.b.1, P.b.2, P.c.2, P.c.3, P.c.4
SCIENCE PRACTICES: SP.1.a, SP.1.b, SP.1.c, SP.2.a, SP.2.b, SP.2.c, SP.2.e, SP.3.b, SP.4.a, SP.5.a, SP.7.a

STUDENT BOOK pp. 70–71

⟩ Preview the Skill

On the board, write these questions: *Will a car's engine run on isopropyl alcohol rather than gasoline? Will a car's engine function better in warm weather than in cold weather?* Ask learners which question can be a source for a scientific investigation and which cannot. Accept answers from several volunteers, and have them explain their reasoning. Ensure that learners understand that only the first question would lead to a valid, testable hypothesis. Because the second question is vague—how warm? how cold? what does *better* mean?—the results of an associated investigation also would be too vague to be of use.

❶ Learn the Skill

Give Examples Read the *Learn the Skill* section on p. 70 with learners. Note that evaluating scientific information helps people determine whether conclusions are valid. Ask learners to brainstorm examples of why valid scientific conclusions are necessary and desirable. Have them consider the effects of accepting invalid conclusions.

❷ Practice the Skill

Decoding Review the following terms from p. 70: *observation, investigation, testable hypothesis, independent variable, dependent variable.* Have volunteers use the words correctly in original sentences.

❸ Apply the Skill

Link to Past Skills Ask learners to examine the diagram on p. 71. As they do, guide them to use the skill *Interpret Complex Visuals* from Lesson 2 of this unit. In particular, ask them to note the column headings and determine the meaning of the arrow on the left side of the diagram. After the class demonstrates an understanding of the diagram, have learners complete item 2.

Answers
1. B; DOK Level: 2; **2.1** A; **2.2** D; **2.3** D; **2.4** A; DOK Level: 2

WORKBOOK pp. 118–121

❶ Review the Skill

SuperSkill Review Invite volunteers to come to the board to list the steps of the scientific method and other information related to scientific investigations (for example, explanations of independent and dependent variables). Discuss how each step or other point relates to the validity of scientific information.

❷ Refine the Skill

Link to Past Skills Recall the skills *Make Inferences* and *Draw Conclusions* from Unit 1, Lessons 14–15. Emphasize that learners must use higher-order thinking skills such as these to evaluate scientific investigations. As a class, read the passage on p. 118, and answer questions 1–2. List the skills that were required to determine the correct answers to the questions. Review those skills before continuing.

❸ Master the Skill

Decoding Instruct learners to scan the phase diagram on p. 119. Note that comprehension of the diagram is crucial for answering question 3 correctly. Advise learners to pay particular attention to the variables measured on each axis of the diagram. Also, encourage them to analyze the labels on the diagram to determine the meanings of its sections. Have learners work in pairs to analyze the diagram and answer question 3.

⟩ LifeLink

Organize learners in pairs. Then have each learner describe scientific information he or she has heard or read about recently. Challenge each partner to evaluate the information to determine its reliability on the basis of its source and how it was determined to be valid. If that background is not known, tell learners to propose a reliable way of forming and testing a hypothesis related to the information.

Answers
1. C; DOK Level: 2; **2.** A; DOK Level: 2; **3.** D; DOK Level: 2; **4.** B; DOK Level: 2; **5.** B; DOK Level: 3; **6.** D; DOK Level 2; **7.** B; DOK Level: 2; **8.** C; DOK Level: 3; **9.** A; DOK Level: 2; **10.** C; DOK Level: 2; **11.** D; DOK Level: 2; **12.** A; DOK Level: 2; **13.** C; DOK Level: 2

Unit 2 Review

SCIENCE CONTENT TOPICS: P.a.1, P.a.2, P.a.3, P.a.4, P.a.5, P.b.1, P.b.2, P.b.3, P.c.1, P.c.2, P.c.3, P.c.4
SCIENCE PRACTICES: SP.1.a, SP.1.b, SP.1.c, SP.2.a, SP.2.b, SP.2.c, SP.2.d, SP.2.e, SP.3.a, SP.3.b, SP.3.c, SP.3.d, SP.5.a, SP.6.a, SP.6.b, SP.6.c, SP.7.a, SP.7.b, SP.8.a, SP.8.b

You may choose to use the Unit 2 Review on student book pp. 72–79 as a mini–practice test. If you wish to time the test, ask learners to complete all items in 95 minutes.

Unit 2 Review Answers

1. A; **2.** A; **3.** C; **4.** C; **5.** Possible answer: The investigation shows that Powder A is sodium chloride because when added to water, this powder does not undergo a visible chemical reaction, only a physical change. The investigation shows that Powder B is copper sulfate because when added to water, it undergoes a chemical change. Evidence of the chemical change includes the visible changes in physical properties: change in color and change in temperature. **6.** B; **7.** B; **8.** D; **9.** A; **10.** B; **11.** D; **12.** A; **13.** A; **14.** D; **15.** C; **16.** A; **17.** +6 m/s^2; **18.** −2 m/s^2; **19.** 0 m/s^2; **20.** vertically oriented arrow; **21.** areas where particles are farther apart; **22.1** A; **22.2** C; **22.3** D; **22.4** C; **23.** B; **24.** D; **25.** increase in kinetic energy—particles speed up, heat is transferred in, volume is increased, temperature is raised; decrease in kinetic energy—temperature drops, particles slow down, heat is transferred out, volume is reduced; **26.** A; **27.** C; **28.** A; **29.** C; **30.** A; **31.** 2,500 kg • m/s eastward; **32.** 125 m/s eastward; **33.** B; **34.** A; **35.** B; **36.** C

Unit 2 Review Item Analysis

SKILL	DOK LEVEL 1	DOK LEVEL 2	DOK LEVEL 3
Understand Scientific Models		4	
Interpret Complex Visuals		20, 21, 24	
Interpret Complex Tables	1		
Understand Chemical Equations	11	12	
Predict Outcomes			13
Calculate to Interpret Outcomes	3, 33	17, 18, 19, 31, 34	
Understand Vector Diagrams	26, 35		
Apply Scientific Laws		30, 32	
Access Prior Knowledge		2	
Link Microscopic and Observable Events		6, 25	
Interpret Observations		10, 22	5
Link Content from Varied Formats		14, 15	16
Draw Conclusions from Mixed Sources		23, 29	
Understand Investigation Techniques		7, 27, 28, 36	9
Evaluate Scientific Information			8

SCIENCE

Unit 2 Review

Use workbook lessons, as identified in the following table, to assist learners who require additional remediation with certain skills or items having certain DOK levels.

Unit 2 Workbook Item Analysis

SKILL	DOK LEVEL 1	DOK LEVEL 2	DOK LEVEL 3
Understand Scientific Models		1, 2, 5, 6, 8, 11	3, 4, 7, 9, 10, 12
Interpret Complex Visuals		3, 4, 6, 8	1, 2, 5, 7, 9, 10, 11, 12, 13, 14
Interpret Complex Tables	1, 3, 4, 9	2, 5, 6, 7, 10	8
Understand Chemical Equations	1, 2, 4, 5	6, 7, 8, 9	3, 10
Predict Outcomes			1, 2, 3, 4, 5, 6, 7, 8, 9, 10, 11
Calculate to Interpret Outcomes	1, 3, 5	2, 4, 6, 7, 8, 9, 10, 11, 12	13, 14
Understand Vector Diagrams	1, 2, 3, 5, 6, 8, 9	4, 7, 10, 11	12
Apply Scientific Laws		1, 2, 3, 5, 6, 7, 8, 9, 10, 11, 12, 14, 15, 16, 17, 18, 19	4, 13
Access Prior Knowledge	11, 12, 13	1, 2, 3, 4, 5, 6, 8, 9, 10, 14, 15	7, 16
Link Microscopic and Observable Events		1, 2, 3, 5, 6, 7	4, 8
Interpret Observations		1, 2, 3, 4, 5, 6, 7, 8, 9, 10, 11, 12	13, 14
Link Content from Varied Formats	1, 11	2, 3, 4, 5, 6, 7, 8, 9, 10, 12, 14	13
Draw Conclusions from Mixed Sources		1, 2, 3, 4, 5, 6, 7	8
Understand Investigation Techniques	8, 9	1, 2, 3, 5, 6, 7, 12	4, 10, 11
Evaluate Scientific Information		1, 2, 3, 4, 6, 7, 9, 10, 11, 12, 13	5, 8

SCIENCE

Unit 3

Earth and Space Science

Earth and space science questions comprise 20 percent of the items that appear on the GED® Science Test. As with Units 1 and 2 of *Steck-Vaughn Test Preparation for the 2014 GED® Test: Science*, Unit 3 mirrors proportionally the amount of Earth and space science test takers will encounter. Mastery of the science content and germane skills presented in Unit 3 will provide your learners with information and strategies they need to succeed on the GED® Science Test and will bolster their confidence as they prepare to take it.

The first lesson in Unit 3 lays the groundwork for comprehension of scientific theories touched on throughout the unit. From that foundation, the remaining lessons in the unit explain Earth's relationship to other bodies in space and then focus on Earth's own patterns and structure. The unit concludes with discussion of issues related to use of Earth's resources.

As learners make their way through Unit 3, they will practice skills related specifically to science, such as understanding scientific theories, applying science concepts, and expressing scientific information. The unit also introduces additional critical thinking skills, such as identifying problems and their solutions and analyzing and presenting arguments.

Table of Contents

LESSON	PAGE
1: Understand Scientific Theories	SCI 40
2: Summarize Complex Material	SCI 41
3: Understand Patterns in Science	SCI 42
4: Interpret Three-Dimensional Diagrams	SCI 43
5: Apply Science Concepts	SCI 44
6: Express Scientific Information	SCI 45
7: Identify Problem and Solution	SCI 46
8: Analyze and Present Arguments	SCI 47
Unit 3 Review	**SCI 48**

SCIENCE

Understand Scientific Theories

SCIENCE CONTENT TOPICS: ES.b.4, ES.c.1
SCIENCE PRACTICES: SP.1.a, SP.1.b, SP.1.c, SP.3.a, SP.3.b, SP.4.a, SP.5.a, SP.7.a

STUDENT BOOK pp. 82–83

Preview the Skill

Relate this scenario: A man is driving on a city street when his car starts to ride unevenly. He gets out to look around and sees several long nails in the road behind his car and one nail sticking out of his front right tire, which is flat. When the tow truck driver asks the man to explain how the flat tire occurred, he says that he ran over a nail. Ask learners to identify the evidence the man has for making this statement *(nails in the road, a nail in his tire).*

1 Learn the Skill

Give Examples Ask a volunteer to read the definition of the term *scientific theory* from the *Learn the Skill* section on p. 82. Then refer to the scenario from the *Preview the Skill* activity, and note that the driver knew how his flat occurred because of the evidence he observed. Lead learners to understand that scientific theories also are explanations based on evidence related to events or processes.

2 Practice the Skill

Use Graphic Organizers As learners read the passage on p. 82, have them use a graphic organizer such as the one shown to list the main pieces of evidence that support the Big Bang theory.

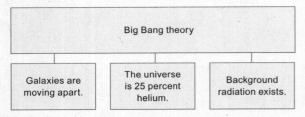

Big Bang theory		
Galaxies are moving apart.	The universe is 25 percent helium.	Background radiation exists.

3 Apply the Skill

Skim and Scan Have learners scan the graph on p. 83 to determine the variable represented by each axis. Note that the graph indicates that the variables increase together at a steady rate. Ask a volunteer to state that relationship *(galaxies move at greater velocities the farther they are from Earth).* Then answer question 2 as a class.

Answers

1. C; DOK Level: 2; **2.** C; DOK Level: 2; **3.** A; DOK Level: 2; **4.** B; DOK Level: 1

WORKBOOK pp. 122–125

1 Review the Skill

SuperSkill Review Write the statements that follow on the board, and have learners identify the scientific theory, the scientific law, and the hypothesis:

- If magma rises and cools at underwater plate boundaries, the ocean floor will gradually spread apart from the boundary *(hypothesis of seafloor spreading).*
- Planets orbit the sun in ellipses *(Kepler's first law of planetary motion).*
- The universe began about 14 billion years ago with the explosion of a hot, dense mass *(Big Bang theory).*

Discuss categorization of the statements.

2 Refine the Skill

Decoding Note that the passage on p. 122 includes statements related to steps of the scientific method. Have learners read the passage and write sentences from it related to questioning, hypothesizing, and investigating. Have learners use their notes to answer questions 1–2.

3 Master the Skill

Spotlighted Item Type Draw attention to the *Spotlighted Item* box on p. 123. Remind learners that the correct answers complete the incomplete passage. Explain that they will have to interpret the diagram, make inferences, and use prior knowledge to determine the correct answers. Then complete drop-down 3.1 as a class.

Cross-Curricular Connection

Help learners relate science to social studies. Display a blank world map, and say that experts expect earthquake catastrophes to increase as the global population increases. Have the class conduct research to determine areas of the world experiencing the highest population growth and then plot these data on the map. As a class, compare the map on p. 125 with the map learners created, and discuss the implications.

Answers

1. B; DOK Level: 1; **2.** B; DOK Level: 2; **3.1** C; **3.2** B; **3.3** D; **3.4** A; DOK Level: 2; **4.** B; DOK Level: 2; **5.** B; DOK Level: 2; **6.** A; DOK Level: 3; **7.** C; DOK Level: 2; **8.** C; DOK Level: 2; **9.** C; DOK Level: 2; **10.** A; DOK Level: 3; **11.** D; DOK Level: 2; **12.** A; DOK Level: 2

SCIENCE

Summarize Complex Material

SCIENCE CONTENT TOPICS: ES.c.1, ES.c.2
SCIENCE PRACTICES: SP.1.a, SP.1.b, SP.1.c, SP.6.c, SP.7.a

STUDENT BOOK pp. 84–85

▶ Preview the Skill

Present this scenario: Stacy tells a friend about a long argument she had with her husband about rules for their teenage children. She says she doesn't think they should be allowed to stay out late on school nights and explains why. She says her husband thinks their staying out late once in a while is okay and explains his reasoning as well. Later, Stacy tells another friend about the situation, stating, "Mark and I argued about rules for the kids. I want to be stricter about their curfew than he does." Explain that Stacy used a summary to relate the situation to the second friend. She gave a short statement containing the main idea and most important details.

❶ Learn the Skill

SuperSkill Review Display the following paragraph: *The municipal tax assessor is required to maintain property record cards. A card contains information about a property, including size of lot, square footage of improvements, number of rooms, and so on. Most assessors will give a property owner a copy of his or her property record card on request.* Then recall the definition of a summary from the *Preview the Skill* activity, and have each learner write a summary of the information. Have volunteers read their summaries.

❷ Practice the Skill

Skim and Scan Have learners skim and scan the passage and illustration on p. 84 to find the main idea of each. Explain that putting these ideas together will help them summarize the information and answer question 1.

❸ Apply the Skill

Decoding Direct learners' attention to the passage in the left column of p. 85. Point out some of the difficult science terms in the passage, such as *radiative zone* and *photosphere*. Engage learners in a discussion of whether such terms should be included in a summary of the passage.

Answers
1. C; DOK Level: 2; **2.** D; DOK level: 2; **3.** B; DOK Level: 2; **4.** A; DOK Level: 2; **5.** B; DOK Level: 2

WORKBOOK pp. 126–129

❶ Review the Skill

SuperSkill Review List the keys to a good summary: brief, focused on the main idea and most important details, in the writer's own words. Then have each learner summarize a paragraph from the local newspaper.

❷ Refine the Skill

Link to Past Skills Ask learners to review the skill *Interpret Complex Visuals* from Unit 2, Lesson 2. Next, have learners work in groups to determine how the model on p. 126 reinforces the main idea and most important details of the passage. Encourage learners to consider their analyses as they answer questions 1–2 and to apply such analysis to other visuals in the lesson.

❸ Master the Skill

Spotlighted Item Type Note that requirements of short answer items vary and that the item on p. 128 requires learners to summarize. Tell students to read the passage with the purpose of learning how to interpret the diagram. Then help learners interpret the diagram by asking what is unusual about the values on its x-axis *(they increase from right to left rather than from left to right)* and challenging them to describe the sun in terms of temperature and brightness *(average temperature and average brightness)*. Emphasize that interpreting the diagram correctly will help learners write their responses to question 6.

▶ LifeLink

Have each learner choose a favorite TV show and write a summary of the show's premise. Have learners working in small groups critique one another's summaries.

Answers
1. D; DOK Level: 2; **2.** B; DOK Level: 2; **3.** C; DOK Level: 2; **4.** A; DOK Level: 2; **5.** C; DOK Level: 2; **6.** The relationships among the traits of color, temperature, and brightness vary depending on the type of star. For example, main sequence stars range from cool, dim stars (represented in the bottom right corner of the diagram) to bright, hot stars (represented in the top left corner of the diagram). Blue giants are large, hot, and bright. Red giants are large, cool, and bright. White dwarfs are small, hot, and dim. DOK Level: 3; **7.** D; DOK Level: 2; **8.** A; DOK Level: 2

SCIENCE

Understand Patterns in Science

SCIENCE CONTENT TOPICS: ES.c.1, ES.c.2
SCIENCE PRACTICES: SP.1.a, SP.1.b, SP.1.c, SP.3.a, SP.3.b, SP.3.c, SP.6.c, SP.7.a

SCIENCE *(side tab)*

STUDENT BOOK *pp. 86–87*

➤ Preview the Skill

Remind learners that a pattern is something that occurs repeatedly, and ask them to explain the pattern of Earth's seasons *(winter, spring, summer, and fall follow each other in a set cycle)*. Explain that patterns relate not only to the occurrence of events but also to objects' structures and movements. Then have volunteers identify everyday objects that have patterns in their structures or movements *(structure example—checkerboard, movement example—clock hand)*.

❶ Learn the Skill

Give Examples Point out that the skill of understanding patterns has real-world applications. As an example, note that we use knowledge of the pattern of seasons to purchase necessary weather-related items or to plan events. Challenge learners to identify a pattern in nature or in a human-made object. Then invite volunteers to share the patterns they have identified. Discuss as a class how an understanding of each pattern is useful in day-to-day life.

❷ Practice the Skill

Skim and Scan Draw learners' attention to the side-by-side diagrams on p. 86. Have them scan the diagrams to recognize the pattern that is shown. Ask how the diagrams differ *(by showing Earth's rotation from two perspectives)*. Explain that a clear interpretation of the diagrams will contribute to their understanding of the information provided in the passage and will help them answer question 1.

❸ Apply the Skill

Link to Past Skills Review the skill *Compare and Contrast* from Unit 1, Lesson 9. Explain that understanding patterns involves comparing and contrasting events, structures, and movements. Note that identifying comparisons and contrasts as they study the illustration and read the passage in the left column of p. 87 will help learners answer questions 2–3.

Answers
1. B; DOK Level: 1; **2.** A; DOK Level: 2; **3.** D; DOK Level: 2; **4.** A; DOK Level: 3

WORKBOOK *pp. 130–133*

❶ Review the Skill

Skim and Scan On the board, write the following phrases describing types of patterns:
- when something happens
- how something looks
- how something moves

Then have partners skim and scan the lesson to identify the pattern type or types associated with each topic addressed in the lesson.

❷ Refine the Skill

Link to Past Skills Explain that the words *illustration*, *diagram*, and *model* often are used interchangeably to describe similar types of visual aids. Have learners review the skill *Understand Scientific Models* from Unit 2, Lesson 1. Then note that the diagram on p. 130 models Earth's orientation and position in relation to the sun at four times during the year. Encourage learners to use the diagram to think about how Earth's orientation and distance from the sun contribute to the local temperatures typically associated with the first day of winter, the first day of spring, and so on. Tell learners to keep this exercise in mind as they answer questions 1–2.

❸ Master the Skill

Spotlighted Item Type Note that the fill-in-the-blank items on p. 132 require sentence completion. Suggest that learners locate key words in each item that will help them identify the answer. Guide learners to find the key words *around Earth* in question 7 and in the passage. Invite a volunteer to explain how finding the key words in the passage is useful in answering the question.

➤ LifeLink

Have learners use the information from the left column of p. 133 to explain why the most recent solar or lunar eclipse looked the way it did from your area.

Answers
1. D; DOK Level: 1; **2.** D; DOK Level: 3; **3.** C; DOK Level: 2; **4.** A; DOK Level: 3; **5.** C; DOK Level: 1; **6.** C; DOK Level: 3; **7.** revolution; DOK Level: 1; **8.** new moon; DOK Level: 2; **9.** larger, smaller; DOK Level: 3; **10.** C; DOK Level: 2; **11.** B; DOK Level: 2; **12.** C; DOK Level: 2

Interpret Three-Dimensional Diagrams

SCIENCE CONTENT TOPICS: ES.b.4, ES.c.3
SCIENCE PRACTICES: SP.1.a, SP.1.b, SP.1.c, SP.3.b, SP.3.d, SP.7.a

STUDENT BOOK *pp. 88–89*

➤ Preview the Skill

Ask learners to imagine cutting open a baseball. Explain that at its core is a rubber or cork sphere. Surrounding that core is a layer of yarn covered with a stitched leather exterior. Ask a volunteer to describe how to draw the interior of a baseball to show its construction. Then have the volunteer draw such an illustration on the board.

❶ Learn the Skill

Give Examples Using the illustration completed during the *Preview the Skill* activity, show how to create accompanying labels. Write boxed names or descriptions of the parts of the baseball, and use lines that link each box to the corresponding structure. Explain that you have created a three-dimensional diagram. Then ask what labels might be found on a three-dimensional diagram of each of the following objects: an egg, a ballpoint pen, a thermos.

❷ Practice the Skill

Skim and Scan Draw attention to the three-dimensional diagram on p. 88. Ask learners to skim and scan the diagram and its labels. Lead learners to understand that some labels can provide detailed information that they can use to interpret functions or characteristics of structures within an object or a system.

❸ Apply the Skill

Link to Past Skills Review the skill *Understand Scientific Models* from Unit 2, Lesson 1. Engage the class in a discussion of how the three-dimensional diagrams on p. 89 are similar to models. Point out that they do not show things as they actually are, and lead the class to recognize that the diagram in the left column represents something that occurs too slowly to observe directly (the formation of rock layers) and the diagram in the right column represents something that is too large to be seen at actual size (Earth's layered structure).

Answers
1. A; DOK Level: 2; **2.** A; DOK Level: 2; **3.** B; DOK Level: 2

WORKBOOK *pp. 134–137*

❶ Review the Skill

Decoding Have learners preview the diagram of the volcano on p. 135. Explain that all the bold text *names* and all the regular text *explains* or *describes*. Remind learners to use all cues, including formatting cues, to understand information presented in a diagram. Then ask volunteers to use their own words to discuss aspects of the diagram.

❷ Refine the Skill

Skim and Scan Ask learners to scan the diagram on p. 134 to differentiate the kinds of information provided by bold text and regular text. Then have learners create an additional label and callout for the diagram in preparation for answering question 2. Suggest the label *Landforms*, and have learners write the callout text. Ask volunteers to share what they have written.

❸ Master the Skill

Spotlighted Item Type Learners may be more likely to select the wrong answer unintentionally for unique item types than for traditional multiple-choice questions. Suggest that learners check their answer to question 12 on p. 137 by using the answer to write a sentence and then comparing that sentence to the information provided. Add that on the GED® Science Test, they will be able to undo a hot spot answer by re-clicking the same area on the computer screen and then clicking the correct area.

➤ Analyze Visuals

Emphasize that the GED® Science Test includes many visuals from which test takers must glean a wide variety of information. Have learners practice analyzing visuals by working in groups to write an additional question related to each diagram on pp. 134–137. Have groups exchange papers and answer the questions. Learners should discuss any differences in their interpretations of the visuals.

Answers
1. D; DOK Level: 2; **2.** C; DOK Level: 2; **3.** D; DOK Level: 2;
4. A; DOK Level: 2; **5.** A; DOK Level: 2; **6.** C; DOK Level: 2;
7. B; DOK Level: 2; **8.** B; DOK Level: 2; **9.** D; DOK Level: 2;
10. A; DOK Level: 2; **11.** C; DOK Level: 2; **12.** features A, B, and C; DOK Level: 2; **13.** D; DOK Level: 2; **14.** B; DOK Level: 3

SCIENCE

Apply Science Concepts

SCIENCE CONTENT TOPICS: ES.a.1, ES.a.3, ES.b.1, ES.b.2, ES.b.3
SCIENCE PRACTICES: SP.1.a, SP.1.b, SP.1.c, SP.3.a, SP.3.b, SP.3.c, SP.7.a

SCIENCE

STUDENT BOOK pp. 90–91

➤ Preview the Skill

Inform learners that applying concepts involves using information they understand, but in a different context. Say that you plan to prepare a new dish for an upcoming meal. Ask what cooking concepts you might need to understand and apply as you make the unfamiliar dish.

❶ Learn the Skill

Give Examples Explain that passing the GED® Science Test requires understanding of basic science concepts. With students, list examples of science concepts that have been addressed in class. Start with the concept mentioned in the introductory paragraph on p. 90: energy transfer among organisms. Ask learners to demonstrate their understanding of the concept by recalling what they have learned about it. Repeat the process for other examples. Explain that applying science concepts involves using what they know about the concepts listed on the board. Note that throughout this lesson, they will use this skill to learn new science material and that on the GED® Science Test, they will use it to demonstrate what they know.

❷ Practice the Skill

Skim and Scan Have learners scan the diagram on p. 90, without reading the passage or callouts on the page. Then have partners apply the concept of energy transfer among organisms to discuss the roles of producers and consumers and the trophic levels in a marine ecosystem.

❸ Apply the Skill

SuperSkill Review After learners study the diagram and read the passage in the left column of p. 91, read question 2 aloud. Have learners identify the concept they must apply to answer it *(transformation of energy)*, and then briefly discuss the concept as a class. Repeat this activity for the other questions on the page.

Answers
1. D; DOK Level: 2; **2.** C; DOK Level: 2; **3.** B; DOK Level: 2; **4.** C; DOK Level: 1

WORKBOOK pp. 138–141

❶ Review the Skill

Give Examples Explain to learners that they use the skill of applying concepts in their daily lives. For example, learners may maintain a checkbook register, requiring that they apply the math concepts of addition and subtraction.

❷ Refine the Skill

Use Graphic Organizers Have a volunteer read callout *a* on p. 138. As a class, use a web such as the one shown to list what learners know about the concept of energy sources. Next, have a volunteer read callout *b*, and use the same type of graphic organizer to list what learners know about the concept of heat transfer. Display the completed webs, and encourage learners to review them before answering questions 1–2.

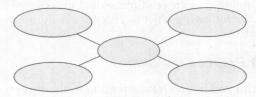

❸ Master the Skill

SuperSkill Review To aid learners in mastering the skill of applying concepts, have them recall that asking questions is often helpful in new situations. For example, suggest that before answering the questions on pp. 139–141, they preview the related passages and visuals and ask the questions that follow for each:
- What is being explained?
- How do science concepts that I have learned about already relate to this topic?

➤ LifeLink

Recall the *Review the Skill* activity about maintaining a checkbook register, and ask learners to provide other examples of ways in which they apply academic concepts in everyday life.

Answers
1. C; DOK Level: 2; **2.** A; DOK Level: 2; **3.1** D; **3.2** D; **3.3** C; **3.4** A; **3.5** B; DOK Level: 2; **4.** C; DOK Level: 2; **5.** A; DOK Level: 2; **6.** B; DOK Level: 2; **7.** A; DOK Level: 2; **8.** D; DOK Level: 2; **9.** A; DOK Level: 2; **10.** C; DOK Level: 3; **11.** C; DOK Level: 3

Express Scientific Information

SCIENCE CONTENT TOPICS: ES.b.1, ES.b.3
SCIENCE PRACTICES: SP.1.a, SP.1.b, SP.1.c, SP.3.b, SP.5.a, SP.6.a, SP.6.c, SP.7.a

STUDENT BOOK pp. 92–93

▶ Preview the Skill

Ask learners whether they have heard a TV meteorologist say that a low pressure system will move into an area. Then ask for a show of hands from those who understand what that statement means. Say that *low pressure system* is a scientific term and that the weather reporter is expressing scientific information. Explain that students will improve their understanding of science concepts, and their ability to demonstrate that understanding, by learning to express scientific information verbally, visually, numerically, and symbolically.

❶ Learn the Skill

Decoding Recall the *Preview the Skill* activity, and explain that a low pressure system occurs where the atmospheric pressure of an area is lower than that of the surrounding area. Add that low pressure systems are associated with clouds and precipitation. Then ask a volunteer to rephrase the weather forecast, expressing the scientific information in a way that is easy for most people to understand *(we're expecting increased cloudiness and rain)*.

❷ Practice the Skill

SuperSkill Review Have learners read the passage and examine the graph on p. 92. Point out that the graph expresses both visually and numerically information about the proportions of gases in the atmosphere. Then challenge learners working in pairs to express the information in another way. Allow them to choose to express the information verbally or in a different visual format.

❸ Apply the Skill

Skim and Scan Instruct learners to skim and scan the passage and map in the right column of p. 93. Have them identify the landmasses shown and locate the United States. Also, make sure learners understand the meanings of the arrows and labels on the map.

Answers
1. D; DOK Level: 1; **2.** D; DOK Level: 2; **3.** A; DOK Level: 2; **4.** B; DOK Level: 2; **5.** B; DOK Level: 2

WORKBOOK pp. 142–145

❶ Review the Skill

Skim and Scan Recall that scientific information can be expressed in several ways. Ask learners to skim and scan pp. 142–145 and list the different ways scientific information is expressed in this lesson.

❷ Refine the Skill

Link to Past Skills Direct learners to review the skill *Interpret Graphs and Maps* from Unit 1, Lesson 5 before answering questions 1–2 on p. 142. Ask what circle graphs show *(the parts of a whole)*. Then have learners interpret the graphs and explain verbally what each graph shows *(the first graph shows the proportion of each material that made up all greenhouse gas emissions in the United States in 2010; the second graph shows the sources of carbon dioxide emissions in the United States in 2010 and the percentage of total carbon dioxide emissions contributed by each source)*. On the basis of their answers, engage the class in a discussion about how choosing a particular format for expressing scientific information can make the information easier to understand.

❸ Master the Skill

Spotlighted Item Type Point out that drag-and-drop items on the GED® Science Test provide the opportunity to express scientific information visually. Explain that a test taker clicks an answer choice, holds down the mouse button and moves the mouse to drag the answer choice to a desired point in a graphic element, and then releases the mouse button. When the test taker releases the mouse button, the answer choice displays at the desired position. To help learners simulate the experience, suggest that they complete question 7 on p. 144 by drawing a line from each answer choice to the appropriate box on the diagram and then writing the answer choice in the box.

Answers
1. C; DOK Level: 2; **2.** B; DOK Level 2; **3.** D; DOK Level: 2; **4.** B; DOK Level: 1; **5.** B; DOK Level: 2; **6.** C; DOK Level: 2; **7.** 3.0—very strong acid precipitation, 5.0—lower end of the range of most acid rain, 5.5—higher end of the range of most acid rain, 5.6—rainwater, 8.0—ocean water, 9.0—higher end of range of freshwater; DOK Level: 1; **8.** C; DOK Level: 2; **9.** D; DOK Level: 2; **10.** B; DOK Level: 3

SCIENCE

Identify Problem and Solution

SCIENCE CONTENT TOPICS: ES.a.1, ES.a.2, ES.a.3, ES.b.1, ES.b.3
SCIENCE PRACTICES: SP.1.a, SP.1.b, SP.1.c, SP.3.a, SP.3.b, SP.3.c, SP.4.a, SP.6.c

STUDENT BOOK pp. 94–95

▶ Preview the Skill

Ask learners to recall movie plots in which a protagonist discovers a problem and then works to solve it. List examples as a class.

❶ Learn the Skill

Give Examples Recall the list you generated during the *Preview the Skill* activity, and have learners working in groups choose a movie to discuss. Groups should identify the main problem, potential solutions tried by the protagonist, and the solution that worked.

❷ Practice the Skill

Decoding Ask a volunteer to read callouts *a* and *b* on p. 94. Then have partners decode a main idea of the passage by working backward to first recognize the situation identified as a problem and then analyze why it is a problem.

❸ Apply the Skill

SuperSkill Review Emphasize that the key to answering question 2 on p. 95 is identifying problem and solution. Suggest that as learners read the passage and examine the map, they record information related to problem and solution in a two-column table. Encourage learners to refer to their tables while writing their responses.

Answers

1. A; DOK Level: 2; **2.** Possible answer: Rebuilding in New Orleans could be a problem if a disaster such as Katrina occurs again. People trying to decide whether to rebuild should take into account what has been done to protect the city from future storms as strong as or even stronger than Katrina. A new system of flood walls and pumps has been set up to shield the city, but is it strong enough? Some businesses might be reluctant to return to the city because the new protective system could still be inadequate. The new system is built to withstand a storm as strong as Katrina but could be overwhelmed by stronger storms that might become more frequent in the future. The loss of wetlands between New Orleans and the Gulf of Mexico continues as well. As this protective barrier against storms disappears, it will be easier for storm waters to surge into the city. A business owner could make a good case for being reluctant to return without additional protective measures. DOK Level: 3

WORKBOOK pp. 146–149

❶ Review the Skill

Give Examples Point out that countries, as well as individuals, face problems. Ask learners to brainstorm examples of science-related problems that the United States faces and possible solutions to those problems.

❷ Refine the Skill

Decoding Ask a volunteer to read callout *a* on p. 146. Help learners understand that although a passage may mention several problems, the main problem is the basic problem—often at the root of the additional problems mentioned. Then have learners skim the first paragraph of the passage to identify problems related to global water supplies. Invite volunteers to suggest which problem mentioned in the paragraph is the main problem *(lack of access to safe drinking water)* and to explain why this is the main problem *(it is the basis for problems such as unsanitary conditions and human fatalities)*.

❸ Master the Skill

Skim and Scan Guide learners to skim the passage in the left column of p. 147 to glean background information and then scan the images to enhance their understanding of the problems mentioned in the passage. Suggest that learners skim and scan in this manner to preview the passages and visuals in this lesson before reading more closely to identify problem and solution.

▶ LifeLink

Remind learners that some plants intended to control erosion, such as kudzu, have become invasive and disturbing to native ecosystems. Point out that a solution that seems feasible initially may lead to new problems. Ask learners to consider new problems that could be created by a solution such as discovery of a method to extend life indefinitely. Have learners suggest and explore other imaginary solutions to existing problems.

Answers

1. B; DOK Level: 2; **2.** D; DOK Level: 1; **3.** A; DOK Level: 3; **4.** C; DOK Level: 2; **5.** C; DOK Level: 1; **6.** D; DOK Level: 3; **7.** C; DOK Level: 1; **8.** D; DOK Level: 2; **9.** C; DOK Level: 2; **10.** B; DOK Level: 2; **11.** C; DOK Level: 1; **12.** C; DOK Level: 2; **13.** B; DOK Level: 2

Analyze and Present Arguments

SCIENCE CONTENT TOPICS: ES.a.1, ES.a.3
SCIENCE PRACTICES: SP.1.a, SP.1.b, SP.1.c, SP.3.a, SP.3.b, SP.4.a, SP.5.a, SP.6.a, SP.6.c

STUDENT BOOK pp. 96–97

➤ Preview the Skill

Have each learner recall making a significant purchase. Point out that they likely analyzed arguments used by salespeople by asking for factual information about the item. Next, have volunteers explain their reasons for making their purchases, and note that the volunteers are presenting arguments.

❶ Learn the Skill

Give Examples Relate this scenario: John's physician tells him that he should participate regularly in physical activity. Have each learner write down a fact that John's doctor might use to persuade him to exercise regularly *(examples: decreased risk of several health problems, weight loss or maintenance, stronger bones and muscles, improved ability to do activities, increased chance of living longer)*. Build an argument by having volunteers present their facts and discussing each as a class.

❷ Practice the Skill

Skim and Scan Have learners find the key words *argument for using renewable energy sources* in question 1 on p. 96. Then have learners skim and scan the passage to identify the parts of the text that present this argument.

❸ Apply the Skill

Link to Past Skills Instruct learners to review the skill *Make Inferences* from Unit 1, Lesson 14. Remind them that an inference is a logical guess based on available information and critical thinking. Then draw attention to question 2 on p. 97. Warn learners that in addition to reading the passage and studying the diagram, they will need to make inferences to determine the correct category for each argument.

Answers
1. D; DOK Level: 2; **2.** pros—it provides jobs in an area that badly needs them; it is safer than mining in deep shafts; it increases domestic supplies of coal, which are preferable to imported oil; cons—diverse forest ecosystems are destroyed and cannot be re-created after mining; removal of forests increases erosion on steep slopes, and flooding results; blasting, mining, and washing the coal can emit unhealthful amounts of coal dust into the air; DOK Level: 3

WORKBOOK pp. 150–153

❶ Review the Skill

SuperSkill Review Say that the government should increase funding for the U.S. space program because no other country can be as successful at space exploration. Then ask learners to explain why your argument is not effective *(it is based in opinion, not fact)*. Emphasize that an argument must be supported by facts.

❷ Refine the Skill

Decoding Draw attention to the word *best* in questions 1–2 on p. 150. Suggest that learners identify the correct answer for each question by trying to determine why each answer choice might *not* be the best answer. Model this strategy with question 1. Ask learners why increasing U.S. imports of oil might not be the argument best supported by the data *(the passage states that the United States must import oil, inferring that this situation is not ideal, so increasing oil imports probably is not the best argument)*. Have partners continue this activity with the remaining answer choices for question 1.

❸ Master the Skill

Link to Past Skills Have learners skim the information in the right column of p. 151. Then guide them in recognizing that the skills *Compare and Contrast* from Unit 1, Lesson 9 and *Interpret Observations* from Unit 2, Lesson 11 can be useful in answering questions 6–7. Have learners preview pp. 152–153 to identify other previously learned skills that might help them answer questions in the lesson.

➤ Enrich and Extend

Organize learners in pairs, and challenge partners to think of a controversial issue. One partner should write a pro argument related to the issue and the other a con argument. Have pairs present their arguments, and have the class determine which argument is stronger and why.

Answers
1. D; DOK Level: 2; **2.** C; DOK Level: 2; **3.** D; DOK Level: 2; **4.** C; DOK Level: 2; **5.** A; DOK Level: 2; **6.** B; DOK Level: 2; **7.** C; DOK Level: 2; **8.** A; DOK Level: 2; **9.** B; DOK Level: 2; **10.** A; DOK Level: 2; **11.** C; DOK Level: 2; **12.** A; DOK Level: 2; **13.** B; DOK Level: 2; **14.** D; DOK Level: 3; **15.** A; DOK Level: 3

SCIENCE

Unit 3 Review

SCIENCE CONTENT TOPICS: ES.a.1, ES.a.2, ES.a.3, ES.b.1, ES.b.2, ES.b.3, ES.b.4, ES.c.1, ES.c.2, ES.c.3
SCIENCE PRACTICES: SP.1.a, SP.1.b, SP.1.c, SP.3.a, SP.3.b, SP.4.a, SP.6.a, SP.6.c, SP.7.a

You may choose to use the Unit 3 Review on student book pp. 98–105 as a mini–practice test. If you wish to time the test, ask learners to complete all items in 80 minutes.

Unit 3 Review Answers

1. C; **2.** A; **3.** B; **4.** B; **5.** B; **6.** Possible answer: The water that drops to the bottom of the falls wears away the rock at the bottom of the cliff. The harder cap rock at the top of the falls does not wear away as quickly as the softer rock under it, creating a ledge of harder cap rock that juts out. Eventually, the harder cap rock breaks off, pushing the falls slightly upstream. **7.** C; **8.** tectonic; **9.** plate tectonic; **10.** landforms; **11.** B; **12.** C; **13.** C; **14.** Possible answer: The fusion reaction starts with two atoms of hydrogen. The atoms fuse to produce one atom of helium. In addition to the helium, the fusion reaction produces one neutron and energy. **15.** D; **16.** D; **17.** evaporation; **18.** B; **19.** C; **20.** A; **21.1** C; **21.2** D; **22.** B; **23.** A; **24.** B; **25.** D; **26.** B; **27.** C; **28.** areas that are on the outside of its meanders; **29.** B; **30.** C

Unit 3 Review Item Analysis

SKILL	DOK LEVEL 1	DOK LEVEL 2	DOK LEVEL 3
Understand Scientific Theories	9, 10	7	
Summarize Complex Material		2, 20, 29	
Understand Patterns in Science	1, 15, 16	12, 18	
Interpret Three-Dimensional Diagrams	3	4, 5	6
Apply Science Concepts		11	17
Express Scientific Information	8	19, 28	13, 14
Identify Problem and Solution		22, 24, 25, 27	26
Analyze and Present Arguments		21, 23	30

Use workbook lessons, as identified in the following table, to assist learners who require additional remediation with certain skills or items having certain DOK levels.

Unit 3 Workbook Item Analysis

SKILL	DOK LEVEL 1	DOK LEVEL 2	DOK LEVEL 3
Understand Scientific Theories	1	2, 3, 4, 5, 7, 8, 9, 11, 12	6, 10
Summarize Complex Material		1, 2, 3, 4, 5, 7, 8	6
Understand Patterns in Science	1, 5, 7	3, 8, 10, 11, 12	2, 4, 6, 9
Interpret Three-Dimensional Diagrams		1, 2, 3, 4, 5, 6, 7, 8, 9, 10, 11, 12, 13	14
Apply Science Concepts		1, 2, 3, 4, 5, 6, 7, 8, 9	10, 11
Express Scientific Information	4, 7	1, 2, 3, 5, 6, 8, 9	10
Identify Problem and Solution	2, 5, 7, 11	1, 4, 8, 9, 10, 12, 13	3, 6
Analyze and Present Arguments		1, 2, 3, 4, 5, 6, 7, 8, 9, 10, 11, 12, 13	14, 15

Glossary

UNIT 1

Categorize: when you choose the criteria for placing organisms, objects, processes, or other items in groups

Cause: an action or object that makes an event happen

Classify: when you put things into groups that already exist based on similarities

Compare: when you identify the ways in which organisms, objects, data, behaviors, events, or processes are similar

Conclusion: a reasoned understanding of something

Content-based tool: a symbol, an equation, a visual element, or another aid used with certain types of subject matter

Context clues: hints in surrounding text or visuals about the meaning of a particular word, phrase, or idea

Contrast: when you focus on ways in which such things are different

Diagrams: drawings that show relationships between ideas, objects, or events in a visual way

Effect: the event that results from the cause

Generalization: a principle, statement, or idea having general application

Graph: a pictorial device, such as a pie chart or bar graph, used to illustrate quantitative relationships

Illustrations: provide information in a visual way

Inference: a logical guess based on facts, evidence, experience, observation, or reasoning

Main idea: the most important point of an informational passage, an article, a paragraph, or a visual element

Scientific evidence: the set of test results and recorded observations that supports a scientific idea

Supporting details: other points that provide additional information about the main idea

Table: a tool used to organize and present information in columns and rows

Thematic map: a type of map or chart especially designed to show a particular theme connected with a specific geographic area

UNIT 2

Chemical equations: use words, symbols, or other components to represent chemical reactions

Complex table: a table that includes several parts or parts organized in a unique way

Complex visuals: show more details than simple illustrations, graphs, or diagrams do

Investigation techniques: observations, measurements, and experiments used in science to determine possible solutions

Outcome: the result that occurs when someone manipulates factors in a scientific investigation

Prior knowledge: the knowledge you already have about a topic

Scientific law: a statement that describes how matter and energy behave

Scientific models: artistic representations that help clarify complex topics. They can represent objects that are too large or too small to be seen at actual size. Also, they can represent processes that occur too slowly or too quickly to be observed directly.

Vector diagrams: arrows that show the direction and magnitude, or strength of forces

Vectors: quantities that have direction and magnitude, such as forces

UNIT 3

Argument: a set of statements in which one follows logically as a conclusion from the others

Concept: a fundamental unit of understanding

Pattern: something that occurs repeatedly

Problem: a question to be considered, solved, or answered

Scientific theory: an explanation that is supported by all the available data

Solution: an answer to a question or problem

Three-dimensional diagrams: illustrations that show part of an object or a structure cut away so that the inside of the object is visible

Correlations/Science

Indicator Codes	Science Practices	*Science* Book Pages
SP.1	**Comprehending Scientific Presentations**	
SP.1.a	Understand and explain textual scientific presentations	**Student Book:** 2, 3, 4, 5, 6, 7, 8, 9, 10, 11, 12, 13, 14, 15, 16, 17, 18, 19, 20, 21, 22, 23, 24, 25, 26, 27, 28, 29, 30, 31, 32, 33, 34, 35, 36, 37, 38, 39, 42, 43, 44, 45, 46, 47, 48, 49, 50, 51, 52, 53, 54, 55, 56, 57, 58, 59, 60, 61, 62, 63, 64, 65, 66, 67, 71, 72, 73, 74, 75, 76, 77, 78, 79, 82, 83, 84, 85, 86, 87, 88, 89, 90, 91, 92, 93, 94, 95, 96, 97, 98, 99, 100, 101, 102, 103, 104, 105 **Workbook:** 3, 4, 5, 7, 8, 9, 10, 11, 12, 13, 14, 15, 16, 17, 18, 19, 20, 21, 22, 23, 24, 25, 26, 27, 28, 29, 30, 31, 32, 33, 34, 35, 36, 37, 38, 39, 40, 41, 42, 43, 44, 45, 46, 47, 48, 49, 50, 51, 52, 53, 54, 55, 56, 57, 58, 59, 60, 61, 62, 63, 64, 65, 66, 67, 68, 69, 70, 72, 73, 74, 75, 76, 77, 78, 79, 80, 81, 82, 83, 84, 85, 86, 87, 88, 89, 90, 91, 92, 93, 94, 95, 96, 97, 98, 99, 100, 101, 102, 103, 104, 105, 106, 107, 108, 109, 110, 111, 112, 113, 118, 119, 120, 121, 122, 123,124, 125, 126, 127, 128, 129, 130, 131, 132, 133, 134, 135, 136, 137, 138, 139, 140, 141, 142, 143, 144, 145, 146, 147, 148, 149, 150, 151, 152, 153
SP.1.b	Determine the meaning of symbols, terms, and phrases as they are used in scientific presentations	**Student Book:** 2, 3, 4, 5, 6, 7, 8, 9, 10, 11, 12, 13, 14, 15, 16, 17, 18, 19, 20, 21, 22, 23, 24, 25, 26, 27, 28, 29, 30, 31, 32, 33, 34, 35, 36, 37, 38, 39, 42, 43, 44, 45, 46, 47, 48, 49, 50, 51, 52, 53, 54, 55, 56, 57, 58, 59, 60, 61, 62, 63, 64, 65, 66, 67, 71, 72, 73, 74, 75, 76, 77, 78, 79, 82, 83, 84, 85, 86, 87, 88, 89, 90, 91, 92, 93, 94, 96, 97, 98, 99, 100, 101, 102, 103, 104, 105 **Workbook:** 2, 3, 4, 5, 6, 7, 8, 9, 10, 11, 12, 13, 14, 15, 16, 17, 18, 19, 20, 21, 22, 23, 24, 25, 26, 27, 28, 29, 30, 31, 32, 33, 34, 35, 36, 37, 38, 39, 40, 41, 42, 43, 44, 45, 46, 47, 48, 49, 50, 51, 52, 53, 54, 55, 56, 57, 58, 59, 60, 61, 62, 63, 64, 65, 66, 67, 68, 69, 70, 72, 73, 74, 75, 76, 77, 78, 79, 80, 81, 82, 83, 84, 85, 86, 87, 88, 89, 90, 91, 92, 93, 94, 95, 96, 97, 98, 99, 100, 101, 102, 103, 104, 105, 106, 107, 108, 109, 110, 111, 112, 113, 118, 119, 120, 121, 122, 123,124, 125, 126, 127, 128, 129, 130, 131, 132, 133, 134, 135, 136, 137, 138, 139, 140, 141, 142, 143, 144, 145, 146, 147, 148, 149
SP.1.c	Understand and explain nontextual scientific presentations	**Student Book:** 2, 3, 5, 6, 7, 8, 10, 11, 12, 13, 14, 15, 16, 17, 18, 20, 21, 22, 23, 25, 26, 27, 29, 31, 32, 33, 34, 35, 36, 37, 38, 39, 40, 41, 42, 43, 44, 45, 46, 47, 48, 49, 50, 51, 52, 53, 54, 55, 56, 58, 59, 60, 61, 62, 63, 64, 65, 66, 67, 71, 72, 73, 74, 75, 76, 77, 78, 79, 80, 81, 83, 84, 85, 86, 87, 88, 89, 90, 91, 92, 93, 95, 96, 97, 98, 99, 100, 101, 102, 103, 105 **Workbook:** 2, 3, 4, 5, 6, 8, 9, 10, 11, 12, 13, 15, 16, 17, 18, 19, 20, 21, 22, 23, 24, 25, 26, 27, 28, 29, 30, 31, 32, 33, 34, 36, 38, 39, 40, 41, 42, 43, 44, 45, 46, 47, 49, 50, 51, 52, 53, 55, 56, 62, 63, 64, 65, 66, 67, 68, 69, 70, 72, 73, 74, 75, 76, 77, 78, 79, 80, 81, 82, 83, 84, 85, 86, 87, 88, 89, 90, 91, 92, 93, 94, 95, 96, 97, 98, 99, 100, 101, 102, 103, 104, 106, 107, 108, 109, 110, 111, 112, 113, 119, 123,124, 125, 126, 127, 128, 129, 130, 131, 132, 133, 134, 135, 136, 137, 138, 139, 140, 141, 142, 143, 144, 145, 147, 148, 149, 150, 151, 152, 153

Correlations/Science

Indicator Codes	Science Practices	*Science* Book Pages
SP.2	**Investigation Design (Experimental and Observational)**	
SP.2.a	Identify possible sources of error and alter the design of an investigation to ameliorate that error	**Student Book:** 69, 74 **Workbook:** 118, 119, 120
SP.2.b	Identify and refine hypotheses for scientific investigations	**Student Book:** 68, 69, 70, 74 **Workbook:** 114, 118, 121
SP.2.c	Identify the strengths and weaknesses of one or more scientific investigation (i.e., experimental or observational) designs	**Student Book:** 71, 74 **Workbook:** 114, 118, 119, 120, 121
SP.2.d	Design a scientific investigation	**Student Book:** 68, 74 **Workbook:** 114, 115, 116, 117
SP.2.e	Identify and interpret independent and dependent variables in scientific investigations	**Student Book:** 69, 78 **Workbook:** 15, 117, 120
SP.3	**Reasoning from Data**	
SP.3.a	Cite specific textual evidence to support a finding or conclusion	**Student Book:** 19, 26, 27, 31, 36, 47, 73, 74, 83, 87, 94, 95, 96, 98, 103, 104, 105 **Workbook:** 20, 29, 31, 35, 36, 37, 52, 53, 56, 59, 60, 61, 88, 93, 103, 113, 123, 137, 141, 146, 147, 148, 149, 150, 151, 152, 153
SP.3.b	Reason from data or evidence to a conclusion	**Student Book:** 7, 11, 16, 17, 24, 25, 27, 28, 29, 30, 31, 32, 33, 34, 35, 36, 37, 38, 45, 47, 51, 60, 61, 62, 63, 65, 66, 67, 69, 71, 72, 73, 74, 75, 76, 78, 79, 82, 87, 88, 89, 91, 93, 95, 96, 97, 98, 99, 100, 101, 102, 103, 104, 105 **Workbook:** 11, 12, 13, 14, 21, 23, 25, 29, 30, 31, 32, 33, 46, 47, 48, 49, 50, 51, 52, 53, 55, 56, 57, 58, 59, 60, 61, 67, 68, 69, 70, 73, 75, 95, 96, 97, 99, 100, 101, 103, 104, 105, 106, 107, 108, 109, 110, 111, 112, 113, 114, 115, 116, 117, 119, 120, 121, 123, 124, 125, 130, 133, 134, 135, 136, 137, 138, 139, 140, 141, 146, 147, 148, 149, 150, 151, 152, 153
SP.3.c	Make a prediction based upon data or evidence	**Student Book:** 29, 50, 51, 63, 74, 95 **Workbook:** 19, 78, 79, 80, 81, 90, 91, 98, 99, 116, 131, 140
SP.3.d	Use sampling techniques to answer scientific questions	**Student Book:** 11, 17, 22, 50, 51, 69, 74, 79 **Workbook:** 25, 30, 31, 32, 33, 42, 70, 73, 79, 81, 115, 137
SP.4	**Evaluating Conclusions with Evidence**	
SP.4.a	Evaluate whether a conclusion or theory is supported or challenged by particular data or evidence	**Student Book:** 67, 71, 83, 94, 96, 99, 104 **Workbook:** 51, 52, 53, 101, 118, 120, 121, 123, 124, 125, 150, 151, 152, 153
SP.5	**Working with Findings**	
SP.5.a	Reconcile multiple findings, conclusions, or theories	**Student Book:** 66, 67, 68, 97 **Workbook:** 110, 111, 112, 113, 115, 117, 119, 120, 121, 124, 125, 144
SP.6	**Expressing Scientific Information**	
SP.6.a	Express scientific information or findings visually	**Student Book:** 15, 19, 37, 47, 65, 77, 78, 97, 102 **Workbook:** 35, 36, 37, 40, 52, 144
SP.6.b	Express scientific information or findings numerically or symbolically	**Student Book:** 75, 79 **Workbook:** 65, 76, 84

SCIENCE

Correlations/Science

Indicator Codes	Science Practices	*Science* Book Pages
SP.6.c	Express scientific information or findings verbally	**Student Book:** 15, 17, 19, 29, 31, 37, 45, 57, 65, 73, 74, 77, 95, 97, 99, 100, 101, 102, 105 **Workbook:** 27, 28, 29, 35, 37, 40, 52, 59, 60, 61, 79, 117, 128, 132, 144
SP.7	**Scientific Theories**	
SP.7.a	Understand and apply scientific models, theories, and processes	**Student Book:** 2, 3, 5, 9, 12, 13, 20, 21, 24, 25, 26, 27, 28, 29, 30, 31, 32, 33, 35, 36, 37, 38, 39, 42, 43, 44, 45, 46, 47, 48, 49, 50, 51, 54, 55, 56, 57, 59, 60, 61, 62, 63, 64, 65, 68, 69, 70, 71, 72, 73, 74, 75, 76, 77, 78, 79, 82, 83, 85, 86, 87, 88, 89, 90, 91, 93, 98, 99, 100, 101, 102, 103, 104, 105 **Workbook:** 2, 3, 4, 5, 7, 8, 9, 14, 15, 16, 22, 23, 24, 25, 38, 39, 40, 41, 46, 47, 48, 49, 50, 51, 52, 53, 54, 55, 56, 57, 58, 59, 60, 61, 62, 63, 64, 65, 66, 67, 68, 69, 70, 72, 73, 74, 75, 76, 77, 78, 79, 80, 81, 86, 87, 88, 89, 90, 91, 92, 93, 98, 99, 100, 101, 102, 103, 104, 105, 107, 108, 109, 111, 114, 115, 116, 117, 118, 119, 120, 121, 122, 123, 124, 125, 126, 127, 128, 129, 130, 131, 132, 133, 135, 136, 137, 138, 139, 140, 141, 145
SP.7.b	Apply formulas from scientific theories	**Student Book:** 52, 53, 55, 57, 59, 72, 75, 78, 79 **Workbook:** 82, 83, 84, 85, 86, 87, 88, 89, 90, 91, 92, 93, 95, 97
SP.8	**Probability and Statistics**	
SP.8.a	Describe a data set statistically	**Student Book:** 69, 79 **Workbook:** 115
SP.8.b	Use counting and permutations to solve scientific problems	**Student Book:** 23, 35, 52, 53, 57, 69, 75, 79 **Workbook:** 12, 41, 42, 43, 44, 45, 53, 74, 75, 76, 77, 82, 83, 84, 85, 86, 87, 88, 90, 91, 92, 93, 118
SP.8.c	Determine the probability of events	**Student Book:** 23, 35 **Workbook:** 42, 43, 45

Correlations/Science

Indicator Codes	Science Content Topics	*Science* Book Pages
Life Science		
L.a Human Body and Health		
L.a.1	Body systems (e.g., muscular, endocrine, nervous systems) and how they work together to perform a function (e.g., muscular and skeletal work to move the body)	**Student Book:** 4, 5, 32 **Workbook:** 7, 8, 9
L.a.2	Homeostasis, feedback methods that maintain homeostasis (e.g., sweating to maintain internal temperature), and effects of changes in the external environment on living things (e.g., hypothermia, injury)	**Student Book:** 8, 9, 36 **Workbook:** 14, 15, 16, 17
L.a.3	Sources of nutrients (e.g., foods, symbiotic organisms) and concepts in nutrition (e.g., calories, vitamins, minerals)	**Student Book:** 6, 7, 32, 34 **Workbook:** 10, 11, 12, 13
L.a.4	Transmission of disease and pathogens (e.g., airborne, bloodborne), effects of disease or pathogens on populations (e.g., demographics change, extinction), and disease prevention methods (e.g., vaccination, sanitation)	**Student Book:** 10, 11, 37 **Workbook:** 18, 19, 20, 21
L.b Relationship Between Life Functions and Energy Intake		
L.b.1	Energy for life functions (e.g., photosynthesis, respiration, fermentation)	**Student Book:** 3, 36 **Workbook:** 4, 5
L.c Energy Flows in Ecologic Networks (Ecosystems)		
L.c.1	Flow of energy in ecosystems (e.g., energy pyramids), conservation of energy in an ecosystem (e.g., energy lost as heat, energy passed on to other organisms) and sources of energy (e.g., sunlight, producers, lower level consumer)	**Student Book:** 12, 13, 33 **Workbook:** 23, 24, 25
L.c.2	Flow of matter in ecosystems (e.g., food webs and chains, positions of organisms in the web or chain) and the effects of change in communities or environment on food webs	**Student Book:** 12, 13, 19, 33 **Workbook:** 22, 23, 24, 25, 36
L.c.3	Carrying capacity, changes in carrying capacity based on changes in populations and environmental effects and limiting resources to necessary for growth	**Student Book:** 16, 17, 32 **Workbook:** 30, 31, 32, 33
L.c.4	Symbiosis (e.g., mutualism, parasitism, commensalism) and predator/prey relationships (e.g., changes in one population affecting another population)	**Student Book:** 14, 15, 34 **Workbook:** 26, 27, 28, 29, 31, 32, 33
L.c.5	Disruption of ecosystems (e.g., invasive species, flooding, habitat destruction, desertification) and extinction (e.g., causes [human and natural] and effects)	**Student Book:** 17, 18, 19, 36, 38 **Workbook:** 34, 35, 36, 37, 61

SCIENCE

Correlations/Science

Indicator Codes	Science Content Topics	*Science* Book Pages
L.d Organization of Life (Structure and Function of Life)		
L.d.1	Essential functions of life (e.g., chemical reactions, reproduction, metabolism) and cellular components that assist the functions of life (e.g., cell membranes, enzymes, energy)	**Student Book:** 2, 3, 33, 36 **Workbook:** 2, 3, 4, 5
L.d.2	Cell theory (e.g., cells come from cells, cells are the smallest unit of living things), specialized cells and tissues (e.g., muscles, nerve, etc.) and cellular levels of organization (e.g., cells, tissues, organs, systems)	**Student Book:** 2, 3, 4, 5, 33, 39 **Workbook:** 3, 4, 6, 8
L.d.3	Mitosis, meiosis (e.g., process and purpose)	**Student Book:** 3, 20, 24, 33 **Workbook:** 3, 38, 39, 40, 41
L.e Molecular Basis for Heredity		
L.e.1	Central dogma of molecular biology, the mechanism of inheritance (e.g., DNA) and chromosomes (e.g., description, chromosome splitting during meiosis)	**Student Book:** 20, 21, 38 **Workbook:** 38, 39, 40, 41
L.e.2	Genotypes, phenotypes, and the probability of traits in close relatives (e.g., Punnett squares, pedigree charts)	**Student Book:** 22, 23, 35 **Workbook:** 42, 43, 44, 45
L.e.3	New alleles, assortment of alleles (e.g., mutations, crossing over), environmental altering of traits, and expression of traits (e.g., epigenetics, color points of Siamese cats)	**Student Book:** 24, 25, 34, 38 **Workbook:** 46, 47, 48, 49
L.f Evolution		
L.f.1	Common ancestry (e.g., evidence) and cladograms (e.g., drawing, creating, interpreting)	**Student Book:** 26, 27, 37, 39 **Workbook:** 50, 51, 52, 53
L.f.2	Selection (e.g., natural selection, artificial selection, evidence) and the requirements for selection (e.g., variation in traits, differential survivability)	**Student Book:** 28, 29, 36 **Workbook:** 54, 55, 56, 57
L.f.3	Adaptation, selection pressure, and speciation	**Student Book:** 30, 31, 35, 39 **Workbook:** 58, 59, 60, 61
Physical Science		
P.a Conservation, Transformation, and Flow of Energy		
P.a.1	Heat, temperature, the flow of heat results in work, and the transfer of heat (e.g., conduction, convection)	**Student Book:** 60, 61, 74, 77 **Workbook:** 98, 99, 100, 101, 115, 118
P.a.2	Endothermic and exothermic reactions	**Student Book:** 48, 73 **Workbook:** 104, 105
P.a.3	Types of energy (kinetic, chemical, mechanical) and transformations between types of energy (e.g., chemical energy [sugar] to kinetic energy [motion of a body])	**Student Book:** 60, 62, 63, 76, 78 **Workbook:** 99, 102, 103, 104, 105, 119
P.a.4	Sources of energy (e.g., sun, fossil fuels, nuclear) and the relationships between different sources (e.g., levels of pollutions, amount of energy produced)	**Student Book:** 66, 67, 69, 75, 79 **Workbook:** 110, 111, 112, 113, 115

SCIENCE

Correlations/Science

Indicator Codes	Science Content Topics	*Science* Book Pages
P.a.5	Types of waves, parts of waves (e.g., frequency, wavelength), types of electromagnetic radiation, transfer of energy by waves, and the uses and dangers of electromagnetic radiation (e.g., radio transmission, UV light and sunburns)	**Student Book:** 61, 64, 65, 76 **Workbook:** 100, 101, 106, 107, 108, 109, 121
P.b Work, Motion, and Forces		
P.b.1	Speed, velocity, acceleration, momentum, and collisions (e.g., inertia in a car accident, momentum transfer between two objects)	**Student Book:** 52, 53, 57, 75, 79 **Workbook:** 82, 83, 84, 85, 91, 92, 93, 116, 119
P.b.2	Force, Newton's laws, gravity, acceleration due to gravity (e.g., freefall, law of gravitational attraction), mass and weight	**Student Book:** 54, 55, 56, 57, 69, 78, 79 **Workbook:** 85, 86, 87, 88, 89, 90, 91, 92, 93, 119, 120, 121
P.b.3	Work, simple machines (types and functions), mechanical advantages (force, distance, and simple machines), and power	**Student Book:** 58, 59, 72 **Workbook:** 94, 95, 96, 97
P.c Chemical Properties and Reactions Related to Living Systems		
P.c.1	Structure of matter	**Student Book:** 42, 43, 68, 72 **Workbook:** 62, 63, 64, 65, 114, 117
P.c.2	Physical and chemical properties, changes of state, and density	**Student Book:** 44, 45, 46, 47, 71, 73, 74, 77 **Workbook:** 66, 67, 68, 69, 70, 72, 73, 77, 114, 116, 118, 119, 120
P.c.3	Balancing chemical equations and different types of chemical equations, conservation of mass in balanced chemical equations, and limiting reactants	**Student Book:** 48, 49, 74 **Workbook:** 74, 75, 76, 77, 114, 120, 121
P.c.4	Parts in solutions, general rules of solubility (e.g., hotter solvents allow more solute to dissolve), saturation, and the differences between weak and strong solutions	**Student Book:** 50, 51, 70, 74 **Workbook:** 78, 79, 80, 81, 116, 117
Earth and Space Science		
ES.a Interactions Between Earth's Systems and Living Things		
ES.a.1	Interactions of matter between living and nonliving things (e.g., cycles of matter) and the location, uses, and dangers of fossil fuels	**Student Book:** 94, 95, 96, 104 **Workbook:** 139, 146, 148, 150, 151, 152, 153
ES.a.2	Natural hazards (e.g., earthquakes, hurricanes, etc.), their effects (e.g., frequency, severity, and short- and long-term effects), and mitigation thereof (e.g., dikes, storm shelters, building practices)	**Student Book:** 95, 103 **Workbook:** 147, 148, 149
ES.a.3	Extraction and use of natural resources, renewable versus nonrenewable resources and sustainability	**Student Book:** 91, 94, 96, 97, 98, 103, 104, 105 **Workbook:** 146, 150, 151, 152, 153
ES.b Earth and Its System Components and Interactions		
ES.b.1	Characteristics of the atmosphere, including its layers, gases and their effects on the Earth and its organisms, including climate change	**Student Book:** 92, 93, 102, 103, 104 **Workbook:** 138, 139, 141, 142, 143, 144, 145, 148

SCIENCE

Correlations/Science

Indicator Codes	Science Content Topics	*Science* Book Pages
ES.b.2	Characteristics of the oceans (e.g., salt water, currents, coral reefs) and their effects on Earth and organisms	**Student Book:** 90, 102 **Workbook:** 138, 140, 141
ES.b.3	Interactions between Earth's systems (e.g., weathering caused by wind or water on rock, wind caused by high/low pressure and Earth rotation, etc.)	**Student Book:** 93, 95, 99, 100, 103, 105 **Workbook:** 138, 144
ES.b.4	Interior structure of the Earth (e.g., core, mantle, crust, tectonic plates) and its effects (e.g., volcanoes, earthquakes, etc.) and major landforms of the Earth (e.g., mountains, ocean basins, continental shelves, etc.)	**Student Book:** 83, 88, 89, 98, 100 **Workbook:** 122, 123, 124, 125, 134, 135, 136, 137
ES.c Structures and Organization of the Cosmos		
ES.c.1	Structures in the universe (e.g., galaxies, stars, constellations, solar systems), the age and development of the universe, and the age and development of stars (e.g., main sequence, stellar development, deaths of stars [black hole, white dwarf])	**Student Book:** 82, 83, 84, 85, 87, 98, 99, 100, 101 **Workbook:** 123, 126, 127, 128, 129, 131, 133
ES.c.2	Sun, planets, and moons (e.g., types of planets, comets, asteroids), the motion of the Earth's motion and the interactions within the Earth's solar system (e.g., tides, eclipses)	**Student Book:** 85, 86, 87, 98, 101, 102 **Workbook:** 130, 131, 132, 133
ES.c.3	The age of the Earth, including radiometrics, fossils, and landforms	**Student Book:** 89, 100 Workbook: 137

SCIENCE

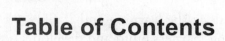

Table of Contents

Table of Contents.. SS 1
About *Steck-Vaughn Test Preparation for the 2014
GED® Test: Social Studies* .... SS 2

UNIT 1 *Geography and the World* .... SS 3
LESSON
1: Understand Geography .... SS 4
2: Understand Map Components .... SS 5
3: Physical Maps .... SS 6
4: Political Maps .... SS 7
5: Movement on Maps .... SS 8
Unit 1 Review .... SS 9

UNIT 2 *United States History* .... SS 11
LESSON
1: Relate Geography and History .... SS 12
2: Interpret Tables .... SS 13
3: Main Idea and Details .... SS 14
4: Categorize .... SS 15
5: Sequence .... SS 16
6: Cause and Effect .... SS 17
7: Interpret Timelines .... SS 18
Unit 2 Review .... SS 19

UNIT 3 *Civics and Government* .... SS 21
LESSON
1: Interpret Diagrams .... SS 22
2: Interpret the Constitution .... SS 23
3: Summarize .... SS 24
4: Compare and Contrast .... SS 25
5: Charts, Graphs, and Flowcharts .... SS 26
6: Make Inferences .... SS 27
7: Interpret Political Cartoons .... SS 28
8: Draw Conclusions .... SS 29
9: Determine Point of View .... SS 30
10: Analyze Information Sources .... SS 31
11: Generalize .... SS 32
12: Identify Problem and Solution .... SS 33
13: Special-Purpose Maps .... SS 34
14: Fact and Opinion .... SS 35
15: Faulty Logic or Reasoning .... SS 36
16: Evaluate Information .... SS 37
17: Analyze Effectiveness of Arguments .... SS 38
Unit 3 Review .... SS 39–SS 40

UNIT 4 *Economics* .... SS 41
LESSON
1: Understand Economics .... SS 42
2: Multiple Causes and Effects .... SS 43
3: Compare and Contrast Visuals .... SS 44
4: Interpret Pictographs .... SS 45
5: Interpret Multi-Bar and Line Graphs .... SS 46
Unit 4 Review .... SS 47

APPENDICES
A: Glossary.. SS 48–SS 49
B: Map of the United States .... SS 50
C: Map of the Western Hemisphere .... SS 51
D: Maps of the Eastern Hemisphere ....SS 52–SS 53

CORRELATIONS/SOCIAL STUDIES
.... SS 54–SS 63

SOCIAL STUDIES

About *Steck-Vaughn Test Preparation for the 2014 GED® Test: Social Studies*

Steck-Vaughn's student book and workbook help unlock the learning and deconstruct the different elements of the test by helping learners build and develop core reading and thinking skills. The content of our books aligns to the new GED® social studies content standards and item distribution to provide learners with a superior test preparation experience.

Our *Spotlighted Item* feature provides a deeper, richer treatment for each technology-enhanced item type. On initial introduction, a unique item type—such as drag-and-drop—receives a full page of example items in the student book lesson and three pages in the companion workbook. The length of subsequent features may be shorter depending on the skill, lesson, and requirements.

A combination of targeted strategies, informational call-outs and sample questions, assorted tips and hints, and ample assessment help to clearly focus study efforts in needed areas.

In addition to the book features, a highly detailed answer key provides the correct answer and the rationale for it so that learners know exactly why an answer is correct. The *Social Studies* student book and workbook are designed with an eye toward the end goal: Success on the GED® Social Studies Test.

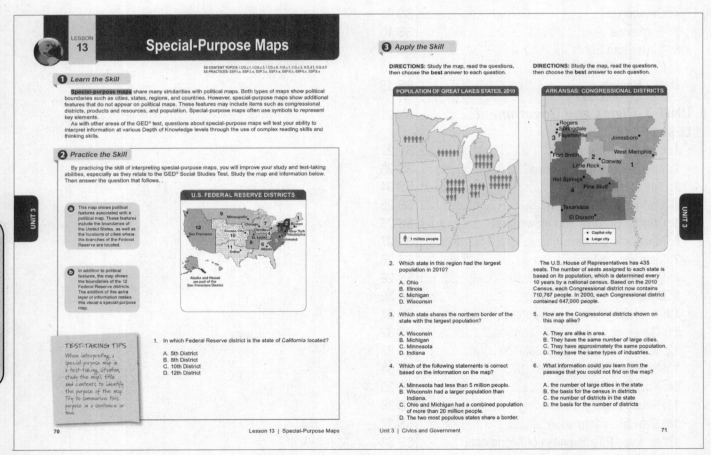

Unit 1

Geography and the World

The two main instructional goals for the geography unit are these: first, learners must be able to read accurately all components on any map; second, learners must be able to use and interpret that information to answer higher-order thinking questions. Using logic and reasoning and making assumptions will be vital to this twofold process. Also, the GED® Social Studies Test requires some basic geographic knowledge, such as names and locations of U.S. states and cities. Several questions in this unit are designed to assess that knowledge.

Geography questions make up 15 percent of all questions on the GED® Social Studies Test. In this unit, learners are first introduced to the key concepts of geography. Then learners are instructed in the fundamentals of analyzing different types of maps, including physical maps, political maps, and maps that show movement.

One of the best ways to prepare learners for geography questions on the GED® Social Studies Test is to have them analyze a wide variety of maps. In addition to the many maps in Unit 1 of the *Social Studies* student book and workbook, a map of the United States and maps of the Eastern and Western Hemispheres appear in the appendices of the *Social Studies* Instructor Edition. You may also want to ask students to bring in any maps they have at home. Street maps, maps showing directions, and maps in brochures from tourist attractions or historic sites may be used to extend learners' knowledge of geography.

Table of Contents

LESSON	PAGE
1: Understand Geography	SS 4
2: Understand Map Components	SS 5
3: Physical Maps	SS 6
4: Political Maps	SS 7
5: Movement on Maps	SS 8
Unit 1 Review	**SS 9**

SOCIAL STUDIES

Understand Geography

SS CONTENT TOPICS: II.G.b.2, II.G.b.3, II.G.b.4, II.G.b.5, II.G.c.1, II.G.c.2, II.G.c.3, II.G.d.1, II.G.d.2, II.G.d.3, II.G.d.4, II.E.d.1, II.E.g, II.E.h, II.USH.e
SS PRACTICES: SSP.4.a, SSP.2.b, SSP.3.c, SSP.6.b

STUDENT BOOK *pp. 2–3*

▶ Preview the Skill

Point to a classroom map or globe. Explain that maps and globes are useful tools for identifying and understanding geographic information. Invite learners to identify geographic terms with which they are familiar, and encourage them to point out examples of these terms that appear on the classroom map or globe.

❶ Learn the Skill

Skim and Scan Review with learners the definitions of geography and the other key geographic terms listed. Then, direct learners to skim and scan reference sources in the classroom or the maps on pp. 2 and 3 to locate geographic information, both in textual and illustrated form.

❷ Practice the Skill

Decoding Direct learners' attention to the Using Logic tip on p. 2, and model for them how to use this feature to decode the question on this page. Explain that the continents on which several answer choices are located (Mexico in North America, Saudi Arabia in Asia, and Italy in Europe) are not shown on the equator on this map, and eliminate them as correct responses. Encourage learners to apply similar geographic understanding to subsequent questions.

❸ Apply the Skill

Spotlighted Item Type Explain to learners that hot spot items enable them to mark their answers directly on maps, tables, charts, etc. Tell learners to read questions 2–6 on p. 3 carefully and identify where and how on the map they will mark their answers for each of the questions.

Answers
1. B; DOK Level: 1; **2.** the Costa and the Galápagos; DOK Level: 1; **3.** Costa Region and Sierra Region; DOK Level: 2; **4.** the Sierra and the Galápagos; DOK Level: 2; **5.** the Sierra and the Oriente; DOK Level: 2; **6.** Sierra Region and Galápagos Islands; DOK Level: 2

WORKBOOK *pp. 2–5*

❶ Review the Skill

Have learners identify the seven continents and any countries they recognize on the map on p. 2. Point learners to Antarctica and discuss why this continent would appear a different size and shape on a globe.

❷ Refine the Skill

Give Examples Ask learners to give examples of what they think of when you say the word *equator*. List their answers on the board. Discuss the concept of the Northern and Southern Hemispheres and ask students to give examples of countries located in each hemisphere. Then direct learners to answer question 1.

❸ Master the Skill

Spotlighted Item Type Point out to learners that on the actual GED® Social Studies Test, they will not be asked to underline, mark an *X*, or circle in a hot spot item. They will instead be asked to click on a spot on the screen to answer.

Answers
1. D; DOK Level: 2; **2.** B; DOK Level: 1; **3.** South America; DOK Level: 1; **4.** Egypt, which is located in Africa; DOK Level: 2; **5.** Argentina; DOK Level: 2; **6.** Limpopo and Mpumalanga provinces; DOK Level: 1; **7.** Kwazulu-Natal, Eastern Cape, and the eastern part of Western Cape provinces; DOK Level: 1; **8.** North West, Gauteng, Mpumalanga, Kwazulu-Natal, Eastern Cape, and Northern Cape provinces; DOK Level: 2; **9.** The Gulf of Mexico and the Pacific Ocean; DOK Level: 1; **10.** the Appalachian Mountains; DOK Level: 2; **11.** the Great Lakes and the Ohio, Mississippi, and Missouri Rivers; DOK Level: 2; **12.** the Rocky Mountains; DOK Level: 3; **13.** the Great Lakes; DOK Level: 2; **14.** Sri Lanka; DOK Level: 2; **15.** China, North Korea, South Korea, Japan, Malaysia, Taiwan, Laos, Vietnam, Thailand, the Phillipines, and Indonesia; DOK Level: 2; **16.** Uzbekistan, Kyrgyzstan, Tajikistan, Afghanistan, Nepal, Bhutan, Laos, and Mongolia; DOK Level: 2; **17.** China; DOK Level: 2; **18.** Mongolia; DOK Level: 2; **19.** Myanmar, Laos, and Vietnam; DOK Level: 2

Understand Map Components

SS CONTENT TOPICS: II.G.b.1, II.G.b.3, II.G.b.4, II.G.b.5, II.G.c.1, II.G.c.2, II.G.c.3, II.G.d.1, II.G.d.2, II.G.d.3, II.G.d.4, I.USH.b.1
SS PRACTICES: SSP.2.b, SSP.3.c, SSP.4.a, SSP.6.a, SSP.6.b, SSP.10.c

STUDENT BOOK pp. 4–5

➤ Preview the Skill

Ask learners to describe a recent experience in which they needed to use a map, an atlas, or GPS. Encourage volunteers to assess whether the information they obtained from these sources proved helpful and to explain why or why not.

❶ Learn the Skill

Link to Past Skills Have learners review the skill *Understand Geography* from Unit 1, Lesson 1. Ask them to list some common geographic features and concepts that they learned about in that lesson. Then direct their attention to maps in the classroom. Invite individuals to take turns identifying various map components that correspond to these core geographic concepts.

❷ Practice the Skill

Decoding Ask learners to decode the map on p. 4. The map key and symbols showing the locations of major cities, as well as the compass rose indicating cardinal directions, provide crucial information needed to answer question 1.

❸ Apply the Skill

Use Graphic Organizers Using the map of Georgia highways on p. 5, instruct learners to complete the following graphic organizer to determine which city's absolute location is closest to 81°W, 32°N, and help them answer question 7.

City	Absolute Location
Athens	83°W, 34°N
Atlanta	84°W, 34°N
Augusta	82°W, 33°N
Macon	84°W, 33°N
Savannah	81°W, 32°N

Answers
1. C; DOK Level: 1; **2.** C; DOK Level: 1; **3.** B; DOK Level: 1;
4. D; DOK Level: 2; **5.** D; DOK Level: 1; **6.** C; DOK Level: 1;
7. A; DOK Level: 1; **8.** B; DOK Level: 1

WORKBOOK pp. 6–9

❶ Review the Skill

Give Examples As a group, ask learners to give examples of useful map components that would help a person travel from the learners' location to your state's capital or statehouse.

❷ Refine the Skill

Skim and Scan Point out that map keys often display colors or shading to distinguish characteristics of geographic areas. Ask learners to skim and scan the map key on p. 6 to identify the meaning of each color or shading found on the map.

❸ Master the Skill

Spotlighted Item Type Using question 10 on p. 8, demonstrate for learners how to interpret multiple map components in order to answer a question correctly. For instance, point out that in order to evaluate the first possible answer choice, learners must locate the symbol for I-90, as well as the symbols and labels for Spokane and Richland. Explain that determining the correct answer choice usually requires learners to locate and decode multiple map components.

➤ Analyze Visuals

Discuss with learners the many symbols that appear on the map on p. 9. Ask them to list correctly the national monuments, museums, and metro stops that appear on the map.

Answers
1. B; DOK Level: 2; **2.** A; DOK Level: 2; **3.** D; DOK Level: 3;
4. B; DOK Level: 2; **5.** C; DOK Level: 3; **6.** A; DOK Level: 3;
7. B; DOK Level: 2; **8.** C; DOK Level: 3; **9.** B; DOK Level: 2;
10. C; DOK Level: 2; **11.** D; DOK Level: 2; **12.** D; DOK Level:
3; **13.** B; DOK Level: 2; **14.** D; DOK Level: 1; **15.** C; DOK
Level: 2; **16.** B; DOK Level: 2; **17.** A; DOK Level: 3; **18.** D;
DOK Level: 2

SOCIAL STUDIES

UNIT 1
LESSON 3

Physical Maps

SS CONTENT TOPICS: II.G.b.1, II.G.b.2, II.G.b.3, II.G.b.4, II.G.b.5, II.G.c.1, II.G.c.2, II.G.c.3, II.G.d.1, II.G.d.2, II.G.d.3, II.G.d.4, II.E.c.7
SS PRACTICES: SSP.2.b, SSP.3.a, SSP.3.b, SSP.3.c, SSP.4.a, SSP.6.b, SSP.6.c

STUDENT BOOK pp. 6–7

▶ Preview the Skill

Ask learners to identify common or notable physical features found in their community or region, such as rivers, lakes, or mountains. Encourage learners to discuss how these features have influenced the area's history and to consider the features' impact on modern life. Explain that physical maps depict the locations of such physical features and may be studied to learn how humans interact with these features.

❶ Learn the Skill

Give Examples Remind learners that map keys will allow them to decode the different types of physical geographic features shown on physical maps. Invite volunteers to give examples of different types of physical features that appear on a physical map. Then discuss how such features could best be shown on a physical map.

❷ Practice the Skill

Decoding Assist learners in decoding the map key of the physical map shown on p. 6. Guide them to determine the types of landforms that might be found in each elevation category shown.

❸ Apply the Skill

Skim and Scan Ask learners to read question 4 on p. 7 and examine each of the possible answers. Then guide them to skim and scan the map of Alabama precipitation, noticing the general precipitation patterns. Demonstrate how learners can use their observations to choose the correct response.

Answers
1. D; DOK Level: 3; **2.** Lake Michigan; DOK Level: 2; **3.** the Au Sable River; DOK Level: 1; **4.** C; DOK Level: 2; **5.** B; DOK Level: 2; **6.** C; DOK Level: 2

WORKBOOK pp. 10–13

❶ Review the Skill

SuperSkill Review Direct learners' attention to a classroom map. Ask students to point out the physical features that are shown on the map. Then have them list some physical features that are not shown on the map.

❷ Refine the Skill

Link to Past Skills Have learners review the skill *Understand Map Components* from Unit 1, Lesson 2, in order to identify the important components of the map on p. 10.

❸ Master the Skill

Use Graphic Organizers Refer learners to the map on the top right of p. 11. Ask them to record in the graphic organizer below the average January temperature range for each state in question 4.

State	Range of Average January Temperatures
Washington	15° to 30°F
Pennsylvania	15° to 45°F
Ohio	15° to 45°F
Maine	0 to 30°F

▶ Analyze Visuals

Discuss with learners the many colors that appear on the map on p. 12. Ask them to list correctly the range of average yearly precipitation North America experiences.

Answers
1. B; DOK Level: 3; **2.** A; DOK Level: 2; **3.** B; DOK Level: 2; **4.** D; DOK Level: 2; **5.** C; DOK Level: 2; **6.** A; DOK Level: 3; **7.** B; DOK Level: 2; **8.** D; DOK Level: 2; **9.** C; DOK Level: 3; **10.** A; DOK Level: 3; **11.** D; DOK Level: 2; **12.** C; DOK Level: 3; **13.** Karachi; DOK Level: 2; **14.** The most mountainous area is north of Islamabad; DOK Level: 2; **15.** the Indus River, the Dasht River, and the Arabia Sea; DOK Level: 1; **16.** India; DOK Level: 2

SOCIAL STUDIES

Political Maps

SS CONTENT TOPICS: II.G.b.1, II.G.c.1, II.G.c.2, II.G.c.3, II.G.d.3, II.G.d.4, II.G.b.2, II.G.b.3, II.G.b.4, II.G.b.5, II.G.d.1, II.G.d.2,, II.E.g
SS PRACTICES: SSP.2.b, SSP.3, SSP.3.a, SSP.3.b , SSP.3.c, SSP.4.a, SSP.6.b, SSP.6.c, SSP.10.c

STUDENT BOOK pp. 8–9

➤ Preview the Skill

Ask learners to name information that might be featured on a political map, such as state name, state capital, counties, population data, and street names. Have learners use this list to sketch political maps of your state.

❶ Learn the Skill

Use Graphic Organizers Help learners compare and contrast political and physical maps by completing a Venn diagram like the one below.

Physical Maps	Both	Political Maps
• Show location of land and water features on Earth's surface • Show physical data such as climate or elevation	• Represent Earth's surface • Include map components	• Show how humans have divided Earth's surface • Show human-made features

❷ Practice the Skill

Give Examples Refer to the second callout for the map on p. 8, and explain to learners that lines of different colors represent county and state borders on this political map.

❸ Apply the Skill

Link to Past Skills Have learners review the skill *Understand Map Components* from Unit 1, Lesson 2, to determine the correct answer to question 5. Encourage learners to study the map key and consider how the map symbols might have been combined to form the symbol located next to Tucson.

Answers
1. B; DOK Level: 2; **2.** D; DOK Level: 2; **3.** A; DOK Level: 2; **4.** D; DOK Level: 2; **5.** B; DOK Level: 3; **6.** B; DOK Level: 2; **7.** D; DOK Level: 3

WORKBOOK pp. 14–17

❶ Review the Skill

SuperSkill Review Instruct learners to work in pairs or small groups. Then distribute classroom reference materials such as atlases, road maps, brochures with maps, or online directions. Ask learners to review and study each map's components to determine whether it is a physical or political map.

❷ Refine the Skill

Decoding Explain to learners that studying the key and title of the map on p. 14 provides the information needed to decode question 2. The title identifies the area shown on the map as the Northeast region. Note that the key provides no information about climate or population density.

❸ Master the Skill

Skim and Scan Have learners read question 5 on p. 15. Then ask them to scan the paragraph for information about Brazil's early period of colonization to help them answer the question.

➤ Enrich and Extend

Ask learners to examine the map on p. 16 and note which areas are most densely populated. Discuss possible problems that may affect people in densely populated areas. Ask learners how conditions might be different for people living in densely populated areas versus people living in sparsely populated areas.

Answers
1. B; DOK Level: 1; **2.** D; DOK Level: 2; **3.** B; DOK Level: 2; **4.** C; DOK Level: 3; **5.** A; DOK Level: 2; **6.** D; DOK Level: 2; **7.** A; DOK Level: 3; **8.** Antarctica; DOK Level: 2; **9.** Asia; DOK Level: 1; **10.** Australia; DOK Level: 1; **11.** South America; DOK Level: 3; **12.** North America; DOK Level: 3; **13.** C; DOK Level: 1; **14.** B; DOK Level: 2; **15.** C; DOK Level: 2; **16.** D; DOK Level: 2; **17.** B; DOK Level: 2

SOCIAL STUDIES

Movement on Maps

SS CONTENT TOPICS: I.G.a, II.G.b.1, II.G.b.2, II.G.b.4, II.G.c.1, II.G.c.2, II.G.c.3, II.G.d, II.G.d.1, II.G.d.2, II.G.d.3, II.E.g, I.USH.b.1
SS PRACTICES: SSP.2.b, SSP.3.a, SSP.3.c, SSP.6.b, SSP.6.c

STUDENT BOOK pp. 10–11

▶ Preview the Skill

Ask learners whether they have always lived in the local city or area. Where were their parents and grandparents born, and did these relatives move to another area? Have learners trace some of these movements on a map. Discuss how movement patterns relate to an area's population and culture.

❶ Learn the Skill

Give Examples Assist learners as they familiarize themselves with the ways in which symbols and colors might be used to convey movement on maps. Then ask learners to list examples of the types of movement that could be shown on a map.

❷ Practice the Skill

Decoding Point out that decoding the map key correctly will help learners find the answer to question 1 on p. 10. Although the routes appear to intersect on the map, the key indicates that these routes actually occurred during three different time periods. Learners can apply this information to help them determine the correct answer choice.

❸ Apply the Skill

Skim and Scan Direct learners to read question 3 on p. 11 and to preview the possible answer choices. Instruct them to locate the cities of Alexandria and Kabul. Learners may then skim and scan along the route to identify cities and landmarks that distinguish the correct answer choice.

Answers
1. D; DOK Level: 2; **2.** D; DOK Level: 2; **3.** B; DOK Level: 2;
4. C; DOK Level: 2; **5.** D; DOK Level: 2

WORKBOOK pp. 18–21

❶ Review the Skill

SuperSkill Review Work as a group to plan the movement of a group of people from one geographic area to another. Ask volunteers to use a map to sketch a few possible routes. Discuss potential benefits of and problems with using different routes and modes of travel.

❷ Refine the Skill

Use Graphic Organizers Direct learners to use the map on p. 18 to complete the graphic organizer below by showing the order of the battles that appear on the map and to answer question 1.

Long Island	
Harlem Heights	
White Plains	
Fort Lee	
Trenton	
Princeton	

❸ Master the Skill

Decoding Assist learners in decoding each of the maps on pp. 18–21. Have volunteers explain each of the keys and map features and describe how each map shows movement. Be sure learners understand how to use each of the different maps.

▶ Spotlighted Item Type

Point out to learners that there is a lot of information on the map on p. 20. Emphasize that they need to study maps carefully for hot spot items and mark exactly where they wish to answer on the map.

Answers
1. C; DOK Level: 1; **2.** A; DOK Level: 2; **3.** B; DOK Level: 2; **4.** B; DOK Level: 2; **5.** D; DOK Level: 2; **6.** D; DOK Level: 2; **7.** D; DOK Level: 2; **8.** B; DOK Level: 2; **9.** Spain and Portugal; DOK Level: 2; **10.** Vikings; DOK Level: 2; **11.** Magellan; DOK Level: 3; **12.** Columbus; DOK Level: 2; **13.** D; DOK Level: 2; **14.** B; DOK Level: 1; **15.** D; DOK Level: 2; **16.** C; DOK Level: 2; **17.** D; DOK Level: 3

SOCIAL STUDIES

Unit 1 Review

SS CONTENT TOPICS: II.G.a, II.G.b.a, II.G.b, II.G.b.1, II.G.b.2, II.G.b.3, II.G.b.4, II.G.b.5, II.G.c.1, II.G.c.2, II.G.c.3, II.G.d.2, II.G.d.3, II.G.d.4, II.E.g, I.USH.b.1, I.USH.b.2, USH.c
SS PRACTICES: SSP.1.a, SSP.1.b, SSP.2.a, SSP.2.b, SSP.3.a, SSP.4.a, SSP.6.b, SSP.7.a, SSP.11.b

You may choose to use the Unit 1 Review on student book pp. 12–19 as a mini–practice test. If you wish to time the test, ask learners to complete all of the items in 75 minutes.

Unit 1 Review Answers

1. B; **2.** D; **3.** C; **4.** D; **5.** A; **6.** B; **7.** D; **8.** A; **9.** B; **10.** C; **11.** D; **12.** C; **13.** southeast, near Ottawa; 14. Iqaluit; **15.** British Columbia, Alberta, Saskatchewan, Manitoba, Ontario, Quebec, New Brunswick; **16.**Yukon; **17.** Yellowknife; **18.** Hudson Bay; **19.** Manitoba and Prince Edward Island; **20.** B; **21.** A; **22.** B; **23.** A; **24.** A; **25.** A; **26.** D; **27.** D; **28.** C; **29.** A; **30.** B; **31.** D; **32.** Burgas; **33.** Slovenia; **34.** Kosovo, Serbia, Romania, Bosnia and Herzegovina, Bulgaria; **35.** Slovenia, Croatia, Bosnia and Herzegovina, Serbia, Montenegro, Kosovo, and Macedonia; **36.** C; **37.** A; **38.** D; **39.** B

Unit 1 Review Item Analysis

SKILL	DOK LEVEL 1	DOK LEVEL 2	DOK LEVEL 3
Understand Geography	25	13, 14, 15, 18, 19, 20, 22, 23, 26, 27, 28, 29, 31, 36	16, 17, 24, 30, 35
Understand Map Components		1, 2, 3	
Physical Maps		20, 22, 23, 37, 38, 39	21
Political Maps		7, 8, 9, 32, 33, 34	10, 11, 12, 35
Movement on Maps	6	4	5

Use workbook lessons, as identified in the following table to assist learners who require additional remediation with certain skills or items having certain DOK levels.

Unit 1 Workbook Item Analysis

SKILL	DOK LEVEL 1	DOK LEVEL 2	DOK LEVEL 3
Understand Geography	2, 3, 6, 7, 9	1, 4, 5, 8, 10, 11, 13, 14, 15, 16, 17	12, 18, 19
Understand Map Components	14	1, 2, 4, 7, 8, 9, 10, 11, 13, 15, 16, 18	3, 5, 6, 12, 17
Physical Maps	15	2, 3, 4, 5, 7, 8, 11, 13, 14, 16	1, 6, 9, 10, 12
Political Maps	1, 9, 10, 13	2, 3, 5, 6, 8, 14, 15, 17	4, 7, 11, 12
Movement on Maps	13, 16	1, 2, 3, 4, 5, 6, 7, 8, 9, 11, 14, 15, 17, 18	10, 12, 19

SOCIAL STUDIES

SOCIAL STUDIES

Unit 2

United States History

Learners may find that the greatest challenge in Unit 2 is the gradual introduction of complex, higher-order thinking skills. The key to success is the ability to master each skill before moving on to the next. Tell learners that the unit begins by building on the geography skills they learned in Unit 1. In Lesson 1, they will connect geography to a historical period or event. As learners move through this unit, initial and intermediate skills are meant to serve as a foundation for more advanced skills. For example, when students understand the concepts of identifying main idea and details, categorizing, and sequencing, they are better equipped to answer questions that address cause-and-effect relationships.

The ability to analyze visual stimuli is essential to success on the GED® Social Studies Test. Unit 2 builds on the map skills taught in Unit 1 and also introduces learners to interpreting tables and timelines. Explain that additional types of visual stimuli will be covered in later units. If possible, provide more examples of tables and timelines so that learners can hone their skill.

The topic of United States history comprises 20 percent of all questions on the GED® Social Studies Test. Although a basic knowledge of history and historical documents (such as a chronology of colonial and early American history and the basic tenets of the Declaration of Independence) is important, students should anticipate an increased emphasis on analysis, application, and evaluation questions.

Table of Contents

LESSON	PAGE
1: Relate Geography and History	SS 12
2: Interpret Tables	SS 13
3: Main Idea and Details	SS 14
4: Categorize	SS 15
5: Sequence	SS 16
6: Cause and Effect	SS 17
7: Interpret Timelines	SS 18
Unit 2 Review	**SS 19**

SOCIAL STUDIES

UNIT 2 / LESSON 1

Relate Geography and History

SS CONTENT TOPICS: II.G.b.1, II.G.b.5, II.G.c.1, II.G.c.2, II.G.c.3, II.G.d.1, II.G.d.2, II.G.d.3, II.G.d.4, I.USH.a.1, I.USH.b.1, I.USH.b.2, I.USH.b.3, I.USH.b.6, II.USH.g.3
SS PRACTICES: SSP.1.a, SSP.1.b, SSP.2.a, SSP.2.b, SSP.3.a, SSP.3.b, SSP.3.c, SSP.4.a, SSP.6.a, SSP.6.b, SSP.6.c, SSP.7.b, SSP.8.a

STUDENT BOOK pp. 22–23

▶ Preview the Skill

Ask learners to work together to craft a definition of the word *context*. Explain that the context of a map includes the historical period in which the map is set. Inform learners that in this lesson, they will learn to connect historical information about time periods or events with geographic information found on maps.

❶ Learn the Skill

Give Examples Brainstorm with learners a list of notable historical periods or events that have taken place in the community, state, or nation. Discuss how these historical events could be reflected on a map. If possible, locate examples of such maps in the classroom, and point out how these maps relate geographic and historical information.

❷ Practice the Skill

Skim and Scan Guide learners in a review of the map on p. 22 in preparation for answering question 1. Point out that the Northwest Territory is a geographical area of the past, but note that the map shows today's state boundaries superimposed on it. Then have students identify the number of complete states formed from the Northwest Territory.

❸ Apply the Skill

Spotlighted Item Type Tell students that fill-in-the-blank responses involve supplying the correct missing word or phrase in a sentence. Note that blanks can appear within a sentence or at the end. Then instruct students to review the skill *Political Maps* from Unit 1, Lesson 4. Have them identify the political information on the first map on p. 23. Point out that they must understand the political information on the map to answer item 2.

Answers
1. C; DOK Level: 2; **2.** MA or Massachusetts; DOK Level: 2; **3.** Santa Fe; Gila; DOK Level: 2

WORKBOOK pp. 22–25

❶ Review the Skill

Link to Past Skills Instruct learners to review the skills *Physical Maps* and *Political Maps* from Unit 1, Lessons 3 and 4. Remind them that they must analyze a map's physical and political features before they can connect geographical information to a historical period or event.

❷ Refine the Skill

Use Graphic Organizers Have students analyze the map on p. 22. Then help them complete a graphic organizer like the one below to identify the rivers, lakes, and whole states that were part of or important to the Northwest Territory. Practice in locating these features will help students answer questions 1 and 2.

Whole States	Lakes	Rivers
Illinois, Indiana, Michigan, Ohio, Wisconsin	Erie, Huron, Michigan, Superior	Mississippi, Ohio

❸ Master the Skill

Spotlighted Item Type Place this sentence frame on the board, and ask each student to complete it: *I was born in the month of _____.* Note that answering fill-in-the-blank items is like filling in a sentence frame with the correct answer.

▶ Analyze Visuals

Ask learners to examine the map on p. 24 showing American and British troop movements leading up to the winter at Valley Forge. Ask learners to identify both the main geographic and historical information. Have learners discuss how both work together on the map.

Answers
1. B; DOK Level: 1; **2.** D; DOK Level: 2; **3.** hills, mountains, vales or valleys; DOK Level: 2; **4.** Mormon; Oregon; DOK Level: 1; **5.** wagon; injury; DOK Level: 2; **6.** Mount Joy; Mount Misery; and the Schuylkill River; DOK Level: 2; **7.** was successful; DOK Level: 3; **8.** temperate or mild; DOK Level: 3; **9.** to protect its shipping rights; DOK Level: 1; **10.** York and the Thames River; DOK Level: 2; **11.** Erie, Michigan, and Ontario; DOK Level: 2

SOCIAL STUDIES

Interpret Tables

SS CONTENT TOPICS: II.E.f, II.E.g, I.USH.b.1, I.USH.b.7, I.USH.c.1, II.USH.e.1, II.G.b.1, II.G.b.2, II.G.b.4, II.G.b.5, II.G.c.1, II.G.c.2, II.G.d.1, II.G.d.2, II.G.d.3, II.G.d.4
SS PRACTICES: SSP.1.a, SSP.1.b, SSP.2.b, SSP.4.a, SSP.6.a, SSP.6.b, SSP.6.c

STUDENT BOOK pp. 24–25

➤ Preview the Skill

Ask learners to think of a favorite sport or TV competition game show they enjoy. Ask them to describe the way the event or game is scored. Explain that tables provide a way to represent such information in an organized manner, making the material easier to understand. Invite volunteers to describe ways in which they have seen tables used to present facts, statistics, and details.

❶ Learn the Skill

Give Examples Direct learners' attention to a calendar, pointing out that it presents information in both rows and columns. Choose several dates on the calendar and review with learners how to identify the rows and columns in which these dates appear. Also, choose a point on the calendar, such as row 2, column 4, and have learners demonstrate how to identify the date that appears at that point.

❷ Practice the Skill

Decoding Work with students to decode the table. Guide them in understanding that reading across each row gives the population for a specific year, and that the years in the first column are in sequence, earliest to latest. Decoding the table will help students answer question 1.

❸ Apply the Skill

Skim and Scan Direct students to skim and scan the second column in the table at the top of p. 25 to identify the way population is listed *(in descending amount from top to bottom)*. Have students analyze geographic location in the left column to determine the location that contributed the largest number of migrants. This will help students answer question 2.

Answers
1. D; DOK Level: 3; **2.** Africa; DOK Level: 1; **3.** the slave trade; DOK Level 3; **4.** B; DOK Level: 3; **5.** D; DOK Level: 3

WORKBOOK pp. 26–29

❶ Review the Skill

SuperSkill Review Ask learners to list all baseball teams in one league and the divisions to which they belong. Discuss ways of organizing the material in a table, including row and column headings.

❷ Refine the Skill

Link to Past Skills Instruct students to review the skill *Understanding Geography* in Unit 1, Lesson 1. The farther north a colony, the harsher its climate and the less likely crops were to survive. The New England colonies were farthest north. Have students recall the names of the New England colonies to answer question 2.

❸ Master the Skill

Use Graphic Organizers Have students complete a graphic organizer like the one below. They can then use it to answer items 8–13.

Conflict	Colonies Involved	Combatants	Reason for Conflict
Pequot Revolt	MA and CT	Pequots vs. English and Narragansetts	Death of an English settler
King Philip's War	MA	Wampanoag vs. English	Land conflict
Yamassee War		Settlers and Creeks vs. Yamassee and Cherokee	Land conflict
Raid on Kittanning	PA	Settlers vs. Delawares	Land conflict

➤ LifeLink

Remind learners that they see tables in many places. For example, a food nutrition label is a table. Ask learners to identify tables and discuss whether, in each case, a table is the best way to organize information.

Answers
1. D; DOK Level: 1; **2.** A; DOK Level: 3; **3.** C; DOK Level: 1; **4.** D; DOK Level: 2; **5.** B; DOK Level: 2; **6.** C; DOK Level: 1; **7.** A; DOK Level: 1; **8.** New England; DOK Level: 1; **9.** Cherokee and Yamassee; DOK Level: 1; **10.** Kittanning; DOK Level: 1; **11.** land; DOK Level: 2; **12.** Pequot attack; DOK Level: 1; **13.** Delaware tribe; DOK Level: 3; **14.** A; DOK Level: 1; **15.** C; DOK Level: 1; **16.** C; DOK Level: 3; **17.** B; DOK Level: 2; **18.** D; DOK Level: 3; **19.** A; DOK Level: 3

SOCIAL STUDIES

Main Idea and Details

SS CONTENT TOPICS: I.USH.a.1, I.USH.b.1, I.E.a, I.E.b, I.CG.a.1, I.CG.b.2
SS PRACTICES: SSP.1.a, SSP.1.b, SSP.2.a, SSP.2.b, SSP.4.a, SSP.5.a, SSP.5.c, SSP.6.b, SSP.7.a

STUDENT BOOK pp. 26–27

▶ Preview the Skill

Ask learners to talk with partners to describe movies or TV shows that they have watched recently. Then lead learners to understand that the key points in their retelling were the main ideas. Explain that points that follow and support the main idea are called supporting details. For example:
- In the movie *Iron Man*, Tony Stark goes from manufacturing weapons to protecting people from them *(main idea)*.
- Terrorists capture Stark and realize they are using weapons made by Stark's company. Stark builds a powerful machine that allows him to fly. Stark's business partner disagrees with his plans *(supporting details)*.

❶ Learn the Skill

Give Examples Review the definition of a main idea and its supporting details. Then use books, stories, news events, or printed forms, and ask learners to name the main idea and at least two supporting details. For example, if examining a credit card application, the main idea involves credit worthiness; supporting details might include income and employment data.

❷ Practice the Skill

Use Graphic Organizers Use the following graphic organizer to determine the main idea and details of the excerpt from *Common Sense*.

The colonies should seek independence from Britain.		
Colonies are young	Population of the colonies is small and can be united	Bravest achievements come in a nation's earliest years

❸ Apply the Skill

Decoding When reading historical documents, learners should use familiar terms to help decode unfamiliar ones. For example, in the excerpt from the Declaration of Independence near the bottom of p. 27, the word *Creator* means "God."

Answers
1. C; DOK Level: 2; **2.** Middle and Southern Colonies; DOK Level: 3; **3.** C; DOK Level: 2; **4.** D; DOK Level: 2

WORKBOOK pp. 30–33

❶ Review the Skill

SuperSkill Review Direct learners to the Using Logic tip on p. 30, and ask them to identify graphics that might provide supporting details for the following events: the American Revolution, the Civil War, and the Great Depression.

❷ Refine the Skill

Link to Past Skills Have learners review the skill *Relate Geography and History* from Unit 2, Lesson 1 to determine the most important detail on the map. This information will help them answer question 2.

❸ Master the Skill

Skim and Scan Ask learners to skim and scan the paragraphs in the left column on p. 32, listing all of the details presented. Then, advise students to use those details to determine the main idea of the passage in order to answer question 7.

▶ Enrich and Extend

Use this brief historical timeline to help learners connect events presented in this lesson:
- **1773:** Boston Tea Party occurs
- **1775:** Battles of Lexington and Concord are fought
- **1776:** Declaration of Independence approved
- **1781-1789:** Articles of Confederation serve as a system of national government
- **1783:** American Revolution ends
- **1787:** Constitutional Convention meets
- **1789:** U.S. Constitution establishes a system of national government

Answers
1. B; DOK Level: 2; **2.** C; DOK Level: 3; **3.** New Jersey; DOK Level: 1; **4.** Battle of New York; DOK Level: 2; **5.** B; DOK Level: 2; **6.** A; DOK Level 2; **7.** C; DOK Level: 2; **8.** B; DOK Level: 2; **9.** D; DOK Level: 1; **10.** A; DOK Level: 3; **11.** A; DOK Level: 2; **12.** C; DOK Level: 3; **13.** D; DOK Level: 2; **14.** B; DOK Level: 2

SOCIAL STUDIES

Categorize

SS CONTENT TOPICS: I.USH.a.1, I.USH.b.1, I.USH.b.3, I.USH.b.4, I.USH.b.6, II.USH.e, I.CG.a.1, I.CG.b.3, I.CG.b.8, I.CG.b.9, II.CG.e.1, II.G.b.1, II.G.c.1, II.G.c.3, II.G.d.1, II.G.d.2, II.G.d.3, II.G.d.4, I.E.a, II.E.g

SS PRACTICES: SSP.1.a, SSP.1.b, SSP.2.a, SSP.2.b, SSP.3.d, SSP.6.b

STUDENT BOOK pp. 28–29

▶ Preview the Skill

Ask volunteers to name some of their favorite television shows. List them on the board. Then ask students to use those responses to identify several genres to which the shows could belong. For instance, you might list the following: *Drama, Science Fiction, Sitcom, Reality, Talk, News* and *Current Affairs*. Discuss in which category each show should be placed.

❶ Learn the Skill

Give Examples Challenge students to brainstorm a short list of important figures in American history. Then ask volunteers to suggest categories into which two or more of those figures could be placed, such as *political leader, military leader, social activist, Founding Father, industrialist,* or *scientist*.

❷ Practice the Skill

Link to Past Skills Have learners review the skill *Interpret Tables* from Unit 2, Lesson 2. Point out that the column headings for the table on p. 28 provide clues about the categories to which various pieces of information are assigned.

❸ Apply the Skill

Decoding Assist learners in paraphrasing the excerpt from *Anti-Federalist Letters from the Federal Farmer to the Republican* on p. 29. Discuss with them how this author views the citizens of the United States. Then help learners decode the possible responses to question 3 and determine which choice best matches the author's view.

Answers
1. C; DOK Level: 2; **2.** B; DOK Level: 3; **3.** D; DOK Level: 2;
4. D; DOK Level 2; **5.** D; DOK Level: 2; **6.** A; DOK Level 3

WORKBOOK pp. 34–37

❶ Review the Skill

SuperSkill Review Direct learners' attention to the categories of history listed on p. 34—social, military, political, and gender histories. Invite learners to use their knowledge of United States history to identify events that could be placed in each of these categories.

❷ Refine the Skill

Skim and Scan Have learners skim and scan the table on p. 34 to review the categories into which the table is divided. This will help them answer questions 1 and 2. Have students note that the title gives a hint as to the categories the table contains.

❸ Master the Skill

Use Graphic Organizers Work with students to analyze the map on p. 35 in order to complete a graphic organizer such as the one below. Students will find this helpful in answering questions 3, 4, and 5.

Democratic-Republican	Federalist	Split
GA, KY, NY, SC, TN	DE, MA, NH, NJ, RI, VT	MD, NC, PA

▶ Enrich and Extend

Guide learners to analyze the information contained in the table on p. 36. Ask them to suggest possible strategies for categorizing the information. Lead a discussion of alternative types of visuals in which the same information could be presented. Ask learners to consider which of these alternatives would make categorizing the information presented easier or more difficult.

Answers
1. C; DOK Level: 1; **2.** A; DOK Level 3; **3.** VA; DOK Level: 1;
4. PA, MD, NC; DOK Level: 2; **5.** Federalist; DOK Level: 1;
6. D; DOK Level: 2; **7.** B; DOK Level 2; **8.** C; DOK Level: 2;
9. A; DOK Level: 2; **10.** B; DOK Level: 3; **11.** B; DOK Level: 3; **12.** D; DOK Level: 2; **13.** B; DOK Level: 2; **14.** C; DOK Level: 2; **15.** D; DOK Level: 1; **16.** A; DOK Level: 3; **17.** C; DOK Level: 1; **18.** B; DOK Level: 2

SOCIAL STUDIES

Sequence

SS CONTENT TOPICS: II.CG.e.3, I.USH.a.1, I.USH.b.2, I.USH.b.6, I.USH.b.7, II.G.b.1, II.G.c.1, II.G.c.2, II.G.d.1, II.G.d.2, II.G.d.3, II.G.d.4
SS PRACTICES: SSP.1.a, SSP.1.b, SSP.2.a, SSP.2.b, SSP.3.a, SSP.3.b, SSP.3.c, SSP.6.b, SSP.10.c

STUDENT BOOK pp. 30–31

▶ Preview the Skill

Ask learners to think about a past experience, such as a vacation, a wedding, or a job interview. Have them list actions associated with the event as shown here:

- Drove to the interview site and arrived early
- Discussed my work experience with the foreman
- Toured the job site with the foreman
- Drove home

Explain that by listing actions in the order in which they occurred, learners are sequencing events.

❶ Learn the Skill

Use Graphic Organizers Explain that a graphic organizer like the one below places historical events in chronological order.

Revolutionary War began
↓
Declaration of Independence signed
↓
U.S. Constitution ratified

❷ Practice the Skill

Give Examples Give learners one minute to list as many words as possible from the passage that indicate sequence. Have volunteers give examples, and explain what the word indicates in terms of sequence. Then note that knowing these words will help learners answer question 1.

❸ Apply the Skill

Skim and Scan Instruct learners to read question 2. Then have them skim and scan the paragraph above for the event that preceded the War of 1812.

Answers

1. C; DOK Level: 1; **2.** B; DOK Level: 2; **3.** D; DOK Level: 3; **4.** B; DOK Level: 2; 5. A; DOK Level: 3

WORKBOOK pp. 38–41

❶ Review the Skill

SuperSkill Review Ask learners to brainstorm a short list of key events from United States history. Then have them sequence these events in chronological order. Explain that sequencing events can help learners make connections among the historical events listed.

❷ Refine the Skill

Decoding Assist learners as they decode the graphic organizer and paragraph on p. 38 to determine the order of main events. This information will help learners correctly answer question 1.

❸ Master the Skill

Link to Past Skills Have learners review the skill *Main Idea and Details* from Unit 2, Lesson 3. Instruct them to read Andrew Jackson's message to Congress at the top of p. 40. Then have them determine the main idea of the passage and one important detail supporting it. This will aid students in answering question 9.

▶ Enrich and Extend

Review the hot spot item at the top of p. 39 with learners. Remind students that hot spot items are visual and require them to locate the correct answers within an illustration, map, graph, chart, photo, or block of text. Challenge volunteers to create a hot spot question for the flowchart on p. 41.

Answers

1. D; DOK Level: 2; **2.** C; DOK Level: 2; **3.** The British give up plans and leave for Britain; DOK Level: 1; **4.** British and American forces arrive near New Orleans in late 1814; DOK Level: 2; **5.** C; DOK Level: 3; **6.** B; DOK Level: 2; **7.** C; DOK Level: 3; **8.** A; DOK Level: 2; **9.** B; DOK Level: 3; **10.** D; DOK Level: 1; **11.** A; DOK Level: 3; **12.** B; DOK Level: 1; **13.** LA; DOK Level 1; **14.** Lewis and Clark expedition; DOK Level: 2; **15.** D; DOK Level: 3; **16.** C; DOK Level: 3

SOCIAL STUDIES

Cause and Effect

SS CONTENT TOPICS: I.USH.1a.1, I.USH.c.1, I.USH.c.2, I.USH.c.3, I.USH.c.4, II.G.b.1, II.G.b.3, II.G.b.4, II.G.b.5, II.G.c.1, II.G.c.2, II.G.d.2, II.G.d.3, I.E.a, I.CG.b.8, I.CG.d.2, II.CG.e.1, II.CG.e.3
SS PRACTICES: SSP.1.a, SSP.1.b, SSP.2.a, SSP.2.b, SSP.3.a, SSP.3.b, SSP.3.c, SSP.4.a, SSP.5.a, SSP.5.d, SSP.6.b, SSP.11.b

STUDENT BOOK pp. 32–33

▶ Preview the Skill

Ask learners to suppose that they have just tuned in to a basketball game on TV. One player is about to shoot a free throw. Ask volunteers to suggest what event or events could have caused this scenario. For example:
- **Cause:** A player commits a foul.
- **Effect:** An opposing player shoots a free throw.

❶ Learn the Skill

Give Examples Explain that in historical accounts, cause and effect are usually described explicitly. Point out, however, that in some cases, causes and effects are merely implied or suggested. Also, make it clear that many single causes can produce multiple effects and vice versa. Ask learners to provide examples of various types of cause-and-effect relationships in history, such as the multiple causes of the American Revolution or the many effects of the terrorist attack on New York City in 2001.

❷ Practice the Skill

Decoding Help learners decode the information in the passage on p. 32 to identify the effects of growing sectional differences on early 19th century America. This information will help them answer question 1 correctly.

❸ Apply the Skill

Skim and Scan Have learners skim and scan the text on p. 33 to identify the contrasting ideas of Jefferson and Stevens on slavery, focusing on how they relate to the causes of the Civil War. This information will help learners answer questions 2 through 5 correctly.

Answers
1. C; DOK Level: 2; **2.** slavery; DOK Level:2; **3.** "the order of Providence"; DOK Level: 2; **4.** new [Confederate] government; DOK Level: 2; **5.** not equal; DOK Level: 2

WORKBOOK pp. 42–45

❶ Review the Skill

Use Graphic Organizers Use the graphic organizer below to show learners how they can understand the relationship between causes and effects.

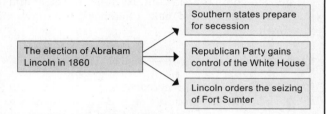

❷ Refine the Skill

Link to Past Skills Have learners review the skill *Political Maps* from Unit 1, Lesson 4. Then, have them analyze how each political division of the country voted in the 1860 election, as shown on the map. This information will be helpful as learners answer questions 1 and 2.

❸ Master the Skill

SuperSkill Review Ask learners to analyze the table and the text on p. 44. For each of the three amendments, model for students how to use a simple diagram to identify cause and effect. This information will help learners correctly answer questions 6 and 7.

▶ LifeLink

Point out that learners can identify cause-and-effect relationships in their personal histories. Instruct learners to work in pairs and share stories from their own lives, such as starting new jobs or getting apartments. Each story should feature a series of causes and effects. Encourage learners to use sentence frames such as *"Because of _____ I decided to _____"; or, "_____ caused me to _____."*

Answers
1. B; DOK Level: 2; **2.** A; DOK Level: 2; **3.** C; DOK Level: 3; **4.** A; DOK Level: 3; **5.** B; DOK Level: 2; **6.** D; DOK Level 2; **7.** B; DOK Level 2; **8.** D; DOK Level: 2; **9.** C; DOK Level: 1; **10.** B; DOK Level: 2

SOCIAL STUDIES

Interpret Timelines

SS CONTENT TOPICS: II.G.b.1, I.USH.c.3, I.USH.d.1, I.USH.d.2, I.USH.d.4, I.USH.d.5, II.USH.f.1, II.USH.f.2, II.USH.f.4, II.USH.f.5, II.USH.f.6, II.USH.f.8, II.USH.f.9, I.CG.b.8, I.CG.c.5, I.CG.d.2
SS PRACTICES: SSP.1.a, SSP.1.b, SSP.2.a, SSP.2.b, SSP.3.a, SSP.3.b, SSP.4.a, SSP.6.b

STUDENT BOOK pp. 34–34

▶ Preview the Skill

Explain that the key to interpreting a timeline is understanding the connection among events, not just the order in which they occur. Emphasize that to interpret a timeline accurately, learners will need to compare and contrast, look for cause-and-effect relationships, make inferences, and draw conclusions.

❶ Learn the Skill

Give Examples Direct learners' attention to the elements on the timeline on p. 34. Ask learners to give examples of how such a timeline suggests relationships between events, as well as overarching trends that are revealed over long periods.

❷ Practice the Skill

Use Graphic Organizers Tell students that Susan B. Anthony was a leader in the movement to grant women the right to vote. Guide them in using a graphic organizer such as the one below to list the states that gave women the right to vote before 1920, in chronological order. This information can help students answer question 1.

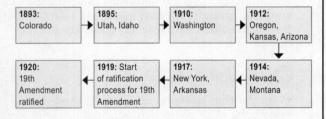

❸ Apply the Skill

Decoding Help students decode the information on the timeline and in the text on p. 35 to better understand major events and legal decisions during the Jim Crow period. Students can then use what they learn to help them answer items 2–5.

Answers
1. C; DOK Level: 3; **2.** 5; DOK Level: 2; **3.** 1913; DOK Level: 2; **4.** equality; DOK Level: 2; **5.** *Plessy v. Ferguson*; DOK Level: 2

WORKBOOK pp. 46–49

❶ Review the Skill

SuperSkill Review Refer learners to the Making Assumptions tip on p. 46, and explain that the title of a timeline will often help clarify the trend to which the events on a timeline relate. Use the timeline on this page to illustrate this point. Then ask volunteers to explain how the individual events listed contribute to the overall trend.

❷ Refine the Skill

Skim and Scan Ask learners to use timeline elements such as benchmarks, labels, and dots or buttons to skim and scan for the year in which *The Blue Book* was published. Point out that students can use this information to answer question 2.

❸ Master the Skill

Link to Past Skills Review the skill *Cause and Effect* from Unit 2, Lesson 6, to help students answer question 7 on p. 48. Explain to students that they can use the skill to determine what caused the rise of the Nazi Party and ensured its victory in the election of 1932. Point out that the events on a timeline can help them to identify cause and effect in a sequence of events.

▶ Enrich and Extend

Have each learner create a simple timeline for an event in his or her life, as shown in this example: *January:* I met Tanya; *February:* Tanya and I began dating; *November:* I proposed to Tanya. Then have learners fill in the gaps to explain the motivations behind each event. This type of analysis helps to establish a timeline's particular trend.

Answers
1. D; DOK Level: 2; **2.** B; DOK Level:2; **3.** B; DOK Level: 2; **4.** C; DOK Level: 2; **5.** A; DOK Level: 2; **6.** B; DOK Level: 2; **7.** A; DOK Level: 3; **8.** C; DOK Level: 2; **9.** C; DOK Level: 1; **10.** B; DOK Level: 3; **11.** B; DOK Level: 3; **12.** C; DOK Level: 2; **13.** D; DOK Level: 3; **14.** B; DOK Level: 3

SOCIAL STUDIES

Unit 2 Review

SS CONTENT TOPICS: I.CG.c.6, II.CG.f, II.USH.e, II.USH.f.2, II.USH.f.3, II.USH.f.4, II.USH.f.5, II.USH.f.9, II.USH.f.10, II.USH.f.11, II.USH.f.12, II.USH.f.13, II.USH.g.1, II.USH.g.2, II.USH.g.3, II.USH.g.4, II.USH.g.5, II.USH.g.6, II.USH.g.9, II.USH.h, I.E.a, I.E.b, II.E.f, II.G.b.1, II.G.b.5, II.G.c.1, II.G.d.1, II.G.d.2, II.G.d.3
SS PRACTICES: SSP.1.a, SSP.1.b, SSP.2.a, SSP.2.b, SSP.3.a, SSP.3.c, SSP.4.a, SSP.5.a, SSP.5.b, SSP.5.d, SSP.6.a, SSP.6.b, SSP.7.a, SSP.10.a

You may choose to use the Unit 2 Review on student book pp. 36–43 as a mini–practice test. If you wish to time the test, ask learners to complete all the items in 60 minutes.

Unit 2 Review Answers

1. D; **2.** C; **3.** A; **4.** C; **5.** B; **6.** D; **7.** D; **8.** D; **9.** B; **10.** A; **11.** Romania; **12.** by rail lines or by railroads; **13.** as the final solution; **14.** espionage or spying; **15.** western; **16.** racism; **17.** B; **18.** C; **19.** D; **20.** D; **21.** B; **22.** B; **23.** C; **24.** C; **25.** D; **26.** B; **27.** A; **28.** A; **29.** D; **30.** A; **31.** B

Unit 2 Review Item Analysis

SKILL	DOK LEVEL 1	DOK LEVEL 2	DOK LEVEL 3
Relate Geography and History		15	
Interpret Tables	3, 4, 10, 11		5, 6
Main Idea and Details		7, 12, 22, 23, 26, 28, 29, 30	8, 9, 16
Categorize			13
Sequence		24	31
Cause and Effect	1, 2, 25	14, 17, 18, 20, 21, 27	
Interpret Timelines		19	

Use workbook lessons, as identified in the following table, to assist learners who require additional remediation with certain skills or items having certain DOK levels.

Unit 2 Workbook Item Analysis

SKILL	DOK LEVEL 1	DOK LEVEL 2	DOK LEVEL 3
Relate Geography and History	1, 4, 9	2, 3, 5, 6, 10, 11	7, 8
Interpret Tables	1, 3, 6, 7, 8, 9, 10, 12, 14, 15	4, 5, 11, 17	2, 13, 16, 18, 19
Main Idea and Details	3, 9	1, 4, 5, 6, 7, 8, 11, 13, 14	2, 10, 12
Categorize	1, 3, 5, 15, 17	4, 6, 7, 8, 9, 12, 13, 14, 18	2, 10, 11, 16
Sequence	3, 10, 12, 13	1, 2, 4, 6, 8, 14	5, 7, 9, 11, 15, 16
Cause and Effect	9	1, 2, 5, 6, 7, 8, 10	3, 4
Interpret Timelines	9	1, 2, 3, 4, 6, 8, 12	5, 7, 10, 11, 13, 14

SOCIAL STUDIES

SOCIAL STUDIES

Unit 3

Civics and Government

The higher-order thinking skill of evaluation is the focus of Unit 3. Lessons include the skills of analyzing information sources, identifying a problem and its solution, distinguishing fact from opinion, evaluating information, and analyzing the effectiveness of arguments. Because of the sophisticated nature of such skills, this unit contains more text passages than visuals. Advise learners to read the text carefully. They will need to use skills learned in previous units to assess the information and answer the questions. Although text passages are the focus of much of Unit 3, the unit also introduces new visual skills. Learners will be asked to evaluate and interpret diagrams, charts, graphs, flowcharts, political cartoons, campaign posters, and special-purpose maps.

Topics relating to civics and the formation of and influences upon the United States government make up 50 percent of all questions on the GED® Social Studies Test. This unit provides a tutorial on interpretation of the Constitution because that document's formal and archaic language can be difficult to understand. Excerpts from editorials, debates, political speeches, and party platforms allow learners to analyze partisan materials for facts, opinions, faulty logic, and effective arguments. You may wish to lead students in a discussion of rhetorical speech. To jump-start your conversation, watch a current televised speech on the Internet. Also, consider reviewing the skill *Analyze Rhetorical Devices* in Unit 2, Lesson 8 of the Reasoning Through Language Arts student edition.

Table of Contents

LESSON	PAGE
1: Interpret Diagrams	SS 22
2: Interpret the Constitution	SS 23
3: Summarize	SS 24
4: Compare and Contrast	SS 25
5: Charts, Graphs, and Flowcharts	SS 26
6: Make Inferences	SS 27
7: Interpret Political Cartoons	SS 28
8: Draw Conclusions	SS 29
9: Determine Point of View	SS 30
10: Analyze Information Sources	SS 31
11: Generalize	SS 32
12: Identify Problem and Solution	SS 33
13: Special-Purpose Maps	SS 34
14: Fact and Opinion	SS 35
15: Faulty Logic or Reasoning	SS 36
16: Evaluate Information	SS 37
17: Analyze Effectiveness of Arguments	SS 38
Unit 3 Review	SS 39–SS 40

SOCIAL STUDIES

Interpret Diagrams

SS CONTENT TOPICS: I.CG.a.1, I.CG.b.1, I.CG.b.5, I.CG.b.6, I.CG.b.7, I.CG.b.8, I.CG.b.9, I.CG.c.1, I.CG.c.2, I.CG.c.3, I.CG.c.4, I.CG.c.6, II.G.b.3, II.G.b.5
SS PRACTICES: SSP.1.a, SSP.1.b, SSP.3.c, SSP.6.b

STUDENT BOOK pp. 46–47

▶ Preview the Skill

Explain that diagrams are a useful way to organize and present information. Ask learners to recall a situation in which they were given information presented as a diagram. Discuss whether the use of a diagram made the information easier to understand.

❶ Learn the Skill

Give Examples Inform learners that diagrams can show relationships between pieces of historical information. Ask learners to examine similarities and differences in political beliefs between two political parties and determine how this information could be presented in the diagram.

❷ Practice the Skill

Use Graphic Organizers Review the features of the Venn diagram on p. 46. Remind learners that each oval contains information specific to one item and that the intersection of the two ovals contains information common to both items. Help learners identify the section of the diagram containing information specific to France so they can answer question 1 correctly.

❸ Apply the Skill

Spotlighted Item Type Have learners look at the drop-down item on p. 47. Explain that they must complete the passage at the bottom of the box by choosing the correct answers for the blanks. Tell learners they will find the answers by analyzing the diagram and the first part of the passage. To allow learners to practice this item type, complete question 2.1 together as a class. Ask: Where will you look to find the answer *(the parts of the diagram on Locke and Rousseau)*? What cue will indicate the correct answer *(We're looking for a term that starts with the word "natural" and is something both men believe all people have.)*? Ask volunteers for the answer *(rights)*, and allow learners to complete the item on their own.

Answers
1. D; DOK Level: 1; **2.1** C; DOK Level: 1; **2.2** B; DOK Level: 1; **2.3** D; DOK Level: 1; **2.4** A; DOK Level: 1; **2.5** A; DOK Level: 3

WORKBOOK pp. 50–53

❶ Review the Skill

SuperSkill Review Explain that the format of a diagram can provide important clues to the type of information the diagram will provide. Point out the two diagrams on p. 50. Explain that the top diagram compares two systems of government and the bottom diagram shows a sequence of events.

❷ Refine the Skill

Decoding To help learners answer question 1, guide them in decoding the first diagram, noting the events associated with the High Middle Ages.

❸ Master the Skill

Spotlighted Item Type Review the drop-down item type with learners. For the items on p. 51, point out that learners must first analyze the diagram carefully to understand where to locate specific pieces of information needed to answer each question. Ask learners to determine what is being compared *(rights and powers of the Articles of Confederation and the Constitution)*. Ask: How does money compare *(made by each state under Articles; made by federal government for whole country under Constitution)*? Ask learners what gray indicates *(same rights and powers under both)*. Then have learners complete the item on their own.

▶ LifeLink

Ask learners to work with a partner to choose one of the diagrams in this lesson. Instruct each pair to brainstorm a way in which the selected visual could be reformatted as a different type of diagram. Then have each pair sketch their new diagram and compare it to the original source. Invite volunteers to explain why their new diagram is more useful than the original visual.

Answers
1. A; DOK Level: 1; **2.** B; DOK Level: 2; **3.1** C; DOK Level: 2; **3.2** D; DOK Level: 1; **3.3** A; DOK Level: 1; **3.4** B; DOK Level: 1; **4.1** B; DOK Level: 1; **4.2** C; DOK Level: 1; **4.3** A; DOK Level: 2; **4.4** D; DOK Level: 1; **5.1** C; DOK Level: 1; **5.2** D; DOK Level: 1; **5.3** C; DOK Level: 3; **5.4** A; DOK Level: 2

SOCIAL STUDIES

Interpret the Constitution

SS CONTENT TOPICS: I.CG.b.2, I.CG.b.3, I.CG.b.5, I.CG.b.6, I.CG.b.7, I.CG.b.8, I.CG.b.9, I.CG.c.1, I.CG.c.2, I.CG.c.3, I.CG.c.4, I.CG.c.5, I.CG.d.1, I.CG.d.2, I.USH.a.1
SS PRACTICES: SSP.1.a, SSP.1.b, SSP.2.a, SSP.3.b, SSP.4.a

STUDENT BOOK *pp. 48–49*

➤ Preview the Skill

Provide learners with an excerpt from the U.S. Constitution, such as the First Amendment (p. 56 of the workbook). Work with learners to examine the language and content of the excerpt. Point out that most government documents contain detailed, formal language that may be difficult to understand.

❶ Learn the Skill

Give Examples Explain that learners can clarify the meanings of unfamiliar terms found in the Constitution by using familiar words and concepts as context clues. Return to the First Amendment and have learners volunteer examples of unfamiliar terms. Then, working together, have the class use context clues to determine their meanings.

❷ Practice the Skill

Decoding Guide learners in decoding the text of the excerpt from the Preamble on p. 48. To help them answer question 1 correctly, instruct learners to look for a word within the phrase that is familiar. Point to the root word *tranquil* within the word *tranquility*, and ask what *tranquil* means. Using that definition, help learners identify what *tranquility* means. Tell learners to use that information as they answer question 1.

❸ Apply the Skill

Link to Past Skills Have learners review the skill *Main Idea and Details* from Unit 2, Lesson 3. Then have learners read the passage in the box on p. 49 and determine the main idea and most important details it contains. When they have clarified this information, instruct them to answer questions 2.1 through 2.4.

Answers
1. C; DOK Level: 2; **2.1** A; DOK Level: 2; **2.2** C; DOK Level: 2; **2.3** D; DOK Level: 2; **2.4** A; DOK Level: 2; **3.** D; DOK Level: 3

WORKBOOK *pp. 54–57*

❶ Review the Skill

SuperSkill Review Invite learners to identify the main ideas and meanings of primary source documents from the late 1700s, such as *Common Sense* on p. 26 and both "The Federalist No. 2" and the *Anti-Federalist Letters* on p. 29 of the Student Edition. Have learners decode a few unfamiliar words in each selection.

❷ Refine the Skill

Use Graphic Organizers Use the following graphic organizer to determine the details of the provisions of Amendment VI on p. 54. Doing so will help learners suggest a title in order to answer question 1 correctly.

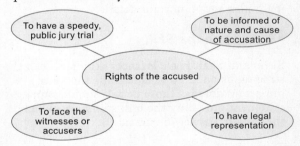

❸ Master the Skill

Give Examples Direct learners' attention to the texts of Amendments I, II, and III on p. 56. Ask learners to give examples of the rights or freedoms guaranteed by each amendment. This exercise will aid learners in finding the answers to questions 9 and 10.

➤ LifeLink

Ask learners to work with a partner to choose one of the amendments from the Bill of Rights and discuss examples that show how the interpretation of the selected amendment has changed over time.

Answers
1. C; DOK Level: 3; **2.** D; DOK Level: 2; **3.** A; DOK Level: 2; **4.** B; DOK Level: 2; **5.** D; DOK Level: 3; **6.** C; DOK Level: 2; **7.** A; DOK Level: 2; **8.** B; DOK Level: 2; **9.** B; DOK Level: 2; **10.** B; DOK Level: 2; **11.** D; DOK Level: 2; **12.** D; DOK Level: 2; **13.** A; DOK Level: 3; **14.** D; DOK Level: 2; **15.** C; DOK Level: 2

SOCIAL STUDIES

Summarize

SS CONTENT TOPICS: I.CG.a.1, I.CG.b.2, I.CG.b.3, I.CG.b.4, I.CG.b.7, I.CG.b.8, I.CG.b.9, I.CG.d.1, I.USH.a.1, I.USH.b.1
SS PRACTICES: SSP.1.a, SSP.1.b, SSP.2.a, SSP.2.b, SSP.3.c, SSP.5.a, SSP.6.b, SSP.9.a, SSP.9.b, SSP.9.c

STUDENT BOOK pp. 50–51

▶ Preview the Skill

Ask volunteers to identify the most recent movies they have seen. Encourage them to describe the plots of these movies briefly and in their own words. Explain that to summarize is to restate in one's own words the main points of an article, an essay, a story, or some other work.

❶ Learn the Skill

Give Examples Explain that a summary is the same as an overview. For example, an overview of the GED® Test would mention the subject areas assessed and the scores required to pass. Have learners provide overviews of current events or historic topics. Remind learners to include only the main idea and important details.

❷ Practice the Skill

Skim and Scan Have learners skim and scan the paragraphs on p. 50 to determine the most important details. Those details should support the statement providing the best summary, which is the correct answer to question 1.

❸ Apply the Skill

Spotlighted Item Type Guide learners in understanding how to answer the Extended Response item on p. 51 by first reviewing the rules for writing a summary. Note that they must first read to understand the main idea and important details of the narrative and the sequence in which important events took place. This information will form the core of their response. Emphasize that learners must use appropriate details from the passage to support the statements that are part of their analysis.

Answers
1. B; DOK Level: 2; **2.** Summaries should include: delegates met in 1787 to overhaul the Articles of Confederation and created a Constitution with a stronger central government. Many states refused to approve it without protection of individual rights from the stronger federal government. States eventually approved the new Constitution with the understanding that a Bill of Rights would be added; DOK Level 3

WORKBOOK pp. 58–61

❶ Review the Skill

SuperSkill Review Explain that one way to organize information for a summary is to think about how to outline the material. In the same way that only the most important main ideas and details are included in an outline, so the same ideas and details would be included in an effective summary.

❷ Refine the Skill

Link to Past Skill Have learners review the skill *Interpret Tables* from Unit 2, Lesson 2, to determine the main ideas communicated by the information in the table on p. 58. Learners can use their interpretation of this information to answer question 1.

❸ Master the Skill

Spotlighted Item Type If necessary, review the rules for writing an Extended Response item on the GED® Test. Tell learners to pay close attention to spelling, punctuation, and grammar, which are important elements of clear, well-composed writing.

▶ Enrich and Extend

Make several magazine and newspaper articles available to learners. Have each learner choose one and read it. When they have finished, direct learners to craft two- or three-sentence summaries of the selected articles.

Answers
1. A; DOK Level: 2; **2.** B; DOK Level: 2; **3.** Summaries should contain: Paine said we feel good about our link with Britain because of the protection it gives us against "enemies" such as France and Spain. But they are not our enemies. They are enemies of Britain. If we cut our ties with Britain, we would be at peace with these nations; DOK Level: 3; **4.** Summaries should include: The Federalist Papers were written to encourage support for the new Constitution and to explain the new government. Federalist No. 37 told how delegates succeeded despite difficulties. Summaries should not include that newspapers published the essays. DOK Level: 3; **5.** Summaries should include: If the colonies joined together, they would have power and success. If they squabbled, they would be powerless and their cause would die; DOK Level: 3

SOCIAL STUDIES

Compare and Contrast

SS CONTENT TOPICS: I.CG.b.7, I.CG.b.8, I.CG.c.1, I.CG.c.3, I.CG.d.2, I.USH.c.1, I.CG.e.2, I.USH.c.3, I.USH.c.4
SS PRACTICES: SSP.1.a, SSP.1.b, SSP.2.a, SSP.2.b, SSP.3.c, SSP.6.c, SSP.3.d, SSP.6.b

STUDENT BOOK pp. 52–53

➤ Preview the Skill

Ask learners to consider two of their favorite musical artists. Invite them to consider the similarities that these artists share. Perhaps both are solo artists or bands, or perhaps they perform within the same genre of music. Ask learners to describe the ways in which these artists are different.

① Learn the Skill

Use Graphic Organizers Remind learners that by comparing and contrasting two or more things, they will consider how those things are both alike and different. Explain that a Venn diagram like the one below can help organize information about the similarities and differences between two items.

```
   Abraham                              Radical
   Lincoln              Both          Rebublicans
  _____        _____     _____
  Hoped to heal       Proposed       Wanted to
  division between    Reconstruction punish harshly
  North and South     plans          the Confederate
                      following Civil States for the
                      War            Civil War
```

② Practice the Skill

Give Examples Direct learners to review the passage on p. 52 and find examples of words that signal comparisons and contrasts. Have them use these words to compare and contrast the two Reconstruction plans and correctly answer question 1.

③ Apply the Skill

Skim and Scan Have learners skim and scan the passage at the bottom of the right column on p. 53 for details relating to the ways Lee and Sherman treated local inhabitants of invaded areas. This information will help them answer question 5.

Answers
1. C; DOK Level: 2; **2.** A; DOK Level: 3; **3.** B; DOK Level: 3;
4. C; DOK Level: 2; **5.** C; DOK Level: 2

WORKBOOK pp. 62–65

① Review the Skill

Link to Past Skills Direct learners' attention to the Test-Taking Tip on p. 62. Then have learners review the skill *Main Idea and Details* from Unit 2, Lesson 3. Remind them to compare and contrast the main ideas of passages as they read historical information.

② Refine the Skill

Decoding Tell learners to read the two passages on p. 62. Then help them decode the meaning of each passage by paraphrasing its content in their own words. This information will help learners answer questions 1 and 2 correctly.

③ Master the Skill

SuperSkill Review Ask learners to read the paragraph about sharecropping on p. 63. Model for learners how to use a simple T-chart to list ways in which sharecropping and slavery were similar and different. This information will help them answer questions 3 and 4 correctly.

Similarities	Differences
•	•
•	•
•	•
•	•

➤ Cross-Curricular Connection

Guide learners in a discussion of the ways in which the skill of compare and contrast is used for scientific information, such as the classification of organisms, and the way it is used in social studies. Discuss how the types of information compared and contrasted are alike and different in the two subjects.

Answers
1. A; DOK Level: 1; **2.** B; DOK Level: 2; **3.** B; DOK Level: 2;
4. D; DOK Level: 2; **5.** C; DOK Level: 2; **6.** A; DOK Level: 3;
7. A; DOK Level: 2; **8.** A; DOK Level: 2; **9.** D; DOK Level: 2;
10. C; DOK Level: 3; **11.** B; DOK Level: 2; **12.** C;
DOK Level: 2; **13.** B; DOK Level: 2; **14.** D; DOK Level: 2;
15. A; DOK Level: 2

SOCIAL STUDIES

Charts, Graphs, and Flowcharts

SS CONTENT TOPICS: I.CG.b.7, I.CG.b.8, I.CG.c.1, I.CG.c.2, I.CG.c.6, I.CG.d.2, II.CG.e.2, II.CG.e.3, II.E.c.7, II.G.b.3, II.G.c.3, II.G.d.1, II.G.d.3, II.G.d.4, I.USH.d.4, II.USH.g.3

SS PRACTICES: SSP.1.a, SSP.1.b, SSP.2.a, SSP.2.b, SSP.3.a, SSP.3.b, SSP.3.c, SSP.6.b, SSP.6.c, SSP.10.a, SSP.10.b

STUDENT BOOK pp. 54–55

▶ Preview the Skill

Ask learners to identify the places in which they usually see charts, graphs, and flowcharts. They might suggest media such as television news programs, newspapers and magazines, or Internet sites. Discuss the benefits of organizing information by using charts, graphs, and flowcharts instead of or in addition to texts.

❶ Learn the Skill

Give Examples Provide learners with examples of the types of visuals that they will learn about in this lesson, such as line graphs and flowcharts. Ask volunteers to describe the information conveyed by each type of visual. Direct learners to identify examples of similar graphs that they have encountered previously.

❷ Practice the Skill

Decoding Assist learners as they decode the graph elements on p. 54. Point out the title, *x*-axis, *y*-axis, and all labels. Tell learners to examine the trend in manufacturing growth between 1890 and 1900 in order to answer question 1 correctly.

❸ Apply the Skill

Link to Past Skills Have learners review the skill *Cause and Effect* from Unit 2, Lesson 6, before analyzing the flowchart at the bottom of p. 55. Point out that connected boxes in the flowchart show a cause and effect relationship between events. Guide learners in understanding the cause and effect relationship between the first and second boxes *(Cause: African American James Plessy sits in a railroad car reserved for whites according to state law; Effect: Plessy sues, charging a violation of the Fourteenth Amendment, and his case reaches the Supreme Court)*. This exercise will help learners answer question 5.

Answers
1. D; DOK Level: 1; **2.** C; DOK Level: 2; **3.** A; DOK Level: 2; **4.** D; DOK Level: 3; **5.** A; DOK Level: 2; **6.** A; DOK Level: 3

WORKBOOK pp. 66–69

❶ Review the Skill

SuperSkill Review Show learners an example of a chart, graph, or flowchart from a newspaper, magazine, pamphlet, or website. Ask volunteers to interpret the various components of the visual, such as a title, label, key, arrow, value on *x* or *y* axis, flowchart box, or graph segment.

❷ Refine the Skill

Link to Past Skills Have learners review the skill *Compare and Contrast* from Unit 3, Lesson 4, to determine the different types of information shown in each graph on p. 66. This review will help learners answer questions 1 and 2.

❸ Master the Skill

Decoding Help learners decode the bar graphs on p. 68 in preparation for answering questions 7 through 10. Review with learners how to read a bar graph. First note that the title of each graph tells what the graph measures. Then point out the axis on each graph that identifies the category measured by its bars *(First graph: x-axis shows the decade for which homestead data is displayed; Second graph: y-axis shows the year for which population data is displayed)*. Tell learners that by reading along the other axis, they can determine the value for each category of data. Note that in the first graph, the values are printed on the graph.

▶ Math Skills

Ask pairs or small groups of learners to use the sample population data below to construct their own simple chart or graph. Then have them ask questions requiring interpretation of the data.
- 1900 – 7,268,894
- 1910 – 10,385,227
- 1920 – 21,588,066

Answers
1. B; DOK Level: 1; **2.** D; DOK Level: 1; **3.** B; DOK Level: 1; **4.** C; DOK Level: 1; **5.** C; DOK Level: 2; **6.** A; DOK Level: 2; **7.** B; DOK Level: 2; **8.** C; DOK Level: 2; **9.** C; DOK Level: 1; **10.** B; DOK Level: 2; **11.1** C; DOK Level: 2; **11.2** A; DOK Level: 2; **11.3** D; DOK Level: 2; **11.4** B; DOK Level: 2; **11.5** C; DOK Level: 2

SOCIAL STUDIES

Make Inferences

SS CONTENT TOPICS: I.CG.b.6, I.CG.b.8, I.CG.c.1, I.CG.c.2, I.CG.c.3, I.CG.c.4, I.CG.c.5, I.CG.c.6, I.USH.d.2, II.CG.e.2, II.CG.e.3, I.USH.d.2, II.USH.d.2, II.USH.f.4, I.USH.f.5, II.USH.f.7, II.USH.g.3
SS PRACTICES: SSP.1.a, SSP.1.b, SSP.2.a, SSP.2.b, SSP.3.a, SSP.3.c, SSP.5.a, SSP.6.b, SSP.9.a, SSP.9.b, SSP.9.c

STUDENT BOOK pp. 56–57

Preview the Skill

Present the following situation to learners: *A friend calls, and you ask how he is doing. Your friend responds sarcastically, "Oh fine, I'm JUST great!"* Using what they know about such sarcastic responses, ask learners what they can infer about the friend? They should be able to infer that the friend is not fine at all and is most likely having a bad day.

❶ Learn the Skill

Give Examples Explain the process of combining two pieces of related information to make an inference. For instance, point out that World War I began in 1914. Then explain that the United States did not enter the war until 1917. From these two pieces of information, learners can infer that initially the United States had hoped to avoid the conflict, but that eventually the country was drawn into the war.

❷ Practice the Skill

Decoding Remind learners that politicians use slogans to reinforce a positive message about a candidate. They tend to choose popular positions that many voters would support, such as "no new taxes." Tell learners to make an inference about public opinion on the war, based on the slogan that Wilson used for his campaign. Learners can use this information to help them correctly answer question 1.

❸ Apply the Skill

Link to Past Skills Instruct learners to review the skill *Summarize* from Unit 3, Lesson 3. Tell them to mentally summarize the information about Elizabeth Cady Stanton and women's suffrage at the turn of the 20th century as they read the passage in the left column of p. 57. Doing so will help learners answer questions 2 and 3.

Answers
1. B; DOK Level: 1; **2.** B; DOK Level: 3; **3.** C; DOK Level: 3;
4. A; DOK Level: 3; **5.** D; DOK Level: 3

WORKBOOK pp. 70–73

❶ Review the Skill

SuperSkill Review Ask learners to review the Test-Taking Tip on p. 70. Then have them read the passage to learn about the U.S. entry into World War I. Have learners combine this information with prior knowledge about World War II to make inferences about similarities between the two conflicts.

❷ Refine the Skill

Skim and Scan Tell learners to skim and scan the excerpt from Wilson's message to Congress on p. 70 for words that express how Wilson feels about going to war. Explain that learners can combine this information with knowledge of Wilson's previous policies on World War I to make an inference and answer questions 1 and 2.

❸ Master the Skill

Decoding Direct learners attention to Susan B. Anthony's speech in the left column of p. 71. Have them decode the speech and note the words and phrases that express her beliefs. This exercise will help them make the inferences needed to answer question 4.

Cross-Curricular Connection

Discuss with learners ways in which making inferences about historical information is similar to making inferences about a work of fiction. Ask learners to recall the story of Superman. Discuss the inferences one has to make about the people around Clark Kent in order to understand how he is able to maintain his secret identity.

Answers
1. D; DOK Level: 1; **2.** A; DOK Level: 2; **3.** A; DOK Level: 3;
4. B; DOK Level: 3; **5.** B; DOK Level: 2; **6.** C; DOK Level: 2;
7. A; DOK Level: 3; **8.** D; DOK Level: 3; **9.** B; DOK Level: 3;
10. D; DOK Level: 2; **11.** D; DOK Level: 3; **12.** Hoover made limited use of the federal government in combating the effects of the Depression. His programs were more likely to target corporations or private organizations to provide help that would trickle down to the public. Roosevelt took a more direct role in providing programs for the average person. Therefore, learners can infer that Roosevelt believed in a more activist role for the federal government than did Hoover.

SOCIAL STUDIES

Interpret Political Cartoons

SS CONTENT TOPICS: I.CG.c.1, I.CG.c.3, I.CG.c.6, I.CG.d.2, II.CG.e.1, II.CG.e.2, II.CG.e.3, II.E.d.7, II.E.d.10, II.USH.f.8, II.USH.f.9
SS PRACTICES: SSP.1.a, SSP.1.b, SSP.2.a, SSP.2.b, SSP.5.a, SSP.5.b, SSP.6.b, SSP.7.a

STUDENT BOOK *pp. 58–59*

➤ Preview the Skill

Ask learners to identify cartoons or comic strips that they enjoy reading. Discuss with learners how these cartoons or comic strips combine compelling images with humor and an interesting story. Explain that political cartoons share these same characteristics while focusing on a current event or issue.

❶ Learn the Skill

Give Examples Locate several examples of contemporary political cartoons and display them for the class. Ask learners to identify the events and issues that these cartoons address, and discuss how each cartoonist expresses an opinion through the images and text of his or her cartoon.

❷ Practice the Skill

Decoding Guide learners to understand that the woodsman in the political cartoon on p. 58 is depicted as strong and heroic, while the politician is portrayed as a caricature of corruption. Help learners decode these symbols and the others in the cartoon in order to answer question 1 correctly.

❸ Apply the Skill

Skim and Scan Have learners skim and scan the cartoon showing President Hoover on p. 59. Instruct learners to look for clues in how the President is depicted, what he is doing, and what the signs around him say in order to determine the cartoonist's point of view about the economic crisis and how Hoover plans to deal with it.

Answers
1. B; DOK Level: 3; **2.** B; DOK Level: 2; **3.** C; DOK Level: 2; **4.** C; DOK Level: 3; **5.** A; DOK Level: 3

WORKBOOK *pp. 74–77*

❶ Review the Skill

SuperSkill Review Direct learners' attention to the cartoon on p. 74. Explain that in political cartoons, cartoonists often make points by using elements such as irony and the juxtaposition of two seemingly unrelated items. Point out the cartoonist's use of these techniques in this cartoon.

❷ Refine the Skill

Skim and Scan Have learners skim and scan the cartoon on p. 74 for details about the man eating apples. Ask learners: Why is he dressed in this way, and what type of person is he? What is he doing, and why? What is his mood? These details will help them determine the correct answers to questions 1 and 2.

❸ Master the Skill

Use Graphic Organizers Invite learners to use the following graphic organizer to analyze the cartoon at the top of p. 75 in order to determine what each of its elements represents. This exercise will help them answer question 3.3.

Sick Old Man	Doctor	Nurse
Uncle Sam/ United States	President Roosevelt	U.S. Congress

➤ Analyzing Visuals

Direct learners' attention to the posters on p. 76. Explain that these images represent propaganda because they are designed to persuade people to behave a certain way. Ask learners what the poster in the left column is meant to persuade people to do *(join the CCC)*. Then ask about the poster in the right column *(support the war)*. As a group, discuss the positive and negative uses and effects of propaganda.

Answers
1. C; DOK Level: 2; **2.** D; DOK Level: 2; **3.1** D; DOK Level: 2; **3.2** C; DOK Level: 2; **3.3** A; DOK Level: 2; **3.4** C; DOK Level: 2; **4.** D; DOK Level: 2; **5.** A; DOK Level: 2; **6.** B; DOK Level: 1; **7.** D; DOK Level: 2; **8.** C; DOK Level: 3; **9.** D; DOK Level: 2; **10.** C; DOK Level: 2; **11.** B; DOK Level: 2; **12.** B; DOK Level: 2; **13.** D; DOK Level: 3; **14.** B; DOK Level: 1; **15.** C; DOK Level: 2; **16.** A; DOK Level: 2

Draw Conclusions

SS CONTENT TOPICS: I.CG.b.3, I.CG.b.9, I.CG.c.1, I.CG.c.2, I.CG.c.3, I.CG.c.4, I.CG.c.6, II.CG.e.2, II.E.f
SS PRACTICES: SSP.1.a, SSP.1.b, SSP.2.a, SSP.2.b, SSP.6.b, SSP.3.c, SSP.4.a, SSP.9.a, SSP.9.b, SSP.9.c

STUDENT BOOK pp. 60–61

➤ Preview the Skill

Instruct learners to think about a detective story from literature, TV, or film. Ask them to describe the ways in which detectives usually solve mysteries. Explain that detectives typically make a series of educated guesses based on evidence, and that when a detective combines several of these inferences to make a judgment, he or she is drawing a conclusion.

❶ Learn the Skill

Link to Past Skills Have learners review the skill *Make Inferences* from Unit 3, Lesson 6. Explain that because drawing conclusions requires learners to combine several inferences, they must be familiar with this earlier skill.

❷ Practice the Skill

Use Graphic Organizers Ask learners to use a flowchart to map out the succession of laws that governed the order of succession in the event that the President is unable to serve.

❸ Apply the Skill

SuperSkill Review Explain to learners that writing the correct response to question 2 requires them to ask and answer certain questions about the situation created by the actions of the steel workers, the threat Truman saw for the country, and the limits of presidential power. Have small groups of learners discuss these topics using the passage, prior knowledge, and the skill of inferring to draw conclusions that will lead to the correct answer. Allow 5 minutes for the discussion. This exercise will help learners focus their thoughts before writing.

Answers
1. D; DOK Level: 3; **2.** The events that unfolded after Truman's actions demonstrate the U.S. government's system of checks and balances, specifically, how the Court limited the powers of the Executive branch. Before 1952 and the Supreme Court decision, the President had considerable power to seize private property; DOK Level: 3

WORKBOOK pp. 78–81

❶ Review the Skill

Use Graphic Organizers Inform learners that they can use a graphic organizer like the one below to organize inferences and combine them in order to draw a conclusion.

Inference	Inference
British rule in India began in the mid-1800s.	India was recognized as an independent nation by 1950.

Conclusion
India experienced an independence movement between the mid-1800s and mid-1900s.

❷ Refine the Skill

Skim and Scan Direct learners' attention to the passage on p. 78. Tell them to skim and scan the passage, asking questions about the Executive Office of the President as they read. Learners should then try to answer the questions they pose, either with material directly from the text or by making inferences. Have learners use this information to respond correctly to questions 1 and 2.

❸ Master the Skill

Decoding Ask learners to look carefully at the table on p. 81. To prepare learners to answer question 10 correctly, discuss shared powers as well as the reasons for the checks and balances.

➤ LifeLink

Discuss with learners real-life instances in which they have had to draw conclusions. Invite volunteers to describe how they went about determining whether their conclusions were correct and logical.

Answers
1. A; DOK Level: 2; **2.** D; DOK Level: 2; **3.** B; DOK Level: 3; **4.** D; DOK Level: 2; **5.** C; DOK Level: 2; **6.** A; DOK Level: 2; **7.** D; DOK Level: 3; **8.** A; DOK Level: 3; **9.** C; DOK Level: 1; **10.** B; DOK Level: 3; **11.** A; DOK Level: 3

SOCIAL STUDIES

Determine Point of View

SS CONTENT TOPICS: I.CG.a.1, I.CG.b.1, I.CG.b.2, I.CG.b.3, I.CG.b.4, I.CG.b.5, I.CG.b.6, I.CG.b.7, I.CG.b.8, I.CG.c.1, I.CG.c.2, I.CG.c.3, I.CG.d.2, I.USH.1.a, II.CG.e.1, II.CG.e.1, II.CG.e.3, II.CG.f

SS PRACTICES: SSP.1.a, SSP.1.b, SSP.2.a, SSP.2.b, SSP.4.a, SSP.5.a, SSP.5.b, SSP.5.c, SSP.5.d, SSP.6.b, SSP.7.a

STUDENT BOOK pp. 62–63

▶ Preview the Skill

Ask learners to think about the many people hired by networks such as ESPN to comment on sports. Explain that unless it is a reporter providing facts, the talking head they see is probably sharing his or her point of view. Discuss with learners the usefulness of this type of information.

❶ Learn the Skill

Give Examples Provide learners with examples of several newspaper editorials. Then lead a discussion in which learners work collectively to identify the point of view from which each editorial is written. Ask volunteers to describe the clues that helped them determine these points of view.

❷ Practice the Skill

Decoding Ask learners to decode the excerpt from President Ford's letter on p. 62. Direct them to look for wording that provides clues to the President's point of view. This information will help them answer question 1.

❸ Apply the Skill

Skim and Scan As learners prepare to answer questions 5 and 6, read the passage aloud one paragraph at a time. At the end of each paragraph, guide learners in pointing out the words or phrases that express the author's point of view. When you have finished reading the passage, ask volunteers to describe the author's point of view. With this background, learners will be better prepared to answer the questions correctly.

Answers
1. B; DOK Level: 2; **2.** D; DOK Level: 2; **3.** B; DOK Level: 2;
4. C; DOK Level: 2; **5.** C; DOK Level: 2; **6.** D; DOK Level: 2

WORKBOOK pp. 82–85

❶ Review the Skill

SuperSkill Review Ask learners to review several of the excerpts from historical documents found in this lesson. Discuss how these excerpts differ from other historical writing, such as that found in textbooks and encyclopedias. Explain that while historical documents usually convey a strong sense of the author's point of view, writings from textbooks and encyclopedias present a more balanced perspective.

❷ Refine the Skill

Skim and Scan Help learners answer questions 1 and 2 by directing them to skim and scan the passage on p. 82 for clues to the author's purpose and point of view.

❸ Master the Skill

Link to Past Skills Have learners review the skills *Make Inferences* from Unit 3, Lesson 6, and *Draw Conclusions* from Unit 3, Lesson 8. Then have learners analyze the list of statements in the right column of p. 83. Tell learners that in cases such as this, the point of view may not be stated directly. They will have to consider the tone of the statements and make inferences about the author's purpose in order to determine the author's goal. By doing this analysis, learners will be better prepared to answer questions 5 and 6 correctly.

▶ LifeLink

Choose a national, state, or local issue with which learners would be familiar. Tell learners to imagine they are writing a letter to a newspaper or website expressing their opinion on this issue. Allow learners five minutes to write their opinion pieces. Invite volunteers on both sides of the issue to share what they have written with the class. Discuss how point of view was expressed in each of the written pieces.

Answers
1. A; DOK Level: 2; **2.** B; DOK Level: 2; **3.** B; DOK Level: 2;
4. D; DOK Level: 3; **5.** B; DOK Level: 2; **6.** C; DOK Level: 2;
7. B; DOK Level: 3; **8.** C; DOK Level: 3; **9.** B; DOK Level: 3;
10. A; DOK Level: 2; **11.** D; DOK Level: 3

SOCIAL STUDIES

Analyze Information Sources

SS CONTENT TOPICS: I.CG.c.2, I.CG.b.5, I.CG.b.9, I.CG.c.1, I.CG.c.3, I.CG.c.4, I.CG.c.5, I.CG.c.6
SS PRACTICES: SSP.1.a, SSP.1.b, SSP.2.a, SSP.3.d, SSP.5.a, SSP.5.b, SSP.6.b, SSP.8.a

STUDENT BOOK pp. 64–65

➤ Preview the Skill

Ask learners to describe the sources they consult when they want to learn about a particular topic, such as the biography of a famous actor or the best driving route to an amusement park. Guide them to understand that, depending on the topic, some sources of information will prove more useful than others. Help learners understand the difference between primary and secondary sources and discuss the situations in which each source is used.

❶ Learn the Skill

Give Examples Have learners list several examples of primary and secondary sources. Explain that learners should always consider the credibility of sources. Ask learners to give examples of ways they can determine whether a source demonstrates excessive bias.

❷ Practice the Skill

Skim and Scan Tell learners to skim and scan the excerpt from Speaker John Boehner's website on p. 64. Encourage them to pay particular attention to any statements that express opinions or beliefs. This information will help them answer question 1.

❸ Apply the Skill

Link to Past Skills Have learners review the skill *Charts, Graphs, and Flowcharts* from Unit 3, Lesson 5, before they study the bar graph on p. 65. Guide them to use the data to evaluate the answer choices for questions 4 and 5.

Answers
1. C; DOK Level: 2; **2.** A; DOK Level: 2; **3.** D; DOK Level: 3;
4. B; DOK Level: 1; **5.** C; DOK Level: 3

WORKBOOK pp. 86–89

❶ Review the Skill

SuperSkill Review Remind learners that information from any source features some degree of bias. Discuss several different news channels or websites, assessing the degree of bias found in each. Have learners consider why the use of multiple sources to verify information could prove valuable to understanding historical events.

❷ Refine the Skill

Link to Past Skills Have learners review the skill *Compare and Contrast* from Unit 3, Lesson 4. Then have them use that skill to help them analyze the way in which information is presented in the two paragraphs on p. 86. Doing so will help learners answer questions 1 and 2 correctly.

❸ Master the Skill

Decoding Direct learners' attention to the table at the top of p. 87 on the different types of federalism. Ask learners to analyze the table, and discuss as a class whether there are examples of bias in the way the information is presented. Have learners suggest the types of information sources in which a table like this might be found. This exercise will help learners answer questions 3.1 through 3.4.

➤ Language Analysis

Review with learners the first passage on p. 88 in order to analyze the sources of bias more closely. Have learners read the passage again and circle any words or phrases that betray the author's bias. As a class, discuss the words and phrases that learners have identified. Talk about the techniques that are used to persuade. Discuss the types of information and sources one might use to counter this author's point of view.

Answers
1. A; DOK Level: 2; **2.** A; DOK Level: 2; **3.1** D; DOK Level: 2;
3.2 B; DOK Level: 2; **3.3** B; DOK Level: 2;
3.4 A; DOK Level: 2; **4.** D; DOK Level: 2; **5.** A; DOK level: 2;
6. C; DOK Level: 3; **7.** B; DOK Level: 2; **8.** C; DOK Level: 2;
9. B; DOK Level: 3

SOCIAL STUDIES

Generalize

SS CONTENT TOPICS: I.CG.b.5, I.CG.c.1, I.CG.c.2, I.CG.c.3, I.CG.c.5, I.CG.c.6
SS PRACTICES: SSP.1.a, SSP.1.b, SSP.2.a, SSP.7.a, SSP.7.b

STUDENT BOOK *pp. 66–67*

➤ Preview the Skill

Ask learners to describe the characteristics shared by many of their favorite athletes. Guide them to recognize that these athletes are likely to exhibit similar traits, regardless of the sports they play. Explain that this fact allows learners to generalize, or make a broad statement about, the selected athletes.

❶ Learn the Skill

Give Examples Review the definition of *generalization*. Remind learners that generalizations typically include clue words such as *most, all,* or *few*. Ask learners to list more clue words and to provide examples of generalizations that include clue words.

❷ Practice the Skill

Decoding Help learners decode the information and find clue words in the passage on p. 66 to determine which generalization the author makes about the U.S. Department of State's Bureau of Energy Resources. This exercise will help learners answer question 1 correctly.

❸ Apply the Skill

Link to Past Skills Have learners review the skill *Summarize* from Unit 3, Lesson 3, as they prepare to answer question 2. Remind learners that a generalization can be proven valid when it is supported by facts and examples. Explain that to answer question 2 correctly, learners must identify the author's beliefs concerning the President's war powers. Ask learners to summarize them, based on the passage. This exercise will help learners answer question 2 correctly.

Answers
1. C; DOK Level: 2; **2.** B; DOK Level: 3; **3.** D; DOK Level: 3;
4. A; DOK Level: 2

WORKBOOK *pp. 90–93*

❶ Review the Skill

Link to Past Skills Have learners review the skill *Determine Point of View* from Unit 3, Lesson 9. Explain that, like a point of view, a valid generalization must be supported by evidence and examples. Remind learners to look for supporting facts when evaluating generalizations.

❷ Refine the Skill

Skim and Scan Ask learners to skim and scan the passage on p. 90 for words and phrases that characterize the duties and powers of the President. Guide learners to understand that the President has executive powers. This fact will help learners choose the correct response when they answer question 2.

❸ Master the Skill

Decoding Have learners start by reading question 3 and its answer choices in the left column of p. 91. Then have them read the passage with that information in mind. Guide learners in evaluating each possible answer as a class, determining whether it is a valid generalization based on the passage or just an opinion or an invalid generalization. This exercise will help learners identify the correct answer to question 3 together.

➤ LifeLink

Have learners brainstorm several generalizations that people in other countries make about the United States or Americans. Talk about why these are generalizations rather than facts, and discuss the probable source of these broad statements. Ask learners if generalizations about a country or a large group of people are ever valid. Have the class listen to and evaluate several learners' opinions.

Answers
1. A; DOK level: 2; **2.** C; DOK Level: 2; **3.** C; DOK Level: 3;
4. A; DOK Level: 3; **5.** The passage argues that the federal government lags behind the rest of the world in use of technology. Responses should clearly identify the enduring issue as the betterment of American society in general and children, the elderly, and minorities in particular; DOK Level: 3; **6.** A; DOK Level: 2; **7.** C; DOK Level: 3

SOCIAL STUDIES

Identify Problem and Solution

SS CONTENT TOPICS: I.CG.b.1, I.CG.b.3, I.CG.b.5, I.CG.c.1, I.CG.c.2, I.CG.c.3, I.CG.c.6, II.CG.e.1, II.CG.e.3, II.CG.f, II.G.b.5
SS PRACTICES: SSP.1.a, SSP.1.b, SSP.2.a, SSP.2.b, SSP.4.a, SSP.5.a, SSP.5.c, SSP.6.b

STUDENT BOOK pp. 68–69

▶ Preview the Skill

Have learners recall situations in which they, either individually or cooperatively, worked to solve a problem in their daily lives. Ask volunteers to describe such situations, and encourage them to identify other solutions that could have been applied to the problems.

① Learn the Skill

Use Graphic Organizers Use the graphic organizer below (about adding lanes to a road) to demonstrate how learners can evaluate the advantages and disadvantages of a proposed solution.

Advantages	Disadvantages
• Increased traffic flow	• Shortage of funds for expansion of current road
• Improved safety for bicyclists and pedestrians	• Increased congestion during lengthy construction phase
• Additional parking during non-peak hours	• Additional traffic signals may offset traffic flow improvements

② Practice the Skill

Decoding Help learners decode the terms and details in the passage on p. 68 to identify the main problem being addressed. This information will help them answer question 1 correctly.

③ Apply the Skill

Link to Past Skills Have learners review the skill *Cause and Effect* from Unit 2, Lesson 6, before they answer questions 5 and 6 on p. 69. Explain that, in terms of question 5, they can assume that one of the answer choices caused a problem that Section 1 of Amendment XXII resolves.

Answers
1. B; DOK Level: 2; **2.** D; DOK Level: 2; **3.** B; DOK Level: 2; **4.** C; DOK Level: 3; **5.** C; DOK Level: 2; **6.** A; DOK Level: 3; **7.** D; DOK Level: 2

WORKBOOK pp. 94–97

① Review the Skill

SuperSkill Review Explain that in examining historical problems and solutions, learners must consider the context of events. Point out that by doing so, learners will be better prepared to identify the causes of historical problems and evaluate the effectiveness of the solutions. Ask learners to brainstorm a list of historical problems and discuss whether those problems were solved effectively.

② Refine the Skill

Give Examples Help learners list the problems that the new fuel efficiency standards are meant to address, as discussed in the passage on p. 94. Then instruct learners to compare the items on the list to the answer choices for question 1.

③ Master the Skill

Skim and Scan Direct learners to skim and scan the excerpt from Franklin Roosevelt's "Fireside Chat" in the left column on p. 97. Ask them to identify the problems described by Roosevelt, as well as his subsequent actions (solutions). This information will help them answer questions 11 through 13 correctly.

▶ LifeLink

Have learners work in small groups, and ask each group to choose a problem facing the community, state, or nation. Have groups list several solutions and evaluate the advantages and disadvantages of each. Then have learners recommend the best course of action. As a class, discuss the process of finding a workable solution.

Answers
1. A; DOK Level: 2; **2.** B; DOK Level: 2; **3.** B; DOK Level: 2; **4.** D; DOK Level: 2; **5.** C; DOK Level: 2; **6.** A; DOK Level: 2; **7.** D; DOK Level: 2; **8.** B; DOK Level: 3; **9.** D; DOK Level: 3; **10.** B; DOK Level: 3; **11.** D; DOK Level: 2; **12.** C; DOK Level: 3; **13.** B; DOK Level: 2; **14.** A; DOK Level: 2; **15.** D; DOK Level: 2; **16.** A; DOK Level: 2

SOCIAL STUDIES

Special-Purpose Maps

SS CONTENT TOPICS: I.CG.c.1, I.CG.c.3, II.CG.e.1, II.CG.e.3, II.G.b.2, II.G.b.4, II.G.c.1, II.G.c.2, II.G.c.3, II.G.d.1, II.G.d.3, II.G.d.4
SS PRACTICES: SSP.1.a, SSP.2.a, SSP.4.a, SSP.6.b, SSP.6.c

STUDENT BOOK pp. 70–71

▶ Preview the Skill

Direct learners' attention to a simple political map (such as the ones in Unit 1, Lesson 4), and point out features such as borders of counties and countries, and the locations of cities. Then ask learners to examine the special-purpose map on p. 70 and compare it with the political maps in Unit 1. Guide learners to determine that although special-purpose maps may show basic political features, they also include additional features related to their special purposes.

❶ Learn the Skill

Give Examples Identify for learners several examples of the features typically found on special-purpose maps. Suggest that these maps may feature electoral districts, population data, or natural resources. As a group, sketch a special-purpose map of your state.

❷ Practice the Skill

Decoding Ask learners to decode the special-purpose map on p. 70. Tell them to use the cities labeled on the map to determine the relative location of California. This information will allow them to answer question 1 correctly.

❸ Apply the Skill

Link to Past Skills Have learners review the skill *Compare and Contrast* from Unit 3, Lesson 4. Help learners list information from the special-purpose map of Arkansas Congressional Districts, and from the text in the right column of p. 71. Explain to learners that contrasting the information in their lists will help them answer question 6 correctly.

Answers
1. D; DOK Level: 1; **2.** B; DOK Level: 2; **3.** A; DOK Level: 2; **4.** C; DOK Level: 2; **5.** C; DOK Level: 2; **6.** D; DOK Level: 3

WORKBOOK pp. 98–101

❶ Review the Skill

SuperSkill Review Direct learners to examine map components such as titles, symbols, labels, and map keys when they interpret special-purpose maps. Explain that these components provide valuable clues to the purpose of each map.

❷ Refine the Skill

Skim and Scan Have learners skim and scan the electoral map on p. 98 to locate the states listed as answer choices for question 1. Assist learners if they are unsure of the state locations. Then have them use their knowledge of United States geography and the map's symbols to determine the correct answer to question 1.

❸ Analyze Visuals

Decoding Help learners decode the map symbols on p. 99 to contrast how the map shows population gains and population losses. In addition, review with learners the regional divisions that are applied in several items on the page: *West Coast, South Atlantic Coast, Great Plains, Northeast, Southwest,* and *Central Plains.* This information is needed for learners to answer questions 4 and 5 correctly.

▶ Optional Activity

Point out that some special-purpose maps use picture icons to represent information, and draw learners' attention to the "Products of Colorado" map on p. 100. Discuss how the picture icons are used. Then have learners suggest other ways in which a special-purpose map might show the same type of information *(Products could be shown with just labels, or with color and pattern symbols.)*.

Answers
1. A; DOK Level: 1; **2.** D; DOK Level: 2; **3.** A; DOK Level: 2; **4.** C; DOK Level: 2; **5.** B; DOK Level: 2; **6.** C; DOK Level: 2; **7.** D; DOK Level: 3; **8.** A; DOK Level: 1; **9.** D; DOK Level: 3; **10.** A; DOK Level: 1; **11.** A; DOK Level: 2; **12.** B; DOK Level: 1; **13.** D; DOK Level: 1; **14.1** A; DOK Level: 2; **14.2** C; DOK Level: 2; **14.3** D; DOK Level: 2; **14.4** B; DOK Level: 2

SOCIAL STUDIES

Fact and Opinion

SS CONTENT TOPICS: I.CG.a.1, II.CG.e.1, II.CG.e.3, II.CG.f
SS PRACTICES: SSP.2 a, SSP.5.a, SSP.5.b, SSP.5.c, SSP.5.d, SSP.7.a, SSP.7.b,

STUDENT BOOK pp. 72–73

▶ Preview the Skill

Invite learners to describe television news programs that they watch regularly. They might watch local news broadcasts, 24-hour cable news channels, or weekly newsmagazine programs. Then lead learners in a discussion of how these programs use both facts and opinions to present information to viewers.

1 Learn the Skill

Give Examples Inform learners that by identifying facts and statements of opinion in social studies information, they will be better able to evaluate the credibility of that information. Have learners provide examples of sources that contain mostly facts, such as atlases, encyclopedias, and scholarly biographies. Then ask learners to offer examples of historical works that are likely to contain many opinions.

2 Practice the Skill

Decoding Remind learners to look for strong or emotional language when they are identifying opinions, as opposed to facts that can be verified. To help them answer question 1, have learners read the passage aloud together, and assist them in locating emotional language in the excerpt from Joe Biden's speech on p. 72.

3 Apply the Skill

Link to Past Skills Have learners review the skill *Determine Point of View* from Unit 3, Lesson 9, to help them identify the opinions of the critics of the Electoral College in the information in the left column of p. 73. They can use this information to answer question 3 correctly.

Answers
1. A; DOK Level: 2; **2.** B; DOK Level: 3; **3.** C; DOK Level: 2;
4. A; DOK Level: 2; **5.** B; DOK Level: 2; **6.** A; DOK Level: 2;
7. B; DOK Level: 2

WORKBOOK pp. 102–105

1 Review the Skill

SuperSkill Review Remind learners that facts are statements that can be proven true, whereas opinions are statements that cannot be proven true. If learners remain unsure about a particular statement, tell them to consider what evidence or details might prove that statement true. If no such evidence exists, explain that the statement is probably an opinion.

2 Refine the Skill

Skim and Scan Tell learners to skim and scan the excerpt from the passage on p. 102 to help them answer question 2. Assist learners in identifying words and phrases in the State of the Union Address that signal the President's opinion about the role of government in health care.

3 Master the Skill

Use Graphic Organizers Tell learners to use a graphic organizer like the one below to help them classify each statement from the passage at the top of p. 103 as either fact or opinion. Instruct learners to use their completed graphic organizers to choose the best responses to the related questions.

Facts	Opinions

▶ Enrich and Extend

Have learners locate editorials in newspapers or magazines. Then instruct them to discuss the balance of facts and opinions in the selected materials. Tell them to evaluate whether the authors support their opinions with convincing evidence or simply present a series of unsupported opinions.

Answers
1. B; DOK Level: 2; **2.** B; DOK Level: 2; **3.** popular vote; DOK Level: 2; **4.** the problem could occur again with the electoral college; DOK Level: 3; **5.** not have as many electoral votes as they do; DOK Level: 2; **6.** should not, or do not; DOK Level: 1; **7.** A; DOK Level: 2; **8.** B; DOK Level: 2; **9.** A; DOK Level: 2; **10.** B; DOK Level: 3; **11.** D; DOK Level: 3; **12.** C; DOK Level: 2; **13.** D; DOK Level: 2; **14.** D; DOK Level: 2; **15.** B; DOK Level: 2; **16.** C; DOK Level: 2; **17.** B; DOK Level: 2; **18.** A; DOK Level: 2

Faulty Logic or Reasoning

SS CONTENT TOPICS: I.CG.b.7, I.CG.b.8, I.CG.c.1, I.CG.c.2, CG.d.2, II.G.d.2, I.USH.b.7, I.USH.d.3, II.USH.g.1, II.USH.g.3
SS PRACTICES: SSP.5.a, SSP.5.b, SSP.5.c, SSP.5.d, SSP.6.b, SSP.7.a, SSP.7.b

STUDENT BOOK pp. 74–75

➤ Preview the Skill

Ask learners to recall a disagreement that they have seen in a movie or television program. Have them describe the positions of both parties in the argument. Guide them to explain each person's strategies for attacking the other person's positions. Suggest that one way in which learners might critique an argument is to look for faulty logic or reasoning.

❶ Learn the Skill

Give Examples Discuss with learners the definition of a hasty generalization, and ask them to give examples of such generalizations *(women are bad drivers; men aren't good with babies)*. Then lead the class in a discussion of why hasty generalizations represent an example of faulty logic or reasoning. Help them recognize that a generalization that cannot be supported by facts is not well reasoned or logical.

❷ Practice the Skill

Decoding Instruct learners to read the passage on p. 74 and to look for instances of faulty logic as they do. Have learners write down one example on a sheet of paper as they read. Then have volunteers read their examples aloud. Have the class discuss and assess the choices. This exercise will help learners answer question 1 correctly.

❸ Apply the Skill

Link to Past Skills Have learners review the skill *Interpret Political Cartoons* from Unit 3, Lesson 7, to help them answer question 3 on p. 75. Direct them to study the text and image within the box to determine the way in which the cartoon criticizes an instance of faulty reasoning linked to the Second Amendment to the U.S. Constitution.

Answers
1. A; DOK Level: 2; **2.** the American public, or the U.S. government; DOK Level: 2; **3.** The Second Amendment guarantees that a well-regulated militia may have the right to own guns, not just a private citizen; DOK Level: 3; **4.** The Second Amendment guarantees that they can; DOK Level: 3; **5.** D; DOK Level: 2; **6.** B; DOK Level: 2

WORKBOOK pp. 106–109

❶ Review the Skill

SuperSkill Review Remind learners to assess logic and reasoning by identifying an author's main argument. Point out that they should next consider whether the argument can be proven true and how it is supported.

❷ Refine the Skill

Skim and Scan Have pairs of learners work together to read the passage on p. 106, looking for faulty generalizations. Have partners discuss the examples they see and describe why the generalizations would be difficult to support with evidence.

❸ Master the Skill

Use Graphic Organizers Instruct learners to use a graphic organizer such as the one below to chart the faulty logic and reasoning highlighted in the text and the cartoon on p. 109. Tell learners that they should identify four events. The first one is given, and the last should be the example of faulty logic and reasoning.

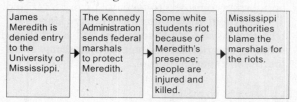

| James Meredith is denied entry to the University of Mississippi. | The Kennedy Administration sends federal marshals to protect Meredith. | Some white students riot because of Meredith's presence; people are injured and killed. | Mississippi authorities blame the marshals for the riots. |

➤ Cross-Curricular Connection

Discuss with learners the fact that they can search for faulty logic or reasoning when analyzing conclusions drawn from the scientific method. A scientist must determine whether his or her results confirm or disprove the experiment's hypothesis. However, if these results are not evaluated logically, the conclusions drawn will not be valid.

Answers
1. D; DOK Level: 2; **2.** B; DOK Level: 2; **3.** B; DOK Level: 2; **4.** B; DOK Level: 2; **5.** C; DOK Level: 3; **6.** B; DOK Level: 2; **7.** C; DOK Level: 2; **8.** D; DOK Level: 2; **9.** D; DOK Level: 2; **10.** A; DOK Level: 2; **11.** D; DOK Level: 2; **12.** B; DOK Level: 2; **13.** C; DOK Level: 3; **14.** B; DOK Level: 2; **15.** C; DOK Level: 3

Evaluate Information

SS CONTENT TOPICS: I.CG.c.2, II.CG.e.1, II.CG.e.2, II.CG.e.3, II.CGf, II.USH.g.7
SS PRACTICES: SSP.1.a, SSP.1.b, SSP.2.a, SSP.3.d, SSP.4.a, SSP.5.a, SSP.5.b, SSP.5.d, SSP.7.a, SSP.7.b, SSP.8.a, SSP.9.a, SSP.9.c

STUDENT BOOK pp. 76–77

▶ Preview the Skill

Have learners recall television commercials for various products. Ask them to consider the claims that these commercials make. Discuss with learners whether the information presented can be considered trustworthy. Explain that, like these commercials, historical information must be carefully evaluated to assess its credibility.

❶ Learn the Skill

Give Examples Have learners list examples of characteristics that they should look for when evaluating the quality of information. These characteristics include purpose, bias, faulty logic or reasoning, and facts and opinions. If necessary, review the definitions of these concepts.

❷ Practice the Skill

Decode Instruct learners to read the Test-Taking Tip on p. 76, and then have them pre-read question 1. Next, tell them to read the passage on the same page, keeping the question in mind. This should help learners determine the correct answer to question 1 as they read.

❸ Apply the Skill

Skim and Scan Direct learners to skim and scan the passage in the left column on p. 77. Ask them to determine which candidate the author endorses and to write down two sentences or phrases that support the author's position. Ask volunteers to share their conclusions and the text that supports them. This exercise should help learners answer questions 2 through 4 correctly.

Answers
1. D; DOK Level: 2; **2.** B; DOK Level: 2; **3.** D; DOK Level: 2;
4. C; DOK Level: 2; **5.** D; DOK Level: 2; **6.** B; DOK Level: 2

WORKBOOK pp. 110–113

❶ Review the Skill

SuperSkill Review Remind learners that all pieces of information feature some degree of bias. Although a reasonable degree of bias does not make a source unreliable, statements that express ideas or beliefs should be supported by facts and evidence.

❷ Refine the Skill

Link to Past Skills Have learners review the skill *Main Idea and Details* from Unit 2, Lesson 3, to determine the main idea and most important supporting details of the passage on p. 110. Explain that learners can use this information to answer questions 1 and 2 correctly.

❸ Master the Skill

Skim and Scan Ask learners to skim and scan the passages on p. 112 to determine how the campaign literature builds support for each candidate. Note that some brochures focus on their candidate's positive attributes while others point out their opponent's negative attributes. Discuss the tactics used and the positive attributes mentioned in each brochure. This discussion will help learners answer questions 4 and 6 correctly.

▶ Language Analysis

Direct learners' attention to the campaign speeches excerpted on p. 113. Note that while the Clinton speech paints a negative picture of his opponent George Bush, the Obama speech takes the opposite tactic in presenting positive achievements. Have learners analyze each speech, circling descriptive words used to achieve its goal. Discuss as a class the contrasting image the language in each speech creates.

Answers
1. A; DOK Level: 2; **2.** D; DOK Level: 1; **3.** LBJ believed Great Society programs would improve the lives of ordinary people. The writer states the program was a success because many problems it tackled improved. Several facts are used to support this point of view; DOK Level: 3; **4.** C; DOK Level: 2; **5.** D; DOK Level: 3; **6.** A; DOK Level: 2; **7.** B; DOK Level: 2; **8.** C; DOK Level: 2; **9.** A; DOK Level: 2; **10.** A; DOK Level: 3; **11.** B; DOK level: 2; **12.** D; DOK Level: 3; **13.** D; DOK Level: 2; **14.** B; DOK Level: 2; **15.** A; DOK Level: 2

SOCIAL STUDIES

Analyze Effectiveness of Arguments

SS CONTENT TOPICS: I.CG.c.1, I.CG.c.2, I.USH.a.1, II.CG.e.1, II.CG.e.3, II.CG.f
SS PRACTICES: SSP.1.a, SSP.1.b, SSP.2.a, SSP.5.a, SSP.5.d, SSP.7.b, SSP.8.a, SSP.9.a, SSP.9.b, SSP.9.c

STUDENT BOOK pp. 78–79

▶ Preview the Skill

Ask learners to suppose that they are debating a question, such as the following one, amongst friends: Who is the greatest NASCAR driver of all time? Then instruct learners to consider how they would construct an argument on behalf of a suggested driver. Guide learners to recognize that convincing arguments provide facts. In this case they would need facts to support the chosen driver, such as statistics, awards, and number of wins.

❶ Learn the Skill

Link to Past Skills Tell learners to read the Test-Taking Tip on p. 78, and review with them the skill *Summarize* from Unit 3, Lesson 3. Explain that summarizing a passage will allow learners to better analyze the effectiveness of arguments in this lesson.

❷ Practice the Skill

Decoding Help learners decode the answer choices for question 1. Guide them in recognizing how Clinton's argument for Obama could best be strengthened.

❸ Apply the Skill

Skim and Scan Instruct learners to skim and scan the excerpt from the Senate debate on the Tonkin Gulf Resolution on p. 79 to identify the main arguments made by the opposing sides. This information will help them answer question 2 correctly.

Answers

1. A; DOK Level: 2; **2.** Neither senator backs up his argument with many facts about what the resolution would authorize the President to do. Fulbright bases his argument largely on what he deems "reasonable" in the situation, while Gruening opposes it with a list of troubling activities of the U.S. armed forces in Southeast Asia. Gruening thinks expanding those activities would escalate military action, and he has facts to support this. Gruening's argument seems more logical and well-reasoned, while Fulbright's seems based mostly on his opinion that the President would be cautious, although he has no facts to back that up and freely admits that he does not know what will happen; DOK Level 3

WORKBOOK pp. 114–117

❶ Review the Skill

Give Examples Ask learners to give examples of weak arguments that are not supported by facts or evidence. Then lead the class in discussing ways in which these weak arguments could be strengthened by specific pieces of evidence.

❷ Refine the Skill

SuperSkill Review Explain that items such as question 1 require learners to analyze the argument strategy of an author. Instruct learners to read the excerpt from Chief Justice Berger's argument in support of the Court's majority opinion in *United States v. Nixon*. Tell them to identify Berger's strategy in order to answer question 1.

❸ Master the Skill

Link to Past Skills Have learners review the skill *Fact and Opinion* from Unit 3, Lesson 14, to determine how arguments are supported. Instruct small groups of learners to read the excerpt from Letter from a Birmingham Jail on p. 115. Ask learners to identify arguments that Dr. King makes to support his belief that demonstrations were justified. Have them address whether King uses valid facts or strong evidence to support his argument. This analysis will help learners answer questions 3 and 5 correctly.

▶ Enrich and Extend

Present a well-known historical argument for learners to evaluate. Use transcripts or videos of a debate (e.g., whether to impeach Richard Nixon). Have learners identify the parties involved in the debates and analyze the effectiveness of each side's argument. As a class, decide which party crafted the most effective argument, and explain the reasoning behind the selection.

Answers

1. C; DOK Level: 2; **2.** D; DOK Level: 3; **3.** B; DOK Level: 2; **4.** C; DOK Level: 2; **5.** D; DOK Level: 2; **6.** C; DOK Level: 2; **7.** A; DOK Level: 2; **8.** D; DOK Level: 2; **9.** C; DOK Level: 3; **10.** A; DOK Level: 3; **11.** C; DOK Level: 2; **12.** D; DOK Level: 2; **13.** D; DOK Level: 3; **14.** B; DOK Level: 2; **15.** C; DOK Level: 3

SOCIAL STUDIES

Unit 3 Review

SS CONTENT TOPICS: I.CG.a.1, I.CG.b.1, I.CG.b.2, I.CG.b.3, I.CG.b.4, I.CG.b.7, I.CG.b.8, I.CG.c.1, I.CG.c.2, I.CG.c.3, I.CG.c.6, I.CG.d.1, I.CG.d.2, II.CG.e.1, II.CG.e.2, II.CG.e.3, II.CG.f, II.G.b.1, II.G.c.1, II.G.c.3, II.G.d.3, II.E.c.4, II.E.c.7, II.E.c.10, II.E.d.3, I.USH.a.1, I.USH.b.1, I.USH.c.1, I.USH.c.2, I.USH.c.4, I.USH.d.3, II.USH.f.1, II.USH.f.8, II.USH.f.9, II.USH.g.1, II.USH.g.3, II.USH.g.8, II.USH.g.9, II.USH.h
SS PRACTICES: SSP.1.a, SSP.1.b, SSP.2.a, SSP.2.b, SSP.3.a, SSP.3.b, SSP.3.c, SSP.4.a, SSP.5.a, SSP.5.b, SSP.5.c, SSP.6.b, SSP.7.a, SSP.10.a

You may choose to use the Unit 3 Review on student book pp. 80-87 as a mini–practice test. If you wish to time the test, ask learners to complete all the items in 60 minutes.

Unit 3 Review Answers

1. B; **2.** C; **3.** B; **4.** D; **5.** B; **6.** B; **7.** D; **8.** D; **9.** B; **10.** C; **11.** D; **12.** B; **13.** A; **14.** C; **15.** B; **16.** A; **17.** C; **18.1** A; **18.2** B; **18.3** C; **18.4** D; **19.** B; **20.** C; **21.** B; **22.** B; **23.** C; **24.** B; **25.** D; **26.** A; **27.** C; **28.** D; **29.** D; **30.** A

Unit 3 Review Item Analysis

SKILL	DOK LEVEL 1	DOK LEVEL 2	DOK LEVEL 3
Interpret Diagrams		7	
Interpret the Constitution	6		20
Summarize		1, 2, 3, 21	
Compare and Contrast		14	
Interpret Charts, Graphs, and Flowcharts		23, 27	24
Make Inferences			5, 15, 28
Interpret Political Cartoons		11	26
Draw Conclusions		12	29
Determine Point of View		9, 22	
Analyze Information Sources		4	
Generalize			8, 30
Identify Problem and Solution		19	
Special-Purpose Maps		18.1, 18.2, 18.3, 18.4	
Fact and Opinion		16, 17	
Faulty Logic or Reasoning			25
Evaluate Information		13	
Analyze Effectiveness of Arguments		10	

SOCIAL STUDIES

Unit 3 Review

Use workbook lessons, as identified in the following table, to assist learners who require additional remediation with certain skills or items having certain DOK levels.

Unit 3 Workbook Item Analysis

SKILL	DOK LEVEL 1	DOK LEVEL 2	DOK LEVEL 3
Interpret Diagrams	1, 3.2, 3.3, 3.4, 4.1, 4.2, 4.4, 5.1, 5.2	2, 3.1, 4.3, 5.4	5.3
Interpret the Constitution		2, 3, 4, 6, 7, 8, 9, 10, 11, 12, 14, 15	1, 5, 13
Summarize		1, 2	3, 4, 5
Compare and Contrast	1	2, 3, 4, 5, 7, 8, 9, 11, 12, 13, 14, 15	6, 10
Interpret Charts, Graphs, and Flowcharts	1, 2, 3, 4, 9	5, 6, 7, 10, 11	8
Make Inferences	1	2, 5, 6, 10	3, 4, 7, 8, 9, 11, 12
Interpret Political Cartoons	6, 14	1, 2, 3.1, 3.2, 3.3, 3.4, 4, 5, 7, 9, 10, 11, 12, 15, 16	8, 13
Draw Conclusions	9	1, 2, 4, 5, 6	3, 7, 8, 10, 11
Determine Point of View		1, 2, 3, 5, 6, 10	4, 7, 8, 9, 11
Analyze Information Sources		1, 2, 3.1, 3.2, 3.3, 3.4, 4, 5, 7, 8	6, 9
Generalize		1, 2, 6	3, 4, 5, 7
Identify Problem and Solution		1, 2, 3, 4, 5, 6, 7, 11, 13, 14, 15, 16	8, 9, 10, 12
Special-Purpose Maps	1, 8, 10, 12, 13	2, 3, 4, 5, 6, 11, 14.1, 14.2, 14.3, 14.4	7, 9
Fact and Opinion	6	1, 2, 3, 5, 7, 8, 9, 12, 13, 14, 15, 16, 17, 18	4, 10, 11
Faulty Logic or Reasoning		1, 2, 3, 4, 6, 7, 8, 9, 10, 11, 12, 14	5, 13, 15
Evaluate Information	2	1, 4, 6, 7, 8, 9, 11, 13, 14, 15	3, 5, 10, 12
Analyze Effectiveness of Arguments		1, 3, 4, 5, 6, 7, 8, 11, 12, 14	2, 9, 10, 13, 15

Unit 4

Economics

Many learners will find that the most difficult and complex skills appear in the economics unit. Explain that economics is the study of the decisions involved in the production, distribution, and consumption of goods and services. To reassure students, point out that most questions on the GED® Social Studies Test require answers based on information that students have just read. Although Unit 4 discusses complex economic concepts, such as capitalism, communism, Gross Domestic Product, supply and demand, trade deficits, and interest rates, all of the basic information necessary to answer the questions is presented in the text, charts, graphs, and pictographs in the unit.

Topics relating to economics comprise 15 percent of all questions on the GED® Social Studies Test. Students must have a strong grasp of all previous skills if they are to complete this unit successfully. Point out that in Lesson 3 cause-and-effect relationships may contain multiple causes and effects, while in Lesson 5 bar and line graphs become multi-line and bar graphs.

Tell learners that many of the questions in this unit relate to visual stimuli. In addition to reading multi-bar and multi-line graphs, students will assess flowcharts, compare and contrast different types of visuals, and interpret pictographs. Completing Unit 4 will help students assess visual information confidently.

Table of Contents

LESSON	PAGE
1: Understand Economics	SS 42
2: Multiple Causes and Effects	SS 43
3: Compare and Contrast Visuals	SS 44
4: Interpret Pictographs	SS 45
5: Interpret Multi-Bar and Line Graphs	SS 46
Unit 4 Review	**SS 47**

SOCIAL STUDIES

Understand Economics

SS CONTENT TOPICS: I.E.a, I.E.b, II.E.c.1, II.E.c.2, II.E.c.3, II.E.c.4, II.E.c.5, II.E.c.10, II.E.d.1, II.E.d.2, II.E.d.4, II.E.d.5, II.E.d.6, II.E.d.7, II.E.d.9, II.E.d.10, II.E.d.11
SS PRACTICES: SSP.1.a, SSP.1.b, SSP.2.a, SSP.2.b, SSP.3.c, SSP.4.a, SSP.6.a, SSP.6.b, SSP.6.c, SSP.10.a

STUDENT BOOK pp. 90–91

▶ Preview the Skill

Discuss with learners the ways in which economics can affect their lives. Point out that economic issues may impact them not only on an individual level, but also on a national (or even global) level.

❶ Learn the Skill

Give Examples Point out that economics includes the exchange of goods and services between people, groups, businesses, and governments. Ask learners to give examples of ways in which they are participants in these exchanges. Possible examples include purchasing food and clothing, paying rent, working at a store, or receiving a paycheck for work.

❷ Practice the Skill

Link to Past Skills Have learners review the skill *Interpret Tables* from Unit 2, Lesson 2 to help them answer question 1 on p. 90. Have them read each answer choice with a partner and determine whether it is an example of microeconomics or macroeconomics based on the table.

❸ Apply the Skill

Use Graphic Organizers Have learners complete the graphic organizer below to help them understand the difference between how a market with monopolies and a competitive market operate.

Competitive Market	Market with Monopolies
competition between sellers	no government regulation
prices kept lower because of competition	monopolies are the only sellers of a particular good
incentives	higher prices because no competition
some regulation	

Answers
1. B; DOK Level: 2; **2.** A; DOK Level: 2; **3.** C; DOK Level: 2; **4.** D; DOK Level: 3; **5.** B; DOK Level: 1

WORKBOOK pp. 118–121

❶ Review the Skill

Skim and Scan Have learners skim and scan the information in this lesson and make a list of the various economics topics covered. Have them revisit their list after they have finished the questions to assess whether they understand each concept.

❷ Refine the Skill

Link to Past Skills Review the skill *Interpret Charts, Graphs, and Flowcharts* from Unit 3, Lesson 5 with learners to help them interpret the graph on p. 118. Point out that this graph is essentially a triple bar graph with the three bars corresponding to different time periods. In addition, it involves both negative and positive numbers to record the average annual percent change. Discuss the various parts of the graph to be sure learners understand it.

❸ Master the Skill

Decoding Help learners decode the correct answer to question 6 on p. 119 by first identifying the views of economists Adam Smith and John Maynard Keyes. Guide them to recognize that Smith supported no interference from the government and Keyes supported government investment to help spur the economy. Then remind them that the United States has a capitalist economic system to help them choose the correct answer.

▶ Analyze Visuals

Direct learners to the graph on p. 120. Have learners discuss with a partner each of the categories of spending and revenues. Have them use reference materials to better understand any of the categories with which they are unfamiliar.

Answers
1. A; DOK Level: 2; **2.** D; DOK Level: 2; **3.** D; DOK Level: 3; **4.** B; DOK Level: 3; **5.** A; DOK Level: 3; **6.** B; DOK Level: 3; **7.** B; DOK Level: 2; **8.** C; DOK Level: 2; **9.** A; DOK Level: 2; **10.** D; DOK Level: 3; **11.** A; DOK Level: 3; **12.** D; DOK Level: 3; **13.** B; DOK Level: 3

SOCIAL STUDIES

Multiple Causes and Effects

SS CONTENT TOPICS: II.E.c.4, II.E.c.6, II.E.c.10, II.E.d.1, II.E.d.2, II.E.d.7, II.E.d.8, II.E.e.2
SS PRACTICES: SSP.3.c, SSP.6.a, SSP.6.b, SSP.10.a, SSP.10.c

STUDENT BOOK pp. 92–93

Preview the Skill

Invite learners to describe some of their proudest moments and accomplishments. Next, ask them to describe the multiple factors that caused them to succeed in these achievements. Finally, invite them to consider that these achievements are likely to have multiple effects on their lives.

1 Learn the Skill

Give Examples Have learners give examples of an economic choice that features multiple causes and effects, such as the purchase of a new cell phone. Perhaps this decision was caused both by a need for improved communications features and by dissatisfaction with an existing service plan. The choice might produce various *effects*—perhaps a higher monthly cell phone bill and less money available to be spent on entertainment.

2 Practice the Skill

Skim and Scan Tell learners to skim and scan the paragraph and bar graph on p. 92 to learn about the causes and effects of inflation and deflation. Tell them to pay particular attention to the effects to help them answer question 1.

3 Apply the Skill

Spotlighted Item Type Point out to learners that they will have an erasable note board to use during the GED® Social Studies test. For drag-and-drop questions such as question 2 on p. 93, they may wish to sketch the diagram and write the options in the diagram on their note board before dragging and dropping the options to ensure that the completed diagram makes sense.

Answers
1. B; DOK Level: 3; **2.** above equilibrium point: demand goes up and supply goes down; below equilibrium point: supply goes down and demand goes up; DOK Level: 3; **3.** D; DOK Level: 2; **4.** A; DOK Level: 2

WORKBOOK pp. 122–125

1 Review the Skill

Give Examples Invite learners to share some of their major purchases. Ask them to describe the thought process that went into the purchase, why they decided to purchase the exact item they did and how the purchase has affected other possible purchases. For example, if they purchased a car, they have less recreational money because some is needed to pay for the maintenance and insurance of the car.

2 Refine the Skill

SuperSkill Review Help learners understand that the changes in holiday spending habits shown in the graph on p. 122 are a direct result of the shift in the economy in 2008-2009. Point out that economic factors that occur at a national or global level have a very direct effect on consumer behavior.

3 Master the Skill

Spotlighted Item Type Have learners scan pp. 123–125 to see the various possibilities for drag-and-drop items. Point out that drag-and-drop items can be used to complete a diagram, label a visual, or complete a table. Ensure learners notice that not all drag-and-drop options are used in each item.

Math Skills

Remind learners of the importance of math skills in everyday life. Direct them to the graph on p. 124. Have them write two questions pertaining to the changes in the prices of gasoline on the graph for which their partner must make calculations to answer.

Answers
1. C; DOK Level: 3; **2.** C; DOK Level: 3; **3.** corn shortage, higher food prices for foods with corn, less land used for wheat and soybeans; DOK Level: 2; **4.** declining demand, low crude oil prices, limited exports of oil; DOK Level: 2; **5.** cause: decrease in housing starts, effect: decrease in construction and carpentry jobs; cause: increase in housing starts, effect: increase in construction and carpentry jobs; DOK Level: 3; **6.** adjustable-rate mortgages and poor economic conditions; DOK Level: 3

SOCIAL STUDIES

Compare and Contrast Visuals

SS CONTENT TOPICS: II.E.c.5, II.E.d.2, II.E.d.3, II.E.d.4, II.E.d.9, II.E.d.10, II.E.e.1, II.E.e.2
SS PRACTICES: SSP.1.a, SSP.1.b, SSP.3.c, SSP.4.a, SSP.6.a, SSP.6.b, SSP.6.c, SSP.10.a, SSP.10.b, SSP.10.c, SSP.11.a

STUDENT BOOK pp. 94–95

➤ Preview the Skill

Point out two visuals in the room for learners to compare and contrast. Ask them to identify how the two visuals are different and similar in the ways they show information and the advantages and disadvantages of each presentation.

❶ Learn the Skill

Link to Past Skills Have learners review the skill *Compare and Contrast* from Unit 3, Lesson 4. Point out that they can observe and compare the ways in which two visuals share a similar theme or main idea. Explain that the details featured in visuals often contain key differences that can be used to contrast the visuals.

❷ Practice the Skill

Decoding Assist learners in decoding the information in the two graphs on p. 94. After they have read about revolving and nonrevolving credit, discuss why the billions of dollars of nonrevolving consumer credit would increase as the same time as the billions of dollars of revolving consumer credit would stay the same. An understanding of these patterns will help them answer question 1.

❸ Apply the Skill

SuperSkill Review Point out that the answer choices for question 4 on p. 95 are lengthy. To most efficiently answer this question, learners should make sure they have a firm understanding of opportunity cost. The question can be answered by looking at the slope of the lines on the graphs. Because the slope of the line for Country A goes steeply to the right, it is clear that its opportunity cost is much greater to produce corn than wheat. The slope of the line for Country B is not as steep, so it is more flexible to produce either crop, although the opportunity cost is slightly lower for corn.

Answers
1. A; DOK Level: 3; **2.** C; DOK Level: 3; **3.** C; DOK Level: 2; **4.** D; DOK Level: 2

WORKBOOK pp. 126–129

❶ Review the Skill

SuperSkill Review Tell learners that one way to compare and contrast visuals is to consider the types of information that the visuals present. Have learners examine the line graph and table on p. 126. Explain that the table shows the basic minimum wage rate in several places within the same year and that the line graph shows how the federal minimum wage has changed over time.

❷ Refine the Skill

Link to Past Skills Have learners review the skill *Make Inferences* from Unit 3, Lesson 6, to help them make an inference about the two visuals and answer question 1 correctly.

❸ Master the Skill

Skim and Scan Have learners scan the visuals on pp. 127–129 to learn how they are related. Discuss each set of visuals as a class and summarize the content of each set of visuals. Use this information to draw conclusions about the data based on the visuals.

➤ Analyzing Visuals

Direct learners to use Internet sources or newspapers to locate articles that feature two or more visuals related to a given economic topic (the G.D.P., the budget for a government program, a company's quarterly earnings). Ask learners to work in pairs to analyze the visuals. As a class, discuss the main ideas of both visuals and consider how the information presented is different, yet related to a similar theme.

Answers
1. C; DOK Level: 3; **2.** B; DOK Level: 2; **3.** A; DOK Level: 2; **4.** D; DOK Level: 2; **5.** B; DOK Level: 2; **6.** C; DOK Level: 2; **7.** A; DOK Level: 3; **8.** D; DOK Level: 3; **9.** B; DOK Level: 3; **10.** B; DOK Level: 3; **11.** D; DOK Level: 2; **12.** D; DOK Level: 3; **13.** A; DOK Level: 3

SOCIAL STUDIES

Interpret Pictographs

SS CONTENT TOPICS: II.E.c.8, II.E.c.9, II.E.c.10, II.E.c.11, II.E.d.1, II.E.d.4, II.E.d.5, II.E.d.10
SS PRACTICES: SSP.3.c, SSP.6.a, SSP.6.b, SSP.10.a, SSP.11.a

STUDENT BOOK pp. 96–97

▶ Preview the Skill

Discuss with learners familiar symbols that they encounter in their daily lives. For instance, learners might suggest symbols such as those used for traffic signs, hospitals, or school and company logos. Explain that pictographs are charts that use symbols to represent data.

❶ Learn the Skill

Give Examples Take a class survey of learners' favorite television shows, sports teams, or cars. Use this information to produce a simple pictograph that shows your findings. Make sure that the pictograph shows key components, including a title, labels for axes, symbols, and a key.

❷ Practice the Skill

Decoding Help learners use the pictograph on p. 96 to decode the correct answer to question 1. Assist them in locating the portion of the graph that represents the value of goods traded between the United States and Japan. Discuss with learners how having a visual representation of the dollar values of trade with U.S. trade partners makes it easier to compare and determine which countries are the biggest trade partners of the United States.

❸ Apply the Skill

Spotlighted Item Type Remind learners that a drop-down item functions much like a multiple-choice item. They will have four answer options for each blank and must click on the correct one. The correct answers to the drop-down items on p. 97 can be found by examining the graph and carefully reading the passage. Help learners decode item 2.2 by explaining the concept of "median" and asking them to identify the state with the median level of production.

Answers
1. C; DOK Level: 2; **2.1** C; **2.2** C, **2.3** D; DOK Level: 2

WORKBOOK pp. 130–133

❶ Review the Skill

SuperSkill Review Direct learners' attention to the Using Logic tip on p. 130. Discuss how considering the purpose of a pictograph can provide valuable clues to interpreting it's meaning. Have learners give examples of different possible reasons for creating a pictograph.

❷ Refine the Skill

Decoding Help learners decode the pictograph so that they will draw the appropriate conclusion and answer question 2 correctly.

❸ Master the Skill

Skim and Scan Have learners skim and scan the pictographs on pp. 131–133. Have them use the skill of comparing and contrasting to analyze the different pictographs and the information they display. Draw attention to the importance of looking at the key for each pictograph as one symbol represents different values on each of the pictographs. In addition, two of the pictographs show positive and negative values. Discuss the advantages of showing deficits and surpluses on pictographs.

▶ Cross-Curricular Connection

Learners can use the mathematics lesson on tables to practice the operations typically required for interpreting pictographs. Have learners use the pictographs in this lesson to formulate and ask questions like those found in the mathematics lesson on tables. Have them trade their questions with a partner.

Answers
1. C; DOK Level: 2; **2.** B; DOK Level: 3; **3.** A; DOK Level: 2; **4.** B; DOK Level: 3; **5.** D; DOK Level: 2; **6.** D; DOK Level: 2; **7.** C; DOK Level: 3; **8.** D; DOK Level: 2; **9.** B; DOK Level: 3; **10.** C; DOK Level: 2; **11.** A; DOK Level: 2; **12.** D; DOK Level: 2; **13.** B; DOK Level: 3; **14.** C; DOK Level: 2; **15.** D; DOK Level: 2; **16.** A; DOK Level: 2; **17.** D; DOK Level: 3

SOCIAL STUDIES

Interpret Multi-Bar and Line Graphs

SS CONTENT TOPICS: II.E.c.4, II.E.c.7, II.E.c.11, II.E.d.4, II.E.d.5, II.E.d.9, II.E.e.1, II.E.e.2, II.E.e.3
SS PRACTICES: SSP.1.a, SSP.6.a, SSP.6.b, SSP.6.c, SSP.10.a, SSP.10.c

STUDENT BOOK pp. 98–99

➤ Preview the Skill

Have learners examine the multi-bar graph on p. 98 and the bar graph on p. 65. As a group, compare and contrast the two graphs. Guide learners to understand that both graphs show how values change over time. However, multi-bar graphs allow users to compare two sets of data during the time period shown.

❶ Learn the Skill

Give Examples Ask learners to give examples of the components that remain the same in single or multi-bar graphs and line graphs, including titles, axis labels, benchmarks, and graph keys. Use the graph on p. 98 to illustrate that multi-bar and multi-line graphs have a graph key that identifies the meanings of the bars or lines.

❷ Practice the Skill

Decoding Help learners decode the graph on p. 98 to answer question 1. Point out that questions about multi-bar or line graphs will often ask for comparisons of data or conclusions about trends and patterns. As learners look at multi-bar and line graphs, they should automatically think about how the graphs compare and contrast data.

❸ Apply the Skill

Link to Past Skills Have learners review the skill *Draw Conclusions* from Unit 3, Lesson 8, to determine the correct answer to question 4. Tell learners to combine inferences based on information in the passage and the multi-line graph to draw a conclusion about the year in which the economy had the most liquidity in total dollars.

Answers
1. B; DOK Level: 2; **2.** C; DOK Level: 2; **3.** B; DOK Level: 2; **4.** D; DOK Level: 2; **5.** B; DOK Level: 3

WORKBOOK pp. 134–137

❶ Review the Skill

SuperSkill Review Remind learners that multi-bar and multi-line graphs add an additional element of comparison. Encourage learners to focus on this comparative element when studying the trends portrayed in such graphs.

❷ Refine the Skill

Skim and Scan Tell learners to skim and scan the graph and paragraph on p. 134 to help them understand the data that the graph displays. Ask them to draw conclusions about whether a greater number of births or deaths in a given year is a sign of a strong economy. Understanding this relationship will help them answer the questions.

❸ Master the Skill

Decoding Assist learners in decoding the text and multi-line graph on p. 136. Help learners determine which interest rates would be most advantageous to borrowers and which would be least advantageous.

➤ Enrich and Extend

Instruct learners to use the data provided below to construct their own multi-bar or multi-line graph for comparing the annual GDP of the New York City and Los Angeles metropolitan areas. Ask learners to use their finished graphs to describe the trends they observe in the data from both areas.

New York- Northern New Jersey-Long Island (annual GDP in millions)	Los Angeles-Long Beach- Santa Ana (annual GDP in millions)
2008: 1,215,348	2008: 749,096
2009: 1,193,868	2009: 717,447
2010: 1,249,076	2010: 720,768
2011: 1,277,228	2011: 747,306

Answers
1. A; DOK Level: 2; **2.** D; DOK Level: 3; **3.** D; DOK Level: 2; **4.** C; DOK Level: 2; **5.** A; DOK Level: 3; **6.** C; DOK Level: 2; **7.** B; DOK Level: 2; **8.** A; DOK Level: 2; **9.** D; DOK Level: 3; **10.** D; DOK Level: 3; **11.** B; DOK Level: 2; **12.** C; DOK Level: 3; **13.** A; DOK Level: 3

Unit 4 Review

SS CONTENT TOPICS: I.E.c.2, I.E.d.9, II.E.c.1, II.E.c.3, II.E.c.4, II.E.c.6, II.E.c.9, II.E.c.10, II.E.c.11, II.E.d.1, II.E.d.2, II.E.d.3, II.E.d.4, II.E.d.5, II.E.d.6, II.E.d.7, II.E.d.8, II.E.d.9, II.E.d.10, II.E.e.1, II.E.e.3
SS PRACTICES: SSP.1.a, SSP.1.b, SSP.2.a, SSP.2.b, SSP.3.c, SSP.4.a, SSP.6.a, SSP.6.b, SSP.6.c, SSP.10.a, SSP.10.c

You may choose to use the Unit 4 Review on student book pp. 100–107 as a mini–practice test. If you wish to time the test, ask learners to complete all the items in 50 minutes.

Unit 4 Review Answers

1. C; **2.** A; **3.** C; **4.** D; **5.** B; **6.** B; **7.** C; **8.** D; **9.** C; **10.** D; **11.** B; **12.** C; **13.** A; **14.** A; **15.** A; **16.** D; **17.** C; **18.** C; **19.** B; **20.** C; **21.** D; **22.** A; **23.** C; **24.** Your Obligation: Managing Credit; Credit Bureau's Obligations: Compliance Under the Act, Error Investigation; Both: Accuracy, Privacy; Working with Lenders; **25.** D; **26.** B; **27.** A

Unit 4 Review Item Analysis

SKILL	DOK LEVEL 1	DOK LEVEL 2	DOK LEVEL 3
Understand Economics		3, 4, 5, 8, 23, 25, 26, 27	1, 2, 24
Multiple Causes and Effects		8, 9, 10, 15	11, 12
Compare and Contrast Visuals		13, 18, 19	14, 16, 17
Interpret Pictographs			6, 7
Interpret Multi-Bar and Line Graphs		22	20, 21

Use workbook lessons, as identified in the following table to assist learners who require additional remediation with certain skills or items having certain DOK levels.

Unit 4 Workbook Item Analysis

SKILL	DOK LEVEL 1	DOK LEVEL 2	DOK LEVEL 3
Understand Economics		1, 2, 7, 8, 9	3, 4, 5, 6, 10, 11, 12, 13
Multiple Causes and Effects		3, 4	1, 2, 5, 6
Compare and Contrast Visuals		2, 3, 4, 5, 6, 11	1, 7, 8, 9, 10, 12, 13
Interpret Pictographs		1, 3, 5, 6, 8, 10, 11, 12, 14, 15, 16	2, 4, 7, 9, 13, 17
Interpret Multi-Bar and Line Graphs		1, 3, 4, 6, 7, 8, 11	2, 5, 9, 10, 12, 13

SOCIAL STUDIES

Glossary

UNIT 1

Borders: lines on maps showing the separation between counties, states, territories, and countries

Climate: the average weather in a place over many years

Elevation: the height of a place

Equator: an imaginary line that runs around the middle of Earth

Geography: the study of Earth

Globe: a model of Earth

Human-made features: roads, buildings, and cities sometimes found on maps

Lines of latitude: used to find exact, or absolute, locations of places and run east-west

Lines of longitude: used to find exact, or absolute, locations of places and run north-south

Map components: the various parts that make up the map such as the key, the scale, etc.

Map: a visual representation of a place that is usually shown on a flat surface

Map key: explains the symbols used on maps

Movement on maps: is shown through the use of symbols such as arrows or lines. These arrows or lines can show the movement, direction, or route of people, goods, or ideas.

Physical map: shows the geographic land and water features of an area, such as mountains, plains, rivers, gulfs, and oceans

Political map: shows all of the usual physical features that you would find on a map, such as mountains, rivers and so on, but rather than the normal country borders that you would see, a political map shows the political and cultural boundaries of countries

Population density on political maps: uses shading or dots to illustrate areas where people live

Scales: on maps help measure real distances

Symbols: such as dots for cities, stars for capital cities, or icons for special events such as battles

UNIT 2

Categorize: to place information in a group of similar or related items

Cause: an action or occurrence that makes another event happen

Effect: something that happens as a result of a cause

Main idea: the most important point of a passage or paragraph

Sequence: the order of events, most often chronologically (from earliest to latest)

Supporting details: additional information or facts about the main idea. Such details include facts, statistics, explanations, graphics, and descriptions.

Tables: a tool used to organize information into **rows** and **columns**. Rows run across the table from the left to the right. Columns run up and down the table from the top to the bottom.

Timelines: present sequences of events in a visual manner

Topic sentence: a sentence that captures the *meaning* of the entire paragraph or group of sentences

UNIT 3

Analyze: to study something closely and carefully

Bias: prejudice in favor of or against one thing, person, or group compared with another, usually in a way considered to be unfair

Caricature: an exaggerated representation of a thing or a person's physical features, to present a point of view

Charts, graphs, and flowcharts: ways to present information visually. Like tables, charts and graphs can present a great deal of numerical information in a relatively small amount of space. A flowchart is a graphic that describes a sequence. It communicates the steps of a process quickly by using concise explanatory text.

Compare: to consider both the similarities and the differences between two or more items

Constitution of the United States: a document that outlines the basis of the federal (national) government of the USA

Contrast: to focus only on the differences between items

Diagrams: drawings that show the different parts of something and how they work together. They are different from other types of graphics, such as charts or graphs, because they can show the relationships that exist between pieces of information

Fact: something believed to be true or real

Faulty logic or reasoning: reasoning that contains a fault or defect and is therefore incorrect

Generalization: a principle, statement, or idea having general application

Generalize: when you make a broad statement that applies to entire groups of people, places, events, and so on. These statements typically contain words such as *usually, all, everyone, many, few, often,* or *overall.* Generalizing is useful when drawing a conclusion about something.

Hasty generalization: a type of fallacy, or a mistake in reasoning, which leaves an argument incomplete or invalid

Inference: a logical guess based on facts or evidence

Information sources: accounts of information. They may be primary or secondary.

Opinion: a viewpoint or a belief that cannot be proven true or untrue

Point of view: the perspective from which he or she writes about a topic

Political cartoonist: an artist who draws editorial cartoons that contain some level of political or social commentary. Their cartoons are usually based upon day to day news and current affair topics. It can also be on a national or international topic.

Political cartoons: drawings that are intended to make political or social statements

Primary sources: original accounts of events written by people who actually experienced them at the time, such as eyewitnesses. These sources may include speeches, documents, journal entries, and letters.

Problem: a question to be considered, solved, or answered

Secondary sources: provide interpretations of primary sources. Encyclopedias, newspaper articles, and history books are secondary sources.

Solution: an answer to a question or problem

Special-purpose maps: political maps that show additional features such as congressional districts, products and resources, and population

Summarize: to restate briefly in your own words the main points of a passage or a visual element

UNIT 4

Economics: the study of the way in which goods and services are exchanged

Multi-bar and line graphs: visuals that can be used to compare values and to show changes over time. However, because they use more than one bar or line, they also allow for the comparison of varied, but connected, data over time.

Pictographs: visuals that use symbols to illustrate data in chart form

SOCIAL STUDIES

MAP OF THE UNITED STATES

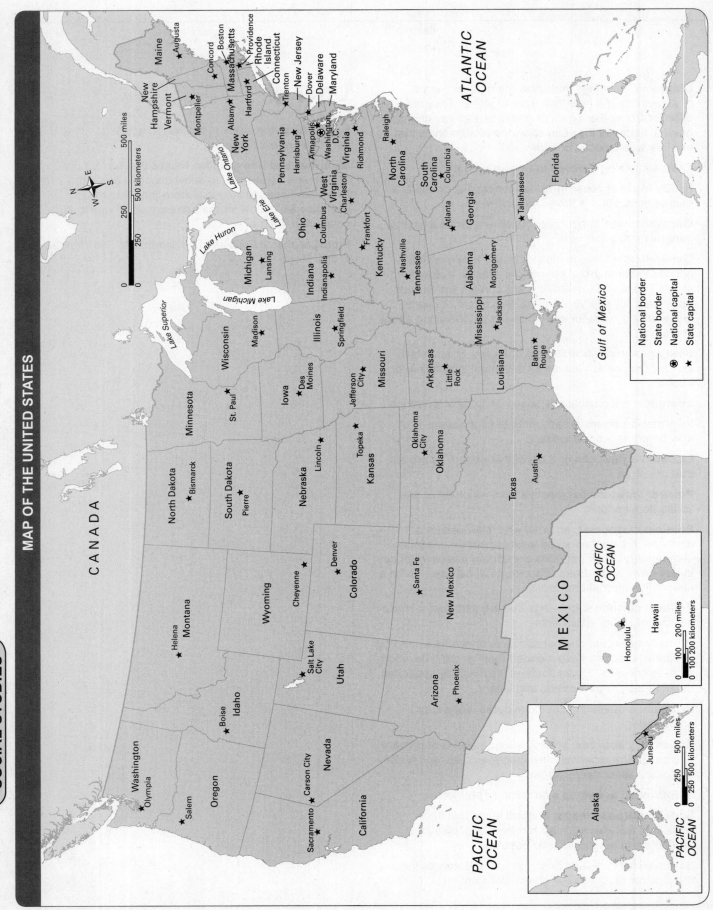

CANADA

ATLANTIC OCEAN

Maine · Augusta

New Hampshire · Concord
Vermont · Montpelier
Massachusetts · Boston
Rhode Island · Providence
Connecticut · Hartford
New York · Albany
New Jersey · Trenton
Delaware · Dover
Maryland · Annapolis

Pennsylvania · Harrisburg
West Virginia · Charleston
Virginia · Richmond
Washington, D.C.
North Carolina · Raleigh
South Carolina · Columbia

Ohio · Columbus
Kentucky · Frankfort
Tennessee · Nashville
Georgia · Atlanta
Florida · Tallahassee

Michigan · Lansing
Indiana · Indianapolis
Illinois · Springfield
Alabama · Montgomery
Mississippi · Jackson

Wisconsin · Madison
Iowa · Des Moines
Missouri · Jefferson City
Arkansas · Little Rock
Louisiana · Baton Rouge

Minnesota · St. Paul
North Dakota · Bismarck
South Dakota · Pierre
Nebraska · Lincoln
Kansas · Topeka
Oklahoma · Oklahoma City
Texas · Austin

Montana · Helena
Wyoming · Cheyenne
Colorado · Denver
New Mexico · Santa Fe

Idaho · Boise
Utah · Salt Lake City
Arizona · Phoenix

Washington · Olympia
Oregon · Salem
Nevada · Carson City
California · Sacramento

Lake Superior · Lake Michigan · Lake Huron · Lake Erie · Lake Ontario

MEXICO

Gulf of Mexico

PACIFIC OCEAN

N E W S

500 miles
500 kilometers
250
250

Legend
- National border
- State border
- ⊛ National capital
- ★ State capital

Pacific Ocean inset
Hawaii · Honolulu
100 200 miles
100 200 kilometers

Alaska inset
Alaska · Juneau
PACIFIC OCEAN
500 miles
250 500 kilometers

MAP OF THE WESTERN HEMISPHERE

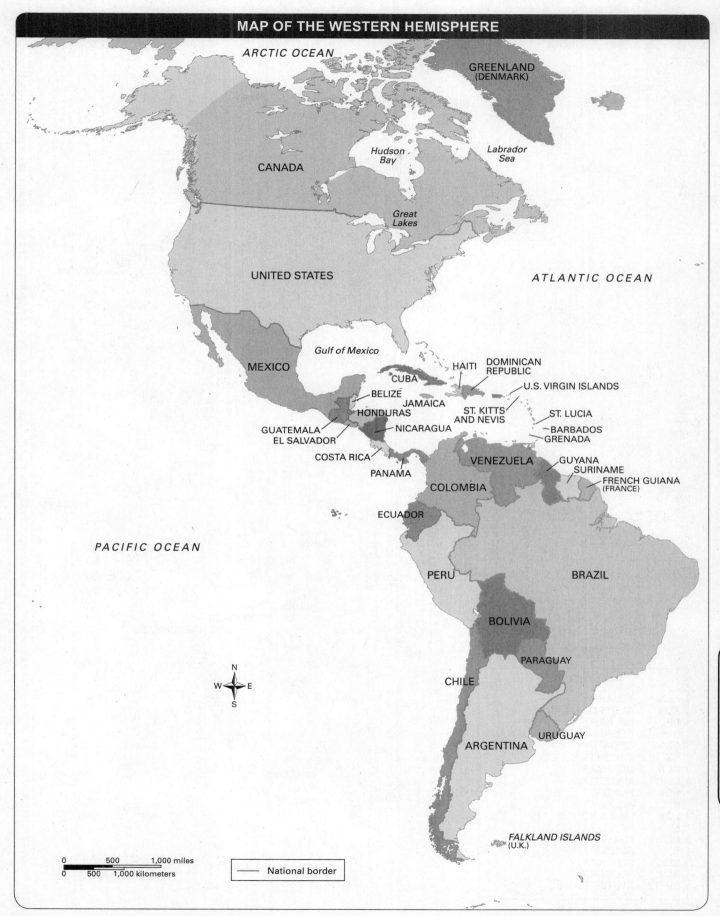

ARCTIC OCEAN

GREENLAND
(DENMARK)

Hudson
Bay

Labrador
Sea

CANADA

Great
Lakes

UNITED STATES

ATLANTIC OCEAN

Gulf of Mexico

MEXICO

CUBA

HAITI

DOMINICAN
REPUBLIC

U.S. VIRGIN ISLANDS

BELIZE

JAMAICA

HONDURAS

ST. KITTS
AND NEVIS

ST. LUCIA

GUATEMALA

NICARAGUA

BARBADOS

EL SALVADOR

GRENADA

COSTA RICA

VENEZUELA

GUYANA

PANAMA

SURINAME

COLOMBIA

FRENCH GUIANA
(FRANCE)

ECUADOR

PACIFIC OCEAN

PERU

BRAZIL

BOLIVIA

PARAGUAY

N
W　E
S

CHILE

URUGUAY

ARGENTINA

FALKLAND ISLANDS
(U.K.)

0　500　1,000 miles

0　500　1,000 kilometers

—— National border

SOCIAL STUDIES

MAP OF THE EASTERN HEMISPHERE

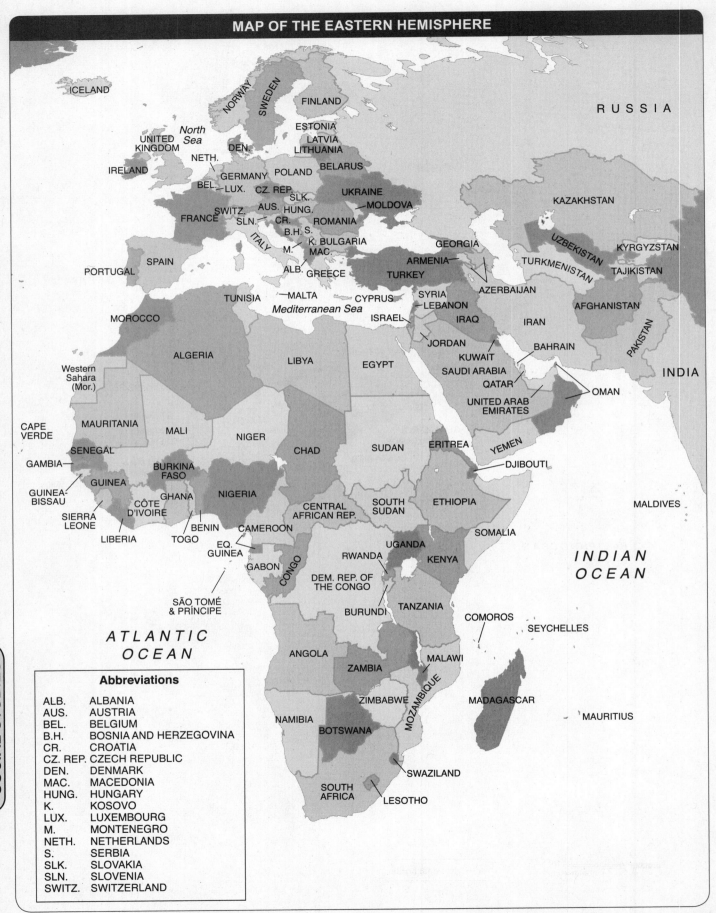

Abbreviations

ALB.	ALBANIA
AUS.	AUSTRIA
BEL.	BELGIUM
B.H.	BOSNIA AND HERZEGOVINA
CR.	CROATIA
CZ. REP.	CZECH REPUBLIC
DEN.	DENMARK
MAC.	MACEDONIA
HUNG.	HUNGARY
K.	KOSOVO
LUX.	LUXEMBOURG
M.	MONTENEGRO
NETH.	NETHERLANDS
S.	SERBIA
SLK.	SLOVAKIA
SLN.	SLOVENIA
SWITZ.	SWITZERLAND

SOCIAL STUDIES

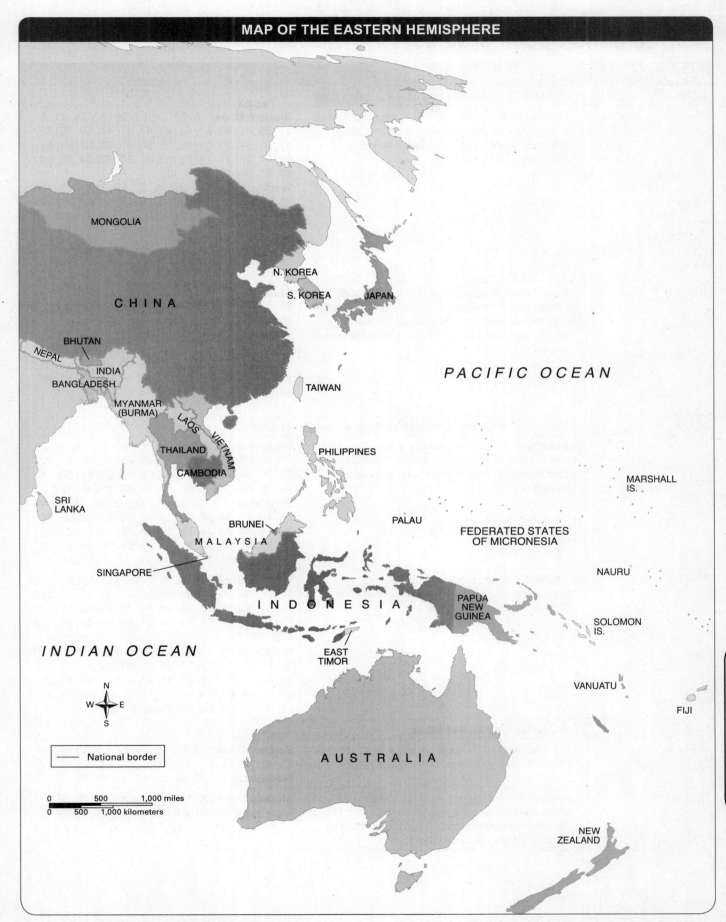

MONGOLIA

CHINA

N. KOREA

S. KOREA

JAPAN

BHUTAN

NEPAL

INDIA

BANGLADESH

MYANMAR
(BURMA)

LAOS

VIETNAM

THAILAND

CAMBODIA

TAIWAN

PHILIPPINES

SRI
LANKA

BRUNEI

MALAYSIA

SINGAPORE

INDONESIA

PALAU

FEDERATED STATES
OF MICRONESIA

MARSHALL
IS.

NAURU

PAPUA
NEW
GUINEA

SOLOMON
IS.

PACIFIC OCEAN

EAST
TIMOR

INDIAN OCEAN

N
W · E
S

VANUATU

FIJI

National border

0   500   1,000 miles
0   500   1,000 kilometers

AUSTRALIA

NEW
ZEALAND

SOCIAL STUDIES

Correlations/Social Studies

Indicator Codes	Social Studies Practices	*Social Studies* Book Pages
SSP.1	**Drawing Conclusions and Making Inferences**	
SSP.1.a	Determine the details of what is explicitly stated in primary and secondary sources and make logical inferences or valid claims based on evidence.	**Student Book:** 16, 22, 24, 25, 26, 27, 29, 31, 33, 37, 38, 39, 40, 41, 42, 43, 46, 47, 48, 49, 50, 51, 52, 53, 54, 55, 57, 58, 59, 60, 61, 62, 63, 64, 65, 66, 67, 69, 71, 78, 79, 80, 81, 82, 83, 84, 85, 86, 87, 91, 99, 103, 106, 107 **Workbook:** 23, 24, 25, 26, 27, 29, 31, 32, 33, 35, 36, 37, 40, 41, 43, 44, 45, 46, 47, 48, 49, 50, 51, 52, 53, 54, 55, 56, 57, 58, 59, 60, 61, 62, 63, 64, 65, 66, 67, 68, 69, 70, 71, 72, 73, 74, 75, 76, 77, 78, 79, 80, 81, 82, 83, 84, 85, 88, 89, 90, 91, 92, 93, 94, 95, 96, 97, 101, 110, 111, 112, 113, 114, 115, 116, 117, 120, 121, 126, 127, 128, 129
SSP.1.b	Cite or identify specific evidence to support inferences or analyses of primary and secondary sources, attending to the precise details of explanations or descriptions of a process, event, or concept.	**Student Book:** 16, 22, 24, 25, 26, 27, 31, 33, 34, 35, 37, 38, 42, 43, 53, 55, 57, 58, 61, 62, 63, 65, 66, 67, 68, 69, 76, 77, 79, 80, 81, 82, 83, 85, 86, 91, 107 **Workbook:** 24, 31, 32, 33, 37, 40, 41, 43, 44, 45, 46, 47, 53, 54, 55, 56, 57, 58, 63, 65, 67, 68, 69, 71, 72, 73, 74, 75, 77, 78, 79, 80, 82, 83, 84, 85, 86, 88, 89, 90, 91, 92, 93, 94, 95, 96, 97, 110, 111, 113, 119
SSP.2	**Determining Central Ideas, Hypotheses, and Conclusions**	
SSP.2.a	Determine the central ideas or information of a primary or secondary source document, corroborating or challenging conclusions with evidence.	**Student Book:** 13, 16, 17, 22, 26, 27, 29, 33, 34, 35, 36, 37, 38, 39, 40, 41, 42, 43, 49, 50, 51, 52, 53, 54, 56, 58, 59, 61, 64, 65, 66, 67, 68, 69, 71, 72, 73, 76, 78, 79, 80, 81, 82, 85, 86, 91, 107 **Workbook:** 23, 24, 30, 31, 32, 33, 40, 41, 43, 44, 45, 46, 47, 54, 55, 56, 57, 62, 63, 64, 66, 68, 69, 70, 71, 72, 73, 74, 75, 76, 77, 78, 79, 80, 82, 83, 84, 85, 87, 88, 90, 91, 92, 93, 94, 95, 96, 97, 101, 102, 103, 104, 105, 114, 115, 116, 117, 121
SSP.2.b	Describe people, places, environments, processes, and events, and the connections between and among them.	**Student Book:** 3, 6, 7, 8, 9, 10, 11, 12, 13, 14, 15, 16, 17, 18, 19, 22, 23, 24, 25, 27, 29, 30, 31, 32, 33, 34, 35, 36, 37, 38, 40, 41, 42, 43, 50, 51, 52, 53, 55, 56, 57, 58, 61, 80, 81, 82, 85, 87, 91, 102, 106, 107 **Workbook:** 2, 3, 4, 5, 6, 7, 8, 9, 10, 11, 12, 13, 15, 16, 17, 18, 19, 20, 21, 22, 23, 24, 25, 26, 28, 31, 33, 34, 35, 36, 37, 40, 41, 43, 44, 45, 48, 49, 53, 60, 63, 64, 67, 68, 70, 71, 72, 73, 75, 76, 79, 80, 82, 83, 84, 85, 88, 96, 99, 100, 119
SSP.3	**Analyzing Events and Ideas**	
SSP.3.a	Identify the chronological structure of a historical narrative and sequence steps in a process.	**Student Book:** 10, 11, 12, 13, 22, 23, 30, 31, 32, 41, 42, 43, 55, 87 **Workbook:** 10, 25, 38, 39, 40, 41, 48, 49, 67, 72
SSP.3.b	Analyze in detail how events, processes, and ideas develop and interact in a written document; determine whether earlier events caused later ones or simply preceded them.	**Student Book:** 22, 23, 31, 34, 35, 55, 85, 87 **Workbook:** 12, 24, 41, 42, 44, 45, 46, 47, 54

SOCIAL STUDIES

Correlations/Social Studies

Indicator Codes	Social Studies Practices	Social Studies Book Pages
SSP.3.c	Analyze cause-and-effect relationships and multiple causation, including the importance of natural and societal processes, the individual, and the influence of ideas.	**Student Book:** 3, 10, 11, 22, 31, 41, 42, 43, 50, 51, 55, 60, 85, 87, 93, 100, 101, 102, 105, 107 **Workbook:** 8, 10, 12, 13, 15, 18, 19, 20, 21, 24, 25, 42, 43, 44, 45, 46, 47, 51, 52, 53, 59, 63, 64, 67, 70, 71, 72, 73, 76, 78, 80, 81, 119, 120, 132
SSP.3.d	Compare differing sets of ideas related to political, historical, economic, geographic, or societal contexts; evaluate the assumptions and implications inherent in differing positions.	**Student Book:** 28, 29, 52, 53, 77, 106 **Workbook:** 86, 88, 111, 113
SSP.4	**Interpreting Meaning of Symbols, Words, and Phrases**	
SSP.4.a	Determine the meaning of words and phrases as they are used in context, including vocabulary that describes historical, political, social, geographic, and economic aspects of social studies.	**Student Book:** 7, 12, 13, 14, 15, 16, 17, 18, 22, 23, 26, 27, 32, 33, 34, 35, 38, 41, 43, 48, 63, 69, 70, 71, 80, 86, 90, 91, 100, 107 **Workbook:** 2, 3, 4, 6, 25, 29, 31, 32, 33, 43, 44, 45, 46, 47, 54, 55, 56, 57, 79, 80, 83, 84, 85, 95, 97, 98, 100, 101, 113
SSP.5	**Analyzing Purpose and Point of View**	
SSP.5.a	Identify aspects of a historical document that reveal an author's point of view or purpose (e.g., loaded language, inclusion or avoidance of particular facts).	**Student Book:** 26, 33, 38, 43, 58, 59, 62, 63, 64, 65, 69, 74, 75, 76, 77, 79, 80, 82, 83, 86 **Workbook:** 61, 71, 74, 75, 76, 77, 82, 83, 84, 85, 89, 94, 95, 97, 106, 108, 109, 110, 111, 113, 114, 115, 116, 117
SSP.5.b	Identify instances of bias or propagandizing.	**Student Book:** 38, 58, 59, 63, 73, 76, 77, 86 **Workbook:** 74, 76, 77, 87, 88, 89, 103, 104, 105, 106, 107, 108, 109, 110, 112, 113
SSP.5.c	Analyze how a historical context shapes an author's point of view.	**Student Book:** 26, 86 **Workbook:** 82, 83, 84, 85, 95, 103, 105, 111, 112, 113
SSP.5.d	Evaluate the credibility of an author in historical and contemporary political discourse.	**Student Book:** 33, 38, 79 **Workbook:** 82, 84, 85, 103, 106, 107, 108, 109, 113, 115, 117
SSP.6	**Integrating Content Presented in Different Ways**	
SSP.6.a	Integrate quantitative or technical analysis (e.g., charts, research data) with qualitative analysis in print or digital text.	**Student Book:** 22, 23, 25, 38, 92, 94, 95, 96, 97, 98, 99, 100, 101, 103, 105, 106 **Workbook:** 23, 30, 118, 120, 122, 123, 124, 125, 126, 127, 128, 129, 130, 131, 132, 133, 134, 135, 136, 137
SSP.6.b	Analyze information presented in a variety of maps, graphic organizers, tables, and charts; and in a variety of visual sources such as artifacts, photographs, political cartoons.	**Student Book:** 2, 3, 4, 5, 6, 7, 8, 9, 10, 11, 12, 13, 14, 15, 16, 17, 18, 19, 22, 23, 24, 25, 27, 28, 31, 34, 35, 37, 39, 46, 47, 54, 55, 57, 58, 59, 65, 70, 71, 75, 80, 81, 82, 84, 86, 87, 90, 92, 96, 97, 98, 99, 100, 101, 102, 103, 104, 105, 106 **Workbook:** 2, 5, 6, 7, 8, 9, 10, 11, 12, 13, 14, 15, 16, 17, 18, 19, 20, 21, 22, 23, 25, 26, 27, 28, 29, 30, 31, 32, 33, 34, 35, 37, 39, 41, 43, 44, 45, 48, 49, 50, 51, 52, 53, 58, 61, 64, 65, 66, 67, 68, 69, 73, 74, 75, 76, 77, 81, 84, 85, 96, 98, 99, 100, 101, 107, 108, 109, 118, 120, 122, 123, 124, 125, 127, 128, 129, 130, 131, 132, 133, 134, 135, 136, 137

Correlations/Social Studies

Indicator Codes	Social Studies Practices	*Social Studies* Book Pages
SSP.6.c	Translate quantitative information expressed in words in a text into visual form (e.g., table or chart); translate information expressed visually or mathematically into words.	**Student Book:** 6, 7, 22, 54, 71, 93, 94, 95, 98, 99, 103, 104, 105 **Workbook:** 2, 3, 4, 18, 19, 20, 21, 29, 33, 43, 63, 66, 67, 68, 86, 87, 101, 120, 126, 127, 128, 129, 134, 135, 136, 137
SSP.7	**Evaluating Reasoning and Evidence**	
SSP.7.a	Distinguish among fact, opinion, and reasoned judgment in a primary or secondary source document.	**Student Book:** 16, 26, 37, 43, 63, 66, 67, 72, 73, 74, 75, 77, 80, 82, 83 **Workbook:** 75, 82, 102, 104, 107, 108, 113
SSP.7.b	Distinguish between unsupported claims and informed hypotheses grounded in social studies evidence.	**Student Book:** 66, 67, 72, 75, 77, 79 **Workbook:** 103, 107, 113
SSP.8	**Analyzing Relationships between Texts**	
SSP.8.a	Compare treatments of the same social studies topic in various primary and secondary sources, noting discrepancies between and among the sources.	**Student Book:** 71 **Workbook:** 23, 86, 111, 113, 116
SSP.9	**Writing Analytic Response to Source Texts**	
SSP.9.a	Produce writing that develops the idea(s), claim(s), and/or argument(s) thoroughly and logically, with well-chosen examples, facts, or details from primary and secondary source documents.	**Student Book:** 61, 79 **Workbook:** 59, 60, 61, 73, 92, 111
SSP.9.b	Produce writing that introduces the idea(s) or claim(s) clearly; creates an organization that logically sequences information; and maintains a coherent focus.	**Student Book:** 51, 61, 79 **Workbook:** 59, 60, 61, 73, 92
SSP.9.c	Write clearly and demonstrate sufficient command of standard English conventions.	**Student Book:** 51, 61, 79 **Workbook:** 59, 60, 61, 73, 92, 111
SSP.10	**Reading and Interpreting Graphs, Charts, and Other Data Representation**	
SSP.10.a	Interpret, use, and create graphs (e.g., scatterplot, line, bar, circle) including proper labeling. Predict reasonable trends based on the data (e.g., do not extend trend beyond a reasonable limit).	**Student Book:** 38, 40, 54, 81, 92, 93, 94, 95, 96, 97, 98, 99, 100, 101, 103, 104, 105, 106 **Workbook:** 66, 68, 118, 120, 122, 123, 124, 125, 126, 127, 128, 129, 130, 131, 132, 133, 134, 135, 136, 137
SSP.10.b	Represent data on two variables (dependent and independent) on a graph; analyze and communicate how the variables are related.	**Student Book:** 54, 94, 95 **Workbook:** N/A
SSP.10.c	Distinguish between correlation and causation.	**Student Book:** 98, 99, 103, 104 **Workbook:** 8, 15, 39, 122, 123, 124, 125, 129, 135
SSP.11	**Measuring the Center of a Statistical Dataset**	
SSP.11.a	Calculate the mean, median, mode, and range of a dataset.	**Student Book:** 97 **Workbook:** 128
SSP.11.b	Identify specific pieces of evidence an author uses in support of claims or conclusions.	**Student Book:** **Workbook:** 43, 44, 45, 82

SOCIAL STUDIES

Correlations/Social Studies

Indicator Codes	Social Studies Content Topics	*Social Studies* Book Pages
Civics and Government		
I. Development of Modern Liberties and Democracy		
I.CG.a	**Types of modern and historical governments**	**Student Book:** 27 **Workbook:** N/A
I.CG.a.1	Direct democracy, representative democracy, parliamentary democracy, presidential democracy, monarchy and other types of government that contributed to the development of American constitutional democracy	**Student Book:** 28, 29, 46, 47, 50, 51, 73, 81, 85 **Workbook:** 31, 33, 50, 51, 64, 83, 105
I.CG.b	**Principles that have contributed to development of American constitutional democracy**	
I.CG.b.1	Natural rights philosophy	**Student Book:** 47, 83 **Workbook:** N/A
I.CG.b.2	Popular sovereignty and consent of the governed	**Student Book:** 26, 27, 48, 50, 51, 83 **Workbook:** 31, 33, 85
I.CG.b.3	Constitutionalism	**Student Book:** 28, 48, 49, 51, 69, 81, 85 **Workbook:** 32, 33, 51, 52, 54, 55, 56, 57, 80, 85
I.CG.b.4	Majority rule and minority rights	**Student Book:** 51, 83, 86 **Workbook:** 33, 63, 82
I.CG.b.5	Checks and balances	**Student Book:** 47, 49, 65, 67, 69 **Workbook:** 33, 52, 85, 88
I.CG.b.6	Separation of powers	**Student Book:** 63 **Workbook:** 33, 51, 52, 70, 84, 85
I.CG.b.7	Rule of law	**Student Book:** 50, 52, 53, 55, 74, 75, 81, 83, 85 **Workbook:** 51, 59, 62, 65, 84, 85, 107, 109
I.CG.b.8	Individual rights	**Student Book:** 29, 33, 35, 47, 49, 50, 51, 55, 57, 63, 74, 75, 80, 81, 83, 85, 86, 87 **Workbook:** 54, 55, 58, 59, 63, 65, 71, 72, 82, 84, 107, 108, 109, 115
I.CG.b.9	Federalism	**Student Book:** 28, 29, 51 **Workbook:** 52, 60, 61, 79, 81, 87, 88
I.CG.c	**Structure and design of United States government**	
I.CG.c.1	Structure, powers, and authority of the federal executive, judicial, and legislative branches	**Student Book:** 49, 52, 53, 55, 59, 60, 61, 65, 67, 69, 70, 71, 74, 75, 79, 82, 84, 85 **Workbook:** 32, 33, 51, 52, 53, 55, 56, 57, 70, 73, 75, 77, 78, 79, 80, 82, 84, 85, 90, 91, 94, 95, 96, 97, 107, 108, 109, 114, 117
I.CG.c.2	Individual governmental positions (e.g., President, speaker of the house, cabinet secretary, etc.)	**Student Book:** 55, 56, 60, 61, 62, 64, 67, 69, 75, 78, 79, 80, 85 **Workbook:** 52, 53, 55, 64, 78, 94, 95, 97, 107, 108, 110, 116
I.CG.c.3	Major powers and responsibilities of the federal and state governments	**Student Book:** 49, 59, 60, 65, 67, 69, 70, 82 **Workbook:** 33, 51, 65, 71, 73, 75, 77, 79, 82, 84, 85, 88, 91, 92, 95, 97
I.CG.c.4	Shared powers	**Student Book:** 49 **Workbook:** 51, 70, 81, 88

SOCIAL STUDIES

Correlations/Social Studies

Indicator Codes	Social Studies Content Topics	*Social Studies* Book Pages
I.CG.c.5	The amendment process	**Student Book:** 34, 57 **Workbook:** 55, 56, 57, 71, 72, 89, 93
I.CG.c.6	Governmental departments and agencies	**Student Book:** 40, 55, 65, 66, 69, 86 **Workbook:** 53, 73, 75, 76, 78, 80, 86, 92, 93
I.CG.d	**Individual rights and civic responsibilities**	**Student Book:** 86 **Workbook:** N/A
I.CG.d.1	The Bill of Rights	**Student Book:** 49, 51, 85 **Workbook:** 33, 54, 55, 58
I.CG.d.2	Personal and civil liberties of citizens	**Student Book:** 33, 35, 49, 55, 57, 58, 74, 75, 80, 83, 85, 86, 87 **Workbook:** 33, 44, 45, 54, 55, 63, 65, 71, 72, 82, 84, 107, 108, 109, 115
II. Dynamic Responses in Societal Systems		
II.CG.e	**Political parties, campaigns, and elections in American politics**	
II.CG.e.1	Political parties	**Student Book:** 63, 72, 73, 76, 77, 78, 80, 83 **Workbook:** 35, 38, 40, 43, 77, 88, 97, 98, 103, 104, 105, 112, 113
II.CG.e.2	Interest groups	**Student Book:** 57, 58, 59, 61, 86 **Workbook:** 63, 67, 71, 97, 111
II.CG.e.3	Political campaigns, elections, and the electoral process	**Student Book:** 58, 63, 72, 73, 76, 78, 83, 86 **Workbook:** 38, 39, 40, 43, 64, 67, 71, 95, 98, 103, 104, 110, 112, 113, 116
United States History		
I. Development of Modern Liberties and Democracy		
I.USH.a	**Key historical documents that have shaped American constitutional government**	
I.USH.a.1	Key documents and the context and ideas that they signify (e.g., Magna Carta, Mayflower Compact, Declaration of Independence, United States Constitution, Martin Luther King's Letter from the Birmingham Jail, landmark decisions of the United States Supreme Court, and other key documents)	**Student Book:** 22, 26, 27, 28, 29, 48, 49, 81, 83 **Workbook:** 31, 32, 33, 39, 40, 44, 45, 54, 55, 56, 57, 59, 114, 115, 117
I.USH.b	**Revolutionary and Early Republic Periods**	
I.USH.b.1	Revolutionary War	**Student Book:** 12, 25, 26, 27, 29, 87 **Workbook:** 6, 18, 19, 20, 21, 24, 31, 32, 33, 59, 61
I.USH.b.2	War of 1812	**Student Book:** 12, 31 **Workbook:** 25, 39, 41
I.USH.b.3	George Washington	**Student Book:** **Workbook:** 24, 35
I.USH.b.4	Thomas Jefferson	**Student Book:** 28 **Workbook:** 35, 36, 37
I.USH.b.5	Articles of Confederation	**Student Book:** 51 **Workbook:** 51
I.USH.b.6	Manifest Destiny	**Student Book:** 23, 31 **Workbook:** 36, 40, 41

SOCIAL STUDIES

Correlations/Social Studies

Indicator Codes	Social Studies Content Topics	*Social Studies* Book Pages
I.USH.b.7	Indian Policy	**Student Book:** 30, 31 **Workbook:** 38, 40, 108
I.USH.c	**Civil War and Reconstruction**	
I.USH.c.1	Slavery	**Student Book:** 32, 33, 80 **Workbook:** 27, 43, 63
I.USH.c.2	Sectionalism	**Student Book:** 32, 33, 80 **Workbook:** 42, 43
I.USH.c.3	Civil War Amendments	**Student Book:** 35 **Workbook:** 44, 45, 62
I.USH.c.4	Reconstruction policies	**Student Book:** 52, 53, 80 **Workbook:** 44, 45, 63
I.USH.d	**Civil Rights**	**Student Book:** **Workbook:** 115
I.USH.d.1	Jim Crow laws	**Student Book:** 35 **Workbook:** 64
I.USH.d.2	Women's suffrage	**Student Book:** 34, 57 **Workbook:** 46
I.USH.d.3	Civil Rights Movement	**Student Book:** 86 **Workbook:** 108, 109, 115
I.USH.d.4	*Plessy v. Ferguson* and *Brown v. Board of Education*	**Student Book:** 35, 55 **Workbook:** N/A
I.USH.d.5	Warren court decisions	**Student Book:** 35 **Workbook:** N/A
II. Dynamic Responses in Societal Systems		
II.USH.e	**European settlement and population of the Americas**	**Student Book:** 25, 37 **Workbook:** 28, 29, 34
II.USH.f	**World Wars I and II**	**Student Book:** 82 **Workbook:** N/A
II.USH.f.1	Alliance system	**Student Book:** 81 **Workbook:** 47, 49
II.USH.f.2	Imperialism, nationalism, and militarism	**Student Book:** 38 **Workbook:** 47
II.USH.f.3	Russian Revolution	**Student Book:** 36 **Workbook:** N/A
II.USH.f.4	Woodrow Wilson	**Student Book:** 37, 56 **Workbook:** 47, 70
II.USH.f.5	Treaty of Versailles and League of Nations	**Student Book:** 37 **Workbook:** 47
II.USH.f.6	Neutrality Acts	**Student Book:** **Workbook:** 48
II.USH.f.7	Isolationism	**Student Book:** 56 **Workbook:** N/A
II.USH.f.8	Allied and Axis Powers	**Student Book:** 81 **Workbook:** 48, 49, 77

SOCIAL STUDIES

Correlations/Social Studies

Indicator Codes	Social Studies Content Topics	*Social Studies* Book Pages
II.USH.f.9	Fascism, Nazism, and totalitarianism	**Student Book:** 38, 39, 87 **Workbook:** 48, 77, 107
II.USH.f.10	The Holocaust	**Student Book:** 39 **Workbook:** N/A
II.USH.f.11	Japanese-American internment	**Student Book:** 39 **Workbook:** N/A
II.USH.f.12	Decolonization	**Student Book:** 38 **Workbook:** N/A
II.USH.f.13	GI Bill	**Student Book:** 40 **Workbook:** N/A
II.USH.g	**The Cold War**	**Student Book:** N/A **Workbook:** 107
II.USH.g.1	Communism and capitalism	**Student Book:** 36, 40, 80, 87 **Workbook:** 106, 107
II.USH.g.2	NATO and the Warsaw Pact	**Student Book:** 42 **Workbook:** N/A
II.USH.g.3	U.S. maturation as an international power	**Student Book:** 37, 41, 42, 43, 81 **Workbook:** 24, 67, 71, 107
II.USH.g.4	Division of Germany, Berlin Blockade, and Airlift	**Student Book:** 41, 42, 43 **Workbook:** N/A
II.USH.g.5	Truman Doctrine	**Student Book:** 40, 41, 42 **Workbook:** N/A
II.USH.g.6	Marshall Plan	**Student Book:** 41 **Workbook:** N/A
II.USH.g.7	Lyndon B. Johnson and the Great Society	**Student Book:** N/A **Workbook:** 111
II.USH.g.8	Richard Nixon and the Watergate scandal	**Student Book:** 85 **Workbook:** N/A
II.USH.g.9	Collapse of the U.S.S.R. and the democratization of Eastern Europe	**Student Book:** 42, 43, 81, 87 **Workbook:** N/A
II.USH.h	**American foreign policy since 9/11**	**Student Book:** 42, 43, 82 **Workbook:** N/A
Economics		
I. Development of Modern Liberties and Democracy		
I.E.a	**Key economic events that have shaped American government and policies**	**Student Book:** 27, 32, 40 **Workbook:** 37, 43, 119
I.E.b	**Relationship between political and economic freedoms**	**Student Book:** 26, 40 **Workbook:** 119
II. Dynamic Responses in Societal Systems		
II.E.c	**Fundamental Economic Concepts**	
II.E.c.1	Markets	**Student Book:** 91, 107 **Workbook:** N/A
II.E.c.2	Incentives	**Student Book:** 105 **Workbook:** 119
II.E.c.3	Monopoly and competition	**Student Book:** 91, 107 **Workbook:** 121

SOCIAL STUDIES

Correlations/Social Studies

Indicator Codes	Social Studies Content Topics	*Social Studies* Book Pages
II.E.c.4	Labor and capital	**Student Book:** 81, 85, 99, 102 **Workbook:** 121, 125
II.E.c.5	Opportunity cost	**Student Book:** 95 **Workbook:** 119
II.E.c.6	Profit	**Student Book:** 104 **Workbook:** 124
II.E.c.7	Entrepreneurship	**Student Book:** 7, 54, 81 **Workbook:** 134
II.E.c.8	Comparative advantage	**Student Book:** 96, 97 **Workbook:** N/A
II.E.c.9	Specialization	**Student Book:** 97, 104 **Workbook:** 131
II.E.c.10	Productivity	**Student Book:** 81, 97, 101, 104 **Workbook:** 118, 119
II.E.c.11	Interdependence	**Student Book:** 96, 104 **Workbook:** 130, 133, 137
II.E.d	**Microeconomics and Macroeconomics**	**Student Book:** 18, 90 **Workbook:** N/A
II.E.d.1	Supply, demand, and price	**Student Book:** 91, 93, 100 **Workbook:** 122, 123, 125, 132
II.E.d.2	Individual choice	**Student Book:** 93, 100 **Workbook:** 119, 122, 123, 124, 127, 129
II.E.d.3	Institutions	**Student Book:** 81, 106 **Workbook:** 120, 129
II.E.d.4	Fiscal and monetary policy	**Student Book:** 99, 100, 101 **Workbook:** 120, 126, 129, 131, 135, 137
II.E.d.5	Regulation and costs of government policies	**Student Book:** 99, 101 **Workbook:** 120, 131, 132
II.E.d.6	Investment	**Student Book:** 91, 103 **Workbook:** N/A
II.E.d.7	Government and market failures	**Student Book:** 100 **Workbook:** 74, 120, 125
II.E.d.8	Inflation and deflation	**Student Book:** 92, 93, 100 **Workbook:** N/A
II.E.d.9	GDP	**Student Book:** 91, 105 **Workbook:** 128, 137
II.E.d.10	Unemployment	**Student Book:** 91, 100 **Workbook:** 74, 127, 132
II.E.d.11	Tariffs	**Student Book:** **Workbook:** 121
II.E.e	**Consumer economics**	
II.E.e.1	Types of credit	**Student Book:** 94, 98, 103 **Workbook:** 128, 136
II.E.e.2	Savings and banking	**Student Book:** 95 **Workbook:** 125, 128, 136
II.E.e.3	Consumer credit laws	**Student Book:** 98, 106 **Workbook:** N/A